Administrative Law

Administrative Law

Timothy Endicott

Fellow of Balliol College
Dean of the Faculty of Law, University of Oxford

OXFORD
UNIVERSITY PRESS

OXFORD
UNIVERSITY PRESS

Great Clarendon Street, Oxford OX2 6DP

Oxford University Press is a department of the University of Oxford.
It furthers the University's objective of excellence in research, scholarship,
and education by publishing worldwide in

Oxford New York

Auckland Cape Town Dar es Salaam Hong Kong Karachi
Kuala Lumpur Madrid Melbourne Mexico City Nairobi
New Delhi Shanghai Taipei Toronto

With offices in

Argentina Austria Brazil Chile Czech Republic France Greece
Guatemala Hungary Italy Japan Poland Portugal Singapore
South Korea Switzerland Thailand Turkey Ukraine Vietnam

Oxford is a registered trade mark of Oxford University Press
in the UK and in certain other countries

Published in the United States
by Oxford University Press Inc., New York

British Library Cataloguing in Publication Data

Data available

Library of Congress Cataloging in Publication Data

Data available

Typeset by Newgen Imaging Systems (P) Ltd., Chennai, India
Printed in Great Britain
on acid-free paper by
Ashford Colour Press Ltd, Gosport, Hampshire

ISBN 978–0–19–927728–5

10 9 8 7 6 5 4 3 2 1

For Peter Endicott

Table of contents

Preface

Comity is the duty of one authority to respect and to support the proper function of other authorities. This book is mostly about comity among public authorities. I aim to explain how administrative law can enable them to work together to give effect to the constitutional principles that support responsible government. I hope that the focus on constitutional principle will help to bring some order to the very diverse topics that you need to deal with, if you are to understand this incredibly complex branch of public law.

Public law imposes duties to serve the public interest. It governs all of us (criminal law and the law of tax and of child protection are parts of public law). The public law of administration is the body of legal standards that establishes institutions of government, and confers governmental powers, and imposes duties on public authorities. It includes the law governing social security, public education, planning, competition, employment, local government, the National Health Service, immigration and asylum, the police, prisons, probation, ASBOs, the armed forces, the ministers of the Crown, and every department of government.

Administrative law consists of a variety of legal processes and techniques for controlling the decisions of public authorities, to require them to use public powers responsibly. It is not a scheme of legal doctrine like contract law or criminal law or the law of trusts; it is more complex, in various ways:

- Since the nineteenth century, Parliament has created a variety of techniques for exercising and for controlling administrative power, such as ombudsmen, auditors, and rights of appeal to the courts.

- In 2008, a new system of tribunals was inaugurated, with appeals to an 'Upper Tribunal' that assumes a new role in the development of large parts of administrative law.

- The law of judicial review of administrative action requires an understanding not only of the powers and duties of administrative authorities, but also of the powers and duties of the courts themselves—powers and duties that the courts are always developing.

- New forms of governmental control of the life of the community have recently created new forms of public power and new challenges for administrative law.

- Special considerations arise in the application to public authorities of the law of tort, contract, restitution, and other forms of civil liability. Those liabilities form part of a system of justice between citizens and government agencies, and it is a very important general principle that public authorities can enter into contracts, and that they are liable for their torts and are capable of bringing claims in tort. But claimants have asked the courts to turn tort and contract liability of public authorities into a source of remedies against uses of public powers that no private defendant has; the law needs to respond in a way that respects the same principles as the other areas of administrative law.

Courses in administrative law need to be complex, because the law is complex. They address various ways in which the law controls public authorities, and various processes and techniques that are available to people who have complaints.

In fact, administrative law courses at university tend to be even more complex than that, because they often address judicial procedure in a way that courses in (e.g.) contract law do not. And some courses cover sociological topics that are important for understanding the work of public authorities, and the context in which legal controls operate, and the impact that legal controls have on administration. Imagine a course in criminal law that requires you to learn criminology, penology, and criminal procedure at the same time as the central doctrines of criminal law. You may face challenges like that in an administrative law course.

Underlying all that variety is a set of principles that ought to be reflected in actual operations of public authorities and in the effects of legal control of the administration. The courts use those principles to justify what they do, and we can use them as standards by which to assess not only the judges' own decisions, but also the schemes by which Parliament has sought to regulate the administration. This book aims to explain those principles and to give you the resources to apply them to the problems of administrative law. The complexity of the subject arises because the general principles need to be applied to a massive variety of government action in widely varying ways.

The book does not even try to cover all techniques for controlling or challenging administration. The most important form of control is managerial control by government ministers and civil servants who have more or less effective techniques for achieving good administration. Another important form of control is scrutiny of administration by Parliament. And related to those forms of control is a very important technique for citizens who have a complaint against the administration: use of the media to bring pressure to bear on the government. But this book addresses parliamentary scrutiny only to explain why it cannot replace legal forms of control of administration (see p 53). And the book does not address managerial control of the administration, or use of the media, or other ways of creating political pressure. Since it aims to explain the principles of administrative law, the book focuses on legal forms of control, and on non-legal forms of control (such as ombudsmen) that are established and controlled by law. The focus is on problems that are distinctively the job of a lawyer (rather than a publicist or a politician) to understand and to solve.

From the mists of time

Administrative law has undergone complex and remarkable developments since the end of World War II. It is easy to forget that its basic structure and principles were partly developed in the middle ages, and partly in the seventeenth and eighteenth centuries. One theme of this book is that the remarkable creative work of English judges in judicial review since the 1960s is deeply woven into the long history of the law. It is a major mistake (encouraged by a small number of unimportant decisions in the first half of the twentieth century, and perpetuated by legal education) to think that administrative law did not exist until Lord Reid invented it in the 1960s. At various points in the book I point out the roots of the 21st-century doctrines that run down through past centuries. In particular, there are several references to the work of one outstanding administrative lawyer, Lord Mansfield.

The point of these illustrations is not to suggest that the law is the same as it was 250 years ago in Lord Mansfield's day. The law has changed deeply and extensively (although on many important points it actually is exactly the same as in the 1750s, and Lord Mansfield was elaborating doctrines that were centuries old). The point is not actually to do history, either—there is no room in a book like this to understand the past fully, by putting the decisions of past generations into their historical and social and legal context. The point of the illustrations is to show the present day vitality of the constitutional principles of the common law. It is important and actually surprising that you can understand exactly what Lord Mansfield and others were trying to do, and the connection to what the judges are doing in the 21st century, *without* being a historian. It shows the durability of some of the principles of legal control of government. Some are permanent, universal principles of what it takes for a community to be governed responsibly, and some are long-enduring principles of our constitution as to how that is to be achieved in the United Kingdom.

As Lord Mansfield said in R v *Bembridge* (1783) 3 Doug 327, 332: 'The law does not consist of particular cases but of general principles, which are illustrated and explained by these cases.'

Judicial review and the rest of administrative law

Some teachers treat administrative law as a course in judicial review; others focus on other legal institutions and processes, on the ground that judicial review plays a limited role in the actual day-to-day resolution of disputes, and in control of government action. I hope this book will be useful for both purposes. The law of judicial review is very complex, and important in itself, but the main role of the account of judicial review in this book is to help you to learn the principles of responsible government that are crucial to *every* area of administrative law. This approach is useful because of one very remarkable feature of judicial review: that the judges have largely created their own powers to control the government, and they continue to develop those powers. Ombudsmen, tribunals, auditors, commissions, and the many other agencies that oversee administration need to develop and elaborate their own role; the judges have largely *invented* their own role.

In the course of doing so, the judges have laboured to articulate the constitutional principles of administrative law in their reasons for decision. If you are interested in how judges create powers and responsibilities for themselves, and how they can do justice with vigilance and creativity, and when their creativity amounts to arrogance instead, then you will love administrative law.

The book points out more than once that judicial review is not the most important technique for preventing abuse of public power, or holding government to account. But the judges' attempts to craft and to justify their role are extremely useful for understanding other accountability techniques. So, for example, the chapter on ombudsmen includes a discussion of judicial review of the reports of ombudsmen, because (I argue) you can understand both ombudsmen and the courts better if you understand the reasons why judicial review of ombudsmen is almost entirely pointless.

Controversy

This book does not tell you the consensus among lawyers. On many surprisingly basic questions of administrative law, there is no consensus. The constitutional principles of administrative law generate deep controversies about some of the simplest practical questions in administrative law. Sometimes the controversies about the law are overtly political controversies (since the law concerns the control of government action). It would be impossible to state the law without saying anything controversial. So I have not tried to avoid stating controversial views; I hope it will be obvious most of the time. And I'm sorry to tell you that there isn't even a consensus as to how to use the terminology. In this book, even the Glossary is controversial.

You will see the fundamental disagreements at every turn; when the judges are not disagreeing with each other, you may find the text disagreeing with all of them. I try to point out the controversies, and to suggest ways for you to reach your own conclusions. But I have not tried to report on the vast and complex body of scholarly work that has accompanied the remarkable developments of the past fifty years. The Online Resource Centre provides a guide to the literature.

The challenge is that you need to develop (and to defend) your own view of the law. I am sure that you will disagree with some of what you read in this book (or in other books, or in the cases). The good news is that you will be able to find the resources, in the cases and legislation discussed in this book, to support an argument in favour of your point of view.

Thanks...

I started this book because I thought that students of English law should know about *habeas corpus*, and because I wanted to put on paper some of the things that I learned from giving tutorials in Balliol College. I have learned from all my students, and I have tried to say 'thank you' by explaining some of the basic lawyer's equipment (rights, precedent, distinguishing, presumptions, exceptions, floodgates arguments... see the Index) that judges and lawyers take for granted.

Several Balliol undergraduates have served as research assistants. I am very grateful to Rosie Davidson (who helped me to start the book), Brydie Bethell, Margaret Price, Craig Looker, Hannah Crowther, Angela Rainey, Fiona Ryan, Laura Findley, and Isabella Costelloe. Emer Murphy made an extraordinary contribution to the project. As well as providing research assistance, she did a large part of the work for the website (including the case summaries), and prepared the chart on p 174. More than that, Emer gave an extremely helpful critical reading of much of the text.

David Phillip Jones, Jeff King, Margaret Lee Grimm, Owen Rees, Anthony J Bellia, Jr gave valuable advice or helped me by showing me their work. Michael Spence saved me from mistakes and managed to encourage me at the same time. Anne Davies gave me some priceless advice in Chapter 15. I have benefited from the opportunity to discuss some of the issues of this book with John Finnis.

I am grateful to the Law Faculty at Oxford for funding for research assistance, and to Oxford University Press for their good advice, support, and patience. Michelle Robb has provided much-appreciated clerical support. For moral support, my thanks to Naomi and Peter Endicott, Orville and Julianne Endicott, Michael Spence, Dan Edwards, and Frank Campbell.

Author's guide to using the book

A look for section at the beginning of each chapter outlines the key ideas that you should aim to understand as you work your way through the chapter.

LOOK FOR • • •

* The purpose of judicial review: is it to police the lawfulness of administra action? To right injustices to claimants?

* The relation between standing (the entitlement to be heard by a court) and purposes of judicial review.

* The increasing potential for political campaigners to use judicial review as a p form to hold the government to account.

* The role of intervenors in litigation against public authorities (and the very rela approach to intervention in the English courts).

From the mists of time boxes can be found within the text. They point out some of the deep and little-known links between administrative law in the 21st century and in past centuries.

> FROM THE MISTS OF TIME
>
> The significant changes in the law of due process since *Ridge v Baldwin* mean that judges sometimes use 'fairness' as a label for new procedural requirements, and 'natural justice' as a label for more traditional procedural requirements. But fairness has been a legal requirement for decision making for centuries, at least for courts of specific jurisdiction. In *R v Cowle* (1759) 2 Burr 834, Lord Mansfield held that any doubt 'whether a fair, impartial, or satisfactory trial or judgment can be had there' was a reason for the Court of King's Bench to quash a decision (861).
>
> The link between fairness and natural justice is that procedural unfairness is injustice: the common law of due process can be summed up by saying that 'a pr

Pop quizzes are interspersed throughout the text. They give you the opportunity to put your critical thinking to work on particular problems.

> But this new form of uncertainty can be extravagant: the legislation may be perfec clear, and yet until a court decides the matter, the parties do not know if a court w treat a widower as *if* he were a widow, or whether a court will treat a person wit partner of the same sex as *if* he were a husband or wife.
>
> ● Pop quiz ●
>
> What do you think of the following argument? Before the Human Rights Act, it was the duty of a court to give a possible interpretation of a statute, if possible. Now it is the duty of a court to give the most Convention-compatible interpretation of a statute. So if the best possible interpretation of a statute is compatible with the Convention, s 3 makes no difference. Therefore, the only effect that s 3 can possibly have is to stop a court from giving the best interpretation of the statute.

A take home message at the end of each chapter lets you check that you have understood the main points.

> TAKE HOME MESSAGE • • •
>
> * **The three main values of procedural participation are:**
>   − the value of promoting good outcomes;
>   − the value of respect for persons affected by a decision; and
>   − the value of imposing the rule of law on public decision making.
>
> * **Due process is proportionate process:** Whether a process is due depends on whet it promotes the three process values, in a way that is justifiable in light of the **proc cost** and any **process danger.**
>
> * The focal concern of the common law of due process is **fairness** to persons affec by a decision, who have something to say on the issues. Fairness requires t

A list of critical reading can be found at the end of each chapter. This points you towards key cases you should read to understand the material covered. The reading is not all cases: you should read the Parliamentary Ombudsman's reports (Chapter 13) and the White Paper on Tribunals (Chapter 12) just as carefully as you would read judicial decisions. A guide to administrative law scholarship is provided on the Online Resource Centre.

Critical reading

R v LCA, ex p Bradford City Council [1979] QB 287
R v LCA, ex p Eastleigh BC [1988] QB 855
R v LCA, ex p Croydon LBC [1989] 1 All ER 1033
R v PCA, ex p Balchin [1997] JPL 917
Bradley v Work and Pensions Secretary [2008] EWCA Civ 36
The Ombudsman's fourth report on the Balchin case: 'Redress in the Round' 11 October 2005, HC 475:
http://www.ombudsman.org.uk/improving_services/special_reports/pca/redress05/index.html
The Debt of Honour report: http://www.ombudsman.org.uk/improving_services/special_reports/pca/interneeso5/index.html

Critical questions are offered at the end of each chapter. These have a similar function to the pop quizzes, but allow for a broader overview of the material covered in the chapter.

CRITICAL QUESTIONS • • •

1   Administrative authorities always ought to make the best available decision. why isn't judicial review generally available on the ground that an authority did make the best available decision?

2   Does the difference between inherent discretions, and discretions conferr expressly by statute, make any difference to judicial review?

3   Are there any unfettered discretionary powers?

4   Can you reconcile judicial control of discretionary power, with the principle th judges are only to strike down an action that the public authority had no power

The glossary at the end of the book explains legal and administrative jargon.

Certiorari ('to be certified'): A prerogative writ developed at common law, wh has been replaced by the order called a 'quashing order' in the Civil Procedure Rul 1998.

Civil servant: A servant of the Crown employed by a department of central gover ment ('public servant' is the term for everyone who works for a public author including civil servants, police, local authority employees, employees of execut agencies and non-departmental public bodies, employees of the armed forces, etc)

Claim: A judicial proceeding in which a claimant seeks a remedy. In an ordin claim, the claimant must establish a right to a remedy; the claimant has no right proceed with the claim if he or she does not assert grounds on which such a right t

A simple approach to learning the law

Administrative law is extremely complex. So you should take a simple approach to learning it. I recommend that you read the 'Critical readings' carefully while you are working on the material in each chapter. Then use other readings cited in the chapter, when revising for an exam or writing an essay. The simple approach allows you to master the principles of the subject first without being overwhelmed by the cases, and then it allows you to put the principles to work when you read the additional cases.

It is generally a good idea to read a chapter from start to finish, because ideas and examples are often introduced and then used throughout a chapter without any further explanation. Where I use an idea from one chapter in another, though, I try to refer you to the place where it is explained. And if I haven't, you can use the Glossary and Index.

Case citations

Square brackets pinpoint the paragraphs in case reports or other documents that have numbered paragraphs. If paragraphs in a report are not numbered, the pinpoint for a quotation is given by page number. Citations are not repeated when it is obvious what source is referred to.

For simplicity, I have used the neutral citation as the only form of citation for recent cases. Here is what to do if you are using the book in a library and you want to read the cases in the law reports. Go to the Law Reports (in most cases, the Appeal Cases) for the right year, and look in the list of contents for the party names. The neutral citation is included at the top of the report, and paragraphs of the reasons are numbered in the reports. Use the same method for the All England Reports. The Weekly Law Reports include the neutral citation in the contents list.

Author's guide to the Online Resource Centre

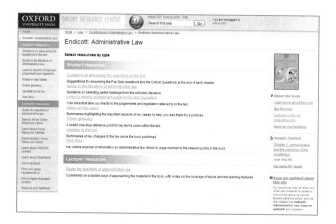

www.oxfordtextbooks.co.uk/orc/endicott/

The website includes links to online reports of judicial decisions and legislation cited in the text, notes on key cases, suggestions for answering the questions in the text, updates to the law, and links to other resources. There is also a guide for teachers, and a guide to the literature of administrative law.

For students

Guidance on the questions

The website offers suggestions for answering the Pop Quiz questions, and the Critical Questions at the end of each chapter of the text. Note that those suggestions are not answers! And they are not meant to replace the work that you will need to do in reading the cases and in making your own arguments. The suggestions are only meant to help you to get into that work.

Judicial decisions and legislation

You will find notes on key cases for each chapter on the website. These are not the same as headnotes, and their purpose is not to save you from reading the case. The purpose is to alert you to the importance of the case for administrative law, so that you can read the case for a purpose. Links to reports of important judgments and legislation cited in the book are also included.

Links to other resources

Many judicial and administrative institutions in England and Europe go out of their way to explain their functions and processes on websites. So there is a wide variety of administrative law resources on the internet, which can be useful in learning the law and in practice. The Online Resource Centre gives links to many of those resources. To find an internet resource mentioned in the text, you only need to go to the links page on the companion website, and find the link by page number in this book.

Keeping up to date

You can use the website to find important new judicial decisions, legislation, and other current material, arranged in the order of the presentation used in the book. But if you are learning administrative law, remember that the point is not to keep up to date – even though the law is alarmingly fast-moving. You won't be able to understand the latest decision unless you have learned the basic principles. The website allows you to find recent developments in the law, but its purpose is the same as the purpose of the text: to help you to understand the principles, and to apply them in solving legal problems. Then in legal practice, you will be ready to deal with the latest decision on a particular issue when it arises.

Guide to the literature of administrative law

The text does not refer to scholarly work on administrative law, because it would have been impossible to do justice to the vast literature. The Online Resource Centre suggests some particularly useful readings. Although the guide is selective, it will not be necessary for you to read everything. But the guide to the literature will show you the breadth of work that has been done on the issues in this book, and the readings will give you a fuller sense of the basic controversies in administrative law.

For lecturers

Guide for teachers

The text and the Online Resource Centre are meant as aids for teaching as well as learning (especially the guidance on questions, the links to cases, and the guide to the literature). There are many possible ways of approaching the material in the text, and the Guide for Teachers is designed to help you to find an approach that suits you. In particular, there are comments on the coverage of topics and the learning features in this book.

Table of cases

Cases are listed by the name of the claimant.

Abbreviations:

ex p = ex parte

LBC = London Borough Council

MBC = Metropolitan Borough Council

QBD = Queen's Bench Division (a branch of the High Court; the part of the Queen's Bench Division that decides judicial review cases has been called the 'Administrative Court' since reforms to the Civil Procedure Rules 1998)

Table of legislation

Introduction

1 Administration and the principles of the constitution

Administrative law includes a complex variety of processes and doctrines that confer and control public power. This chapter outlines the underlying principles that make it into more than just a miscellaneous jumble.

LOOK FOR • • •

- **Good administration**: what it is, and how it is related to constitutional principles.

- The fundamental constitutional principle of **responsible government**, and the **system principles** that promote it.

- **Arbitrary government**, and the **rule of law**.

- The different roles of different institutions in restraining arbitrary government.

- The particular responsibilities of the courts: the **principle of legality**, and the requirement of **due process**.

- The **principle of relativity**: the requirements of constitutional principles are related to the context in which they are applied.

> ❛The King hath no prerogative, but that which the law of the land allows him. ❜
>
> **Case of Proclamations (1611) 12 Co Rep 74 (Lord Coke)**

> ❛...the King was greatly offended, and said, that then he should be under the law, which was treason to affirm, as he said; to which I said, that Bracton saith, That the King ought not to be under any man but under God and the law. ❜
>
> **Prohibitions del Roy (1607) 77 ER 1342, 12 Co Rep 64 (Lord Coke)**

1.1 Arbitrary government and the core of administrative law

After the invasion of Afghanistan at the end of 2001, United States forces captured more than 600 men suspected of links to Al Qaeda. They were imprisoned in Guantánamo Bay, a naval base in Cuba that the Americans hold on an indefinite lease. The point of keeping the men in Guantánamo Bay was to avoid interference from judges, which the American administration knew would follow if they imprisoned men on American soil. The President claimed the constitutional authority to detain the men as long as he chose, in conditions that he chose, with no recourse except what he chose to give them.

The families of the detainees claimed that the men should have access to an independent legal process. They also claimed that some of the detainees were aid workers; innocent visitors to Afghanistan and Pakistan, sold to the American forces by villagers for bounty money. In November 2002, the mother of Feroz Abbasi, a British detainee in Guantánamo Bay, asked the English courts to declare that the Foreign Secretary had a duty to take steps to get the government of the United States to release him (R (Abbasi) v Foreign Secretary [2002] EWCA Civ 1598). In the Court of Appeal, the judges concluded that Abbasi's detention was arbitrary:

> ❛in apparent contravention of fundamental principles recognised by both jurisdictions and by international law, Mr Abbasi is at present arbitrarily detained in a "legal black-hole" ❜. [65]

It was strong language for judges. By calling the detention 'arbitrary', they were saying that the United States government was claiming an uncontrolled power that lends itself to abuse. The detainees were being held at the say-so of the President, when the decision ought to be controlled by law. But although the judges frankly condemned the detention, they refused to tell the Foreign Secretary to say anything to the Americans, or even to give reasons for his decision not to say anything.

Meanwhile, the families' claims were going through the U.S. federal courts. The Bush administration argued that the courts should not listen to complaints by a foreigner detained outside the U.S. The justices of the United States Supreme Court were deeply divided; they held 5–4 that the U.S. Constitution required that the detainees in

Guantánamo Bay should be able to challenge their detention in the U.S. federal courts through *habeas corpus*, the ancient remedy for arbitrary detention that the Americans inherited from English law (*Boumediene v Bush*, 553 US (2008)).

1.1.1 *Habeas corpus*

What if the British government tried to create an enclave abroad, like Guantánamo Bay, for uncontrolled executive detention? English law still includes *habeas corpus*. The phrase 'habeas corpus' ('that you produce the body') was used in a variety of early judicial writs (directions from a court issued in the name of the King), designed to get a person into the court to give evidence, or to respond to a claim. In the 1300s, the judges developed one such writ into an order to an official to explain why a person is being detained. If the official did not give a lawful reason for the detention, the court could order the detainee released.

The writ read as a command of the King, as follows:

> 'We command you to produce before us the body of ___, with the day and the reason of his detention, to undergo and receive whatever our court then and there may order concerning him.'[1]

It gave the judges power to order the release of a person who was being detained unlawfully. They still have that power today—so long as there is jurisdiction to hear the claim.

The late medieval English judges were able to invent *habeas corpus* because they could issue writs in the King's name. Their role as the King's judges gave them a far-reaching power of constitutional invention. But that role also endangered their independence. In *Darnel's Case* (1627) 3 Howell's State Trials 1, the judges refused to issue *habeas corpus* for detentions ordered by the King himself. It can't have helped that the King had just dismissed an uncooperative Lord Chief Justice, and replaced him with a supporter. It would take an Act of Parliament to extend *habeas corpus* to control detention ordered by the King: the Habeas Corpus Act 1640. Since 1640, the courts have been able to review the lawfulness of any detention by the government. But English judges have never faced a situation like Guantánamo Bay. There is no settled law as to whether the courts have jurisdiction to hear a claim from a foreigner detained abroad. How would an English court decide the matter, if the British government set up a British version of Guantánamo Bay?

The decisions on *habeas corpus* show that the judges have a very wide discretion to decide their own jurisdiction. In the 18th century, Lord Mansfield held that the writ was available in Berwick–upon-Tweed, even though the town was outside the regular jurisdiction of the High Court. If the court did not give *habeas corpus*, he held, 'there must, in many important cases, be a total failure of trial, and consequently, of justice'

---

[1]   J H Baker, *An Introduction to English Legal History* (4th edn, 2002) 552.

(R v Cowle (1759) 2 Burr 834, 860). Lord Mansfield was uncertain whether *habeas corpus* was available to control detentions overseas, saying that where the judges 'cannot judge of the cause, or give relief upon it, they would not think proper to interpose'. But they *would* listen to a claim, 'where a writ of *habeas corpus* out of this Court would be the properest and most effectual remedy' (856).

If people were detained in a British Guantánamo Bay, we could expect that the judges today would follow the lead of Lord Mansfield, and would assert *habeas corpus* jurisdiction if that was the only way to provide an effective remedy. The Court of Appeal suggested that view in the *Abbasi* decision. But the strongest reason for expecting the House of Lords to take the approach suggested in *Abbasi* is the decision in *A and X v Home Secretary* [2004] UKHL 56, on the effect of the European Convention on Human Rights.

In *A and X*, nine men were detained without trial, on suspicion of involvement in international terrorism. The men were held in Belmarsh Prison; the media called it Britain's Guantánamo Bay, but it was different—and not just in the number of detainees. Belmarsh is in south London, not on foreign soil. The Belmarsh detainees had access to review hearings from the start (though not to the ordinary process of the courts). What's more, they could have left the country. They were foreign nationals, whom the British government could not lawfully deport.[2] Unable to deport them, and not wanting to release them in Britain, the British Government decided to derogate from the right to liberty in Art 5 of the Convention (that is, they decided to make an exception to it). Parliament authorized detention without trial of people in that situation, in the Anti-terrorism, Crime and Security Act 2001 s 23.

The European Convention provides for derogations from Art 5, but only 'in time of war or other public emergency threatening the life of the nation', and only 'to the extent strictly required by the exigencies of the situation'. The Home Secretary thought that the situation strictly required indefinite detention without trial. The Law Lords decided 8–1 that the detentions were not strictly required; Lord Hoffmann did not even think that the emergency was a threat to the life of the nation. Lord Walker alone thought that the judges ought to defer to the Home Secretary's judgment as to whether the situation required the detentions. The majority thought that they could hold that the detentions were unnecessary, without interfering illegitimately with the Home Secretary's work.

How does *A and X* relate to *habeas corpus*? It shows that if the British government created a Guantánamo Bay, the Law Lords would regard it as legitimate judicial business to question the detention. The history of *habeas corpus* gives the judges power to determine the extent of their own jurisdiction. If they are to use it responsibly, the judges have to use it with respect for the constitutional role of the Home Secretary— that is, with **comity** toward the Home Secretary. In the Guantánamo Bay litigation, the dissenting U.S. Supreme Court justices thought that they had to defer to the

---

2   They would have faced inhuman or degrading treatment if they had been deported to their own countries, and the European Court of Human Rights has held that deportation in that situation would violate the right under Art 3 of the Convention, not to be subjected to torture or to inhuman or degrading treatment (*Chahal v UK* (1996) 23 EHRR 413).

Commander-in-Chief's judgment as to how to run a campaign that he called a 'war' (*Boumediene v Bush* (Scalia J)). *A and X* shows that the majority in the House of Lords would not defer to the Home Secretary's judgement as to whether it is necessary to detain people indefinitely.

Convention rights

If terrorism suspects were detained in a British Guantánamo Bay, the **European Convention on Human Rights** (see Chapter 3) would apply. The European Court of Human Rights has held that the Convention applies if a state 'exercises effective control of an area outside its national territory' (*Loizidou v Turkey* (1997) 23 EHRR 513 [62]). In *R (Al-Skeini) v Defence Secretary* [2005] EWCA Civ 1609, the Court of Appeal held that the Convention and the Human Rights Act 1998 apply in respect of a death in a British military prison in Iraq, though not in respect of a death in the streets of Basra patrolled by British troops.

So unless the United Kingdom derogated from Art 5, detainees in a British Guantánamo Bay would have a remedy under the Human Rights Act in the English courts. And if the Government did derogate from Art 5, *A and X v Home Secretary* [2004] UKHL 56 shows that the courts would decide whether the detentions were necessary, rather than deferring to the Home Secretary.

1.1.2 What is arbitrary government?

A decision is arbitrary if the decision maker is unresponsive to reasons for giving one decision rather than another. Sometimes arbitrary decision making is all right. In the National Lottery, the techniques for deciding the winning number are deliberately made as arbitrary as possible. That is all right because there *are no* reasons for picking a particular ticket holder as the winner of the lottery. An election is a public decision that leaves it up to the voters to respond to the reasons on which they ought to base their decision. It is not a lottery, and the voters shouldn't flip coins; they ought to decide on the relevant political considerations. But the law leaves it entirely up to them to decide what those considerations are. And because it leaves that up to them, it leaves them free to ignore the relevant considerations, and so it leaves them free to act arbitrarily. But of course, the freedom of the ballot box is legitimate—in fact, it is necessary for democracy. The law must treat the voter's decision as not needing any justification other than the fact that the voter made it.

A decision-making arrangement does not count as arbitrary government, if there is a good reason for leaving the decision maker free to act the way that he or she wishes, without requiring any justification for the decision other than the fact that the decision maker made it. To identify arbitrary government, we must be able to identify acts that call for—and lack—a technique for *other institutions* to decide what justification the acts may have, aside from the mere will of the initial decision-maker. So, for example, Parliament's power to levy an income tax is not an example of arbitrary government, just because other institutions have no legal power to control it; that exercise of power needs to be controlled by the people, and control by any other institution would not make the decision less arbitrary. But a decision-making arrangement is arbitrary if it needs to be controlled by other institutions, and it is not. That would be a failure in the rule of law. And a particular decision is arbitrary, if legal institutions can identify it as a departure from responsible government.

- **Arbitrary government is government that is contrary to the rule of law.**
- **A decision is arbitrary in the sense relevant to the rule of law, if it is one that other institutions can identify as not responding to the relevant considerations.**

In *Abbasi's* case, why wasn't it arbitrary for the Foreign Secretary to refuse to demand the release of a man who was being arbitrarily detained abroad? If the court does not need to leave it to the government to decide whether detentions are necessary in a case like *A and X*, why leave it to the government to decide whether to demand Abbasi's release by a foreign power?

The judges held that the considerations at stake in the Foreign Secretary's decision included the answers to questions such as whether Britain ought to stand shoulder-to-shoulder with the Americans in combating terrorism and, if so, whether demanding the return of British detainees would damage the alliance, and how it would affect relations with other countries besides the Americans. The Court of Appeal held that those questions are not **justiciable** (see p 239). That is, they are not suitable for judges to decide. There were two crucial issues in both *Abbasi* and *A and X*: the first is whether there are considerations at stake that the courts cannot assess. The second is whether the interests of the claimant need to be protected by the court in spite of any such issues. If the British government is detaining suspects, as in *A and X*, the decision may affect relations with other countries in ways that the court cannot pass judgment on. But the court can still identify indefinite detention as arbitrary, regardless of the other issues at stake. A court is able to decide whether the Home Secretary is acting arbitrarily if he detains people indefinitely without a trial; but a court cannot determine whether the Foreign Secretary is acting arbitrarily, if he refuses to make representations to a foreign government.

Some of the most important executive decisions are simply not controlled by law (such as the decision to put a bill before Parliament), or are barely controlled by law (such as the decision to wage war, or to sign treaties). They can be exercised capriciously and with no regard to the relevant considerations, and then they are arbitrary in a sense. But they are not arbitrary in the sense that is contrary to the rule of law, because legal institutions are not capable of determining whether they respond to the relevant considerations, without damaging the constitutional function of the executive.

The core of administrative law is the provision of processes independent of the government, for the prevention of government action that can be identified as

> arbitrary with no breach of comity. That is, the core task of administrative law
> is to impose the rule of law on public authorities.

The main point of administrative law is to stand against arbitrary government, by imposing the rule of law on executive action. The law can often do more than that to promote good government. What more can the law do? There is no general answer to this question. The reason is that administration is extremely complicated.

FROM THE MISTS OF TIME

Under Henry VIII, Commissioners of Sewers were given statutory power to provide public services such as drainage ditches, and power to charge landowners for the expense. The Privy Council ordered that no actions should be entertained in the courts against the Commissioners of Sewers. Two centuries later, William Blackstone looked back on the early development of judicial review as follows: 'The pretense for such arbitrary measures [preventing claims against the Commissioners] was no other than the tyrant's plea, of the necessity of unlimited powers in works of evident utility to the public, "the supreme reason above all reasons, which is the salvation of the king's lands and people." But now it is clearly held, that this (as well as all other inferior jurisdictions) is subject to the discretionary coercion of his majesty's court of king's bench.' *Commentaries on the Laws of England* (1765–1769), Book 3 Chapter 6.

● *Pop quiz* ●

The 'tyrant's plea' was an argument of **comity**—i.e., an argument that judicial interference with the executive would damage the ability of the executive to carry out its constitutional function. If courts ought to act with comity toward the executive, what was wrong with that argument?

1.2 Administration

'Administrative' is used in a very broad sense in administrative law. Administration is more than just the operation of government departments and the carrying out of government programmes. The **executive** includes all public authorities except the courts and Parliament.[3] **Administration** includes all the conduct of the executive except conduct in Parliament, such as presenting bills to the House of Commons or the House of Lords, or answering questions in the House of Commons. Administrative law controls decision-makers who are more or less independent from the government, such as the Crown Prosecution Service (see p 254), and decision makers who are almost as independent from the government as judges (such as tribunals (see Chapter 12) and ombudsmen (see Chapter 13).

---

3   What about private agencies doing work for the government? See Chapter 15.

> **Jargon alert**
>
> 'Government' is organized action on behalf of a political community; the phrase
> 'the government' can be used very widely to include all the agencies engaged in
> government, but it is usually used for the political leadership of the executive in
> an independent state. So in Britain, 'the government' usually means the Prime
> Minister and the other ministers of the Crown who are appointed on the advice the
> Prime Minister.

What's more, 'administrative law' includes the legal control of much decision making that is not administrative at all, and is not done by the executive. It controls the operation of the courts that are traditionally called 'inferior courts'—courts that have been created by statutes that specify their jurisdiction (I will call them 'courts of specific jurisdiction'; the High Court, by contrast, has a general inherent jurisdiction over the administration of justice).

The sturdy skeleton of 21st-century administrative law was created in the 13th to 17th centuries, as the judges in the court of King's Bench developed techniques for monopolizing the administration of justice. After the King's special courts disappeared in the Glorious Revolution of 1688, the King's Bench exercised supervisory jurisdiction over all other public authorities except Parliament and the courts of equity, in a process that has come to be called 'judicial review'. For centuries more it was still thought that the prerogatives of the Crown could not be controlled by the judges. After the 17th century, prerogatives were always exercised on the advice of the ministers of the Crown. 'On the advice of' the ministers means, in effect, by the ministers, and it was long thought that the ministers' responsibility to Parliament was the only constitutional control on prerogative. But in a line of cases running from the 1980s into this decade, the judges have asserted jurisdiction to decide the lawfulness of *any* exercise of government power, where the issues at stake are suitable for a court to determine.

So the 'administrative' in 'administrative law' refers to all public action that is not taken in the High Court or in Parliament. And in the 21st century, the judges use techniques that they developed in the Middle Ages to control almost all government action, including the government's responses to terrorism.

1.3 The principle of relativity

Because administrative law controls such a vast and complex diversity of exercises of power, its effect depends quite radically on various features of a particular exercise of power. The way in which the law ought to control a decision —if at all—depends on:

- the type of power being exercised;

- the nature of the body (the expertise of its members and the degree to which they are independent of government, etc.);

- the processes by which it acts;

- the sorts of considerations that need to be taken into account if the power is to be exercised with integrity; and

- the way it affects particular people,

—and more. The variety of these features of decisions has two important consequences. First, it has led to the development of a complex assortment of institutions and legal processes for controlling the exercise of public powers. Secondly, it means that any particular legal process for the control of government must operate with attention to the diversity of forms of public power that may be under control. As a result, it is very hard to generalize about the rules that ought to govern the courts' general jurisdiction first, to control different powers and secondly, to supervise other techniques for controlling the exercise of power.

The requirements of administrative law, and the processes that it provides, must not depend on the whims of the government, or on the likes and dislikes of the judges. But they must depend on the context—on the nature of the body that makes an administrative decision, and on the type of decision, and on the nature of the impact it has on people who want to complain about it, and on the circumstances in which it is made. Lord Steyn said in R (Daly) v Home Secretary [2001] 2 AC 532, 548 that 'In law context is everything.' In R (Persey) v Environment Secretary [2002] EWHC 371 [43], Simon Brown LJ called that 'the most quoted dictum in all of administrative law'.

But Lord Steyn must have been speaking ironically: context is not everything. Contexts are the sets of circumstances in which everything plays out. The basic reasons for the rules of administrative law are, for the most part, very general constitutional principles that are just as sound in other countries and, as we will see, in the European Union (EU) (see e.g., p 293). And for the most part, those principles have been recognized for centuries. Administrative law has undergone significant transformations not only in the past century but in each of the past six decades. Even the abstract principles of the constitution have changed since the Middle Ages. But the common strands are remarkable.

The rest of this chapter outlines the principles; the rest of the book will explain how their application by various institutions, through various processes, depends on the contexts in which official power is exercised.

1.4 The principles of the constitution

Principles are abstract, basic rules—starting points for reasoning about what is to be done. A principle is a *constitutional* principle if:

- it regulates what constitutions regulate (that is, the framework of government), and

- it does so in the way that constitutions regulate things (that is, by putting issues off the agenda of day-to-day politics).

Freedom of expression is a principle of our constitution. What makes it so? First of all, the principle regulates the framework of government, since it protects the ability to criticize the government, and promotes accountability.[4] But what takes political censorship off the agenda in day-to-day politics? Not just the fact that Britain has signed the European Convention on Human Rights, or that the Human Rights Act gives certain forms of legal effect to the Convention (see Chapter 3), or that it would be a tort for the government to close down a printing press by force for criticizing the government (see Chapter 14). In fact, a treaty (like the European Convention), a statute, and a rule of the common law cannot by themselves make anything into a constitutional principle, because Parliament can repeal its statutes, and change the common law, and the constitution does not prohibit the government from violating its treaty commitments. A constitutional principle cannot be repealed by a statute, and it must bind the government. Our unwritten constitution has no principles at all, unless the institutions of government adhere to them to some extent. But then, a country with a written constitution is the same—the institutions of government must adhere to the principles set out in the document to some extent, or they are only a sham.

Freedom of expression is a principle of the British constitution because the authorities that have power under the constitution regulate themselves and each other, to some extent, in a way that is guided by the principle. To identify a principle of a country's constitution, you must find support for it in the constitutional institutions' conduct. You must be able to say that it is *their* principle. Saying that can be consistent with a great deal of conduct that is contrary to the principle. So, for example, the separation of powers was already a British constitutional principle, even when the Home Secretary had the legal power to decide how long prisoners on life sentences would stay in prison (a power that violated the principle).

Parliamentary sovereignty (a law-making power that is not limited by law) is a principle of our constitution. Does that mean that the constitution has no other principles, because nothing is put off the ordinary political agenda? No: it only means that Parliament has lawful power to decide to what extent British law adheres to the principles of the constitution. Parliament has the power to infringe freedom of speech, or to empower others to do so.[5] If it did, it would act against a constitutional principle. If Parliament infringes freedom of speech so extravagantly that the framework of our government is no longer generally committed to freedom of speech, then freedom of speech will no longer be a principle of the constitution at all.

Why have constitutional principles? The point of regulating the framework of government in a way that puts some issues off the political agenda is to support good government.

4   Freedom of speech protects much more than just speech criticizing the government; it is not just a constitutional principle.

5   Doing so might infringe the European Convention on Human Rights; that would violate Britain's treaty obligations, and would give judges a power under the Human Rights Act to declare that Parliament had acted incompatibly with the Convention, but Parliament's action would still have force in English law. See Chapter 3.

1.4.1 Good government

Government is organized action on behalf of the community. *Good* government acts justly on behalf of the community, and makes the community a good community. Or at least, it does the limited things that can be done for that purpose by organized action. The principles of good government include efficiency and compassion. They include the duty to pay attention to everything that is necessary for government to serve a community well.

Administrative law has a very important role in securing good government, but it is a strictly limited role. Administrative law only supports good government indirectly, by doing what the law can effectively do to secure *responsible government*. The first constitutional principle of administrative law is that good government requires responsible government.

1.4.2 Responsible government

Responsible government responds to the considerations that make for good government. So, for example, instead of pursuing the personal benefit of the rulers, responsible government responds to the needs of the community (for everything from good roads, to social security, to integrity in foreign relations). Responsible government means, primarily, that government action is taken in the interest of the governed (and not for the personal advantage of the officials). But it is only *primarily* in the interest of the governed, because responsible government does not abuse strangers to serve the interests of the governed. If military attacks on other countries and unjust policies toward refugees are in the interest of the people of this country, that does not mean that our officials are acting responsibly if they take those actions. And if abusing a few of us would benefit most of us, that does not mean that we will have responsible government if our officials do it. Responsible government, while acting in the interests of the governed, also responds to the community's duties of justice to the powerless, and to visitors, and to outsiders. Even then, you might say, it is still responding to the interests of the governed in a sense, since they need a way in which their community can act with justice.

What is the difference between responsible government and good government? The added ingredient in good government is simply success. Responsible government aims in good faith to serve the community; good government serves the community well.

> **Responsible government** is **reasonable government** (see p 227 on what reasonableness is).

Irresponsible government, of course, is arbitrary government. Administrative law only indirectly promotes good government; it directly promotes responsible government, by standing against arbitrary government.

The constitutional principles of administrative law justify much of the law that is stated in this book. They also give good grounds for criticizing some important aspects of the law. And they explain its limitations. This chapter will outline two basic, interwoven groups of principles: **system principles**, and **principles of accountability**.[6] Both types of principle are against irresponsible government, so they indirectly promote good government. The two types are interwoven for various reasons: partly because adhering to the system principles makes government more accountable, and partly because non-legal forms of accountability can support that especially famous system principle, the rule of law.

1.5 System principles

1.5.1 The separation of powers

Like any good constitution, the British constitution allocates power to various distinct state institutions. It is very important (especially for administrative law) that the point of the separation of powers is not merely to spread power around among various bodies, but to create *two particular branches of government*—the courts and the legislature—that are distinct from the executive branch. And the separation of powers gives the executive, the courts, and the legislature *particular functions*.

In every constitution, the executive is the primary branch of government. The functions of the executive are open-ended, while the core judicial function (passing judgment on legal claims), and the core legislative functions (passing judgment on legislative proposals, and, in our constitution, scrutinizing and endorsing or removing the government) are much more limited functions of government action. The courts and the legislature can close down for the vacation, but the executive cannot.[7] Neither the courts nor the legislation handle guns. So it is the executive that is chiefly responsible for the rule of law. In Britain, Parliament can change the constitution, and the courts can determine the law of the constitution, but it is the government that must uphold the constitution. And all the powers of the separate branches of the state are inherited from the unified executive power of the Crown. At the time of the Norman Conquest, the Crown was a symbol for the person of the monarch, who really did control the executive, judicial, and legislative power of the state. Today, the Crown is a symbol for a symbol. It is a symbol for the Queen, who is herself a symbol for the power of the state, which is exercised by the government. The judges are called the Queen's judges, and legislation is said to be passed by the Queen in Parliament. But even in countries like the United States and South Africa, the

---

[6] Further principles, of less generality, are explained throughout the book; they mostly represent facets of the broad principles outlined here. Note, also, that many general substantive principles of the law are relevant to administrative law. For example, the principle of freedom of speech, discussed above, affects the way in which administrative law should regulate the use of public power.

[7] But the courts cannot *altogether* close down: it is important for the rule of law that you should be able to find a judge in the vacation, or in the middle of the night, to issue a writ of *habeas corpus*: this was first achieved in the Habeas Corpus Act 1679.

executive is the primary branch of government. While these countries adopted constitutions approved through deliberation in assemblies, it took executive acts to set up the processes and to convene the assemblies.[8]

Why are powers separated into these three particular functions (judicial, legislative, and executive)? In any process of constitution formation, the executive has reasons to allocate powers to special institutions that are more or less independent of the executive, and to which the executive will be accountable:

- **Responsible government needs an effective agency for making clear, open, prospective, stable, general rules for the community.** So in the *Case of Proclamations* (1611) 12 Co Rep 74, Lord Coke held that the Crown has no prerogative to change the common law or statute, or to create new offences.

- **Responsible government needs an independent and effective agency to resolve disputes over the rules.** So in *Prohibitions del Roy* (1607) 12 Co Rep 63, Lord Coke held that the King could not decide cases in the courts. Coke explained it on the basis that the 'artificial reason and judgment of law' take special training, but he was being polite: if the King trained as a common lawyer, it would still be inappropriate for him to sit as a judge. The reason is the constitutional need to prevent the executive from certain sorts of abuse of power. The constitution does so by authorizing independent judges to determine the requirements of the law.

Finally, each branch needs to be well organized for its own tasks. That means, incidentally, that *all three* branches must carry out executive, legislative, and judicial tasks:

	Executive functions	Judicial functions	Legislative functions
Executive branch	...	Deciding some complaints against government departments	Delegated legislation, legislation under the prerogative
Judicial branch	Keeping order in the court and managing facilities	...	Making rules governing procedures and the costs of litigation
Legislative branch	Policing order in Parliament, administering the process for voting on bills	Deciding disputes over contempt and breach of privilege	...

Figure 1.1 Examples of the varied functions within branches of the state

Powers need to be separated *within* branches, and not just between branches. This is one reason for the complexity of administration. In the executive branch, it is

---

[8]   We can actually put England in the same category: after the Glorious Revolution in 1688, William of Orange summoned the irregular Parliament that declared him to be King and passed the Bill of Rights.

extremely important that police and prosecutors are able to operate independently of the government; some agencies act at arm's length from government with various forms of accountability to ministers (see Chapter 15), while departments act at the direction of ministers. The chambers of the legislature need speakers who can exercise executive power on behalf of the chamber. The courts need judges and administrators to carry out the legislative work of making rules and the executive work of allocating judges to cases, and so on.

The separation of powers has an importance to the constitution that is wider than its role in controlling the executive. What role does it have in administrative law? It has two roles: first, some administrative decision-making power needs to be separated from control by the government; separation of powers *within* the executive branch of government is a crucial feature of the statutory creation of a multitude of quasi-independent tribunals in the 20th century. The reconstruction of tribunals in the Tribunals, Courts and Enforcement Act 2007 has enhanced their independence, and made them more like courts (see Chapter 12).

Secondly, the separation of powers requires good decisions as to the limits of administrative power. It is a reason for taking certain decisions away from executive officials (and, therefore, right out of the domain of administrative law), and giving them to judges. The most dramatic example is the judges' use of the Human Rights Act to declare that it was incompatible with the European Convention on Human Rights for the Home Secretary to decide the 'tariff' of time to be spent in prison by a prisoner on a life sentence (see p 50). The executive should not have excessive legislative power, and it should not have powers that ought to be exercised by judges.

1.5.2 Subsidiarity

Subsidiarity is familiar to students of European law, because of the special role it has played both in political debates about European integration, and in the legal development of the effect of European law in member states. The principle is that government power ought to be assigned at the right level. Larger, more remote organizations should not take over tasks that can be carried out more effectively and justly at a level that is closer to the people whom the organizations ought to serve. So, for example, subsidiarity explains the dominant role that the EU plays in the international trade of member states, and the peripheral role that the EU plays in criminal law and family law.

But subsidiarity is not simply a European principle. It explains the special tasks of local authorities. And it is a principle of law in general: the law's role in regulating your action and mine ought to be subsidiary to our own responsibility for our lives, rather than treating us like slaves. As a constitutional principle, subsidiarity promotes responsible government. It is a guide to allocating power to the institutions that can exercise it most responsibly.

> **Margin of appreciation**
> The principle of subsidiarity can be seen at work in the leeway that the European Court of Human Rights in Strasbourg allows to the authorities of contracting states, in passing judgment on what the Convention rights require in the context of particular countries (see p 96).

1.5.3 Comity

Separation of powers and subsidiarity are principles of power allocation; comity is the respect that a public authority ought to show for the work of another public authority. You might say that it is respect for the separation of powers, and for subsidiarity. It is not enough to have separate branches of the state; we also need each public authority to act in a way that is compatible with the roles of other public authorities.

Article 9 of the Bill of Rights 1689 is a requirement of comity: 'That the freedom of speech and debates or proceedings in Parliament ought not to be impeached or questioned in any court or place out of Parliament'. The courts would be interfering with the constitutional function of Parliament if they allowed lawsuits for defamation against MPs for what they say in the House of Commons. The irony is that it is no better for someone to tell damaging lies about you in the House of Commons than it is anywhere else. The Bill of Rights thus prevents certain injustices from being remedied by the courts. That is not as shocking as it sounds, because although everyone has a right not to be defamed, no one has a right to a *remedy against* defamation that would interfere with the representation of the people. Comity always has this ironic effect: it prevents one institution from doing justice, in order to preserve the capacity of another institution for good government.

Comity is a crucially important principle of administrative law, because of the judges' remarkable ability to invent powers for themselves. They have a general, inherent jurisdiction over the administration of justice, which we saw in the story of *habeas corpus*. Why shouldn't they use that jurisdiction to replace all administrative decisions with their own decisions? The answer is complex, but bits of it are all too obvious: they wouldn't necessarily be better at it than other public authorities (and they might be worse), they do not represent the people, and their processes are only good for resolving legal disputes. And, most obvious of all, the constitution forbids it. Comity is a principle of the constitution, because the framework of government is regulated by the principle that a public authority (such as a court) ought to respect the constitutional functions of other public authorities.

> **A judicially enforceable rule that official action is unlawful if it is contrary to good government would transform a court into a governing council.**

1.5.4 The rule of law

A community is not ruled by law unless:

- the life of the community is governed by clear, open, stable, prospective, general standards,

- government officials adhere to those standards, and

- there are independent tribunals (i.e. courts) that regulate the conduct of the other institutions.

Two facets of the ideal of government by law are easily overlooked, and they are especially important for administrative law. First, the rule of law requires not just standards, but also processes. Secondly, the rule of law does *not* require that *everything* be controlled by clear, open, stable, prospective, general standards, or by legal processes. We cannot decide whether the community attains the ideal, unless we know which aspects of the conduct of government must be regulated by law.

The importance of process

The rule of law requires not just a set of standards, but also a set of processes. The processes must be designed to give effect to the standards, but that is not their only purpose. The processes must also serve the same purpose that the standards serve: that is, to support responsible government. Consider the change in setting a tariff of imprisonment for life prisoners, which used to be decided by politicians and is now decided by judges (see p 50). The change is a step toward the rule of law, but not because life sentences are now governed by rules. The standards that judges use in determining the tariff are no more definite than the standards that the Home Secretary used to use. But the new process is less arbitrary, because the decision is made by someone who, unlike the Home Secretary, is under no pressure to respond to public opinion as to what should happen to a particular murderer. In this respect, the life of our community is no longer ruled by politics.

What is to be ruled by law?

For a community to attain the rule of law (and to escape arbitrary government), the law must control some executive functions of government—but not all. Which functions need to be controlled by law, and how?

Why does the rule of law demand that judges decide the time that life prisoners spend in prison, when it does not demand that judges decide government expenditure, or appoint ministers, or set the income tax? The answer is that we can attain the rule of law without everything being controlled by law. The point of the rule of law is to prevent arbitrary government,[9] and for *that* purpose, we do not need legal standards or legal processes to control every governmental function. The rule of law

---

[9]   The rule of law is also opposed to *anarchy*, which means that effective executive decision making (and, e.g., the capacity to respond to emergencies without being prevented by legalities) is itself a requirement of the rule of law.

only requires a decision to be controlled by legal standards or processes if that will help to prevent arbitrary government.

As Lord Steyn put it, 'In our system of law the sentencing of persons convicted of crimes is classically regarded as a judicial rather than executive task.' (R v Home Secretary ex p Anderson [2002] UKHL 46 [39]). A sentencing decision by the executive is arbitrary, but the appointment of a minister on the mere say-so of the Prime Minister is not arbitrary. Not that it is all right for him to make bad appointments! But legal control of his decision cannot improve the appointment of ministers.

So the separation of powers and the rule of law are linked, in a way that is very important to administrative law. Attaining the rule of law requires that *some* official decisions be controlled by legal standards and processes; we cannot decide which decisions those are, without a clear understanding of the rationale for the separation of powers. And because the rule of law does not require all official decisions to be controlled by law in the same way, **comity** between the courts and the executive is a requirement of the rule of law. The executive branch must accept judicial decisions; conversely the law should not give legal institutions forms of control over the executive that they cannot exercise with respect for the function of the executive.

The judges' role in achieving the rule of law is more limited than it is sometimes thought to be. Yet they still have a critically important role, because the rule of law is a *reflexive* ideal: it requires the system to regulate itself. The judges' independence and effective power enable them to provide the self-regulation that a system of government needs, if it is to attain the rule of law. And for the same reason, the rule of law demands that the judges craft and abide by rules for their own conduct that will distinguish their actions from their arbitrary say-so. So, for example, *habeas corpus* gives judges a wide discretionary power, since it provides for a detainee to undergo 'whatever our court then and there may order concerning him'. But it gives the judges no power to release a detainee who is lawfully imprisoned.

The rule of law is not necessarily improved when judges interfere with administrative decisions. *More judicial control* of official action, and *more legal regulation* of the life of the community, do not necessarily bring the community closer to the ideal. In fact, excessive interference with administration at the whim of judges will actually detract from the rule of law. That is why comity is a requirement of the rule of law.

1.5.5 Principles allied to the rule of law

The principle of legality

An obvious, central requirement of the rule of law is that public officials should be bound by the law. That means that no administrative authority has discretion to violate the law or to suspend it. One aspect of this principle was enacted in Art 1 of the Bill of Rights 1689: 'the pretended power of suspending the laws or the execution of laws by regal authority without consent of Parliament is illegal.' The rule applies even to national defence: the government has a very wide discretionary power under the royal prerogative to defend the United Kingdom, but it cannot do so by raising taxes, or using land, or conscripting people, unless Parliament authorizes it by statute.

This principle of legality has a much broader application that is of great importance in the law of judicial review. First, if a statute sets out to protect administrative
action from judicial review, judges will bend over backwards to apply the legislation
restrictively, so that they can still prevent abuse of power (or even, so that they can
simply quash a decision that is incompatible with their interpretation of legislation;
see p 63). Secondly and more generally, the courts will read down general grants of
administrative power, so that the power must be used in a way that is compatible
with certain basic legal values. It is a 'familiar and well-established' principle that
'general words . . . should not be read as authorising the doing of acts which adversely
affect the basic principles on which the law of the United Kingdom is based' (*Jackson
v Attorney General* [2005] UKHL 56 [28]).

Which values do those basic principles protect? This is an aspect of the question
of what must be ruled by law, and what can justly be left to executive decision. There
is no authoritative catalogue of legally protected values, and the result is that judicial review is dynamic: it is up to the judges to decide which basic values should be
protected against the general powers of public authorities. The foremost examples
involve the value of access to the courts themselves: it is the sphere in which the judges
feel most able to interfere with a general executive power. So the courts have quashed
a decision to raise the fees for commencing litigation and to remove the exemption
from fees for claimants on income support (R v Lord Chancellor, *ex p Witham* [1998] QB
575). And because prisoners may need access to their solicitors, and even to journalists, in order to pursue a campaign to right a miscarriage of justice, it has been held
unlawful for the Home Secretary to use a general power to regulate prisons in a way
that interferes disproportionately with a prisoner's correspondence with a solicitor
(R *(Daly) v Home Secretary* [2001] UKHL 26), or to impose a blanket ban on journalists
using interviews with prisoners (R v *Home Secretary ex p Simms* [2000] 2 AC 115 (HL)).

Even though there is no authoritative catalogue, the principle of legality protects
other values besides access to the courts. English law has always had a special regard
for property rights, and general powers to interfere with property have been controlled since the Commissioners of Sewers cases of the 1600s. We can add freedom of
expression to the list of protected values (not only in a case like *Simms* where it affects
access to the courts, but generally), but with a proviso: the protection that the judges
give to it varies widely depending on the other interests at stake in an administrative
decision that controls the media (R v *Home Secretary, ex p Brind* [1991] 1 AC 696). It is an
instance of the principle of relativity: varying forms of protection are given to different legally protected interests in varying circumstances.

The principle of legality has been 'expressly enacted', as Lord Hoffmann put it, in
the Human Rights Act 1998:

> s 3(1) So far as it is possible to do so, primary legislation and subordinate
> legislation must be read and given effect in a way which is compatible with the
> Convention rights.[10]

---

[10]   R v Home Secretary ex p Simms [2000] 2 AC 115, 132.

That applies to legislation granting general administrative powers, so that they cannot be used to violate Convention rights, unless the legislation authorizes it. And there is an authoritative catalogue of the protected values for the purpose of the Human Rights Act: they are the values protected by the Convention rights (see Chapter 3). But even under the Convention, the context is still essential: the protection given to freedom of speech, for example, depends on the other interests at stake in a decision.

> **On the role of the principle of legality in judicial review, see** p 266.

Due process

All governmental decisions ought to be made by processes that put the relevant considerations effectively before the decision makers. Very often, the only effective way to achieve that goal is to give people affected by the decision an opportunity to participate in the process. If a public authority is deciding whether you committed murder, you ought to be able to participate in ways that would be superfluous or damaging when a public authority is deciding whether to build a new school in your town. The role that you ought to have in the process varies radically, depending on the nature of the decision, and the way in which it affects you, and whether the decision maker needs your input in order to grasp the relevant considerations. There is no general right to any form of participation in official decisions, but there is a right to a form of participation that is due, in the circumstances.

┌─ FROM THE MISTS OF TIME ─────────────────────────────────

Due process (see chapter 4) is an ancient English idea. If you are familiar with the phrase 'due process' from Hollywood lawyer movies, that is because the Americans inherited it from the time of the Plantagenets, and wrote it into their Bill of Rights: the Fifth Amendment provides that 'No person shall be...deprived of life, liberty, or property, without due process of law.'

By the Middle Ages, it was already an accepted legal principle that a person should be given the form of participation in a decision-making process that is due—that is, appropriate in the context. In the Petition of Right 1628, Parliament reminded King Charles that Parliament had guaranteed 'due process of law' nearly 300 years earlier: 'And in the eight-and-twentieth year of the reign of King Edward III, it was declared and enacted by authority of parliament, that no man, of what estate or condition that he be, should be put out of his land or tenements, nor taken, nor imprisoned, nor disinherited nor put to death without being brought to answer by due process of law.'[11]

---

11   '...nul homme, de quel estate ou condicion q'il soit, ne soit oste de titre ne de tenure, ne pris, n'emprisone, ne desherite, ne mis a la mort, saunz estre mesne en repons par due process de lei' 28 Ed III c 3 (1354).

There is an especially close relation between due process and the principle of legality. Courts protect legally recognized values not only by reading down general powers, but also by conferring special procedural protections on persons when a decision affects a basic legal value. So, for example, where a statute undeniably gives a public authority power to destroy property, the courts hold that the common law requirement of due process calls for the public authority to give a hearing to the person who owns the property (see p 108).

As a result of the close relationship between due process and the principle of legality, the law of due process gives us a deeper understanding of the values that both principles protect. For example, we can find a catalogue of legally protected values in the 1354 statute of due process: it protected title, land tenure, personal liberty, inheritance, and life. Compare the values protected 700 years later, in the European Convention on Human Rights: life, freedom from torture[12] and from slavery, personal liberty, freedom from retrospective punishment, privacy, family life, freedom of religion, expression, and association, freedom from discrimination, and (in the Protocols), property, education, free elections, freedom of movement, and freedom from expulsion. The Protocols also prohibit the death penalty.

What about the Bill of Rights 1689?

Its catalogue of protected values was a response to abuses of executive power under the Stuart Kings, and its focus was on protecting Parliament from the King. The Bill of Rights prohibited suspension of laws by the executive, taxation without approval by Parliament, prosecutions of people who bring petitions to the Crown, and the raising of a standing army. It protected the bearing of arms by Protestants, free elections, free speech in Parliament, freedom from excessive bail, freedom from cruel and unusual punishment, the proper use of juries, and frequent Parliaments. It was mostly a bill of Parliament's rights.

Access to justice

The legal processes for controlling government will be no good if people cannot get at them. Since they are legal processes, they are cumbersome and expensive. The challenge is partly for legal aid to provide public funding to challenge public authorities (which is outside the scope of this book), and partly for advocacy groups to undertake litigation in the public interest (see section 11.2 on campaign litigation).

---

[12]   Torture was inflicted before the Civil War on warrants issued by authority of the King. In *A and others v Home Secretary* [2005] UKHL 71, Lord Bingham said that the common lawyers had regarded torture as '"totally repugnant to the fundamental principles of English law" and "repugnant to reason, justice, and humanity"' [12]. Lord Bingham said that no warrant authorizing torture had been issued since 1640. The House of Lords unanimously held in *A and others* that the common law allows no admission of evidence obtained by torture.

Legal certainty

In R v Bolton (1841) 1 QB 66, the parish claimed that Bolton was occupying one of its houses as a pauper, and threw him out; he claimed that he had been paying rent for it. The magistrates decided against him, and in judicial review the court of Queen's Bench refused to hear evidence that the magistrates had got the facts wrong. Lord Denman CJ said, 'It is of much more importance to hold the rule of law straight than, from a feeling of the supposed hardship of any particular decision, to interpose relief at the expense of introducing a precedent full of inconvenience and uncertainty in the decision of future cases.'

English judges today lack Lord Denman's relish for leaving an injustice unremedied. Instead, they would rather run the risk of downplaying the value of legal certainty—'the principle that parties should know where they stand' (R (Thomas) v Central Criminal Court [2006] EWHC 2138 [20]). Legal certainty is one of the general principles of EC law developed by the European Court of Justice (ECJ).[13] It is especially important in the European Court of Human Rights,[14] because the Convention could be read to give the Court an open-ended power to revisit administrative decisions in a way that would have shocked Lord Denman. For example, the requirement of hearings by an independent tribunal in Art 6 of the Convention could have been read to require judges to review the merits of a vast range of administrative decisions. But the courts have declined to do so (see p 87–9). And in R (Beeson) v Dorset County Council [2002] EWCA Civ 1812, Laws LJ said, 'There is some danger, we think, of undermining the imperative of legal certainty by excessive debates over how many angels can stand on the head of the Art 6 pin' [15]. Lord Hoffmann added, 'Amen to that, I say' in Begum v Tower Hamlets LBC [2003] UKHL 5 [59].

The more power that judges are given to generate uncertainty, the more attention they need to pay to the principle of legal certainty. It is not generally an overriding value, but it is enough to generate a **presumption of non-interference** (see p 222)— that is, a rule that a decision made by a body to whom a power has been allocated is not to be interfered with merely because a different decision ought to have been made. There has to be some justification for undoing what has been done. In the High Court, such a justification is a 'ground of judicial review'.

1.5.6 What happened to justice?

Think of Mr Bolton, thrown out of his house and told by the Lord Chief Justice that it is more important to hold the rule of law straight than to do justice in a way that might create uncertainty. And let's suppose for the moment that the parish council's decision was unjust (we don't know, because the Court never heard the matter). Should the court have done justice in the case, or held to the rule of law?

....

[13] See, e.g., Case C-61/05 Commission v Portugal [2006] 3 CMLR 36, and Case C-310/04 Spain v Council [2006] ECR I-7285 [141].

[14] See Evans v United Kingdom (2006) 43 EHRR 21.

It is an injustice for a government agency to fail in its duty to act with due regard for the public interest and for the private interests that are at stake in public decisions. But not all injustices are controlled by law. And they cannot all be put right by judges. Every police officer, housing officer, teacher, politician—and in one way or another every one of our 6,000,000 public sector employees—has a responsibility for justice. So have decision-making institutions such as school boards and local councils. The role of the law in controlling all that is extremely important *and* strictly limited. Its importance can lead people to discount the limits or to forget them. The role of courts is *even more strictly limited* than the role of the law, because there are so many other legal institutions for controlling administration, and resort to the courts is meant to be a last resort (see p 60).

Imagine that the Prime Minister were to choose a crony as Chancellor of the Exchequer, instead of a person who could do the job much better. That would be an injustice to the whole nation, but the rule of law does not require a remedy for it. In fact, comity would forbid the High Court to interfere. If a politician who had been overlooked went to the High Court and asked the judges to quash the Prime Minister's decision on the ground that the decision was unjust, the Court should not even give permission for the claimant to seek judicial review. Even in the face of an allegation of injustice, the court's role is limited by its responsibility for the rule of law. It would be a breach of comity, and not an assertion of the rule of law, for judges to review the decision. This limitation on the courts' role allows judges to remedy many injustices, but not all.

So in Mr. Bolton's case, the Court was right to refuse to consider the magistrates' decision, if it would have been a breach of comity to question their decision on the facts. But if the Court could have reviewed the decision without damaging the magistrates' ability to do their job, then the Court missed an opportunity to do justice according to law.[15]

How to reconcile justice and the rule of law

Comity is a system principle that requires constitutional institutions *not* to act on principles of justice! But the reasons for the principle of comity are themselves reasons of justice: it will promote just government under the constitution, if the institutions allow each other to function without undue interference. And interference with a decision can be inappropriate, even if the decision itself was unjust. Comity is a requirement of responsible government.

Consider **proportionality** (see section 8.3). It is a crucial principle of justice: a decision maker must not impose a greater burden on someone than is justified by the attainment of some good goal. All government action ought to respect this principle. But its *legal* effect is strictly limited, and its limited role in the law reflects the limited role of administrative law in doing justice. The judge or other legal authority

---

[15]   The courts today would take a different approach from Lord Denman's; they would hear the case, but would quash the magistrates' finding of fact only if it were plainly untenable (see section 9.2.4).

applying the principle of proportionality may not be best placed to decide what is proportionate.

Proportionality is a principle of good government, but it is not a principle of the constitution, because the framework of government cannot generally be regulated by giving one institution authority to pass judgment on whether decisions of another institution are proportionate. And the circumstances in which courts can quash an administrative decision purely on grounds of proportionality are limited: they depend on the requirements of due process and the principle of legality. The separation of powers is a fundamental principle of the constitution that requires that different kinds of decision as to what is proportionate be allocated to different institutions. The judges have no general jurisdiction to impose justice on other officials.

1.6 Accountability

An accountable government faces up to people. Accountability is a fundamental requirement for responsible government, because public officials cannot be trusted to act responsibly if they don't have to face up to anyone.

The principle of accountability is unspecific. The reach of the principle is much broader than law: the most constitutionally important accountability techniques are the political techniques of democracy. At the national level, democracy is secured through the combination of:

- elections to Parliament;

- the constitutional rule that entrusts the government to the party with the confidence of the House of Commons;

- the rule that ministers of the Crown must answer questions in Parliament;

- the practice of debating policy in Parliament as well as deliberating over legislation; and

- the rule that the power of the Crown is to be exercised on the advice of the ministers.

Democracy is also secured at different levels, through different democratic mechanisms, in the European Union[16] and in local government. At all these levels of government the law regulates elections, and gives legal effect to legislative decisions. But effective government accountability depends on much more than just law. It depends on party politics, on participation by voters, on independent and critical media, and on the commitment and integrity of Members of Parliament and other representatives. The role of the media gives a healthy reminder of the limited role of

---

[16] Those mechanisms are not found chiefly in the role of the European Parliament (it is not the legislature; it shares legislative power with the Council). Democracy in the EU depends on democratic processes in the Member States, whose representatives make up the Council; Member States also nominate Commissioners (subject to approval by the European Parliament). See http://europa.eu/abc/12lessons/lesson_4/index_en.htm.

law in the accountability of the government: the law needs to protect the newspapers from political censorship, but the government will not be held to account unless the companies that run the newspapers actually allow journalists to do their job, and the journalists are committed to their work. And all that will happen only if people buy the newspapers that criticize the government.

Accountability needs to take diverse forms in a complex 21st-century state. Parliament imposes certain forms of political accountability on government and the courts impose certain forms of legal accountability, but accountability has to reach far beyond the courts and Parliament. Auditors hold public authorities to account for their finances, and their decisions may be backed by massive financial penalties for officials involved in corruption. Rewards (such as promotion processes) provide a form of accountability. Other accountability techniques are effective because they create publicity that has crucial political effects. Some are effective merely because they are embarrassing to the individuals involved who make decisions on behalf of public authorities. Public authorities ought to be accountable in a wide variety of ways to a wide variety of people and institutions—to ombudsmen, to public inquiries, to police investigations, to school inspectors, to a variety of tribunals, to the voters, to the media, to the courts, to the institutions of the European Union, to the states that are party to the Geneva Conventions, to the United Nations...

This book is about a limited set of accountability techniques: the legal ones. Legal accountability is imposed by laws that give one institution or public official legal power to call another to account. It encompasses a relatively limited yet still vast array of accountability techniques. Legal accountability is neither more nor less important than other forms of accountability. It is often thought that Parliament is failing to provide proper political accountability, and that the courts have had to step into the breach, through judicial review. But that depressing view of parliamentary control of the executive is actually irrelevant to public law. Judicial control of government decisions has a limited scope, but it is not secondary to Parliament's very different power to control government (see p 53). Parliament and the courts each have distinct supervisory functions over the government. So the political and legal processes serve as complementary accountability techniques.

Securing accountability

Special legal problems arise when the government contracts out operations to private companies. If a local authority provides housing, the law controls its decisions. For example, Art 8 of the European Convention requires the authority to respect the tenants' privacy. Tenants can challenge the lawfulness of the local authority's decisions, under the Human Rights Act. What happens if the local authority pays a private company to provide housing, and the service provider invades the tenants' privacy? The local authority will say that it has not invaded the tenants' privacy, and the company will say that the Human Rights Act does not apply to it because it is not a public authority. Chapter 15 deals with the ways in which legal accountability can be disrupted by contracting out.

1.6.1 Open government: a new constitutional principle?

In *Local Government Board v Arlidge* [1915] AC 120, the court refused to order a government department to disclose advice it had received from a planning inspector. Lord Shaw said that a court order of disclosure would be inconsistent 'with efficiency, with practice, and with the true theory of complete parliamentary responsibility for departmental action' (137). In 1947, Lord Greene approved of the *Arlidge* approach, saying that 'the idea that a Minister can be compelled to disclose to anybody information…which he has obtained as a purely administrative person, is alien to our whole conception of government in this country' (*B Johnson & Co v Minister of Health* [1947] 2 All ER 395, 401).[17] The theory of parliamentary responsibility for departmental action, and in fact 'our whole conception of government', have changed since those cases were decided. The result is a massive gain in accountability, because a minister becomes more accountable, if he or she has to disclose the information on which a governmental decision is based. The change has partly been the result of legislation.

The **Freedom of Information Act 2000** (it only came into full effect in 2005) provides a right to *some* government information. Before that, no one outside Parliament had any right to demand information from the government, except (1) under the duties that public authorities have to give reasons for some decisions (see Chapter 6), and (2) in litigation (if they are given permission to seek judicial review, claimants can get disclosure of information relevant to their claims).[18] The new right to information is general: that is, you don't need a reason for asking for it. You have a right to information *unless* the public authority has some reason not to give it to you. But statutory exemptions restrict the right, and they give public authorities some dangerous grounds for withholding information.

After an initial rush, the volume of requests under the Freedom of Information Act has averaged just over 2,500 per month, adding up to more than 60,000 in the first two years;[19] just over 60% of requests are granted initially. Most refusals have been based on the exemptions for personal or confidential information, or for information on investigations by public authorities. But hundreds of requests have been refused on the basis of the rather worrying exemptions: for information on 'the formulation or development of government policy' (s 35(1)(a)), and information that might 'inhibit the free and frank provision of advice, or the free and frank exchange of views for the purposes of deliberation', or might 'prejudice the effective conduct of public affairs' (s 36(2)). Those exemptions are tailor-made to preserve a culture of secrecy in government; they mirror the objections that governments used to make to passing freedom of information legislation at all.

---

[17] He approved of the approach of the House of Lords in *Arlidge*.

[18] Another exception was audit information; see below.

[19] Statistics are available at http://www.foi.gov.uk/reference. Note that we have no measure of how much information has been made publicly available as a result of the Act, by public authorities that know they will need to release it if a request is made.

Rejected

The following are examples of requests turned down under the exemption for dis-
closures that would harm the development of government policy (s 35(1)(a)):

- Home Office reports on 'the impact of its plans for compulsory ID cards';
- the Health Department chief economic adviser's report into the relation
  between MRSA and bed occupancy; and
- policy discussions on the future of school funding.

Information on the public cost of guarding Prince Charles and Camilla Parker
Bowles was refused on the ground of the potential threat to royal security, and
Tony Blair's Christmas card list was withheld on the ground that disclosure would
be harmful to international relations.[20]

The 'policy' and 'prejudice' exemptions are a bar to accountability, and they give
public authorities a potentially arbitrary power. Is the power adequately controlled?
You can ask for an internal review if a public authority does not disclose information you request. If you are still not satisfied, you can complain to the Information
Commissioner, who can issue a notice requiring disclosure. You and the public
authority can appeal to the Information Tribunal if you are not satisfied with the
Commissioner's decision.[21] The Tribunal's decision can be appealed on a question of
law to the High Court (Freedom of Information Act 2000 s 59). The 'policy' exemption and the 'prejudice' exemption will provide a cloak for the embarrassing things
that secretive officials would really rather not disclose, unless the Information
Commissioner, the Information Tribunal, and, ultimately, the courts, are prepared
to act on their own judgment on the effect of the disclosure on administration.

The **Public Interest Disclosure Act 1998** supplements public access to information—and public accountability—by protecting 'whistleblowers' who disclose
information about malpractice. Malpractice includes a criminal offence, a failure
to comply with any legal obligation, a miscarriage of justice, a danger to health or
safety, or environmental damage (s 1).[22] If the disclosure is to the media, though,
it is only protected if the whistleblower first raised the matter internally or with a
regulator, or reasonably believed that doing so would result in victimization or a
cover-up. Victimization in breach of the Act entitles a complainant to damages in an
employment tribunal. In July 2005, an employment tribunal awarded Carol Lingard
£470,000 in compensation for constructive dismissal, after she was victimized for
telling her superiors of claims that prisoners were being bullied at Wakefield high-
security jail.

---

[20]   *The Independent* (London 28 December 2006) 2.

[21]   See http://www.dca.gov.uk/foi/guidance/proguide/chap09.htm.

[22]   The Act does not protect members of the armed forces, intelligence services, or police forces.

As with the Freedom of Information Act, there are still tensions in the government's moves toward openness. In 2000, a whistleblowers' charity successfully asked the High Court to order that Employment Tribunal records of cases should provide enough information for them to be able to identify whistleblower cases that had settled before a hearing.[23] The Department of Trade and Industry played for time by appealing, while they prepared regulations that would cancel the effect of the decision. The Parliamentary Ombudsman investigated the DTI, and reported 'I strongly criticise them for that.'[24]

The **Audit Commission Act 1998** governs the independent inspection of the accounts of local authorities, health authorities, and police and fire authorities. The audits themselves open a window on the public authorities, because the reports are public, and the authorities must consider them at meetings which are at least partly open. But the Act also provides that 'any persons interested may…inspect the accounts to be audited and all books, deeds, contracts, bills, vouchers and receipts relating to them' (s 15). The provision has been interpreted broadly to include as a 'person interested' a local TV company wanting to use the information for a programme on a private landlord who provided care services funded by the local authority for vulnerable people: R (HTV Ltd) v Bristol City Council [2004] EWHC 1219.

In spite of the tensions, these three new statutes form one aspect of a general trend toward more open government. The courts have also taken important steps; the most notable are described in the account of the changes in the law of due process in Chapters 4 and 6: the increase in availability of oral hearings, duties of disclosure of information before a hearing, and enhanced duties to give reasons for decisions. And since the 1970s, the doctrine of legitimate expectations (see Chapter 8.4) has made it much more difficult for the government to make secret changes in its policies and practices. In one leading case, Lord Mustill identified a general trend: 'I find in the more recent cases on judicial review a perceptible trend towards an insistence on greater openness, or if one prefers the contemporary jargon "transparency", in the making of administrative decisions' (R v Home Secretary, ex p Doody [1994] 1 AC 531, 561).

What's more, judicial review itself has become an aspect of the trend. Public interest litigation (bringing a claim to pursue a campaign in the public interest rather than to obtain personal benefit) has turned the court into a new kind of forum in which political activists can hold the government to account (see section 11.2). And remarkably, the courts have given permission to seek judicial review to claimants who have no prospect of success, just because they raise issues so important that they deserve an airing (such as the government's refusal to hold a public inquiry into its decision to invade Iraq: R (Gentle) v Prime Minister [2006] EWCA Civ 1078; see p 370).

---

[23] R v Employment Tribunals, ex p Public Concern at Work [2000] IRLR 658.

[24] Parliamentary Commissioner for Administration report PA-3002/0058, 1 August 2005 [85]. On ombudsmen, see Chapter 13.

> ### Public interest immunity
> Until *Conway v Rimmer* [1968] AC 910, public authorities had a 'Crown privilege' to
> withhold documents in litigation (see *Duncan v Cammell Laird and Co Ltd* [1942] AC
> 624). It was a legally uncontrolled power (like the privilege of private parties not
> to disclose correspondence with their solicitors). In *Conway*, the House of Lords
> held that the courts' responsibility for the administration of justice required
> them to decide whether there was a sufficiently urgent public interest to justify
> non-disclosure. The decision in *Conway* increased disclosure in litigation, and was
> a landmark in the dismantling of the generalized deference to government that
> judges had (sometimes) shown in the first half of the 20th century.

Consultation

The government has contributed to its own openness, partly through the expanded
use of public consultation in policy development. The Cabinet Office has a code of
practice for consultation on plans for central government policies and regulations.
It recommends clear, concise, and widely accessible consultation involving 'a minimum of 12 weeks for written consultation at least once during the development of
the policy'. The code also calls for departments to give feedback on the responses
received and to explain how the consultation process influenced the policy.[25] Statutes
often require consultation on proposals that affect a group of people in such a way
that they ought to have a say in the policy decision (such as a proposal to close a
school (R v Leeds City Council, ex p N [1999] ELR 324), or to close a coal mine (R v Trade
and Industry Secretary, ex p Vardy [1993] 1 CMLR 721), or to sell a council estate (R v
Environment Secretary, ex p Walters (1998) 30 HLR 328)).

In principle, consultation offers a better democratic connection between government and the people, because it focuses specifically on an urgent problem for the
community, and gives the people affected a chance to give information and to make
argument. It is only meant to contribute to the government's policy formation, and
not to turn it into a judicial process. As Lord Woolf has said,

> It has to be remembered that consultation is not litigation: the consulting
> authority is not required to publicise every submission it receives or (absent some
> statutory obligation) to disclose all its advice. Its obligation is to let those who
> have a potential interest in the subject matter know in clear terms what the pro-
> posal is and exactly why it is under positive consideration, telling them enough
> (which may be a good deal) to enable them to make an intelligent response. The
> obligation, although it may be quite onerous, goes no further than this.[26]

---

[25] http://www.berr.gov.uk/whatwedo/bre/consultation-guidance/page44420.html.

[26] *R v North and East Devon Health Authority, ex p Coughlan* [2000] 3 All ER 850 [112].

But consultation *generates* litigation, because the people consulted often end up thinking that the 'consultation' was window-dressing for a decision that had already been taken. The classic administrative mistake is to make the decision before the end of the so-called consultation. That will be held to be procedurally unfair (R (*Parents for Legal Action Ltd*) *v Northumberland County Council* [2006] EWHC 1081). In judicial review, the courts will consider whether consultation required by statute was carried out in accordance with the statute, and will add duties of fairness not specified in the statute. But they will not overturn a decision where there is a technical defect in the consultation, if the purpose of the consultation has been accomplished (see *Walters*).

Consultation is a form of openness that the government brings upon itself. But the courts in the 21st century have made their auxiliary role in supervising consultations into a real nuisance for the government:

- if consultation is undertaken, it must be done properly (*Coughlan* [108]);

- if the government promises to consult before taking a decision, the courts will quash the decision if the consultation does not happen or is inadequate (R (*Greenpeace*) *v Trade and Industry Secretary* [2007] EWHC 311); and

- the United Kingdom has entered into a treaty requiring consultation before taking certain decisions with serious environmental impact,[27] and it seems that the courts will hold that such decisions are unlawful if the consultation has not been taken: 'in the development of policy in the environmental field consultation is no longer a privilege to be granted or withheld at will by the executive' (*Greenpeace* [49]).

Consultation in Europe

The European Commission has guidelines for consultations on policy initiatives before the adoption of a proposal; the principles of the scheme are 'participation, openness and accountability, effectiveness and coherence'. Its minimum standards include allowing eight weeks for written contributions from the public, the holding of public meetings, and response to contributions.[28]

Is openness a new constitutional principle?

We should not exaggerate the transforming effect of these developments: openness in government is not altogether new, and it is not guaranteed. To get things in perspective, keep in mind the forms of openness that the government has had

---

[27] Convention on Access to Information, Public Participation in Decision-making and Access to Justice in Environmental Matters ('the Aarhus Convention').

[28] http://ec.europa.eu/civil_society/consultation_standards/index_en.htm#_Toc46744748.

to live with for centuries. The most important is the power of MPs to ask questions of ministers in Parliament. The openness of the courts themselves is an important aspect of open government, and it is much older than the effective scrutinizing role of MPs. The independence of police and prosecutors is more recent, but it predates the 20th century.

And various forms of public inquiry are ancient. Since 1276 coroners—independent judicial investigators—have had a statutory duty to investigate 'the deaths of persons slain, drowned, or suddenly dead' (see R (Amin) v Secretary of State [2004] 1 AC 653 [16]), and even that statutory rule only confirmed the common law of the time. In Amin's case, Lord Bingham said that the point of the coroner's inquiry is 'to ensure so far as possible that the full facts are brought to light; that culpable and discreditable conduct is exposed and brought to public notice; that suspicion of deliberate wrongdoing (if unjustified) is allayed; that dangerous practices and procedures are rectified; and that those who have lost their relative may at least have the satisfaction of knowing that lessons learned from his death may save the lives of others' [31]. In this century, the European Court of Human Rights has enhanced the 'transparency and effectiveness' that are needed for public confidence in the investigation (Jordan v United Kingdom (2003) 37 EHRR 2 [144]).

Public inquiries have been required for decisions on land use planning for generations—both for government projects, and for the approval of private projects. In hearing the many challenges from opponents of planning decisions, the judges have enhanced procedural rights in inquiries.

And in certain respects, the role of judicial review in promoting open decision making goes back centuries. In Bentley's Case (1748) Fort 202, the court of King's Bench held that the University of Cambridge had to comply with natural justice by giving a doctor a hearing before depriving him of his degree. Fortescue J cited a decision of 1470 by the Chancellor and Judges, 'that it is required by the law of nature that every person, before he can be punish'd, ought to be present' (206). For more than five hundred years, it has been unlawful (unless specially authorized by statute) for the government to use administrative means to make a secret decision to punish anyone for anything.

Open government is only partly new, and cannot be taken for granted. But the principle that administrative information in general is to be open (subject to exemptions) really is a radically new principle, which has only developed since the 1990s. It is of constitutional importance. The value of transparency is partly that it can contribute to political control of government (by giving the opposition the opportunity to embarrass the government, and by letting MPs know what questions to ask in Parliament). It can also contribute to the rule of law (by exposing unlawful official conduct, and specifically by giving a potential claimant useful information in deciding whether to bring a legal claim against a public authority). But it has a more basic importance, because it makes the government face up to people: it is in itself an accountability technique.

1.7 Europe and the principles of the constitution

A breach of European Community law is unlawful in English law,[29] so acting incompatibly with Community law is a ground of judicial review. But Community law has a much broader significance for administrative law, because of the sophisticated techniques that the EJC uses in controlling the action of the institutions of the European Union. The EU has borrowed freely from the traditions of member states, and has developed new devices and doctrines aimed at enhancing the effectiveness of Community law, while imposing the rule of law on the EU institutions. In this book, you will find those devices and doctrines in sections on some of the trendiest topics—the role of ombudsmen (Chapter 13), the doctrine of proportionality (section 8.3), the protection of legitimate expectations (section 8.4), the practice of consultation on policy, and the very un-English doctrine of state liability to compensate for loss caused by unlawful state conduct (see p 553). These developments have become integral parts of the practice of administrative law in this country; they originate in the administrative law doctrine of the ECJ, and lawyers and judges have used them as sources of analogies to support arguments in the English courts.

The administrative law of the EU institutions is a creature of the treaties, and of the decisions of the ECJ. The ECJ reviews the legality of some acts of the institutions (the European Parliament, the Council, the Commission and the European Central Bank). An EU institution or a member state can bring a claim in the ECJ to annul a decision or measure taken by an institution (including the making of regulations). And any person can challenge a decision that is 'addressed to that person' or 'is of direct and individual concern' to him or her. This test for **standing** for private persons to challenge a decision is more demanding than the test of standing in English judicial review (see section 11.6). The restrictive test corresponds to the legislative nature of many of the measures that private parties might want to challenge; the ECJ has not wanted to offer a forum for the continuation of political battles that the EU law-making process was designed to resolve.

Article 230 of the EC Treaty provides that, 'the Court of Justice shall declare the act concerned to be void' if a claimant succeeds in showing that any of the following grounds apply:

- 'lack of competence,
- infringement of an essential procedural requirement,
- infringement of this Treaty or of any rule of law relating to its application, or
- misuse of powers'.

These grounds reflect the same concern for the rule of law that underlies the English law of judicial review. 'Essential procedural requirements' are the demands of due

---

[29] European Communities Act 1972, s 2; see *Bourgoin SA v Ministry of Agriculture, Fisheries and Food* [1986] QB 716.

process. Lack of competence (called 'jurisdiction' in English law) and infringement of any rule of law are grounds of review for the same reason in Community law as in English law: the judges are given jurisdiction to impose the law on the other institutions of the Community.

The really interesting problems of judicial review in the ECJ are remarkably similar to those in the English courts. 'Misuse of powers' gives the ECJ an opportunity to craft for itself the same sort of far-reaching supervision of *some* acts of the institutions that the English courts have crafted. And in its case law, the ECJ has developed 'general principles of Community law' that enhance its supervisory jurisdiction: they include the protection of fundamental rights, proportionality, and protection of legitimate expectations.[30] There are really crucial differences between the work of the ECJ and the work of the English courts: the ECJ determines the validity of legislative instruments made by European institutions, and (very importantly) those instruments are all meant to be passed for the accomplishment of limited objectives specified in the treaties. But one similarity with English judicial review is really striking: the case law of the ECJ reveals the same tension over the requirements of comity. This one basic question of constitutional principle poses the same challenges in Luxembourg as in London: how can a court promote responsible government without taking over a responsibility that the constitution gives to other institutions?

When we look at the doctrines of legitimate expectations and proportionality (in which English judicial review has been particularly influenced by the analogies with Community law) we will look closely at one recent case on judicial review of reforms to the Common Agricultural Policy, in order to see how the ECJ copes with the same problems of comity and accountability that English courts face.[31]

> ### European laws
> Don't confuse European law with the law of the European Convention on Human Rights. Both are European, but if you use the term 'European law' at all, it is best kept for the law of the European Union (also commonly called 'Community law'). The European Convention is the creature of a set of institutions under a separate treaty organization, the Council of Europe. See section 3.3.

1.8 Conclusion: 'the properest and most effectual remedy'

The main task for law-makers and judges in developing administrative law is to fashion what Lord Mansfield called 'the properest and most effectual remedy' against irresponsible government.[32] Over the past eight centuries, the judges have developed

---

[30]   Under Art 230, decisions that breach the general principles of Community law will be held to have been a misuse of a power, or to have infringed a rule of law.

[31]   Case C-310/04 *Spain v Council*; see section 8.6.

[32]   R v Cowle (1759) 2 Burr 834, 856.

a variety of techniques for controlling administrative decisions. Over the past century, Parliament and the government have created an enormous variety of new institutions and processes for the same purpose. The most effectual remedy depends on the context. So the requirements of administrative law depend very substantially on the context.

For judges (in courts and in tribunals), for ombudsmen, and for other people who have the opportunity to right injustices in public administration, giving a proper and effectual remedy means doing justice while acting with comity toward other public authorities. That is why the new techniques of administrative law vary in their application: they are tailored to the complexity of modern administration. The courts retain (in fact, they have enhanced) their role of intervening, but as in Lord Mansfield's day, their job is to do so only when their techniques for controlling government provide the properest remedy. So you cannot generally say that judges will or will not substitute their own judgment for that of an administrative official: it depends on the circumstances.

Administrative law cannot guarantee good government. In fact, it cannot even guarantee responsible government. But it does have a core role of curtailing exercises of public power that can be identified as arbitrary by the institution given power to interfere with official action. The story of *habeas corpus* reflects that core role, and also reflects the remarkable power that the judges have to confer powers on themselves. By restraining the arbitrary use of power, administrative law can give effect to the constitutional principles that support responsible government (system principles and principles of accountability). The core role of administrative law is to impose the rule of law on the executive.

Administrative law can improve administration in various ways that go beyond its core role. So, for example, ombudsmen promote good administration directly, by investigating complaints of bad administration. But like judicial review, that can only succeed if the ombudsmen who are interfering with an administrative decision do so with respect for the role of the public authorities in question. Comity is a general principle that applies to ombudsmen and tribunals as well as to judicial review, and also to the processes for enforcing liabilities of public authorities in ordinary claims.

Judicial review has a special importance for understanding those general principles. That is not because the judges control everything. In fact, judicial review is of limited importance as a process for resolving disputes with the government (see section 2.7). But two features of the judges' work are important for learning administrative law. First, the judges give reasons for their conclusions as to what the law requires. The courts have tried to articulate the principles of public law in a way that no other public institution has the capacity or the authority to do.

Secondly—and most remarkably—unlike any other institution, the courts have power to determine the nature and the scope of their own power. That is why we began with the story of *habeas corpus*, which is perhaps the most dramatic instance of that constitution-making power. It is a power that has pervasive importance in the law of judicial review. In judicial review, the judges not only have to resolve a dispute between two parties; they have to work out the limits of their own power to interfere with the work of another public authority. The case law of judicial review determines the court's own power to control the administration. So judges do not have the luxury of simply quashing a decision if there was something wrong with it. When they interfere with another public authority's use of its power, they are crafting standards for the control of their own power. And even if a decision was unlawful, the common law gives them a discretionary power to decide whether to interfere (see p 381).

The special importance of comity in that process means that the study of judicial review is a good way to approach the general problem of administrative law. Chapter 2 introduces that problem: how can one public authority interfere with another, in a way that promotes responsible government?

TAKE-HOME MESSAGE • • •

- The real objective is good government (that is, just government that makes the community better). But administrative law promotes good government indirectly, by providing techniques for achieving responsible government.

- Administrative law can promote responsible government by giving effect to constitutional principles: a general principle of **accountability**, and system principles (that is, principles that govern the role of government decisions in a system of institutions): **the separation of powers, subsidiarity, comity, the rule of law (which includes the principle of legality and due process), access to justice, and legal certainty**.

- The core task of administrative law is to impose **the rule of law** on public authorities. But the institutions that impose the rule of law on other public authorities must do so with **comity**—that is, with respect for the capacity of another public authority to do its job.

- The application of those principles to governmental decision making depends on the type of decision that needs to be controlled, and on the context in which it is made. But not everything depends on the circumstances: the general principle of **accountability**, and the **system principles** of the constitution, are very old and are recognized (though they are applied in varying ways) in the law of many countries and in European Community law.

Critical reading

R (Abbasi) v Foreign Secretary [2002] EWCA Civ 1598

A and X v Home Secretary [2004] UKHL 56

CRITICAL QUESTIONS • • •

1   Why do you suppose that *habeas corpus* is used very little in Britain today? Why didn't the Belmarsh detainees ask for *habeas corpus* in *A and X v Home Secretary* [2004] UKHL 56?

2   Suppose that the government detains people without statutory authority, and says in *habeas corpus* proceedings that there is reason to think that they are terrorists, that the reason for the suspicion is not something that can be put to the court in evidence, and that the court should not interfere because the freeing of the men would create a catastrophic danger to the United Kingdom. What should the court do?

3   Are tribunals (Chapter 12) and ombudsmen (Chapter 13) part of the executive branch of government?

4   Should one public authority ever *abandon* comity toward another public authority?

Further Questions:

5   Could there be responsible government in an absolute monarchy?

6   Who decides what is to be ruled by law?

online resource centre

Visit the online resource centre to access the following resources which accompany this chapter: links to legislation and online reports of judicial decisions, summaries of key cases and legislation, updates in the law, suggestions for answering the pop quizzes and questions, and links to useful websites.

2 The rule of law and the rule of judges

At common law, the judges will hold administrative conduct to be unlawful on any of three grounds: error of law, lack of due process, and improper exercise of discretionary power. Chapters 4 through 9 will address those grounds in detail. This chapter raises the basic question of how the three grounds of judicial review are supported by constitutional principle. Each ground must be controlled by the principle of comity.

LOOK FOR • • •

- The question that the public authority must answer in order to do its job.

- The court's approach to that question: will the court impose its own answer, or review the public authority's decision on some other ground?

- Deference by judges to administrative authorities, and its limits.

- The difference—and the connections—between the rule of law and the rule of judges.

- The core rationale for judicial review.

> ‘ It may be misfortune for the applicant that the court... cannot begin to evaluate the comparative worth of research in clinical dentistry; but it is a fact of life. ’
>
> **R v Higher Education Funding Council, ex p Institute of Dental Surgery**
> **[1994] 1 WLR 242, 262 (Sedley J)**

2.1 *Walker's* case: an introduction to the grounds of judicial review

In May 1995, a Serbian tank fired a shell at the accommodation block in Bosnia where British members of the United Nations Peace-keeping Force were staying. Trevor Walker was one of the peacekeepers sleeping in the compound. The shell injured his right leg so badly that it had to be amputated above the knee.

Walker applied for compensation under a criminal injuries compensation scheme that the Ministry of Defence had introduced in 1979. The scheme was not enacted in a statute, and did not create any legal right to compensation; the Ministry merely decided, and announced, that the Army Board would make payments to members of the armed forces injured abroad in crimes of violence. The Ministry published special guidelines for peacekeepers in Bosnia, which stated that compensation was *not* available if a peacekeeper was injured as a result of 'military activity by warring factions'.

The Ministry rejected Sergeant Walker's application for compensation, on the ground that the attack on the accommodation block was military activity by a warring faction. Sergeant Walker applied for judicial review of the decision, and his application was rejected by a High Court Judge. The Court of Appeal and (in a split decision) the House of Lords upheld the decision to dismiss his challenge (R v Ministry of Defence, ex p Walker [2000] 1 WLR 806).

Think of the question *whether Sergeant Walker should receive compensation*. If the Law Lords rejected his appeal only because they agreed with the Ministry on *that* question, then the court in judicial review simply replaces the administrative decision with the decision that the judges would have made. That is not what the Law Lords claimed to do in *Walker*. Instead, they claimed to apply the three traditional grounds for judicial review. Understanding those grounds means understanding the difference between the rule of law, and the rule of judges.

Remember the restriction on compensation: injuries caused by 'military activity of warring factions' did not qualify. Walker claimed:

(1) that the Ministry misinterpreted the restriction, so that the decision was based on an **error of law**;

(2) that it had been **'irrational'** for the Ministry to introduce the restriction at all; and

(3) that the restriction had been introduced by an **unfair process**.

These three complaints in Walker's case illustrate the three general grounds of judicial review.

Note on styles of cause

Why wasn't *Walker's case* called **Walker v Ministry of Defence**? The answer is that Sergeant Walker had no cause of action—that is, he could assert no legal right to a remedy in an ordinary claim. So he could not bring an ordinary claim, but he was able to bring a claim for judicial review to ask the High Court to review the lawfulness of the decisions of the Ministry of Defence. The case is styled **R v Ministry of Defence, ex p Walker** because the idea is that the Crown initiates the proceeding (on the application of Walker) to ask the Court to review decisions of the Ministry of Defence to decide whether they were lawful. The court was not asked whether Sergeant Walker had a right to compensation, but whether the ministry misinterpreted its own rules, or used its discretion unlawfully in making its rules, or made the rules by a process that was unfair to Sergeant Walker. On the differences between a claim for judicial review and an ordinary claim, see section 10.3.

Since the Civil Procedure Rules 1998 came into force, the courts have stopped using 'ex parte', and started using 'on the application of'. E.g.: R (on the application of Begum) v Denbigh High School [2005] EWCA Civ 199.[1] The reason is that the initial application for permission to seek judicial review is no longer heard *ex parte* (that is, without the defendant being involved in the process). But the new style of cause maintains the medieval heritage: the Queen, in an exercise of her ancient prerogative to administer justice, brings the claim for judicial review on behalf of the claimant, in order to ask her judges to determine the lawfulness of official conduct.

These are not just technicalities; they reflect a feature of judicial review that has great practical importance: a claimant in judicial review *does not need to assert any right to a remedy.*

2.2 Error of law

Walker's lawyers said that the attack that injured him was a crime, and that it could not count as 'military activity' if it was criminal. Lord Slynn said that the issue was 'whether the Ministry of Defence has correctly interpreted the scheme . . . or whether its decision involves an error of law' (810). Along with the majority, he decided against Walker on this point because 'in my opinion the exclusion from compensation as a matter of interpretation covers the injury to Sergeant Walker' (812).

Lord Hobhouse dissented because he interpreted the scheme differently: 'My Lords, Sergeant Walker is right to say that applying the Government's own criteria his case falls on the right side of the line and he should be compensated. . . . The attack was a criminal act not an act of war' (819).

---

[1]   The citation of cases is abbreviated in this book by omitting 'on the application of'.

When a public authority applies a scheme of standards to a case in order to decide whether to confer benefits or to impose burdens on a person, judicial review is available to correct an error in the agency's understanding of those standards. So the judges in *Walker* asked: How are the guidelines for the scheme to be interpreted? The majority agreed with the Ministry's interpretation of the guidelines, and Lord Hobhouse dissented because he agreed with Walker's interpretation.

This ground of judicial review is remarkable. It is unlike the approach that judges in other common law countries take to interpretations of the law by public authorities (see p 317). In England, the judges will not merely ask if other authorities' interpretations are unreasonable or arbitrary; a decision will be quashed if it runs contrary to the judges' own interpretation of the standards the agency is applying. In English law, judges are to show no deference to other public authorities on questions of law.

Jargon alert

Judges and academics sometimes use 'deference' in various ways—they sometimes use it to mean a spineless attitude. Everyone agrees judges shouldn't be spineless. Here, 'deference' is used, instead, for the judge's view that a decision should be given some kind of respect because of the fact that it was made by another public authority. The fact that another public authority made the decision can require the judges to keep their hands off the decision altogether (as, e.g., when the Queen appoints a cabinet minister), or to scrutinize the decision and the reasons for it very closely (as they used to do when the Home Secretary set tariffs of imprisonment (see p 50)). So judges can and do defer *more* or *less* to other public authorities, depending on the type of decision. If the decision is purely a matter for the judge, then the judge does not defer at all.

Chapter 9 explains the doctrine of review for error of law, and why administrative authorities still have some leeway in applying their rules. On a question of **how to interpret** the standards that other public authorities apply, the judges will impose their own view. As long as those standards are correctly interpreted, though, the judges may defer to other public authorities on particular questions of **how to apply** them to the facts of a case (the difference between interpreting and applying a scheme of standards is explained in section 9.3). The judges are *not* meant to impose their own conclusion on the question of how to apply a scheme of standards to the particular case.

Was Walker's injury caused by military activity of warring factions? *That* was a question for the Ministry and not for the Court. But if the Ministry decided it on the basis of a misinterpretation of the restriction, then the Court would strike down the decision.

The role of the courts in imposing their own interpretations on administrative authorities is not very well defined, and it is pulled in two different directions, as the judges describe their own role in modest or immodest ways. On the one hand, judges sometimes say that they will quash a decision because the law has been incorrectly applied in the case, and not only on the ground that it has been misinterpreted. So Lord Hobhouse said in *Walker*, 'If the ministry fails correctly to interpret and apply the terms of the scheme, the decisions it takes are open to judicial review' (817). Taken literally, those statements would make the administrative decision in a case like *Walker* merely provisional—to be replaced by the decision of a judge.

On the other hand, judges often suggest that review for error of law leaves flexibility for public authorities to answer a question of law one way or another. Because the ground of review is *error of law*, the court has to decide that the public authority interpreted the law wrongly (and not merely differently from the way the judges would have interpreted it), before there is ground for judicial review. And sometimes the judges suggest that they cannot hold that a public authority has erred in law, unless there was something *very* wrong with their interpretation of the law. As Lord Slynn put it:

> ❛ If I had come to the view that this phrase was imprecise enough for several meanings to be adopted, then I would not accept that the minister's interpretation of it was such as to be "so aberrant that it cannot be classed as rational" (*R v Monopolies and Mergers Commission, ex p South Yorkshire Transport Ltd* [1993] 1 WLR 23, 32, Lord Mustill). ❜ (813)[2]

On the question of how to apply the law to the case, the judges often make it clear that they really won't impose their own view. The public authority's decision can go either way without being quashed on judicial review, as long as it is reasonable. Consider Lord Hoffmann's reason for rejecting Walker's argument on error of law:

> ❛ He was fired upon by a Serbian tank. I do not see how it can be said that the ministry could not reasonably take the view that this was military activity by a warring faction. ❜ (815)

This statement suggests that in order to succeed, Walker would have had to persuade the judges that 'the ministry could not reasonably take the view' that it took—either because the Ministry misinterpreted the rules, or because the Ministry could not reasonably apply the rules (correctly interpreted) to his case in the way that it did. Essentially, administrative law requires reasonable application of the rules, and Chapter 9 explains the way in which the judges give effect to that requirement.

Isn't it odd that there were no legal rights at stake in Walker's case?

Lord Slynn asked 'whether the Ministry of Defence has correctly interpreted the scheme...or whether its decision involves an error of law'. But the Ministry was

---

[2]   On the *South Yorkshire Transport* case, see p 334.

not interpreting the *law*; it was only interpreting a scheme of payments made *ex gratia* (i.e. given as a favour, not as a right). This remarkable fact about *Walker* shows two respects in which the judges' approach to judicial review is very broad: they will review a decision that does not affect the legal position of the claimant in any way, and they will quash a decision for 'error of law' if it is based on a misinterpretation of standards that create no legal rights and, in fact, have no legal status at all apart from the legal status that they derive from the judges' willingness to control their application.

2.3 Improper use of discretionary power

Sergeant Walker also argued that if the restriction *did* apply, the Ministry never should have adopted it in the first place. But this argument was different; he could not simply claim that the Ministry had made an error in adopting the restriction, because error in the use of a discretionary power *is not a ground of judicial review*. The Ministry had no legal duty to create a particular sort of compensation scheme, or to create a scheme at all. So when the Ministry decided to offer compensation, the terms on which it would do so were up to the Ministry. It had discretion (see p 230). The courts had no legal power to choose the terms on which compensation ought to be awarded. But they did have legal power to *control* the choices that the Ministry made. The courts supervise the exercise of discretionary powers.

Lord Slynn explained this ground of review in *Walker* by saying that 'It is not for the courts to consider whether the scheme with its exclusion is a good scheme or a bad scheme, unless it can be said that the exclusion is irrational or so unreasonable that no reasonable minister could have adopted it' (812). That is the traditional approach to supervising the exercise of discretionary powers, and it gave Sergeant Walker a difficult test to meet. He argued that the restriction was 'irrational' because troops in Northern Ireland were entitled to compensation if they were injured by a terrorist attack, and there was no rational basis for distinguishing between their situation and his. But Lord Slynn said, 'the line may be fine, but to adopt it as a general rule cannot be said to have no rational base despite what seemed to me to be common features between the two situations' (812).

So the judges' approach to discretion, to *some* extent, is to keep their hands off it. They won't interfere merely because they would have made a different decision, and they will not even interfere *generally* on the ground that the wrong decision was made. So Lord Hoffmann suggested that the Ministry of Defence used its discretion in the wrong way—and there *still* was no ground for interfering with its decision: 'Speaking entirely for myself, I find the distinction a fine one ... in neither Northern Ireland nor Bosnia were the British soldiers engaged in warfare. ... But I cannot say that the distinction drawn by the ministry is irrational. That is too high a hurdle to surmount' (816).

What does it take to surmount that high hurdle? It takes a special flaw in the exercise of discretion—a flaw that allows judges to say that the decision was improper *even though* the public authority had a discretion. Sometimes this notion of a specially flawed exercise of discretion is summed up as an 'unreasonable' exercise of discretion. But as Lord Greene pointed out in the famous case of *Associated Provincial Picture Houses Ltd v Wednesbury Corporation* [1948] 1 KB 223 (CA), this word 'unreasonable' has to be treated carefully, in a way that is consistent with the lawful discretionary power of the public authority. Lord Greene explained the special defects that justify interference with discretionary power, by saying that an administrative decision maker must 'direct himself properly in law' (that is, there must be no error of law). And in addition, the decision maker must:

- 'call his own attention to the matters which he is bound to consider'; and

- 'exclude from his consideration matters which are irrelevant to what he has to consider' (229).

Doing otherwise is acting 'unreasonably' in the sense that justifies judicial interference with a decision. Then Lord Greene added:

> Similarly, there may be something so absurd that no sensible person could ever dream that it lay within the powers of the authority. Warrington L J in *Short v Poole Corporation* [1926] Ch 66 gave the example of the red-haired teacher, dismissed because she had red hair. That is unreasonable in one sense. In another sense it is taking into consideration extraneous matters. It is so unreasonable that it might almost be described as being done in bad faith; and, in fact, all these things run into one another . (229)

The 'something so absurd' ground of review is often called '*Wednesbury* unreasonableness'. Remember that *Wednesbury* unreasonableness is just one of the various grounds of review Lord Greene mentioned, which are often collectively called 'the *Wednesbury* principles'. He explained *Wednesbury* unreasonableness in three different ways. The exercise of a discretionary power must be *so* unreasonable that:

- 'no sensible person could ever dream that it lay within the powers of the authority' (229);

- 'it might almost be described as being done in bad faith' (229); and

- 'no reasonable authority could ever have come to it' (230).

He added that 'to prove a case of that kind would require something overwhelming' (230). Lord Greene was responding to the argument that unreasonable exercises of discretion are unlawful—and he did not simply accept that argument. He held that certain *especially* unreasonable decisions are to be struck down in judicial review.

This means that there is *no general rule that unreasonable actions of public authorities are unlawful*. Only certain sorts of unreasonableness are grounds for judicial review. The reason is **comity** (see p 17). No one should ever make an unreasonable decision, but a rule that judges should quash any unreasonable decision would give the judges a role in the work of other public authorities that would not actually improve administration; it would shift administrative decision making into the courts. It is not generally the judges' job to decide which administrative decisions would be reasonable. Before there is ground for judicial interference, an action has to be unreasonable in a way that enables the judges, from their detached perspective on the court, to see that no person *in the position of the public authority in question* can seriously defend the action as the authority's legitimate use of a lawful power.

What is reasonableness?

To act reasonably is simply to be guided by the reasons that ought to guide your action. Some of the reasons on which public decisions ought to be based can best be identified and assessed by the public authorities to whom a decision-making responsibility was assigned, rather than by the judges (who are responsible for the rule of law, and not for good government in general). An action is unreasonable in the special, restricted sense that provides a ground of judicial review, if it is not guided by reasons *that the law authorizes judges to insist on.*

Lord Greene's speech is the most important and influential statement of the judicial control of discretionary power in English legal history. In Chapters 7 and 8, we will see the ways in which the law has developed since Lord Greene's decision, and why (in spite of many premature announcements of the death of *Wednesbury*) his statement is still an integral part of the law today. The crucial point to keep in mind is that '*Wednesbury* unreasonableness' was only *one* of the *Wednesbury* principles, which also include the doctrine of relevance, and the rule against bad faith.

Twenty years after the *Wednesbury* decision, in *Padfield v Minister of Agriculture* [1968] AC 997, Lord Reid added another item to the list of special flaws that call for a discretionary decision to be quashed by the judges. It was a remarkable decision in which the House of Lords quashed a decision that a politician had made for political purposes (see p 268). The *Padfield* addition was that a statutory power can only be used 'to promote the policy and objects of the Act'—and that determining those purposes 'is always a matter of law for the court' (Lord Reid, 1030).

Padfield was a striking and creative decision (and controversial: Lord Morris dissented vehemently). And yet, it relied on two very old principles that, presumably, Lord Greene was taking for granted in his speech in *Wednesbury*: that a person who has a discretion must **genuinely consider exercising it** (see p 264), and that it must be used **for the 'objects' of the statute** and not for the public authority's extraneous purposes: 'The question whether a judge, or a public officer, to whom a power is given...is bound to use it upon any particular occasion, or in any particular manner, must be solved...from the context, from the particular provisions, or from the general scope and objects of the enactment conferring the power' (*Julius v Bishop of Oxford* (1880) LR 5 AC 214, 235 (Lord Selborne)).

Special flaws in a discretionary decision may justify judicial interference:

- **genuine exercise:** a public authority must not refuse to consider exercising a power, or merely pretend to exercise it;
- **relevance:** matters that are 'irrelevant' or 'extraneous' must not form the basis of the decision, and matters that the authority 'is bound to consider' must be considered;
- **proper purposes:** the authority must not use the power for purposes that are incompatible with the reasons for which it was given the power;
- the judges will quash a decision that is '**so absurd** that no sensible person could ever dream that it lay within the powers of the authority'; and
- the judges will quash a decision that is made in **bad faith**. See Chapters 7 and 8.

As Lord Greene pointed out, these grounds of review tend to run into one another. More precisely, acting for improper purposes, *Wednesbury* unreasonableness, and bad faith *are all instances of acting on irrelevant considerations*. If a public authority uses a power for some object that the legislation excludes, it is acting on irrelevant considerations. And without acting on irrelevant considerations, a public authority cannot do 'something so absurd that no sensible person could ever dream that it lay within the powers of the authority'. And acting in bad faith is simply an extreme instance of acting on irrelevant considerations: the fact that an action may hurt your enemies may seem appealing to you, but it is irrelevant to your exercise of a public power.

So the common threads in all these grounds of judicial review of discretionary action are (1) the doctrine of relevance, and (2) the judicial determination to identify a hands-off way of controlling the considerations on which public authorities must act.

Now return to *Walker's* case, and consider whether he had a good argument that the Ministry of Defence had used its discretion unlawfully. The Ministry had discretion as to whether to set up a scheme and, if so, as to what restrictions to impose. So the court could only quash the decision if it was contrary to the *Wednesbury* principles. What were the considerations on the basis of which the Ministry introduced the restriction? It decided that the original restriction (ruling out compensation for injuries from acts of violence 'committed by an enemy' in war) was too generous, since the peacekeeping role in Bosnia exposed the troops not to enemies, but to two hostile factions. The consideration that the scheme should not be too generous was a relevant consideration, and because of the Ministry's discretion on the question of how generous it should be, the court deferred to the Ministry.

Statute and prerogative

Does it matter that the powers in *Padfield* and *Wednesbury* were statutory powers, rather than prerogative powers? It seemed to make a difference when those cases were decided, because it was not until *Council of Civil Service Unions v Minister for the Civil Service* [1985] AC 374 (see p 238) that the House of Lords unequivocally held that the courts could review the exercise of the prerogative on the same broad grounds as the exercise of statutory powers. Today, grounds of judicial review of the exercise of prerogative power are not generally different from grounds of review of statutory powers: it is unlawful for a Minister of the Crown to use a pre-rogative power for improper purposes. The House of Lords held for the first time in *R (Bancoult) v Foreign Secretary* [2008] UKHL 61 that even legislation for a colony by Order in Council can be judicially reviewed on the usual standards described in this chapter. But note that the judges may need to exercise special forms of defer-ence in assessing the purposes for which some prerogative powers may be used, as the House of Lords did in *Bancoult* (see p 240).

2.4 Due process

Sergeant Walker did not persuade the House of Lords that the Ministry had misinter-preted the restriction, or that it was an abuse of power for the Ministry to adopt the restriction. But he also challenged the *process* by which the Ministry had adopted the restriction.

The criminal injuries scheme was introduced with fanfare. The Ministry announced it to service commanders, to let armed forces personnel know that a generous new benefit was being created for them. When the Ministry decided to *restrict* the scheme in 1994 by excluding compensation for injuries caused by mili-tary activity of warring factions, the Minister announced the change in the House of Commons, with no fanfare. It was not announced directly to soldiers or to their commanders. Sergeant Walker argued that this process was unfair. He claimed that he had a **legitimate expectation** (see section 8.4) that he would be compensated under the scheme as it had originally been announced, and that it was unfair to disappoint that expectation without having first communicated the new restriction to the ser-vices as openly as the original scheme was communicated.

Walker was arguing that the Ministry's conduct was unlawful because it was procedurally unfair. A decision is unfair if it wrongly neglects the interests of someone affected by the decision. The substance of the decision here was **the new restriction.** The procedure that Walker complained of was **adopting the restriction without communicating with services personnel.** The decision was *substantively* unfair if it was unfair for the Minister to restrict the scheme; it was *procedurally* unfair if it was unfair for the Minister to do so without announcing it to services personnel.

Decisions cannot be quashed for *substantive* unfairness in general. Unfairness is a form of unreasonableness, and we have seen that unreasonableness is not a general ground of judicial review. To ask a court to quash a substantively unfair decision, it is necessary to use the standards for the control of discretion (the special, restricted forms of reasonableness) that are addressed in Chapters 7 and 8. Public authorities should not make decisions that wrongly neglect the interest of an affected person, but that does not mean that judges should replace the administration's assessment of people's interests with their own assessment. That is the basic reason for the restrained standards of control of discretionary power outlined above.

Procedural unfairness, by contrast, is the clearest and least controversial ground of judicial review—although in Chapter 4 we will see fierce controversies about just what counts as unfair. Procedures are steps that a public authority takes in the course of making and announcing decisions, to communicate with people affected, or people who might have information to contribute or opinions that ought to be taken into account. *Fair* procedures give the persons affected an appropriate role in the process. Think of the decision to convict an accused person of murder. To treat the accused fairly, a criminal court needs to make sure that the accused is told what allegations he is facing and what offence he is charged with. The accused needs to be present when the prosecution makes its case, and needs to have an opportunity to respond to the evidence by challenging it and by introducing contrary evidence of his own. And if the accused is not able to do that himself, he needs help from someone who is competent to do it. In English criminal law, those requirements take the remarkable form of a jury trial with elaborate rules of indictment, disclosure before trial, a right to lead evidence and to choose whether to testify, a right to cross-examine prosecution witnesses, and a right to be represented by counsel and to have legal aid.

Associated with these demands of fairness is the requirement that the decision maker not be biased. In an English murder trial that requirement is met mainly by the jury system, in which the accused has a right to challenge any juror on grounds that he or she is prejudiced against him.

Fairness to a person affected by a decision is not the only reason for the law to impose procedural requirements. Good procedure in a murder trial is important to the public, too. It promotes good decisions, and makes the process open to the public, in a way that helps to hold the criminal justice system accountable.

Administrative decisions are all more-or-less radically different from the decision to convict a defendant of murder. And the procedures that are necessary for good decision making differ correspondingly. They depend on the nature of the decision, and on the relevant considerations (section 4.4). That is why administrative law only requires *due* process, and not the equivalent of a murder trial to test every action a public authority takes. The interests in participation, in openness, and in fairness call for different procedures in different decision-making regimes. But in each regime, a court can oversee the public authority's *procedures* with somewhat more confidence than it oversees the *substance* of the decision.

So we can return to *Walker's* case with an understanding of the special role for judicial review on grounds of due process: a court that is concerned not to usurp the Ministry's discretion to decide the terms of the compensation scheme can still decide its *procedures*. And Lord Slynn said that 'it would have been better if the ministry had given a degree of publicity of the change similar to that given to the original proposal' (814). If judges can impose procedural requirements without usurping the public authority's role, and if they thought it would have been better for the Ministry to announce the change to services personnel, why didn't Walker succeed on this ground of judicial review? Why didn't the House of Lords hold that the Ministry's procedure was unlawful?

The answer is that the requirement of due process does not mean that a court will interfere simply because the process could have been better. Lord Hoffmann said, 'I do not think that your Lordships are concerned to decide in general terms whether it would have been better administration to make the announcement in a different way' (815). The Law Lords' conclusion was that the process was not unfair to Sergeant Walker. He did not know the 1980 policy, and he had not been told that his case would be treated under it. There is no doubt that the Ministry would have been acting in a more open *and accountable* fashion if it had publicized the new restriction as widely as it had publicized the new scheme. But judicial review is not a general technique for improving administrative process.

2.5 Constitutional principles and judicial review

The **system principles** of the constitution (see section 1.5) ought to govern judicial review: in particular, parliamentary sovereignty, the separation of powers, comity among public authorities, and the rule of law. What is the link between grounds of judicial review, and constitutional principles? **Parliamentary sovereignty** requires that judges pass judgment on the lawfulness of administrative decisions if Parliament directs them to do so (and requires them not to do so if Parliament has directed them not to do so). The **separation of powers** requires judges not to take over powers of the administration, and judges can promote the separation of powers by holding it unlawful for administrative authorities to act contrary to statute or to the common law. **Comity** requires judges to support the ability of administrative authorities to do their job.

The most important principle behind judicial review is **the rule of law**, and its demands are related to the demands of all the other system principles. The rule of law requires that public authorities adhere to consistent, open, prospective, non-arbitrary standards, and it *also* requires decision-making processes that distinguish government action from the mere arbitrary whim of the people in power. But why should courts interfere? Why not leave administrative agencies to construct and follow their own consistent, open, prospective, non-arbitrary standards, and to devise their own processes?

Here is an easy answer, which may seem plausible: law is for the judges, you may think, so that any question of the standards administrative agencies ought to follow is a question for judges. The main point of this chapter is that it would be a mistake to think that. Judicial review *can* promote the rule of law. But we are not necessarily closer to the rule of law just because a question—even a question of law—is decided by a judge, rather than another public official.

2.5.1 How judicial review can promote the rule of law: the imprisonment of murderers

Replacing the decision of one official with the decision of another does not necessarily promote the rule of law. But it *can* do so. We can find the best examples in the courts' claims to have imposed the rule of law on the imprisonment of murderers. Parliament gave the Home Secretary power to decide how long to imprison under-age murderers (detained 'at Her Majesty's pleasure' (Children and Young Persons Act 1933 s 53(1))), and in the case of adults the power to decide the 'tariff', or period to be served for the purposes of retribution and deterrence before consideration for parole (The Crime (Sentences) Act 1997 s 29). In the 1990s, the judges, who openly opposed what amounted to a sentencing decision by a politician, imposed a variety of restrictions on its exercise. Each restriction promoted the rule of law. They held that:

- the Home Secretary could not impose a secret tariff (R v Home Secretary, ex p Doody [1994] AC 531);

- the prisoner had a right to make representations (Doody);

- the prisoner had a right to be given reasons for the decision (Doody);

- the tariff could not ordinarily be increased retrospectively (R v Home Secretary, ex p Pierson [1998] AC 539); and

- it was unlawful for the Home Secretary to base his decision on public clamour (including petitions in favour of a long tariff for two child murderers, and 20,000 coupons that readers had clipped out of a newspaper that had said that two under-age murderers 'must rot in jail') (R v Home Secretary, ex p Venables and Thompson [1998] AC 407).

It is not only the English judges who have imposed the rule of law on the Home Secretary. First, the European Court of Human Rights declared that detention of child murderers at Her Majesty's pleasure is contrary to the guarantee of an independent tribunal in the European Convention on Human Rights Art 6 (V v United Kingdom (App no 24888/94) (2000) 30 EHRR 121).[3] Then, after the Human Rights Act came into effect, the House of Lords held that it is incompatible with Art 6 for the Home Secretary to decide the tariff for an adult murderer (R v Home Secretary, ex p Anderson [2002] 3 WLR 1800). The Government responded to Anderson by asking Parliament to amend the legislation, and the power to set the tariff was given to the judges.

Why say that these developments in English law promote the rule of law, rather than merely the rule of judges? Because each of them, in varying ways, stands in the way of **arbitary** (see p 7) decisions about imprisonment. The judges did what they could to insulate the Home Secretary's decision from the pressures from the media that are liable to motivate a cabinet minister. And taking the power away from the Home Secretary under the Human Rights Act detached it from those pressures. The result is that what happens to a murderer is ruled by a process of decision making that can be distinguished from a whim of the Home Secretary.

....

3   To carry out the United Kingdom's treaty obligation to comply with declarations of the European Court of Human Rights, the Home Secretary immediately announced that he would exercise his statutory power in Venables' and Thompson's cases and in future cases on the basis of the recommendation of the Lord Chief Justice.

The rule against secret tariffs and the prohibition on retrospective increases promote the rule of law values of openness and prospectivity; the right to make representations promotes the rule of law by requiring the decision maker to face up to the factual claims and the arguments of the offender. The right to reasons supports that function of representations. A requirement of reasons increases openness, and also opposes arbitrary decisions, through the pressure it puts on the decision maker who has no rationale to offer. And the control on the considerations on which the Home Secretary may act promotes the rule of law by insulating the decision, to some extent, from political influence.

Note that there are more straightforward ways in which sentencing could be ruled by law: a simple minimum tariff, like the minimum of 25 years before parole in Canada for first-degree murder (Criminal Code s 745), would achieve legal control of the sentencing decision much more simply and effectively than all the subtle judicial developments in the English cases.

The idea that the English judicial and legislative developments and the Canadian legislative tariffs promote the rule of law depends on an assumption. The assumption is that the period an offender spends in prison is the sort of decision that ought to be controlled by law. There are many sorts of decisions which the judges will not review on the grounds they used in the life sentence cases, and to which Art 6 of the European Convention has no application: decisions about government expenditure, the appointment of ministers, and the disposition of the armed forces are the obvious examples. Why should the law control the time that life prisoners spend in prison, in a way in which it does not control decisions about government expenditure, or the appointment of a minister, or the disposition of the armed forces? A good understanding of the rule of law requires an understanding of which governmental decisions need to be controlled by artificial and cumbersome legal processes, in order to achieve responsible government. For the appointment of ministers, we can achieve responsible government through parliamentary control on the Prime Minister, and through general elections; judicial review of the decision would add nothing. In fact, judicial interference would *detract* from responsible government. To achieve responsible government in the imprisonment of murderers, on the other hand, the control that Parliament and the electorate can exert on government would not be enough. It would be arbitrary to subject a particular murderer's life to political forces. We need the decision to be made by an independent tribunal.

We saw that although all administrative decisions should be reasonable, a *legal* requirement of reasonableness would require courts to decide (to some extent) what reasons are good reasons (see p 17). The courts have no general jurisdiction to do that, and it would be a breach of comity for them to invent one for themselves. Yet it is *not* a breach of comity for them to invent for themselves powers to control administration, where (1) they are capable of controlling a decision without damaging another public authority's capacity to carry out its tasks, and (2) the alternative is to leave a public authority free to engage in arbitrary government. The invention of *habeas corpus* (see p 5) is perhaps the oldest example of the use of the judges' creative role, and in the 21st century the courts retain a dynamic jurisdiction to decide what new forms of judicial control are required for responsible government. Like any governmental power, the courts' jurisdiction will itself be a tool for arbitrary government, if the judges do not use it responsibly.

● *Pop Quiz* ●

Judges, unlike administrative officials, are **independent** (see section 5.3). Does that mean that replacing another public authority's decision with the decision of a judge generally promotes the rule of law?

2.5.2 Judicial deference to administrative authorities

In Walker's case, why were the judges reviewing the compensation decision at all, when the rules of the scheme had always said that 'whether or not to make such a payment, and, if so, the amount, shall be wholly within the discretion of the Army Board'? On the one hand, it seems that the courts should respect the fact that a decision has been committed to another public authority (whether the power is conferred by a statute or, as in Walker's case, by a prerogative act by the government). On the other hand, a very wide grant of power should not be turned into a tool for abuse. These two principles are in tension, but they do not contradict each other. In *Walker*, Lord Hoffmann pointed out that the scheme gave discretion to the Army Board, and simply added, 'But the discretion may not be exercised arbitrarily' (815). The central challenge for judges in judicial review is to prevent other public authorities from using their powers arbitrarily—which the judges need to do in order to impose the rule of law—without imposing their own judgment as to how public authorities should use the discretionary powers that have been allocated to them. That means that judges must very often defer to other public authorities—to some extent—on the question of how to use a power. To **defer** to (e.g.) the ministry on (e.g.) the question of whether injuries caused by military activity of warring factions should be excluded from the compensation scheme, is to treat *the fact that the ministry decided that those injuries are to be excluded*, as a reason why they should be excluded.

Courts cannot do everything. They have a **supervisory jurisdiction** over public bodies such as the Ministry of Defence, but they are not a defence agency. They have a supervisory jurisdiction over the Higher Education Funding Council, but they are not a higher education funding agency. So in R *v Higher Education Funding Council, ex p Institute of Dental Surgery* [1994] 1 WLR 242, the Court of Appeal refused to evaluate the worth of research in dentistry; they could not decide that the funding council had or had not made the right decision, so they would not interfere with it. They deferred to the Funding Council on the question of how to evaluate dentistry research.

How far should the courts defer to an administrative decision? Very radically or not at all, depending on the type of decision, the body that is making it, and the context in which it is made. This feature of judicial review explains why courts will quash administrative decisions for certain forms of unreasonableness, but not for unreasonableness in general. Much of Chapters 7 and 8 will be concerned with the considerations requiring greater or lesser deference to exercises of discretionary power.

2.5.3 Isn't it Parliament's job to control the executive?

There is a myth in modern British constitutional lore: that it is generally the job of the sovereign Parliament, and not of the courts, to control the government. And the associated myth about judicial review is that courts have been taking over that controlling role (since, roughly, the 1960s), because Parliament has been failing in its task. The first-past-the-post election system tends to create strong majorities, and the party Whips control the backbenchers through threats and promises, with the result that the House of Commons is under the control of the executive, instead of the executive being under the control of Parliament.

But it is a myth to think that judicial review is a substitute for proper parliamentary control, for two reasons:

(1) judicial review is **ancient** (older than the tradition of parliamentary supervision of administration), and

(2) judicial review and parliamentary control of administration are **complementary**.

The roots of the courts' authority to control administration are medieval. And by the 17th century the courts were asserting that authority in a very creative way. It was only after the 17th century that Parliament was able to exercise any reliable and creative control over the government. It is certainly more than three hundred years since English judges doubted their power to supervise the legality of executive action (though they have dramatically revised their view of what makes executive action unlawful).

┌─ FROM THE MISTS OF TIME ─────────────────────────────

Nearly four hundred years ago, the Chief Justice could claim that 'to this Court of King's Bench belongs authority, not only to correct errors in judicial proceedings, but other errors and misdemeanors extra-judicial, tending to the breach of peace, or oppression of subjects, or to the raising of faction, controversy, debate or any manner of misgovernment' *Bagg's Case* (1615) 11 Co Rep 94 (Coke CJ). That was putting it too high, because it has never been the judges' job to correct 'any manner of misgovernment'; Lord Coke's statement has to be read as subject to the requirements of **comity**.

Lord Chief Justice Holt put it less extravagantly in *Groenvelt v Burwell* (1700) 1 Ld Raym 454, holding that 'by the common law', 'this court will examine if other courts [including statutory authorities such as, in Groenvelt's case, the censors of the College of Physicians of London] exceed their jurisdiction'.

The judges who developed judicial review were not making up for Parliament's failings. Judges and MPs have different capacities and different opportunities to supervise the executive. Judges have special competence for controlling certain forms of misgovernment (unlawful uses of power), and Parliament has special competence for controlling other forms (the pursuit of policies that are contrary to the national interest).

Parliament has control over administration, first, because the Prime Minister is the leader of the party that has the confidence of the House of Commons, and he or she needs to conduct the administration in a way that helps to keep that confidence. More specifically, too, the practice of Parliament allows MPs to ask questions of ministers concerning administration in departments and executive agencies for which they are directly or indirectly responsible. The possibility of asking embarrassing questions in the House of Commons supports a practice of written questions from MPs to departments, which helps the MP to get a response to complaints on behalf of constituents. Since the 1960s, MPs have been able to refer complaints to the Parliamentary Commissioner for Administration or 'Parliamentary Ombudsman' (see Chapter 13). And the work of the Parliamentary Ombudsman is supported by the Public Administration Select Committee of the House of Commons, which receives reports from the Ombudsman and makes recommendations to the House.

Apart from the role of individual MPs in responding to complaints, since the late 1970s select committees of MPs have had the task of overseeing the administration of departments. There are now sixteen departmental select committees. They are made up of backbench MPs, and they help Parliament to control the executive by examining policy, expenditure, and administration in each of the main government departments and their associated agencies. Even though each committee has a government majority, the committees provide a technique for general scrutiny of administration that is more effective than debates in the House of Commons itself. Select committees do for the House of Commons what it cannot do for itself, by taking written and oral evidence. They can summon witnesses to give evidence or to produce documents. A select committee report can generate political pressure in the House of Commons, and the onus of responding to a report can itself change government policy.

Judicial review of the lawfulness of executive action is different, and it is a central judicial function. If it is done right, it is perfectly consistent with parliamentary control of the government. The work of the select committees and debates in the House of Commons impose an important control on administration in the public interest (or at least they *can* do so, depending on political pressures), but they do not provide effective redress for the complaints of particular persons about administrative action.

Of course, one difference between Parliament and the courts is that while courts can only interfere with the government on legal grounds, Parliament can hold the government to account on *any* good grounds. Courts only promote good government indirectly; Parliament can do so directly. Parliament can also insist on the rule of law. A complaint of unlawful administrative action *could* (like any complaint of bad government) be good material for questions in the House of Commons, or even grounds for a vote of no confidence. Or it could play a role in a parliamentary election campaign. But that does not mean that controlling unlawful behaviour is a parliamentary function that courts have had to take on. Elections and debates in the House of Commons are not remotely as well-designed as a claim in the High Court, for responding to a particular person's complaint, for identifying the facts, or for deciding a dispute as to what counts as unlawful. MPs' questions and the Parliamentary Ombudsman provide a worthwhile way of seeking a response to some complaints about the administration, but neither mechanism offers what judicial review offers: that is, an independent decision maker with authority to make a binding decision that government action is unlawful.

Consider R v Bolton (1841) 1 QB 66 (see p 23), in which Mr. Bolton's council threw him out of his house. He could have complained to his MP, who could have raised the matter in the House of Commons; the government could have taken executive action to help Mr. Bolton in response to clamour in the House, or Parliament could have passed a statute retrospectively benefiting him and imposing new duties on the parish council (or new duties on the courts to control the parish council). All that is fanciful, though, as a way of dealing with a particular person's complaint—especially in the case of a pauper thrown out of a council house. When particular personal problems end up being discussed in Parliament, it is because of more-or-less random media frenzies that may have nothing to do with the justice of the case. Parliament is just not an effective forum for securing justice according to law for particular individuals. The courts have access problems too (the expense of legal services is the most noticeable). But once Mr. Bolton is in court, he has an opportunity to make an argument to a person independent of government, and the public authority is put in the predicament of having to meet his argument with a lawful justification of its action. That arrangement is a necessary technique for imposing the rule of law on the executive, even if Parliament is doing its job well. Administrative law does not make up for any modern failure by Parliament to carry out its responsibility; Parliament never did the things that we need the courts to do.

And on the other hand, judicial review can never be a remedy for inadequate parliamentary control. Parliament controls the executive in the national interest, as a representative assembly. Legal institutions impose the rule of law on the executive, and hear particular cases. So if Parliament is not doing its job well, the legal institutions *cannot* solve that problem. Judges do not have any techniques to fill a constitutional vacuum left by spineless backbenchers, excessive party discipline, or a weak opposition.

The *ultra vires* controversy

If the legal control of administrative authorities is not a job for Parliament, perhaps it is a job that Parliament has given to the courts? It is obviously unlawful for a public authority to do something that it has no lawful power to do.[4] Such an action is *ultra vires* (outside the authority's powers). An action is *ultra vires* whether it is a rule of the common law, statute law, or any other source of law that deprives the authority of power to take the action. But English judges and scholars have often used the phrase *ultra vires* as if it meant 'contrary to the statute that grants

---

4   Although the question of what, if anything, a court should do about it is a separate question: see Chapter 10.4.6 on the judges' discretion over remedies against unlawful administrative action.

a power'. And some of them have argued that judicial authority to quash actions of public authorities is conferred by statutes that the judges ought to construe as requiring judicial review for error of law, due process, and to prevent abuse of power. Others say that the source of that judicial authority is, in general, the common law.

● *Pop quiz* ●

What do you think? Did Parliament give the judges power to interfere with the exercise of a statutory power? Or did the courts take it upon themselves in the development of the common law? Does the controversy make any difference to the grounds of judicial review?

2.6 The 20th-century judicial adventure

The story so far is that the judges are prepared to pass judgment on other public authorities' interpretation of the law, to impose due process on them, and to quash a decision that they can identify as an abuse of power. This dynamic pattern of judicial law making is compatible with the role of Parliament in the constitution, and it can potentially be justified by the constitutional principle of the rule of law. Whether it is actually justified always depends on whether the judges exercise their power with comity toward other public authorities, which requires the judges to defer to the initial decision maker on many questions, sometimes very radically. But if the judges find a lack of **due process**, or if they can identify a decision, from their rather isolated point of view, as an **abuse of power**, they do not need to defer to another public authority's view that it was the right thing to do.

In the development of their role, the judges repeatedly need to assess what deference is due to other public authorities on particular questions; they make a mistake if they think that they must *generally* defer to administrative decision makers, or if they think that they can *generally* decide for themselves the grounds on which administrative decision makers should act.

In the first half of the 20th century, the courts developed a tendency toward general deference to administrative authorities. After World War II, the courts went through a remarkable period of expansion and new articulation of the grounds of judicial review, which was so far-reaching that it has seemed to many lawyers as if administrative law was invented in the second half of the 20th century. It should already be apparent that many of the most dramatic judicial inventions are centuries old. But the developments in the decades after the 1940s are remarkable, and even a partial list will give you a picture both of the capacity of the courts to develop new rules of administrative law, and also of the state of the law in the 21st century:

Timeline of the 20th-century judicial adventure

- *Ridge v Baldwin* [1964] AC 40: an administrative body needn't have a duty to act judicially, in order to be subject to the law of due process (see p 116).

- *Conway v Rimmer* [1968] AC 910: instead of having a 'Crown privilege' against disclosing documents in litigation, the government must ask a court to decide whether documents should be given public interest immunity from disclosure.
- *Anisminic v Foreign Compensation Commission* [1969] 2 AC 147: the courts will not give effect to a statutory provision that an administrative decision is not to be brought into question in a court (note that this is *not* the way the House of Lords described what it was doing in *Anisminic*! See p 310.).
- *O'Reilly v Mackman* [1983] 2 AC 237: any decision based on an error of law will be quashed.
- *Council of Civil Service Unions v Minister for the Civil Service* [1985] AC 374: the three grounds of judicial review apply to an exercise of prerogative power.
- *Gillick v West Norfolk and Wisbech Area Health Authority* [1986] AC 112: judicial review extends to guidance circulars issued by a department of state without any specific authority and without any legal effect (compare the application of the three grounds of judicial review to a decision with no legal consequences, in *Walker*).
- *R v Panel on Take-overs and Mergers, ex p Datafin Plc* [1987] 1 QB 815 (CA): judicial review can be available against a body that is not a government agency (see p 585).
- *M v Home Office* [1993] 3 WLR 433: the courts can award injunctions against ministers of the Crown, and declare them to have acted in contempt of court.
- *R v Home Secretary, ex p Doody* [1994] 1 AC 531: cases on disclosure and duties to give reasons have developed a general trend toward openness in the making of administrative decisions.

In the control of discretionary powers, there has been a marked move away from general deference to administrative authorities, toward deferring only for specific reasons. The *Wednesbury* principles can be traced back generations before the 1940s. But after the 1940s the courts gave them further articulation, and in the course of doing so, they have extended them. That movement includes the *Padfield* case, and the prisoner cases discussed above. It also includes:

- *Inland Revenue Commissioners v Rossminster* [1980] AC 952: the House of Lords held that *Liversidge v Anderson* [1942] AC 206, in which a majority of the House of Lords decided that the courts must defer radically to the Home Secretary's judgment as to whether there is good reason for a detention under a statutory power, was wrongly decided (see Lord Diplock (1011));

- the development of a doctrine of **legitimate expectation** that to some degree protects substantive interests (and not only interests in consultation or a hearing) against changes to or deviations from government policy (see section 8.4);

- *R v Home Secretary, ex p Ahmed and Patel* [1998] INLR 570: the signing of a treaty can create a legitimate expectation that government will act in conformity to the treaty;[5] and

---

5   The effect is limited because a minister can lawfully adopt and act on a contrary policy.

- *R v Home Secretary ex p Simms* [2000] 2 AC 115: the courts have articulated the **principle of legality**, which is a rule that general statements of powers in statutes do not confer power to act contrary to certainly legally protected values.[6]

FROM THE MISTS OF TIME

The judges sometimes seem to think that judicial review was invented in the 20th-century adventure. So in the *Page* case, Lord Browne-Wilkinson referred to 'the great development that has recently taken place in the law of judicial review whereby the courts have asserted a general jurisdiction to review the decisions of tribunals and inferior courts' (*R v Lord Chancellor, ex p Page* [1993] AC 682, 700). There certainly had been great developments in the law of judicial review, in the forty years leading up to *Page*. But the tradition of general judicial supervision was already old when *Keighley's Case* (1609) 10 Co Rep 139 imposed judicial control over the Commissioners of Sewers, who had been given legal power by a statute that said nothing about judicial control. The *Keighley* decision implicitly asserted a general jurisdiction to review the decisions of tribunals and inferior courts.

In fact, English judicial history is unified across the centuries by *excessive* judicial claims of responsibility for controlling administrative decision making (on why the claim in the *Page* case is excessive, see p 309).

Since 1998, this judicial creativity has not diminished; the barristers' (and therefore the judges') energy has turned to the development of claims based on the Human Rights Act. Chapter 3 will discuss ways in which grounds of judicial review are affected by the application of doctrines applied under the European Convention on Human Rights, and under European law.

In addition to their role in developing grounds of judicial review, the judges have reformed the *process* for seeking judicial review, through:

- a complex pattern of decisions on access to judicial review (see Chapter 10), and

- a series of judicial decisions elaborating a very relaxed approach to **standing** (see Chapter 11), which has facilitated claims by campaign groups.

The Civil Procedure Rules 1998 were also the result of judicial advisory work (see p 347).

Much of this book is concerned with the good achievements and the drawbacks of the judicial adventure. The most *important* achievement has been an array of very wide-ranging and far-reaching improvements in the fairness and openness of administrative decision-making processes. The more *dramatic* achievement has

---

[6]   The courts' control of discretionary powers has also been extended since the 1940s in the development of tort liabilities of public authorities. It is not a straightforward matter to assess this development; it is complex, and the judges have (with notable exceptions) been very cautious not to turn causes of action into tools by which claimants can get courts to decide what administrative decisions ought to have been taken. See Chapter 14.

been a judicial willingness to stand against abuse of power even in very political contexts that would have been considered out of bounds for judges in the 1940s. The drawbacks include the creation of a massively expensive litigation industry in the pursuit of pointless complaints against administrative decisions on grounds that the courts are not equipped to apply. And occasionally, the drawbacks include a form of judicial imperialism as the judges succumb to the temptation constantly offered to them by claimants' barristers—to replace administrative decisions with decisions the judges think would have been better.

With these dramatic advantages and drawbacks, judicial review gives us a way of understanding the constitutional principles of administrative law. The judges' supervisory jurisdiction is an important feature of English administrative law, and it is the most useful way into the subject. The irony is that we can only understand its place in the constitution, if we see that judicial review actually plays a very limited role in controlling administrative action.

2.7 Judicial review isn't everything

Other techniques for controlling administrative decisions are much more important to millions of people in practice: most important of all are discussion and negotiation with public authorities themselves over their decisions and policies and plans. And during the same period in which the judges have reinvigorated judicial review, Parliament has enhanced existing techniques and instituted new techniques for resolution of disputes and for supervision of administration, which have restructured the law and practice of administration:

- administrative **tribunals** have been reconstructed into a highly judicialized system by the Tribunals Courts and Enforcement Act 2007 (Chapter 12);

- **ombudsmen** schemes have been created to investigate complaints of maladministration in some departments of central government and local government (Parliamentary Commissioner for Administration Act 1967 and Local Government Act 1974) (Chapter 13).

- a system of **parliamentary select committees** has been created to enhance supervision of administration by the House of Commons; and

- the economy, efficiency, and effectiveness of government spending has been subjected to greatly enhanced scrutiny by the **Audit Commission** (for local government) and the **National Audit Office** (for central government). See p 578.

Ombudsmen and parliamentary committees and auditors have far-reaching powers of investigation that courts do not have. Their ways of getting a result for the complainant are more flexible than the court's remedies. And they are better equipped than courts to achieve worthwhile general changes in administrative practice. Judges are restricted to identifying unlawful procedures. Ombudsmen, committees, and auditors can recommend better procedures.

As for adjudication of legal claims, far more cases are resolved in tribunals than in courts. And if a claim reaches a court, it is far more likely to do so in a statutory appeal from a tribunal or directly from a government decision[7] than in a claim for judicial review.

A lawyer who only knew about judicial review would be very badly prepared to assist a client with a complaint against a government decision. The alternatives to judicial review are not simply used more often than judicial review; their role is essential to the principles of the subject. You cannot understand judicial review itself, if you think it is the primary form of legal control of administrative action. It is not even the *secondary* technique. It is a last resort. As Lord Scarman put it, 'a remedy by way of judicial review is not to be made available where an alternative remedy exists. This is a proposition of great importance. Judicial review is a collateral challenge: it is not an appeal' (R v Inland Revenue Commissioners, ex p Preston [1985] AC 835, 852). In that case, the House of Lords held that judicial review should not generally be used when a statutory appeal process was available. This approach to judicial review has survived the judicial adventure of the past 50 years.

It may seem tempting to think that the judges must be prepared to pass judgment on any allegation of unlawful administrative decision. And if the allegation is made out, it may seem that the court must hold that because it was unlawful, the decision is a nullity. But something more is needed to justify the bringing of a claim for judicial review. And the fact that a decision was unlawful does not automatically lead to the conclusion that a court should strike it down. Bringing a claim for judicial review is only justified if the operation of the process of judicial review, and the remedies the judges can order, are proportionate to the nature of the complaint. And justifying a remedy requires not only showing that a decision was unlawful, but *also* an explanation of *why the court should interfere.*

In *Evans v University of Cambridge* [2002] EWHC 1382, a Cambridge University lecturer was refused permission to apply for judicial review of a refusal to promote her. She claimed that the University was a public institution in which she held a public office, so that its decisions were amenable to judicial review. So far as it goes that was right: universities are amenable to judicial review. But the court held that because she had an employment contract, the decision was not subject to judicial review. She had a right to go to an employment tribunal; of course, the reason she was seeking judicial review was that she knew that on the facts of her case, she would not succeed in an employment tribunal. That in itself is no reason for judicial review: the ordinary standards of employment law were sufficient to subject the University to the rule of law, so that there was no reason for judicial interference.

Tribunals (see Chapter 12) are not the only alternative to judicial review. In *Cowl v Plymouth City Council* [2001] EWCA Civ 1935, Lord Woolf emphasized the 'paramount importance' of avoiding litigation through alternative dispute resolution. The Court

---

7   To give one important example, the Housing Act 1996 s 204 gives a right of appeal to a county court on a point of law from an internal review of decisions as to what housing is suitable for homeless people. See *Begum v Tower Hamlets LBC* [2003] UKHL 5.

of Appeal held that permission should not be given for judicial review, if the claimant has not pursued other means of resolving the dispute before litigating. That important decision simply rejects the idea that all complaints of unlawful conduct are to be heard by a court, with a view to quashing the decision if the judges find that it was unlawful. Similarly, a claim for judicial review cannot be brought alongside a claim in tort (see Chapter 14), if the remedy in the tort claim would address the reasons for bringing the claim for judicial review.

Any dispute with a government agency can, in principle, be resolved through reconsideration by the agency, and many disputes can be resolved through other legal processes than judicial review. Whether judicial review should be allowed in *any* case is itself a question of **due process**: and as we will see in Chapter 4, a question of due process is a question of proportionality. If there is another way to resolve a dispute with the government, due process does not require judicial review.

— **FROM THE MISTS OF TIME** —————————————

In *R v Barker* (1762) 3 Burr 1265 (see p 395), Lord Mansfield held that 'A *mandamus*…ought to be used upon all occasions where the law has established no specific remedy, and where in justice and good government there ought to be one' (1267). Note the last part of that decision: a *mandamus* (today, a mandatory order requiring a public authority to exercise a legal power) *will not be issued* unless justice and good government require the order to be made.

Chapter 10 will address the judicial review process. For now, it is worth outlining some of the restrictions on judicial review, to put it in its place as an extraordinary process:

Restrictions on judicial review

- No one has a right to seek judicial review; a claimant must ask the court for **permission**, first.[8]
- The claimant must proceed within a very restrictive three-month **time limit** for claims for judicial review. Even more stringent time limits are imposed by statute in some particular fields.
- The claimant will not be given **standing** (Chapter 11) to bring a claim for judicial review, unless a court decides that he or she has a 'sufficient interest' in the matter of the claim.
- The courts have **discretion in remedies**: even if they find that a decision was unlawful, they do not need to quash it if there are good grounds for giving it effect (see p 381).
- **An unlawful process is not in itself a reason for quashing a decision.** So, for example, if a hearing does not meet lawful requirements, it will not be

---

8 Note that an ordinary claim, such as a claim in tort, is different: a claimant has a right to bring a claim, although a court can strike it out on the defendant's application if the claim does not present an arguable right of action. See Chapter 14.

quashed if the irregularity was not substantial enough to make it unfair (NJ
v Essex County Council [2006] EWCA Civ 545). And when a tribunal rejects evidence for a number of reasons, if some of the reasons it gives were unlawful,
the court will not quash the decision if it is confident that the decision would
have been the same if it had been made only on lawful grounds: *HK v Home
Secretary* [2006] EWCA Civ 1037.

- Judicial review is a **last resort**: the judges will not give permission to seek judicial review, if there is another adequate way in which the claimant can seek a
  remedy.
- **Power to remit:** If the judges find that a decision was unlawful, they have very
  wide power under the Civil Procedure Rules to send the matter back to the
  initial decision maker, for it to make a lawful decision. For example, if a body
  owes a duty to give reasons, it is unlawful for the body to give a decision without adequate reasons. But the Court of Appeal has held that it may be disproportionate to quash a decision for which inadequate reasons were given; the
  decision should be remitted to the decision maker for further explanation if
  possible (*R (Adami) v Ethical Standards Officer of the Standards Board for England*
  [2005] EWCA Civ 1754).[9]

In spite of these basic restrictions on judicial review, the government has sometimes wanted to set up bodies whose decisions cannot be challenged in the courts.
But when Parliament has enacted provisions designed for that purpose (called 'priv-
ative clauses' or 'ouster clauses'), the courts have offered no cooperation at all.

2.7.1 Ouster clauses

At the beginning of the 20th-century judicial adventure, it was not obvious that the
courts had jurisdiction to give judicial review, if a statute stated that the decision of an
administrative body was 'final'. But in *Pyx Granite Co Ltd v Ministry of Housing and Local
Government* [1960] AC 260 it was clarified: Viscount Simonds said, 'It is a principle not
by any means to be whittled down that the subject's recourse to Her Majesty's courts
for the determination of his rights is not to be excluded except by clear words' (286).
The decision was right, because the fact that an administrative decision is final does
not mean that the courts should not interfere when it has been made unlawfully. But
Viscount Simonds' statement of the principle comes dangerously close to suggesting
that it is the courts' job to determine all questions of right—when it is actually their
job to ensure that authorities that have power to determine questions of right do so
with due process, and do not abuse their power.

Far from being whittled down, Viscount Simonds' principle became overex-
tended in the following years. Lord Steyn suggested, in *Jackson v Attorney General*
[2005] UKHL 56, that the courts might disregard an attempt by Parliament 'to abolish

---

9   But conversely, the Civil Procedure Rules include a far-reaching provision for the Admin-
     istrative Court to step in and make the decision that the public authority should have made if
     'there is no purpose to be served in remitting the matter to the decision-maker' (CPR 54.19(3)).

judicial review or the ordinary role of the courts' [102]. That approach does not treat Parliament as sovereign. And the same approach was taken (though not stated so openly) forty years ago. In *Anisminic v Foreign Compensation Commission* [1969] 2 AC 147 HL, Parliament had provided that:

> 'The determination by the Commission of any application made to them under this Act shall not be called in question in any court of law.' [10]

Yet the House of Lords quashed the Commission's determination of an application made to them under that Act, on the ground that the Commission had misinterpreted the legislation it was to apply, in such a way that its decision did not count as a genuine determination for the purpose of the statute (see p 304). *Anisminic* shows a judicial tendency to inflate the importance of judicial review: if the minority in the House of Lords had prevailed in the case, the result would simply have been that foreign compensation would have been governed by the commission's interpretation of the legislation (an interpretation with which one of the Law Lords agreed), rather than by the interpretation of the majority of the judges. It would still have been possible for courts to interfere—in spite of the ouster clause—with an abuse of power by the administrative decision maker.

The very skeptical approach that judges take to ouster clauses has a long tradition. William Blackstone wrote in the 1760s that tribunals with administrative jurisdictions, 'derogating from the general jurisdiction of the courts of common law, are ever taken strictly, and cannot be extended farther than the express letter of their privileges will most explicitly warrant' (*Commentaries on the Laws of England* (1769), Book iii Chapter 6). It would be a mistake to think of jurisdictions created by statute as automatically derogating from the courts of common law. When a new administrative scheme is created (to award compensation from a foreign compensation fund, for example, or to provide social security, or to award criminal injuries compensation to soldiers ...), Parliament is taking nothing away from the common law courts if it creates a new tribunal to operate the scheme, or to resolve disputes over its operation. We will see in Chapter 12 that one central feature of the reconstruction of tribunals is that finally, after centuries, English law has escaped from the presumption that the ordinary courts are the appropriate forum to determine all legal disputes. Administrative tribunals do not necessarily take away anything at all from the role of the courts, and the role that the courts can play in controlling administrative tribunals should be worked out by asking what they can do to improve decision making—and not by presupposing that the rule of law requires them to interfere with a decision that derogates from their jurisdiction. [11]

---

[10]   Foreign Compensation Act 1950, section 4(4).

[11]   Note the strategy in the reconstruction of tribunals, which is—wisely—not to try to insulate the tribunal system from the ordinary courts by means of an ouster clause, but to allow statutory appeals to the Court of Appeal—see p 452.

This development reflects the tension between a judicial tendency to excessive legalism on the one hand, and the legitimate judicial concern not to leave arbitrary public decisions uncontrolled. The **principle of legality** (see p 19) creates a standing temptation for courts to exaggerate their responsibility for the administration of justice. The temptation is to think that the principle of legality requires that judges quash a decision of another public authority merely on the ground that it is incompatible with the judges' interpretation of the public authority's standards, even if Parliament has said that the courts are not to do so.

That would be a failure of due process. The courts *do* have a general jurisdiction to control the lawfulness of decisions by other public authorities; but the decision-making power of other public authorities is not a derogation from any general jurisdiction of the courts to decide all legal disputes. The creation of any jurisdiction creates a risk of abuse of power. And the court does have a responsibility for restraining abuse of power, to the extent that it can lawfully do so. The courts should do whatever they can lawfully do to prevent other public authorities from turning an ouster clause into a cloak for abuse of power. But if Parliament has decided that determinations of a commission are not to be questioned in court, there is no justification for judges quashing a determination of the commission on the ground that is based on a misinterpretation of its rules. Yet we will see in Chapter 9 that the law of English judicial review requires judges to do just that. In developing that rule, the English judges have gone beyond their responsibility to impose the rule of law, and have—to a limited extent—imposed the rule of judges. And there is one rule-of-law consideration that always weighs *against* judicial review: the interest in the finality of proceedings. Litigation actually works against the rule of law, because it reduces legal certainty (see p 23). The availability of litigation over the lawfulness of an executive decision always leaves matters up in the air, and makes it impossible, for a time, to take an official decision at face value. And litigation often creates incidental risks that the relevant information will no longer be available, or will be misunderstood, in the judicial hearing.

As the European Court of Human Rights held in *Pullar v United Kingdom* (1996) 22 EHRR 391, it is 'an important element of the rule of law' that 'the verdicts of a tribunal should be final and binding unless set aside by a superior court on the basis of irregularity or unfairness' [32].[12] In cases of 'irregularity or unfairness', as the Strasbourg Court called it, judicial review is essential to the rule of law, in spite of the drawbacks of litigation. To justify judicial review, we cannot simply say that the rule of law must subject everything to the rule of courts. We need to find special reasons of constitutional principle that make the litigation a proportionate response to the claim.

Grounds of unlawfulness—grounds of judicial review

An administrative decision made without due process is subject to judicial review because it is unlawful. The three grounds of judicial review (error of law, improper

---

[12]   Cited in *Montgomery v HM Advocate* [2003] 1 AC 641 (PC), 669. The comment concerned a judicial tribunal, but the same reasoning applies to administrative decision makers.

exercise of discretionary power, and lack of due process) are grounds of unlaw-fulness. There is an unlimited number of grounds of unlawfulness that do not concern us because they are not general rules of administrative law, but simply rules of public law: a tax demand is unlawful if there is no legislation to authorize it, and so on.

The grounds of judicial review are not *only* grounds of judicial review; they may provide a defence to criminal prosecution (*Boddington v British Transport Police* [1999] 2 AC 143 (HL)), or to possession proceedings (*Poplar Housing v Donoghue* [2001] EWCA Civ 595). Or they may make an entry to property into a trespass rather than a lawfully authorized act (*Cooper v Board of Works* (1863) 14 CB (NS) 180). Our focus on them as grounds of judicial review is due to this remarkable fact about them: they were invented by the courts as grounds for quashing decisions of other public authorities.

2.8 Conclusion: the core rationale for judicial review

The core rationale for judicial review may seem to be that, if an administrative action is unlawful, courts must step in to impose the law. But that would be a mistake. It is an easy mistake to make, because judges are absolutely essential to justice and the rule of law. Not just judges, but independent, active judges. The judges' capacity is limited, however, and so their constitutional role is limited, too. They 'cannot begin to evaluate the comparative worth of research in clinical dentistry' (R v Higher Education Funding Council, ex p Institute of Dental Surgery [1994] 1 WLR 242), for example. Where fidelity to the law requires an administrative authority to evaluate research in clinical dentistry, the judges are not well equipped to improve the authority's fidelity to law.

The **core rationale** for judicial review: Where there is no other process for impos-ing the rule of law, independent judges should support the rule of law by interfer-ing with another public authority's decisions (if the judges can do so effectively and without damaging the public authority's capacity to do its own job), to impose due process, and to oppose arbitrary government.

So the developments in the English law of imprisonment for murder have been steps toward the rule of law; similar judicial controls on decisions as to the appointment of ministers would not take steps toward the rule of law, but would only give Britain the rule of judges. Where is the boundary between imposing the rule of law and impos-ing the rule of judges? If we keep in mind that all executive decisions ought to be reasonable, but that they cannot necessarily be made more reasonable by legal con-trols, we will see that legal control of an executive decision is not *generally* valuable. Executive action uncontrolled by law is not *generally* arbitrary. Legal control of the executive always needs the justification that it can help the executive to act with just-ice and for the public good.

Control of administrative action by law goes well beyond the core rationale for judicial review. For example, the law sets up ombudsmen to *improve* administration directly, and it establishes tribunals with expert membership to resolve disputes with public authorities, and auditors to improve economic efficiency in administration. But the core rationale for judicial review identifies a central set of tasks for judges— tasks that they are justified in taking on themselves (as they took upon themselves the *habeas corpus* jurisdiction in the Middle Ages). If the courts leave behind the limited role that is supported by that rationale, they may or may not make better decisions than the administrators, but they will not be imposing the rule of law. It is a challenge for judges to articulate a form of supervision of administration that holds to the rule of law. Because of the judges' ongoing struggle to respond to that challenge, judicial review is the best way in to studying administrative law.

The central problems for administrative law are these: what processes ought to be available for the control of one public authority's decision by another public authority? On what grounds ought the second public authority to interfere with a decision of the first public authority? And how can that interference be reconciled with the comity that one public authority owes toward another? All these problems are addressed (articulately, with remarkable results) in the law of judicial review, and that is why Chapters 4 through 9 will unpack the grounds of judicial review outlined in this chapter.

TAKE-HOME MESSAGE • • •

- Respect for **parliamentary sovereignty** requires judges to interfere with other public authorities on any grounds on which Parliament enacts that they should do so.
  - See **Chapter 3** on the Human Rights Act 1998 s 6: Parliament has made it unlawful for a public authority to act in a way which is incompatible with a Convention Right (unless the action is required by an act of Parliament).

- Respect for the **rule of law** justifies judges in imposing due process on other public authorities in their decision making (Chapter 4). Because the rule of law is opposed to the arbitrary use of power, the ideal also justifies judges in developing a doctrine of review for abuse of power (Chapter 7).

- The rule of law also requires judges to control the way in which administrative authorities **interpret** the law. But the judges' duty to impose the rule of law on the administration does not justify the doctrine of review for error of law (on whether there is any other justification for it, see Chapter 9).

- While certain forms of unreasonableness provide grounds for judicial review, **there is no general principle that unreasonable decisions are unlawful**. Every public decision ought to be reasonable, *not* every decision can be made more reasonable by judicial review.

- **Comity** requires judges to supervise decisions of other public authorities in a way that shows respect for their role, and that reflects the reasons why the power to make those decisions was given to a body that is not a court.

> ### Critical reading
>
> Associated Provincial Picture Houses Ltd v Wednesbury Corporation [1948] 1 KB 223 (CA)
> R v Ministry of Defence, ex p Walker [2000] 1 WLR 806

CRITICAL QUESTIONS • • •

1 What is the purpose of judicial review: is it to police the lawfulness of administrative action? To right injustices to claimants?

2 Can you explain the difference between review for error of law, and review for the proper use of discretionary power?

3 Can you find examples of judges explicitly basing their decisions in judicial review on the rule of law?

4 Do judges play a political role in judicial review? Should they?

Further questions:

5 Can you think of *any* grounds on which a court ought to be prepared to review a decision by the Prime Minister to recommend the appointment of a particular person as a minister of Crown?

6 Would judicial review become unnecessary, if Parliament had better techniques for scrutinizing the executive?

online
resource
centre

Visit the online resource centre to access the following resources which accompany this chapter: links to legislation and online reports of judicial decisions, summaries of key cases and legislation, updates in the law, suggestions for answering the pop quizzes and questions, and links to useful websites.

3 Convention rights and administrative law

The **European Convention on Human Rights** is a remarkable treaty that not only guarantees certain rights, but also creates an international Court. The **Human Rights Act** gives English judges *dramatic* but *limited* techniques for vindicating the Convention rights. Those techniques will be seen at work throughout this book. This chapter surveys what the judges in Strasbourg and in England have made of the power they have been given to develop their own role in protecting fundamental rights.

LOOK FOR • • •

- The content and the structure of the Convention rights.

- The ways in which those rights are protected in English administrative law, particularly through the Human Rights Act.

- Tests of proportionality required by the Convention, and the extraordinary role that it gives to judges.

- The role of the Strasbourg Court, and the role of the English courts.

> ❛The Human Rights Act 1998 was no doubt intended to strengthen the rule of law but not to inaugurate the rule of lawyers.❜
> *R (Alconbury) v Environment Secretary* [2001] UKHL 23 [129] (Lord Hoffmann)

> ❛The Convention respects the general principle of the separation of powers between the executive and the courts, including the principle that there remain some areas which are essentially matters for the executive and not the courts.❜
> *R (Gentle) v Prime Minister* [2006] EWCA Civ 1689 [75]

3.1 *Venables and Thompson*: the difference the Convention makes

When they were 10 and 11 years old, Jon Venables and Robert Thompson killed Jamie Bulger, who was two years old. After they were convicted of murder, the Home Secretary had a statutory power[1] to set a tariff (the time they would spend in prison before they could be considered for release; see p 50). The Bulger family and others campaigned for a long tariff. The Home Secretary received thousands of letters, a petition signed by 278,300 people, and 21,281 coupons clipped out of *The Sun*, in favour of imprisoning the boys for the rest of their lives. The coupons read, 'Dear Home Secretary, I agree with Ralph and Denise Bulger that the boys who killed their son James should stay in jail for LIFE.' The coupons followed a campaign under headlines such as '80,000 call TV to say Bulger killers must rot in jail' (*R v Home Secretary, ex p Venables and Thompson* [1998] AC 407, 525). The Home Secretary set a tariff of 15 years, rather than the 8 years that the trial judge had recommended. And because the Home Secretary wanted the world to know that he was responding to the popular clamour, the announcement of his decision said that one of his reasons was 'the public concern about this case, which was evidenced by the petitions and other correspondence'.

When Venables and Thompson challenged the tariff decision in judicial review, a controversy over the separation of powers divided the House of Lords. The majority held that it was unlawful for the Home Secretary to take the coupons into account. Lord Steyn said:

> ❛In fixing a tariff the Home Secretary is carrying out, contrary to the constitutional principle of separation of powers, a classic judicial function.... Parliament must be assumed to have entrusted the power to the Home Secretary on the supposition that, like a sentencing judge, the Home Secretary would not act contrary to fundamental principles governing the administration of justice. Plainly a sentencing judge must ignore a newspaper campaign designed to encourage him to increase a particular sentence. It would be an abdication of the rule of law for a judge to take into account such matters.❜ (526)

---

[1]   Under the Criminal Justice Act 1991.

Lord Lloyd dissented, arguing that:

> ' It is to the Home Secretary that Parliament has entrusted the task of maintaining public confidence in the criminal justice system, and as part of that task gauging public concern in relation to a particular case when deciding on the earliest release date. I do not regard it as the function of the courts to tell him how to perform that task. ' (517)

The judges had to work out whether the principles of the separation of powers and the rule of law (see p 14 and p 18) *prohibited* the Home Secretary from acting on the basis of public clamour—or whether Parliament had deliberately given him the power *because* politicians respond to popular opinion. It was not the judges' job to prevent him from doing the job Parliament gave him. But did Parliament give him the job of deciding like a judge? Or the job of deciding on the basis of public opinion about the child murderers? The question raised an especially controversial problem of **comity** (see p 17), because the courts had to decide whether the Home Secretary—a politician—could act on political considerations.

How much simpler it became when the lawyers for Venables and Thomson took their case to the European Court of Human Rights in Strasbourg. In two sentences, the Court observed that the European Convention on Human Rights guarantees a fair hearing by an independent tribunal, and held that 'independent' means independent *of the executive*. Since the Home Secretary is a member of the executive, the boys' punishment was not decided by an independent tribunal, so that their Convention right under Art 6 had been violated (*V v United Kingdom* (2000) 30 EHRR 121).

Why was the Strasbourg decision so much simpler? Because the decision raised no question about the Court's own power. The Strasbourg Court did not need to invent for itself a creative way of controlling another public authority's power; the Convention gave the Court the task of deciding whether the boys' rights had been violated. Today, in limited ways, the Human Rights Act gives English courts the same task.

Some problems of comity are solved, when the law gives judges the job of enforcing fundamental rights. Their task is prescribed by law, when a Convention right has been violated. Yet deciding *whether* a Convention right has been violated often requires a court to work out and to justify its own role in protecting fundamental rights. Really difficult problems of comity emerge in litigation over Convention rights, when courts need to decide whether to defer to other public authorities in deciding the content of the rights.

We need to deal with those problems throughout this book; in this chapter we will start with a sketch of the institutions that give effect to the Convention rights, the processes by which they do so, and the content of the rights themselves.

3.2 The European Convention, the European Court of Human Rights, and the English courts

In 1950, Britain signed the European Convention on Human Rights. In 1966, Britain allowed petitions to the European Court of Human Rights in Strasbourg. The Convention empowers the Strasbourg Court to interpret and to apply the Convention, in deciding complaints either by another contracting state, or by a person who claims to have been the victim of a violation of a Convention right (Arts 32, 33, 34). Judgments of the European Court of Human Rights bind the state against which a complaint is made (Art 46). But they are not directly binding in English law. They are binding in *international* law, which requires states to abide by treaty obligations. The British government has a regular practice of complying with its treaty obligations, but those obligations cannot be enforced in an English court.

Before the Human Rights Act 1998 came into force in October 2000, Convention rights had a very important impact on administration, because the government took steps to meet its treaty obligation. The Convention had no direct effect in English law. But since 1966, the British government has consistently responded to declarations of the Strasbourg Court by providing a remedy. So, for example, as soon as the European Court of Human Rights declared that Venables and Thomson's right under Art 6 had been violated, the Home Secretary announced that he would ask the Lord Chief Justice to decide the tariff, and the Lord Chief Justice reinstated the eight-year tariff set by the trial judge. If the Home Secretary had not done that, the UK would have been in violation of its treaty obligation. But Venables and Thompson would not have been able to ask an English court to do anything about it.

Even before the Human Rights Act, though, the Convention had an indirect effect in English administrative law: Lord Bingham said that 'the Convention exerted a persuasive and pervasive influence on judicial decision-making in this country, affecting the interpretation of ambiguous statutory provisions, guiding the exercise of discretions, bearing on the development of the common law' (R v Lyons [2003] 1 AC 976 [13]). The judges used it as a way of deciding what actions counted as an abuse of discretion. But the *Smith* case shows how limited that effect was: Convention rights provided a background to applying the *Wednesbury* principles of judicial review (see p 226), and did not provide a different ground of review.

Jeanette Smith was discharged from the Royal Air Force under a policy that homosexuals could not serve in the armed forces, regardless of their conduct. She claimed that the policy infringed her right to privacy in Art 8 of the Convention. But the Human Rights Act was years in the future, and she could not argue that the policy was unlawful on the ground that it infringed a Convention right. In judicial review, she used Art 8 as a ground for arguing that the policy was an unlawful use of discretion under the ordinary English doctrines of control of discretionary power.

Lord Justice Simon Brown said that the protection of fundamental rights is a responsibility of the courts, but that they could only interfere 'if it were plain beyond sensible argument' that the policy was pointless (R v Ministry of Defence, ex p Smith [1996] QB 517, 541).

> ❝ If the Convention for the Protection of Human Rights and Fundamental Freedoms were part of our law and we were accordingly entitled to ask whether the policy answers a pressing social need and whether the restriction on human rights involved can be shown proportionate to the benefits then clearly the primary judgment (subject only to a limited 'margin of appreciation') would be for us and not others: the constitutional balance would shift. ❞ (541)

That is, the questions for an English court in 1996 remained the Wednesbury questions: whether the Ministry of Defence had acted on relevant considerations, and whether the decision was one which a reasonable decision maker could make. Smith made it clear that the courts would not turn Convention rights into legal limits on administrative action. That was up to Parliament.

The European Court of Human Rights has never been subject to the constitutional bounds that the English courts observed in Smith. The Convention gives it a jurisdiction to interpret and to apply the Convention rights. Jeanette Smith's complaint was upheld in Strasbourg: the Court held that the blanket ban on homosexuals violated Art 8. The Court reached that decision by addressing the question that the English courts had declined to address: whether the impact of the policy on the interests protected by Art 8 was **proportionate** to the benefits that the Ministry of Defence was trying to achieve by banning homosexuals. The Court emphasized that the English law of judicial review had prevented the English courts from considering 'whether the interference with the applicants' rights answered a pressing social need or was proportionate to the national security and public order aims pursued, principles which lie at the heart of the Court's analysis of complaints under Article 8 of the Convention' (Smith v United Kingdom (2000) 29 EHRR 493 [138]).

The Venables and Thompson and Smith cases show the two crucial respects in which the work of the European Court of Human Rights differs from the protection of fundamental rights in the common law:

(1) At common law, a statutory power could be controlled in ways that promote the rule of law and the separation of powers, but the power could not be taken away even if it conflicted with those principles (Venables and Thompson).

(2) At common law, fundamental rights were relevant to the legal control of a statutory or prerogative power only if the fact that such rights were violated was a reason to hold that an action was unlawful under the Wednesbury principles (Smith).

Under the Convention:

(1) No infringement of rights can be justified on the ground that the legislature of a state authorized it.

(2) Interferences with the interests protected by Convention rights must be *proportionate to the pursuit of legitimate purposes.*

But until 1998, those special effects of the Convention could only be pursued legally by a complaint to the European Court of Human Rights. The Human Rights Act would indeed shift the constitutional balance, through four quite specific devices.

3.3 The four techniques of the Human Rights Act

The Human Rights Act 1998 does not incorporate the Convention into English law; it uses four techniques to give specific effects to some[2] of the Convention rights:

- a new technique for reading and giving effect to statutes (s 3),

- a new ground on which administrative action can be unlawful (s 6),

- a new power to give a remedy in relation to acts that are unlawful under s 6, including an award of damages if 'necessary to afford just satisfaction' (s 8) (see section 14.6), and

- a new governmental power to amend statutes that the judges declare to be incompatible with Convention rights (ss 4, 10).

Under s 6, 'it is unlawful for a public authority to act in a way which is incompatible with a Convention right'—except that it is not unlawful to do so, if the public authority 'was acting so as to give effect' to an incompatible provision in primary legislation.[3]

'So far as it is possible', primary and subordinate legislation 'must be read and given effect in a way which is compatible with Convention rights' (s 3). If that is not possible, the court can declare that the primary legislation is incompatible with a Convention right (s 4). A declaration of incompatibility does not affect the validity or change the legal effect of the incompatible provision (s 4(6)). Instead, it triggers a fast-track amendment procedure (s 10), by which the government can make a remedial order. A remedial order can amend a statute if each House of Parliament approves it by a resolution—a process that is simpler and faster than the passage of a new statute.

If the government has infringed a Convention right, the Human Rights Act gives a simple basis for judicial control of executive power. Remember the difference the European Convention made in *Venables and Thompson*. Compare the controversial and elaborate reasoning in the House of Lords decision (quashing the Home Secretary's decision on the ground that he had acted on an irrelevant consideration by

2   The duty of contracting states under Art 1 to 'secure to everyone within their jurisdiction the rights and freedoms defined in Section I of this Convention' was omitted, as was the Art 13 right to an effective remedy; in both cases the drafters wanted to control the techniques that were invented for the Human Rights Act, rather than authorize judges to give effect to the Convention on its own terms. This is one reason why it is misleading to say that the Act 'incorporated' the Convention into English law.

3   'Primary legislation' includes not only acts of Parliament, but also orders in Council under the prerogative (s 21(1)). So those exercises of executive authority cannot be quashed under s 6, even though they are not protected from judicial review on common law grounds.

basing it partly on coupons from *The Sun*), with the simple decision in the European Court of Human Rights (Art 6 was infringed because the Home Secretary was not an independent tribunal). Under the Human Rights Act, the English courts can—like the European Court of Human Rights—declare that the statute giving the Home Secretary such a power is incompatible with the Convention. A declaration to that effect from the Strasbourg Court has no legal effect on the operation of the statute in English law, but is binding on the United Kingdom in international law. A declaration of incompatibility from the English courts has no legal effect on the operation of the statute, but it makes it easy for the government to change the legislation. And it has the effect of imposing an obscure sort of political onus on the government to do so—though the Human Rights Act itself does *not* say that the government must change the legislation.

A popular misconception

When the courts declare that a statute is incompatible with the Convention, as in *A and X v Home Secretary* [2004] UKHL 56 (see p 6), politicians and reporters often say that the courts have held that the statute, or the government's actions under the statute, are unlawful. That is a misconception. The Act leaves it to Parliament to decide *whether to change* a law after a court declares that it is incompatible with a Convention right.

This blind spot in the media corresponds to a very strong expectation that has developed in political circles: the expectation that when the courts declare that a statute is incompatible with a Convention right, the government will present a remedial measure to Parliament, and Parliament will approve it. In fact, there is nothing in English law to require any remedial measure even to be considered. But the developing political expectation that it will happen is bolstered by a sobering fact: if the government does not respond to a declaration of incompatibility by changing the statute, the complainant can still go to the European Court of Human Rights. And then the government will be bound in international law to honour any declaration that is made in Strasbourg.

After the Human Rights Act, in *R (Anderson) v Home Secretary* [2002] UKHL 46, the House of Lords did the same thing for adult murderers that the European Court of Human Rights had done for child murderers in *V v UK*. Once the House of Lords accepted that deciding the tariff for a life prisoner was a sentencing function, the case was as straightforward in the English courts as Venables and Thompson's case had been in the European Court of Human Rights: Art 6 requires an independent tribunal for sentencing decisions, and the Home Secretary is not an independent tribunal.[4]

---

4   The fate of a life prisoner *after* the tariff is still governed by an administrative process carried out by the Parole Board, with representations made by the Home Office and the prisoner. See p 124.

Anderson's case is a good example of the effect that the Human Rights Act has on English public law. It also shows the effect that the Act does *not* have. Given the interpretative tool in s 3, and the tool for direct control of official action in s 6, the judges could have remodelled the law dramatically, either by giving a Convention-compatible effect under s 3 to statutory provisions that seem clearly incompatible, or by taking a restrictive view of the circumstances in which a public authority is acting 'so as to give effect' to an incompatible statutory provision, under s 6. The impact of the Act on judicial review is limited because the House of Lords is not willing to use either s 3 or s 6 to interfere directly with a public authority's decision in a case like *Anderson*. Instead, a declaration of incompatibility will be issued. And yet, we will see that in the right circumstances, the Law Lords will actually use s 3 to give an effect to a statute that is contrary to what Parliament has enacted.

A cure for the American disease?

The United States courts can quash an Act of Congress that violates the Bill of Rights, and the only democratic technique for overruling the judges is a very stringent constitutional amendment procedure (U.S. Constitution Art V). In Canada, the courts can quash statutes that violate the Charter of Rights. But the federal and provincial legislatures can put a statute beyond the judges' reach by expressly providing that it is to have effect notwithstanding the Charter.

In formulating the Human Rights Act, the Labour government was keen not to give judges the power to quash statutes at all (and the English judges did not generally want that role).

But note

(1) The less direct techniques of the Human Rights Act do not free the judges from making the policy judgments that American and Canadian judges must make, because the issues that underlie a decision in Britain to declare a statute incompatible with the guarantee of freedom of expression are the same as the issues that underlie a decision in the U.S. or Canada to quash a statute. The English judges' role is *no less political* than the role of the U.S. and Canadian Supreme Courts. But the power of Parliament is less restricted than the power of the American and Canadian legislatures, because the legal effect of the judges' decisions is different.

(2) The techniques of the Human Rights Act mitigate the separation of powers problem by giving the government (and Parliament) control over remedial measures, and by giving the government no legal obligation to do anything at all to respond to a declaration of incompatibility. But those techniques put pressure on the interpretative obligation in s 3 (which has no parallel in the U.S. or Canada), and on decisions as to whether an administrative act counts as 'giving effect' to a statute, under s 6.

3.3.1 Section 3: the art of the possible

> **3. Interpretation of legislation**
>
> (1) So far as it is possible to do so, primary legislation and subordinate legislation must be read and given effect in a way which is compatible with the Convention rights.....

A claimant challenging action under a statute will generally want to use s 3 if possible (and ask the court to give the legislation an effect that is compatible with the Convention), instead of asking for a declaration of incompatibility (which does not affect the operation of the legislation or the lawfulness of action taken under it). The government may prefer it, too. If the court can remove an apparent incompatibility by interpreting it away, the government will not need to make a remedial measure. A declaration of incompatibility means that the government controls the form of any change in the law (subject to approval by each House of Parliament), but the government may not want that control. The courts have said repeatedly that a declaration of incompatibility is 'a measure of last resort' (e.g. Lord Steyn in R v A (No 2) [2001] UKHL 25 [44] and *Ghaidan v Godin-Mendoza* [2004] UKHL 30 [39]), and that s 3 is 'the principal remedial measure' (*Ghaidan* [39]).

So, when a statute seems to be incompatible with a Convention right, both parties *and* the court may be in favour of finding a way to give the statute an effect that conforms to the Convention rights. But the courts are to do so only 'so far as possible'. Claimants often ask courts to push the boundaries of the possible, and public authorities may ask the courts to push the boundaries too, as an alternative to a declaration of incompatibility.[5] Where are the boundaries?

Judges still have to 'read and give effect' to legislation. Legislation does not have effect *subject to* Convention rights, as legislation has effect subject to rules of European Community law.[6] Instead, legislation is to be given effect in a way that is compatible with Convention rights, so far as it is possible to do so. Section 3 'does not affect the validity, continuing operation or enforcement of any incompatible primary legislation' (s 3(2)(b)). So this may seem easy: if a statute can be read in more than one way, then a court must choose a Convention-compatible reading, if there is one. If the statute is clearly incompatible with a Convention right, then it

---

5   In *R (H) v London North and East Region Mental Health Review Tribunal* [2001] EWCA Civ 415, and *Ghaidan v Godin-Mendoza* [2004] UKHL 30, the Government's counsel argued that the statutes in question should be interpreted so as to make them comply—so that a declaration of incompatibility was not necessary.

6   European Communities Act 1972 s 2(4) provides that 'any enactment passed or to be passed, shall be construed and have effect subject to' provisions requiring the recognition and enforcement of EC law. In *R v Transport Secretary, ex p Factortame (No 2)* [1991] 1 AC 603, the House of Lords held that 'Under the terms of the Act of 1972 it has always been clear that it was the duty of a United Kingdom court, when delivering final judgment, to override any rule of national law found to be in conflict with any directly enforceable rule of Community law' (Lord Bridge, 659).

is impossible to read it and to give effect to it in a way that is compatible with the Convention (and the court can only declare that it is incompatible).

But no, it is not that simple—the judges have decided that s 3 must have some more far-reaching effect than that. The Act did not need to do anything merely to let them resolve ambiguities in a Convention-compatible manner, for they could do that already.[7] It is common ground both that s 3 changes the effect of legislation, *and* that it does not give the judges a licence to ignore a statute. But because the Human Rights Act does not say what change it is making, it is unclear what would count as ignoring a statute.

At first the judges showed restraint. Consider *Anderson*, an important early case on s 3. The Home Secretary had power under a statute to set a tariff of imprisonment for murderers (Crime (Sentences) Act 1997 s 29). But Art 6 requires a hearing by an independent tribunal. The Law Lords made a declaration of incompatibility under s 4. Why couldn't they have held that it was possible to give effect to the Act in a way that is compatible with Art 6? The Act did not require the Home Secretary to use his power to impose a longer tariff than the trial judge or the Lord Chief Justice had recommended. So you might think that s 3 of the Human Rights Act required the court to give effect to the Act subject to a duty implied by Art 6 not to set a longer tariff than an independent tribunal (i.e., the trial court) had recommended. The prisoner would not be disadvantaged by the fact that the power was held by a politician, and there would be no Art 6 complaint. Yet the legislation would not be contradicted.

The Law Lords all rejected that approach: it 'would not be judicial interpretation but judicial vandalism' (Lord Bingham [30]); 'It would not be interpretation but interpolation inconsistent with the plain legislative intent' (Lord Steyn [59]); it would be 'to engage in the amendment of a statute and not in its interpretation' (Lord Hutton [81]). The conclusion is that it is not possible to give effect to an act conferring a power on the Home Secretary *as if* it imposed an obligation to use the power on the advice of the judges.

That is the restrained approach; it holds on to the distinction between interpreting what Parliament has enacted, and giving effect to a statute *as if* Parliament had enacted something else. But then what is the point of s 3, and what effect does it have on legislation? In *Ghaidan*, the House of Lords gave a revolutionary answer. Section 3 may result in a change in the effect of legislation, and it is the judges' job to decide what the change is to be.

The 'fundamental features' approach

Since 1920, legislation has protected a widow from being thrown out of her home if her late husband had a protected tenancy. Widowers gained similar protection in 1980, and unmarried survivors of cohabiting heterosexual relationships gained it in 1988 (*Ghaidan* [14]). Juan Godin-Mendoza claimed the same protection when his same-sex partner died. He claimed a statutory right to succeed to the tenancy as a

---

7   See e.g. Lord Steyn in R v A (No 2) [2002] 1 AC 45 [44], and Lord Millett in *Ghaidan* [60].

surviving spouse under the 1988 amendment to the Rent Act 1977. The legislation counted a person 'living with the original tenant as his or her wife or husband' as a spouse [4]. The House of Lords held that treating survivors of long-term homosexual partnerships less favourably than survivors of long-term heterosexual partnerships infringed their rights under Arts 8 and 14 of the Convention.

But Godin-Mendoza was not living with the original tenant as his or her wife or husband.[8] So he was not a 'spouse' under the statute. When the House of Lords held that it was contrary to his Convention rights for his relationship to be treated differently from a heterosexual relationship, you might think that the result would be a declaration of incompatibility under s 4. But the House of Lords revolutionized s 3 by using it to give the Rent Act an effect that was compatible with their conclusion on Godin-Mendoza's Convention rights—an effect that was incompatible with the legislation.

How could they give Godin-Mendoza statutory protection, if the statute only provided protection for a person living with the original tenant as his or her wife or husband? Lord Steyn built on his earlier decision in R v A (No 2) [2002] 1 AC 45, in which, he said, the House of Lords had 'rejected linguistic arguments in favour of a broader approach' [47]–[48].[9] He suggested that 'linguistic arguments' are picky and technical and should not stand in the way of 'bringing rights home' [46]. Similarly, Lord Rodger insisted on 'concentrating on matters of substance, rather than on matters of mere language' [123]. But legislation is nothing but the authoritative decision of the legislature to enact the mere language of a bill into law. The task of judges in interpretation has always been to decide the effect of that decision in the context in which it is taken. The opposition to 'linguistic arguments' should not obscure the fact that the House of Lords has decided that it must use s 3 to depart from what Parliament enacted. Lord Nicholls said, 'to an extent bounded only by what is "possible", a court can modify the meaning, and hence the effect, of primary and secondary legislation' [32]. As Lord Rodger put it, 'where the court finds it possible to read a provision in a way which is compatible with Convention rights, such a reading may involve a considerable departure from the actual words' [119]. He might have said, 'a considerable departure from the act of Parliament'.

Once the courts will treat a statute as if it meant something different from what it means, where will it all end? The Ghaidan answer is that the courts should not 'adopt a meaning' that is inconsistent with 'a fundamental feature of legislation' [33], or 'an important feature expressed clearly in the legislation' [34], or 'essential

---

[8]   Not only is it clear from the words of the legislation; the House of Lords had decided that a person does not live with his or her homosexual partner 'as his or her wife or husband' in Fitzpatrick v Sterling Housing Association Ltd [2001] 1 AC 27, a case in which the original tenant had died before the Human Rights Act came into effect.

[9]   A statute excluded evidence of the sexual conduct of the alleged victim in a rape trial, unless the similarity between the conduct in the evidence and the facts of the alleged offence 'cannot reasonably be explained as a coincidence'. In R v A (No 2), the House of Lords gave effect to that provision so as to allow evidence that is 'so relevant to the issue of consent that to exclude it would endanger the fairness of the trial under article 6 of the Convention' (see Ghaidan [46]).

principles' [121], or the 'substance of the measure which Parliament has enacted' [123], or a 'cardinal principle' [128]. The effect given to the legislation must 'go with the grain of the legislation' [121]; it must not 'remove the very core and essence, the "pith and substance" of the measure that Parliament had enacted' [111]. It must be consistent with 'its cardinal principles' [114].

Ghaidan has the potential to make the effect of statutes very unclear, and to give the courts an unprecedented responsibility for deciding what is essential, important, fundamental, or cardinal in the legislation. This approach still does not give the Convention the overriding effect on legislation that EC law has. But it gives the courts a vaguely defined power to give a statute an effect that is incompatible with what Parliament enacted.

And because public authorities will often prefer a novel 'interpretation' to a declaration of incompatibility, s 3 can generate really striking, unargued changes in the effect of a statute. The decision in R (Hammond) v Home Secretary [2005] UKHL 69 treated a statutory provision that a life prisoner's tariff 'is to be determined by a single judge of the High Court **without an oral hearing**' [5] as giving the judge a discretion to **require an oral hearing** where fairness required it (Criminal Justice Act 2003 Sch 22 para 11(1)). The Home Secretary accepted that the provision ought to be read that way if it would otherwise be incompatible with the Convention, and because the Home Secretary took that position, the Law Lords treated it as an issue that they did not need to decide (Lord Bingham [17]). Lord Hoffmann said, 'Neither side challenged this proposition and your Lordships are therefore not asked to decide whether such a bold exercise in "interpretation" is permissible' [29]. So if the government does not contest it, statutes can actually be given an effect that is flat contrary to their terms, with no consideration of the issue by the judges.

Yet the judges still like to say, as they did in *Anderson*, that they are interpreting legislation and not amending it. Lord Rodger insisted in *Ghaidan* that the majority decision did not cross 'the boundary between interpretation and amendment' [113].

> ❛ When the court spells out the words that are to be implied, it may look as if it is "amending" the legislation, but that is not the case. If the court implies words that are consistent with the scheme of the legislation but necessary to make it compatible with Convention rights, it is simply performing the duty which Parliament has imposed on it and on others. ❜ [10] [121]

If Parliament has imposed on courts a duty to do it, that does not mean that the courts are not amending statutes. The *Ghaidan* approach has the same effect as a rule that the courts must amend legislation to make it compatible with the Convention, as long as they can do it without amending any fundamental feature. According to

----

[10]   Cf. Lord Nicholls in In re S [2002] 2 AC 291 [39], 'Interpretation of statutes is a matter for the courts; the enactment of statutes, and the amendment of statutes, are matters for Parliament.'

Ghaidan, it really does not matter whether a proposed 'interpretation' is patently incompatible with what Parliament enacted, as long as it does not go against something fundamental or important or cardinal in the legislation. And the courts are to judge what is fundamental.

In *R (Wilkinson) v Inland Revenue Commissioners* [2005] UKHL 30, Lord Hoffmann preserved the notion that s 3 requires interpretation. And he helpfully described interpretation as the process of deciding what meaning 'the reasonable reader would give to the statute read against its background, including, now, an assumption that it was not intended to be incompatible with Convention rights' [18]. He held that a bereavement allowance payable only to *widows* was incompatible with the Convention, but refused to use s 3 to interpret the statute so as to extend the allowance to a *widower*. He said that 'The contrary indications in the language...of the 1988 Act[11] are too strong' [19]. Is that a step back from Lord Steyn's approach in *Ghaidan*, which rejects 'linguistic arguments'? Not necessarily: Lord Hoffmann claimed that his judgment in *Wilkinson* was consistent with *Ghaidan*. To reconcile the cases, we need only conclude that giving benefits to widows and not to widowers was a fundamental feature of the legislation in *Wilkinson*. Yet Lord Hoffmann's own account of *Ghaidan* shows that the House of Lords in that case had 'interpreted' the words 'as his or her wife or husband' 'to refer to a relationship...not limited to the heterosexual relationship of husband and wife' [18]. The reasonable reader—even assuming that Parliament does not intend to infringe Convention rights—would not conclude that Parliament meant to use 'wife or husband' to refer to a different relationship from that of wife and husband.

Section 3 does not *say* that courts should modify statutes: it is headed 'Interpretation of legislation', and it requires that statutes be 'read and given effect'. So have the courts illegitimately taken on themselves a legislative power to *modify* statutes, rather than to interpret them? Lord Millett, dissenting in *Ghaidan*, evidently thought so: 'any change in a fundamental constitutional principle', he said, 'should be the consequence of deliberate legislative action and not judicial activism, however well meaning' [57]. But it is possible to say the following in favour of the approach that the judges took to using s 3 to modify statutes in *Ghaidan*: it is **limited,** and there are **considerations in favour** of treating the Human Rights Act as authorizing changes in the effect of statutes.

Limits on the impact of *Ghaidan*

(1) Under the *Ghaidan* doctrine, judges cannot change statutes as they see fit; they can only change a statute so as to make it compatible with Convention rights.

(2) *Ghaidan* limits the judges' power to change statutes not only through the 'fundamental features' doctrine, but also by insisting that even where no fundamental feature is at stake, s 3 cannot be used to solve a problem of incompatibility with Convention rights, if doing so would require courts 'to make decisions for which they are not equipped' [33].

----

[11]   Income and Corporation Taxes Act 1988.

(3) *Ghaidan* has a limited impact, because if the courts issued a declaration of incompatibility instead, the government would promptly make a remedial measure to conform to the court's declaration. Given the strong political tradition that has already developed (of taking such measures in response to declarations of incompatibility) the *Ghaidan* approach may achieve the same change in the law as a remedial measure, without taking Parliamentary time.[12]

(4) Adventurous interpretations under s 3 can be controlled by Parliament. After a decision like R *v* A (No 2), there is nothing to stop Parliament from passing legislation in which, in Lord Steyn's words, 'a *clear* limitation on Convention rights is stated *in terms*' [68].[13] In litigation over the effect of the new legislation, the judges could do nothing but declare it to be incompatible with a Convention right.

Considerations in favour of changing the effect of a statute under s 3

(1) Parliament implied in s 3 that the effect of statutes was to change *somehow*, and did not say how. So Parliament invited the judicial activism that Lord Millett opposed.

(2) The *Ghaidan* approach does not stop Parliament from legislating contrary to Convention rights, if it chooses to do so.

(3) The 'so far as it is possible' technique in s 3 is borrowed from EC law, and by that borrowing, the Human Rights Act implicitly authorizes some sort of change in the effect of statutes.

This last point is particularly important. When statutes or regulations are enacted for the purpose of implementing EC law, the English courts under European Communities Act 1972 s 2 have long been construing the legislation so as to make it consistent with EC law, 'however wide a departure from the *prima facie* meaning of the language of the provision might be needed in order to achieve consistency' (*Garland v British Rail Engineering* [1983] 2 AC 751, Lord Diplock 771). In order to achieve consistency with the Treaty (*Pickstone v Freemans* [1989] AC 66) or a directive (*Litster v Forth Dry Dock & Engineering* [1990] 1 AC 546), the House of Lords was willing to give the legislation an effect that 'may involve some departure from the strict and literal application of the words which the legislature has elected to use' (*Litster*, Lord Oliver 559).

Then, in a landmark 1990 decision, the ECJ held that EU directives must affect the interpretation of the law of member states in this dramatic fashion, whether the

---

[12]   But note that the *Ghaidan* approach can make all the difference for a particular claimant; in *Ghaidan* itself the dispute was between two private parties, and a remedial measure would not have helped Godin-Mendoza.

[13]   Cf. 'If Parliament disagrees with an interpretation by the courts under section 3(1), it is free to override it by amending the legislation and expressly reinstating the incompatibility.' Lord Steyn in *Ghaidan* [43].

member state has tried to implement the directive or not, and whether the member state law was adopted before or after the directive was issued. A national court interpreting national law 'is required to do so, **as far as possible**, in the light of the wording and the purpose of the directive' (Case C-106/89 *Marleasing SA v La Comercial Internacional de Alimentación SA* [1990] ECR I-4135 [8].[14] The idea was that the European Treaty required all the authorities of member states, including the courts, 'to ensure the fulfilment' [8] of a directive. Similarly, the Human Rights Act was designed to include the English courts in the project of securing the Convention rights, by giving them a new authority (and duty) to 'read and give effect' to primary legislation in a way that is compatible with Convention rights. The power to change the effect of statutes under *Ghaidan* is supported by the fact that the Human Rights Act borrows this 'so far as it is possible' idea from *Marleasing*.

We can summarize the effect of s 3 on administrative law by saying that Parliament did not tell the courts what they can do to make statutes compatible with the Convention rights; Parliament told the courts to do what they can. The phrase 'so far as it is possible to do so' in s 3 is best understood to mean 'so far as it can be done without undermining the control over changes to statutes that the Human Rights Act reserves to the government and to Parliament through s 3(2) and s 4'. So you cannot work out how statutes are to be interpreted, without answering a question about the separation of powers under the Human Rights Act between judges and Parliament. And the judges have authority to decide the effect of s 3, so the Human Rights Act gives them an ill-defined (but not unlimited) power to change the effect of statutes.

Dramatic uncertainties result in cases like *Ghaidan* and *Wilkinson*. We should not exaggerate the uncertainties. Public authorities have always faced uncertainties as to how the courts might interpret legislation. And it may conceivably be quite clear that a fundamental feature of a statute is incompatible with a Convention right (so that s 3 will not solve the problem)—or, conversely, that a novel reading of a statute would solve a problem of incompatibility with Convention rights, without departing from a fundamental feature (so that s 3 requires the problem to be solved that way). But this new form of uncertainty can be extravagant: the legislation may be perfectly clear, and yet until a court decides the matter, the parties do not know if a court will treat a widower *as if* he were a widow, or whether a court will treat a person with a partner of the same sex *as if* he were a husband or wife.

● *Pop quiz* ●

What do you think of the following argument? Before the Human Rights Act, it was the duty of a court to give the best possible interpretation of a statute. Now it is the duty of a court to give the most Convention-compatible interpretation of a statute. So if the best possible interpretation of a statute is compatible with the Convention, s 3 makes no difference. Therefore, the only effect that s 3 can possibly have is to stop a court from giving the best interpretation of the statute.

---

[14]   Lord Steyn comments on the *Marleasing* case in *Ghaidan v Godin-Mendoza* [2004] UKHL 30 [45].

3.3.2 Section 6: the effect of 'effect'

> **6. Acts of public authorities**
>
> (1) It is unlawful for a public authority to act in a way which is incompatible with a Convention right.
>
> (2) Subsection (1) does not apply to an act if—
>
>   (a) as the result of one or more provisions of primary legislation, the authority could not have acted differently; or
>
>   (b) in the case of one or more provisions of, or made under, primary legislation which cannot be read or given effect in a way which is compatible with the Convention rights, the authority was acting so as to give effect to or enforce those provisions....

Don't mix up the Human Rights Act s 6 with Art 6 of the Convention!

In *Anderson's* case (see p 77), the House of Lords declared the Crime (Sentences) Act 1997 s 29 incompatible with the right to a fair trial under Art 6 of the Convention, as the Act gave power to the Home Secretary (rather than to an independent and impartial tribunal) to set the minimum tariff for an adult mandatory life prisoner. When the Home Secretary set a longer tariff than that recommended by the judiciary, why didn't the House of Lords use the Human Rights Act 1998 s 6 to quash the decision as an unlawful exercise of his statutory power, rather than declaring that the statute was incompatible with the Convention? The Home Secretary would still have been giving effect to primary legislation if he had *not* increased the tariff, but accepted the judge's recommendation. The Crime (Sentences) Act 1997 did not require him to depart from what the trial judge had recommended. So you might think that the House of Lords could have achieved compatibility with Art 6 without declaring the statute incompatible, by ordering the Home Secretary to abide by judicial recommendations as to tariff.

The House of Lords rejected that approach. Parliament had decided to give the choice to the Home Secretary, and that was the Art 6 problem. If the House of Lords had ordered the Home Secretary not to act on his own judgment, it would have been rejecting Parliament's decision. As Lord Hutton said, 'in forming his own view whether to accept the recommendation of the judiciary as to tariff or to fix a longer tariff period and when to refer a case to the Parole Board, the Home Secretary is acting in accordance with the intention of Parliament' [82].

That does not mean that, under the Human Rights Act 1998 s 6(2), public authorities are free to exercise discretionary powers contrary to Convention rights. But if the very fact that a public authority *has* a statutory power is incompatible with Art 6, the courts will issue a declaration of incompatibility, and will not use s 6 to quash an exercise of the power.

Remember that in *Wilkinson*, the House of Lords held that a bereavement allowance payable only to widows was incompatible with the Convention, and made a declaration of incompatibility instead of using the Human Rights Act 1998 s 3 to remove the incompatibility. In a case decided on the same day as *Wilkinson*, another widower argued that the Work and Pensions Secretary could solve the Art 14 discrimination problem by making payments to widowers to match the statutory widows' benefits (*R (Hooper) v Work and Pensions Secretary* [2005] UKHL 29). The government can always just write a cheque to someone, and the Court of Appeal held that the Secretary of State had a duty under the Human Rights Act 1998 s 6 to write cheques to widowers, in order to treat them in the same way as the widows to whom the statute required the government to make payments. The House of Lords reversed the decision, holding by a majority that s 6(2) 'gives primacy to Parliamentary sovereignty over the Convention rights' (Lord Hope [78]). If Parliament established a discriminatory scheme of benefits for widows, the Minister could not avoid that act of lawmaking by paying out benefits to widowers.

Impact on judicial review

How does the Human Rights Act 1998 s 6 affect the three common law grounds of judicial review?

- **Due process:** Most complaints of a violation of the requirements of natural justice can now be argued under the Convention, and Art 6 has had a special impact on the law of bias (Chapter 5). Yet apart from the distinct requirement of independence for some decisions, the procedural requirements of Art 6 are ordinarily the same as the common law requirements of due process.
- **Error of law:** The Act does not change the doctrine of review for error of law in any way at all. But it does change the law. By s 3, if it is possible to interpret a statute in a way that makes it compatible with Convention rights, then it is an error of law for a public authority (including a court) to interpret the statute incompatibly. The effect is to extend the pattern of the past forty years (since *Anisminic v Foreign Compensation Commission* [1969] 2 AC 147), by giving the courts an even more open-ended and creative way of determining the standards that bind public authorities (see Chapter 9).
- **Control of discretionary powers:** Perhaps the most important way in which the Act has affected administrative law is by adding a new form of proportionality that is distinct from the *Wednesbury* principles. But it is important to remember: (1) that the Act has no direct effect on an administrative decision that does not violate a Convention right,[15] (2) that under the *Wednesbury* doctrine, many acts of public authorities that infringe Convention rights were already unlawful (see, e.g., *R v Home Secretary, ex p Simms* [2000] 2 AC 115), and

---

[15] See section 8.3 on whether the Human Rights Act will have a more far-reaching indirect effect, by encouraging the courts to develop new, more generally applicable tests of proportionality.

(3) that judicial interference with public authorities under the Act will turn out to be more or less restrained, to the extent that judges defer to public authorities (executive authorities and Parliament) in making judgments of proportionality (see below, section 3.8).

3.4 Rights, human rights, and the content of the Convention rights

Consider the main provisions of the Convention, and you may find it odd to call them 'human rights'. You have a right if others owe you a duty to promote or to respect your interests regardless (to some extent) of (some) other considerations. Your right is a *human* right if you have it simply because you are a human being. The right not to be tortured and the right to life are human rights: just because you are a human being, everyone always owes you a duty not to torture you or to murder you, regardless of what they could achieve by doing so. Of course, you have human rights no matter what the law says. You have a *legal* right, when *the law requires* others to promote or to respect your interests regardless (to some extent) of (some) other considerations. The effect of protecting the rights not to be killed or tortured in Arts 2 and 3 of the Convention is to give them a particular legal effect, with associated processes for remedying violations.

But most of the rights provisions in the Convention do not enshrine ways in which everyone ought to treat people merely because they are human. Most of the rights enshrine ways of protecting people from arbitrary acts of state power in a community with a legal system. Arts 5, 6, and 7 promote crucial requirements of **the rule of law**: they prohibit arbitrary executive detention, require fair procedures in the determination of criminal charges and civil rights, and prohibit retrospective criminal penalties. The Convention could more accurately have been called 'the European Convention on the Rule of Law'. The same is true of the Universal Declaration of Human Rights, adopted by the United Nations in 1948, which served as a model for the European Convention. Most of the provisions of the Universal Declaration set out principles for a good legal system, rather than universal human rights.[16] Lord Steyn has said that 'the rule of law...underlies all human rights instruments' (R (Ullah) v Special Adjudicator [2004] UKHL 26 [43]). As Lord Hope of Craighead said in *Montgomery v H M Advocate* [2003] 1 AC 641, 673, 'the rule of law lies at the heart of the Convention'.

The Preamble to the European Convention on Human Rights states that the governments of signatory states entered into it, 'as the governments of European countries which are like-minded and have a common heritage of political traditions,

---

[16]   See http://www.un.org/Overview/rights.html.

ideals, freedom and the rule of law'. In *Golder v United Kingdom* (1979–80) 1 EHRR 524, the European Court of Human Rights held that it is 'natural' to bear in mind this commitment to the rule of law 'when interpreting the terms of Art 6(1) according to their context and in the light of the object and purpose of the Convention' [34].

3.4.1 Fundamental freedoms: beyond the rule of law

But the Convention does protect more than just the rule of law. The **fundamental freedoms** in the Convention include not only the freedom from arbitrary detention (Art 5), but also the 'political freedoms' of thought and religion, expression, and association (Arts 9, 10, 11). Like the rule of law provisions, these three articles promote a certain sort of community, rather than merely guaranteeing human rights.[17] Similarly, the Articles protecting private and family life and marriage (Art 8 and 12) regulate relations in a community, rather than merely protecting persons from inhuman treatment or protecting the rule of law. Art 8, in particular, regulates those relations in ways that are quite new to English law.

So the Convention protects certain human rights, and protects the rule of law, and protects fundamental freedoms. All that unifies the Convention rights is the fact that they represent the Council of Europe's judgment concerning rights which should not only be protected in law, but should be put outside the ordinary law-making processes, and should be interpreted and applied by an international tribunal. This background is important for administrative law, because it explains the tensions that arise in Convention litigation both in the European Court of Human Rights and in English courts under the Human Rights Act. The Convention commits decisions as to how (for example) to protect privacy and freedom of expression to the Strasbourg Court. But crucial community interests are at stake in deciding when it is legitimate to interfere with people's privacy, or expression. The job of assessing those community interests is committed to a court, because they need to be assessed if the rights are to be applied. Yet the assessment involves the sort of reasoning that is a central task of government officials and legislatures. The court, then, needs to decide how, if at all, to defer to the judgment of other officials on those issues. Deference in certain respects is essential. The need for deference, ironically, arises from the fact that the Convention requires the Strasbourg Court to assess whether the value of an administrative decision in the public interest is proportionate to its impact on the interests that the Convention protects (and not merely whether the decision was made through proportionate processes). The Human Rights Act requires English courts to make the same assessments of proportionality. So it requires the English courts to decide

---

[17] Note that even these provisions are related in various ways to the rule of law. For example, freedom of expression promotes the rule of law because it makes it possible for the media to expose infringements of the rule of law. But Art 9 protects many forms of speech that have no relation to the rule of law.

how, if at all, to defer to the judgment of other officials on the value of an administrative decision.

3.5 The special role of Article 6: proportionate process

' **Article 6—Right to a fair trial**
1. In the determination of his civil rights and obligations or of any criminal charge against him, everyone is entitled to a fair and public hearing within a reasonable time by an independent and impartial tribunal established by law.... '

Article 6 of the Convention has the potential to remodel administrative law. Unlike the rest of the Convention rights, it affects all administrative decision making that determines 'civil rights and obligations'. The European Court of Human Rights has interpreted that phrase broadly enough to apply to a vast range of administrative decisions including, for example, applications for licences (*Benthem v Netherlands* (1986) 8 EHRR 1) and claims for some social security benefits (*Feldbrugge v Netherlands* (1986) 8 EHRR 425). In all such decisions, 'everyone is entitled to a fair and public hearing within a reasonable time by an independent and impartial tribunal established by law'.

In R (*Alconbury Developments Ltd*) *v Environment Secretary* [2001] UKHL 23, the Divisional Court of Appeal made a dramatic declaration that it was incompatible with Art 6 for the Secretary of State to make decisions which affect rights to the ownership or use of land. The case shows the potential for courts to use Art 6 to overhaul the administration of government, by taking such decisions out of the hands of administrative authorities and assigning them to independent authorities such as courts. Think about the impact of that approach: the Court of Appeal decision would have meant that the whole business of deciding on planning permission and compulsory purchase would no longer be a matter for elected officials, but for judges (for an overview of the planning process, see p 173). But in a landmark display of judicial restraint under the Human Rights Act, the House of Lords overturned the Court of Appeal's decision in *Alconbury*, holding that it is not unfair for a minister to have an overriding power in planning decisions, and that the Art 6 right is satisfied by the availability of judicial review.

How is that possible, when Art 6 requires an independent hearing? Once the court held that planning decisions determined 'civil rights and obligations', you might think that would be the end of it, just as *Venables and Thompson* and *Anderson* were straightforward because the Home Secretary is not independent. The Environment Secretary is not independent, either. The Court of Appeal certainly thought that was the end of it: a politician is not independent, so it must be incompatible with the Convention for him or her to determine civil rights and obligations.

It might seem, that is, that *Alconbury* is no different from *Anderson*. But in fact there is a very important difference. As Lord Brown has put it, 'so far as administrative or disciplinary tribunals are concerned, there is compliance with article 6 so long as the requisite guarantees (of an independent and impartial tribunal, a fair and public hearing and the like) are provided, if not at the initial decision-making stage, then on a subsequent review or appeal (by a tribunal with the jurisdiction to undertake a sufficient merits hearing)' (R (Hammond) v Home Secretary [2005] UKHL 69 [41] (emphasis added)). The decision in Anderson was not the decision of an administrative or disciplinary tribunal. It was a sentencing decision. A defendant convicted of an offence needs to be protected from the agenda that a Home Secretary may have to respond to public clamour about a particular case; a developer hoping to build a shopping mall cannot expect to be protected from the government's agenda—or from public views—concerning the use of land.

What then is the difference between Alconbury's case, and Anderson's case? If Art 6 only gives Alconbury a right to seek judicial review of a minister's decision, why wasn't judicial review enough to satisfy Anderson's right under Art 6? It is not that there is a right to an independent hearing in sentencing decisions but not in planning or housing decisions. The difference is that the right to an independent hearing is fulfilled in *different* ways depending on the nature of the matter being determined. The right to an independent hearing in the housing case is fulfilled if an independent court has a jurisdiction to review the housing decision, on standards sufficient to guarantee the procedural fairness of the way in which Alconbury was treated. Anderson's case is different because only an independent *initial* decision on sentencing can guarantee procedural fairness—and protect the rule of law. The effect of Art 6 is to implement a principle of proportionality in administrative processes, which is very closely aligned with the principle of proportionality that has emerged in the common law doctrine of due process (see Chapter 4 and Chapter 5).

Article 6

As the nature of a decision on civil rights becomes more and more of the type the judiciary normally deals with (involving fundamental rights and liberties), the requirements of Art 6(1) become more stringent and an independent tribunal is more likely to be required as the primary decision maker.

As the nature of a decision on civil rights becomes more and more of the type the government normally deals with (involving public policy and the community's interests), the requirements of Art 6(1) become less stringent and judicial review by an independent tribunal is more likely to satisfy Art 6.

The moral of the story is that in order for a community to be ruled by law, it is not necessary for every aspect of government action to be controlled by legal processes, or for every dispute to be resolved by a court. What is essential for the rule of law is that a dispute should be resolved by an independent decision maker when that is what it takes to prevent arbitrary government (see p 7).

The result of Alconbury is that even under the Human Rights Act, the law's procedural requirements will be kept in proportion to the kind of decision. And as we will see in Chapter 4, the common law of due process itself requires (subject to any statute providing otherwise) that same form of proportionality. In *R (Smith) v Parole Board* [2005] UKHL 1, Lord Bingham pointed out that the Court will not even need to address questions of the effect of Art 6, where it would not 'afford any greater protection' than the common law duty of procedural fairness [44] (see p 130). So Art 6 will not revolutionize administrative law, even after the Human Rights Act. But *Anderson* shows that it will lead to major changes in particular areas, where statutes establish processes that are incompatible with the Convention.

What to remember about *Alconbury*

(1) the House of Lords was willing to interpret Convention rights by using the principles of the common law. So, for example, to Lord Clyde it was very important that the minister was not *judex in sua causa* (a judge in his own cause), but was acting in the public interest [142].

(2) the Law Lords played up the intrusive reach of judicial review, to support their conclusion that judicial review satisfied Art 6. So the decision includes some of the most expansive statements of the grounds of judicial review that the Law Lords have made (e.g. Lord Slynn [51]–[53]). They said that it was not necessary to make judicial review more intrusive to meet the requirements of Art 6.

3.6 Proportionality and the structure of Convention rights

The Convention rights protect fundamental interests—in freedom and privacy and so on. But the protection is limited, because it can be perfectly legitimate to interfere with someone's freedom or privacy. For example, it is quite right for the police to be able to break into a house to stop an assault. It is right to limit freedom of speech through criminal laws against communicating state secrets to an enemy, or through tort liability for publishing damaging lies about other people. But a power for police to go into any house for any reason they choose would violate Art 8. And laws on state secrets that are too restrictive (or laws on defamation that make it too dangerous to publish critical opinions) would violate Art 10. Laws and official decisions that are too burdensome for some purpose are **disproportionate**.

The need to make judgments of proportionality can arise in applying all the Convention rights. The Art 3 right not to be subject to torture allows no justification at all for torture, yet judgments of proportionality are needed in applying the **positive duties** that the Strasbourg Court has interpreted Art 3 as imposing (e.g., to investigate complaints of police brutality). Once the courts use the Convention to impose positive duties on the state to promote the interests protected by Convention rights, they create remarkable challenges for themselves in deciding what is proportionate.

Positive duties

The effect of the Convention rights has developed further than the representatives of the states could have foreseen when they designed the Convention. Article 2 says that 'Everyone's right to life shall be protected by law.' The Strasbourg Court has interpreted it to impose positive duties on states, 'not only to refrain from the intentional and unlawful taking of life ("Thou shalt not kill") but also to take appropriate steps to safeguard the lives of those within its jurisdiction' (*Van Colle v Chief Constable of Hertfordshire* [2005] UKHL 14 [28], Lord Bingham). There are other positive duties: for example,

- to protect children from inhuman treatment, under Art 3 (*Z v UK* (2002) 2 FLR 612),
- to protect the media from violence under Art 10 (*Ozgur Gundem v Turkey* (2001) 31 EHRR 49), and
- not to deport an illegal immigrant to a country where there is a serious risk that he will suffer inhuman treatment, under Art 3 (*Chahal v UK* (1996) 23 EHRR 413).

What about the right to respect for private and family life in Art 8? Its reach is remarkable and may seem almost unlimited: anything that is against a person's interests in any way can affect his or her private and family life. The Strasbourg Court has held that Art 8 'protects a right to personal development' (*Pretty v UK* (2002) 35 EHRR 1 [61]).

A state that has respect for private and family life will not just refrain from interfering with people in certain ways; it will take all sorts of positive measures to support families and individuals, and their personal development. Is it now the job of the courts to decide what the state should do to promote your personal development? No. Art 8 does not authorize courts to decide what measures the state should take out of respect for private and family life, but only to interfere when the state shows disrespect. Article 8 does generate positive duties that the Strasbourg Court will enforce, but 'this is an area in which the contracting parties enjoy a wide margin of appreciation' (*Abdulaziz v UK* (1985) 7 EHRR 471; see also *Botta v Italy* (1998) 26 EHRR 241 [33]). See section 3.7 on the margin of appreciation.

The courts have to distinguish between protecting the right to respect for persons (which is their role), and requiring the state to do the right things to promote personal development (which is not the courts' role). The results can seem random. Any decent European state provides housing for the homeless and social security, but 'The Court of Human Rights has always drawn back from imposing on states the obligation to provide a home, or indeed any other form of financial support' (*Anufrijeva v Southwark LBC* [2003] EWCA Civ 1406 [19]; cf *Harrow LBC v Qazi* [2003] UKHL 43).[18] On the other hand, the Strasbourg Court has taken it upon itself to impose duties on states to admit family members of immigrants in particular circumstances (*Sen v Netherlands* (2003) 36 EHRR 7). And it was held in *R (Bernard) v Enfield LBC* [2002] EWHC 2282 that people entitled to local authority support under

---

[18] But 'where the welfare of children is at stake, article 8 may require the provision of welfare support in a manner which enables family life to continue' (*Anufrijeva* [43]). And Art 3 may require welfare support, if it would amount to inhuman treatment to leave someone without support (*Anufrijeva* [35]).

National Assistance Act 1948 s 21 (because they need special care because of age, illness, disability, or other circumstances) 'are a particularly vulnerable group. Positive measures have to be taken (by way of community care facilities) to enable them to enjoy, so far as possible, a normal private and family life' [32].

An unfair trial is never compatible with the Convention, no matter what objective the state is pursuing. But *what counts as fair* depends on proportionality between procedures and the purposes for which they are provided. So the European Court of Human Rights has held that 'the right of access to the courts is not absolute but may be subject to limitations...a limitation will not be compatible with Article 6 para. 1 if it does not pursue a legitimate aim and if there is not a reasonable relationship of proportionality between the means employed and the aim sought to be achieved' (*Ashingdane v United Kingdom* (1985) 7 EHRR 528 [57]).

The role of proportionality is easiest to see in the two parts of Arts 8 to 11, which protect privacy and family life, freedom of religion, freedom of expression, and freedom of assembly (I will call those freedoms the **Convention freedoms**). The Convention freedoms are protected by **qualified rights**—that is, rights that are subject to express provisos. The qualified rights have the following structure:

Right to X (e.g., to Freedom of Expression)

1. Everyone has the right to X.

2. There shall be no interference by a public authority with the exercise of this right except such as is in accordance with the law and is **necessary in a democratic society** in the interests of {**A, B, or C**}.

'Interference by a public authority with the exercise' of the right is an awkward way of saying, 'restriction of the freedom that the right protects'. The test of necessity for such restrictions on freedom may sound very demanding. But the Convention contemplates that a limit on freedom of expression may be legitimate if it is:

> 'necessary...in the interests of national security, territorial integrity or public safety, for the prevention of disorder or crime, for the protection of health or morals, for the protection of the reputation or rights of others, for preventing the disclosure of information received in confidence, or for maintaining the authority and impartiality of the judiciary (Article 10.2). '[19]

Those provisos in Arts 8 to 11 are the **public interest limitations**[20] on Convention freedoms. What limitations are *necessary* to protect such open-ended, undefined

---

[19] Not all Convention rights use necessity as a test for limits: the protection for property in Art 1 of the First Protocol allows that a person may be deprived of possessions 'in the public interest and subject to the conditions provided for by law and by the general principles of international law'.

[20] But note that they include limitations based not only on the public interest but on the interests of other individuals.

interests of society and of other individuals? The Strasbourg Court developed the doctrine of proportionality to deal with that question. Perhaps the drafters of the Convention used the word 'necessary' simply to underscore that the rights are fundamentally important. The judges' response has been to soften the test of necessity into a requirement that an interference with an interest protected by the Convention must be **proportionate** to an objective that the Convention acknowledges as legitimate.

Proportionality is a relation between two things. In the application of Convention rights, those two things are (1) the value of pursuing a legitimate state purpose by some course of action, and (2) some resulting detriment to an interest that is protected by a Convention right. So a judgment of proportionality starts with (or takes for granted):

- a legitimate interest (of the community or of individuals) that an action would promote, and

- detriment that the action would cause to an interest that a Convention right protects.

The public interest limitations on Convention freedoms recognize interests that can justify some detriment to the interests that the Convention freedoms protect. An action is proportionate if it does not cause *too much* detriment to a protected interest (that is, detriment that is out of proportion to the value of the objective).

The English courts' approach to proportionality has been based on the Canadian Supreme Court's approach to the limits on the rights protected by the Canadian Charter of Rights and Freedoms, a constitutional bill of rights adopted in 1982. The Charter guarantees the rights and freedoms that it sets out 'subject only to such reasonable limits prescribed by law as can be demonstrably justified in a free and democratic society' (s 1). Early in the development of Charter case law, the Supreme Court of Canada held that deciding what limits are reasonable involves 'a form of proportionality test' (R v Big M Drug Mart [1985] 1 SCR 295 [140]). In R v Oakes [1986] 1 SCR 103, the Chief Justice, Dickson CJC, held that a limit on a Charter right must have an objective that is not 'trivial or discordant with the principles integral to a free and democratic society' [73]. And then the test of whether it is reasonable to pursue the objective in a particular way has 'three important components'.

Three components of proportionality:

(i) ... 'the measures adopted ... must be rationally connected to the objective. ...'
(ii) ... 'the means ... should impair "as little as possible" the right or freedom in question. ...'
(iii) ... 'there must be a proportionality between the effects of the measures which are responsible for limiting the Charter right or freedom and the objective. ...' [70]

The first and second components mean that the limitation can only be justified by *the legitimate objective*—so that if the restriction of a freedom does not promote the objective, or if the objective can be promoted as well without restricting the freedom (or without restricting it as much), then the objective does not justify the restriction of the freedom. Notice the third component, which really *is* the proportionality test. It means that even if a measure promotes a legitimate objective, and the objective cannot be achieved with less restriction of a freedom, the measure is still unjustified (and therefore, an infringement of the right) if it restricts the freedom *too much*.

In the early English case law on the Human Rights Act, the third component was omitted from Lord Steyn's classic discussion of the proportionality test in R (Daly) v Home Secretary [2001] UKHL 26 [27]. In *International Transport Roth v Home Secretary* [2002] EWCA Civ 158, Lord Justice Simon Brown added another requirement that he said was 'implicit in the concept of proportionality':

> that not merely must the impairment of the individual's rights be no more than necessary for the attainment of the public policy objective sought, but also that it must not impose an excessive burden on the individual concerned. [52]

That is Chief Justice Dickson's third component.

The third component in EC law and in the law of the Convention

The same component appears in explanations of proportionality in the European Court of Justice, where it is called 'proportionality in the narrow sense'. Article 5 of the EC Treaty provides that 'Any action by the Community shall not go beyond what is necessary to achieve the objectives of this Treaty.' The ECJ has crafted a principle of proportionality to give effect to that requirement, just as the European Court of Human Rights has crafted its principle of proportionality to deal with the public interest limitations on Convention rights. A long line of ECJ cases have taken the doctrine of proportionality more or less verbatim from the decision in Case 265/87 *Schräder v Hauptzollamt Gronau* [1989] ECR 2237 [21], which asserted that 'the Court has consistently held that the principle of proportionality is one of the general principles of Community law'. EC measures are invalid if they impose burdens on private persons that are disproportionate to their aims. The Court held that the principle of proportionality involves the following requirements:

(1) European Community measures must be 'appropriate and necessary for meeting the objectives legitimately pursued by the legislation in question';

(2) 'when there is a choice between several appropriate measures, the least onerous measure must be used'; and

(3) burdens imposed 'must not be disproportionate to the aims pursued'.[21]

---

[21] On the general scope of the principle see R *(FEDESA) v Minister of Agriculture, Fisheries and Food* [1991] 1 CMLR 507 [13], and see the discussion of proportionality in the ECJ in section 8.6.

Notice two features of proportionality reasoning that give judges a potentially intrusive role:

1. It requires them to pass judgment on the value of pursuing a public objective in a particular way.
2. There are no scales! That is, there usually no units in which the value of pursuing a public objective in a particular way can be measured against the impact on a protected interest. So there is nothing like a precise answer to the proportionality question of *how much* interference with an interest is too much. That gives judges a resultant discretion.*

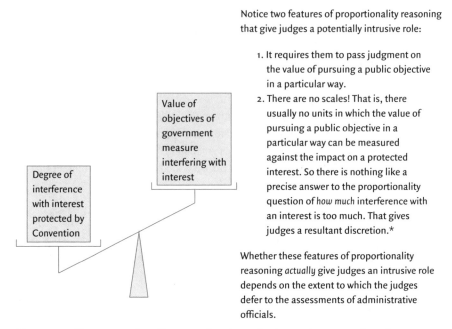

Whether these features of proportionality reasoning *actually* give judges an intrusive role depends on the extent to which the judges defer to the assessments of administrative officials.

Figure 3.1 The proportionality question: how do the scales come down?

In Convention rights litigation under the Human Rights Act, that third component in proportionality reasoning brings a small revolution to English administrative law. The revolution is that in order to determine the lawfulness of acts of public authorities that restrict the Convention freedoms, the English courts must *assess the aims* for which the public authorities act, and weigh the value of pursuing those aims against the impact on interests protected by the Convention.

Immigration control and Article 8

We can see how far-reaching the judicial role can be, if we consider how proportionality reasoning unfolds in the most delicate and contentious area of Convention rights litigation in the 21st century: immigration control. The Convention provides no right for persons to choose where to live. But the right to respect for family life in Art 8 has become a very common recourse for would-be immigrants. Whether seeking asylum or applying for ordinary immigration, candidates spend long enough in the country that they may develop family ties, if they did not already have family in the U.K. Then, refusal of leave to remain in the country will be detrimental to their family life. The issue will be whether the detriment to their family life is proportionate to an interest that the Convention recognizes. How is the Immigration Appeal Tribunal to decide such questions? The House of Lords decided in R (Huang) v Home Secretary [2007] UKHL 11 that the Tribunal must ask the following question:

---

*   That is, a discretion that results from the vagueness of the standard they are meant to apply. See p 232.

> whether the refusal of leave to enter or remain, in circumstances where the life of the family cannot reasonably be expected to be enjoyed elsewhere, taking full account of all considerations weighing in favour of the refusal, prejudices the family life of the applicant in a manner sufficiently serious to amount to a breach of the fundamental right protected by article 8. [20]

This question does not provide the Immigration Appeal Tribunal with a *test* of proportionality; the Tribunal judges have no guide to their decision, except that the impact on a claimant's family life must not be out of proportion to public purposes that are unspecified. The House of Lords drew attention to Chief Justice Dickson's third component, holding that the judges need to balance the interests of society with the interests of claimants [19]. The question is not just whether the burden on the claimant is necessary to achieve a legitimate objective; even if it is, the Tribunal must still ask whether the detriment to an interest protected by the Convention is *too much* to be justified under Art 8.

The House of Lords did not specify the 'considerations weighing in favour of the refusal' of leave to remain in the UK. If the question is whether refusal would be *proportionate*, and a claimant shows that refusal would cause some detriment to her family life, what state purpose could make the refusal legitimate in spite of the detriment? Part 2 of Art 8 was not designed with immigration control in mind: it recognizes that an interference with family life may be justifiable 'in the interests of national security, public safety or the economic well-being of the country, for the prevention of disorder or crime, for the protection of health or morals, or for the protection of the rights and freedoms of others'. And the government's agenda in trying to limit immigration through the immigration rules is not very articulate.

The result is that the judges of the Immigration Appeal Tribunal (and courts on appeals from the Tribunal) really are in charge of immigration decisions in particular cases. If a claimant does not satisfy the rules that give some immigrants a right to remain in the UK, but refusal of leave to remain would be detrimental to their family life, then the Tribunal must make a proportionality judgment that amounts to weighing the immeasurable (the gravity of the impact of deportation on someone's family life[22]) against the unspecified (legitimate state purposes in having immigration rules). That leaves the judges with a mind-boggling, open-ended task not merely of weighing up the unweighable, but of deciding what has to be weighed against what.

But the result is revolutionary not because it is so unclear, but because it requires judges to do something that they do not do in ordinary judicial review: to assess for themselves the value of pursuing public purposes in the way that a public authority has done or proposes to do. In cases such as *Huang*, the Human Rights Act hands to judges the whole job of achieving just state action.

You might think, then, that proportionality reasoning will hand government of the country over to judges. But it will not, for several reasons. In the next section, 3.7,

---

[22]   In *Huang's* case, refusal of leave would have forced her to leave the country where her daughter and her family lived.

we will see one reason why the judges of the European Court of Human Rights are not going to take over the government of this country: they apply a 'margin of appreciation' to state action. And in the Conclusion of this chapter, section 3.8, we will see why the *English* judges are not going to take over the government, even under the Human Rights Act.

The limits of constitutional rights

Constitutional bills of rights such as the Canadian Charter authorize 'reasonable' limits on rights. The United States Bill of Rights is silent on the limits to the rights it protects: the 'First Amendment' provides that 'Congress shall make no law respecting an establishment of religion, or prohibiting the free exercise thereof; or abridging the freedom of speech...' The fact that no limitations are stated does not mean that Americans have the right to slander people or to communicate secrets to the enemy. The courts have had to determine the implicit limits on 'the freedom of speech' with no guidance from the U.S. Constitution. But the attempts to identify the limits on rights in the European Convention and the Canadian Charter are so vague, that they leave a responsibility to judges that is similar to the responsibility that the U.S. judges have.

● *Pop quiz* ●

Are Convention rights constitutional rights?

3.7 Subsidiarity and the margin of appreciation

The European Court of Human Rights gives public authorities in contracting states a **margin of appreciation**—a leeway for them to act as they see fit, to some extent, on some issues as to the limits of Convention rights (*Handyside v UK* (1976) 1 EHRR 737; *Smith v UK* (2000) 29 EHRR 493). This form of deference may seem strange, because a Court of Human Rights is meant to give remedies against violations of rights, and not to decide whether a contracting state has acted reasonably in deciding what counts as a violation. But the Convention freedoms are subject to the public interest limitations. The application of those limitations may legitimately vary, since national security (for example) may make some restriction on a Convention freedom necessary in one country that is unnecessary in another, and the same form of expression may be shocking and offensive in one community, and not in another. Applying the Convention rights means deciding what limitations are legitimate in particular communities. Some things are illegitimate in *any* community (such as torture); but some forms of defamation law may be legitimate in one country and illegitimate in another.

As the Strasbourg Court put it in *Sahin v Turkey* (2005) 41 EHRR 8, 'the national authorities are in principle better placed than an international court to evaluate local needs and conditions' [100].[23] Leyla Sahin insisted on wearing an Islamic headscarf,

---

[23]   The same views were upheld by the Grand Chamber of the Court in *Sahin v Turkey* (2007) 44 EHRR 5 [121].

which was against the rules of her medical school. When she was excluded from lectures, she complained to the European Court of Human Rights. The issue was whether the medical school's dress code was necessary for protecting the rights and freedoms of others. The Strasbourg Court deferred to the judgment of the Turkish authorities on that question, holding that 'the role of the Convention machinery is essentially subsidiary' [100]. **Subsidiarity** is justice in the division of powers between levels of government (see p 16). A public decision should be made by an institution at the level at which it can most effectively be made—and that means at a level close to the person it affects, unless there is some reason why a more remote set of institutions can pursue a just purpose more effectively. Not all decisions about life in Europe can be made by the European Court of Human Rights. Its role is to support the contracting states in protecting fundamental rights.

An international court would not be supporting contracting states in respecting the Convention rights, if it imposed its own judgments as to the extent of the public interest limitations. A court in Strasbourg (with judges drawn from more than 40 different countries) does not have the appreciation of conditions in a particular contracting state that would enable it to make sound judgments on all questions of whether government action is protected by the public interest limitations. Its role is to interfere when the contracting state authorities make judgments that pass beyond the margin of appreciation: judgments that interfere with Convention interests in a way that is so clearly illegitimate that that the European Court of Human Rights must interfere in order to carry out its supporting role. So the margin of appreciation tempers proportionality reasoning under the Convention. The European Court of Human Rights will not interfere unless government action can be seen to be clearly disproportionate, from the Court's detached point of view.

In 1979, Richard Handyside was convicted under the Obscene Publications Act 1959 of publishing material 'such as to tend to deprave and corrupt' children who were likely to read it. He had published The Little Red Schoolbook, a Danish sex education manual intended for school children from the age of 12. When he challenged his conviction in the European Court of Human Rights as a violation of Art 10, the Strasbourg Court did not simply decide for itself whether banning The Little Red Schoolbook was necessary for the protection of morals. Its role was to ensure that the English courts acted within the margin of appreciation. The Court based that view of its role on the principle of subsidiarity: 'The Convention leaves to each Contracting State, in the first place, the task of securing the rights and liberties it enshrines' [48]. The reason for the principle is that:

> ‘ By reason of their direct and continuous contact with the vital forces of their countries, State authorities are in principle in a better position than the international judge to give an opinion on the exact content of these requirements as well as on the 'necessity' of a 'restriction' or 'penalty' intended to meet them. ’
> (Handyside [48])

This reasoning led to the conclusion that the European Court of Human Rights has a *supervisory* jurisdiction, rather than an original jurisdiction to decide how freedom of expression should or should not be restricted. Its responsibility is to *review* decisions rather than to replace them: 'it is in no way the Court's task to take the place of the competent national courts but rather to review under Article 10 the decisions they delivered in the exercise of their power of appreciation' [50].

3.7.1 How wide is the margin of appreciation?

There is no clear or definite answer to this question. But it ought to be limited, because the margin of appreciation is dangerous: by leaving national authorities free, to some extent, to act on their own judgment, it leaves them free to act on *misjudgments*.

And we can identify limits to the margin of appreciation. The European Court of Human Rights will decide 'whether the reasons given by the national authorities to justify the actual measures of "interference" they take are relevant and sufficient under Article 10 para. 2' (*Handyside* [50]). By contrast, in judicial review of administrative conduct under the *Wednesbury* doctrine, English judges will decide whether a public authority's reasons for an exercise of discretion are relevant, but *not* whether they are *sufficient* to justify the decision (see p 269). So the Strasbourg Court uses a more intensive form of review of interferences with freedom of expression, in spite of the margin of appreciation.[24] Richard Handyside lost his claim because the Strasbourg Court decided that 'the competent English judges were entitled, in the exercise of their discretion, to think at the relevant time that the Schoolbook would have pernicious effects on the morals of many of the children and adolescents who would read it' [52]. The Strasbourg Court defers to English authorities to the extent that it asks whether *their* reasons for interfering with freedom of expression are legitimate, rather than directly deciding whether freedom of expression should be interfered with. But the deference is limited by the requirement that there must be *sufficient* reason—that is, the reason for interfering with a Convention interest must be proportionate to the pursuit of a purpose that the Convention recognizes as legitimate.

The Human Rights Act gives English courts the responsibility for doing what the European Court of Human Rights had been doing for decades: deciding the sufficiency of reasons for interfering with the interests that the Convention protects. A large part of the rationale for the Act was to end the embarrassing predicament of litigants who had to go to Strasbourg for the vindication of rights that the United Kingdom had committed itself to respecting. But the shift was potentially huge, because English courts do not have the same reasons of subsidiarity that the European Court of Human Rights has for restrained review.

With no margin of appreciation, does the Act leave all the questions raised by the public interest limitations to the English judges? The answer, as we will see, is 'no'.

----

[24] See also *Smith and Grady v UK* [88] 'The Court recognises that it is for the national authorities to make the initial assessment of necessity, though the final evaluation as to whether the reasons cited for the interference are relevant and sufficient is one for this Court. A margin of appreciation is left to Contracting States in the context of this assessment, which varies according to the nature of the activities restricted and of the aims pursued by the restrictions.'

The English Courts and the European Court of Human Rights

The English courts 'must take into account' decisions of the European Court of Human Rights (Human Rights Act 1998 s 2(a)). They have no legal duty to *follow* those decisions. But the judges know that if they hold against a claimant when the European Court of Human Rights would have held in his or her favour, the claimant can go to Strasbourg and ask the European Court of Human Rights to follow its own case law. And then the United Kingdom will be bound in international law to give effect to the Strasbourg decision, even if the English judges took a different view of the Convention.

In *Alconbury*, Lord Slynn said: 'it seems to me that the court should follow any clear and constant jurisprudence of the European Court of Human Rights' [26]. Lord Bingham followed that statement in *Anderson*, and suggested that there is a presumption in favour of following European Court of Human Rights decisions: '. . . the House will not without good reason depart from the principles laid down in a carefully considered judgment of the court sitting as a Grand Chamber' [18].[25]

Note, however, that the County Courts, the High Court, and the Court of Appeal must abide by a precedent of a higher court even if it is clearly incompatible with a later decision of the European Court of Human Rights (*Leeds City Council v Price* [2006] UKHL 10 [40]–[45] (Lord Bingham)).

3.8 Conclusion: what the Human Rights Act doesn't do

Remember *R v Ministry of Defence, ex p Walker* [2000] 1 WLR 806, from Chapter 2. If the Human Rights Act had been in force when he was denied an award under the army's criminal injuries compensation scheme, it would have been of no use at all to him. Like many decisions of public authorities, the decision he complained about did not affect any interest that the Convention protects. The judicial role under the Human Rights Act seems exciting and interventionist, because of the remarkable new responsibility under s 6 to quash some administrative decisions that interfere disproportionately with fundamental interests. But that role is limited, and in several ways the judicial role in common law review is much more adventurous. The old law of judicial control of discretionary powers gives judges a much more wide-ranging jurisdiction to control government action than the Human Rights Act gives them.

Remember, too, that English courts were already doing some of what the Human Rights Act says that they should do: as Lord Hoffmann has put it, s 3 'expressly enacts' the principle of legality that was already part of our law (*R v Home Secretary, ex p Simms* [2000] 2 AC 115, 132).

---

[25] The Grand Chamber is composed of 17 judges who hear cases referred from a 'Chamber' of seven judges.

But, subject to those limitations, the Human Rights Act does give courts a new responsibility that challenges the principles of judicial control of administration that we encountered in Chapter 2. This new responsibility is to assess the value of a public authority's policy objective, and to determine whether it is legitimate for the authority to pursue the objective in a particular way, at a particular cost to the claimant's privacy or freedom. The Human Rights Act would pose no serious challenge to the separation of powers if it only prohibited torture and arbitrary killings by public authorities. But the cases discussed in this chapter show how the Act requires judges to decide whether the public interest justifies a huge variety of interferences with people's fundamental interests. And in applying Article 6 of the Convention (right to a fair trial), the judges have a new responsibility for administrative processes. (See section 4.1.)

The need to make judgments of proportionality in applying the qualified rights creates a potential failure in the separation of powers (see section 1.5.1), because it invites judges to answer questions that the legislature or the executive are better equipped to answer. The emerging doctrine of deference is the judges' answer to that problem. It is the major element in the English judges' cautious approach to their dramatic powers under the Human Rights Act. The courts have shown that they are ready to use the power the Act gives them, but they are not ready to expand those powers in ways that would remodel English public law.

English law has had deferential proportionality requirements for centuries. Under the *Wednesbury* principles, it is generally unlawful for a public authority to act *so* disproportionately that no reasonable public authority would do the same. Lord Ackner pointed that out in the *Brind* case, but he also concluded that there was no basis to apply the doctrine of proportionality that had been developed by the European Court of Human Rights, 'unless and until Parliament incorporates the Convention into domestic law'.[26] The Human Rights Act has not *incorporated* the Convention into domestic law, but under s 6, the Strasbourg form of proportionality has indeed become a control on those administrative decisions that affect the interests protected in the Convention.

Judicial review under the *Wednesbury* principles is certainly different from judicial application of Convention rights under the Human Rights Act 1998 s 6. The *Wednesbury* doctrine was designed as a way for judges to justify interfering with someone else's discretionary power. By making it unlawful to act incompatibly with Convention rights, s 6 gives a power to judges to *apply* the rights. So it may seem that the difference is that the *Wednesbury* doctrine requires that judges defer to other public authorities, and that s 6 requires them *not* to defer in deciding what counts as a violation of a Convention right. But the situation is more complicated. The very reasons that require proportionality reasoning (e.g., the fact that a decision affects fundamental interests) can also, in some situations, give judges a reason to defer.

The 'margin of appreciation' (the European Court of Human Rights' doctrine of deference) is based on reasons of subsidiarity. The Strasbourg Court defers to

---

[26] See R v Home Secretary, ex p Brind [1991] AC 696, 762–3; also Lord Lowry, 766.

Turkish authorities on the question of whether a dress code is a proportionate restriction on freedom of religion, and the reason is that the Court is so distant from Turkish life. When an English court gives effect to Convention rights under the Human Rights Act, those reasons of subsidiarity vanish, because the court is part of the British legal system. So the Human Rights Act offers the possibility that English judges will be more intrusive than the European Court of Human Rights: the Court in Strasbourg has reasons to defer which do not apply to the High Court on the Strand in London.

But there are also reasons of comity (see p 17) for deference. Those reasons apply to an English court, and not just to an international court. Even though it does not face the Strasbourg Court's problem of subsidiarity, the House of Lords has other reasons for deferring to an English school on the question of whether a dress code is a proportionate restriction on freedom of religion (R (Begum) v Denbigh High School Governors [2006] UKHL 15; see p 275). The extent to which English judicial scrutiny under the Human Rights Act will be more intrusive than European Court of Human Rights scrutiny will depend on the way in which the English judges develop their own doctrine of deference. This crucial aspect of the impact of the Convention on administrative law will be addressed in Chapter 8.

When is it o.k. to infringe a Convention right?

Writers and judges sometimes say that a contracting state can legitimately infringe a Convention right when the Convention itself provides a justification.[27] The suggestion is that, e.g., the 'right to freedom of expression' in Art 10.1 *includes* the right to slander people and to communicate military secrets to the country's enemies, but that the right can legitimately be *infringed* 'in the interests of national security' and 'for the protection of the reputation or rights of others' (Art 9.2).

But the Convention does not say that the right may be infringed; it says that freedom of expression may be restricted (Art 9.2). If you are convicted of treason for selling state secrets, or if you are held liable in defamation for slandering someone, your right under Art 9 is not infringed, because Art 9 itself allows the exercise of freedom of expression to be restricted. The right of freedom of expression is a right to a restricted freedom, which does not include selling state secrets or slandering people.

It is *always unlawful* for a public authority to infringe a Convention right, except to give effect to an act of Parliament (Human Rights Act 1998 s 6(2)).

---

[27] Examples can be found in Lord Bingham's speech in R (Daly) v Home Secretary [2001] 2 AC 532 [17]. Cf. Lord Hoffmann: 'Even if there had been an infringement of Shabina's rights under article 9, I would … have been of opinion that the infringement was justified under article 9.2' (R (Begum) v Denbigh High School [2005] EWCA Civ 199 [58]). That statement is best read as a conclusion that a restriction on Shabina's *freedom* was justified under Art 9.2, so that there *was no infringement* of the right. The Chief Justice of the Canadian Supreme Court took the same approach as Lord Hoffmann to describing 'infringements' of rights in Oakes [75].

TAKE-HOME MESSAGE • • •

- The Convention has not become part of English law; the Human Rights Act gives **specified, limited legal effects** to the rights protected in the Convention.

- What the Human Rights Act does:
  - it changes the effect of statutes, requiring them to be read and given effect in a way that is compatible with Convention rights, 'so far as possible'. And it leaves judges to decide what is possible (s 3);
  - it creates a new ground for quashing administrative action as unlawful, if the action infringes a Convention right, and is not required by statute (s 6));
  - if a statute cannot be read and given effect in a way that is compatible with a Convention right, it empowers judges to declare a statute incompatible (s 4). A declaration of incompatibility triggers a fast-track amendment process;
  - it gives English judges new ways of imposing the rule of law on the government, because it gives effect in English law to the provisions against arbitrary detention (Art 5), the right to a fair hearing before an independent and impartial tribunal (Art 6), and the prohibition on retrospective criminal liability (Art 7);
  - it requires judges to decide whether interferences with some fundamental interests are proportionate to legitimate objectives; and
  - it leaves it to judges to find a middle way between leaving other public authorities to violate Convention rights, and imposing their own views of the public interest on other public authorities in a way that would damage the separation of powers.

- What the Human Rights Act does not do:
  - it **does not replace the common law** standards **of judicial review**; and
  - it **does not** undermine **the principle of parliamentary sovereignty**.

- The House of Lords has used **s 3** of the Act to give some statutes an effect that is contrary to their meaning.

- But the courts have declined some of the opportunities offered to them by claimants' barristers, to use the Act to remodel English law:
  - the House of Lords' interpretation of **s 6** has protected exercises of a Convention-incompatible statutory power from being quashed on judicial review;
  - the courts have developed a **doctrine of deference** to executive and legislative authorities in making the assessments of the public interest that they need to make to apply the qualified Convention rights (the role of deference is dealt with in Chapter 8); and
  - the House of Lords has refrained from using **Art 6** of the Convention (right to a fair trial) to restructure administrative decision making.

- Decisions of the **European Court of Human Rights** have the same effect in international law as they had before the Human Rights Act: its decisions bind the United Kingdom. Those decisions have a *new* effect in English law under the Human Rights Act, because English courts must take account of them (s 2). Keep in mind that any litigant who loses on a Convention issue in the English courts will have to decide whether to go to Strasbourg to seek a different decision.

··· Critical reading ···
Handyside v UK (1976) 1 EHRR 737
R v Home Secretary, ex p Venables and Thompson [1998] AC 407
V v United Kingdom (2000) 30 EHRR 121
R (Daly) v Home Secretary [2001] UKHL 26
R (Alconbury) v Environment Secretary [2001] UKHL 23
R (Anderson) v Home Secretary [2002] UKHL 46
Ghaidan v Godin-Mendoza [2004] UKHL 30
R (Wilkinson) v Inland Revenue Commissioners [2005] UKHL 30

CRITICAL QUESTIONS • • •

1   Is judicial review for incompatibility of administrative action with Convention rights justified by constitutional principle?

2   How does the Human Rights Act promote the rule of law? Does it pose dangers to the rule of law?

3   Should English courts be *less* deferential than the Strasbourg Court in applying the qualified Convention rights?

4   Are there proportionality tests for the application of all Convention rights?

Further questions:

5   Neither House of Parliament is a 'public authority' for the purposes of the Human Rights Act (s 6(3)). Why not?

6   Why does the Human Rights Act define 'primary legislation' to include an 'Order in Council made in exercise of Her Majesty's Royal Prerogative' (s 21(1))? How does that provision affect judicial review of the prerogative?

7   The Human Rights Act 1998 s 19 provides that 'A Minister of the Crown in charge of a Bill in either House of Parliament must...(a) make a statement to the effect that in his view the provisions of the Bill are compatible with the Convention rights; or (b) make a statement to the effect that although he is unable to make a statement of compatibility the government nevertheless wishes the House to proceed with the Bill.' Suppose that a Minister makes a statement that in his view a bill is compatible with Convention rights, but in fact the bill is incompatible with Convention rights. Does a person aggrieved by the minister's conduct have any legal remedy?

8   Could you get judicial review of a governmental decision not to ask Parliament to amend legislation that a court has declared to be incompatible with a Convention right?

9   Can a remedial order under the Human Rights Act 1998 s 10 be quashed by a court as *ultra vires*?

10   Why do the privacy and political freedom articles (Art 8, 9, 10, 11) allow only those limits on freedom and privacy that are '*necessary* in a democratic society'? Why not allow those limits that are just or reasonable?

online resource centre

Visit the online resource centre to access the following resources which accompany this chapter: links to legislation and online reports of judicial decisions, summaries of key cases and legislation, updates in the law, suggestions for answering the pop quizzes and questions, and links to useful websites.

Also see the Online Resource Centre for a list of the convention rights to which the Human Rights Act gives effect in English law.

Process

4 Due process

Due process requires a variety of procedures for different decisions in different contexts. Good procedures are essential for responsible government. But they also increase the cost of administration. And procedural requirements may actually prevent good administration. The attempt to achieve *due* process is essential to good administration, and to the administration of justice. The law of due process is the judges' best contribution to administrative law.

LOOK FOR • • •

- **Proportionality** in procedural duties of public authorities.

- The three **process values**: procedural requirements can improve decisions, treat people with respect, and subject the administration to the rule of law.

- **Process cost** and **process dangers**.

- **The problem of comity**: can the judges improve decision making by requiring particular procedures? Or will they actually damage the process by doing so?

- The **irony of process**: the law must sometimes require procedures that impose *disproportionate* burdens on administrative authorities, in order to protect due process.

- The cases on executive decisions concerning detention (in parole, mental health, asylum, and terrorism), which raise questions at the frontiers of due process.

> '... the Board of Education will have to ascertain the law and also to ascertain the facts. I need not add that in doing either they must act in good faith and fairly listen to both sides, for that is a duty lying upon every one who decides anything. But I do not think they are bound to treat such a question as though it were a trial. '
>
> *Board of Education v Rice* [1911] AC 179 (HL), 182 (Lord Loreburn LC)

4.1 The justice of the common law

Mr Cooper started building a house. He got as far as the second floor, when the Wandsworth Board of Works 'sent their surveyor and a number of workmen, at a late hour in the evening, and razed it to the ground' (*Cooper v Board of Works* (1863) 14 CB (NS) 180, 182).

Cooper sued the Board for the tort of trespass to property (see section 14.1). The Board's defence was that the demolition was no trespass, because it was authorized by statute. The statute required seven days' notice to the Board before any new building could be started. If a building was started without the seven days' notice, the statute said, 'it shall be lawful for the ... board to cause such house or building to be demolished' (Metropolis Local Management Act, 1855 s 76). The Board had received no notice; Cooper said he had sent one in but admitted that he had started work five days after giving notice.

The Board of Works lost. The court held that the demolition was unlawful. How is that possible, if Cooper had not given seven days' notice, and a statute of Parliament said that demolition 'shall be lawful' if seven days' notice was not given? The answer is that 'although there are no positive words in a statute requiring that the party shall be heard, yet the justice of the common law will supply the omission of the legislature' (Byles J, 194). The demolition was unlawful *because the Board had not given Cooper a hearing*; that is, the common law required the officials to give Cooper notice of what they had in mind, and to listen to what he had to say, before they could lawfully exercise the power that Parliament had given them.

Why did the justice of the common law require a hearing? Byles J took something for granted in his famous statement, which the other judges spelled out: 'no man is to be deprived of his property without his having an opportunity of being heard' (Erle CJ, 187). 'A tribunal which is by law invested with power to affect the property of one of Her Majesty's subjects, is bound to give such subject an opportunity of being heard before it proceeds' (Willes J, 190).[1] Willes J called it a rule 'of universal application, and founded upon the plainest principles of justice' (190).

To reach that decision, the judges needed to deal with two problems raised by counsel for the Board of Works in *Cooper*. The first is whether the Board of Works was right to think that its public role demanded that it get on with the job of demolishing

---

[1] Is due process restricted to British subjects? No: for example, today as in the 1860s, the availability of *habeas corpus* does not depend on nationality.

Cooper's house without giving a hearing. The second is whether it is appropriate for judges to impose the processes they consider appropriate on an executive agency. So we need to address a question of **procedural justice**, and also a question of **comity**:

- what are the 'plainest principles of justice' (Willes J at 190) on which the rule of due process is founded? (See section 4.2.)

- granted that justice *sometimes* requires a hearing, why shouldn't the judges leave it to the administration to decide when? (See section 4.3.)

'Hearing' is used metaphorically for any procedure in which a decision maker considers what a person affected has to say, before making a decision. In an **oral hearing** (see section 4.8), the decision maker listens to the person face to face.

A **procedure** is a step taken for the purpose of making or justifying or communicating or explaining or reconsidering a decision.

A **process** is the set of procedures taken in the making of a decision.

A **proceeding** is a set of procedures for the determination of a particular case before a tribunal or court.

4.2 Natural justice

For centuries before *Cooper's* case, English lawyers had been using **'natural justice'** as a technical term for the procedural duties owed by a court, or by an administrative body that makes decisions that are similar to those of a court ('quasi-judicial' decisions).[2] When you are deciding whether to pull down someone's house, it is unjust to act as if they had nothing to say on the matter.

It was wrong to pull down Cooper's house without talking to him for a reason the judges pointed out: since the Board's decision was based on Cooper's failure to give notice, he might have had new information relevant to the decision. He might have been able to show that it was only by accident (or due to the fault of a third party) that his notice hadn't reached the Board. Or, if he really had not given notice, he might be able to tell them something relevant to the discretionary power that they had to exercise (for example, that the construction met their standards). It would be unjust for the Board to pull down his house if there is good reason not to, so it is *procedurally unjust* to do so without knowing all the information or argument that might show a good reason not to. It also went against the public interest for which the Board had been set up. The Board was not doing its job of protecting people from dangerous buildings (and not demolishing buildings that are not dangerous), if it pulled down houses on partial or faulty information.

---

2   But the phrase 'natural justice' had earlier been used more generally for what is naturally just, in substance or in process: in *Moses v Macferlan* (1760) 2 Burr 1005, 1012, Lord Mansfield CJ said of what is now called a claim in restitution that 'the defendant, upon the circumstances of the case, is obliged by the ties of natural justice and equity to refund the money'.

But there is also another reason why it was unjust to pull down Cooper's house without talking to him about it. Even if he had *no* information to give, tearing down someone's house without telling him ahead of time shows disrespect. Counsel for the Board in *Cooper's* case asked, 'What necessity can there be for giving the party notice, when he well knows that he is doing an illegal act, and that the board have power to prostrate his house?' (186). The court's answer was that the Board owed him the respect that it would have shown him if it had given notice of the plan—even if that way of proceeding could make no difference to the outcome. The men from the Board of Works came at night. Erle CJ said that there was evidence that they were not on 'amicable' terms with Cooper. The lack of notice and lack of a hearing were in themselves ways of abusing Cooper, by treating him as if he didn't matter.

> ### FROM THE MISTS OF TIME
>
> Byles J cited the 1748 case of R *v Chancellor of Cambridge ex p Bentley* (1748) 2 Ld Raym 1334. Dr. Bentley had been expelled from the University of Cambridge: Fortescue J held that before being deprived of rights as a punishment for misconduct, 'The laws of God and man both give the party a right to make his defence, if he has any'. And he observed that 'even God himself did not pass sentence upon Adam before he was called upon to make his defence' (*Cooper*, 195). The point of the story is that God already knew the facts of the case. So even if nothing can possibly be learned from the person affected by a decision, the decision maker can, and sometimes must, treat such a person decently by letting him or her have a say. Byles J said that Fortescue J's judgment 'is somewhat quaint, but it . . . has been the law from that time to the present' (195). It is still the law in the 21st century.

Finally, apart from showing respect for Cooper, and even if the person affected has nothing to say, the requirement of a hearing subjects the power of the Board of Works to the **rule of law**, and promotes the allied value of **accountability**. Uncontrolled public decision making doesn't just lead to poor outcomes and show disrespect for the people affected; it lacks the regularity and transparency that could distinguish it from the mere say-so of the people on the Board of Works. Procedural participation by people affected by a decision promotes the rule of law by making it more difficult for a public authority to act arbitrarily. And it is an accountability technique in itself, because it puts the public authority in the predicament of having to face up to the people affected by a decision.

These benefits are *related* to the outcome goal of getting the right houses pulled down, and to the value of showing respect for Cooper. Protecting him from an uncontrolled process is a way of showing him respect, and so is a rule making someone from the Board of Works look him in the eye before pulling down his house. But the rule-of-law value of procedures is distinct from their value in improving outcomes and showing respect. Think of an armed robber who is caught red-handed by police, and who wants no procedural protection. The police cannot just take him off to prison—English law still insists on a criminal trial, with the cumbersome procedures that it involves even when the accused pleads guilty. The reason is to impose the rule of law on the community's response to crimes, and to provide accountability to the community, and not just to the person affected.

Process value: the advantages of procedural participation

- **The value of promoting good outcomes:** to improve the capacity of the decision maker to act on all the relevant considerations. That is just good administration, which is in the public interest.
- **The value of respect:** to treat a person who is involved in certain ways in the outcome of a decision as someone who should be involved in the process.
- **The value of imposing the rule of law on the administration:** to promote integrity in public decision making by controlling the process.

But notice the drawbacks of making the Board of Works give a hearing to people like Cooper. First, it **costs public money**. It is cheaper to decide whether to pull down a house without paying someone to spend time giving notice to Cooper (and finding him in the first place), and listening to what he may have to say. Secondly, **it may actually be dangerous to the public interest**. Requiring hearings will make the officials' work less convenient, and that actually carries a risk of damaging the public interest. Remember that the point of the Board's powers was partly to protect the public against dangerous building practices, and a dangerous building can fall down in the time it takes to give notice and to give a defaulter the opportunity to explain. As counsel for the Board in *Cooper* pointed out, 'in many cases the object to be attained would be utterly frustrated unless done promptly' (187). No doubt, the court would not have held the action in *Cooper* to be a tort if the Board of Works had acted in an emergency to prevent the house from falling on passers-by. But the decision in *Cooper* puts pressure on officials to be concerned with the risk of liability that they may face in pulling down a house without lawful procedures—and not just about the risk that the house will fall down.

Process cost and process danger: the disadvantages of procedural rights

- **Process cost:** the expense of procedural steps, in time and money.
- **Process danger:** the risk that by requiring a particular procedure, the law will damage the capacity of the public authority to carry out its functions justly and effectively.

Natural justice demanded a hearing in the *Cooper* situation, in spite of the drawbacks. The danger was inconsequential, and the value of a hearing in that situation was worth the cost.

Process and substance

In *Cooper's* case, the Board of Works decided to pull down the house, and they decided that Cooper's failure to give notice justified them in doing so. The **substance** of the Board's decision is what they decided: *both* the action they decided to take, and the reasons for which they decided to take it. The defect in the **process** by which the Board made the decision was the failure to listen to Cooper. Substance and process are distinct, but are connected to each other. Because of the connections, the distinction can seem either mind-bending or non-existent. So hold onto the simple idea that the substance of a decision is *what was decided*. If you can write down, 'the public authority decided **that**...', then the three dots stand for the substance of the decision (in *Cooper's* case, the Board decided **that** his house was to be demolished because of his lack of notice); the process is the sum of the steps by which that decision was reached. But 'steps by which a decision was reached' is ambiguous! It could refer to steps in the public authority's *reasoning*, or to things that the public authority *did* to enable it to do that reasoning. Steps in the public authority's reasoning are actually part of the substance of its decision (see section 6.9).

Due process requires a decision maker to take the steps (in particular, listening to people who have something to say on the issues) that are suited to making a good decision. It *further* requires actions that promote responsible decision making, such as communicating the decision, giving reasons for it (Chapter 6), and being prepared to reconsider it or to provide an appeal from it. And it requires those things to be done by people who can be seen by a reasonable observer to be unbiased (Chapter 5).

Of course, people like Cooper are only concerned with process when the substance of the decision is adverse to their interest; if, without giving him a hearing, the Board had made a decision not to pull down Cooper's house, he would have no complaint. The point of procedural protection is subsidiary to good decisions.

4.3 Comity between the judges and the Board of Works

The Board ought to have listened to Cooper. But what gives the judges jurisdiction to right the wrong? More recent cases take the judge's jurisdiction for granted. But it was at issue in *Cooper*. The Board of Works made an argument of comity (see p 17): that even if natural justice required a hearing, it was the *court's* job to impose it only when an official was acting 'judicially'. And the Board argued that it had acted 'ministerially' (that is, its function was to administer a public programme, rather than to adjudicate Cooper's rights). The Board had a job to do in the public interest, and while it is possible for administrators to abuse their power, 'the great safe-guard against abuses in the administration ... is that the members of which these boards are composed are elected by the rate-payers of the district' (186). The lawyer for the Board of Works might have said something similar for *any* public authority: that the appropriate form of control is through management by an executive that is democratically accountable. In support of the argument that the Board was acting ministerially and not judicially, Counsel for the Board said something that no English lawyer would say today: 'An arbitrary power is conferred upon the board, which is necessarily to be exercised without any control' (186).

The failure of that argument is the most important development in modern administrative law. It is the founding principle of the modern law of due process: even when the functions of a public authority are administrative or 'ministerial', rather than judicial, they must be exercised with due process, and the judges have a general jurisdiction to require due process. In the rest of this chapter, we will see that the principle is justified by the **core rationale** (see p 65) for judicial interference with other public authorities: the judges can improve the administration of justice by taking this power on themselves. It is required, as Byles J put it (194), by the justice of the common law—that is, by the judges' responsibility for the administration of justice.

4.3.1 Due process in judicial *and* administrative decisions

In *Cooper*, the argument that natural justice is restricted to judicial or quasi-judicial functions failed. But the judges' response to the argument was muddled. It would take *Ridge v Baldwin* [1964] AC 40, a century later, to clear away the muddle. Erle CJ could not quite decide whether the decision in *Cooper* was judicial (189). Byles J said 'I conceive that they acted judicially', but also, 'It seems to me that the board are wrong whether they acted judicially or ministerially' (194). If they acted ministerially, he thought that they owed Cooper no hearing, but still were bound to give notice of the demolition before they carried it out (195). Willes J said, 'it is clear that these boards do exercise judicial powers' (191), but did not say how a ministerial power would differ. After *Cooper*, it was unclear whether hearings are required in the exercise of administrative functions, and what the difference is between administrative functions and quasi-judicial functions.

One solution would be for the judges to decree (as Byles J did) that the decision was 'judicial' or 'quasi-judicial', because of the way it affected Cooper. The Court of Appeal took that approach in *Hopkins v Smethwick Local Board of Health* (1890) 24 QBD 712 (CA). But that approach led to confusion over how a decision had to affect a person in order to be judicial or quasi-judicial. It also led to procedural injustice. In *Nakkuda Ali v Jayaratne* [1951] AC 66, the Privy Council allowed such an injustice. The Ceylon Controller of Textiles had power to revoke a licence if there were reasonable grounds to believe that a dealer was unfit. Lord Radcliffe held for the Privy Council:

> ❛ In truth, when he cancels a licence he is not determining a question: he is taking executive action to withdraw a privilege because he believes, and has reasonable grounds to believe, that the holder is unfit to retain it. ❜ (78)

That was a **process failure**. It may seem that the problem is that there is no distinction between judicial/quasi-judicial and administrative functions. But the distinction is actually quite clear: an administrative decision is designed to give effect to the policy of the government, while a judicial or quasi-judicial decision is designed to decide a dispute as to the legal position of the parties. The problem is that these types of decision overlap: a decision to give effect to a policy of the government often determines someone's legal position—as it did in *Nakkuda Ali*. The decision in *Nakkuda Ali* was a process failure because the judges wrongly thought that no decision giving effect to government policy requires procedural participation by the people it affects. But the administrative ('executive' as Lord Radcliffe called it) task of preventing textile trading by unfit dealers cannot be done fairly without listening to what the dealer in question has to say.

The right solution is for the common law to require due process in the exercise of administrative functions, *as well as* judicial and quasi-judicial functions. One early statement of this solution to the problem lies in Lord Denning MR's reasons in the Court of Appeal in *Padfield v Minister of Agriculture, Fisheries and Food* [1968] AC 997: 'It is said that the decision of the Minister is administrative and not judicial. But that does not mean that he can do as he likes, regardless of right or wrong. Nor does it mean that the courts are powerless to correct him' (1006). In making administrative decisions, due process may require a hearing, because of (1) the process value of a hearing, and (2) the possibility of requiring a hearing without damaging the public authority's performance of its administrative functions. Judicial decisions may call for special procedures. But the difference between administration and adjudication does not mean that it is acceptable to make administrative decisions with no procedural participation for people affected.

If judges can impose due process on the executive without stopping them from doing their job, then it is not a breach of comity for the judges to do so. Erle CJ commented in *Cooper*, 'I cannot conceive any harm that could happen to the district board from hearing the party before they subjected him to a loss so serious as the demolition of his house; but I can conceive a great many advantages which might arise in the way of public order, in the way of doing substantial justice, and in the way of fulfilling the purpose of the statute, by the restriction which we put upon them' (188). He exaggerated just a little, because harm *would* result from a requirement of a hearing: the Board would face the process cost of paying officials to deal fairly with people before pulling down their houses. And it would face a possible process danger of failing to protect people effectively from dangerous houses. So there *is* a problem of comity, because the decision interferes with the administration. And the judges in *Cooper* took it upon themselves to judge the value or detriment of interference. Judges who take that attitude might end up imposing fussy, expensive, and damaging procedures on a body that could and would act justly without them. But in cases like *Cooper*—and *Nakkuda Ali*—the readiness to impose due process on the executive is essential for the rule of law.

English administrative law since the twelfth century has been prepared to impose these costs in *some* cases. The process danger in *Cooper* was so small, and the process cost was so obviously worth paying, that the judges were justified in imposing it in the interest of the rule of law. Even though the Chief Justice was a judge and not a works expert, he could see that the Board would be 'fulfilling [its] purpose' better, not worse, if it gave a hearing. It was not a breach of comity for the judges to impose procedures on the Board of Works, because the independent judges could see that the process danger was trivial and the process cost worth paying.

The principle of legality at work

The requirement of due process is based on the principle that the requirements of the law are to be understood in light of certain legally protected values, and are limited by those values (see p 19). Courts subject the general statutory power to demolish a house to a qualification that the legislature did not impose. So Lord Mustill said in R v Home Secretary, ex p Doody [1994] 1 AC 531, 'where an Act of Parliament confers an administrative power there is a presumption that it will be exercised in a manner which is fair in all the circumstances' (560). The presumption is a rule of the common law that gives effect to the principle of legality.

But because public authorities need only give *due* process, the courts will not use the principle of legality, for example, to add procedures to a statutory process by which central government can limit spending by local councils.[3] The reason is not that public authorities are sometimes free to act unfairly, but that fairness does not always require a hearing.

The judges who decided cases like *Nakkuda Ali* did not think that it was o.k. for the administration to act unfairly: in *B Johnson & Co v Minister of Health* [1947] 2 All ER 395, Lord Greene said that 'every Minister of the Crown is under a duty, constitutionally, to the King to perform his functions honestly and fairly' (400). Then he added, 'but his failure to do so, speaking generally, is not a matter with which the courts are concerned.' In his decision in *Associated Provincial Picture Houses v Wednesbury* [1948] 1 KB 223 (see p 44) later the same year, Lord Greene MR said that the courts will quash an exercise of discretion only for certain *restricted* forms of *unreasonableness*, and in *B Johnson & Co*, he insisted that only certain *restricted* forms of *unfairness* are the courts' concern. A minister's decision in planning matters 'cannot be challenged and criticised in the courts unless he has acted unfairly in another sense, *viz.*, in the sense of having, while performing quasi-judicial functions, acted in a way which no person performing such functions, in the opinion of the court, ought to act' (400).

Today, you need to remove the words 'while performing quasi-judicial functions' from his statement of the law. *Any* kind of decision is now unlawful, if it is made by a process that no person performing such functions ought to adopt. Since the 1940s, it has become a basic principle that administrative functions, as well as judicial functions, must be carried out with due process. The differences among decisions do not mean that some decisions are not subject to due process; they mean that different processes are due. Even in the landmark case of *Ridge v Baldwin*, this principle was not very clearly stated. But it was firmly established as a result of Lord Reid's approach to the case.

---

3   R v Environment Secretary, ex p Hammersmith LBC [1991] 1 AC 521 (598–9), Lord Bridge; on this important decision, see p 247.

4.3.2 *Ridge v Baldwin*: a general requirement of due process

Charles Ridge was the Chief of Police in Brighton, and had served 23 years on the police force, when he was prosecuted on corruption charges. He was acquitted, but at the end of the trial the judge said first that he was a bad example because of his association with men suspected of bribing police, and secondly that his evidence would not be trusted in future prosecutions. The day after this damaging scene, the police authority told Ridge that he was sacked. His lawyer immediately complained to the Home Secretary that the decision was contrary to natural justice, because the authority had given Ridge no hearing. The Home Secretary upheld the decision, and Ridge brought an action for a declaration that the decision was unlawful.

The police authority's defence was that 'For those who are responsible for a police force such a dismissal is a matter of the policy of the borough and therefore in acting they need not apply the principles of natural justice' (58). It is the argument that the Board of Works had made against Cooper, and it combines the arguments of necessity and comity. The argument is that because of the public need for effective policing, it is not unfair to proceed without a hearing, and it would be a breach of comity for the courts to require one. Counsel for Ridge had an answer to the argument:

> ‘ It is accepted that when administrative actions are to be considered, policy is always a factor. But the rules of natural justice are concerned with a fair form of procedure, not with controlling policy. ’ (61)

That argument succeeded, and transformed administrative law. In a landmark opinion, Lord Reid harked back a century to *Cooper*, and said that if Ridge's case had come a few decades earlier, it would have been plain that he had to be given a hearing. Lord Reid thought that the courts had lost track of the scope of natural justice because 'insufficient attention has been paid to the great difference between various kinds of cases' (65). In cases of dismissal, he held, a hearing was required if, as in *Ridge's* case, the decision had to be made on grounds of neglect of duty.

Lord Reid's approach reconciled comity with due process, by applying the **principle of relativity** (see p 10). The crucial point in his opinion is his response to the police authority's claim that *because it was implementing policy on behalf of Brighton, the principles of natural justice did not apply*. Lord Reid made no use of the old distinction between ministerial and judicial powers, but just pointed out the varied roles that policy might play in different decisions, and the ways in which an administrative decision might still resemble the work of a judge, even when a public authority is implementing policy. He said that the police authority 'was not deciding, like a judge in a lawsuit, what were the rights of the person before it. But it was deciding how he should be treated—something analogous to a judge's duty in imposing a penalty. No doubt policy would play some part in the decision—but so it might when a judge is imposing a sentence' (72). So the police authority's responsibility for effective policing was perfectly consistent with a duty to listen to Ridge. In fact, Lord Reid might have pointed out, good policy *required* that it proceed in a manner that would put all the relevant considerations on the table. The importance of doing so is worth the **process cost** of giving the police chief a hearing.

It may have seemed to the police authority that there was a **process danger** (a risk that policing would be damaged if they listen to the Chief Constable). They may have thought that maintaining public confidence in the police demanded a summary dismissal as a statement. If it really were necessary for the good of the community, it would not be unfair to dismiss Ridge without a hearing. Compare the position of cabinet ministers, who can be sacked without a hearing at the mere say-so of the Prime Minister. And the minister cannot get judicial review! Why not? It is not because the Prime Minister does not need to act fairly, but because of (1) the nature of job, and (2) the constitutional value served by committing the decision to the leader of the executive alone. So a court will not ask whether the Prime Minister has proceeded unfairly in dismissing a minister.

The decision in *Ridge* was a good one, because the judges could interfere without doing the sort of damage they would do if they tried to supervise the dismissal of ministers. There is no need for the police authority to be able to proceed without a hearing, or to be free from judicial interference. And there is a genuine danger in that context, that officials free from judicial interference will fail to give due process because of the pressures they may be under, and because they actually bear the process cost of a hearing.

The effect of Lord Reid's decision was something that *Cooper* and the other cases had not said: it imposed due process generally on administrative authorities. And Lord Hodson simply decided that the principles of natural justice apply to 'persons acting in a capacity which is not on the face of it judicial but rather executive or administrative' (130). The distinction between administrative and quasi-judicial decisions had only been distracting. Administrative decisions, like judicial decisions, should be made with due process (though the form of process that is *due* will be affected by the administrative nature of the decision).

The requirement of a hearing in *Ridge v Baldwin* created an obstacle to arbitrary use of the power to dismiss, by making the process of its exercise more open, and by requiring the authority to listen to Ridge. It forced the authority to treat Ridge decently: as someone who had something to say on the matter of whether he should be sacked for misconduct, and as someone who was entitled to know what was said of him to his superiors. The question of how to proceed was one that the court could answer without usurping the authority's power to decide whether Ridge was fit to be a police chief. So fairness and the rule of law counted in favour of the decision. The House of Lords' decision was a just use of judicial power to check the arbitrary use of executive power: it fits the **core rationale** for interference by judges with another public authority.

The problem of comity has been solved for tearing down houses, and for sacking police chiefs. The solution is that the process values of better outcomes, showing respect to the people in question, and subjecting the administration to the rule of law are worth pursuing, in spite of the process danger and the process cost. But the

Board of Works in *Cooper's* case was a 19th-century precursor of a regulatory state that has grown massive, making decisions that affect people in very diverse ways, requiring very different forms of procedural involvement for people who want a say in the process. And the problem of comity becomes fraught in executive decision making over detention of persons.

Like most bad arguments, the arguments of the public authorities in *Cooper* and *Ridge* (and the successful argument of the public authority in *Nakkuda Ali*) were based on a kernel of good sense: that administrative decisions do not require the same procedures as judicial processes. The mistake was the idea that justice does not demand *any* procedural protections when a decision is administrative. Even after *Ridge*, the judges had not quite finished putting the mistake to rest. Three years later, Lord Parker CJ sorted it out again, from first principles, without even mentioning *Ridge*:

> ...even if an immigration officer is not in a judicial or quasi-judicial capacity, he must at any rate give the immigrant an opportunity of satisfying him of the matters in the subsection, and for that purpose let the immigrant know what his immediate impression is so that the immigrant can disabuse him. That is not, as I see it, a question of acting or being required to act judicially, but of being required to act fairly. Good administration and an honest or bona fide decision must, as it seems to me, require not merely impartiality, nor merely bringing one's mind to bear on the problem, but acting fairly; and to the limited extent that the circumstances of any particular case allow, and within the legislative framework under which the administrator is working, only to that limited extent do the so-called rules of natural justice apply, which in a case such as this is merely a duty to act fairly. [4]

Lord Parker pointed out with some embarrassment that it was difficult to reconcile this view with Lord Radcliffe's opinion for the Privy Council in *Nakkuda Ali*: 'I very much doubt, however, whether it was intended to say any more than that there is no duty to invoke judicial process unless there is a duty to act judicially' (631). That generous approach to *Nakkuda Ali* retains the kernel of good sense behind a mistaken decision: that fairness demands procedures that are proportionate to the issues at stake in the administrative process.

In the rest of this chapter, and in Chapter 5, we will see how the law determines that proportion.

Latin lesson

- ***audi alteram partem***: 'listen to each side of the story'
- ***nemo judex in causa sua***: 'no one is to decide his own case'

Those two maxims encompass much of procedural justice, including the common law rule against bias and the right to a fair hearing. Requiring reasons is *partly* an

---

[4]   *In re HK (an infant)* [1967] 2 QB 617.

instrument for requiring the decision maker to hear both sides and to decide without bias. A right to an administrative or judicial appeal (or to judicial review) bol-
sters the *audi alteram partem* rule, by guarding the integrity and soundness of the
initial determination.

4.4 Due process is proportionate process

Can we say that, since *Ridge's* case, there is a general duty to give hearings before
making administrative decisions? No. Remember R *v Ministry of Defence, ex p Walker*
[2000] 1 WLR 806 (see section 2.1). One of the challenges to the Army's criminal
injuries compensation scheme was that it lacked due process—specifically, that it
was unfair for the Ministry to restrict the criminal injuries compensation scheme,
without announcing the change directly to soldiers or to their commanders. But the
argument was unsuccessful. Walker did not even claim that he ought to have had a
hearing, but only notice—and the court held that he had no right even to that. The
decision to restrict the scheme is an example of the sort of administrative action that
yields *no legal right to any procedural participation* by the people affected.[5]

Due process does not mean *giving a hearing*. It means *giving a hearing when the
person affected ought to have a way of participating in the making of the decision.* As Lord
Reid emphasized from the beginning in *Ridge*, that depends on the circumstances.
In Lord Denning MR's words, 'The rules of Natural Justice—or of fairness—are not
cut and dried. They vary infinitely' (R *v Home Secretary, ex p Santillo* [1981] QB 778, 795).
There is no general answer to the question, 'what procedures does the common law
require for an administrative decision?'—except that it requires *due* or *proportionate*
procedures.

A question of proportionality is a question of how much of something is enough
to achieve or protect something that must be achieved or protected. Proportionality
does not require a jury trial on a parking ticket, because it would be superfluous for
the purpose. Proportionality is a relation between two things (see p 92)—in this case,
a relation between the procedural involvement of a person affected by a decision, and
the issues at stake in the decision. A decision without a jury trial on a charge of murder would fail to give the defendant the procedural protection that is proportionate
to the nature of the charge.

So what determines the variation in procedural protections? What should they be
proportionate to? Lord Denning MR in *Santillo* held that the Home Secretary did *not*
have to give a man a hearing when he decided to deport him at the end of his imprisonment for rape, after the trial judge had recommended deportation. It did not even
matter if the Home Secretary had received new information that reinforced his judgment that the man should be deported. This part of Lord Denning's decision puts a
limit on the **duty of respect**: you do not have a right to a hearing merely because you

---

[5]   But even where there is no right to procedural *participation*, the fairness doctrine provides procedural *protection*: the decision must be made without bias (see p 152).

might be able to set the record straight when a public authority has heard something derogatory about you. However, Lord Denning did not hold that a convict *generally* has no right to a hearing before deportation: if a 'new adverse factor may turn the scale against the man', the Home Secretary 'should invite him to deal with it' (374). In that sort of case, the Home Secretary *would* have a duty to give notice of the adverse factor, and a duty to give a hearing.

Whether a particular procedure is *due* depends on the three process values: promoting good outcomes, showing appropriate respect for a person affected, and imposing the rule of law on the process. A procedure is due if it is the right way to pursue those purposes, given the process cost and any process danger that may be involved.

The common law of due process has largely addressed these considerations in terms of the second process value, *fairness to the claimant*, because showing respect for the person affected is the courts' special concern. After all, in judicial review, they hear complaints *by the persons affected by decisions*. Promoting the public interest in good outcomes (the first process value) and imposing the rule of law on the administrative process are typically the result of requiring procedures that are fair to the claimant. So we can say that in English law, a hearing (or some other form of procedural participation) is due:

- when **legislation** (including the Human Rights Act) or a public authority's own rules require it, and

- when **fairness** (in Lord Greene MR's restricted sense in *B Johnson & Co v Minister of Health* [1947] 2 All ER 395) requires it.

But there is one proviso, which Lord Greene had in mind in *B Johnson & Co*, and which is often forgotten: the requirements of procedural fairness are subject to the principle of comity. A procedure is not required unless it is possible for judges to require it without damaging the decision maker's ability to do its job. There are many ways in which public authorities could act unfairly without being subject to any judicial control. The Prime Minister might dismiss a Cabinet minister unfairly and the minister would have no legal recourse.

Subject to that proviso, fairness to the claimant is the chief focus of the law of due process. In fact, fairness is sometimes spoken of as if it were the entire reason for procedural duties. But remember that the public interests in the rule of law and in good administration also require that public authorities be subjected to procedural duties.

4.4.1 Legislation

The decision-making processes in *Cooper*, *Ridge*, and *B Johnson & Co* were all governed by legislation. It may seem that a court faces no problem of comity in giving effect to legislative procedural requirements: it is simply enforcing the rules made by Parliament (or by a minister in delegated legislation, or through the use of the prerogative). But there is still a problem for the courts: when the parties contest the interpretation of the legislative procedures, or their applicability to the case, should the court defer to the public authority's interpretation of the rules? And do the legislative processes exclude other procedural requirements? The judges' answer to both questions is 'no'. In *Cooper*, *Ridge*, and *B Johnson & Co*, the public authorities argued each time that the courts should not impose additional procedures that the legislation had not required. In *Ridge*, the police authority argued that it did not need to give a hearing because by statute, the Home Secretary had power to overturn its decision. That argument always fails, as it did in *Lloyd v McMahon* [1987] 1 AC 625: 'when a statute has conferred on any body the power to make decisions affecting individuals, the courts will not only require the procedure prescribed by the statute to be followed, but will readily imply so much and no more to be introduced by way of additional procedural safeguards as will ensure the attainment of fairness' (Lord Bridge, 703). Here again the principle of legality is in action, ensuring that statutory schemes are not treated as implicitly displacing the constitutional principle of due process.[6]

4.4.2 Fairness

A decision is **unfair** if it wrongly neglects the interest of a person it affects. It is **procedurally** unfair if it wrongly neglects a person's interest in participating in the process; it is **substantively** unfair if its outcome wrongly injures a person's interest (see p 205 on the difference substance and process).

Since *Ridge v Baldwin*, the judges have used 'procedural fairness' as a general term for the procedural requirements that the common law imposes.[7] Even after *Ridge*, until the 1980s, the judges sometimes suggested that natural justice involves a more demanding set of procedures, and is only required if a decision is quasi-judicial. So in *Bushell v Environment Secretary* [1981] AC 75, Lord Diplock said of a local planning inquiry, 'rather than use such phrases as "natural justice" which may suggest that the prototype is only to be found in procedures followed by English courts of law, I prefer to put it that... it must be fair to all those who have an interest in the decision' (95).[8] But Lord Denning's approach has largely taken over—he used 'natural justice' and 'fairness' interchangeably (e.g. in *Santillo*, above; and Lord Slynn did the same in *R (Alconbury) v Environment Secretary* [2001] UKHL 23 [50], and in *R v Criminal Injuries Compensation Board, ex p A* [1999] 2 AC 330, 345). Lord Bridge said that the phrase 'the requirements of fairness' better expresses the 'underlying concept' than 'natural justice' (*Lloyd v McMahon* [1987] 1 AC 625, 702).

---

[6]   Compare also the giving of reasons for decision (section 6.6): we will see that, when a statute requires the giving of reasons, the courts will imply the same criteria of adequacy as in common law requirements of reasons: *In re Poyser and Mills' Arbitration* [1964] 2 QB 467, 478.

[7]   But the roots of the doctrine go back long before the 1960s: see Lord Loreburn's remark in *Board of Education v Rice* [1911] AC 179 (HL), at the beginning of this chapter.

[8]   And see Megarry VC's discussion of the two terms in *McInnes v Onslow-Fane* [1978] 1 WLR 1520, 1530.

┌─ FROM THE MISTS OF TIME ────────────────────────────

The significant changes in the law of due process since *Ridge v Baldwin* mean that judges sometimes use 'fairness' as a label for new procedural requirements, and 'natural justice' as a label for more traditional procedural requirements. But fairness has been a legal requirement for decision making for centuries, at least for courts of specific jurisdiction. In R *v Cowle* (1759) 2 Burr 834, Lord Mansfield held that any doubt 'whether a fair, impartial, or satisfactory trial or judgment can be had there' was a reason for the Court of King's Bench to quash a decision (861).

The link between fairness and natural justice is that procedural unfairness is an injustice: the common law of due process can be summed up by saying that 'a procedure that involves significant injustice' is unlawful, unless it is expressly authorized by statute (R *(Roberts) v Parole Board* [2005] UKHL 45 [83], Lord Woolf). If such an injustice is authorized by statute, the statute may be incompatible with Art 5 or 6 of the European Convention on Human Rights (ECHR).

Fairness to whom?

Note that the courts will require a public authority to act fairly not just toward the parties to a dispute, or even just toward those affected by the outcome of a decision, but also toward those affected *by the process*: e.g. to witnesses at a public inquiry, or in parole board hearings, or a coroner's inquest, who might be endangered by disclosure of their identity and/or testimony (R *(A) v Lord Saville of Newdigate* [2002] 1 WLR 1249).

4.5 What's at stake in the outcome, and what's at stake in the process?

So, due process requires a hearing when the person affected by a decision ought to have a way of participating in the making of the decision, and that will depend on proportionality between the process values that a procedure would serve (good outcomes, respect, the rule of law) and any process costs and process danger.

When does fairness require a person to be able to participate in the decision-making process? It may seem that what's fair depends on the impact of the decision on the person affected. After all, the prospect of the destruction of his property is what entitled Cooper to a hearing. And Ridge stood to lose his position as Chief Constable.

But some decisions that have an enormous impact on someone's life can be made fairly without involving that person in the decision-making process. If the government sends an aircraft carrier to the other side of the globe, the decision will affect the liberty of the sailors, and the property of merchants in Southampton, and the private and family life of the sailors' children, and the life of people on the other side of the globe. None of them has any legal right to advance notice of the plan, or the reasons for it, or to have an opportunity to put a case to the government as to why the aircraft carrier should not be sent to sea.

Rights to involvement in a decision-making process do not depend merely on the impact of the decision on a person, but on *whether the person has something to say on the issues that are relevant to the decision*. Lord Mustill summed up the law of fair procedures accurately in R *v Home Secretary, ex p Doody* [1994] 1 AC 531, by saying, 'Fairness will very often require that a person who may be adversely affected by the decision will have an opportunity to make representations' (560). If a person is adversely affected, fairness requires such an opportunity *very often*, but not *generally*. It is unfair to make a decision that adversely affects someone without a hearing only *if* there is a **process value** that justifies a particular procedure.

> ### A classic statement of what it is that procedural fairness depends on
> 'what the requirements of fairness demand…depends on the character of the decision-making body, the kind of decision it has to make and the statutory or other framework in which it operates' *Lloyd v McMahon* [1987] AC 625, 702 (Lord Bridge).

To see why procedural fairness does not depend merely on the impact of a decision on a person adversely affected, consider the difference between parking tickets and parole decisions. If a public authority is deciding whether to fine you £40 for parking on a double yellow line, you have a right to an oral hearing before an adjudicator.[9] If the Parole Board is deciding whether you should go free, or stay in prison for many months, you may have no right to an oral hearing (see section 4.8).

But we can generalize in one way: a public authority must give some form of hearing before deciding to deprive a person of property (*Cooper*). And although Ridge had no right to continue as police chief if his conduct was damaging the police force, he had a right to be heard on the question of whether that was the case. There is a general duty to give a hearing to a person whom the decision will **deprive of a legally protected interest** as in *Ridge*; it is a duty to the person who stands to be deprived. A person will *always* have something to say on the issues relevant to the decision whether to deprive him of an interest protected by law, because his participation may contribute to good decision making, will treat him with respect, and will uphold the rule of law.

> ### Lord Denning's answer to the question of what determines the variation in the requirements of fairness
> '[A]n administrative body may, in a proper case, be bound to give a person who is affected by their decision an opportunity of making representations. It all depends on whether he has some right or interest, or, I would add, some legitimate expectation, of which it would not be fair to deprive him without hearing what he has to say.'[10]

---

9   See: www.parkingandtrafficappeals.gov.uk/yourhearing.htm.

10   *Schmidt v Home Secretary* [1969] 2 Ch 149, 170.

Fairness depends not on whether the decision is important to the person affected, but on how the law protects the particular kind of interest that is at stake. The fact that a decision affects my interests does not mean that making it without consulting me is unfair to me. It is not even unfair when my interest is relevant to the issue. It is unfair when the way the decision affects my interest makes my participation relevant to the process. My participation will generally be deemed necessary if a public authority is deciding whether to deprive me of my rights, or of an interest protected by law.

Personal liberty, of course, is one interest that the law is especially concerned to protect. So Lord Denning also said, 'where a public officer has power to deprive a person of his liberty or his property, the general principle is that it is not to be done without his being given an opportunity of being heard and of making representations on his own behalf' (Schmidt v Home Secretary, 170). We can say something stronger about a decision to deprive a person of liberty: it is not even a matter for **administrative justice;**[11] it has required judicial process ever since habeas corpus developed into a general remedy against arbitrary government in the seventeenth century. This general principle explains the political and legal opposition to special legislation that derogates from it—such as the Terrorism Act 2006, allowing detention by the Home Secretary for up to 28 days, and the provision for detention for up to 42 days without charge under the Counter-Terrorism Bill 2007–08.[12]

No one can lawfully be imprisoned without a judicial hearing, unless an act of Parliament specifically authorizes it. Special procedural protection against arbitrary detention is not just part of our history; it is also guaranteed by the ECHR. Article 5 requires a prompt explanation of the reason for an arrest, and a prompt hearing by a court that can decide whether the detention is lawful. So legislation authorizing administrative detention would have to be accompanied by a derogation from the Convention, or it would be incompatible with Art 5. And the legislation would still be incompatible, if the derogation was not lawful (see p 6 on A and X v Home Secretary [2004] UKHL 56).

Sentencing of prisoners is a task for judges, and not for the administration. Yet the Parole Board is an administrative body. It can decide how long someone will stay in prison (and it can do so without an oral hearing), because (1) the person is subject to a sentence of imprisonment and so has no legal right to be at liberty, and (2) the issues relevant to the decision concern the protection of the public, and not the guilt of the prisoner. A Parole Board decision can mean the difference between immediate release, and years behind bars. So its impact can be greater than the impact of a criminal trial. But the parole process offers procedural protections for the prisoner that are much less than the protections of a criminal trial.

---

[11]   'Administrative justice' is an increasingly popular term for processes run by the administration, yet designed to achieve justice between the administration and a complainant (see Chapters 12 and 13).

[12]   The Government abandoned the 42-day provision after defeat in the House of Lords in October 2008.

All three reasons for process rights depend on the value of a person's participation in the determination of an issue:

- **the interest in good outcomes:** a hearing can only improve the capacity of the decision maker to act on all the relevant considerations if a person has something to say on the issues at stake;
- **the duty of respect:** it shows no disrespect if the public authority makes a decision without involving you in the process, if there is no value in your participation; and
- **the rule of law:** process rights can protect the integrity of public decision making by standing in the way of arbitrary decisions and forcing decision makers to listen to those who have something to say on the issues relevant to the decision.

4.6 The elements of process

If you do have a right to participation in a decision-making process, what does it give you? It varies, of course. But we can find the basic elements of fair procedure in *Ridge*. Lord Reid held that the power of dismissal cannot be exercised until the police authority 'have informed the constable of the grounds on which they propose to proceed and have given him a proper opportunity to present his case in defence' (79). Lord Hodson said that 'three features of natural justice stand out—(1) the right to be heard by an unbiased tribunal; (2) the right to have notice of charges of misconduct; (3) the right to be heard in answer to those charges' (132).

We can take these elements out of the dismissal situation and generalize: a person with a legally protected interest in the outcome of a decision is presumed to have something to say on the issues that are relevant to the decision, so that procedural fairness demands (1) no bias, (2) notice, and (3) an opportunity to make representations. You might say that the first and second follow from the entitlement to make representations: a hearing is a sham if the tribunal is biased, and a person will not be able to make representations effectively without notice of the issues.

To support these basic elements, a person affected by a decision may want some or all of the following procedural benefits.

The Menu

Disclosure of information held by the public authority or others

• • •

An oral hearing

• • •

Openness or confidentiality, depending on the situation

• • •

Representation (by a lawyer or other advocate)

. . .

An opportunity to present evidence

. . .

An opportunity to challenge contrary evidence (possibly by
cross-examining witnesses)

. . .

Reasons for the decision

. . .

All steps in the proceedings to be held in a convenient location, and
within a reasonable time

. . .

The option of waiving procedures

. . .

Reconsideration of an adverse decision, and/or an appeal,
and/or judicial review

The role of judicial review

Remember that from the complainant's point of view, judicial review forms part
of the whole process. *Alconbury* (see p 87) shows the role of judicial review in fair
administrative procedures: that role is *not* to do what the administrative processes
were meant to do, but only to provide judicial control that is sufficient to ensure
an independent and impartial determination of the legality of the administrative
decision and procedures [49].

Procedural schemes adopted by legislation or by internal guidelines in government
departments can be unspecific and leave the details to the persons responsible for
giving a hearing (a judicial decision like *Ridge* or *Cooper* does that, too). But some
such schemes regulate all the details on the menu.[13] In sections [4.7]–[4.10], we will
see how the courts have addressed the problem of procedural justice and the problem of comity in dealing with selected items from the menu: notice and disclosure
(section 4.7), oral hearings (including the availability of cross-examination, and the
openness of hearings) (section 4.8), waiver (section 4.9), reconsideration and appeals
(section 4.10).

---

[13]   For an example of an elaborate scheme, see the Parole Board rules, 2004: http://www.
paroleboard.gov.uk/policy_and_guidance/parole_board_rules/.

4.7 Notice and disclosure

> Since the person affected usually cannot make worthwhile representations without knowing what factors may weigh against his interests fairness will very often require that he is informed of the gist of the case which he has to answer. [14]

The requirement of informing the person affected of the 'gist of the case' is designed to serve the three purposes of a hearing:

- **the interest in good outcomes:** the person with an interest can only make a useful contribution to the process if he knows the issues *and* the information on which the public authority may proceed to act;

- **the duty of respect:** it is not enough for this purpose to tell the person affected that there will be a hearing; he needs to know what is at stake; and

- **the rule of law:** notice of issues and disclosure of information to the person affected opens up the operations of the public authority to public scrutiny.

In *B Johnson & Co v Minister of Health* [1947] 2 All ER 395 (CA) (see p 115), a Minister had a statutory duty to consider objections to a compulsory purchase proposed by a local authority, before deciding whether to confirm the plan. Lord Greene MR held that the Minister had a duty to disclose statements to the claimants (the owners of the property) that the local authority made to him *while he was considering the objections*: 'it has always been naturally said that information of that kind must be disclosed to the other party to give that other party an opportunity of controverting it, or making comments upon it' (401). It is a long-established rule that a public authority (here the Secretary of State) resolving a dispute between two parties (the claimants and the local authority) must disclose to each the information provided by the other.

But *before he received the objections*, the local authority had told the Minister that the claimants were 'speculative builders', implying that the claimants would make ill-founded objections to the plan. Lord Greene MR held that the law did not require the Minister to disclose information 'which he has obtained as a purely administrative person' (401). *Doody's* case, a landmark of due process, shows how the law on disclosure has changed since Lord Greene's day. Lord Mustill said, 'I find in the more recent cases on judicial review a perceptible trend towards an insistence on greater openness, or if one prefers the contemporary jargon "transparency", in the making of administrative decisions' (561).[15] Doody was a life prisoner for whom the Home Secretary was setting a tariff—a period of time which must be spent in prison for punitive purposes, before the prisoner can be considered for parole. The issue in *Doody* was disclosure of the judge's recommendation. The Home Secretary was still

---

[14]   *R v Home Secretary ex p Doody* [1994] 1 AC 531, 560 (Lord Mustill).

[15]   See section 1.6.1 on the Freedom of Information Act 2000, and on other aspects of the trend toward open government.

clinging to a lack of transparency in 1994, when *Doody* was decided; and here we can see a hangover of the distinction between administrative and judicial decisions. For transparency had long been the rule in decisions that the courts considered to be judicial; disclosure is tightly connected to the commitment to judgment in open court, which goes back to the common law's roots in the twelfth century.

> *It seems to be fundamental to any judicial inquiry that a person…must have the right to see all the information put before the judge, to comment on it, to challenge it and if needs be to combat it, and to try to establish by contrary evidence that it is wrong. It cannot be withheld from him in whole or in part.* [16]

When *Re K* reached the House of Lords, Lord Devlin agreed that 'the ordinary principles of a judicial inquiry' include the rule 'that judgment shall be given only upon evidence that is made known to all parties' (*Re K (Infants)* [1965] AC 201, 238). That rule has moved into administrative law for judicial, quasi-judicial, and administrative decisions, with a proviso and an exception.

General rule: if a party has a right to a hearing, the decision must be based on information that has been disclosed to that party.

Proviso: an interested person cannot expect disclosure that is not necessary for the purposes of his participation in the process.

Exception: the law may forbid disclosure of information which *does* affect the complainant's participation in the process. But by the principle of legality, that can only happen when statute or valid secondary legislation authorizes it. For a serious crisis over this exception to the requirement of disclosure in administrative law, see below on the withholding of sensitive information before the Parole Board (section 4.12).

Since participation is the point of disclosure, the disclosure has to come in time for the party to be able to use it in the administrative process (*R v Criminal Injuries Compensation Authority, ex p Leatherland, Bramall and Kay* [2001] ACD 13 (Turner J)). And participation as the point of disclosure also explains the 'gist of the case' rule, and also one further restriction on the disclosure that can be expected: the decision maker does not have to disclose *what he or she is thinking*, before making a decision. Lord Diplock pointed out that 'Even in judicial proceedings in a court of law, once a fair hearing has been given to the rival cases presented by the parties the rules of natural justice do not require the decision maker to disclose what he is minded to decide so that the parties may have a further opportunity of criticizing his mental processes before he reaches a final decision. If this were a rule of natural justice only the most talkative of judges would satisfy it and trial by jury would have to be abolished' (*Hoffman-La Roche v Trade and Industry Secretary* [1975] AC 295, 369).

---

[16]   *Re K (Infants)* [1963] Ch 381 (CA), 405–6 (Upjohn LJ).

> **The crucial connection between disclosure before a decision, and reasons for decision**
> Reasons for a decision at one stage in a complex process act as disclosure, to inform a complainant of the issues that need to be addressed at the next stage in the process. See p 185.

4.8 Oral hearings

4.8.1 Oral hearings are exceptional

Even when a hearing is due, there is no general requirement that the decision maker meet the complainant face to face. That is, an *oral* hearing is not generally required. 'Natural justice does not generally demand orality' (R *(Morgan Grenfell & Co Ltd) v Special Commissioner of Income Tax* [2001] EWCA Civ 329 [47] (Blackburne J)). In that case, a tax inspector asked a Special Commissioner (i.e., a tax tribunal) for permission to require disclosure of documents from a taxpayer; the taxpayer sought judicial review of the Special Commissioner's refusal to give him an oral hearing on the question of whether to order disclosure. The Court of Appeal held that an oral hearing would be 'worth little without knowledge of the case that has to be met' [50]. And the taxpayer had no right to know the reasons why the tax inspector was asking for permission. So giving an oral hearing would be useless if the taxpayer learned nothing. And it might be worse than useless: it would be 'destructive of the whole purpose of the procedure', if it led to disclosure of the reasons for the inspector's request. So **because of the process danger** that an oral hearing would involve, the Court of Appeal held that the Special Commissioner must not give an oral hearing.

But an oral hearing is not guaranteed even when there is no such process danger, and the consequences of the decision are serious. It depends on whether an oral hearing would make a difference on the issues at stake. In the classic case of *Lloyd v McMahon* [1987] 1 AC 625, the House of Lords held that an oral hearing was unnecessary for a decision by an auditor that 49 councillors should reimburse Liverpool Council for a loss of more than £100,000 caused by their misconduct in delaying setting a rate (they were trying to pressurize central government into increasing the Council's funding). The case is a reminder that procedural rights do not simply depend on the impact of a decision on the claimant. They depend, instead, on the nature of the public authority making the decision, the decision, and the statutory framework in which it was made. And as a result, they depend on whether the claimant has something to say on the issues. The auditor found misconduct and bad faith, and those findings will often cry out for an oral hearing (*In re Smith and Fawcett Ltd* [1942] Ch 304, 308 (Lord Greene MR)). Yet none was called for in *Lloyd's* case, because an oral hearing would have made no difference to the facts on which the auditor properly based his decision, after considering the councillors' written response.

Even when a Parole Board decides to revoke parole and return a prisoner to jail, the common law duty of fairness may not require an oral hearing. But it often will do so, as in R (Smith and West) v Parole Board [2005] UKHL 1. Smith and West had got into trouble while on parole; the facts were messy and obscure (West had been breaking his parole rules by visiting his former partner and not staying at the required address, and Smith had been using illegal drugs), and both prisoners wanted to do a lot of explaining. The House of Lords held that they should have been given an oral hearing, and that the duty to do so was wider than the Parole Board had thought, even though it depended on the circumstances.

> Even if important facts are not in dispute, they may be open to explanation or mitigation, or may lose some of their significance in the light of other new facts. While the board's task certainly is to assess risk, it may well be greatly assisted in discharging it (one way or the other) by exposure to the prisoner or the questioning of those who have dealt with him. It may often be very difficult to address effective representations without knowing the points which are troubling the decision-maker. The prisoner should have the benefit of a procedure which fairly reflects, on the facts of his particular case, the importance of what is at stake for him, as for society. (Lord Bingham [35])

Like the common law duty of fairness, the ECHR Art 6 does not generally demand an oral hearing for administrative decisions, either. Its title in the Convention is 'Right to a fair trial', but it gives a right to a trial only for certain sorts of determinations of civil rights and obligations. And though it gives a right to a trial on a criminal charge, it allows some decisions determining length of custody to be made without an oral hearing. For example, in R v Home Secretary, ex p Dudson [2005] UKHL 52, the House of Lords dealt with the procedure adopted by the government following a decision of the European Court of Human Rights that the tariff for young offenders convicted of murder had to be determined by an independent decision maker (V v United Kingdom (2000) 30 EHRR 121; see p 70). The Home Secretary asked the Lord Chief Justice to review Dudson's tariff. Under the Home Secretary's scheme, the Lord Chief Justice decided the matter on written representations, and recommended a reduction from 18 years to 16. Dudson claimed that the Lord Chief Justice's decision had been unlawful because Art 6(1) of the Convention gave him a right to an oral hearing. The House of Lords held that his original trial satisfied the right to a fair and public hearing on a criminal charge; after that, he had to be dealt with fairly, but:

> ...the application of [Article 6(1)] to proceedings other than at first instance depends on the special features of the proceedings in question. Account must be taken...of the role of the person or persons conducting the proceedings that are in question, the nature of the system within which they are being conducted and the scope of the powers that are being exercised. The overriding question...is whether the issues that had to be dealt with at the stage could properly, as a matter of fair trial, be determined without hearing the applicant orally. (Lord Hope [34])

That requirement of fairness depended on whether any information the applicant could have provided at an oral hearing would have added anything. The decision was a firm endorsement of the **principle of relativity**, even in the application of a Convention right. In fact, the requirements of Art 6 even depend, in one respect, on **process cost**: the House of Lords held that because the Lord Chief Justice had an obligation under Art 6(1) to carry out the exercise within a reasonable time, he did not have to give hearings that would be bound to delay the review of tariffs unreasonably for no good purpose.

Oral hearings for people seeking permission to visit their family in the UK?

In 2005, the Government announced in its five-year strategy for asylum and immigration, 'We will retain appeals for family visits because we recognise the importance of family life. But we will remove the possibility of an oral hearing and deal with all appeals on papers only; and we will limit the right of appeal to cases where the proposed visit is to a close family member. This will discourage speculative appeals.'[17] It will discourage well-founded appeals, too. The Government runs the risk of denying justice if it is not prepared to give hearings that encourage speculative appeals. If there is a justification for the policy, it is that an oral hearing is generally superfluous (and therefore, not required by due process) in the case of an adverse decision when a foreign national is refused permission to visit a UK resident in the UK.

Oral hearings are:

Generally required for:

- deprivations of legal rights or legally protected interests, and in particular:
  - any serious disciplinary or other penalty;[18] and
  - dismissal from a public office 'where there must be something against a man to warrant his dismissal' (*Ridge v Baldwin* [1964] AC 40, 65 (Lord Reid)) and, therefore, a hearing is not required in dismissing a minister from office.

Routine for:

- parole revocation for life sentence prisoners (R (*Smith and West*) v Parole Board [2005] UKHL 1 [27]).

Only required if fairness demands it for:

- refusals of release on parole;
- objections to a grant of planning permission (R (*Adlard*) v Environment Secretary [2002] EWCA Civ 735);

---

17   'Controlling our borders', February 2005, Cm 6472 [34].

18   But *Lloyd v McMahon* [1987] 1 AC 625 is an exception.

- review of tariff for young offenders (R (Dudson) v Home Secretary [2005] UKHL 52);
- applications for licences (R v Gaming Board, ex p Benaim and Khaida [1970] 2 QB 417, 430); and
- decisions of the Law Society arising out of complaints by former clients (R (Thompson) v Law Society [2004] EWCA Civ 167).

The judges have a fondness for oral argument, and they are aware of the difference it can make to the decision maker.[19] But the common view is that oral hearings are not 'the very pith of the administration of natural justice' (R v Local Government Board, ex p Arlidge [1914] 1 KB 160, 192–3, endorsed by Woolf LJ in Lloyd v McMahon [1987] 1 AC 625, 670). They are required when the issues can only be dealt with justly and effectively if the decision maker sees the parties face to face.

Public authorities generally have discretion to give an oral hearing in the operation of statutory schemes; this is one instance of the principle of legality (see p 19). A public authority will be treated as having a discretion to give an oral hearing even if the statute does not confer the power to do so, and the public authority will have a duty to do so where it would be unfair to proceed without one. We can see the principle tested almost to its limit in R (Hammond) v Home Secretary [2005] UKHL 69. The Criminal Justice Act 2003 provided that a life prisoner's tariff 'is to be determined by a single judge of the High Court without an oral hearing' (see [5]). The House of Lords held that this rule was subject to the judge's discretionary power to give an oral hearing if fairness required it. This remarkable decision was only possible because of the Human Rights Act 1988 s 3, and the issue was not argued because the Home Secretary accepted the idea. But the fact is that the House of Lords accepted that it was 'possible' to interpret a statute prohibiting oral hearings as allowing an oral hearing where fairness requires it (see p 79).

Addressing the principles behind the variability of procedural fairness in R (Thompson) v Law Society [2004] EWCA Civ 167, Clarke LJ said:

> An oral hearing should be ordered where there is a disputed issue of fact which is central to the Board's assessment and which cannot fairly be resolved without hearing oral evidence. [46]

That simply frames the problem of when an oral hearing is required, since it still uses the term 'fairly'. But it frames it in the right way: the question is not whether the decision affects the claimant, but whether the participation of the claimant (in this case, through an oral hearing) is needed for the resolution of an issue. The conclusion was that the Law Society, in deciding complaints against a solicitor of inadequate professional services and ordering compensation to a client, could proceed without giving the solicitor an oral hearing unless it was necessary. The Court of Appeal has pointed out that the court can even conduct the necessary oral hearing itself, in

[19] Compare the importance that oral hearings have in tribunal proceedings: section 12.4.5.

exceptional circumstances (R (Wilkinson) v Broadmoor Special Hospital [2001] EWCA Civ 1545).

> **Flexibility generates judicial review**
>
> Flexibility in processes enables administrators to give *due* process; it also leads to litigation. In *Thompson*, Clarke LJ held that some processes involving no oral hearing are compatible with Art 6(1) only because the court has an open-ended jurisdiction in judicial review to quash the decision and require an oral hearing to be held where fairness requires it 'in any particular case' [67]–[69]. So in *every* case where a person is disadvantaged by an administrative decision taken without an oral hearing, it is worth considering seeking judicial review on the ground that particular circumstances required one. But the cases refusing to order oral hearings (such as *Thompson*) make it clear that it would take something extraordinary to require an oral hearing before decision makers that do not generally have to give an oral hearing.

4.8.2 Opportunity to cross-examine

Complainants who are dissatisfied with a decision of a public authority will often claim (sometimes rightly) that the process was unfair because the information before the decision maker ought to have been tested through the same sort of demanding, adversarial procedures as in the courts. Cross-examination is the best example of such a procedure, and it is not easy to get a court to order it.

There is no general right to cross-examine witnesses who give evidence before a public authority (Bushell v Environment Secretary [1981] AC 75 (HL)). The government's duty to investigate deaths under the ECHR has not changed that principle: in R (D) v Home Secretary [2006] EWCA Civ 143, the Court of Appeal overturned a High Court decision that there was a right to cross-examine in a public inquiry concerning an attempted suicide in prison. There is no general right to cross-examination in the relevant legislation (Inquiries Act 2005), and the Court of Appeal held that it should be up to the chair of an inquiry. That principle concerning inquiries has a more general application: cross-examination is not a general requirement of a fair hearing, but a public authority conducting an oral hearing will generally have discretion to allow cross-examination, and must do so if it is necessary for the purposes that require the hearing.

4.8.3 Open hearings

Among the fundamental rules of judicial decision making, Lord Devlin included the rule 'that all justice shall be done openly' Re K (Infants) [1965] AC 201, 237. It is one respect in which open government is a very old principle (see p 31). There are many exceptions, even in the High Court (e.g., in family law proceedings involving children). But we can take it as a general rule that any oral hearing by an administrative authority is to be held in public unless there is reason to do otherwise.

The same imperative was written into the requirement of a 'fair and *public* hearing' in the ECHR Art 6. That requirement seems to be presented as a necessity for any determination of civil rights. But as with the rest of the seemingly categorical requirements of Art 6, the Strasbourg Court and the English courts have found a way to recognize the principle of relativity, and to dilute this apparent essential into a default requirement that can be overridden. For example, public inquiries are *on behalf* of the public, but they need not be *held* in public, even after the Human Rights Act (R (*Persey*) v *Environment Secretary* [2002] EWHC 371).

4.9 Waiver

If you have a right to a hearing, and the public authority offers to hear you, and you decline, then you cannot get judicial review on the ground that you weren't given a hearing. A process is not due to the claimant, if the claimant waives it. So in claims for judicial review on the ground that the claimant was not given a hearing, public authorities often argue that the claimant waived a hearing; they seldom succeed.

In *Smith and West*, Lord Slynn said, 'On any view the applicant should be told that an oral hearing may be possible though it is not automatic; if having been told this the applicant clearly says he does not want an oral hearing then there need not be such a hearing unless the board itself feels exceptionally that fairness requires one' [50]. So it is possible to waive an oral hearing in revoking parole (a context in which the decision maker ought to be 'predisposed in favour of an oral hearing' [50]). An informed and express waiver will evidently be effective unless there are exceptional reasons. The principles are tolerably clear: you can waive a hearing in an administrative process, but:

- you will not ordinarily be taken to have waived a hearing just because you did not insist on having one;

- an ill-informed waiver will not count as a genuine waiver; and

- there may be exceptional circumstances in which a process is improper because a procedure ought to have been taken even though it *was* waived.

Showing respect for the claimant means taking his or her word at face value in deciding what procedures to take. In fact, to give no effect to a well-informed waiver is to treat the claimant as incapable of making a responsible decision.

Even without a waiver, there can be circumstances in which a claimant cannot complain of the lack of a procedure that he did not ask for. In *Thompson*, the Court of Appeal held that a solicitor who did not ask for an oral hearing could not ordinarily complain that none was given [46]. The difference from the parole situation is important: if the person in question had the necessary resources and understanding of the situation, it can be fair to expect him to ask for a hearing if he wants one.

> ### Compare, also, the criminal process
> You cannot waive a trial on a serious criminal charge, but you can plead guilty, and if you plead not guilty you need offer no evidence. You cannot appeal from a conviction merely on the ground that you did not have a fair hearing because you pleaded guilty. These features of the process give the defendant a measure of control over his situation that is compatible with the administration of justice.
>
> ### Compare waiver of a complaint that a decision may have been biased
> (see p 162): waiver is impossible if the integrity of the process is put in doubt.

4.10 Reconsideration and appeals

Here is one fundamental difference between administrative process and judicial process: administrative decision makers have no general doctrine of *res judicata* (the rule that a judicial decision cannot be challenged or reopened, except in an appeal or a lawful challenge to the court's jurisdiction). The High Court ordinarily has no jurisdiction to reconsider its decisions. But administrative decision makers do have that power:

> Fairness will very often require that a person who may be adversely affected by the decision will have an opportunity to make representations on his own behalf either before the decision is taken with a view to producing a favourable result; or after it is taken, with a view to procuring its modification; or both. [20]

A decision in your favour may give you a legitimate expectation (see p 278) that the public authority's stance will *not* be modified. But if the decision is adverse, you may be able to ask for reconsideration (if no one else has a legitimate expectation, and there is no public interest that makes it fair to refuse the request). And very commonly, legislation will also give you a right to appeal a decision to another decision maker (typically to a tribunal, sometimes to the High Court).

Reconsideration and administrative appeals must be conducted with due process, and the complainant will ordinarily need to make use of any such process before seeking judicial review. It may seem that an administrative appeal would make judicial review on due process grounds unnecessary—and it *ought* to do so, because judicial review is not available if it is superfluous. But in fact, the availability of an administrative appeal often does not block judicial review on due process grounds, because (1) any irregularity in the appeal will itself be ground for judicial review, and (2) a process failure in the initial decision will not necessarily be cured by an appeal.

---

[20]   *R v Home Secretary, ex p Doody* [1994] 1 AC 531, 560 (Lord Mustill).

Remember that in *Ridge*, the police chief had actually benefited *both* from recon-sideration by the police authority, and an appeal to the Home Secretary. When Ridge brought his action for a declaration of illegality, the police authority argued that each of these procedures cured the defect in the initial decision to sack Ridge without a hearing. Lord Reid held that a proper reconsideration would have solved the defect:

> ❛I do not doubt that if an officer or body realises that it has acted hastily and reconsiders the whole matter afresh, after affording to the person affected a proper opportunity to present his case, then its later decision will be valid. ❜ [21]

But the police authority's reconsideration was 'very inadequate' (79), because there was no disclosure of the case against Ridge. As for the appeal to the Home Secretary, the Law Lords' explanation of its role is complicated by their conclusion that the ini-tial decision was a nullity (see p 384 on the effect of nullity). That approach obscures the real problem with the appeal to the Home Secretary, which is suggested in Lord Reid's speech: the Home Secretary merely decided that there was 'sufficient material on which the watch committee could properly exercise their power of dismissal' (81). Because the appeal did not give Ridge the opportunity to contest that material, it did not correct the process failure in the initial decision. Ridge would have had no case if he had been given either a genuine rehearing with proper disclosure from the police, or a decision from the Home Secretary remitting the matter to a differently consti-tuted committee of the authority for a proper hearing. Ordinarily, an administrative appeal can only cure a procedural defect in the original hearing if the appeal itself amounts to a whole new hearing with fair procedure, or results in the matter being sent back to the initial decision maker to be dealt with fairly.

> **A duty to inquire**
> In *Rahman v Home Secretary* [2005] EWCA Civ 1826, Laws LJ said, 'the adjudicator and the AIT owed at least some duty of enquiry to consider what was the true issue … and to establish the relevant facts' [13]. If it is not possible in an adminis-trative appeal to find those facts, the appeal authority must remit (i.e. send back) the matter for decision after a new hearing that will identify the relevant facts.

4.11 Discretion in process

Do public authorities have discretion in deciding what procedures to follow (see p 230 on what discretion is)? The court can impose procedural requirements without interfering with the substance of the considerations for which an authority is respon-sible. So the court requires public authorities to give the *right* procedures. It may seem that there is no room for discretion.

---

[21]   *Ridge v Baldwin* [1964] AC 40, 79.

But in fact there can be a great deal of discretion in deciding on procedures, because there may be different ways of proceeding that are fair and are compatible with legislation. As Lord Mustill said in *Doody*, 'it is not enough...to persuade the court that some procedure other than the one adopted by the decision-maker would be better or more fair. Rather, they must show that the procedure is actually unfair. The court must constantly bear in mind that it is to the decision maker, not the court, that Parliament has entrusted not only the making of the decision but also the choice as to how the decision is made' (560–1). In addition, the House of Lords has identified an 'implied power of an administrative body to *enhance the fairness* available to a person who otherwise would be adversely affected by the lack of that power' (R *(Roberts) v Parole Board* [2005] UKHL 45 [65] (Lord Woolf)). That power implicitly gives public authorities in general a discretionary power to invent procedures that are required neither by legislation nor by the common law. But as the *Roberts* case itself shows, those inventions may be extremely controversial, and will be subject to judicial supervision, and will be ruled unlawful if the judges decide that they are unfair. So, as Lord Woolf had put it in an earlier decision, even if a public authority 'is master of its own procedure and has considerable discretion as to what procedure it wishes to adopt, it must still be fair. Whether a decision reached in the exercise of its discretion is fair or not is ultimately one which will be determined by the courts' (R *v Lord Saville of Newdigate, ex p A* [2000] 1 WLR 1855 [38]).[22]

In summary, since proportionality is the organizing principle of due process, the judges' role in controlling procedural decisions is the same as their role in controlling those decisions of substance for which proportionality is the standard of judicial control (see p 273). Even though it can be a very intrusive form of review, it still leaves considerable free choice to the public authority.

4.12 Process danger: special advocates

In the borderlands between administrative justice and criminal justice lie the problems of detention of people with a mental illness who have committed violent crimes, detention of asylum seekers, detention of terrorism suspects, and detention of life prisoners who have completed their tariff.

Harry Roberts was involved in the bloody murder of three policemen in London in 1966—a year after Parliament suspended the death penalty. He shot two of the officers. He was given an especially long tariff of 30 years; in periodic reviews since the tariff had expired in 1996, the Parole Board had to decide whether his detention 'is no

---

[22]   Inquiries, as in the *Lord Saville* case, have extra latitude in deciding how to proceed: *Bushell v Environment Secretary* [1981] AC 75 (HL) ('wide discretion as to the procedure' (96) in a local inquiry under Highways Act 1959 with no statutory rules of procedure); R *(Persey) v Environment Secretary* [2002] EWHC 371 (discretion whether to receive evidence in private in a public inquiry into the outbreak of foot and mouth disease); R *v SS Transport, ex p Gwent CC* [1988] 1 QB 429 (433) (Lord Woolf; 'wide discretion' over what issues to investigate in a local inquiry).

longer necessary for the protection of the public',[23] in which case he must be released. In a deeply divided decision in *Roberts*, the House of Lords approved a **special advocate** scheme that the Parole Board had invented for itself. The Home Secretary gave the Board information that the Board withheld from Roberts, in order to protect the sources [3]. But the Board appointed a lawyer to make representations on Roberts' behalf, and disclosed the information to the lawyer. Roberts sought judicial review of the decision to appoint a lawyer for him, whom he wasn't allowed to talk to.

The House of Lords held by a majority that the invention of the scheme was within the powers of the Board to take steps incidental to its decisions. The majority approval of the special advocate scheme depended on a crucial condition: the ability of the Board to withhold relevant information from prisoners. Rules made by the Home Secretary under the Criminal Justice Act 1991 s 32(5) provided that the Board could do so on the ground of 'national security, prevention of disorder or crime or the health and welfare of the prisoner or others' [22]. The majority reckoned that if the Board could lawfully withhold evidence, then giving the prisoner a special advocate is better than nothing. So Lord Woolf said that the scheme 'can only enhance the rights of a life sentence prisoner' [67]. He saw the power to arrange special advocates as an instance of a public authority's implied discretion to 'enhance the fairness' of its process [65].

So why was there a vehement dissent by Lord Bingham and Lord Steyn? Lord Bingham appealed to the **principle of legality**: access to an adversarial hearing had a value to the prisoner which the law protects. So in their general power to make and apply procedural rules, the Home Secretary and the Board should not be able to detract from that value, unless the statute expressly authorized it (and by contrast, Parliament *has* authorized special advocate schemes in other fields).

Lord Steyn called the Parole Board's proceedings a 'phantom hearing' [88], and an 'evisceration of the right to a fair hearing' [89]. He too relied on the principle of legality [93], and said that the majority decision was 'contrary to the rule of law' [97]. He even called Roberts' situation 'Kafkaesque'.

The Kafka Test for due process: What Josef K didn't know

Franz Kafka's 1925 novel, *The Trial*, portrays the terror and helplessness of a defendant who is arrested and not told the case against him. In fact, Josef K doesn't know:

- what the charges are;
- who is pressing the charges;
- which court is hearing the charges;
- where the court is;
- when he is supposed to appear; or
- what decisions, if any, are made during the proceeding.

---

[23]   By the combined effect of the Crime (Sentences) Act 1997 s 28(6), and the decision of the House of Lords in R v *Lichniak* [2002] UKHL 47 [8], [29].

Josef has a lawyer, but the lawyer talks nonsense. When Josef actually finds the court after wandering through a confusing block of flats, there are many officials doing nothing in particular, and every session ends inconclusively. *The Trial* is a nightmare in the form of a novel. Look away from the footnote if you don't want to know the ending.[24]

In *Roberts'* case, Lord Rodger said that the problem the House of Lords faced in *Roberts* is trivialized by 'inapposite references to Kafka' [110].

The emotional argument reflects the suspect role of special advocates. The word 'special' should make the hairs stand up on the back of a lawyer's neck: it means a departure from the basic responsibility to the client, which gives a certain integrity to the lawyer's job. And the link isn't only important to the advocate. Without it, the person 'represented' does not have the slightest reason to have confidence in his advocate. Any appointment of a special advocate represents a disruption in the ethical basis of the profession, and a departure from its history.

Our 21st-century legacy: special advocate schemes

There were no special advocates until 1997.[25] Now just look at the variety of schemes in which they may be used:

- **Special Immigration Appeals Commission:** for decisions to remove foreigners from Britain on national security grounds when some of the evidence is top secret (Special Immigration Appeals Commission Act 1997 s 6, and SIAC (Procedure) Rules 2003 SI 2003/1034, r 35–6).[26] A special advocate 'shall not be responsible to the person whose interests he is appointed to represent' (SIAC Act 1997 s 6(4)). The advocate can see evidence that is withheld from the appellant, and can cross-examine secret witnesses, but cannot communicate with the appellant without permission from SIAC after seeing secret material.
- **Proscribed Organisations Appeal Commission:** set up to hear appeals from bodies outlawed as terrorist organizations (The Proscribed Organisation Appeal Commission [Procedure] Rules 2001 SI 2001/443 rule 10).
- **Racial discrimination claims:** Special advocates can be appointed on national security grounds to 'represent the interests' of a claimant in proceedings under the Race Relations Act 1976 (Race Relations Amendment Act 2000 s 8).

---

[24] The officials stab him to death without telling him why. It could have been worse: among Kafka's other protagonists, one commits suicide on the say-so of his father, one is transformed into a hideous insect and dies slowly, and one is mutilated by his own torture machine.

[25] See *Roberts* [28], where Lord Bingham catalogues the schemes listed here.

[26] SIAC's role was extended in the Anti-Terrorism, Crime and Security Act 2001 to consider appeals by foreigners indefinitely imprisoned without charge because they are suspected of involvement in terrorism; that regime was declared incompatible with the Convention in *A v Home Secretary* [2004] UKHL 56—see p 6. The Government's scheme was embarrassed by two high-profile resignations of special advocates in 2004 and 2005: http://www.guardian.co.uk/guardianpolitics/story/0,,1392057,00.html.

- **Pathogens Access Appeal Commission:** the Attorney General may appoint 'a person to represent the interests of any person who will be prevented from hearing or inspecting any evidence' on grounds of national security (Pathogens Access Appeal Commission (Procedure) Rules 2002 SI 2002/1845; Anti-Terrorism, Crime and Security Act 2001, Sch 6).
- **Local planning inquiries:** If the Secretary of State decides a local planning inquiry is to be held in secret on national security grounds the Attorney General may appoint a special advocate to represent the interests of any person prevented from being there (Planning and Compulsory Purchase Act 2004 s 80).
- **The making of Control Orders** under the Prevention of Terrorism Act 2005 may involve special advocates (The Civil Procedure (Amendment No 2) Rules 2005 SI 2005/656).[27]
- And now, **Parole Board hearings:** where the Board can lawfully withhold evidence from the prisoner, it may appoint a special advocate to make representations on behalf of the prisoner (*Roberts*).

The courts have appointed special advocates

- in an appeal against a decision of the Special Immigration Appeals Commission: *Home Secretary v Rehman* [2003] 1 AC 153 [31]–[32]. It is only to be done 'in the most extreme circumstances. However, considerations of national security can create situations where this is necessary. If this happens, the court should use its inherent power to reduce the risk of prejudice to the absent party so far as possible.' (Lord Woolf [31]);
- when examining 'very sensitive material' on an application for judicial review by a member or former member of a security service in *R v Shayler* [2003] 1 AC 247 (HL) [34], the House of Lords was prepared to allow the procedure where necessary; and
- for deciding whether the public interest requires information to be withheld from the defence in a criminal prosecution in *R v H* [2004] UKHL 3, if 'no other course will adequately meet the overriding requirement of fairness to the defendant' [22].

There are two possible interpretations of the dissent in *Roberts*, and perhaps Lord Steyn and Lord Bingham had both in mind. One is that they thought that the Home Secretary's rule allowing the Board to withhold evidence from the prisoner was unlawful.[28] The other is that they considered a special advocate arrangement in itself

---

[27] Introducing a new Part 76 to the Civil Procedure Rules (Proceedings under Prevention of Terrorism Act 2005). Rules 76.23–76.25 cover the appointment of special advocates.

[28] In fact, Lord Bingham implies it, though he does not say it: 'There is ... nothing in either Act which expressly authorises the Board to make a decision adverse to a prisoner without disclosure to the prisoner of the case against him ...' [24] Note that the majority did not hold that it was lawful to withhold the information in Roberts' case—the issue was not before the court. But the majority did hold that the Home Secretary could authorize the withholding of information.

to be contrary to a fundamental legal value, so that it would take express statutory authorization (of the kind that Parliament has given in asylum and anti-terrorism cases).

There is a **process danger**—not mentioned in the speeches—that may lie behind the dissent: a special advocate scheme risks making non-disclosure manageable, and therefore normal. It will be easier for the Board to persuade itself to withhold information from a prisoner, if it has a scheme to help out the prisoner when it does so. But it should always be a crisis, when a decision maker acts on secret information that is adverse to a party who has a right to a hearing. Withholding the information clashes with the reasons for process rights—the interest in good outcomes, the duty of respect, and the rule of law.

The case for the majority decision in *Roberts* lies in the arguments that the public authorities tried to make in *Cooper* and *Ridge*: that the responsibility of a public authority to serve the public interest can make it appropriate to limit procedural protections that involve a process danger. In the special advocates schemes, there is:

(1) A process danger which **motivates** the scheme (if an open hearing was conducted, the public interest might be harmed by the publication of sensitive information), and

(2) A process danger which **results from** the scheme (appointing a special advocate risks sacrificing the benefits of due process, i.e. good decisions, respect, and the rule of law).

Roberts was controversial because it concerned an administrative decision about detention. Like the Parole Board, the criminal process tries to protect witnesses— and it is a struggle, because English criminal law has never accepted that anyone can be convicted of a crime or sentenced on information that is kept secret to protect the informant. But Harry Roberts had been convicted in an open trial, and was sentenced to life in prison. Roberts' situation is *different* from the situation of Josef K in Kafka's novel, because Roberts knows exactly why he was sent to prison, *and* that he was sent to prison for life, subject to a non-judicial process for considering early release, *and* that the protection of the public is the only issue in the parole decision. So if there is a justification for the majority decision, it is that in administering that life sentence, it is fair to act on secret information, in the interest of protecting informants.

The Law Lords in *Roberts* were at least united by an attitude: that the question they faced was the question of fairness to Harry Roberts. The issue in his case was not *whether* the Parole Board should act fairly toward him, but what fairness required (whether it is fair to keep him in prison on secret information and, also, whether a special advocate scheme endangers the administration of justice by normalizing that sort of secrecy).

That approach is an advance in English law, which has come about while Harry Roberts has been in prison: compare the attitude of a great judge 30 years ago, in *R v Home Secretary, ex p Hosenball* [1977] 1 WLR 766. The Home Secretary ordered

Hosenball deported on national security grounds, after a hearing before a panel that heard evidence that was kept secret from Hosenball. Lord Denning MR said: 'When the public interest requires that information be kept confidential, it may outweigh even the public interest in the administration of justice' (782). It was a fundamental mistake for a court to put any value at all above the administration of justice. If it is o.k. to withhold information about his parole from Harry Roberts, that is not because the public interest outweighs the importance of dealing justly with him. It is because there is no injustice for Roberts to complain of.[29]

This change in outlook is not just a change in a manner of speaking, because it demands that the judges pay attention to what is good for Roberts (and reconcile it with the other interests at stake). Lord Denning's approach would license the judges to disregard his interests. That would mean being prepared, in principle, and within a limited sphere, to abuse him.

Obviously, the change in outlook did not resolve the problem in *Roberts*. At least it means that the deep division in the House of Lords was a division over the right issue. Lord Denning should not have talked as if justice needn't be done for people like Hosenball—or Harry Roberts.

4.13 Conclusion

The justice of the common law has often misfired; when it works, it imposes due process on the administration even where Parliament (and the administration itself) failed to do so. Imposing due process on the administration is the best thing that judges can do for it. The **dangers** of process are not serious dangers, if process is kept in proportion. The **costs** of administrative processes are massive, but they are, generally, a bargain for the public. And in any case, justice often demands them: **process failure** is an invitation to arbitrary government. So process cost has a very strictly limited relevance to the question of what procedures a court should impose: 'The most that can be said is that the more burdensome and far-reaching the consequences, the more carefully must be scrutinised the rule that is said to produce them. . . . The concepts of natural justice and the duty to be fair must not be allowed to discredit themselves by making unreasonable requirements and imposing undue burdens' (*McInnes v Onslow-Fane* [1978] 1 WLR 1520, 1533–1535). So undue process is a costly mistake; due process is necessary, regardless of the cost.

The **core rationale** (see p 65) for judicial review supports the wide-ranging common-law techniques of due process. So it is not necessarily a breach of comity for courts to invent their own ways of interfering with other public authorities. It is a breach of comity for them to interfere unduly—that is, in a way that damages the public authority's capacity to do its job. The courts do not generally do that when, e.g., they require the public authority to listen to both sides, or to decide impartially, or to give its own reasons for decision. But even these basics are not required of every

---

[29]   And in Hosenball's case, the question ought to have been whether a foreigner suspected of being dangerous to the country had a right to know everything that was put to the Home Secretary's panel—not whether to abandon the administration of justice.

executive decision: when the Prime Minister is thinking of dismissing a minister, he ought to listen to people who have something to say on the issues, and it may be important for him to talk to the minister first (depending on the issues), and in any case he shouldn't be biased, and he should have good reasons. But *the law* does not require him to listen to anyone, or to tell anyone his reasons, or even to decide impartially. If procedural requirements are pointless, or if imposing them would damage the public authority's function, then comity requires the court to stay out of it.

The law has to respond to the **principle of relativity** (see p 10). But look at the consequences: if process rights depend on the type of decision and the context in which it is made, there is considerable room for litigation over the particular requirements of the case. In R *(Thompson) v Law Society* [2004] EWCA Civ 167, the Court of Appeal held that fairness may require an oral hearing for a complaint of inadequate service against a solicitor: 'What is fair depends upon the circumstances of the particular case. I can imagine circumstances in which an adjudicator or appeal panel might think it appropriate to hold an oral hearing and there may even be cases in which the court would intervene to quash a decision refusing to do so' [45]. The result is a litigation trap: any solicitor who loses without an oral hearing can think of judicial review as potential recourse. The extent of the litigation trap depends first of all on how clearly potential claimants can see from a case like *Thompson* whether judicial review is pointless or promising, and secondly on how stringent the judges are in granting permission for a claim for judicial review. Certainty would be gained by a blanket rule requiring oral hearings, or a blanket rule that they are not required. But either approach would fail to offer proportionate process. So the cost of *proportionate* process is the *disproportionate* process that is generated by the litigation trap.

The irony of process

Any obstacle to arbitrary use of power will also pose a potential obstacle to the sensible use of the power. In order to guarantee *due process*, it may be necessary to provide processes that will be *undue* in some cases. And the availability of judicial review compounds the irony.

Here is an illustration of the irony of process, from the Government's strategy for asylum and immigration:

> Some types of application raise fundamental issues. In these cases it is right that it should be possible to appeal against a decision to refuse the application. This applies to asylum applications, where the person concerned claims that they face persecution or death in their own country, and to marriage and family cases. However, applicants should not be able to abuse that right by making unmeritorious appeals to frustrate our efforts to remove them. [30]

---

[30] Controlling our borders (Five year strategy for asylum and immigration), February 2005, Cm 6472 [32].

The tragedy is that there is no fair way to decide which appeals are unmeritorious, without some form of hearing. Sometimes, the entire appeal needs to be heard before it can be seen to be unmeritorious.

Because of this problem, process is extremely important. No one ever brought a procedural challenge to a decision in their favour. And no one needs the court to hold that procedures were unfair, if they can get the court to interfere with the substance of a decision. And the result of a procedural challenge may be merely that the decision maker does the same thing again with a different process.

Yet the control of process is the most important and most successful part of administrative law: the judges and the legislature do not suffer the same disabilities that they face in questions of substance, and they can do justice by imposing due process on the administration.

For one thing, if it's too late for a new process to set things right, a procedural challenge gives the claimant a substantive outcome. So in *Cooper*, the house had been pulled down, and Cooper got damages in tort because it was too late for the court to order the public authority to make the decision again using the right process.

Also, a claimant may bring a procedural challenge in order to get the decision made by a different person or body: if a decision is quashed because the process was flawed, the new decision will generally need to be made by a differently constituted decision maker. So in *Ridge*, the decision gave the police chief a fair crack at getting his pension.

What is more, it is a wrong in itself (a breach of the **duty of respect**) for a public authority to tear down a house or sack an employee without hearing the other side of the story first. Even if you have had a hearing, if a decision goes against you, it is very easy to get the feeling (and it is sometimes true) that you have not *really* been listened to at all. And so a holding that a decision was made unfairly can give a claimant a sense of vindication. Allied to that potential for vindication is the simple, direct opportunity for accountability, which motivates many judicial review challenges: the judicial process gives people who feel they have not been listened to the remarkable opportunity to drag the public authority in front of an independent body.

Although some of its principles are as old as (and in fact, much older than) *Bentley's* case of 1748, the law on process has seen major advances since *Ridge*. It is still in flux. As Lord Mustill said in *Doody*, 'The standards of fairness are not immutable. They may change with the passage of time, both in the general and in their application to decisions of a particular type' (560).[31] Amid all this change, it is worth remembering when people have (and will presumably continue to have) *no* right to a hearing, even though an executive decision affects them very significantly. In the following cases,

---

[31] 'Standards and perceptions of fairness may change, not only from one century to another but also, sometimes, from one decade to another', according to Lord Bingham: R *v* H [2004] 2 AC 134 [11].

the affected person will ordinarily have no right to procedural participation:

- a Cabinet minister who is dismissed;

- a sailor whose ship is sent to sea;

- a farmer from Ghana who is opposed to British agricultural policy;

- a soldier, when the Army's compensation scheme is changed; and

- a celebrity who is not nominated for an honour.

So you do not have a right to any particular form of participation in a decision-making process, just because you are affected by an executive decision.

And still, the most important development in modern administrative law is the principle that administrative decisions must be made with due process.

TAKE-HOME MESSAGE • • •

- **The three main values of procedural participation are:**
  - the value of promoting good outcomes;
  - the value of respect for persons affected by a decision; and
  - the value of imposing the rule of law on public decision making.

- **Due process is proportionate process:** Whether a process is due depends on whether it promotes the three **process values**, in a way that is justifiable in light of the **process cost** and any **process danger**.

- The focal concern of the common law of due process is **fairness** to persons affected by a decision, who have something to say on the issues. Fairness requires that the public authority abide by its **duty of respect** for people affected by its decisions, and that it act on all the **relevant considerations**. But fairness is not the only concern:
  - due process also promotes the public interest in responsible decision making, in which the outcome is based on all the relevant considerations; and
  - due process includes procedures laid down by valid legislation, and may require conformity to procedures that a public authority has announced or has used.

- **The irony of process:** to guarantee due process, it may be necessary to afford more process than is due.

- There is no general reason to involve someone affected in the making a decision. British farm policies affect farmers in Ghana, and British and EU policies that oppress those farmers are unjust. But farmers in Ghana have no legal right to participation in the policy-making process.

CRITICAL QUESTIONS • • •

1   Why shouldn't it be up to the public authority to decide what process is appropriate? Why should judges decide?

2   The law of due process is in flux. Considering (1) the 'continuing momentum in administrative law towards openness of decision-making' (Lord Mustill in R v Home Secretary, ex p Doody [1994] 1 AC 531, 566), and (2) the effect of the Human Rights Act, do you think the procedures that were refused in the following decisions would be ordered by the courts today:

   • B Johnson & Co v Minister of Health [1947] 2 All ER 395

   • Nakkuda Ali v Jayaratne [1951] AC 66 (PC)

   • McInnes v Onslow Fane [1978] 1 WLR 1520

3   Can you reconcile the following two views?

   • Lord Greene's view in B Johnson & Co v Minister of Health [1947] 2 All ER 395, that a minister's duty to perform his functions honestly and fairly, 'speaking generally, is not a matter with which the courts are concerned' (400), and

   • Lord Loreburn's view in Board of Education v Rice [1911] AC 179 (HL) that listening to both sides fairly 'is a duty lying upon every one who decides anything' (182)?

Further Questions:

4   The government has considered abolishing oral hearings when a person is refused leave to enter the UK to visit a family member, and using 'paper hearings' instead. Would that be compatible with Art 6 of the Convention?

5   No one complains about lack of due process when they get the outcome they want. Sergeant Walker (see section 2.1) would not have been bothered if the military had adopted a more generous compensation scheme without consulting soldiers; Charles Ridge would not have minded if the police authority had considered the matter without listening to him, and decided not to dismiss him; Cooper would have had no complaint if the Board of Works had decided not to tear down his

house, after considering it without talking to him. Does that mean that judicial review over mere procedures is pointless?

online
resource
centre

Visit the online resource centre to access the following resources which accompany this chapter: links to legislation and online reports of judicial decisions, summaries of key cases and legislation, updates in the law, suggestions for answering the pop quizzes and questions, and links to useful websites.

5 Impartiality and independence

There is an ancient common law rule against bias in judicial and administrative decision making, and its requirements are surprisingly close to those of the European Convention guarantee of impartiality in the determination of civil rights. But the Convention adds a requirement of independence. Impartiality and independence have an important but limited role in administration: they don't stop a public authority from the fair pursuit of its policy objectives.

LOOK FOR • • •

- The difference between bias (which is unlawful), and a lack of impartiality (which may be lawful).

- When bias will be presumed.

- The relation between independence and impartiality.

- The difference—and the connection—between substance and process.

- Bias as a lack of due process, **and** as a flaw in the substance of a decision maker's reasoning.

> ‘ Every body in the town has already pre-engaged his opinion. The burgesses have all taken sides: the justices have already declared him so heinously guilty, that he ought to be immediately disfranchised, without waiting for a trial of the indictment. I dare say they were of that opinion, without prejudice to the man, but from indignation at his guilt: and perhaps very justly; for a man may judge impartially even in his own cause. However, we must go upon general principles. ’
>
> R v Cowle (1759) 2 Burr 834, 862–3 (Lord Mansfield)

5.1 Impartiality and bias

A decision maker is impartial if he or she is not inclined to decide one way or the other, before hearing from the people who ought to be heard. Lord Mansfield thought there were no justices left in Berwick who could hear Cowle's case impartially. After a riot, the justices had charged Cowle with assault and had also, before the trial, applied for him to be deprived of his voting rights. Because the law requires criminal prosecutions to be decided impartially, Lord Mansfield decided that it would be unlawful for the Berwick justices to try Cowle, and the court of King's Bench gave *habeas corpus* to get the man's detention examined (and the criminal charges heard) outside Berwick. Lord Mansfield explained the law of bias as follows:

> ‘ If a witness in a cause has an **interest**, though it be small, he must be rejected: or if a juryman has declared his opinion by a former verdict, he may have done it very justly, but yet is liable to be challenged for this cause, on a subsequent trial. In the present case, it is impossible but that all the persons who would be concerned in trying this matter at Berwick, must be **biassed** by their **preconceived opinions**. I do not speak this, with the least imputation upon the magistrates of Berwick: but it is not fit that they should be judges in their own cause, and after having already gone so far as they have done. ’ [1]

We long ago abandoned the notion that a *witness* must be impartial, but for jurors and judges we have the same rule today as in 1759. Yet impartiality is *not* a general requirement of lawful decision making. Administrative officials ought to be partial to their policies. A **biased** decision, on the other hand, is unlawful at common law, whether it is made by a judge or an administrative official.

A bias is a bad attitude. It is a disposition to make a decision against a party's interest, regardless of how it ought to be decided.[2] As Lord Goff put it, a biased

---

[1]   R v Cowle (1759) 2 Burr 834, 862–3.

[2]   What about dispositions to decide against the *public* interest? There is no legal remedy for that, *unless* a claimant in judicial review has standing to challenge the relevance of considerations on which the public authority acts. See the discussion of R v Foreign Secretary, ex p World Development Movement [1995] 1 WLR 386, p 270.

decision maker 'unfairly regard(s)...with favour, or disfavour, the case of a party to the issue under consideration by him' (R v Gough [1993] AC 646, 670).

If the decision maker has that sort of unfair attitude, no hearing can be fair. In fact, a hearing isn't really a hearing at all, if the decision maker is going to decide against you regardless of what he hears. The 'hearing' becomes a sham. So the rule against bias is part of the law of due process (see Chapter 4).

An administrative or judicial decision will be quashed for lack of due process if a decision maker had:

(1) an **improper interest** in the outcome, or

(2) a **relation** to one party to a dispute that makes it **unfair** for the decision maker to decide between the parties, or

(3) an **improper preference** for one outcome (or, as Lord Mansfield called it 'a preconceived opinion').

It is not impossible for a person to make a fair decision in spite of their interests and relations. A mom, for example, *can* resolve a dispute between her own child and someone else's child without leaning in favour of her own child. But it is not easy, and the law does not trust judges or jurors to do it. As Lord Mansfield said, 'a man may judge impartially even in his own cause. However, we must go upon general principles.' So it would be unlawful for a mom to sit as a judge in a claim in tort brought by her child against someone else.

If a decision maker has the wrong sort of interest in the outcome, or the wrong sort of relation to a party, or the wrong sort of opinion about the facts, the law **presumes** that the decision maker was influenced by it. That is, without any proof that a judge decided against the complainant because of the unfair interest or relation, the law deals with the situation as if it were proved. An improper preference is an **actual** bias; it is a ground for the decision maker to recuse himself or herself (i.e., to withdraw from the proceeding and leave it to someone else to make the decision), and it is ground for a decision to be quashed in judicial review, if the decision maker does not do so. A decision maker should recuse (and the decision should be quashed for failure to do so), if the decision maker has **relations** or **interests** or **preconceived opinions** that create a real possibility of a bias (i.e., a real possibility of a bad attitude toward one side).

Jargon alert!
The House of Lords has used 'actual bias' differently, to mean 'a disqualifying interest of any kind' (*Davidson v Scottish Ministers* [2004] UKHL 34 [19] (Lord Bingham)). On disqualifying interests, see p 154.

A presumption of bias cannot be rebutted: that is, if a decision is challenged on the ground of a real possibility of bias, the decision cannot be rescued by proof that the decision maker was actually being perfectly fair-minded. We must go upon general principles, as Lord Mansfield said. And if there is one biased member of a decision-making body, all the members will be disqualified, at least if the proceeding reached a point at which the members discussed the issues.[3] So Lord Mansfield was not prepared to hear that some particular justice from Berwick had no preconceived opinion about Cowle.

5.1.1 Judicial bias

The judges have not hesitated to strike down decisions by their fellow judges, to protect both the integrity of their own process and the *appearance* of integrity. In the past ten years, the House of Lords has been extraordinarily willing to uphold complaints of bias or of the possibility of bias by lower court judges. And both the House of Lords[4] and the Court of Appeal[5] have invented judicial review of their own processes, when a party wants to complain of bias or the appearance of a possibility of bias in one of their decisions. In an extraordinary process to hear a complaint that a House of Lords decision was tainted by the appearance of a possibility of bias,[6] the Law Lords overturned the decision (R v Bow Street Metropolitan Stipendiary Magistrate, ex p Pinochet Ugarte (No 2) [2000] 1 AC 119). Lord Hoffmann had been the unpaid chairman of Amnesty International's fundraising organization. Amnesty International was given leave to intervene in a case over whether General Pinochet had immunity from extradition as former head of state of Chile. Amnesty, a human rights advocacy group, intervened because of their agenda to prevent (and to improve recourse against) state torture of the kind that Pinochet was accused of perpetrating. Amnesty had no material interest in the outcome of the litigation, but the Law Lords decided that it might not look right to the public, for a judge to have an institutional connection with an organization that had hired lawyers to make representations to the judges. As we will see, the House of Lords since *Pinochet* has found the appearance of a possibility of bias in very remote connections to the matter of a dispute.

5.1.2 Administrative bias

Cowle was a criminal prosecution; *Pinochet* was an extradition appeal in the House of Lords. So what do these cases have to do with administrative law? The rule against bias governs both judicial and administrative decision making. And the courts have

---

3   In re Medicaments (No 2) [2001] EWCA Civ 1217 [99].

4   R v Bow Street Metropolitan Stipendiary Magistrate, ex p Pinochet Ugarte (No 2) [2000] 1 AC 119 (HL).

5   Taylor v Lawrence [2002] EWCA Civ 90.

6   Note that judges often use the phrase 'apparent bias' as a shorthand for 'the appearance of a possibility of bias' (e.g. Davidson v Scottish Ministers [2004] UKHL 34 [1], [25], [44]).

long considered the application of the doctrine to judges as an example for administrative decision makers:

> '…it will have a most salutary influence on these tribunals when it is known that this high court of last resort, in a case in which the Lord Chancellor of England had an interest, considered that his decree was on that account a decree not according to law, and was set aside. This will be a lesson to all inferior tribunals to take care not only that in their decrees they are not influenced by their personal interest, but to avoid the appearance of labouring under such an influence.'[7]

Why is the law on bias in *administrative* decision making linked to the cases on bias in *judicial* decision making? Partly, it is because in **administrative justice** (that is, in the resolution of disputes by an independent body that is not part of the court system, such as a tribunal or an ombudsman or an auditor), the problems of bias are much the same as the problems in courts.

Tribunals and courts differ in one way: tribunals often have members who are there because of a technical expertise, or as representatives of the community (see section 12.4.3). Contrast judges, who are meant to apply the law on the basis of the evidence before the court, without acting on any technical expertise in deciding the facts, and without representing any interest except the public interest in the administration of justice. So does tribunal membership raise problems of bias? Not according to the House of Lords: Lord Hope has held that the integrity of the tribunal system 'is not compromised by the use of specialist knowledge or experience when the judge or tribunal member is examining the evidence' (*Gillies v Work and Pensions Secretary (Scotland)* [2006] UKHL 2 [23]). Basically, the rules on bias for tribunal judges are the same as the rules for jurors, and the rules for judges in the High Court or, for that matter, in the House of Lords (*R v Gough* [1993] AC 646, 670). This section and sections 5.2 and 5.3 address the decisions of bodies that are governed by the same test as judges.

And in fact, you might say that *all* administrative decision making is governed by the same rule: that decisions must be *unbiased* (where bias is a bad attitude against one side). But it is critically important that not all administrative decision makers have to be *impartial*; some public authorities not only may, but must have some sort of 'preconceived opinion' at the point when they hear from parties who have a right to a hearing. The application of the rule against bias raises *much* more interesting problems in some fields of administrative decision making, such as in the planning process, than it does in courts. There are two interrelated reasons:

The two-body problem

(1) Many public authorities, *unlike* courts and tribunals, do not hear a dispute between parties, but hear responses to their own (tentative or even concluded)

---

7 *Dimes v Proprietors of Grand Junction Canal* (1852) 3 HL Cas 759, 793–4.

decisions or policies or plans. So they are already involved in the issues, rather than serving as a neutral third party resolving a dispute between two sides.

That lack of independence does not in itself create a presumption of bias. But it generates difficult problems in deciding what sort of involvement with the issues creates a real possibility of a bad attitude against a claimant. Even for administrators who do not resolve a dispute between two parties but simply have to consider the view of a person affected by their decision before acting (such as the Board of Works in *Cooper v Board of Works* (1863) 14 CB (NS) 180; see p 108), *some* interests, relations, and preconceived opinions will be improper. But the question of which are improper will be different from the question of whether a judge in a tribunal or in the High Court is biased.

The policy problem

(2) In the two-body cases, administrators, unlike judges, *ought* to bring their policy agendas to their work.

It is all right for a person who has a policy that goes against your interests to make a decision after hearing you. But *some* dispositions are still improper. Essentially, those will be dispositions to decide against the claimant regardless of how the matter ought to be decided. In sections 5.4 and 5.5, we will see how the law must do something to control the preconceived opinions of administrators in the two-body cases, and we will see how difficult it is for the court to do so without a breach of comity (see pp 178–9). And in section 5.5, we will see the deep, important connection between the law on bias (for all decision makers), and the doctrine that discretionary decisions must be made on the basis of the relevant considerations. Like the law on the giving of reasons (see Chapter 6), the law on bias is a point of connection between legal control of decision-making processes, and legal control of the substance of decisions.

    The law of bias on the part of tribunal judges really is simply part of the law on judicial bias, and we will start with that in this chapter. Then we will come to grips with the ways in which the two-body problem and the policy problem create special difficulties for administrative decision makers who do not resolve a dispute between two parties, but simply have to give a hearing in their decision making-process.

5.1.3 The basic rule for courts and tribunals

When a court or a tribunal decides a dispute between two parties, it is unfair, and therefore unlawful, for a particular judge to participate in the decision if he or she has a hostile attitude toward one side. Of course, judges don't generally recuse themselves on the ground that they are against one of the parties. They do not generally announce in court or in their reasons that they were against one party, and decisions are not generally struck down on that basis. In an appeal or in a complaint of bias brought to a different judge of the same court, incidentally, there is simply no way to get the allegedly biased judge into a witness stand to face questioning as to what his or her views actually were. No English court has ever heard testimony from one of its judges as to what attitude he or she had toward the complainant.[8] Bias is a bad attitude, remember, and there simply are no reported cases of actual bias.

Behave yourself

Even a judge who behaves badly may decide impartially, as Lord Mansfield pointed out. Judges never quite express an opinion that a particular party ought to get it in the neck. But they have to be extremely careful about expressing attitudes of other kinds that may be prejudicial, or the Court of Appeal will throw out a decision. In *El Farargy v El Farargy* [2007] EWCA Civ 1149, the judge in a civil dispute involving an Arab Sheikh came up with a variety of digs at the Sheikh, such as, 'if he chose to depart on his flying carpet never to be seen again', '...to see that every grain of sand is sifted', '...at this I think relatively fast-free time of the year', and a joke that the Sheikh's case was 'a bit like Turkish Delight' [28]. The Court of Appeal quashed the judge's decision because the remarks could be seen 'to be mocking and disparaging...for his status as a Sheikh' [30]. The Court of Appeal will not even ask whether a party actually got a fair hearing from a judge who said regrettable stuff about him.

What are the grounds on which there is some practical chance of challenging a judge's role in a dispute? A judge is **automatically disqualified** if he or she has a substantial financial interest in the outcome of a case (*Locabail v Bayfield* [50]). There is no official list of the grounds for automatic disqualification, but aside from financial interests they certainly extend to any **relationship** that, on general principles, is incompatible with the neutrality of a judge (such as being the mom of a defendant or claimant, or having decided the dispute that is being appealed). The Court of Appeal has extended automatic disqualification, roughly, to *any* personal connection between the judge and a party, holding that a judge was automatically disqualified when he realized that he knew an expert witness for one party. The Court of Appeal held that he could not proceed to hear the case by proposing that they call a different witness (*AWG Group Ltd v Morrison* [2006] EWCA Civ 6 [29]). Automatic disqualification is appropriate where the judge's involvement in a decision would reflect badly on the integrity of the system, regardless of what the parties to the dispute might think about it. *AWG* shows that the courts will be quick to decide that there is a problem if a judge has anything to do with one of the parties.

If a judge is not automatically disqualified, it is still unlawful for him or her to decide the matter if an interest, relation, or opinion makes it unfair to do so. And as there is no viable way for a court in appeal or judicial review to consider the judge's actual attitudes, the law needs general principles for deciding whether a process was

---

[8]   Although a judge may say something about the matter in a court transcript, which would be available to an appeal court, and the judge may give reasons for a decision when a party complains of bias directly to the judge. And a court considering a complaint of bias may accept a statement from a judge or juror (*Locabail v Bayfield Properties* [2000] QB 451, 477). In all of these cases, the complainant has no way of challenging what the judge says.

fair. When a party complains about an interest or relation or opinion of a judge, the basic question is this:

When bias will be presumed

'The question is whether the fair-minded and informed observer, having considered the facts, would conclude that there was a real possibility that the tribunal was biased.'

Porter v Magill [2001] UKHL 67 [103]

In this standard formulation, 'biased' has the meaning explained above—i.e., a judge is biased if he is disposed to decide against a party regardless of the merits.[9] And bias will be presumed if the fair-minded, informed observer would think that there is a possibility of it.

The *Porter* formulation has been unanimously and repeatedly endorsed by the House of Lords (in *Lawal v Northern Spirit Ltd* [2003] UKHL 35 [14], *R (Al-Hasan) v Home Secretary* [2005] UKHL 13 [30], and *Gillies* [3]). It was devised, though, in the Court of Appeal, in *Re Medicaments No 2* [2001] 1 WLR 700, as a modification of a different test that Lord Goff had set out in *Gough*. He held that the question was whether 'there was a real danger of bias on the part of the relevant member of the tribunal in question' (670).

How could the Court of Appeal modify a test that was adopted by the House of Lords? By using the Human Rights Act. The Act requires the English courts to take into account decisions of the European Court of Human Rights, and Lord Philips in the *Medicaments* case held that the Strasbourg jurisprudence required the courts to pay more attention to what an observer would think, and not just to whether there really was a danger of bias. The Strasbourg court had held that:

It must be ascertained whether sufficient guarantees exist to exclude any legitimate doubt. . . . Even appearances may be important; what is at stake is the confidence which the court must inspire in the accused in criminal proceedings and what is decisive is whether the applicant's fear as to a lack of impartiality can be regarded as objectively justifiable. [10]

So here are three tests for the presumption that a decision was biased:

- the *Gough* test: whether there is a real danger of bias;

- the **Strasbourg test:** whether the applicant's fear as to a lack of impartiality can be regarded as objectively justifiable; and

---

9 The House of Lords in *Porter* was presupposing this, on the basis of Lord Goff's speech in *Gough* 670, discussing the possibility that a tribunal member might be biased 'in the sense that he might unfairly regard (or have unfairly regarded) with favour, or disfavour, the case of a party to the issue under consideration by him' (670).

10 *Gregory v United Kingdom* (1998) 25 EHRR 577. Similarly, the Court had held in *Pullar v United Kingdom* (1996) 22 EHRR 391, 402–3, that 'no member of the tribunal should hold any personal prejudice or bias', but also, the tribunal 'must offer sufficient guarantees to exclude any legitimate doubt in this respect' [30]. See also *Findlay v United Kingdom* (1997) 24 EHRR 221.

- **the *Porter* test:** whether a fair-minded and informed observer, having considered the facts, would conclude that there was a real possibility that the tribunal was biased.

You might say that all three are the same: if there is no real danger of bias, an applicant's fear as to a lack of impartiality is not objectively justifiable, and a fair-minded and informed observer, having considered the facts, would conclude that there was no real possibility that the tribunal was biased. But the courts see the change from *Gough* to *Porter* as shifting the emphasis from how things are, to how things look. Why quash a decision for mere appearances?

5.2 Appearance and reality

In *Cowle*, Lord Mansfield held that 'a doubt whether a fair, impartial, or satisfactory trial can be had there' is a reason to remove a case from the Berwick justices (861). It didn't have to be proved that a trial there would not be fair. It was enough if it was doubtful. But whose doubt counts? The judge's, or Cowle's, or that of the people of Berwick? Or of the country? Is a misguided doubt enough? We need to work out the reasons for quashing a decision without proof of actual bias.

It is very commonly said that justice must not only be done, but be seen to be done.[11] A rule that a decision will be quashed if there is an appearance of bias (or even better, the appearance of a *possibility* of bias) has advantages:

- it is a guard against actual bias, which is more or less impossible to prove;

- where a decision maker was acting in good faith but had an unfair relation or interest, it enables judges to quash an unfair decision without having to condemn the decision maker;[12] and

- it can help to enhance public respect for the court.

In fact, being prepared to quash decisions for the appearance of a possibility of bias is absolutely crucial, because of Lord Mansfield's simple point that 'we must go upon general principles'. A connection with the case of a kind that might influence someone to decide it unfairly is embarrassing for the judge as well as alarming for the parties, and there is no way of working out whether the judge actually decided with an open mind.

The drawback, of course, is that quashing decisions for the mere appearance of bias gives a party an opportunity to try to get rid of a decision maker who may quite fairly decide against them. Or it gives an opportunity to overturn a process after the outcome goes the wrong way, on the ground that something didn't look right. Either way, a rule designed to protect a party from the mere appearance of bias potentially

---

[11]   E.g. *Davidson v Scottish Ministers* [2004] UKHL 34 [7] (Lord Bingham).

[12]   As the Court of Appeal put it in *Re Medicaments No 2* 'It is invidious for the reviewing Court to question the word of the Judge . . . but less so to say that the objective onlooker might have difficulty in accepting it' [67].

gives that party a way of stitching up the process if they don't like the way things are going, or the way things have gone.

> ### The irony of process (see p 143)
> Good process can demand that the decision maker give a party a technique for overturning a process that was not actually unfair, if they don't like the result.

The *Porter* test, and the Strasbourg cases it is based on, seem to be concerned with raw public opinion. According to the unanimous House of Lords in *Lawal v Northern Spirit Limited* [2003] UKHL 35, 'Public perception of the possibility of unconscious bias is the key' [14]. Perhaps the strongest statement of judicial anxiety about appearances comes in an Australian High Court decision rejecting the *Gough* test: 'Both the parties to the case and the general public must be satisfied that justice has not only been done but that it has been seen to be done' (*Webb v The Queen* (1994) 181 CLR 41, 52. Either the judges were taking it for granted that the parties and the general public must be reasonable, or they were holding that a decision can be quashed because someone might have a misconception that it was unfair.

Take the *Gough* question: whether there is a real danger (which only means a possibility) that the decision was biased. There is nothing that the role of public perception can add, unless the public perception is *mistaken*. This is why the difference between *Gough* and *Porter* is unclear. In *Porter*, the hypothetical observer, who could presumably be either a party or the general public, must be fair-minded and informed, and must have considered the facts—and the fair-minded and informed observer will not think that there is a real possibility of bias, when there is no real possibility of bias. In *Lawal*, the Law Lords did not say that public misconceptions mattered. But if the role of public perception is the key, perhaps they ought to? After all, respect for the courts can be affected by a totally misguided public opinion that a decision was biased.

Public perception of the courts is undoubtedly important, but the raw facts of what people will think are a dangerous ground for controlling judicial or administrative processes. Suppose that the vast majority of the British public think:

(1) that a court must be biased against the prosecution, if a particular defendant is not convicted of murder;

(2) that a judge in a civil claim between two private parties is biased against the claimant;

(3) that a judge in a criminal prosecution is biased against the defendant; and

(4) that a public authority is biased against a person complaining about an administrative decision.

In (1), the public perception should not weigh even a nanogram in the jury's decision. An acquittal will result in public hostility toward the courts, and that is completely irrelevant to the juror's task. Similarly, in (2), the courts should refuse to let one side use the fact of public perception as a ground for attacking the judge's decision if there is no good reason for it (and if there is good reason, the fact that the public perceives it is irrelevant). In (1), the reason for ignoring public perception is justice to the defendant in a criminal prosecution; in (2), the reason for ignoring public perception may be a combination of **process cost** (see p 111), and fairness to the other party, who should be able to rely on the decision of a judge unless there is good reason for the public's perception.

What about (3) and (4)? Examples of cases in which the courts have allowed claims of bias in such circumstances include *Davidson v Scottish Ministers*. Here, you might say that there is less at stake in quashing the initial decision and requiring it to be made by another decision maker because of the public perception. All that we have to lose is the process cost. But actually there is more: we lose finality. There is a process danger in giving people disappointed with a criminal conviction or an administrative decision a weapon to fight a fair decision.

In any case, the judges in cases like *Davidson* or *Pinochet* have only the roughest ways of judging what public perception actually is. They need to guard respect for their processes very carefully, but they have little access to information on what people think. Widespread ignorance of what goes on in court means that public opinion does not form very predictably.

Like any public authority, a court must be accountable to the public. But the accountability they owe is to be transparent, to guard the integrity of their processes, to promote access to justice, and to give clear and candid reasons for their decisions. They should not give the public good reason to doubt the fairness of their process. But they owe nothing at all to raw public misconceptions. If we start with the entirely necessary rule that decisions will be quashed for an appearance of a possibility of bias, and *add* a rule that the key is the public's perception, then the drawbacks of quashing decisions because of appearances are worsened, because the court must be prepared to quash decisions made through a process that it can see was fair, because somebody might have the misconception that it might have been unfair. The remedy ought to be for the court to explain the situation in its reasons, rather than to quash a fair decision.

In *Porter* itself, an auditor was investigating politically charged complaints that Conservative councillors had been selling off council housing at a loss, in an attempt to move Conservative voters into key wards before an election. The auditor held a televised press conference after the preliminary phase of his investigation, and posed for the cameras beside high stacks of documents in ring binders with a security guard watching over them. The Law Lords called it an error of judgment: 'The main impression which this would have conveyed to the fair-minded observer was that the purpose of this exercise was to attract publicity to himself, and perhaps also to his firm. It was an exercise in self-promotion in which he should not have indulged. But it is quite another matter to conclude from this that there was a real possibility that he was biased' [105]. So according to *Porter*, it isn't enough that a process looks bad, or that someone might suffer from a misconception. If a decision is to be quashed, it must have looked bad in such a way that a complainant has a justifiable fear that the decision maker was biased.

5.2.1 The judge's opinion on the law

In the rash of bias decisions over recent years, have the judges been *too* ready to quash decisions for an appearance of bias? It depends on what they have been expecting from the 'fair-minded and informed observer' in the *Porter* test, and whether they have been too concerned with public perceptions, and not enough with justifiable public perceptions. In one respect, though, they have gone beyond the true rationale for a rule against bias, which is to secure due process.

The fact that a decision maker—judge or administrator—has previously expressed a view that has adverse implications for a party to a dispute does not necessarily indicate bias. Otherwise, a judge would not be able to sit in a case in which one party wanted to rely on a precedent decided by that judge. Even though the fair-minded observer might think that a judge would be inclined to take the same view of the law that he or she took in a previous case, that would not be enough to make the fair-minded observer think that the judge was biased. It would be fruitless to complain that a Law Lord should recuse himself, when you need to ask for a precedent that he decided to be overruled. You might think that the court is predisposed to decide against you—and it might be true—but the judge is not disqualified on that ground. Lord Bingham has said that 'adherence to an opinion expressed judicially in an earlier case does not of itself denote a lack of open-mindness' (*Davidson v Scottish Ministers* [10]).

Moreover, the judges may quite appropriately form a view of a case, based on the papers submitted by the parties and their own reading, before an oral hearing. That really does give the judges a predisposition before the barristers stand up to make their arguments, but there is nothing unfair about it. As Ward LJ has said, 'The business of this court would not be done if we were to recuse ourselves for entering the court having formed a preliminary view of the prospects of success of the appeal before us' (*El-Farargy v El-Farargy* [2007] EWCA Civ 1149).

The reason why these forms of potential or actual predisposition are fair is not simply that judges are expected to be open-minded enough to listen to arguments as to why they should change their view (though we need judges who can do that). The really important reason is that a judge *ought* to have views on what the law is (and, e.g., on whether a precedent ought to be overruled).

It would, however, be improper for a judge elevated from the High Court to the Court of Appeal to decide an appeal from his or her own decision.[13] There ought to be a simple rule, that the expression of a *general* view as to the law by a judge is never good ground for a claim that there is the appearance of bias (whether it was in a law journal, or a previous decision, or an after dinner speech). It would be different if a judge had committed himself or herself to a *particular application* of the law to the complainant's case (e.g., by writing in a law journal or saying on TV that a particular party ought to lose a particular claim). But even if a general point of law is crucial to a party's case, it should be simply no objection at all that a judge has expressed a view on it.

---

[13] Judges are also automatically disqualified from sitting in disputes that they were involved with in legal practice before becoming a judge.

But in *Davidson*, the House of Lords unanimously quashed a decision for no more reason than that. Davidson wanted an injunction ordering a Scottish minister to move him to a different prison, and a three-judge court held that no injunction was available under the Scotland Act against a Scottish minister. Lord Hardie, one of the judges, had been a Government Minister three years earlier, and during the passage of the Scotland Bill, he had expressed the opinion in Parliament that the Bill along with the Crown Proceedings Act 1947 would prevent injunctions against Scottish ministers. Lord Bingham held that 'The fair-minded and informed observer, having considered the facts, would conclude that there was a real possibility that Lord Hardie, sitting judicially, would subconsciously strive to avoid reaching a conclusion which would undermine the very clear assurances he had given to Parliament' [17]. The House of Lords' decision can be explained partly by the connection with party politics: it may be thought to look bad that the judge had been speaking on behalf of the Government when he expressed his opinion in Parliament. The House of Lords' decision can also be explained as a zealous attempt to follow two decisions in which the European Court of Human Rights had suggested that involvement in the passage of legislation disqualified a judge from later interpreting it, and held that a 'doubt in itself, however slight its justification, is sufficient to vitiate the impartiality' of the tribunal in question.[14]

No ground is offered in the *Davidson* case for thinking that the fair-minded observer (as the *Porter* test puts it) would believe that there was a possibility that Lord Hardie was biased. In the light of the Law Lords' references to the Strasbourg cases, the conclusion must be that the possibility of an *unreasonable* perception of bias may be treated as a ground for quashing a decision. Given the process havoc that results, a decision should only be overturned if the integrity of the judicial process is at stake; and its integrity is not endangered by unreasonable misperceptions of bias.

As Lord Hope said, while concurring with the rest of the Law Lords,

> 'It would be easy, were we permitted to take a more robust view, to deplore a system which permits an unsuccessful litigant to challenge a judge's decision that has gone against him by searching after the event for previously undiscovered material, like a needle in a haystack, that might be thought to undermine his objectivity. One might think that the cost and delay of rehearing the case would only be justified if there was a real possibility that the wrong decision had been reached because of the alleged bias.' [46]

That shows the price we pay for a rule that decisions can be quashed for the appearance of a possibility of bias. There is no genuine sense in which Davidson had not got a fair hearing of his claim for an injunction against a Scottish minister. And the guarantee of impartiality in Art 6 ought to be interpreted in light of its purpose of securing due process. Although it is the judges' obligation under the Human Rights

---

[14]   *Procola v Luxembourg* (1995) 22 EHRR 193 [45], *McGonnell v UK* (2000) 30 EHRR 289 [57].

Act to take account of Strasbourg decisions, *Davidson* would have been a good case in which to depart from *obiter dicta* from the Strasbourg Court suggesting that a decision can be quashed because of the possibility of a misconception that there was a possibility of bias. The European Court of Human Rights' view that 'doubt in itself, however slight its justification, is sufficient to vitiate the impartiality' of a tribunal is, potentially, damaging to the administration of justice.

Decision maker	Relations to a party	Appearance of a possibility of bias?
Juror in a burglary trial	—she realized after the conviction that the defendant was the brother of her former next-door neighbour (with whom the defendant was accused of conspiracy).	No[15]
Lay member on a tribunal	—during the hearing she applied for a job with a company, forgetting that one party's main witness was a director of the company.	Yes[16]
Lay member on a tribunal	—had sat on other tribunals with a lawyer for one party.	Yes[17]
Medical member of a three-person tribunal, hearing a claim against the Benefits Agency	—she provided expert reports on behalf of the Benefits Agency in other cases.	No[18]
Judge	—conducted a summary trial for contempt, for the defendant's outrageous behaviour in her court.	No[19]
	Conduct	
A judge in a theft trial	—repeatedly criticized defence counsel's competence and integrity (accusing her of 'silliness', 'nonsense', and 'being ridiculous').	Yes[20]

Figure 5.1 House of horrors: is it bias?

[15] *R v Gough* [1993] AC 646. But note that Lord Goff in his reasons suggested that the court should only quash the conviction if there was a real possibility of bias; in his view, an appearance of a possibility was not enough. *Porter* departs from that approach.

[16] *Re Medicaments (No 2)*: 'a fair-minded observer would apprehend that there was a real danger that Dr Rowlatt would be unable to make an objective and impartial appraisal of the expert evidence' [98].

[17] *Lawal v Northern Spirit* [2003] UKHL 35.

[18] *Gillies v Work and Pensions Secretary* [2006] UKHL 2.

[19] *Wilkinson v Lord Chancellor's Department* [2003] EWCA Civ 95.

[20] *R v Lashley* [2005] EWCA Crim 2016: 'repeated and unnecessary demonstrations of inappropriate personal animosity towards counsel' interfered with 'the normal due process required at every trial' [48].

Decision maker	Relations to a party	Appearance of a possibility of bias?
	Conduct	
A judge in a civil claim	—joked about whether an Arab Sheikh would disappear on his flying carpet (etc.).	Yes[21]
A coroner	—called relatives of the deceased 'unhinged' and 'mentally unwell'.	Yes[22]
An auditor	—held a press conference to show off how thorough his investigation was, with a security guard posing by the ring binders of documents.	No[23]
Deputy prison governor	—had been present when the governor approved an order for prisoners to undergo a squat search; in disciplinary proceedings he ruled that the governor's order was lawful.	Yes[24]
A judge	—decided in the Scottish Court of Session that injunctions could not be granted against the Scottish ministers (after giving advice to the House of Lords, as Lord Advocate, that injunctions could not be granted against the Scottish ministers).	Yes[25]
A judge in a commercial trial	—realized that an expert witness for one party was a friend of his, and proposed that the party call another witness.	Yes[26]

Figure 5.1 House of horrors: is it bias? *Continued*

5.2.2 Waiver

Can a person waive the right to an unbiased tribunal? It would be wrong to allow it, if bias is a blot on the integrity of the court. And we have seen that *some* interests, relations, and opinions are inherently objectionable. The relations and interests that lead to automatic disqualification are unwaivable: it would just be improper for a judge to preside in a claim in tort against her son, even if the claimant did not object. The grounds for automatic disqualification should simply result in a judge recusing himself or herself, rather than asking the party who might suffer detriment if they mind.

[21] *El-Farargy v El Farargy* [2007] EWCA Civ 1149.

[22] *R v HM Coroner for Inner London West District, ex p Dallaglio* [1994] 4 All ER 139.

[23] *Porter v Magill* [2002] 2 AC 357.

[24] *R (Al-Hasan) v Home Secretary* [2005] UKHL 13.

[25] *Davidson v Scottish Ministers (No 2)* [2004] UKHL 34.

[26] *AWG Group Ltd v Morrison* [2006] EWCA Civ 6.

But since decisions can be quashed merely because of an appearance of the possibility of bias, we really need a good doctrine of waiver. Some relations with a party that would lead to disqualification of a judge can certainly be waived. For example, if the judge is a solicitor whose firm has acted for a party, he or she has a relation that is improper unless it is disclosed; if it is disclosed, and the other party has no objection, then the judge is not disqualified, if he or she has not acted for one of the parties (*Locabail (UK) Ltd v Bayfield Properties* [2000] QB 451, 486).

A good doctrine of waiver must start with a duty on the judge to give full and early notice of any relation with the parties (although it needs to be flexible enough to deal with the situation in which a judge learns during a hearing that he or she has a relation to a party). And the next requirement is that, as with any waiver of procedural protections (see p 134), a waiver of the right to a hearing that does not raise the appearance of a possibility of bias 'must be clear and unequivocal, and made with full knowledge of all the facts relevant to the decision whether to waive or not' (*Locabail v Bayfield*, 475).

In spite of the need for clear and unequivocal waiver, it may be possible to waive by doing nothing. The Chief Justice saw this problem coming in 1924: in R v Sussex Justices, ex p McCarthy [1924] 1 KB 256, the clerk who advised the justices in a criminal conviction for dangerous driving was a solicitor from the firm that was suing the defendant for injuries to the victim of a collision. Lord Hewart held that 'In those circumstances I am satisfied that this conviction must be quashed, unless it can be shown that the applicant or his solicitor was aware of the point that might be taken, refrained from taking it, and took his chance of an acquittal on the facts, and then, on a conviction being recorded, decided to take the point. On the facts I am satisfied that there has been no waiver of the irregularity, and, that being so, the rule must be made absolute and the conviction quashed' (289). So it appears that a reviewing court may hold that an appearance of a possibility of bias is waived by a party who does nothing. But they would presumably have to do nothing in circumstances that make it abusive for them to complain about the irregularity later. The mere fact that a party could have complained earlier will not be enough to count as a waiver (*Millar v Dickson* [2001] UKPC D 4).

5.3 Independence

In order for a community to achieve responsible government, powers need to be separated not only among the executive, judiciary, and legislature, but also *within* each branch of government (see p 15). The independence of judges is a crucial part of the separation of powers between the judiciary and the executive. The independence of some administrative decision makers is a separation of powers within the executive branch of government.

Independence is a structural feature of decision makers that tends to improve their capacity to act with impartiality. It means 'not only a lack of hierarchical or institutional connection but also a practical independence' (*Ramsahai v Netherlands*

(App no 52391/99) ECHR 15 May 2007 [325]). In *Findlay v United Kingdom* (1997) 24 EHRR 221 [73], the European Court of Human Rights said: 'in order to establish whether a tribunal can be considered as "independent", regard must be had inter alia to the manner of appointment of its members and their term of office, the existence of guarantees against outside pressures and the question whether the body presents an appearance of independence'.

In England, administrative tribunals have been designed for more than a century to achieve more-or-less independent review of many forms of administrative decision; the **reconstruction of tribunals** is designed to enhance their independence (see Chapter 12). A lack of independence can be ground for judicial review of an administrative decision, if it amounts to 'the effective surrender of the body's independent judgment' (*R v Environment Secretary, ex p Kirkstall Valley Campaign Ltd* [1996] 3 All ER 304 (QBD), 321 (Sedley J). An administrative body that has been given responsibility for a decision must genuinely exercise that responsibility (see p 264), and cannot surrender its judgment or be overridden by any other government agency that is not specifically authorized to do so. But at common law, there has never been a distinctive legal requirement of institutional independence in administrative decision making, and no administrative decision could be challenged as biased merely on the ground that the decision maker was not independent of government. One reason for this is that if Parliament gives a decision-making power to a public authority that is not independent of government, the courts cannot hold it to be unlawful for that authority to exercise the power.[27] The other reason is that many administrative decisions do *not* require an independent tribunal. The Board of Works in *Cooper* is a good example of the sort of administrative decision maker that decides people's rights, without being independent of government. And the police authority in *Ridge v Baldwin* [1964] AC 40 is a reminder of the varieties of independence: police authorities have an independence *from ordinary administration* by elected government at both national and local level. It is a form of separation of powers within the executive that is essential for the rule of law. But the authority that sacked Ridge was responsible both for policy and administration of the police, and also for deciding whether he had a right to serve as chief of police. So Ridge had not yet had an independent hearing, when he was sacked. But the defect in the process was not that the police authority was not independent; it was just that they had not heard his side of the story.

In the European Convention on Human Rights (ECHR), independence is a distinct, additional protection for impartial decision making. So the right to an *independent* tribunal under the ECHR brought something new to English law. Art 6(1) provides that:

> In the determination of his civil rights and obligations or of any criminal charge against him, everyone is entitled to a fair and public hearing within a reasonable time by an independent and impartial tribunal established by law.

---

[27]   See the discussion of *R v Home Secretary, ex p Venables and Thompson* [1998] AC 407, p 70.

So, for example, investigation of government wrongdoing must be independent from government (*Edwards v United Kingdom* (2002) 35 EHRR 487 [70]).

You might think that Art 6 would revolutionize English administrative law, requiring all decisions determining rights to be made by someone (such as a judge) who is independent of government. The decision makers in *Cooper* and *Ridge* lacked independence, since the Board of Works in *Cooper* and the police authority in *Ridge* were administrative bodies that were *part of* the government. If their decision-making role is incompatible with Art 6, it would revolutionize administrative law.

But there has been no revolution. The change has been significant, but limited. In *R (Anderson) v Home Secretary* [2002] UKHL 46, the House of Lords declared under the Human Rights Act that the Home Secretary's statutory power to determine tariffs for adult prisoners was incompatible with Art 6(see section 3.5). Sentencing decisions and decisions over parole must be made by persons who are independent of government. The result is that the Act shifted tariff setting into the courts. That change in the law is important because the inadequacy of judicial review to preserve a proper separation of powers in tariff setting was exposed in *R v Home Secretary, ex p Venables and Thompson* [1998] AC 407 (see p 70). Before the Human Rights Act, the judges could only tell the Home Secretary what considerations he could lawfully take into account; in *V v United Kingdom* (2000) 30 EHRR 121, the European Court of Human Rights simply held that it was a breach of the Convention for a tariff to be decided by a government minister, because he is not independent.

Now the English judges can do what the Strasbourg judges can do, and declare that a statute is incompatible with the ECHR. But the Act has not brought any *general* requirement of independence to administrative law. Unlike in *Anderson* or in *Venables and Thompson*, most administrative decision making does not determine how long someone stays in prison. Article 6 does not even apply to all administrative decisions, but only to those determine 'civil rights and obligations or...any criminal charge.' That vague phrase was used with a technical meaning that restricts the effect of Art 6. And where Art 6 *does* apply, if an initial decision maker is not independent, compound decision making (that is, the combination of the initial decision plus appeal or review) can provide the independent control over the decision that is necessary for due process (see p 167).

┌─ **FROM THE MISTS OF TIME** ─────────────────────────────────────

The independence of **judges** has been protected for more than three hundred years in England. In 1628, King Charles I dismissed Sir Ranulf Crew, for 'shewing no zeal' for the King's scheme to force nobles to give him loans,[28] and his successor, Sir Nicholas Hyde, promptly decided *Darnel's Case* (1627) 3 Howell's State Trials 1 (KB), 1 (see p 5) in favour of the King, and against the knights who refused to make the loan. No judge has been dismissed since then for lacking zeal for the administration's projects. The Act of Settlement 1700 provided that 'judges commissions

---

[28] Sir Edward Coke, too, had been removed from office in 1616 by the Privy Council, partly for disrespect toward the King.

be made *quamdiu se bene gesserint* [while they behave themselves well], and their salaries ascertained and established; but upon the address of both Houses of Parliament it may be lawful to remove them' (art III). Before that, they had held their commissions so long as the king saw fit. Today, there is a 'guarantee of continued judicial independence' in s 3 of the Constitutional Reform Act 2005.

Temporary judges with no job security who rely on the government for promotion are not independent for the purpose sake of Art 6 (*Ruxton v Starrs* [2000] HRLR 191).

5.3.1 Determining civil rights

The drafters of the ECHR actually *missed* an opportunity to impose due process on administration. By using the slightly mysterious phrase 'determination of his civil rights', they meant to exclude decisions that they thought of as administrative; they meant to protect the sort of rights that were typically asserted in the private law courts, in European countries that had separate courts for disputes over administrative decisions.[29] The rest of Art 6(1) regulates the publicity of 'the trial', and the whole article is titled 'Right to a fair trial'. So the article was drafted for the sort of disputes that are typically resolved in a trial.

FROM THE MISTS OF TIME

Article 6 was cribbed from the International Covenant on Civil and Political Rights of the United Nations.[30] In UN negotiations in 1949 over the drafting of the International Covenant, the French and Egyptians proposed a guarantee of process rights for the determination of 'rights and obligations' in general. The Danes responded that such a guarantee would be too broad: 'it would tend to submit to judicial decision any action taken by administrative organs exercising discretionary power conferred on them by law....the individual should be ensured protection against any abuse of power by administrative organs but the question was extremely delicate and it was doubtful whether the Commission could settle it there and then. The study of the division of power between administrative and judicial organs could be undertaken later' (*Feldbrugge*, 444–5). As a result, the UN resolved to guarantee 'rights and obligations in a suit of law', which became 'civil rights and obligations' in the ECHR. And 'the study of the division of power between administrative and judicial organs' has been carried out by the Strasbourg Court in applying Art 6, which was not built for that purpose.

---

[29] See *Feldbrugge v Netherlands* (1986) 8 EHRR 425, cited by Lord Hoffmann in *Begum v Tower Hamlets LBC* [2003] UKHL 5 [28].

[30] Article 14 now provides: 'In the determination of any criminal charge against him, or of his rights and obligations in a suit at law, everyone shall be entitled to a fair and public hearing by a competent, independent and impartial tribunal established by law.' The International Covenant lacks the adjudication and enforcement facilities of the European Convention.

In the cases on the applicability of Art 6, the European Court of Human Rights has explained a 'civil' right as a right in private law (see *Albert and Le Compte v Belgium* (1983) 5 EHRR 533 [28]). The guarantee of independence in Art 6(1) applies to tort claims against government (*X v France* (1992) 14 EHRR 483), to planning disputes (*Bryan v UK* (1995) 21 EHRR 342, *R (Alconbury) v Environment Secretary* [2001] UKHL 23), and to disputes as to whether a claimant is entitled to a welfare benefit (*Schuler-Zgraggen v Switzerland* (1993) 16 EHRR 405). It does not apply to discretionary criminal injuries compensation schemes (*Masson v Netherlands* (1996) 22 EHRR 491), or to decisions in tax disputes (*Ferrazzini v Italy* (2001) 34 EHRR 1068). But the idea of a civil right is 'autonomous', meaning that a member state cannot deprive a person of a civil right by making it enforceable only in administrative courts (*Begum* [85]–[87]). If legislation entitles you to a specific economic benefit in a precisely specified situation, your claim to it will be a claim to a 'civil right' (with the resultant Art 6 procedural protections); by contrast, a claim that a public authority unlawfully failed to use its discretion in your favour is not likely to be treated as a claim to a civil right.

It is peculiar that the law of social security benefits is covered by Art 6, and the law of taxation is not; that is one of the peculiar features of the European background to Art 6. Note that the main cases on the applicability of Art 6 have concerned complaints of delay (*Salesi v Italy* (1998) 26 EHRR 187, *Mennitto v Italy* (2002) 34 EHRR 48, *Ferrazzini v Italy* (2001) 34 EHRR 1068). The determination of 'civil rights' is the condition for the availability of *all* the protections in Art 6(1). But while we have seen important reasons for not requiring some administrative decisions to be made by an independent tribunal, those are *not* reasons for allowing unreasonable delay. And they are not reasons for allowing an unfair hearing or a biased decision, either.

There is a simple design flaw in this aspect of Art 6. The Convention should have prohibited unreasonable delay and bias and other forms of unfairness in the determination of rights generally. It should have required an independent tribunal in a more narrowly restricted range of decisions (those decisions, such as the determination of sentences, in which independence in the initial decision is necessary for due process). As it is, the structure of Art 6 puts pressure on the Strasbourg Court to widen its applicability in order to extend the protections against unreasonable delay, and bias, and refusal to give a hearing when fairness requires a hearing. In dealing with this problem, coming up with a good interpretation of 'determination of civil rights' is not enough, because the extent of a guarantee against delay or bias ought to be different from the extent of a guarantee of independent decision making. So the courts have had to develop a complex account of the role that independence ought to play in a compound decision-making process, when due process does not demand that the initial decision maker should be independent.

5.3.2 Compound decision making

If a body doesn't comply with Art 6, an appeal to another body, or judicial review, may prevent a breach of Article 6. Art 6, like the common law, shouldn't really do more than protect *due* process, which means proportionate process (see p 119). The courts have occasionally (as in *Davidson*) given claimants disproportionate protection against bias. But otherwise, their elaboration of Art 6 has given effect to the principle of proportionate process. So in *Porter v Magill* [2002] UKHL 67, a local government auditor acted as investigator, prosecutor, and judge. That would infringe the separation of powers within administration, if it were uncontrolled. And ordinary judicial review would not be enough to vindicate Art 6. But Lord Hope held that the councillors' rights under Art 6 were protected by the availability of an appeal to the divisional court, which could confirm, vary, or quash a decision.[31] The court 'can exercise afresh all the powers of decision which were given to the auditor' [92].

Compound decision making can protect the interests at stake, while allowing a non-independent initial decision maker to pursue the public interest. For some decisions, it may be best to get a body with a policy agenda to make the initial decision, because appeal or review by an independent body may be enough to protect those interests of a complainant that ought to be protected by law. And the jurisdiction of the court in review or appeal need not be as intrusive as the court's jurisdicion was in *Porter v Magill*.

Think of the police authority in *Ridge v Baldwin* [1964] AC 40. A police authority is responsible for preserving the reputation of the police. A threat to that reputation might lead them to a conclusion that Ridge had to be sacked for the good of the police force, without due regard for Ridge's own interests. If the decision were left to an independent body that could pass judgment on the situation without trying to push through a policy agenda, the decision as to whether Ridge should be the chief of police would be deeply detached from management of the police. Since the role of the chief of police is critical to the management of a police service, an independent body set up to decide whether a police chief should be dismissed would either become the real police service management (and then it wouldn't be independent any more), or else it would make uninformed decisions. Ridge has no right to a system that detaches decisions as to his position from the management of the force. And because the managers of a police service ought to have a say in the discipline and dismissal of police officers, there is no injustice to Ridge in a general scheme that gives the police authority a power to dismiss, as long as there is independent and effective review on grounds of due process and abuse of power.

But compound decision making undoubtedly creates risks:

(1) a risk of **particular injustices**, if the independent reviewer fails to identify or to remedy an injustice in the decision of the initial decision maker, and conversely:

(2) a risk that the independent reviewer will **interfere with sound decisions**, in the mistaken view that it knows what decision the initial decision maker ought to have made.

Today, the requirements of Art 6 of the Convention are met if a public servant who is dismissed has access to an independent tribunal that can reverse the decision.

---

[31] He also held that this view was consistent with the interpretation of Art 6 by the Strasbourg Court in *Bryan v UK* (1995) 21 EHRR 342, 360.

Neither common law fairness nor the ECHR forbids administrative bodies to determine people's rights, as long as an independent tribunal has power to determine the lawfulness of the decision.

In *Begum v Tower Hamlets LBC* [2003] UKHL 5, the Tower Hamlets Council had a legal duty to house Ms Begum, who was homeless. She complained that the home they offered her was in a drug- and crime-infested area, that she had been robbed when she went to visit it, and that her estranged husband frequented the neighbourhood. The Council's decision was reviewed by one of the Council's own housing officers, who rejected her complaint; the housing officer decided that Ms Begum had not been robbed, that the other complaints were not serious, and that the alternatives available in the borough were no better. Ms Begum claimed that the process infringed her Art 6 right to an independent tribunal.

The housing officer certainly was not independent. But Ms Begum had a statutory appeal to the County Court. Her right to determination of her civil rights by an independent tribunal was not infringed, if it was the County Court that determined them. But she claimed that her rights were already determined before she could get to the court, because she could only appeal on a question of law (see Chapter 9) and her complaint was against the housing officer's determination of the *facts* of her situation. So her case raised two questions: (1) did the decision as to whether she had been offered reasonable housing determine her civil rights? And if so, (2) had her civil rights been determined by an independent tribunal?

There would be two drawbacks in a scheme providing Ms Begum with a fully independent tribunal on the question of whether the housing offered to her was reasonable:

- **Process cost (see p 111):** the Council (or some other public authority) would need to pay for an independent agency to hear evidence and determine the facts of the situation.

- **Process danger (see p 111):** a truly independent decision maker would not be in a position to appreciate some of the considerations relevant to the decision, which include the needs of other homeless people, and the alternatives available to the Council in housing Ms Begum.

Given those drawbacks, the Law Lords thought it appropriate that the Council's housing officer should decide whether the housing was reasonable, subject to Ms Begum's right of appeal. But how can that be squared with Art 6? It would be simplest to treat the housing officer's decision *Begum* as a decision that did not 'determine civil rights' for the purpose of the Convention. There would still be an independent tribunal (the County Court) that could determine and protect Ms Begum's civil right *not to be the victim of an abuse of power* by the Council.

But the Strasbourg jurisprudence had moved a long way to bring welfare benefits under Art 6. If she had a right to housing in a different home, it might count as a civil right for the purposes of Art 6, and then it was determined (subject to judicial review) by the non-independent decision of the Council's housing officer. Lord Bingham and Lord Hoffmann *assumed* that Art 6 applied, perhaps in order to leave the British government free to argue in similar cases in Strasbourg that it did not apply. Lord Millett held that Art 6 ought to be extended to such cases, but (1) only because otherwise the Convention would provide no protection at all for impartiality in administrative process, and (2) only 'hand in hand with moderating its requirements in the interests of efficient administration where administrative decisions are involved' [94].

So instead of holding Art 6 inapplicable, they held that the farther its applicability extends, the more relaxed the requirement of independence must become. The relaxation comes in the role of the reviewing court. The Strasbourg Court has held that 'either the jurisdictional organs themselves comply with the requirements of Article 6(1), or they do not so comply but are subject to subsequent control by a judicial body that has full jurisdiction and does provide the guarantees of Article 6(1)' (*Albert and Le Compte v Belgium* (1983) 5 EHRR 533 [29]). That suggests, of course, that 'full jurisdiction' is compatible with a scheme in which a reviewing court does not replace the initial decision maker's view on all points with its own, but imposes control. And the House of Lords has taken up this suggestion. Lord Hoffmann held in *Alconbury* that ' "full jurisdiction" does not mean full decision-making power. It means full jurisdiction to deal with the case as the nature of the decision requires' (*Alconbury* [87]; unanimously approved by the Law Lords in *Begum*). 'Full jurisdiction' means jurisdiction that is sufficient for the purpose of vindicating the due process rights in Art 6.

The Convention cries out for another technique for restricting the requirement of an independent tribunal, besides the Strasbourg Court's flexible approach to the identification of civil rights. The technique lies in the line of House of Lords cases from *Alconbury* to *Begum*. As Lord Bingham put it, 'the more elastic the interpretation given to "civil rights", the more flexible must be the approach to the requirement of independent and impartial review if the emasculation (by over-judicialization) of administrative welfare schemes is to be avoided' (*Begum* [5]).

This means that the **principle of relativity** (see p 10) is a principle of the interpretation of an international human rights instrument like the Convention. Even under Article 6, the need for independent decision making depends on the context. For example, the right to an independent decision maker is violated if the Home Secretary decides a tariff (R (Anderson) v Home Secretary [2002] UKHL 46), but not if the Home Secretary *reviews* a tariff during the prisoner's term of imprisonment (R (Smith) v Home Secretary [2005] UKHL 51).

Common law procedural protections extend more broadly than the protections in Article 6

The common law of due process is not restricted to decisions that determine 'civil rights'. Determination of civil rights is only one consideration that goes into the due process calculation at common law (it is a ground for the right to a hearing). English courts have sometimes imposed on themselves a similar classification problem, by holding that natural justice must be given in judicial and quasi-judicial decisions, but not in administrative decisions (see p 113). But the House of Lords in

> *Ridge v Baldwin* re-established a more flexible approach to due process at common law, which makes it unnecessary for English courts to define a boundary between decisions that do and do not require due process. So Lord Justice Sedley has said, 'One relevant divergence [between the Convention and the common law] is that the common law sets high standards of due process in non-judicial settings to which the European Court of Human Rights at Strasbourg declines to apply Art 6 of the Convention for the Protection of Human Rights and Fundamental Freedoms. Here a claimant can derive better protection from the common law than from the Convention, and the Human Rights Act 1998 s 11(a) expressly preserves his right to do so' (R (Wooder) v Feggetter [2002] EWCA Civ 554 [46]).

In these compound decision-making cases, shouldn't the complainant still get a fair hearing before the first body? Yes, of course they should, and that is why a biased decision before an initial decision maker is always a breach of Art 6. But the guarantee of *independent* decision making in Art 6 has to be interpreted in a way that promotes due process, and independence is simply not a general requirement of fair governmental decision making.

5.3.3 The value of independence

We can conclude with three basic points about the value of independence. First, **independence is not necessarily a good thing.** It tends to improve the capacity to act with impartiality, so it may not be valuable if a decision maker need not or should not act impartially. That follows from the *Alconbury* and *Begum* cases. As Lord Hoffmann has said, 'Independence makes the courts more suited to deciding some kinds of questions and being elected makes the legislature or executive more suited to deciding others' (R (ProLife Alliance) v British Broadcasting Corporation [2003] UKHL 23 [76] (Lord Hoffmann)).

Secondly, independent decision making can sometimes be a good idea not because decisions as to rights need to be insulated from policy making, but because **independence may improve policy making.** One of the first initiatives of the new Labour Government in 1997 was to give away the role of setting interest rates to the Monetary Policy Committee (MPC) of the Bank of England. Under the Bank of England Act 1998, the Committee is to support the government's economic policy; but that duty is subject to a *primary* duty to maintain price stability (i.e., to keep inflation under control (s 11)). And questions as to what those duties require are questions for the MPC. The government cannot ordinarily give directions to the Bank as to monetary policy, though it can take over in 'extreme economic circumstances' (s 19). The idea has been that independence would enhance policy making by insulating interest rate decisions from political pressures that might influence the government to take bad risks with decisions that might boost inflation. More generally, over the past ten years, Labour governments have expanded a trend that the Conservatives started in the 1980s, toward policy implementation by 'non-departmental public bodies' that operate with substantial independence from government (see p 562). The Prisons Service, the Child Support Agency, the Benefits Agency, NHS trusts, and many other bodies are designed to achieve good delivery of public services in partial autonomy from government departments.

Finally, we should note that the **independence of judges** is part of the **core rationale** (see p 65) for judicial review. Judicial review can be a good way of securing responsible government partly because of the protection that independent judges are able to provide *for* due process and *against* abuse of power. And by the same token, the independence of tribunal judges is part of the rationale that successive Parliaments have had over a century, for committing the resolution of complaints over a wide variety of government acts to specialist tribunals (see Chapter 12).

5.4 Policy and prejudice

There is a puzzle about impartiality and independence in administrative decision making: why even bother requiring the Board of Works to give Cooper a hearing, before they tear down his house? The Board of Works is obviously predisposed against the complainant, if they even reach the point of listening to him. They only get to that step if they think there is a reason to tear down his house. Or why require the police authority to give Ridge a hearing, when they are predisposed to sack him?

The answer to the puzzle is partly that officials are not incapable of responding to objections to a plan of action that they have in mind. And it is partly that compound decision making can do something to protect Cooper[32] or Ridge from unfairness. But the more important part of the answer lies in the fact that neither independence nor impartiality is necessarily a good thing. A predisposition in favour of a course of action is *not necessarily improper*. There is a rule against bias in all administrative decision making, but *not* a rule requiring impartiality in all administrative decision making. It depends on what kind of decision is being made, and on what kind of predisposition the decision maker has. Partiality is a predisposition (i.e., a disposition that a decision maker has before hearing from people affected). Bias is a bad form of partiality, and not all predispositions are bad.

In a criminal trial, a predisposition to convict *or* to acquit would be improper. A court should also begin the hearing of a civil claim with no predisposition in favour of either party. But an administrative decision maker can formulate a very particular, provisional policy objective (e.g., to tear down Cooper's house for non-compliance with safety legislation), and then *ask what someone involved* (e.g., the homeowner) has to say about it. That explains why it is not unfair for the police authority to have power to dismiss Ridge. This is not to say that there can be no bias on the part of a police authority. Bias would be presumed, and members of the authority automatically disqualified, if

---

[32] *Cooper v Board of Works* was a claim in tort. A claim in tort against a public authority represents a form of compound decision making, because the public authority has a defence if its action was lawful. So tort claims against public authorities involve a review of the lawfulness of administrative action. See section 14.1.

they had any financial interest in Ridge's dismissal, or if they were prejudiced against him on racial grounds, or if Ridge was in the course of a messy divorce from a member's sister. But it would not be bias, e.g., for them to go into a disciplinary hearing thinking that the damage from his alleged conduct, if he actually did it, is so damaging to the reputation of the police that he should be sacked if he has no good explanation.

In a criminal trial, the prosecution puts the case to decision makers (jurors) who must start out with no suspicions. A disciplinary decision is different, and it is not impossible for a decision maker who suspects someone of misconduct to give them a fair hearing. Some kinds of decision are different again, and are in fact the implementation of a policy as to how to pursue the public interest. In *Ridge v Baldwin*, Lord Reid pointed out 'the great difference between various kinds of cases' in which the courts have had to decide what due process requires. 'What a minister ought to do in considering objections to a scheme may be very different from what a watch committee ought to do in considering whether to dismiss a chief constable' (*Ridge v Baldwin* [1964] AC 40, 65).

The most striking challenges for the law of bias arise where a public authority has a scheme, and needs to consider objections to it. If an official has a policy that counts against your argument, can that *ever* count as bias? We will address that question by looking at decisions whether to approve plans for development of land. They are decisions that generate masses of litigation because there is a lot of money at stake, and also because people have such strong feelings in favour of projects that they reckon will improve their neighbourhoods, and bitter feelings against projects that threaten them.

5.4.1 Planning

Here is a much-simplified account of the elaborate system of compound decision making in England for approval of proposals to build housing, shopping malls, leisure centres, and other developments. 'Planning permission is required for the carrying out of any development of land' (Town and Country Planning Act 1990 s 57(1)). The standard way of getting planning permission is to apply to the local planning authority: a committee of local councillors, who hold public consultations before deciding whether (and on what conditions) to give permission. In England, the Secretary of State for Communities and Local Government can call in an application (s 77), which means that she decides (in place of the local planning authority) whether the project should go ahead. Planning decisions are guided by the local authority's plan (Planning and Compulsory Purchase Act 2004). The Planning Inspectorate[33] (an executive agency (see p 563) of the Department of Communities and Local Government) hears appeals from local planning authority decisions and holds inquiries into local development plans.

An applicant can appeal to the Secretary of State (Town and Country Planning Act 1990 s 78) against a refusal of permission by the local planning authority, or

---

[33] http://www.planning-inspectorate.gov.uk/.

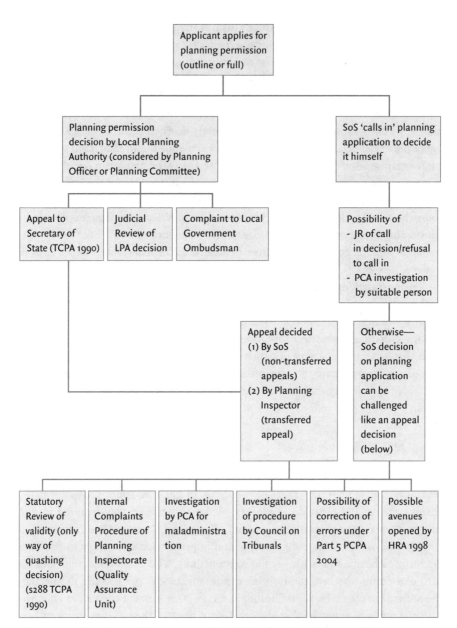

Figure 5.2 Overview of the process of applying for planning permission

against conditions imposed on a permission. The Secretary of State decides the appeal after getting a report from a Planning Inspector. The Secretary of State may 'deal with the application as if it had been made to him in the first instance' (s 79(1)). Only the applicant for planning permission has this appeal right (s 78), but third parties who want to complain that the local planning authority gave permission unlawfully can seek judicial review (R v Hammersmith and Fulham LBC, ex p Burkett [2002] UKHL 23). The Secretary of State's decision on an appeal can be challenged through a statutory judicial review process with a special (very short!) six-week time limit (Town and Country Planning Act 1990 s 288). A decision by the Secretary of State not to call in an application is subject to judicial review. When the Secretary of State does call in an application, there is no appeal from her decision (s 77), but the s 288 review process is available.

Where does the law of bias fit into that scheme of compound decision making? Here is a starting point. At *every single step* in that very complex diagram, a decision maker should be automatically disqualified if he or she has personal financial stake in the development proposal under consideration (or if her child owns the property...). With a financial stake in the project, a local councillor on the planning committee should step aside and should not even play any role in discussions. A local or parliamentary ombudsman with a financial interest should leave it to someone else to investigate. The Secretary of State should declare her interest and the Prime Minister should ask someone else to take the decision. A judge should recuse himself or herself. And so on. The integrity of the process would be damaged at *any* point if a decision were made by a person with a private interest in the development.

What about a decision maker with another sort of interest—a person whose policy or whose aims for the area in question are in favour of the development, or against it, or are in favour of imposing particular conditions? Or a person whose political party has such policies or aims?

R v Hillingdon LBC, ex p Royco Homes [1974] QB 720 was the first decision in which the courts quashed a local authority's decision under the modern planning system.[34] The council granted the builder permission to build houses on the condition that ten years' accommodation in the homes would be given to homeless people whom the council had a legal duty to house. The Divisional Court quashed the permission, in a decision that the judges regarded as 'a strong step' (Bridge J, 732). Their decision was only justified because the conditions were 'the equivalent of requiring the applicants to take on at their own expense a significant part of the duty of the council as housing authority' (Lord Widgery CJ, 731). The conditions were *Wednesbury* unreasonable, and therefore unlawful.

But the applicant did not argue that the council had been biased in its consideration of the application for planning permission. Why not? The council had obviously not been impartial in imposing the conditions; it had been pursuing its policy agenda of getting the homeless housed at minimum cost. But there is a simple reason why bias wasn't alleged: pursuing a policy agenda is a form of partiality, but the judges can only call it a *bad* form of partiality (and therefore it only counts as bias) if the judges are in a position to hold that it is an unlawful policy. And then the decision is unlawful anyway, and the claimant does not need the law of bias.

Yet increasingly in this century, people challenging planning decisions (disappointed applicants for permission, or competitors who want to stop a successful applicant from building new shops or homes, or local residents who opposed a project unsuccessfully in the planning process) have been trying to use the law of bias,

---

[34]   In the Town and Country Planning Act 1947; now the Town and Country Planning Act 1990.

to argue that a councillor who has expressed views about the project is biased, or that a committee is biased if a political party endorses or opposes the project, or if the council itself, as opposed to a councillor in his or her personal capacity, has an interest. Opponents of a council's agenda have used the doctrine of bias to take their battle to the courts, after losing in the planning committee.

R v Amber Valley DC, ex p Jackson [1985] 1 WLR 298 is a classic of administrative law: the first attempt to argue that a planning decision was biased because of the policy of the controlling party. Woolf J held that the Labour group controlling the council was indeed 'politically pre-disposed' in favour of the development that they proceeded to approve, but that there was nothing unlawful about it even though the objectors might well think that the planning committee would act on that political agenda:

> The rules of fairness or natural justice cannot be regarded as being rigid. They must alter in accordance with the context. Thus in the case of highways, the department can be both the promoting authority and the determining authority. When this happens, of course any reasonable man would regard the department as being pre-disposed towards the outcome of the inquiry. The department is under an obligation to be fair and carefully to consider the evidence given before the inquiry but the fact that it has a policy in the matter does not entitle a court to intervene. (307–8)

The caveats to this statement are (1) that Woolf J made it clear that the rules of fairness *are* rigidly against involvement of a councillor with a private interest in the decision (307), and (2) that he insisted that the planning committee had a duty to consider the objections to the planning application on their merits (308). But if the committee members took the view that the objections were not good objections *to their own policy*, there was nothing unlawful in that.

In R v Environment Secretary, ex p Kirkstall Valley Campaign Ltd [1996] 3 All ER 304 (QBD), Sedley J asserted 'the principle that a person is disqualified from participation in a decision if there is a real danger that he or she will be influenced by a pecuniary or personal interest' (325). But he also held that 'the law recognises that members will take up office with publicly stated views on a variety of policy issues' (325), and that (as Woolf J had held in *Amber Valley*), those views do not count as bias unless the councillor refuses to consider objections.

Those classic cases have not stopped angry opponents of developments from alleging political bias. In R (Lewis) v Redcar and Cleveland [2008] EWCA Civ 746, the Court of Appeal has taken a half-measure to keep the law on bias in proportion. In a challenge to a local planning authority's approval of an application to build a leisure centre and housing on land owned by the council, the Administrative Court held that the fair-minded and informed observer in the *Porter* test for bias 'will not take it amiss that councillors have previously expressed views on matters which arise for decision'. But the observer will conclude that there is a real possibility of bias if there are 'additional and unusual circumstances which suggest that councillors may have closed their minds before embarking upon a decision' [11]. The judge found such circumstances because the project had become an issue in an upcoming election, the councillors who voted for the project pushed it through in the run-up to the election, they made 'forceful public statements in support of the project', and the governing coalition on the council voted unanimously for it [12]. The Court of Appeal allowed an appeal by the developer, Pill LJ holding that 'The notion that a planning decision is suspect because all members of a single political group have voted for it is an unwarranted interference with the democratic process' [38].

There is no doubt that the *Porter* test is the right way to decide whether there is the appearance of a possibility of bias arising from a personal interest on the part of a council member. But is it the right way to decide whether the party politics behind a council decision reflect bias? Lord Justice Pill actually suggested that the *Porter* test does not apply to *that* question:

> The danger of the "notional observer" test [i.e. the *Porter* test] is that the role of elected Councillors may not fully be taken into account. That could lead to any Councillor, elected on a pro-scheme manifesto, creating a serious risk of a Council's grant of permission being quashed if he participated in the decision to grant. That would not be in the public interest or accord with the law. It is for the court to assess whether Committee members did make the decision with closed minds or that the circumstances give rise to such a real risk of closed minds that the decision ought not in the public interest be upheld. The importance of appearances is, in my judgment, generally more limited in this context than in a judicial context. [70]–[71]

But Longmore LJ and Rix LJ held that appearances matter, and that the *Porter* test does apply—though it must be applied in a way that is sensitive to the circumstances. They both considered that it is a very hard test to satisfy when the claimant alleges that the party politics showed a predisposition in favour of a project [96], [109]–[110].

Start from a point that all the judges agreed on (a point established by *Amber Valley* and *Kirkstall Valley Campaign*): that the local council was 'an elected body entitled to make and carry out planning policies' [15]. Then there can be no bias in a predisposition that arises from the councillors' policies. Any of the following can be a ground for judicial review:

(1) a danger to the integrity of the process that arises, e.g., from a personal financial interest, and

(2) a refusal to pay attention to the relevant considerations ('predetermination', as Sedley J had called it in *Kirkstall Valley Campaign* (325), and

(3) policies so unreasonable that no reasonable planning authority could pursue them.

(1) certainly is a matter of bias, and the *Porter* test applies to it. But (2) and (3) are grounds for the control of the substance of discretionary decisions, which we will address in Chapters 7 and 8. Note that for predetermination, it is not enough that a councillor stuck to his or her preconceived policy; there would have to be evidence of a refusal even to consider objections. Now, there is no harm in calling (2) and (3) forms of bias, as long as that doesn't make you think that the *Porter* test should apply to the policy views of planning authorities. A person who refuses to listen to your objections is in a sense biased against you. Their refusal to listen to you is a bad attitude. And a person who does something so unreasonable that no reasonable person could do it clearly has a bad attitude, too. But that does not mean that the *Porter* test of appearances should be applied to the *Royco Homes* situation. If it were, we might as well say that the test for all grounds of judicial review is whether the fair-minded and informed observer would think that there is ground of judicial review.

For predetermination in particular, there should be no *Porter*-style appearance test, any more than there is an appearance test for *Wednesbury* unreasonableness. For the same reasons that bias was not alleged in *Royco Homes*, the court should not even listen to an argument of bias based on the notion that council members stuck too closely to party lines.[35] The court should not ask whether it might appear to an observer to be possible that a councillor's mind was closed: as Pill LJ held, 'the question is whether in fact their minds were closed' [41]. But the majority in the Court of Appeal has left it open to claimants to say that the party politics of a planning committee might appear to an observer to involve a possibility that the councillors' minds were closed.

Imagine that Councillor Jones owns the company that wants to develop a piece of land, and Councillor Smith thinks that a development will be a great improvement to a town, or is a member of a party that supports the proposal. The law should presume that Councillor Jones is biased. But bias is quite irrelevant in the case of Councillor Smith. Councillor Smith must still listen to objections. If he thought before the hearing that the proposal was brilliant, it may be difficult or impossible for an objector to persuade him that it ought to be rejected. But that is not a closed mind in the sense that is relevant to the law. Councillor Smith would only have a closed mind *if he refused to consider the merits*—his opinion that the merits are in favour of the proposal is anything but a refusal to consider the merits. The planning business should never have been confused by litigation over bias in the politics of planning. The Court of Appeal could have done more in *Lewis* to stop litigation in which an opponent to a scheme alleges that the pattern of voting by party members in a local planning committee might appear to an observer to involve a possibility of bias.

Of course, the opponents may be right in their view that the approval of a project is a disaster for their community, *and* that the politicians were not really listening to them because they were just toeing the party line. But that is not bias in a sense

---

[35] Not that party political behaviour cannot be unlawful, or cannot amount to bias. If a political party bribed a council member, that would be bias, and if it ordered its members not to consider objections, that might result in predetermination.

that the law can cope with. It is actually a breach of comity for the courts to be asking, as the Administrative Court asked in *Lewis*, whether a local planning decision was too political. And the Court of Appeal leaves the door ajar for claimants to argue that a decision may be biased if it was *very* political. The controls on malfunctioning political decisions over planning are only (1) local democracy (which sometimes works very well in recognizing and promoting genuine local interests, and sometimes doesn't), and (2) the Secretary of State's power to call in an application (and to hear appeals from a disappointed applicant). If that political process doesn't work well, the judges cannot fix it. Litigation is an effective way to slow projects down and to spend the other side's money in a dispute, but it is not an effective way to resolve the very difficult questions a community may face about whether houses should be allowed on a common, or a shopping mall on the edge of town.

5.5 Conclusion

When is it bias (that is, a bad attitude), for a public authority to act on its policy? Only when it results in a closed mind (so that the authority is not paying attention to the merits at all), or when pursuit of the policy is *Wednesbury* unreasonable (that is, so unreasonable that no public authority would do it). So, e.g., if a police authority had a policy of eliminating officers of a particular race, its decision to sack a police officer of that race would be biased. Notice that the problem is one of due process (because the police authority wouldn't be giving the officer a fair hearing) *and* substance (because the authority would be acting on an irrelevant consideration). In Chapter 6, we will be looking more closely at the difference between, and the relation between process and substance. Here, they come together. A public authority that sacks a police officer on racist grounds is *both* deciding on substantively improper grounds, *and* failing to treat the officer with due process. The decision is biased, but the doctrine of bias has nothing to add to the doctrines of control of discretion that we will address in Chapters 7 and 8.

> **It is unlawful to rely on irrelevant considerations, and a bias is a disposition to rely on irrelevant considerations.**
> Bias plays a distinct role in the judicial control of administrative decisions, when the judges do not have to decide what the relevant considerations are, in order to identify a possibility that a decision maker will rely on irrelevant considerations (such as when the decision maker has a personal financial interest).

This fact about bias shows, incidentally, why the entire law of due process is connected with the substance of decision making: the main point of requiring procedures, like the point of outlawing bias, is to get decisions made on the relevant considerations. As Sedley J said in *Kirkstall Valley Campaign Ltd*, the *audi alteram partem* ('listen to each side'—see p 118) principle is 'one application of the wider principle that all relevant matters must be taken into account' (324).

Any obligation to give a hearing of any kind implies some sort of rule against bias, because a biased decision maker isn't listening. Alertness to the considerations that a party may offer is an essential part of a hearing. In *Stansbury v Datapulse Plc* [2003] EWCA Civ 1951, when an Employment Tribunal member had been drinking alcohol and fell asleep, the Court of Appeal found 'an analogy with cases of bias' [28]. Relying on the *Porter* test, the Court quashed the decision because 'the hearing should be by a tribunal each member of which is concentrating on the case before him or her' [28].

Note, though, that the rule against bias applies without regard to any entitlement to a hearing, or to any procedural participation in a decision. In *McInnes v Onslow-Fane* [1978] 1 WLR 1520, it was held that even where there was no right to a hearing or to reasons for a decision not to award a boxing manager's licence, 'the board were under a duty to reach an honest conclusion, without bias, and not in pursuance of any capricious policy' (Megarry VC, 1530).

TAKE-HOME MESSAGE • • •

- A **bias** is a disposition to decide against a party for some improper reason, regardless of the merits of the question being decided.

- A decision maker must be **impartial** when fairness requires it. Unfair partiality is bias, but not all decisions must be made impartially.

- The rule against bias applies to all decisions by public authorities, but impartiality is only required in decision making that is relevantly similar to the role of judge or juror in a court:
  - judges and jurors need to start their hearings with no predisposition to decide one way rather than another (except that a judge may quite properly hear a case even if she starts out with a strongly held view that goes against the argument that one of the parties wants to make on a general question of law); and
  - it is not unfair (e.g.) for a public authority who suspects an employee of misconduct to make a disciplinary decision, after hearing a public servant's side of the story, or for planning authorities to pursue their planning policies in a responsible way.

- The **principle of relativity** determines when impartiality is required: the fairness or unfairness of a particular sort of predisposition depends on the nature of the decision.

- **Relations** or **interests** that might lead to an improper disposition are enough to disqualify a decision maker automatically.

- The appearance of the possibility of an unfair disposition is enough to disqualify a decision maker.

···· Critical reading ···

R v Amber Valley DC, ex p Jackson [1985] 1 WLR 298

R (Alconbury) v Environment Secretary [2001] UKHL 23

Porter v Magill [2001] UKHL 67

Begum v Tower Hamlets LBC [2003] UKHL 5

Davidson v Scottish Ministers [2004] UKHL 34

R (Al-Hasan) v Home Secretary [2005] UKHL 13

R (Lewis) v Redcar and Cleveland [2008] EWCA Civ 746

CRITICAL QUESTIONS • • •

1   Is the point of quashing decisions for the mere appearance of a possibility bias to avoid damage that would be done to the good repute of the legal system, if bystanders are shocked at an unfairness? Or is it to protect the affected party from abuse?

2   Can it ever count as bias, for an administrative authority to base a decision on its policy?

3   The common law of due process applies broadly, but flexibly, to administrative decisions, and that is 'one relevant divergence' between the common law and the European Convention (R (Wooder) v Feggetter [2002] EWCA Civ 554 [46]). What other divergences are there?

4   What difference is there, if any, between making an unreasonable decision, and being biased?

5   It would have taken a 'study of the division of power between administrative and judicial organs', in order for the framers of the European Convention to deal explicitly with the role that independence ought to play in administrative decision making (see section 5.3.1). What would that study have to accomplish? How could Art 6 be redrafted to address the problem explicitly?

Further question:

6   In 2004, Amnesty International campaigned against the Belmarsh detentions,[36] and Lord Hoffmann gave the most strongly worded condemnation of the detentions in the House of Lords decision holding the detentions to be unlawful (A and X v Home Secretary [2004] UKHL 56—see section 1.1.1). The House of Lords held that it had been unlawful for Lord Hoffmann to sit in the Pinochet decision, because of his work as a fundraiser for Amnesty International. But it would have been unthinkable for him to be ruled out of A and X v Home Secretary. Why?

---

[36]   http://news.bbc.co.uk/1/hi/magazine/3714864.stm.

online resource centre

Visit the online resource centre to access the following resources which accompany this chapter: links to legislation and online reports of judicial decisions, summaries of key cases and legislation, updates in the law, suggestions for answering the pop quizzes and questions, and links to useful websites.

6 Reasons: process and substance

This chapter illustrates the principle of relativity (see p 10), by explaining why public authorities may or may not be required to give reasons for their decisions, depending on the type of decision and its context.

The chapter will conclude with an explanation of the difference, and the connection, between the substance of a decision and the process by which it is made. That discussion will prepare the way for the discussion of how judges review the substance of decisions in the following chapters.

LOOK FOR • • •

- The reasons why public authorities should *sometimes* explain their reasons for a decision:
  - requiring reasons may improve decisions;
  - it may be unfair (to a person affected by the decision) for the decision to be unexplained; and
  - reasons may support judicial review, and may improve transparency and accountability in government in other ways.

- The link between duties to give **reasons for** a decision, and duties to give **disclosure before** making a decision.

- The *Padfield* Practicality Principle: even where no one has a right to reasons, a public authority may need to give reasons, in order to avoid a conclusion on judicial review that it acted unlawfully.

- Reasons why public authorities do not always need to give reasons.

- The difference, and the relationship, between process and substance.

> ❛ (T)he duty to give reasons...is a function of due process, and therefore of just-
> ice. Its rationale has two principal aspects. The first is that fairness surely requires
> that the parties especially the losing party should be left in no doubt why they have
> won or lost....The second is that a requirement to give reasons concentrates the
> mind; if it is fulfilled, the resulting decision is much more likely to be soundly based
> on the evidence than if it is not....Transparency should be the watchword. ❜
> Flannery v Halifax Estate Agencies [2000] 1 WLR 377 (CA), 381 (Henry LJ)

6.1 Giving reasons for decisions

The giving of reasons is a procedural step that informs people affected by a decision (and, potentially, the public) of the substance of a decision. It seems to be a very
attractive general notion that public authorities ought to explain their decisions. It
is an advance in accountability in itself. It is a step toward open government, and
it can show respect for the persons affected by a decision. And it seems that a court
can require a public authority to give reasons with no breach of comity (see p 114),
because a requirement of reasons does not tell the public authority how to decide, but
only requires it to be candid about its own reasons. Even here, though, the requirements of the law ought to depend on the context. Sometimes there is just no reason
for the law to require administrative authorities to explain themselves.

Public authorities have no general legal duty to give reasons for their decisions.[1]
It has often been suggested that this is an outdated idea, and that the remarkable
advances in procedural protections since the 1950s have reversed it, so that reasons
must be given for administrative decisions unless there is some exceptional excuse.[2]
But in fact it is a very important and durable principle, for two reasons:

- **Standing before the public authority:** A public authority has no duty to explain a
  decision to people who are not affected by it. So for example, Lord Bridge's classic
  statement of the doctrine of fairness in Lloyd v McMahon [1987] AC 625 concerns
  'decisions affecting individuals', and does not give rights to one individual to be
  told the reasons for a decision as to another individual's position.

  Standing to insist on reasons is an implicit, seldom discussed restriction on
  legal duties of public authorities to explain themselves. Even where there is a duty
  to give reasons, it will only be owed to persons whose legally protected interests
  are affected by the decision.[3]

---

[1]   McInnes v Onslow-Fane [1978] 1 WLR 1520, 1531 (Megarry V-C), R v Home Secretary, ex p Doody [1994]
   1 AC 531, 564 (Lord Mustill). As Sedley J said in R v Higher Education Funding Council, ex p Institute
   of Dental Surgery [1994] 1 WLR 242 (DC), 'there being no general obligation to give reasons, there
   will be decisions for which fairness does not demand reasons' (258).

[2]   See, e.g., R (Wooder) v Feggetter [2002] EWCA Civ 554, below.

[3]   On standing before courts, see Chapter 11.

Open standing under the Freedom of Information Act 2000
The Act gives a *general* right of access to information to 'Any person making a request for information to a public authority' (s 1(1)). That right gives general access to reasons for a decision if the public authority has a record of them, and if the information is not exempt from disclosure under Part II of the Act (see p 27).

- **The principle of relativity** (see p 10): Even individuals directly affected by a public authority's decision may have no right to know the reasons for it, depending on the context. Examples:
  - general policy announcements by government departments will often be accompanied by reasons, but the government has no legal duty to give reasons just because it has decided on a policy; and
  - even decisions that directly affect particular people do not necessarily carry a duty to give reasons. If 100 people apply for a job in the civil service, the 99 unsuccessful applicants have no legal right to be told the reasons why the department decided to hire someone else.

The absence of a general duty to give reasons does not simply mean that public authorities do not always have to explain themselves. It also means that before a court imposes any requirement of reasons on any public authority, there has to be a specific, legal reason for reasons. Reasons must have some legally recognized **process value** (see p 111), or the law does not require them.

It is important to remember these points from the start, because they can easily be forgotten when you see the remarkable judicial extension of duties to give reasons since *Ridge v Baldwin* [1964] AC 40. The rationale for this extension is the same as the rationale for the extension of disclosure (see p 127). In fact, a duty to give reasons at one stage in the administrative process is a duty to disclose useful information for the next stage, when a complainant seeks recourse in a complaint within a government department, or in a tribunal. Reasons for an administrative decision also have the effect of advance disclosure for judicial review, enabling a person to formulate a challenge before seeking permission to apply for judicial review. Reasons are *especially* important because the grounds of judicial review are restricted. If the judges simply gave a new hearing and re-decided the issue that an administrative decision maker had addressed, the court would not need to know the decision maker's reasons.

So *R v Home Secretary, ex p Doody* [1994] 1 AC 531 is both the leading case on reasons for administrative decisions, and the leading case on disclosure: the House of Lords required the Home Secretary both to *disclose* the judges' recommendation regarding the tariff to be served by a life sentence prisoner, and to *give reasons* for his own decision. Then the prisoner would be able to use those reasons as the basis for an application for judicial review. The extension of duties to give reasons is part of a trend that Lord Mustill described in that case, toward greater transparency in administration.

The same things that make a hearing desirable can make the giving of reasons desirable. Lord Justice Sedley has given a pithy statement of some of the benefits and drawbacks of reasons, and it could equally be a statement of benefits and drawbacks of hearings:

> ‘The giving of reasons may among other things concentrate the decision-maker's mind on the right questions; demonstrate to the recipient that this is so; show that the issues have been conscientiously addressed and how the result has been reached; or alternatively alert the recipient to a justiciable flaw in the process. On the other side of the argument, it may place an undue burden on decision-makers; demand an appearance of unanimity where there is diversity; call for the articulation of sometimes inexpressible value judgments; and offer an invitation to the captious to comb the reasons for previously unsuspected grounds of challenge’.[4]

So, like hearings, reasons can have:

- **process value** (the values of promoting good outcomes, showing respect for persons affected, and subjecting the administration to the rule of law),

- **process cost** (they are an expensive chore to produce, and they may generate pointless litigation over the wrong choice of words), and even

- **process danger** (the danger of distorting good decision making).

It may seem that the value of reasons is only superficial, because the public authority can simply say what it knows will sound proper, since there is no way of getting at its *real* reasons. But a right to be given reasons can be really valuable. Even a losing party who deeply disagrees with the explanation for a decision is in a better position than a losing party who is given no explanation. Reasons give the losing party something to criticize in public. The mere fact that the public authority had to give reasons confers a gesture of respect on the losing party. The **value of respect** is equally important in both judicial and administrative decision making: reasons treat a person affected by a decision as someone to whom an account must be given.

Reasons may **promote good outcomes** by focusing the mind of a decision maker who knows that the decision must not only be made, but also *explained*. What is more, giving reasons can promote good outcomes by controlling future decisions. Consider the giving of reasons *by judges* in the common law: it shows the outcome value of reasons, because it allows the courts to use a sophisticated doctrine of precedent to control the law. If judges did not give reasons, they could not make law. Publicizing their reasons gives the courts a way of developing and improving the standards that they use to decide disputes, and achieving more uniform adherence to those standards. In administrative decision making, the importance of that value is generally more limited than it is in the common law courts. But in the work of certain appeal tribunals, such as the Employment Appeals Tribunal, it has the same value as in the courts. And the new Upper Tribunal will have the opportunity to use its reasons to control the work of tribunals (see p 446).

---

4   *Institute of Dental Surgery*, 257–8.

More important in administrative decision making is the **rule-of-law** value of giving an open account—not only to persons affected, but to the public—of administrative conduct. A duty to give reasons creates a direct and significant way of holding a public authority to account for its adherence to the law. And reasons, therefore, facilitate judicial review, which in turn is designed to uphold the rule of law. So *Doody* was a major step in the process by which the judges attempted to impose the rule of law on the Home Secretary's power to set tariffs for life sentence prisoners, before the power was taken away under the Human Rights Act (see p 50).

In *judges*' decisions, reasons can promote the rule of law because the public explanation of a decision is the most important technique of judicial accountability. Courts give reasons not just for the benefit of the parties, and not only to facilitate the development of the law, but also to show the community that the judges are themselves ruled by law. Responsible judicial conduct depends on the judges' integrity, and therefore on the various institutional and cultural factors that sustain their integrity (such as a good appointments process, good legal education, and an independent-minded bar). Accountability supports responsible judging in the same way that it supports other aspects of responsible government. But in the courts, the giving of reasons is the judges' *only* form of accountability, since their independence forbids any other way of calling them to account for the soundness of their decision making. In administrative decision making, by contrast, reasons play a part in a complex system of accountability involving appeals to tribunals, judicial review, investigations by ombudsmen, and inspection and regulation by auditors and other authorities.

Finally, it is worth noting the reflexive value of requiring reasons: they promote due process. Reasons vindicate a person's participation in the process, by requiring the public authority to *respond* to the representations that a person made in a hearing. And reasons may expose a process failure by showing that the decision was based on considerations that a party had no opportunity to address.[5]

When does a public authority need to give reasons? As with hearings, the only general statement we can make about reasons is that they are required if:

- legislation (including the Human Rights Act) requires reasons (see sections 6.1.1–6.1.3), or

- it would be unfair not to explain the decision to the person seeking reasons (see section 6.1.4).

6.1.1 Legislation: the Tribunals and Inquiries Act 1958

Even before *Ridge v Baldwin*, the Tribunals and Inquiries Act 1958 required tribunals to give reasons for decisions, and in this century reasons are a deep-rooted feature of the system that is emerging from the reconstruction of tribunals (see Chapter 12). The effect of the 1958 Act was dramatic: in R *v IRC, ex p Federation of Self-Employed and Small Businesses* [1982] AC 617, Lord Diplock pointed out that the Act

---

5   The plaintiff made this claim, unsuccessfully, in *Lloyd v McMahon* [1987] 1 AC 625, 697.

had made a statement of reasons mandatory for 'many administrative decisions that had previously been cloaked in silence; and the years that followed...witnessed a dramatic liberalisation of access to the courts.' The development was part of 'that progress towards a comprehensive system of administrative law that I regard as having been the greatest achievement of the English courts in my judicial lifetime' (640, 641).

After the 1958 Act, scrutinizing a tribunal's reasons became the stock in trade of lawyers acting for people with a complaint against a public authority, both because the reasons might disclose that the decision was based on an error of law or an irrelevant consideration, *and also* because an inadequacy in the reasons became a ground of judicial review in itself. And this development encouraged the development, in *Doody*, of common law duties to give reasons in decisions not governed by the 1958 Act.

6.1.2 The Human Rights Act 1998

Article 5(2) of the European Convention requires reasons to be given for an arrest. Article 6 only states that, in the determination of civil rights and obligations, 'Judgment shall be pronounced publicly'. But the European Court of Human Rights has held that pronouncing judgment generally requires reasons (*Helle v Finland* (1998) 26 EHRR 159). So, where Art 6 applies to an administrative decision (see p 166), there is a general right to reasons. 'Judgment' must normally be 'a reasoned judgment' (*English v Emery Reinbold & Strick Ltd* [2002] EWCA Civ 605 [7]).

The European Court of Human Rights has linked the requirement of reasons to 'the proper administration of justice' (*Garcia Ruiz v Spain* (2001) 31 EHRR 22 [26]). It has also been linked to fairness (*English* at [7]), and to the need to make appeal rights meaningful (*Hadjianastassiou v Greece* (1992) 16 EHRR 219 [33]). So the right to reasons under Art 6 has the same complex basis as rights to reasons at common law. And like duties to give reasons in the common law, 'The extent to which this duty to give reasons applies may vary according to the nature of the decision' (*Ruiz Torija v Spain* (1995) 19 EHRR 553 [29]).

Aside from the impact of Art 6, reasons may be required for interferences with the interests protected by other Convention rights. Lord Justice Sedley has held that Art 8 (the right to respect for private and family life) 'recognises a standard of protection of personal autonomy' (*R (Wooder) v Feggetter* [2002] EWCA Civ 554 [47]), which requires reasons for decisions that interfere with that autonomy. But he also held that the common law development since *Doody* provides the very same basis for requiring reasons. It shows that reasons requirements, like much of the law of administrative procedures, are essentially the same in the common law and under the Human Rights Act.

As a result, the principles of reason-giving are the same under the Convention as at common law, and the Human Rights Act only makes a difference to the law of reasons in two ways:

- decisions of the Strasbourg Court as to when the principles apply must be taken into account by English judges (Human Rights Act 1998 s 2), and

- by the Human Rights Act 1998 s 4, a statutory provision that reasons need not be given for such interferences with personal autonomy could be declared incompatible with the Convention.

6.1.3 European Community law

Article 253 of the EC Treaty provides that:

> ‘ Regulations, directives and decisions adopted jointly by the European Parliament and the Council, and such acts adopted by the Council or the Commission, shall state the reasons on which they are based and shall refer to any proposals or opinions which were required to be obtained pursuant to this Treaty. ’

Like reasons under the European Convention on Human Rights, the reasons for this EC reasons requirement lie in the same combination of fairness, the rule of law, and transparency, as in English law: ‘[Art 253] ... seeks to give an opportunity to the parties of defending their rights, to the court of exercising its supervisory functions and to Member States and to all interested nationals of ascertaining the circumstances in which the Commission has applied the Treaty’ (Case 24/62 *Germany v Commission* [1963] ECR 63, 69). And here, too, the principle of relativity is recognized: ‘the statement of reasons required by Article [253] of the Treaty must be appropriate to the nature of the measure in question’ (Cases C-71/95, C-155/95, C-271/95 *Belgium v Commission* [1997] ECR I-687 [53]).

The question whether a statement of reasons meets the requirements of Art 253 ‘must be assessed with regard not only to its wording but also to its context and to all the legal rules governing the matter in question. Moreover, the degree of precision of the statement of the reasons for a decision must be weighed against practical realities and the time and technical facilities available for making the decision’ (Case C-180/96 *UK v Commission of the European Communities* [1998] ECR I-2265).

6.1.4 Fairness

As for the common law of fairness, it is in flux. We can best understand the flux as a developing attempt to give effect to the **process values** of showing respect for persons, promoting good outcomes, and supporting the rule of law. There is a common law duty to give reasons when it would be unfair not to do so. By focusing on fairness to the claimant, the common law also promotes the rule of law and good decision making.

But the value of reasons is limited, and fairness does not require reasons that would be pointless or worse. Suppose that a police authority has to appoint a chief of police. Suppose that a good outcome will be the choice (other things being equal) of the candidate with the best combination of leadership ability, expertise in police work, and organizational skills. Achieving that outcome depends on the sensitivity of the committee members, and the grasp of the candidates' abilities that they can develop in the appointment process. It may be possible for the committee members to explain their sense of the candidates' abilities. But requiring them to do so would not promote a good outcome. Giving reasons would not actually promote the rule of law, either: you might say that an assessment of the leadership ability of a candidate need not and cannot be ruled by law, except by the doctrine of impartiality (Chapter 5), and by substantive controls aimed against abuse of power (Chapter 7). And while it is extremely important for the selection committee to act with respect toward the candidates, the law cannot improve its conduct by requiring the committee to explain to an unsuccessful candidate why it came to the conclusion that another candidate would make a better chief of police. The crucial issue in the decision is the comparison of the abilities of the candidates, and an unsuccessful candidate has no right to an account of the talents of the successful candidate. It would be pointless to give reasons for a decision, and so it is fair to refuse to do so. Reasons are not required if they would not help with an appeal, would not help you to understand what had happened to you, and would not make the decision more transparent.

The requirements of fairness are very different if a police authority is deciding to *dismiss* a chief of police. In *Ridge v Baldwin*, one of the Chief Constable's complaints was that when the police authority dismissed him, it only stated a general finding of 'negligence', with no particulars. Lord Reid said, 'I fully accept that where an office is simply held at pleasure the person having power of dismissal cannot be bound to disclose his reasons' ([1964] AC 40, 66). The House of Lords held that there *was* a duty to give reasons in Ridge's case, because the police authority only had lawful authority to dismiss on grounds of negligence or unfitness. A dismissal on those grounds must be explained. The requirement of reasons in *Ridge* reflects all three of the process values: the value of respect, the interest in good outcomes, and the rule of law. The difference between a hiring decision and a dismissal decision is that the issues are different: the question in hiring is whether someone is the best candidate; in dismissal, the question is whether someone's misconduct or incapacity has made it impossible for the employment relationship to be sustained.

Not all public servants have a right to reasons for being dismissed. Like duties to give a hearing, duties to give reasons do not simply depend on the impact of a decision on a person. We can see this from Lord Reid's statement about offices held 'at pleasure': a dismissal from such an office has just as great an impact as the dismissal in *Ridge* (and is just as capable of being unfair), but that does not mean that the law requires reasons. It is an open question, to be resolved on the general principles of fairness. Lord Reid said that a person holding an office at pleasure 'has no right to be heard before he is dismissed' (65); but we cannot expect that courts would treat that as a general rule today. Lord Reid said that there was a clear reason for the rule: 'As the person having the power of dismissal need not have anything against the officer, he need not give any reason' (65–66). But if that person purports to dismiss for misconduct, why shouldn't he or she have to hear the officer, and give reasons? Doing so might contribute to the fairness, outcome, *and* rule of law reasons for reasons. In Canada, the Supreme Court has held that the requirements of procedural fairness, including duties to give reasons, apply in the same context-dependent fashion to dismissal from offices held 'at pleasure', as in the rest of administrative law (*Knight v Indian Head School Division* [1990] 1 SCR 653). But that means that, *depending on the context*, there may be no duty to give reasons for a dismissal. The clearest example is the dismissal of a Cabinet minister; even though Lord Reid's general rule is in doubt, it is very clear that a minister has no legal right to be told the reasons for a dismissal.[6] The judges would be failing in the duty of comity they owe the Prime Minister (i.e., the respect that they owe for his role as Prime Minister), if they ordered him to give reasons for recommending that the Crown dismiss a minister. The reason is the nature of the Cabinet minister's job: the community needs him or her to be accountable to the Prime Minister in a way that is controlled by no other institution. Even by requiring reasons, the judges would be interfering with the Prime Minister's political responsibility.

What fairness depends on

Lord Bridge insisted in *Save Britain's Heritage v Number 1 Poultry Ltd* [1991] 1 WLR 153 that the duty to give reasons does not 'depend on the **degree of importance** which attaches to the matter falling to be decided' (166), but 'entirely on the **nature of the issues** falling to be decided' (167).[7]

The lack of a general duty to give reasons is not a special concession that the law gives to the executive. Reasons are not required for some of the most crucial decisions made in courts, either. In a criminal trial, juries give no reasons for a conviction. Contrast this with the decisions a trial judge makes on legal issues. Here, reasons are required to improve the decision by requiring the judge to explain it, to help the defendant with an appeal, and to improve the transparency of the decision. Yet although a murder trial is the paradigm of procedural protection for a person affected by the decision, reasons are not required for a jury conviction. They would have no process value. The instrument of a jury trial makes a conviction depend on whether ten out of twelve impartial citizens are convinced that the defendant committed murder; their judgment typically depends on their assessment of the credibility of witnesses, and always depends on judgments that might be very hard to explain. The jurors may have different reasons, and there is no reason to think that their explanation would tell the defendant anything he needs in order to understand what was happening to him, or give him any legitimate basis to appeal from a conviction.

---

[6]   'Apart from judges and others whose tenure of office is governed by statute, all servants and officers of the Crown hold office at pleasure.' *Ridge*, 65), Lord Reid. Most Crown servants today have a tenure of office governed by statute, and statutory access to tribunals for resolution of disputes. But Cabinet ministers do not.

[7]   Approved in *South Buckinghamshire District Council v Porter (No 2)* [2004] UKHL 33 [42].

> **A reminder of the limited value of reasons**
> Fairness does not require reasons for the crucial findings in a murder trial.

Judges do generally give reasons for their conclusions on the main issues in a claim or appeal, but not for all decisions (*Flannery v Halifax Estate Agencies Ltd* [2000] 1 WLR 377). Reasons are not generally given for a refusal of leave to appeal, or for some procedural decisions (*McInnes v Onslow-Fane* [1978] 1 WLR 1520, 1533). Those decisions can be crucial to the parties; yet no reasons are required unless reasons would have a distinct process value that justifies imposing a duty on the public authority. Likewise, judges do not generally need to explain why they believe one eyewitness over another. But reasons *are* to be given for preferring one expert witness over another, if the decision between them depends on argument that the judge could articulate (*Flannery*, 377).

And the judge's duty to give reasons develops with the law: reasons were generally not given for an award of costs before the Civil Procedure Rules 1998, since costs went to the winner of the litigation except in exceptional circumstances. But the new rules gave the courts wider grounds on which to use costs to encourage parties not to waste time and money in litigation, with the result that judges may have more explaining to do. If a costs award needs explanation, the Court of Appeal may send it back for the judge to give reasons (*English v Emery Reimbold & Strick* [2002] EWCA Civ 605).

The conclusion is that the question of whether fairness requires reasons does not depend on the *impact of the decision*, but on **the process value of giving the reasons.**

6.2 The deprivation principle

The process value of reasons generally does lead to a duty to explain administrative decisions that deprive a person of a right, or of a legitimate expectation. So there is a general duty to give reasons for disciplinary or punitive decisions. *Ridge v Baldwin* is an example, but the rule extends more broadly today than it did in 1964. This requirement matches the requirement of disclosure before a decision in such cases (see p 127). The prospect of a deprivation of a right or a legitimate expectation means that the persons affected are entitled to know the case against them:

- through disclosure, in order to know what the public authority is thinking of doing to them, and to participate in the decision-making process, and

- through reasons, in order to understand what has been done to them, and also to pursue any available recourse (in administrative justice or through the courts).

Disclosure and reasons vindicate the right to a hearing in such cases.

In *McInnes v Onslow-Fane*, the plaintiff wanted to know why he was refused a licence to work as a boxing manager; Megarry VC pointed out that 'There may be no "case against him" at all, in the sense of something warranting forfeiture or expulsion' (1532). But how could McInnes know whether there *was* a case against him, without reasons? The result of *McInnes* is that, if a decision *needn't* be based on a case against the applicant, he has no right to the reasons that would let him know whether the decision *was* based on a case against him. Is that unfair? The solution to this puzzle is that because the public authority was deciding *whether to give* a licence, rather than *whether to revoke one*, it did not matter whether the decision was based on a case against McInnes. His case was not a deprivation case: he was only applying for a licence, and did not even have a legitimate expectation of being given one. Megarry VC pointed out that 'A man free from any moral blemish may nevertheless be wholly unsuitable for a particular type of work.' He concluded that McInnes had no right to reasons 'in the absence of anything to suggest that the board have been affected by dishonesty or bias or caprice, or that there is any other impropriety' (1535).

6.3 The duty of respect

The courts have made it clear that reasons will very often be required in order to facilitate judicial review. The point was made explicitly in the landmark decision of *R v Home Secretary, ex p Doody* [1994] 1 AC 531:

> ❝ the decision of the Home Secretary on the penal element is susceptible to judicial review. To mount an effective attack on the decision, given no more material than the facts of the offence and the length of the penal element, the prisoner has virtually no means of ascertaining whether this is an instance where the decision-making process has gone astray. I think it important that there should be an effective means of detecting the kind of error which would entitle the court to intervene, and in practice I regard it as necessary for this purpose that the reasoning of the Home Secretary should be disclosed. ❞ (565)

This important holding does *not* mean that reasons must be given for every decision that could be judicially reviewed (if that were the case, there *would* be a general duty to give reasons for an administrative decision). Lord Mustill's remark depended on the facts in *Doody*.[8] In *McInnes v Onslow-Fane*, Megarry VC had held that the Boxing Board of Control did not even need to give the gist of its reasons for refusing a license (if there was no legitimate expectation of receiving a licence). Discouraging litigation actually counted in favour of the decision: 'I can well see that the board would be...reluctant to give reasons (whether full or in outline) which might provide ammunition for litigation against the board' (1536). Are *McInnes* and *Doody* inconsistent, since *McInnes* used the prospect of litigation as an argument against reasons, and *Doody* required reasons to *assist* the claimant in litigation? No: consider the difference

---

[8]   As Lord Justice Sedley pointed out in *R v Higher Education Funding Council, ex p Institute of Dental Surgery* [1994] 1 WLR 242, 257.

between the application for a boxing manager's licence in *McInnes*, and the setting of a tariff in *Doody*. The **relevance doctrine** (see p 267) required the courts to scrutinize the tariff-setting decision in a way that an application for a licence is not scrutinized. So the mere fact that a decision is subject to judicial review does not mean that a public authority has a duty to give reasons. Reasons are required *when a claimant for judicial review needs the public authority's reasons in order for the process of judicial review to be fair*. Even that restricted requirement places a very significant onus on public authorities to give reasons for decisions that **penalize**, or **discipline**, or **deprive a person of a legitimate expectation**.

We can generalize further, in fact: 'one of the classes of case where the common law implies a duty to give reasons is where the subject matter is an interest so highly regarded by the law (for example, personal liberty) that fairness requires that reasons, at least for particular decisions, be given as of right' (R *(Wooder) v Feggetter* [2002] EWCA Civ 554 [24], Lord Justice Brooke). In *Wooder's* case, a psychiatrist decided to give an anti-psychotic drug to a patient who had been detained in a mental health institution since he had killed a man in 1985. The patient did not consent; the psychiatrist prescribed the drug, and then asked for the second opinion that the law requires before drugs can be forced on a patient without consent. The second doctor agreed that the drug treatment was needed, but the patient was not given the second doctor's reasons for agreeing. The Court of Appeal held that reasons had to be given.[9]

Notice two ways in which *Wooder* goes beyond the approach that had been suggested in *Ridge*, and affirmed in *Doody*. First, there was no allegation of misconduct, for which Wooder ought to be heard in his own defence. In *Ridge's* case, there were suggestions (though not in Lord Reid's speech) that Ridge might not have been entitled to reasons if the police authority had dismissed him for unfitness, rather than for neglect of duty. Secondly, the relevant considerations in *Wooder* were a matter for professional expertise. It might seem that there is no process value in giving reasons for a decision, when a layperson would have no relevant contribution to offer to the process. Note also that because the decision was based on the doctor's professional judgment, the value of reasons to the patient in judicial review would be very limited: the court is not in a position to second-guess the second opinion. Requiring a second opinion is itself the chief legal protection against arbitrary use of the power to force drug treatment on an unwilling patient.

The duty of **respect** (see p 110) calls for reasons in such a case: some decisions cannot fairly be made without the best attempt at an explanation, even if the person subject to the decision has nothing to contribute to the making of the decision. The only process value in disclosure is the important value of treating the person as someone to whom an explanation is due. Lord Justice Brooke based his decision on 'the social justice benefit' of explaining the decision [28]. And Lord Justice Sedley held that the decision was 'so invasive of physical integrity and moral dignity that it

---

9   The Court of Appeal made the duty to give reasons subject to an *exception*, where the giving of reasons itself would be 'likely to cause serious harm to the physical or mental health of the patient or any other person' [30].

calls without more for disclosure of the reasons for it' [37]. We can still say that the duty of respect does not require reasons to be given when they would be pointless; but they are not pointless when refusing to explain would itself be abusive.

● *Pop Quiz* ●
In *Wooder*, should the doctors be required to give the patient their reasons *before* administering the drug? Or is it good enough to explain afterwards?

6.4 Trigger factors for reasons

The *Wooder* approach is an important further step in the trend toward open decision making (see p 127); it raises a question as to how much further the courts will go in requiring reasons for professional assessments. Eight years before *Wooder*, a limit had been drawn in *Institute of Dental Surgery*. The Funding Council's grants to educational institutions were based on its assessment of their research quality, for which it gave no reasons. In the Divisional Court, Sedley J held that in cases like *Doody*, 'the nature and impact of the decision itself call for reasons as a routine aspect of procedural fairness' (262). Where that is *not* the case, 'some trigger factor is required to show that, in the circumstances of the particular decision, fairness calls for reasons to be given'.

Compare requirements to give a *hearing*. A similar divide can be made between cases in which there is a right to a hearing because of the nature and impact of the decision (such as *Ridge* or *Cooper* (1863) 14 CB (NS) 180), and cases in which there is a right to a hearing *only if* some particular feature of the claimant's case makes it unfair for the public authority to proceed without hearing from the claimant.

Let's call the the latter kind of cases 'trigger-factor' cases; *McInnes v Onslow-Fane* is an example of a trigger-factor case in which no such feature could be made out, so that it was *not* unfair to refuse to give reasons. In cases like *Ridge* (which discipline, penalize, deprive of a legal right or legitimate expectation etc.), the common law requirement of reasons is like a statutory requirement of reasons: it makes reason-giving part of the administrative routine. In trigger-factor cases, the public authority has to be ready to explain itself only if some special consideration makes it necessary.

Sedley J's example of a 'trigger factor' case was R v Civil Service Appeal Board, ex p Cunningham [1992] ICR 816 (CA). The Appeal Board in that case had power to order compensation for unfair dismissal, and without giving reasons it awarded Cunningham less than half what he would have received from an employment tribunal; that discrepancy provided the trigger factor that called for an explanation. In *Institute of Dental Surgery*, Sedley J held that 'purely academic judgments' are in the *Cunningham* category rather than the *Doody* category: the Funding Council had no legal duty to give reasons unless a trigger factor made it unfair to proceed without an explanation. He held that 'an apparently inexplicable decision may be a sufficient but is not a necessary condition for requiring reasons' (*Institute of Dental Surgery*, 259). That possible trigger factor must be restricted to decisions that are *justiciably* inexplicable, or the judges would not be able to determine that it is unfair for the public authority not to give reasons. The court must be able to identify a trigger factor in the decision without passing judgments that it cannot legitimately pass (on justiciability, see p 239). Suppose that a university student and her teachers have good reason to think that the student must have performed better on an exam than the grade reflects; that in itself gives no ground to demand reasons for the assessment from the university.

If the trigger factor is, as in *Institute of Dental Surgery*, an apparently inexplicable feature of a decision, it must be something that the court can itself properly identify as so peculiar that it is only fair for the person affected to have an explanation. That feature may arise from the context in which the decision is made. In R v DPP, *ex p Manning* [2001] QB 330, Lord Bingham CJ held that neither the common law nor the Convention impose an 'absolute' obligation on a prosecutor to give reasons for a decision not to prosecute. But where an inquest gives a verdict of unlawful killing by an identifiable person, 'the ordinary expectation would naturally be that a prosecution would follow. In the absence of compelling grounds for not giving reasons, we would expect the Director to give reasons in such a case' [33].

Can you get reasons for academic judgments?

Universities and colleges can grade undergraduate exam papers without giving reasons for the grade. But in examining graduate research degrees, the universities have a general and consistent practice of asking for reports from the examiners explaining the reasons for the examiners' recommendations, and those reports are regularly given to the student. If a university failed a doctoral candidate without providing reasons, a court in judicial review would presumably require reasons, even if the university's own rules did not require it—either because of the student's **legitimate expectation** based on the practice, or because of the unfairness of giving no explanation for the rejection of a thesis that represents years of work. So reasons can be expected for one of the most difficult forms of academic judgment. This is the case even though the court would defer (more or less completely) to the examiners' judgment as to whether the thesis met the standard for the degree. The reasons for reasons in such a case are analogous to the reasons in *Wooder*: to show respect for the person on whom judgment is being passed, and to bring openness and a form of accountability to a decision that would otherwise be dangerously secret.

The contrasting unavailability of reasons for undergraduate grades can be explained partly by the massive **process cost** that it would take to give a similar report on the strengths and weaknesses of each examination script.[10] There is no feasible method for controlling the unavoidable forms of arbitrariness in undergraduate grading, except for careful use of double marking, and review by an

---

[10]   Compare the grading of GCSE and A Level examinations, for which no reasons are given. There is a clerical checking service, a re-marking process, you can get your script back, and there is an appeal following a re-mark—but you do not get reasons for the mark.

internal committee and by external examiners. Students and universities (and for that matter, employers reading a transcript) have to rely on the skill, commitment and integrity of markers. Administrative law has hardly anything to contribute.

In the *Institute of Dental Surgery* case, Sedley J pointed out that undergraduate marking decisions are not insulated from judicial review, even though the court will have to defer to the academic judgment of the examiners: '…where what is sought to be impugned is on the evidence *no more* than an informed exercise of academic judgment, fairness alone will not require reasons to be given. This is not to say for a moment that academic decisions are beyond challenge. A mark, for example, awarded at an examiners' meeting where irrelevant and damaging personal factors have been allowed to enter into the evaluation of a candidate's written paper is something more than an informed exercise of academic judgment' (262). That approach does not mean that reasons will be required for an unexpectedly low grade on an examination.[11]

Awarding of grades in university is a reminder of the basic principle that public authorities have no general duty to give reasons for decisions—even decisions that affect a person profoundly.

After *Doody, Institute of Dental Surgery*, and *Wooder*, there is still a wide variety of decisions—even decisions that shape a particular person's future—for which no reasons need be given. There is no general duty to give reasons, but the cases in which reasons must be given are not exceptional, either, because there is no general power to make a decision *without* giving reasons. It all depends on the purpose of the decision, and on the context. And reasons can be required in contexts where they had previously been considered unnecessary. In *Wooder*, Lord Justice Brooke suggested that 'it should not be taken for granted that the HEFC [*Institute of Dental Surgery*] case would be decided in the same way today. Indeed, it might well have been decided a different way [i.e., if it had gone to the Court of Appeal] in 1993' [23].

Who or what deserves respect?

Do Cooper[12] or McInnes[13] or Ridge,[14] who are human beings, deserve a form of respect that the Institute of Dental Surgery does not deserve? The courts have not differentiated between personal claimants and businesses, and they do not generally need to. Giving process rights to business organizations shows respect for the human beings they serve, and promotes good outcomes, and serves the rule of law (cf. the **standing** of public interest organizations to seek judicial review—see

---

[11] The new ombudsman service for higher education does not interfere on grounds of academic judgment, but is prepared to scrutinize a university's operation of its examination system very closely—see p 495.

[12] *Cooper v Wandsworth Board of Works* (1863) 14 CB (NS) 180.

[13] *McInnes v Onslow-Fane* [1978] 1 WLR 1520.

[14] *Ridge v Baldwin* [1964] AC 40.

p 405). But there are some special duties owed only to human beings, because the duty of respect puts special burdens on public authorities that do certain things that can only be done to human beings—such as detention, and dismissal from employment.

6.5 The *Padfield* practicality principle

Since *Padfield v Minister of Agriculture* [1968] AC 997 (see p 45), it has been well established that where a public authority has no duty to give reasons, it cannot use its own silence to insulate a decision from judicial review. The Law Lords all agreed. Lord Hodson put it most strongly: if the circumstances suggest that one of the grounds of review is made out, a minister 'would not escape from the possibility of control by mandamus through adopting a negative attitude without explanation' (1049). The result is that public authorities with no *duty* to give reasons may *need* to give the aggrieved person reasons in order to explain why their conduct is not unlawful.

Before *Padfield* reached the House of Lords, Lord Denning had paved the way in his judgment in the Court of Appeal, which is a classic of administrative law. The Minister of Agriculture had decided not to refer a complaint from farmers to a committee for investigation. Lord Denning said,

> If the Minister is to deny the complainant a hearing—and a remedy—he should at least have good reasons for his refusal: and, if asked, he should give them. If he does not do so, the court may infer that he has no good reason. If it appears to the court that the Minister has been, or must have been, influenced by extraneous considerations which ought not to have influenced him—or, conversely, has failed, or must have failed, to take into account considerations which ought to have influenced him—the court has power to interfere. (1006–7)

This practicality principle is expressed most neatly by Lord Keith in R *v Trade and Industry Secretary, ex p Lonrho plc* [1989] 1 WLR 525: even where there is no duty to give reasons, 'if all other known facts and circumstances appear to point overwhelmingly in favour of a different decision, the decision-maker, who has given no reasons, cannot complain if the court draws the inference that he had no rational reason for his decision' (540). But that was not the case in *Lonrho*, and 'the absence of reasons for a decision where there is no duty to give them cannot of itself provide any support for the suggested irrationality of the decision' (539–40).

So the cases where the practicality principle calls for reasons are similar to trigger-factor cases: the public authority's need to show that there was reason for the decision will only arise where some feature of the decision, in its context, raises a question as to whether there was any reason for it. The difference is that in a trigger-factor case, the question is whether (because of something inexplicable in a decision) it was procedurally unfair for the public authority to proceed without giving reasons. The practicality principle concerns challenges to the substance of a decision, and it applies even where the public authority has not acted unfairly: if the decision appears to be extremely unreasonable until it is explained, then the public authority had better explain. Since the possibility that a decision will appear to be unreasonable can be unpredictable to the initial decision maker (as in *Padfield*), the practicality principle means that it is good policy to explain a decision wherever it is feasible to do so, if there is someone who may seek judicial review. For this reason, *Padfield* itself has indirectly led to an increase in open government: those developments have given public authorities more cause to explain what they do.

6.6 The content of reasons

When there is a duty to give reasons, it is a duty to give *sufficient explanation, for the purpose for which reasons are required*. It was not enough for the police authority to tell Ridge that he was sacked for negligence; the authority had to explain why they held that he had been negligent.

> **Proportionality alert**
> The content of reasons provides another instance of proportionate process (see p 119). Reasons must be explicit and detailed *enough* for the purpose. Notice how proportionality acts as a *limit* on what the law requires of a public authority: the public authority need not say more than the purpose requires.

The content of reasons ought to depend on the purposes for requiring reasons, and those purposes are multiple. If the purpose is simply **transparency**, then reasons must be sufficient to demonstrate that the decision maker is acting responsibly. If the purpose is to show **respect** to a person affected, then the reasons will need to address the arguments (if any) that a claimant made. Reasons may also be given in the interest of **good outcomes** or to provide **fair disclosure** to a claimant who may wish to seek recourse against a decision. In those cases, grounds of appeal or of judicial review partly determine the extent of the reasons that a decision maker must give. The *Doody* principle means that the decision maker needs to give sufficient explanation of a decision to enable the court to decide whether there has been a process failure, or an error of law, or an unlawful use of a discretionary power. So reasons may need to:

- facilitate judicial review (R *v* Home Secretary, ex p Doody [1994] 1 AC 531[15]),

- explain the decision maker's response to representations made by a party,

- bring transparency to a decision on which there were no representations and on which the court will defer (R *(Wooder) v Feggetter* [2002] EWCA Civ 554, and doctoral examinations by universities).

---

[15] Note that in R *v* Home Secretary, ex p Venables and Thompson [1998] AC 407 (see p 69), it was the Home Secretary's reasons (the reasons that the *Doody* case required) that led to the decision being quashed on the ground of irrelevant considerations.

Reasons required under the Tribunals and Inquiries Act 1958 must not only be intelligible, but must 'deal with the substantial points that have been raised' (*Re Poyser and Mills' Arbitration* [1964] 2 QB 467, 477–8, approved by the House of Lords in *Westminster City Council v Great Portland Estates* [1985] AC 661). *Poyser and Mills* can in fact be treated as stating the general requirement for any decision given after a hearing (including under the reconstruction of tribunals—see Chapter 12): the reasons need not address 'every particular point that has been raised at the hearing', and it takes 'something substantially wrong or inadequate in the reasons' to justify interference on judicial review (478). But the decision will be unlawful if the reasons given do not address the substance of the parties' arguments. So in *Poyser and Mills*, the decision maker's statement of reasons was held to be inadequate when he identified the relevant issues and simply stated that the facts were sufficient to justify his resolution of the issues.

When reasons are required, their purpose is not to show the reviewing court that the decision was correct. Demanding reasons that show the decision to be the correct decision would presuppose a judicial power to replace another public authority's decision with its own. Correctness is not a general ground of judicial review.

And the courts have not generally demanded perfect or even complete reasons. As *Ridge v Baldwin* and *Poyser and Mills* show, it is a big mistake for a public authority merely to refer to a legislative standard that must be applied, and to state that the reason for the decision is that the standard is or is not met. On the other hand, no reasons will be required that are unnecessary in the circumstances. If someone who knows the evidence given and the submissions made at a hearing can understand why the decision was made, that is enough. So in *S v Special Educational Needs Tribunal* [1995] 1 WLR 1627 (QBD), the High Court held that reasons have to enable a party to establish whether there had been an error of law. A legal duty to give reasons may be satisfied, even if the reasons given would not adequately explain the decision to someone who was not familiar with the making of the decision. The duty to give reasons only requires an explanation that will serve the purpose for which the law requires it.

6.6.1 Reasons for planning decisions

The House of Lords has given extensive consideration to reasons requirements in controversial planning decisions, and in doing so it has established a rule against 'excessive legalism' that ought to apply generally to reasons for administrative decisions (*Save Britain's Heritage v Number 1 Poultry Ltd* [1991] 1 WLR 153; for an explanation of the planning process, see p 173).

When planning inspectors decide whether a complaint about a proposed project is well founded, and when ministers decide whether to approve a project, their reports and decisions often generate anger and resentment. But it is very hard to challenge the substance of a report or a decision. So the controversies have often taken the form of challenges to the adequacy of the reasons given. It is an example of the fact that claimants resort to procedural challenges when it is hard to challenge the substance of a decision they oppose (see p 144).

In *Bolton v Environment Secretary* (1996) 71 P&CR 309, the House of Lords unanimously overturned a Court of Appeal decision that the Environment Secretary had to address every material consideration, when giving reasons for granting planning permission for a shopping centre:

> ❛ What the Secretary of State must do is to state his reasons in sufficient detail to enable the reader to know what conclusion he has reached on the "principal important controversial issues". To require him to refer to every material consideration, however insignificant, and to deal with every argument, however peripheral, would be to impose an unjustifiable burden. ❜ (Lord Lloyd, 314)

The Law Lords have held that reasons for planning inspectors' conclusions may be brief, and need only explain what needs to be explained to people who are aware of the issues and the arguments made in the inquiry. Reasons do not need to mention every material consideration. Hoffmann LJ put it that 'The inspector is not writing an examination paper' (*South Somerset District Council v Environment Secretary* [1993] 1 PLR 80, 83, approved in *South Buckinghamshire District Council v Porter* (No 2) [2004] UKHL 33 [29], Lord Brown). Lord Bridge held in *Save Britain's Heritage* that even a *deficiency* in reasons will not be enough to justify quashing a planning report, unless the interests of the claimant 'have been substantially prejudiced by the deficiency' (*Save Britain's Heritage*, 167, approved in *Porter* [29], [36]).

But, of course, a public authority that does not address material considerations in its reasons is leaving itself a hostage to fortune. The impetus against excessive legalism may mean that a decision is safe from being quashed on a procedural challenge for inadequate reasons, but on a challenge to the substance of a decision, the court determines with hindsight which material considerations had to be addressed in order for the claimant to know whether there is ground for judicial review. So the *Padfield* Practicality Principle extends to planning inspectors: they need to explain anything that may look unreasonable in their report.

As Lord Bridge pointed out in *Save Britain's Heritage*, inadequate reasons themselves can cause substantial prejudice if 'the lacuna in the stated reasons is such as to raise a substantial doubt as to whether the decision was based on relevant grounds and was otherwise free from any flaw in the decision-making process which would afford a ground for quashing the decision' (168). That means—as Lord Mustill suggested in *Doody*—that reasons must be tailored to the grounds of judicial review. So in order to avoid excessive legalism, the courts should keep in mind the limits on those grounds, when they decide whether adequate explanation has been given for an administrative decision.

Public reasons

There are many situations in which public authorities need to explain their actions to other public authorities; the examples that have special constitutional importance are the responsibility of ministers to answer questions in Parliament about the conduct of their department, and the ministers' managerial capacity to ask questions of civil servants in their departments, and of agencies that carry out public functions on behalf of the government. But departments and other public authorities may also have to explain the reasons for their decisions to independent investigators such as ombudsmen (see Chapter 13) and auditors (see p 579).

Compare the European Convention on Human Rights Art 15(3), which imposes a control on derogations from Convention rights in time of war or other public emergency. The government must 'keep the Secretary General of the Council of Europe fully informed of the measures which it has taken and the reasons therefor'.

6.7 How to remedy inadequate reasons

If no reasons were given where they ought to have been given, or inadequate reasons have been given, should the court on judicial review allow the decision to stand and require the public authority to give reasons for it? Or should the court quash the decision? It is a basic principle of judicial process that no unnecessary proceeding should be ordered, and the same principle should apply to administrative decisions. No new hearing is necessary if the public authority can legitimately give reasons for the decision being challenged (*Flannery v Halifax Estate Agencies* [2000] 1 WLR 377 (CA)). But that may no longer be possible by the time of judicial review.

In R (O) v West London Mental Health NHS Trust [2005] EWHC 604, the defendant had a common law duty to give reasons for refusing to discharge a paranoid schizophrenic patient. When the patient pointed out that the stated reasons did not address the crucial question of whether he would be a danger to himself or others, the Trust gave further reasons addressing that point. On judicial review, the court held that in a case involving personal liberty, 'the adequacy of the reasons is itself made a condition of the legality of the decision' [18]. If that means that the court must automatically quash a decision as to personal liberty where the decision maker adds further explanation after giving inadequate reasons, it is too broad. Even if adequate reasons are a condition of the legality of a decision, the court has discretion not to give any remedy (see p 381). How should that discretion be exercised? There are two points in favour of the decision in (O), which are addressed in the decision. First is the risk that the giving of new reasons after a patient complains may amount to mere rationalization (i.e., phoney reasons) for a decision that was not made on the relevant considerations (but then, mere rationalization is a risk whenever anyone gives reasons for anything). Secondly, for decisions of the kind involved in the case, it is important for the claimant to have complete reasons not at the point when he seeks judicial review, but when the decision is made (and invalidating the decision for lack of reasons is a way of recognizing that need for timely reasons).

But if a defect in reasons can be cured by the giving of a proper explanation in response to a query or an objection to the reasons given, then there is no good reason to invalidate a decision, even if a decision is only lawful if reasons are given. It is worth considering that the *courts* are very flexible about the remedying of their own reasons: if a party applies to a trial judge for permission to appeal on the ground of lack of reasons, the judge can give additional reasons. If a party applies to an appellate court for permission to appeal on the ground of lack of reasons, the appellate court can adjourn the application and invite the trial judge to give additional reasons (see *English v Emery Reimbold & Strick Ltd* [2002] EWCA Civ 605 [25]).

6.8 Reasons and process danger

It is a very attractive idea that, as Lord Justice Henry put it, 'transparency should be the watchword' (*Flannery*, 381). But it is dangerous. In *Flannery*, the Court of Appeal ordered a retrial after a High Court judge said that he preferred the evidence of the defendant's expert witness, but did not explain why the other party's expert was wrong. Within a few months, the decision in *Flannery* led to a 'rash of applications for permission to appeal', which the Court of Appeal described as 'an industry which is an unwelcome feature of English justice' (*English* [3], [2]). In *English*, the Court dismissed three appeals in spite of 'shortcomings' in two of the sets of reasons, and held that:

> an unsuccessful party should not seek to upset a judgment on the ground of inadequacy of reasons unless, despite the advantage of considering the judgment with knowledge of the evidence given and submissions made at the trial, that party is unable to understand why it is that the judge has reached an adverse decision. [118]

It is meant to be a high hurdle: claimants have to convince the appellate court that they cannot understand why they lost. Shortcomings in the reasons are not enough.

Since the common law requirement of reasons is based on fairness, it should only require a fair explanation, not a complete or perfect explanation. The danger is that the requirement of reasons itself, if turned into a requirement of *good* reasons, will distort the legal process by generating pointless litigation by disappointed appellants who know why they lost. This danger can be kept under some sort of control through the approach in *English*, and the same approach should be taken to judicial review of administrative decisions for inadequacy of reasons. And the same approach has been taken in the European Court of Human Rights concerning the right to reasons under Art 6. That requirement has been interpreted not to require a detailed answer to every argument of a party (*Ruiz Torija v Spain* (1995) EHRR 553, 562). And in European law, the requirement of reasons in Art 253 does *not* mean that the Commission must 'discuss all the issues of fact and law raised by every party during the administrative proceedings' (Joined Cases 240–242, *Stichting Sigarettenindustrie v Commission* [1985] ECR 3831 [88]).

So the law needs to avoid the danger of demanding too much in the giving of reasons for a decision. Can it ever be dangerous to require reasons *at all*? Yes. In *R (Abbasi) v Foreign Secretary* [2002] EWCA Civ 1598 (see p 4), Abbasi's mother claimed that it was unlawful for the Foreign Secretary to complain to the Americans about the detention of a British national in Guantánamo Bay. The Court of Appeal rejected the claim, on the ground that there were potential disadvantages in complaining to the Americans, which the Foreign Secretary had to take into account, but which the judges could not assess. If that is the right decision, one question remains about *Abbasi*: why did the Court of Appeal also refuse to require the Foreign Secretary to give reasons? Here, there is no problem of justiciability: the Court would not have to answer any question it is ill-suited to answer about the disadvantages of complaining to the Americans. It need only impose on the Foreign Secretary a duty to explain *his own* reasons for not doing so. The rationale for the Court's refusal to require reasons is that *communicating reasons* would itself affect relations with the United States and other countries. Then, the mere fact of telling a public official to explain a decision might interfere illegitimately with his or her role. And then a judicial requirement of reasons would be a breach of comity between the courts and the government.

There can be process danger in ordering reasons to be given for a decision. Of course, process dangers should not be exaggerated. In *Ridge v Baldwin*, the police authority doubtless thought that the requirement of reasons was damaging to its function in serving the public interest. The House of Lords' decision in the case is a rejection of any *general* notion that it is damaging to require a public authority to explain itself.

Summary of reasons for reasons

- to **vindicate other forms of procedural participation**, by requiring the public authority to respond to representations of parties;
- to show **respect** for a person by explaining what the public authority is doing to them;
- to provide **disclosure** that may be needed for a challenge to a decision in an administrative justice process, or on judicial review;
- to increase **openness** of decision making in the public interest; and
- to provide a direct form of **accountability** by requiring a public explanation of a decision.

These reasons may or may not arise, depending on the type of decision and the circumstances. When they do arise, they reflect the three general **process values** (promoting good outcomes, showing respect, and imposing the rule of law on the administration) (see section 4.2). Unless legislation requires reasons to be given for a particular decision, the legal duty to give reasons arises only when it would be **unfair** to refuse to give reasons, in spite of the process costs involved—and in spite of any process dangers.

The act of giving reasons is a *procedural* step. It tells the person affected the *substance* of the decision. Reaching a decision for the right reasons is a matter of the substance of the decision. The rest of this chapter explains the difference between process and substance.

6.9 The difference between process and substance, and why it matters

6.9.1 The ambiguity of 'process'

Calvin's mom finds a lamp broken in the living room. She asks Calvin if he knocked it over. He says that Hobbes did it. She thinks that Hobbes can't have done it, and there is no one else on the scene. So she decides that Calvin did it, and she sends him to his room for breaking the lamp.

The *substance* of her decision is *what* she decided; it can be stated like this: 'Calvin's mom decided that ___'. So the conclusion that Calvin broke the lamp is part of the substance of the mom's decision (Calvin's mom decided *that he did it*[16]). The punishment is also part of the substance of her decision: she decided *to send him to his room*, and if (like public authorities) she is responsible for her decisions, that entails a decision *that sending him to his room was an appropriate response.*

The *process* by which she decided is the way in which she decided, so it can be stated like this: 'Calvin's mom decided by ___.' There is an ambiguity in this idea of the *way* in which a decision is made; it is an ambiguity in the idea of process. A decision is made:

(1) **by taking steps** to obtain information relevant to the decision (typically, steps that involve others in the making of the decision, such as the step of asking Calvin whether he did it), and

(2) **by reasoning**, e.g., by concluding that Hobbes can't have done it, and by reasoning that Calvin must therefore have done it.

In a 'process' in the first sense, the steps taken are procedures (see section 4.6). Other, allied actions by which a decision maker carries out its responsibility for a decision are also procedures (they include giving reasons for the decision, reconsidering it, or providing an appeal, and so on[17]). A 'process' in the second sense is a process of reasoning.

What about Calvin's mom's decision *that* Hobbes can't have broken the lamp? It is a step in reasoning to the conclusion that Calvin did it. It is part of 'process' in the sense of a process of reasoning. But it is very different from 'process' in the first sense, because *it is also part of the substance of the decision.* It is (part of) what she

---

[16] The decision *to ask Calvin* (and to listen to what he had to say) is the substance of a decision as to what procedure to use.

[17] And procedural flaws may include not only the fact that a decision maker proceeded in the wrong way, but that it is improper for the decision to be made by the person or body that made it. See Chapter 5.

decided. **The reasons for which she reaches her conclusion, and not merely the conclusion, are the substance of the decision. They are (part of) what she decided: she
decided *that* Hobbes can't have done it, and *that*, therefore, Calvin must have done it.**

The reasoning process is part of the substance of the decision. Process in the first
sense is not. Does the difference matter? It doesn't matter in Calvin's case. His mom
ought to give fair procedures, *and* the substance of her decision ought to be fair. She
shouldn't base her conclusions as to what Calvin did on assumptions that she ought
to know are false. She shouldn't punish him if he doesn't deserve it. And if he does
deserve it, she shouldn't punish him disproportionately.

But the difference matters in a system of law, in which we need one institution to
control the decisions of another. The reasons for a court to defer to another public
authority on issues of substance (which include issues of the way in which the authority reasoned) are generally different from—and more extensive than—the reasons
for a court to defer on issues of process in the first sense.

We saw in Chapter 4 that courts can generally impose due process on administrative authorities without any breach of comity. They could not generally impose *due substance* without a massive breach of comity. But throughout Chapter 4, the discussion
was of 'process' in the first, procedural sense, in which a decision maker's *reasoning*
is not part of the process at all. Difficulty has often arisen, in English administrative
law, from a confusion between the two senses of 'process'. Although it is possible for
a decision to be unlawful because of the reasoning process by which it was reached,
it is actually a fundamental principle of administrative law (seldom stated and often
disregarded), that the law does *not* require public authorities to engage in the correct
reasoning process.

6.9.2 Begum's case

Shabina Begum was sent home from school for wearing the jilbab, a long dress
designed to hide the shape of a girl's body. Her family said that her Muslim faith
demanded it. The school's uniform policy allowed the headscarf and shalwar kameeze
(a smock over a long-sleeved shirt, along with tapered trousers), but not the jilbab.
The school reasoned that her freedom of religion was not at stake, because main-
stream Muslim opinion allowed the shalwar kameeze. She claimed that the school
had infringed her right to manifest her religion under Art 9 of the Convention.

The Court of Appeal held that her freedom of religion was affected (R (Begum) v
Denbigh High School [2005] EWCA Civ 199). And the appeal judges concluded that the
school had unlawfully excluded her, even though forbidding the jilbab might be a
proportionate restriction on the freedom of religion. The school had not used the
appropriate process, because it ought to have *reasoned* that her freedom of religion
was at stake, and asked itself whether there were interests that justified a restriction
on her freedom. Begum's case is the most striking example of the potential confusion between the two senses of 'process'.

The House of Lords rejected what Lord Bingham called 'the Court of Appeal's
procedural approach', because 'what matters in any case is the practical outcome, not

the quality of the decision-making process that led to it' (*Begum* [31]). He pointed out that the Strasbourg Court takes a 'pragmatic approach', and does not find a violation of the Convention 'on the strength of failure by a national authority to follow the sort of reasoning process laid down by the Court of Appeal' [29]. And Lord Hoffmann concluded:

> ❛ In domestic judicial review, the court is usually concerned with whether the decision-maker reached his decision in the right way rather than whether he got what the court might think to be the right answer. But article 9 is concerned with substance, not procedure. It confers no right to have a decision made in any particular way. What matters is the result: was the right to manifest a religious belief restricted in a way which is not justified under article 9.2?...Head teachers and governors cannot be expected to make such decisions with textbooks on human rights law at their elbows. ❜ [68]

The Law Lords' conclusion about the Convention must be right, because Art 9 does not confer a right to a reasoning process: its purpose is to protect freedom of religion. If the school's uniform policy had the good purpose of protecting the rights and freedoms of others (by fostering an inclusive and non-competitive culture in the school), and the school pursued it without interfering disproportionately with Shabina Begum's manifestation of her religion, then the school did not infringe her right under the Convention, even if the school authorities did not follow the correct reasoning process.

But head teachers and governors cannot be expected to make their decisions with textbooks on judicial review at their elbows, either. The strange thing about the decision in Begum's case is the suggestion that 'conventional judicial review' (Lord Bingham [28]) or 'domestic judicial review' (Lord Hoffmann [68]) is 'procedural', in a way that requires that decisions be based on the right reasoning. The idea sounds like a way of expressing the role of courts in imposing due process—which, as we have seen, they can do without any breach of comity. But if 'process' and 'procedural' are taken to include the way in which a decision maker *reasons*, and if the court is considered to have responsibility for due 'process' in *that* sense, then the right to have a decision made in the right way becomes a right to the right reasoning. The Law Lords in *Begum* cannot have meant that any incorrectly reasoned decision can be set aside on judicial review. Lord Hoffmann expressly denied it by saying that judicial review is not concerned with 'whether he got what the court might think to be the right answer' [68]. A duty to *follow the correct reasoning process* would yield a right to the right answer.

In fact, conventional judicial review does not require that decisions be based on the correct reasoning process. It is true that a decision can be unlawful if it is based on an irrelevant consideration, or if a public official does not 'direct himself properly in law' (*Associated Provincial Picture Houses v Wednesbury Corporation* [1948] 1 KB 223, 229). It is these powerful techniques of judicial review, combined with the ambiguity of 'process', that lead judges to suggest that a claimant in judicial review has a right to a decision that is made by the correct reasoning process. But it should be obvious that a flawed reasoning process is not a ground for judicial review. Suppose that a local council has the misconception that its by-laws are not controlled by the rule in the *Wednesbury* case, so that it can decide on any ground it chooses. Its decisions are made on the basis of flawed reasoning. That would do nothing, in itself, to invalidate the council's by-laws. And similarly in Begum's case: if the school thought that its uniform policy was not subject to judicial review, it would be making an error of law, but *that* error would not give a ground for judicial review. Or suppose that a school formulated its uniform policy partly on the basis of a patent error of fact (see section 9.2), but it was also apparent to the court in judicial review that the school had other reasonable grounds for its policy. The policy would not be unlawful, in spite of the flaw in the school's reasoning.

But now, suppose that a high school prohibited the jilbab for racist reasons. *Then*, both on the conventional rules of judicial review and under the Human Rights Act,[18] the policy would be unlawful. And that would be the case even if reasonable school authorities might have prohibited the jilbab in the same circumstances, in order to protect the rights and freedoms of others.[19] So a public authority's reasoning *can* make a decision unlawful, all by itself. But that can happen only when the mere fact that the public authority reasoned that way is an abuse of power (e.g., because it expresses contempt for the people affected by it). There is ground for judicial review only when leaving the decision to stand would damage values that the law protects— and ordinarily, a flaw in reasoning (whether in a Human Rights Act case or under conventional judicial review) only makes a decision unlawful when the decision injures values that the law protects. Judicial control of the reasoning of an administrative authority should be (and generally is) exercised only on the grounds of irrelevance and extreme unreasonableness. That is because it is part of the judicial review of the substance of decision.

6.9.3 *Venables*: substance and process

The ambiguity of 'process' is not the only obstacle to understanding the distinction between substance and process. Another obstacle is the fact that some judicial review decisions control *both at once*, so that it can seem that there is no distinction between substance and process. In *R v Home Secretary, ex p Venables and Thompson* [1998] AC 407 (see p 69), the fact that public opinion was in favour of a long tariff of imprisonment for the child murderers was an irrelevant consideration and the House of Lords struck down the Home Secretary's decisions in its control over the *substance* of his decision. But the boys' lawyers also put *the same* complaint in terms of procedural impropriety, on the ground that the Home Secretary should not have taken

---

[18]   And also under the Race Relations Act 1976 ss 1(1)(a), 17, 18, and 71.

[19]   Cf. *Roncarelli v Duplessis* [1959] SCR 121: a minister's malicious motivation for taking away Roncarelli's liquor licence would have made the decision unlawful even if there happened to be other grounds on which a reasonable minister might take away the licence (see section 7.1).

account of 'expressions of opinion' from newspapers (538). So was it unfair for the Home Secretary to listen to the clamour in the media (which is a procedural defect)? Or was the media clamour an irrelevant consideration (which is a substantive defect)? The answer is that it was both; but that does not mean that there is no distinction between process and substance.

The House of Lords quashed the Home Secretary's decisions for lack of natural justice, *as well as* for irrelevant considerations. After holding that the doctrine of irrelevant considerations applied, Lord Steyn held that 'the decisions of the Home Secretary were also procedurally flawed by the credence and weight which he gave to public clamour for an increase in the level of the tariff' (519). Lord Hope held that 'Natural justice requires' that petitions and newspaper campaigns 'be dismissed as irrelevant to the judicial exercise, as it would be unfair for the judge to allow himself to be influenced by them' and that the decisions were 'procedurally unreasonable on this ground' (538–9).

Part of the procedural problem, as Lord Hope pointed out, is that the expressions of opinion in the media 'cannot be tested by cross-examination or by any other form of inquiry in which the prisoner for his interest can participate' (538). But it was procedurally unfair for the Home Secretary to rely on what the newspapers said for a more basic reason: the clamour was irrelevant. As Lord Steyn put it, the problem of procedural unfairness 'overlaps' with the problem of irrelevant considerations. Paying attention to the newspapers (a procedural step) had nothing to contribute to the making of the decision except a potentially prejudicial consideration (that the public opinion was in favour of a long tariff) which the law forbids the decision maker to take into account.

The overlap between process and substance is not an accident. The standard reason for a procedural step is *that it will contribute to putting the relevant considerations before the decision maker.* As we have seen over the past three chapters, that is not the only reason for procedures. Giving a hearing, and giving reasons for decision, also serve the value of treating a person subject to the decision with respect, and the value of imposing the rule of law on the decision by making it more transparent. The variety of reasons for procedures does not detract from the basic, standard connection between good administrative procedures and the substance of good decisions: the procedures should be designed to promote good decisions. A claimant who wants procedures that put irrelevant considerations before the decision maker has no right to them, and procedures that put adverse irrelevant considerations before the decision maker are unfair. The reason is that irrelevant considerations cannot contribute anything worth having to the substance of the decision.

6.10 Conclusion

Procedural requirements ought to contribute to good substance. The point of procedures is to provide accurate fact finding, faithful application of the law, and responsible exercise of discretionary powers, by the best-placed decision maker, on the basis of all the relevant considerations. This is true even when a procedure is required because of the value of respect: the procedure would be a sham, rather than a step that shows respect for the person, if it had no potential to contribute to the making of a good decision.

This deep connection between process and substance can make the distinction seem obscure. But it is actually fairly simple. A fair procedure is, typically, an action designed to achieve a good outcome. It would be a mistake to think that the law's concern is only with procedures: its concern for procedures ought to be based on a concern for substantive justice. Remember the paradigm case of a legal requirement of due process: *Cooper v Wandsworth Board of Works* (1863) 14 CB (NS) 180 (see section 4.1). Erle CJ thought that a hearing should be given before the use of the power to tear down houses, *because* that power 'seems to me to be a power which may be exercised most perniciously' (188). He suggested that if the Board had listened to Cooper, he might have been able to show that although he hadn't given notice, the building work conformed to the standards that the Board applied to new buildings. And then, Erle CJ said:

> I cannot conceive any harm that could happen to the district board from hearing the party before they subjected him to a loss so serious as the demolition of his house; but I can conceive a great many advantages which might arise in the way of public order, in the way of doing substantial justice, and in the way of fulfilling the purposes of the statute, by the restriction which we put upon them, that they should hear the party before they inflict upon him such a heavy loss. (188–9)

Suppose the Board had given Cooper a hearing, and he admitted he had contravened the statute by not giving notice, but proved that the work had been done strictly in accordance with the statute. Then, it might seem that they could lawfully exercise the statutory power to demolish the house. But as Keating J asked, 'can any one suppose for a moment that the board would have proceeded to inflict upon the man the grievous injury of demolishing his house? I cannot conceive it for a moment' (196). And Erle CJ said, 'if he explained how it stood, the proceeding to demolish, merely because they had ill-will against the party, is a power that the legislature never intended to confer' (188).

There in 1863 is the ancestry of the control of discretionary powers outlined in *Wednesbury*, which we saw at work in R v Ministry of Defence, ex p Walker [2000] 1 WLR 806 (see p 39), and which is explained further in Chapter 7. It is a form of control over the substance of an administrative decision. And it *also* provides the standard rationale for the law of due process.

TAKE-HOME MESSAGE • • •

- You cannot get reasons for every administrative decision. But you have a right to reasons if it would be unfair for a public authority not to give them, or if legislation requires them.

- As with other procedural protections for persons affected by a decision, reasons are required if they have a **process value** that is worth pursuing in spite of the **process cost**, and in spite of any **process danger**.

- But they can only be required by someone with standing to ask for reasons.

- There is no general duty to give reasons for public decisions, because the giving of reasons may have no process value.

- The substance of a decision is what was decided. The process is the set of steps by which the decision was reached.

- Judicial review is available to quash decisions made without *due process*, but the fact that a decision was made by the wrong *reasoning process* is not in itself a ground of judicial review. The requirement of due process applies to procedural steps to support the making of a decision, and does *not* require the correct reasoning process.

··· Critical reading ···

Ridge v Baldwin [1964] AC 40

Save Britain's Heritage v Number 1 Poultry Ltd [1991] 1 WLR 153

R v Home Secretary, ex p Doody [1994] 1 AC 531

English v Emery Reinbold & Strick Ltd [2002] EWCA Civ 605

R (Wooder) v Feggetter [2002] EWCA Civ 554

R (Begum) v Denbigh High School [2005] EWCA Civ 199

CRITICAL QUESTIONS • • •

1   **Can the court demand reasons without demanding correct reasoning?**

2   **Can you give an example of a situation in which a person would have no standing to require a public authority to give reasons for a decision?**

3   **What difference has the Human Rights Act made to the law on administrative authorities' duties to give reasons?**

4   **Should judges be more deferential in reviewing matters of substance, than in reviewing matters of procedure?**

Further questions:

5   **Would the courts today hold that a minister has a duty to give reasons in a situation like that in *Padfield v Minister of Agriculture* [1968] AC 997?**

6   **Should the law require the giving of reasons for undergraduate examination marks in universities and colleges?**

online resource centre

Visit the online resource centre to access the following resources which accompany this chapter: links to legislation and online reports of judicial decisions, summaries of key cases and legislation, updates in the law, suggestions for answering the pop quizzes and questions, and links to useful websites.

Substance

7 Discretion and deference

The common law controls the substance of administrative decisions, through the doctrine of abuse of power. The point of the doctrine is to promote responsible government. If a court is to control other public authorities, it has to do so with comity. The challenge of comity is to work out the difference between an arbitrary decision (which the judges should remedy), and a bad decision (which may be none of the judges' business).

LOOK FOR • • •

- **Deference**—a requirement of comity that depends on:
  - justiciability;
  - process impact; and
  - the value of second-guessing by an independent decision maker.

- The three principal reasons for allocating power to an administrative body:
  - expertise;
  - political responsibility; and
  - effective processes.

- The resulting **four reasons for a court to defer:** expertise, political responsibility, effective processes, along with the mere fact that the law has allocated the power to an administrative body.

- The variation in the amount of leeway that the courts leave to other public authorities in various situations, and the resulting cluster of standards of reasonableness.

> ' . . . the task of the court is not to decide what it thinks is reasonable, but to decide whether what is prima facie within the power of the local authority is a condition which no reasonable authority, acting within the four corners of their jurisdiction, could have decided to impose. '
>
> *Associated Provincial Picture Houses v Wednesbury Corporation* [1948]
> 1 KB 223, 233 (Lord Greene MR)

> ' It is not the constitutional role of the court to regulate the conditions of service in the armed forces of the Crown, nor has it the expertise to do so. But it has the constitutional role and duty of ensuring that the rights of citizens are not abused by the unlawful exercise of executive power. While the court must properly defer to the expertise of responsible decision-makers, it must not shrink from its fundamental duty to "do right to all manner of people . . . " '
>
> *R v Ministry of Defence, ex p Smith* [1996] QB 517, 556
> (Sir Thomas Bingham MR)

7.1 Abuse of power: the how-to guide

In the 1940s, Jehovah's Witnesses started knocking on doors in Montreal, seeking converts. The government of Quebec wanted to keep them off the streets. The police tried arresting hundreds for selling their magazines without having peddlers' licences. The Jehovah's Witnesses challenged this use of the peddling byelaws. While the challenges went through the courts, the Jehovah's Witnesses would have been off the streets in police custody, if not for Frank Roncarelli. Roncarelli was frustrating the police action. More than three hundred times, he paid bail money into court to get the Jehovah's Witnesses out of jail. Once they were out on bail, they were knocking on doors again.

So Maurice Duplessis, the Prime Minister of the province, ordered the director of the Liquor Commission to cancel the liquor licence at Roncarelli's restaurant. Roncarelli's liquor was seized, his business was ruined, and he brought a claim for damages against Duplessis.

Roncarelli claimed that the cancellation of his licence had been unlawful. But the liquor control legislation said that 'The Commission may cancel any permit at its discretion' (*Roncarelli v Duplessis* [1959] SCR 121, 155). It said nothing about the grounds on which the power was to be used. In the Supreme Court of Canada, Cartwright J thought that the Commission had an 'unfettered discretion', since the legislation mentioned no restrictions on the power. But the majority disagreed, and Roncarelli won a huge damages award. In a classic judicial manifesto for controlling administrative discretion, Rand J explained why he disagreed with Cartwright J:

> ' In public regulation of this sort there is no such thing as absolute and untrammelled "discretion", that is that action can be taken on any ground or for any reason that can be suggested to the mind of the administrator; no legislative Act can, without express language, be taken to contemplate an unlimited arbitrary power exercisable for any purpose, however capricious or irrelevant, regardless of the nature or purpose of the statute. ' (140)

Notice, first, the role of **reasons**: as we saw in the last chapter, the law requires public authorities to *state* their reasons for some decisions (that is a procedural constraint on decision making). But some reasons cannot lawfully be acted on (that is a constraint on the substance of a decision).

Secondly, notice that Rand J was using what English judges now call the **'principle of legality'** (see p 19): even if no limits on a discretionary power are stated in the legislation that confers it, the law subjects the power to limits. These limits protect certain values (in Roncarelli's case, the pursuit of his livelihood, his freedom to give bail money, and his freedom to adhere to a religious group even if some members were accused of crimes) from certain sorts of interference (in Roncarelli's case, the cancelling of his liquor licence).

Finally, notice the crucial role of the notion of **arbitrary power** (see p 7). The judges' role is not to do the Prime Minister's job, but to protect responsible government. It is not the courts' job to prevent *all* irresponsible governmental acts. A reckless spending decision on a weapon system that the army does not need is irresponsible, but it is not the judges' job to quash the decision (unless the legislature has assigned that job to the judges). Decisions need to be ruled by law where the law can help to prevent arbitrary government. A decision is arbitrary in the relevant sense, if it is one that other institutions can identify as failing to respond to the relevant considerations. What sort of failures can the courts identify? That is, what must be wrong with a use of power for it to be prohibited by the common law? *Very many* cases offer their own versions of **The List** of substantive features of a decision that make it unlawful. Listing the sort of things that the courts stand against is the judges' favourite way of explaining a decision whether to interfere with somebody else's power in a particular case. The judges have offered various versions of The List; we will see that all versions have a lot in common. Here is Rand J's version:

The List of substantive features that make an exercise of power unlawful: *Roncarelli* version

- **Fraud** and **corruption**: they 'are always implied as exceptions' to an undefined power (140).
- **Bad faith** or **malice**: ' "Discretion" necessarily implies **good faith**' (140).[1]

---

[1]   Is bad faith a matter of *procedure* rather than the substance of a decision? See section 6.9 on the difference, and the relations, between procedure and substance. Every decision made in bad faith was made by a *biased* decision maker, and that certainly is a procedural defect. And every

- Use of a power for a **purpose that is contrary to the statute** conferring the power: clear departure from the objects of the statute is 'just as objectionable as fraud or corruption' (140).
- **Irrelevant considerations**: acting on considerations '**irrelevant** to the *Liquor Act*' is unlawful (141).

The **rule of law**—which is opposed to arbitrary government—is the constitutional principle that justifies these grounds of interference. In Rand J's peculiar words, 'that an administration according to law is to be superseded by action dictated by and according to the arbitrary likes, dislikes and irrelevant purposes of public officers acting beyond their duty, would signalize the beginning of disintegration of the rule of law as a fundamental postulate of our constitutional structure' [44]. Judges face a huge, complex challenge: to work out the difference between imposing the rule of law on public authorities, and imposing the rule of judges.

You can see that challenge emerging in Rand J's version of The List. The forms of unlawful behaviour include the obvious (corruption), and the provocative: acting on irrelevant considerations. The really interesting thing about Duplessis's nasty scheme is that he hadn't taken a bribe, and he didn't even have anything personal against Roncarelli. He did something that he really thought was in the public interest. He thought that cancelling Roncarelli's liquor licence would help to protect the community from a religious campaign that he thought was offensive and insulting to the people of Quebec. Duplessis thought that Roncarelli's behaviour in supporting Jehovah's Witnesses was *highly* relevant to the question of how he should use a discretion that the people of Quebec had given him to use on their behalf. In a press release the day after the liquor licence was cancelled, Duplessis announced:

> '...the Provincial Government had the firm intention to take the most rigorous and efficient measures possible to get rid of those who under the names of Witnesses of Jehovah, distribute circulars which in my opinion are not only injurious for Quebec and its population, but which are of a very libellous and seditious character....A certain Mr. Roncarelli has supplied bail for hundreds of witnesses of Jehovah. The sympathy which this man has shown for the Witnesses, in such an evident, repeated and audacious manner, is a provocation to public order, to the administration of justice and is definitely contrary to the aims of justice.' (137)

In his defence to Roncarelli's damages action, Duplessis not only pointed out that the statute set no limits to the discretion it gave him; he added an argument of **justiciability** (see p 239): that it was the task of a politician to decide whether, e.g., the community needed protection from Jehovah's Witnesses, and that the courts were in no position to make that judgment.

What was wrong with that justiciability argument? The legislature had good reason for giving the liquor licensing power to a government minister, and not to judges. Of course, the reason the power was given to the government was not to let

----

such decision is made on the basis of an irrelevant consideration, which is a defect in the substance of the decision. So decisions made in bad faith are defective in procedure *and* substance.

the officials take bribes, or destroy their own personal enemies (which explains why corruption and malice belong on The List). The reasons had to do with (at least) the familiarity that political officials have with the public interest in liquor control, and their political responsibility to the community for promoting that interest, and their ability to find out what was really going on in a restaurant without the restrictive fact-finding process of a court.

Three potential reasons for allocating a power to an administrative decision maker

- expertise;
- political responsibility; and
- effective processes.

Given the reasons for allocating the liquor licensing power to the Prime Minister, how could it be right for the court to step in and *contradict* the Prime Minister's opinion as to how to use a power that the public had entrusted to him to exercise on its behalf?

The answer is that even though the power was given to a minister, judges must prevent *some* injustices in its use. Not all injustices, or courts would have to review all exercises of discretionary powers to decide what ought to have been done. Instead of that, the judges' duty is to **defer** to the person to whom the law allocates the power, in a way and to an extent that reflects the point of that allocation of power. And it is possible to defer more or less, and on some issues but not on others. So it is possible to defer in the way that the allocation of power demands, without leaving the power uncontrolled. None of the three reasons for allocating a *power* to an administrative official is a reason for allocating *uncontrolled* power to the official.

A court that defers to the holder of discretionary power (in the way the allocation of the power demands) can still intervene to remedy fraud and corruption, *and also abuse* of the power. This is a crucial starting point in understanding the judicial control of discretionary power: the court in *Roncarelli* did not need to claim (and it could not claim) to be able to do the Prime Minister's job better than the Prime Minister could do it. It had to claim that the Prime Minister wasn't really doing his job at all when he cancelled Roncarelli's liquor licence. But for that purpose, since the power had been given to the Prime Minister in the interest of just public order, the judges *did* have to disagree with him about the merits of his decision (that is, about how to do his job), or they could not have protected Roncarelli or anyone else from an abuse of power.

Remember this, if ever you find someone saying that judicial review does not control the merits of an administrative decision. The classic example is what Lord Brightman said in *Chief Constable of the North Wales Police v Evans* [1982] 1 WLR 1155, 1173:

> Judicial review is concerned, not with the decision, but with the decision-making process. [2]

---

[2]   Cited with approval by Lord Fraser in *Council of Civil Service Unions v Minister for the Civil Service* [1985] AC 374, 401. See p 238 on the decision in that case.

The implication is that there is no review of the substance, or the merits of a discretionary decision. But in virtually every case discussed in this chapter, and Chapter 8, and Chapter 9, the judges display a willingness to concern themselves with the decision—its substance, and not merely the process.

The *substance* of a decision is what was decided (see p 205). A question as to the *merits* of a decision is a question as to how good or bad its substance was. Judicial review *must* be concerned with the decision—its substance, and its merits—or it would leave the executive free to abuse its discretionary powers. If a court is to prevent abuse of power without taking over the use of the power, it has to find an approach to controlling the substance of exercises of discretionary power that gives the initial decision maker a leeway that corresponds to the reasons why the power was allocated to that person or institution. The judges must, to some extent, keep their hands off the decisions of other public authorities, without allowing abuses.

In England in the 21st century, the judges never suggest that judicial review is not concerned with the decision. But they still refer constantly to Lord Greene's attempt to find a hands-off approach to the substance of administrative decisions, in *Associated Provincial Picture Houses v Wednesbury Corporation* [1948] 1 KB 223. That attempt was not new in 1948: Lord Russell had sketched the same approach 50 years earlier, in *Kruse v Johnson* [1898] 2 QB 91. And *Kruse* was not new; it was based on *Slattery v Naylor* (1888) 13 App Cas 446—which wasn't novel either. The decision in *Slattery* upheld a byelaw prohibiting the burial of bodies in cemeteries within 100 yards of a dwelling. *Kruse* was also a challenge to a local authority byelaw (providing that 'No person shall sound or play upon any musical or noisy instrument or sing in any public place or highway within fifty yards of any dwelling-house' after being asked to desist). *Wednesbury* was a challenge to a local authority decision to license a cinema to show movies on a Sunday subject to a condition that children under 15 not be admitted. So these three landmark cases, like *Roncarelli*, concerned the exercise of statutory powers to regulate public order and conduct in the community, which local authorities had exercised for purposes that they took to be in the public interest. Unlike *Roncarelli*, all three were unsuccessful challenges to the substance of a governmental decision. And the judges in each case tried to articulate a form of legal control that judges can apply with no breach of comity.

The two common strands are (1) that the judges are *not* generally to quash such decisions on the ground that they are unreasonable, but (2) that there are *forms* of unreasonableness that do give a ground for judges to interfere. The ground of review is not unreasonableness in general. The ground of review is that, in spite of their disadvantages in reviewing someone else's judgment, the judges can see that the decision is unreasonable. So the unreasonableness must be 'manifest' to a reviewing authority.

	Grounds for quashing a decision:	Not grounds for quashing a decision:
Slattery v Naylor (1888) 13 App Cas 446, 452–3 (Lord Hobhouse)	'a merely fantastic and capricious bye-law, such as **reasonable men could not make in good faith**' (452), 'capricious or oppressive' (453).	A byelaw cannot be quashed 'merely because it does not contain qualifications which commend themselves to the minds of judges' (452).
Kruse v Johnson [1898] 2 QB 91, 94–5 (Lord Russell)	'partial and unequal in their operation...manifestly unjust;...bad faith;...such oppressive or gratuitous interference with the rights of those subject to them as **could find no justification in the minds of reasonable men**' (99–100).	'A by-law is not unreasonable merely because particular judges may think that it goes further than is prudent or necessary or convenient' (100).
Associated Provincial Picture Houses v Wednesbury Corporation [1948] 1 KB 223, 230–1 (Lord Greene)	'...unreasonable in the sense that the court considers it to be **a decision that no reasonable body could have come to**' (230).	'It is not what the court considers unreasonable, a different thing altogether' (230).

Figure 7.1 The classic cases: an attempt at comity

7.1.1 The four basic reasons for deference

That hands-off approach to the initial decision is a **deferential** form of control. To defer is to leave the answer to some question, to some extent, to the initial decision maker, so that it takes some special reason for the court to interfere with that decision maker's answer to it. There are **four basic reasons** for this approach; in Lord Russell's reasons in *Kruse*, three are mentioned and the other is implicit:

> '...the question of reasonableness or unreasonableness is one which must be decided by the **representative** body **entrusted with the power** to make by-laws, and **knowing the locality** in which they are to take effect and the needs and wishes of its inhabitants' (95).[3]

(1) **Legal allocation of power**: the mere fact that Parliament *entrusted the power* to the local council means that the council should decide what byelaws the town should have, and the court should not interfere just because the judges would have made a different byelaw.

That is important both because of the rule-of-law value of finality (that is, there shouldn't be a further proceeding to upset a decision unless there is a good reason

---

[3]   Cf. 'the local authority are entrusted by Parliament with the decision on a matter which the knowledge and experience of that authority can best be trusted to deal with' (*Wednesbury*, 230, though Lord Greene did not mention *Kruse v Johnson*).

for it), and also because the court ought to presume that the allocation of a decision-making power to a public body was done for some good reason. The three potential reasons for allocating a power to an administrative decision maker generate the second, third, and fourth reasons for deference.

(2) **Expertise**: the council's familiarity with the locality may give them a better grasp than the judges can have of the considerations that are relevant to the question of what byelaws the town should have.

(3) **Political responsibility**: as representatives, the councillors, unlike the court, are accountable to the inhabitants and have the job of acting responsibly as their representatives.

In *Kruse*, the fourth consideration is implicit in the better grasp of the relevant considerations that Lord Russell presumed the councillors to have: it is not just that they are more skilled at assessing those considerations, but also that they have techniques for going about the task that are more effective than the limited and artificial fact-finding techniques that are available in a court:

(4) **Processes:** the councillors have ways of learning what is relevant that represent no failure of due process, and are better tuned to the decision-making task than the courts' heavily restricted processes.

The four reasons for deference are all interrelated. For example: a good power-allocation decision (by Parliament, or the Crown, or by an administrative authority with delegated power) (reason 1) is one that gives the power to a decision maker that ought to have political responsibility for it (reason 3). And it is important that responsibility for some decisions be given to people who have the expertise (reason 2), and have the decision-making processes and resources (reason 4), to make good decisions.

The first reason (legal allocation of power) alone is enough for a **presumption of non-interference by courts**. That is, if the law allocates responsibility for a decision to an administrative authority, you can never go to a court simply on the ground that the authority ought to have reached a different conclusion. Judicial review is not a second chance at the right decision; the process is a last resort (see p 60) in which the claimant can ask the court for permission to argue that a decision was unlawful. You need a ground of *review*—a reason for a court to overturn someone else's decision. Otherwise, administrative decisions would be merely provisional, and if you did not like the result, you would be able to ask a court to do the administrative task instead.

What does it take to establish a ground of review that will overcome the presumption of non-interference by courts? It depends! The presumption of non-interference may be very weak or very strong, and its strength is determined by the widely varying ways in which the other three basic reasons for deference apply in a variety of circumstances. All we can say in general is that, if Parliament has decided that responsibility for a decision ought to rest with an administrative official, then the court ought to respect that allocation of power. So, in an important restatement of the *Wednesbury* approach, in R *v* Home Secretary, *ex p* Hindley [1998] QB 751, Lord Bingham CJ said:

> '...responsibility for making the relevant decision rests with another party and not with the court. It is not enough that we might, if the responsibility for making the relevant decision rested with us, make a decision different from that of the appointed decision maker. To justify intervention by the court, the decision under challenge must fall outside the bounds of any decision open to a reasonable decision maker.' (777)

Administrative **expertise** (the second reason for deference) comes in an extremely wide variety of forms—some quite technical and some (as in *Kruse*) a matter of having a thorough grasp of the situation in which a decision is to be made. And the **processes** by which relevant information can be found and assessed (the fourth reason for deference) vary, too. By comparison to the processes available to the initial decision maker, the judicial review process may be very effective *or* very poor at putting the relevant information in front of the judges, depending on the issues at stake.

Even the forms of **political responsibility** (the third reason for deference) are various—from the constitutional responsibility of Parliament, which makes its decisions unreviewable, to the constitutional responsibility of the Crown for national security, to the managerial responsibility of government departments for their own operation. Political responsibility in these varying forms is tied to similarly varying forms of political **accountability**: to the voters in the case of Parliament, and to superiors and ultimately to ministers in the case of civil servants. Local authorities like those in *Slattery*, *Kruse*, and *Wednesbury* are democratic but they have none of the constitutional status of Parliament, and judges have a variable record in deferring on the ground of the local voters' mandate.

The reasons for deference depend radically on the type of decision, the nature of the initial decision maker, and the context in which the decision is made. Not only do the forms of allocation of power, expertise, political responsibility, and decision-making process vary widely; their importance as reasons for deference varies too, depending on the issues at stake in a particular decision. So the principle of relativity (see p 10) is a central principle of the control of discretionary power. What does not vary, though, is the court's constitutional responsibility for preventing administrative authorities from abusing their power, when it can be done with no breach of comity. None of the four reasons for deference is a reason for administrative decisions to be unreviewable.

7.1.2 Abuse of power and arbitrary government

The one general feature of a decision that justifies review in spite of the reasons for deference is **abuse of power**, which is, as Lord Russell put it in *Kruse v Johnson*, 'such oppressive or gratuitous interference with the rights of those subject to [a decision] as could find no justification in the minds of reasonable men' (94–5). This formula, echoing *Slattery* and echoed in *Wednesbury*, makes a very important constitutional move: it offers a programme for preventing arbitrary government, while preserving the principle that it is not for the judges to decide what byelaws would be reasonable.

> ### Bad government, arbitrary government, abuse of power
>
> Bad government in general does not respond well to the considerations that ought to guide it. **Arbitrary government** does not respond *at all* to the considerations that ought to guide it. **Abuse of power** is the use of power for bad purposes; maliciously, for example (e.g., imprisoning someone just to prevent them from criticizing the government), or for private gain rather than in the public interest (e.g., taking a bribe to release a prisoner).
>
> What is the difference between arbitrary government and abuse of power? Abuse of power is an example of arbitrary power, because an official who abuses his power is not responding to the considerations that ought to guide its use, at all. You might say that arbitrary government is randomness, and abuse of power is randomness that hurts.
>
> There are many bad government decisions that do not count as arbitrary government, and are not abuses of power. If the argument in favour of a decision is not as strong as the argument against it, then the decision is a bad decision. If there is no real argument in favour of it at all, then the decision is an act of arbitrary government. So here is what makes it difficult to identify arbitrary government: it can be hard, in some cases, to distinguish between a decision that is only supported by a bad argument, and a decision that is not supported by any argument at all.

Because it can be hard to distinguish between a bad argument and no argument, it may seem impossible or paradoxical to try to prevent arbitrary use of a power, without deciding how a power should be used. But here is the judges' attempt in the three classic cases of *Slattery*, *Kruse*, and *Wednesbury*:

> **If the judges are able to say that no one in the position of the public authority could present the action in good faith as a genuine exercise of their discretion, then the judges can interfere with someone else's decision with no breach of comity.**

And they *must* do so, because in that scenario it becomes the judges' responsibility to interfere to prevent or to remedy arbitrary government. The judges cannot take that responsibility without assessing the merits of the decision. But the judgment they pass on the merits is restrained. The question is whether the merits of the decision are *so* bad that no one in *the position of the initial decision maker* could present it in good faith as an exercise of discretion. The result is a restrained, flexible, vague standard of review.

There, in a nutshell, is the core of the doctrine of abuse of power in English administrative law. As a standard of judicial review for very many administrative decisions, it is justified by the **core rationale for judicial review** (see p 65). Its vagueness gives judges a tool that they can misuse, by striking down reasonable decisions that they do not like, or by leaving abuses of power unremedied. But it also gives them the opportunity to control arbitrary use of power while acting with comity toward other public authorities.

However, there remains one further point to note about the scope of this doctrine in *Slattery*, *Kruse*, and *Wednesbury*. Like any precedent, the effect of those cases on the law depends on their facts. In fact, this point is crucial, because *Wednesbury* has taken on such a legendary role that sometimes it seems like a code for the control of discretionary powers. And then because it does *not* offer a code, people sometimes suggest that it must be abandoned.

Slattery, *Kruse*, and *Wednesbury* each concerned more or less democratic decisions of local councils; so the *ratio* in each case is limited in two ways. First, there is good reason, in reviewing some other sorts of decision, for judges to be even more restrained than in *Slattery*, *Kruse*, and *Wednesbury*. So the ways of controlling licensing decisions that Lord Greene set out in *Wednesbury* do *not* apply to all administrative decisions (see section 7.3).

Secondly (and conversely), the doctrine of abuse of power leaves all sorts of room for courts to substitute their judgment for that of the public authorities with less restraint, concerning different sorts of decisions. Lord Greene refused to accept that 'the ultimate arbiter of what is and is not reasonable is the court and not the local authority', but *that* conclusion depends on the role of the local authority. Sometimes it is an extremely good idea for the courts to set themselves up as ultimate arbiter of what is reasonable, when public authorities carry out tasks that are very different from the task of making byelaws. The classic example is *habeas corpus* (see p 5): in inquiring into an administrative decision to detain a person, the court will not merely ask whether the decision to detain was 'a decision that no reasonable body could have come to'. The court actually *will* set itself up as the arbiter of what is reasonable. This is not a historical peculiarity of *habeas corpus*; in R v Home Secretary, ex p Khawaja [1984] AC 74, an application for a declaration and *certiorari* (a quashing order), the House of Lords decided that the court could substitute its own view for the decision of an immigration officer as to whether a person was an illegal immigrant, rather than merely asking whether any reasonable immigration officer could have reached that conclusion.

Didn't the *Wednesbury* approach apply to *Khawaja*? No: Lord Scarman agreed with the Home Secretary that if Lord Greene's approach applied to *Khawaja*, it would prohibit the court from substituting its own judgment for that of the immigration officer. But for that very reason, the whole House of Lords refused to take that restrained approach. 'Such exclusion of the power and duty of the courts runs counter to the development of the safeguards which our law provides for the liberty of the subject' (109–10). It may sound as if *Khawaja* partly overruled *Wednesbury*, but that is not the case at all: Lord Scarman said that Lord Greene's approach 'is undoubtedly correct in cases where it is appropriate' (109).[4] *Wednesbury* does not require a restrained judicial approach to the detention of an alleged illegal immigrant, because the reasons for

---

[4]   But the decision did overrule R v Home Secretary, ex p Zamir [1980] AC 930 (HL), which had held that the Home Secretary's decision to remove an immigrant could only be reviewed on the ground that no reasonable person could have reached it.

Lord Greene's restrained approach depend on its facts: he was reviewing the regulation of cinemas by local byelaws, not the detention of a person by an immigration officer.

More generally, we can say that the courts will take a more intrusive approach to review of an administrative decision, whenever they do not have the same reasons for deference (reasons of administrative expertise, political responsibility, and effective process) as in *Slattery*, *Kruse*, and *Wednesbury*. So consider Lord Greene's view, in *Wednesbury*, that it 'would require something overwhelming' before a court could hold that a decision was so unreasonable that no reasonable authority could have come to it (230). Like the *ratio* of any decision of the common law, the effect of this rule is to be understood as applied to the facts of the case. There is no general rule that it 'would require something overwhelming' before a court can interfere with an administrative decision; it is a rule that applies in a challenge to the content of a town byelaw. The general rule is that the court has to be able to see that the decision is unreasonable, *in spite of* the fact that the decision-making power was allocated to another authority, and in spite of any superior expertise or better process that the initial decision maker may have, and in spite of the political responsibility that the initial decision maker may have for the decision. When it comes to overruling town byelaws, that *would* take something overwhelming. But the standard is flexible enough to allow judges a much more intrusive role in other sorts of decisions, when the four reasons for deference apply with lesser force.

> ### The List of substantive features that make an exercise of power unlawful: *Wednesbury* version
>
> - **Error of law** (A person entrusted with a discretion must, so to speak, direct himself properly in law.)
> - **Irrelevance** (He must call his own attention to the **matters which he is bound to consider**. He must exclude from his consideration matters which are **irrelevant** to what he has to consider.)
> - Something so **absurd** that no sensible person could ever dream that it lay within the powers of the authority—a decision that no reasonable body could have come to.
> - **Bad faith** (225).[5]

The judges often call Lord Greene's version of The List the '*Wednesbury* principles' or '*Wednesbury* grounds',[6] and they often isolate the third of those principles, and call it '*Wednesbury* unreasonableness'. That phrase is a label for what Lord Greene called 'a decision that no reasonable body could have come to' (230). It is simply the use of

---

[5]   Bad faith is the most powerful but the hardest to prove of any ground of judicial review; note that bad faith is a ground of judicial review even if the substance of the decision is *not* so unreasonable that no public authority would have done it. Compare the role of bad faith in the tort of misfeasance in a public office; see section 14.5.

[6]   See, e.g., R v *Environment Secretary, ex p Nottinghamshire County Council* [1986] AC 240, 249 (Lord Scarman).

a discretionary power in a way that gives judges special reason to identify it as unreasonable, even though it is not generally their job to say whether someone else's decision is reasonable. It is not a general control on administrative decisions, because sometimes—as in *Khawaja*—it *is* the judges' job to say whether someone else's decision is reasonable.

● *Pop Quiz* ●

Lord Russell's version of The List in *Kruse v Johnson* is largely the same as Lord Green's in *Wednesbury* except that Lord Russell *also* mentioned conduct that is manifestly unjust, capricious, inequitable, or partial in its operation, and oppression. Are those separate grounds of review that were missing from Lord Greene's version of The List in *Wednesbury*?

When he cancelled Roncarelli's liquor licence to punish him for helping Jehovah's Witnesses, Duplessis' behaviour was arbitrary. But the judges could only reach that conclusion because he was so badly wrong about what the public interest required, that they could responsibly say so even though they were not ministers with responsibility for liquor licences. The judges were right to interfere because the minister went *extremely* wrong in the very job that had been committed to him.

So if you want to abuse your power, you have to make do with only vague guidance from the law: it will undoubtedly be enough if you act corruptly, or maliciously. Or it may be enough to act on an irrelevant consideration, at least if it is badly irrelevant, so that the court can identify it as improper without taking over your job. The only general guide available is that what you do must be identifiable, from the perspective of a court, as an abuse of the power.

7.1.3 The unreasonable and the irrational

An unreasonable decision is one that does not properly respond to the reasons that the decision maker should be acting on. Unreasonableness is a very flexible thing: on the one hand, it isn't reasonable to do the wrong thing. On the other hand, even if a decision is quite wrong, people often say that it was reasonable, as a way of saying that there is some sort of strength in the reasoning that led to it. This huge flexibility in the idea of reasonableness makes the standards of judicial review rather vague, but not as vague as you might think. For as we saw from *Wednesbury*, there is *no general judicial review for unreasonableness*. A public authority should never use its power unreasonably, but a court will not interfere unless it finds a kind of unreasonableness that it can act on, while showing respect for the fact that the power to make the decision was allocated to the initial decision maker.

The court can do that if, as Lord Greene put it, a byelaw is 'so unreasonable that no reasonable authority could ever have come to it' or, more simply, if it is 'a decision that no reasonable body could have come to' (229). Picking up on Lord Greene's insistence that in the case of local byelaws it would take something 'overwhelming', judges have often been at pains to emphasize that judicial control of discretionary powers may be *very* restrained, so that they will only interfere with an *extremely* unreasonable decision. The favourite way of emphasizing that point is to refer to *Wednesbury* unreasonableness as 'irrationality'.[7] That started with Lord Diplock's speech in *Council of Civil Service Unions v Minister for the Civil Service* [1985] AC 374, 410, in which he tried to shoehorn the grounds of judicial review of exercises of discretionary power into the words 'illegality', 'irrationality', and 'procedural impropriety'.[8]

'Irrationality' is a misleading term. To everyone except English public lawyers, an irrational decision is one that cannot be understood as having any intelligible purpose. A decision is reasonable if it is arguable that it is the right decision; just as the argument in favour of a decision can be stronger or weaker, a decision can be more or less reasonable. If a decision is *totally* unreasonable—so that there is no argument in favour of it at all—then it is irrational. Irrational action is inexplicable. Extremely unreasonable actions can be highly rational; irrational actions are just mad.

It should not and does not take an administrative decision that is irrational in the ordinary sense (i.e., mad), before the judges will interfere. The decision in *Roncarelli v Duplessis* was *Wednesbury* unreasonable (no reasonable Prime Minister would cancel a liquor licence in order to punish a man for lawfully helping the Jehovah's Witnesses). But it was all too rational. Like many abuses of public power, the Prime Minister's vendetta was directed to an intelligible purpose, which he had adopted in an attempt to serve the public, but which the law prohibited.

There is probably not a single case in this book, or even in the law reports, in which government action was irrational in the ordinary sense. So if Lord Diplock wanted to explain *Wednesbury* unreasonableness, it would have been better for him to say that the exercise of a discretionary power may be quashed if the courts can identify it as an abuse of power. Yet it has become very common for judges to say that 'irrationality' is a ground of review, and to quash administrative decisions on that ground. When you see the word 'irrational', you have to view it as code for a complex form of review, in which the courts for a variety of reasons decide that there is something *so* wrong (or so unreasonable) with a decision that it is no breach of comity for them to interfere with the substance of another public authority's decision.[9] In other words, when the judges say that 'irrationality' is a ground of review, they mean that abuse of power is a ground of review.

---

7   R v Ministry of Defence, ex p Walker [2000] 1 WLR 806 is one example among hundreds: Lord Slynn said that the courts would only interfere with a term of a compensation scheme if it was 'irrational or so unreasonable that no reasonable minister could have adopted it' (812), and Lord Hoffmann said that the standard was irrationality (816). Sometimes the judges speak of 'Wednesbury irrationality': Tesco Stores v Environment Secretary [1995] 1 WLR 759, 780 (Lord Hoffmann).

8   Lord Russell had suggested that unreasonableness is irrationality, in Education Secretary v Tameside [1977] Ac 1014 (HL), 1074.

9   Brooke LJ has said, 'far too often practitioners use the word "irrational" or "perverse" when these epithets are completely inappropriate' (R (Iran) v Home Secretary [2005] EWCA Civ 982 [12]). Cf. Sedley LJ's view in R (Bancoult) v Foreign Secretary (No 2) [2007] EWCA Civ 498, that it is a mistake to call a decision 'irrational', if the decision maker's reasoning 'reveals no true flaw of logic but rather an inadmissible or collateral purpose' [59].

The flexibility of the *Wednesbury* principles is important, and it will be the theme of the rest of this chapter and the next. The danger of the word 'irrationality' is that it suggests that a court can only interfere with a public authority that has gone mad (and done something 'merely fantastic', as Lord Hobhouse called it in *Slattery*). It would indeed take a fairly mad byelaw to justify judicial review in a case like *Slattery*, *Kruse*, or *Wednesbury*. Treating those cases as if they held that only irrational decisions can be quashed, judges have often suggested that the law has changed to go beyond 'irrationality' to allow more intrusive control of discretionary powers. But there never was a rule that a court can only interfere with the substance of a decision if it is irrational. It is dangerous (even though it is popular) to try to divide the grounds of review into 'illegality, irrationality, and procedural impropriety' (see p 339).

Wednesbury unreasonable asylum decisions

In this century the courts have held more than a dozen decisions of immigration officers and of successive Home Secretaries in dealing with asylum seekers to be *Wednesbury* unreasonable.[10] It may seem either that the immigration officers and the Home Secretaries have been insane, or that the judges have illegitimately taken over asylum policy under the pretence that rational decisions were irrational. In fact it's neither one nor the other. It is not the judges' job to replace the initial decisions on asylum with their own, but it is compatible with *Wednesbury* for the courts to show less deference to the Home Secretary in asylum decisions than they show to local councils in claims that a byelaw is unlawful. The **four basic reasons for deference** (allocation of power, expertise, political responsibility, and processes) apply very differently in different types of claim.

Because the reasons for deference have little force in these cases (cf. *Khawaja*, above) the judges can justifiably interfere with the Home Secretary's decision *without* it being an extreme case. You could say that *Wednesbury* unreasonableness is too hands-off a standard, in these cases. But the judges still often say that they are applying *Wednesbury* unreasonableness.

Before tackling the details of judicial control of the substance of administrative decisions, we need to sort out the tools of the trade. Sections 7.2.1–7.2.3 explain what *discretion* is, what *discretionary powers* are, and how discretion is related to *powers and duties*. Section 7.2.4 explains *deference*, and its relation to discretion.

Section 7.3 explains why the courts allow massive deference to public authorities in certain areas of administration: spending decisions, decisions involving technical expertise, planning decisions, decisions approved in Parliament, investigations and prosecutions, and decisions based on impressions.

---

[10] Examples: *R (Ahmadzai) v Home Secretary* [2006] EWHC 318, *R v Home Secretary, ex p Elshani* [2001] EWHC Admin 68 [24], *R (Zeqiri) v Home Secretary* [2001] EWCA Civ 342 [70], *R (Javed) v Home Secretary* [2001] EWCA Civ 789, *R v Home Secretary, ex p Senkoy* [2001] EWCA Civ 328, *R v Home Secretary, ex p Mersin* [2000] INLR 511.

Chapter 8, conversely, explains when and why the courts allow minimal deference—or none at all. Don't think that there are simply two categories of case; there is an indefinite variety of cases, and there is even a range of ways in which they differ. The reasons for deference are correspondingly diverse, and there is not even a single continuum of degrees of deference.

Yet in order to understand judicial control of executive power, it is very useful to focus on some of the reasons courts can have for deferring quite radically on some issues (this chapter), and some of the reasons they can have for deferring very little—or not at all—on other issues (Chapter 8).

7.2 Discretion

'Discretion' is a useful word, because it is ambiguous. It refers to a freedom of choice on the part of a decision maker; but on the other hand, it is also a sort of synonym for propriety and decency. The double aspect of discretion is that:

(1) the decision maker has a choice to make, and yet

(2) since it is a *discretion*, the decision maker is to act responsibly and not arbitrarily.

So the choice is not to be made for the decision maker's own personal benefit, but for purposes that the decision maker is responsible for pursuing on behalf of the community. Having a discretion means having a choice; having no discretion means having no choice. Having a discretion does *not* mean that anything goes. Every public power must be exercised responsibly, and every public decision ought to be made reasonably. That means deciding in the public interest, and with respect for the private interests of persons affected by the decision. But for a public authority to have a discretion means that it is *up to that authority to decide* what is in the public interest, and to determine what is required by respect for private interests.

Here is one crucial point that is easy to forget: the fact that a power is to be used responsibly does not in itself mean that anyone else ought to have power to interfere with an irresponsible use of the power. A reviewing court must work out how—if at all—to control a freedom of choice that has been given to another public authority. And we have already seen that it is possible to control a public authority's freedom, without taking it away.

7.2.1 Varieties of discretion

There are various ways in which a decision maker can be free to decide as he or she sees fit.

Express discretion: a law maker may say that a decision maker is to have a discretion.

- **Example:** *Roncarelli v Duplessis* [1959] SCR 121, 155: the Quebec Alcoholic Liquor Act 1941 provided: 'The Commission may cancel any permit at its discretion.'

Implied discretion: The same thing can be done implicitly, by saying that a decision maker *may* do something, or that it has power to do it, without saying how (or even whether) the power must be used:

- **Example:** *Cooper v Wandsworth Board of Works* (1863) 14 CB (NS) 180: 'it shall be lawful for the...board to cause such house or building to be demolished' (Metropolis Local Management Act, 1855 s 76).

The Act implies that the Board has a choice, because it does not say that the Board must demolish the building. Of course, since they give an *implied* discretion, such provisions state no limits on the discretion; but as *Cooper* shows, the common law may 'supply the omission of the legislature' (194) (see section 4.1), and impose limits on the discretionary power. So, for instance, the Board of Works acted unlawfully by failing to give Cooper a hearing before demolishing his house.

Grants of power in subjective terms: a law maker may say that a decision maker's own view is to prevail.

- **Example:** *Associated Provincial Picture Houses v Wednesbury Corporation* [1948] 1 KB 223: the local authority could give licences 'subject to such conditions as the authority think fit to impose'.

That may seem to be the ultimate grant of discretion. The local authority in the *Wednesbury* case *did* think fit to impose the condition that the cinema challenged. So how could the cinema ask the court to pass judgment on whether the condition was reasonable? The answer is that, since World War II, legislation making a public authority's powers depend on what the public authority *thinks* has consistently been read to require the public authority to have legitimate *grounds* for what it thinks. So the legal effect of that legislation ('...such conditions as the authority think fit to impose') is exactly the same as it would be if it simply read that the authority may impose conditions. A notorious case during World War II treated an objective restriction on the Home Secretary's power to detain enemy aliens (requiring him *to have reason* for suspicion of association with the enemy) as if it was satisfied if the Home Secretary *thought* he had reason (*Liversidge v Anderson* [1942] AC 206). That approach has been categorically rejected since: see e.g., R *(Guisto) v Governor of Brixton Prison* [2003] UKHL 19 [41] (on the difference between objective and subjective tests, see p 539).

Inherent discretion: A power is *inherent* if a body has it simply because the power is essential if the body is to carry out its role. Inherent powers typically involve some substantial degree of discretion.

- **Example:** *R v Ministry of Defence, ex p Walker* [2000] 1 WLR 806: the Ministry of Defence had a power to create a compensation scheme that had not been conferred on it by any statute or other lawmaking act: it could decide to give compensation, but it had no legal duty to do so.

All the major authorities of the state in our constitution have certain powers without which they could not fulfill their responsibilities. Parliament's inherent power to legislate gives it discretion of a scope that is not limited by any legal rule (and it has inherent discretionary power to control its own proceedings). The power of the High Court to control its own process (through contempt of court and through decisions concerning procedures[11]) is an inherent discretionary power.

Administrative authorities have inherent discretionary powers, too. The **prerogative** of the Crown is an inherent discretionary power (but it is limited by law, and is subject to judicial review). And public authorities that do not exercise the prerogative of the Crown may have all sorts of powers of legal persons (such as the power to contract) even if Parliament has not acted to give them such powers. Finally, since they need to adopt decision-making procedures if they are to be decision makers at all, administrative authorities have an inherent discretionary power to invent procedures. That power is recognized by the common law, but it is also limited by the duties imposed by the common law of due process.

What is and is not prerogative, and why it doesn't matter

The royal prerogative includes a variety of distinctive powers of the Crown. In *R (Heath) v Home Office Policy and Advisory Board for Forensic Pathology* [2005] EWHC 1793, a forensic pathologist challenged a decision of the Board to refer a complaint to a disciplinary tribunal on the ground that there was no statutory power to do so, and that the referral was not an exercise of prerogative. The challenge failed because an action of a public authority does not have to be an exercise of statutory or prerogative power in order to be lawful; the court held that the referral of the complaint could be 'executive action'.

The 'executive action' label does not explain why the board had lawful power to make the decision. *Everything* that the government does (whether lawful or unlawful) is executive action. The reason why the Board had lawful power to make the decision in *Heath* is a legal principle that has been acted upon but never very clearly stated in the cases: any public authority has **inherent power** (i.e., a power not conferred by any lawmaker) to act with legal effect where it is necessary for the proper fulfillment of its lawful functions (e.g., by entering into contracts—see section 15.3). Prerogative powers are inherent powers of the Crown.

For the purpose of deciding the standard of judicial review, it doesn't matter in a case like *Heath* whether a public authority is exercising a statutory power, or a prerogative power of the Crown, or some other inherent power, because the standards of review for error of law, due process, and the prevention of abuse of power do not depend on the legal source of the power.

Resultant discretion: Suppose I ask you to come to my party, and you ask when you should turn up. I just say, 'oh, please come early'. It may not be clear *how early is*

---

[11]   Today, the Civil Procedure Rules 1998 preserve these discretions: section 10.1.

early.[12] Then my request is vague (because there is no sharp boundary to the actions that count as complying). I have not simply asked you to come whenever you please; I am giving you a standard for your behaviour, and if you don't come early, you won't have done what I asked. But the vagueness of my request (that is, the uncertainty as to when 'early' starts and stops) gives you some degree of choice (even though there will be times that clearly are *not* early).[13] Discretion results because the vagueness of the request leaves you a choice of how to comply, even though you are acting according to a standard that regulates your conduct.

- **Example:** *R v Monopolies and Mergers Commission, ex p South Yorkshire Transport* [1993] 1 WLR 23 (see p 334), in which the Commission could inquire into mergers that affected a 'substantial part of the United Kingdom'.

Where the law is vague, the power to apply the law is a discretionary power, because the vagueness of the law will leave the administrative authority a choice in some cases that is not determined by law. There is a difference between enacting that a public authority shall have discretion in awarding licences, and enacting that it shall give licences to persons who are suitably qualified. But both legislative techniques give discretion.

> **'What to justice shall appertain'**
> The World's Greatest example of a resultant discretion was conferred on *judges* by the Habeas Corpus Act 1640, which provided that on the issue of a *habeas corpus*, the court 'shall proceed to examine and determine whether the cause of such commitment... be just and legal, or not, and shall thereupon do what to Justice shall appertain, either by delivering, bailing or remanding the prisoner'.
>   When the law tells judges to do what to justice shall appertain, and doesn't say what *does* appertain to justice, it gives them a wide-ranging discretion.

Note that all these varieties of discretion are compatible with the principle that **they must be exercised responsibly.** And that is compatible with control by a reviewing authority on the *Wednesbury* grounds. But to the extent that a reviewing authority imposes standards that require the initial decision maker to use a discretionary power in a particular way, its discretion is taken away.

7.2.2 Discretion and discretionary power

A discretion is a choice that the law leaves up to you, and a discretionary power is a power that gives you that choice in *some* cases, on *some* grounds. Having *discretion in a particular case* is different from having *a discretionary power*. If you have discretion, the

---

[12]   Note that I also give you an implied discretion: if there is *a range of times that clearly count as early,* my request implies that you can choose among them. An unspecific request confers an implied discretion, and a vague request confers a resultant discretion.

[13]   The discretion may be very wide or very narrow, depending on the situation and on what else I do. My reason for asking you to come early may be obvious (or I may state it), and that reason may or may not make it quite clear just what time you should come.

law (while potentially ruling out all sorts of things you might wish to do) does not require a particular decision.

Many discretionary powers can only be used in one particular way in many cases: in *those* cases, the agency has no discretion.

Jargon alert

People often use the word 'discretion' as shorthand for 'discretionary power'. And the phrase 'control of discretion' is popular shorthand for control of the exercise of discretionary powers.

Consider the power in *Roncarelli*: the Prime Minister had a discretionary power to cancel liquor licences, but he had no discretion to cancel Roncarelli's liquor licence to punish him for helping Jehovah's Witnesses (i.e., the law didn't give him that choice). Yet there would be many cases in which the law would leave it to him to decide (for example) just how much disorder in a tavern would justify cancelling a liquor licence. The power is a discretionary power because it leaves him a choice in those cases.

Similarly, although the Privy Council in *Slattery v Naylor* (1888) 13 App Cas 446 decided that the council had discretion to ban burials within 100 yards of a dwelling, they suggested that there would be no discretion to ban Roman Catholics from conducting burials. The powers to cancel liquor licences or to make byelaws are discretionary, but they do not give you discretion to wage a religious war.

Note, finally, that it may be very controversial *whether* a power is discretionary, and whether the decision maker has discretion in a particular case. In *Slattery*, *Kruse*, and *Wednesbury*, each dispute was as to *whether* the public authority had discretion to do what it had done.

A discretion is a freedom of choice (among options that may limited) that is to be exercised responsibly. A public authority has that freedom of choice when it has no legal duty to make one decision rather than another. When a court holds that an exercise of a discretionary power was unlawful, as in *Roncarelli*, it is deciding that the initial decision maker had no discretion to make the decision it made.

FROM THE MISTS OF TIME

The idea that discretionary powers are to be controlled by the High Court is very old. In *Keighley's Case* (1609) 10 Co Rep 139 (140a), Lord Coke said that the statutory power of the Commissioners of Sewers to act 'according to your wisdoms and discretions' (Statute of Sewers 1531, 23 Henry VIII c 5, s III) was 'to be intended and interpreted according to law and justice, for every Judge or commissioner ought to have *duos sales, viz. salem sapientiae, ne sit insipidus, & salem conscientiae ne sit diabolus*' ['two gifts: the gift of wisdom—not to be stupid—and the gift of conscience—not to be a devil']. Coke, like the modern judges, thought that the wisdom of the common law was a special preserve of judges, which gave them a special responsibility to supervise administrative agencies. But even Coke did not think that good conscience was the special gift of judges.

7.2.3 Powers and duties

Giving a power to a public authority always confers discretion, unless the public authority is duty-bound to use the power in a particular way. If the law requires the authority to exercise the power in a particular way, then it imposes a legal duty, and there is no discretion. The Parole Board has a discretionary power to release a prisoner after the completion of the tariff period, if the prisoner poses no danger to the public. The House of Lords (following the lead of the European Court of Human Rights in *Stafford v UK* (2002) 35 EHRR 32) has turned that power into a duty to release a prisoner who poses no danger. The law requires parole in that situation (R v Lichniak [2002] UKHL 47 [20]).

Yet a public authority may have **discretion** in the performance of a **duty**. In *Lichniak*, the House of Lords only imposed a duty to release a prisoner after the tariff if the prisoner posed no danger to the public, so the Parole Board had a duty to act according to a vague standard. In *deciding whether* that duty applies, the Parole Board will have a resultant discretion whenever it is unclear whether a particular prisoner poses a danger.

A public authority has discretion whenever it has a duty to provide a service, but has a range of choices available as to how to provide the service.

> **But is it really discretion?**
> Can a public authority really have a *discretion*, when there are principles at stake (so that it must exercise its judgment responsibly and not just act on a whim)? If not, there are no discretions, because all public powers must be used responsibly. Sedley J suggested in *R v Tower Hamlets, ex p Tower Hamlets Combined Traders Association* [1994] COD 325 '…an administrative decision-making power may be 'a matter of judgment according to the legal principles and not to discretion'.
>
> But if those principles themselves allow the public authority the leeway to choose one way or another, then the public authority has discretion: rather than determining the outcome, the law leaves it to the public authority (to some extent) to decide what the principles require. The making of that choice does indeed require judgment, but the law does not require a particular judgment to be made. Lord Keith took this approach in *R v Devon CC, ex p G* [1989] AC 573, 604, in deciding whether a local authority had a discretion in deciding if free transportation was 'necessary' for school students: 'The authority's function in this respect is capable of being described as a "discretion," though it is not, of course, an unfettered discretion but rather in the nature of an exercise of judgment' (604).

7.2.4 Deference

Deferring to someone else means going along with their answer to a question. The ultimate in deference is obedience to a person or institution that has authority over you: the deference of courts to Parliament is one instance, and the fact that the government must defer to the order of a court is another. But deference becomes much more interesting and problematic when a decision maker *could* interfere with someone else's decision, and decides not to do so because there is some reason to leave the resolution of the question to the original decision maker. As Lord Slynn put it in *Walker*'s case, as regards the deference of courts to a ministry's decisions in setting up a compensation scheme, 'It is not for the courts to consider whether the scheme with its exclusion is a good scheme or a bad scheme, unless it can be said that the exclusion is irrational or so unreasonable that no reasonable minister could have adopted it' (*Walker*, 812).

You may think that deference of any kind is dangerous: it can work to protect things done in bad faith. Bad faith is a ground of judicial review of every administrative decision, but it is very hard to identify. If the judges decided for themselves whether an administrative decision was the right decision, then they would have the opportunity to correct injustices in cases where a public authority has acted in bad faith, but the claimant cannot prove it. If the courts defer to the executive on questions of substance, the effect will be that some decisions made in bad faith will stand uncorrected. But that only reflects the fact that judges cannot completely secure justice in public administration (see p 23). The danger of leaving a decision to an authority that might act unjustly is not a reason for judges to take over all public decision making; they should only interfere where judicial review will itself improve public decision making. Their duties of comity toward other public authorities require them not to start from scratch and do the initial decision maker's job. And a court does not have to choose between refusing to review a decision, and making a new decision in place of the original. It can defer more or less, and on some questions and not others.

Deference and discretion

What is the connection between deference and discretion? First of all, a public authority can have discretion even if a reviewing court shows no deference at all to its decision, because there may simply be no right answer to the question. In *Moyna v Work and Pensions Secretary* [2003] UKHL 44, the question was how to apply a statute that entitled a person to a disability allowance if 'he cannot prepare a cooked main meal for himself if he has the ingredients'. Mrs Moyna could prepare a cooked main meal some of the time, but not regularly. The resulting dispute over £15 per week went to the House of Lords,[14] and Lord Hoffmann held that the Court of Appeal should not have tried 'to sharpen the test to produce only one right answer' [20]. He thought that there was no error in a decision either way. To reach that decision, Lord Hoffmann did not have to defer to the initial decision maker; there was simply no ground of review, because there was no error in the initial decision. The presumption

---

[14] Mrs Moyna lost before the adjudication officer, the disability appeal tribunal, and the social security commissioner, won in the Court of Appeal, and finally lost in the House of Lords—see p 450.

of non-interference cannot be overcome if the court can identify nothing wrong with the decision.

Secondly, deference by courts does not itself give discretion to administrative authorities. Think for a moment about the questions of fact that public authorities must decide. A court will defer to the initial decision maker on such questions, but that does not mean that the public authority can decide the facts as it chooses; its legal duty is to do its best with the processes available to find the facts as they are. But the courts can only interfere to correct a finding of fact when it is blatantly obvious that the initial decision maker got it wrong (see section 9.2).

So discretion does not depend on deference, and deference does not necessarily give discretion. Yet there is, of course, a very important connection between deference and discretion. After all, a discretion is a freedom to answer a question in more than one way, and judicial deference ordinarily leaves an administrative authority free, to some extent, to answer a question in more than one way. Every act of deference by a court toward a public authority amounts to a judicial decision not to craft legal standards that would restrict the discretion of the public authority. So deference has the opposite effect from the **principle of legality** (see p 19). When the court applies the principle of legality, it is crafting a standard that restrains an authority's discretion. When the court defers, it is deciding not to do so.

But is it really deference?

In R (ProLife Alliance) v British Broadcasting Corporation [2003] UKHL 23, Lord Hoffmann denied that the court should defer to other public authorities: 'although the word "deference" is now very popular in describing the relationship between the judicial and the other branches of government, I do not think that its overtones of servility, or perhaps gracious concession, are appropriate to describe what is happening. In a society based upon the rule of law and the separation of powers, it is necessary to decide which branch of government has in any particular instance the decision-making power and what the legal limits of that power are....when a court decides that a decision is within the proper competence of the legislature or executive, it is not showing deference. It is deciding the law' [75]–[76].

But deference is not necessarily servile, or a concession: an army general is a superior officer who may need to defer to a sergeant on the question of how to get a platoon across a river. The general could override the sergeant's decision (and there might even be some special reason to do so). But it may be better for the sergeant to answer the question of how to cross the river than the general (the sergeant may know the terrain, and the abilities of each soldier, or it may be damaging to his relations with the soldiers if the general steps in...). A good general will then defer to the sergeant (to some extent), even if he can't see the point of what the sergeant is doing. The general is not servile, and is not making a gracious concession; the reason for deference is that in order to do his own job well, the general has to respect the sergeant's role. That is, **the reason for deference is comity.**

> A court, of course, is not a commanding general, any more than it is servile. Like the general, a court will often need to defer to the expertise of other decision makers in order to do its own job well. But unlike the general, the court also has reasons of political responsibility to defer to other decision makers, and its supervisory jurisdiction may even be restricted by law.
>
> By contrast, think of the attitude a judge ought to take to *legal argument* made by the lawyers for a public authority: the judge should listen with respectful attention, and with an open mind, and should then decide the matter with no deference at all to either party's legal argument.

7.3 Massive deference and non-justiciability

7.3.1 Foreign affairs and national security

In 1984, Prime Minister Thatcher decided to ban the trade union at the government's intelligence communications centre, Government Communication Headquarters ('GCHQ'). And she decided to do it without consulting the union first. The House of Lords held that the union had a legitimate expectation that she would consult the union before banning it from the workplace (*Council of Civil Service Unions v Minister for the Civil Service* [1985] AC 374; the Prime Minister is also the Minister for the Civil Service). As we will see in Chapter 8, the courts will quash a decision of a public authority that disappointed a legitimate expectation (on grounds of unfairness), *unless* it was fair to do so in the circumstances. Mrs Thatcher said that consultation would create a risk of industrial action by the union, which would endanger national security. Once her Cabinet Secretary gave evidence that she had based her decision on national security, the House of Lords was not prepared to hold that it had been unfair for the Prime Minister to disappoint the union's legitimate expectation of consultation.

If consulting the union would create a serious danger to the nation, then it was not unfair for the Prime Minister to go ahead and ban the union without consulting first. If the danger that would be caused by union consultation was trivial (or even imaginary, so that the Prime Minister was really just trying to make the unions look like enemies of the nation), then it was unfair to proceed without consultation. And that is what the Law Lords refused to decide: whether consulting the union would create a serious danger to the nation. So the House of Lords would not hold that Mrs Thatcher had acted unlawfully.

There are three key points to take from the GCHQ case:

GCHQ: key points

(1) The decision established clearly, for the first time, that **the courts can control the exercise of the royal prerogative**, using the same grounds of judicial

review that they use when they control the use of statutory powers.[15] For that reason, the decision is a milestone in the movement away from general deference to the executive, towards deference on specific issues (see section 2.6).

(2) The judges, nevertheless, retained the idea that **some powers are non-justiciable**.

(3) The case treats the four basic reasons for deference as considerations that *may* lead the court to consider a question to be non-justiciable.

'Justiciable' means 'suitable for a court to decide'. Lord Diplock held that the question of what would pose a danger to national security is a *non*-justiciable question, because 'the executive government bears the responsibility and alone has access to sources of information that qualify it to judge what the necessary action is' (413).

The importance of political responsibility for protecting the nation is the third of the four basic reasons for deference. Judges ought to leave the resolution of some questions to politicians because the people's ability to remove the politicians is a good control on the decision, and because otherwise the responsibility of politicians would be diluted by judicial control. An understanding of justiciability must also involve an understanding of what judges are good at (the second reason for deference) as well as what the judicial *process* is good for (the fourth reason for deference): an issue is not justiciable if the way in which courts make decisions is the wrong way to resolve that issue.

Deference and terrorism

Expertise, process, and political responsibility can be pressing reasons for deference, and they have come to seem more urgent since the September 11, 2001 attacks on New York and Washington. In October 2001, in reviewing a Home Office decision that it was in the public interest to deport a terrorism suspect, Lord Hoffmann pointed out the government's 'access to special information and expertise in these matters' and added that decisions on how to combat terrorism 'require a legitimacy which can be conferred only by entrusting them to persons responsible to the community through the democratic process' (*Home Secretary v Rehman* [2001] UKHL 47 [62] (Lord Hoffmann).

Similarly, the House of Lords unanimously held in R (*Corner House Research*) v *Director of the Serious Fraud Office* [2008] UKHL 60 that it was lawful for a serious fraud investigation to be halted on the ground that Saudi Arabia was threatening to withdraw its cooperation with anti-terrorism measures—a possibility allegedly creating a risk to British lives. Neither the judges nor the Director of the Serious Fraud Office could assess that risk, and the judges accepted that the Director could act on the views of the government.

---

[15] There had been suggestions to the same effect in *Chandler v DPP* [1964] AC 763, and a decision under the criminal injuries compensation scheme, set up under the prerogative, was actually reviewed in R *v Criminal Injuries Compensation Board, ex p Lain* [1967] 2 QB 864.

And in R (Bancoult) v Foreign Secretary (No 2) [2008] UKHL 61, the House of Lords reviewed the Foreign Secretary's decision to ban the Chagos Islanders—whose families had been moved from their islands in the Indian Ocean to Mauritius in the 1970s—from returning to the Islands. The Law Lords held 3–2 that it was not an abuse of power for the Foreign Secretary to base the decision on his assessment of the value of military cooperation with the United States. The Americans did not want any Islanders living within hundreds of miles of their airforce base on Britain's Indian Ocean territories, and the majority of the Law Lords left it to the Foreign Secretary to decide how pressing a consideration that was.

Does this approach to the 'war on terror' amount to an abandonment of the rule of law? Not necessarily, because the rule of law does not require that judges decide what would be good for national security or public safety. The role the judges play has to reflect their disadvantages in assessing dangers to the public, and it has to reflect the risk of abuse of power by a government that claims to be protecting the public from danger. There will be a failure in the rule of law if the government abuses the freedom that comes with the judges' deference. And the judges give the government a technique for abuse, if their deference on issues of public safety is too great, or if it stops them from asserting the rights of a claimant, or from protecting those aspects of the public interest that judges *can* assess.

The most important tensions in the control of discretionary powers result from a clash between issues on which judges need to defer, and the highly justiciable values that the courts insist on protecting. These things are controversial among the judges, and there is no easy overall way of assessing their success in standing up for the rule of law. In *Corner House Research*, the judges in the Divisional Court were adamant that surrendering to a threat from the Saudis was an abandonment of the rule of law; the House of Lords unanimously held that the need for investigators to consider a risk to the public (and their need to rely on assessments by government officials) was compatible with the rule of law. In *Bancoult*, the House of Lords was itself deeply divided over whether the judges needed to defer to the Foreign Secretary's assessment of the security considerations that, he said, gave reason to ban the Islanders from the Islands. The courts could not assess the United Kingdom's need to cooperate with the Americans, but all three Court of Appeal judges and two of five Law Lords were prepared to protect the Chagos Islanders' interest in living on the Chagos Islands regardless. They concluded that no matter how important it is to create a safe base for the U.S. Air Force (that was the question on which judges needed to defer), no reasonable Foreign Secretary would ban the Islanders from the Islands. Lord Bingham and Lord Mance dissented on the ground that the Islanders had a fundamental right not to be deprived of their place of abode. It seems clear that the Law Lords in the majority would have concurred in quashing the decision if the Islanders had actually been living on the Islands; the majority thought that since there had been no economically viable prospect for decades of resettlement of the Chagos Islands, the litigation for practical purposes concerned the Islanders' campaign for more support from the government, and the government's concern to be able to control visits to the Islands. If there had been a consensus among the judges that the ban on return to the

Islands was a violation of a fundamental right, there would have been a consensus that the Foreign Secretary could not violate it in order to please the Americans.

And the Belmarsh Prison case (A and X v Home Secretary [2004] UKHL 56, see p 6) shows that in spite of their need to defer on issues of public safety, the judges will almost unanimously line up against government action in the right conditions. Those conditions arise where, as in A and X, persons are detained on the basis of the judgment of politicians as to what emergency steps the 'war on terror' requires.

Why justiciability?

The GCHQ case represented a failure to attain the rule of law if the judges, in spite of their relative inability to assess the alleged danger to national security, could still have decided whether it was unfair for the Prime Minister to ban the union without consultation (if, for example, it should have been obvious to the judges that consultation could be conducted with no detriment to the operation of GCHQ). If that was the case, we might ask, why did the Law Lords put the problem in terms of justiciability, rather than simply pointing out some strong reasons for deference? All of the four basic reasons for deference arose in GCHQ. But they all arose in Slattery, Kruse, and Wednesbury, too. Why didn't the judges in those cases hold that the claims were non-justiciable?

Some entire claims are non-justiciable, because courts have no jurisdiction to hear them.

Non-justiciable claims

- The court will not hear a defamation claim that requires it to pass judgment on the acts of another country, because 'the court would be in a judicial no-man's land' (Buttes Gas and Oil Co v Hammer (No 3) [1982] AC 888, 938).
- The court will not ordinarily pass judgment on whether foreign legislation should be respected, although it will do so, exceptionally,
  - where the legislation is extremely abusive (Oppenheimer v Cattermole [1976] AC 249—a decree depriving German Jews of their German nationality), or
  - where the legislation is undeniably contrary to international law (Kuwait Airways v Iraqi Airways (Nos 4 and 5) [2002] UKHL 19—an Iraqi Government decree purporting to dissolve Kuwait Airways and transfer its airplanes to Iraqi Airways).
- Civil claims for damages for torture cannot be brought in the English courts against states and their representatives: state immunity is 'an absolute preliminary bar, precluding any examination of the merits' (Jones v Saudi Arabia [2006] UKHL 26 [33] (Lord Bingham)).
- A claim for judicial review of an act of Parliament on the ground that it was unreasonable would be non-justiciable.
- A claim in defamation against an MP for what he or she says in the House of Commons is non-justiciable, because of parliamentary privilege.

In all these cases, justiciability restricts the courts' jurisdiction: they have no power to determine the reasonableness of an act of Parliament, or to award damages for torture against a foreign state. But in *GCHQ*, the court did have jurisdiction to decide whether the Prime Minister's decision was *Wednesbury* unreasonable. Applying that standard requires the court to defer, but the question of *how much* to defer is one of degree. As Lord Bingham said in *R v Ministry of Defence, ex p Smith* [1996] QB 517:

> ‘ The greater the policy content of a decision, and the more remote the subject matter of a decision from ordinary judicial experience, the more hesitant the court must necessarily be in holding a decision to be irrational. That is good law and, like most good law, common sense. Where decisions of a policy-laden, esoteric or security-based nature are in issue even greater caution than normal must be shown in applying the test. . . . ’ (556)

Given that explanation of the duty to defer in controlling certain discretionary powers, what does it add to say that an issue is non-justiciable (and not merely that the judges must defer)? The answer is that an issue is non-justiciable if comity requires that judges not even address it. The puzzling part is this: if the courts won't second-guess an administrative judgment *at all*, aren't they abandoning their responsibility for the administration of justice? The key to the puzzle is to understand just which questions are non-justiciable.

Justiciability in administrative law is a feature of issues

In the *GCHQ* case, Lord Diplock concluded that 'what action is needed' to protect national security is 'a matter upon which those upon whom the responsibility rests, and not the courts of justice, must have the last word' (412). That makes it sound as if it is the question of *how to use a power* that may be non-justiciable. And Lord Roskill offered a non-exhaustive list of 'excluded categories' of prerogative power that are not susceptible to judicial review, 'because their nature and subject matter are such as not to be amenable to the judicial process': his instances were 'the making of treaties, the defence of the realm, the prerogative of mercy, the grant of honours, the dissolution of Parliament and the appointment of ministers' (418). That list was whittled down in later decisions,[16] but it took the decision in R (Abbasi) v Foreign Secretary and Home Secretary [2002] EWCA Civ 1598 (see p 4) to clarify the meaning of this list. Abbasi, like *GCHQ* itself, was a landmark case concerning the control of the prerogative, even though the claimant lost.

---

[16]   So in R v Home Secretary, ex p Ruddock [1987] 1 WLR 1482, Taylor J made it plain that a claim that national security was at stake did not (in itself) prevent the court from exercising its supervisory jurisdiction. And in R v Home Secretary, ex p Bentley [1994] QB 349, the court reviewed the exercise of the prerogative of mercy.

> ### Losers' landmarks
> Watch for landmark cases that push the law dramatically in the direction of the *losing* party's argument! It happens quite often, not only because the judges are sympathetically trying to give the loser some consolation, but because in giving reasons for their decision, conscientious judges will strive to state the argument for the losing side as favourably as it can be put, and then to explain why the case *still* needs to go the other way.

The decision in *Abbasi* pushed the imposition of the rule of law on the executive well beyond what was decided in GCHQ. The Court of Appeal decided that Abbasi was being arbitrarily detained in Guantánamo Bay, yet declined to reach the conclusion that the Foreign Secretary was acting unlawfully in refusing to demand Abbasi's release. The reason was that the proper exercise of the discretionary power to make representations to another country on behalf of the Crown involved considerations that were not justiciable. The Court of Appeal decided that it was inappropriate for judges even to ask the questions that they would need to answer, if they were to decide whether the Foreign Secretary had exercised the discretion properly. Those questions include whether and how Britain ought to co-operate with the Americans in their 'war on terror'. The repercussions for relations with the Americans (and for that matter with France and Pakistan) were relevant considerations and were non-justiciable.

If those questions are not for judges to answer, then whether the Foreign Secretary's decision was wise or foolish, just or unjust, the English judges have no jurisdiction to tell the Foreign Secretary how to respond to the relevant considerations. They lack the expertise, the techniques of inquiry, and the political accountability that are all essential for taking responsible decisions based on those considerations. *Abbasi* is a demonstration of the fact that judges have no general jurisdiction to do justice. Comity forbids them to impose a just foreign policy on the government.

In reaching its decision in *Abbasi*, the Court of Appeal clarified two points:

- no prerogative power is unreviewable, but

- judges cannot interfere with the exercise of a discretionary power (statutory or prerogative) if they would need to decide a non-justiciable issue in order to apply the grounds of review.

It is not a *power*, or the exercise of a power, that is justiciable or non-justiciable; what may be non-justiciable is a particular *issue* that would need to be decided, in order to give effect to the grounds of judicial review.

The Court of Appeal dismissed the claim for judicial review because, even after deciding that Abbasi was being arbitrarily detained, the judges were not in a position to find that the Foreign Secretary's refusal to complain to the Americans was itself an abuse of power. The new step in *Abbasi* was that the court *was* prepared to apply the doctrine of **relevance** (see section 8.2) to an exercise of the prerogative power to conduct relations with other states. The court held that Abbasi's arbitrary detention in a foreign country was relevant to the Foreign Secretary's decision. It is implicit in the Court of Appeal decision that, if the Foreign Secretary:

(1) had refused to consider a request that he challenge the Americans, or

(2) had denied that Abbasi was being arbitrarily detained, or

(3) had denied that the conditions of Abbasi's detention were relevant to his decision,

the court would have declared that he had reached his decision unlawfully, and would have required him to make the decision again on the basis of the relevant considerations (see *Abbasi* [99]–[100]). The point is emphasized by another Court of Appeal decision following *Abbasi*: in R (Al Rawi) v Foreign Secretary [2006] EWCA Civ 1279, the court rejected an argument that the Foreign Secretary had failed to attend to all the relevant considerations when he refused to demand the release of detainees from Guantánamo Bay. Laws LJ held that 'The court's role is to see that the government strictly complies with all formal requirements, and rationally considers the matters it has to confront. Here, because of the subject-matter, the law accords to the executive an especially broad margin of discretion' [148]. But, Laws LJ implied, judicial review is still available to require the government to *consider* 'the matters it has to confront'.

Abbasi made it clear that no administrative power is exempt from judicial review for abuse of power. But in the exercise of some powers, there are virtually always non-justiciable considerations at stake, which means that the courts will not interfere except on grounds such as corruption. So, even though no administrative power is beyond review in principle, the result of *Abbasi* is that certain forms of exercise of power will be largely unreviewable in effect, because they will always involve non-justiciable considerations. It is an inescapable conclusion, implicit in *Abbasi*, that non-justiciable issues are always at stake in the decision whether to make demands to another country. So it seems that the court will never tell the Foreign Secretary what representations to make to another government.

It is primarily *issues* that are justiciable or non-justiciable. A *claim* is non-justiciable if it cannot succeed unless the court passes judgment on a non-justiciable issue. But no power or action is non-justiciable. How, then, can we understand the remarkable justiciability case of R v Prime Minister, ex p Campaign for Nuclear Disarmament [2002] EWHC 2712? The CND asked the court to declare that the Prime Minister would be acting contrary to international law, if he sent troops into Iraq without a resolution from the United Nations Security Council specifically authorizing it. The Court of Appeal held that the issue of whether the Prime Minister would be acting contrary to international law was non-justiciable. But why? It is *not* beyond the ability of judges to decide whether it was lawful in international law to invade Iraq. In terms of expertise (the second basic reason for deference) and processes (the fourth), the judges were in a better position than the executive to determine this question. So why was this issue (and thus the claim) non-justiciable?

The courts will decide questions of international law whenever they need to (as in *Kuwait Airways v Iraqi Airways (Nos 4 and 5)* [2002] UKHL 19). But they only do so in order to determine some question of rights and duties between two parties; they will not determine what international law requires without a dispute under English law. There was no such dispute in the CND case. So the court refused to decide the international law issue, because doing so would take it beyond a court's role. In fact, since international law binds other nations too (but the orders of English courts do not), it would be 'an exorbitant arrogation of adjudicative power' (CND [37]). Even though the issues were quite manageable for judges, it is not their role to make a declaration of their opinion on a point of international law that does not need to be decided for any purpose of English law. The English judges cannot authoritatively determine the British government's obligations in international law.

And the court had a further reason for holding that the international law issue was non-justiciable: as Simon Brown LJ put it, 'The plain fact is that even to argue the substantive issue here, let alone to decide it, would be contrary to the national interest' [45]. That is, a hearing of the issues would embarrass the British government by forcing its lawyers to state its views in court on an issue of international relations. And if the court went on to decide the international law issue, even though the British government would not be violating English law if it ignored the court's opinion, the national and international politics of the Iraq war decisions would have been affected by the court's involvement. The court decided that it should stay out of all that, *even if international law prohibited the invasion.* If the British government invades another country in violation of international law, the CND case shows that the English courts will not interfere.

Similarly, in *Corner House Research*, the House of Lords rejected an argument that the judges should require the Director to act on the judges' interpretation of the UK's obligations under the international Convention on Combating Bribery of Foreign Public Officials 1997. There were two reasons: the Convention established an international working group that could discuss the interpretation and application of the Convention. More importantly, the House of Lords held that it would not be unlawful in English law for the Director of the Serious Fraud Office to act incompatibly with the Convention (Lord Bingham [47]).

Discretion or jurisdiction?

In CND, Simon Brown LJ said that it was immaterial for the court's purposes 'whether as a matter of juridical theory such judicial abstinence is properly to be regarded as a matter of discretion or a matter of jurisdiction.' [47] In fact, deciding that an issue is non-justiciable can be **both**. The High Court is a remarkable public authority partly because it has power to determine its own jurisdiction. That power is a discretionary power, which does not mean that the judges can exercise it any way they like; there are rules that bind the courts not to hear certain claims (see above on claims that contest the validity of a statute of Parliament, or that rely on the invalidity of foreign legislation). Where it is not clear what those rules require (see the *Oppenheimer* and *Kuwait Airways* cases above), the court may have a discretion to choose either way; that discretionary choice determines the courts' jurisdiction. Non-justiciability can leave public authorities with a wide discretion in some matters. In R *v Jones* [2006] UKHL 16, the House of Lords held that defendants charged with aggravated trespass in a protest against the Iraq war could not plead that they were trying to prevent the United Kingdom from committing the crime of aggression in international law. Lord Hoffmann said that, 'The decision to go to war, whether one thinks it was right or wrong, fell squarely within the discretionary powers of the Crown to defend the realm and conduct its foreign affairs. To say that these matters are not justiciable may be simply another way of putting the same point' [66]–[67]. Lord Hoffmann's link between justiciability and discretion is important. A public authority with responsibility for determining non-justiciable issues has a massive freedom of decision.

The non-justiciability of the issue in CND, then, is rather different from the non-justiciability of the issues in the GCHQ case. The whole question of what international law required was, in the circumstances of the case, not for the English judges to decide.

Non-justiciability is a special reason for complete deference, but only for complete deference *on some particular issue*. Conversely, remember that if an issue *is* justiciable, that does not mean that judges ought to decide it! Non-justiciability is a limit on judicial review; justiciability is not a *reason for* judicial review. If an issue is perfectly justiciable (e.g., a question of fact that a housing agency decides[17]), there is still no ground of judicial review unless the court, in spite of not being the initial decision maker, can identify a decision as unreasonable.

Even though non-justiciability seems like an all-or-nothing matter, it is surprisingly flexible, because it can be generated by the four basic reasons for deference. Even the question of what is necessary in responding to a national security emergency is not necessarily non-justiciable.

Political questions in the U.S.A.

In 2004, a court in California dismissed the complaint in *Taxpayers of United States of America v Bush*, without a trial. The plaintiffs claimed that the Bush Government had conspired with the Government of Saudi Arabia to conduct the September 11, 2001 attacks on the World Trade Center and Pentagon, in order 'to gather public support for the military invasion of Iraq and persuade Congress to enact the U.S.A. Patriot Acts' (2004 WL 3030076 (N.D.Cal.), Illston J, December 30, 2004). The court struck out the claim on the ground that the issues were non-justiciable under the 'political questions' doctrine.

In a classic statement of that doctrine in *Baker v Carr*, 369 US 186, 210 (1962), the U.S. Supreme Court held that the court should refuse to answer a question on the

---

[17]   See *Begum v Tower Hamlets London Borough Council* [2003] UKHL 5, p 327.

ground of 'a textually demonstrable constitutional commitment of the issue to a coordinate political department; or a lack of judicially discoverable and manageable standards for resolving it; or the impossibility of deciding without an initial policy determination of a kind clearly for non-judicial discretion; or the impossibility of a court's undertaking independent resolution without expressing lack of the respect due coordinate branches of government; or an unusual need for unquestioning adherence to a political decision already made; or the potentiality of embarrassment from multifarious pronouncements by various departments on one question' (217).

7.3.2 Money

Massive deference and local council funding

The best examples of massive deference in the English law of judicial review are the cases on local council funding under the Thatcher Government: R v Environment Secretary, ex p Nottinghamshire County Council [1986] AC 240 and R v Environment Secretary, ex p Hammersmith and Fulham LBC [1991] 1 AC 521. Parliament had authorized the Environment Secretary to assess whether local authorities were setting excessive budgets. The Government could control local expenditure by reducing the support grant to local authorities (Nottinghamshire), and by capping the community charges that local authorities could impose (Hammersmith and Fulham). The Conservatives punished dozens of Labour councils for spending too much, and the local authorities went to court to challenge the decisions on the Wednesbury grounds. Lord Scarman hinted in Nottinghamshire that there was no justiciable issue (247), and in Hammersmith and Fulham, Lord Bridge said that, 'the merits of the policy underlying the decisions are not susceptible to review by the courts and the courts would be exceeding their proper function if they presumed to condemn the policy as unreasonable' (597). The House of Lords held in both cases that the Wednesbury grounds of review were unavailable. The Minister's decisions could not be challenged on the ground of Wednesbury unreasonableness, according to Lord Scarman in Nottinghamshire, but only on the ground of bad faith or improper motive, or on the ground that the decision was 'so absurd that he must have taken leave of his senses' (596). If that sounds like irrationality, it just shows why the popular use of the term 'irrationality' for Wednesbury unreasonableness is dangerous and confusing. 'So absurd that he must have taken leave of his senses' is a very good synonym for 'irrational', but Lord Scarman was deliberately trying to identify a way of controlling the financial control discretion that was more restrained than the way of controlling local byelaws that was set out in Slattery, Kruse, and Wednesbury. It is hard to identify a form of control on an exercise of discretionary power that is more restrained than the control that Lord Greene imposed on city byelaws, when the Wednesbury standard is called 'irrationality'. In Hammersmith and Fulham, Lord Bridge said that not just any irrationality would do as a ground of judicial review of a decision to cap the community charge: 'it is not open to challenge on the grounds of irrationality short of the extremes of bad faith, improper motive or manifest absurdity' (527).

These cases show that *Wednesbury* does not offer a general set of standards of review of executive action.[18] No clearer illustration could be given of the **principle of relativity** (see p 10). The courts do not necessarily have power to quash a *Wednesbury*-unreasonable decision; it depends on the issues at stake. Even in *Hammersmith and Fulham*, the House of Lords did not say that the decision was unreviewable: the local authorities would have won if they could have shown bad faith (for example, that the Environment Secretary had taken a bribe, or that he had targeted Labour councils on grounds other than their spending plans). But it is not the judges' job to decide whether a government grant to a local authority is so unreasonable that no reasonable politician could have decided to make it.

Justiciability check

Remember that it is a particular question or issue that is justiciable or non-justiciable (see p 242). *Decisions* are neither justiciable nor non-justiciable. So Lord Scarman suggested in *Nottinghamshire* that while the interpretation of a statute giving a wide discretion over public expenditure is 'justiciable', the 'matters of political judgment' which have to be decided in exercising the discretion are for the ministers and the House of Commons, and 'are not for the judges or your Lordships' House in its judicial capacity' (247). A decision in bad faith could still be quashed on judicial review (as *Roncarelli v Duplessis* [1959] SCR 121 and *Wednesbury* state), because the court would not need to pass judgment on anything non-justiciable in order to quash the decision.

When can a public authority take the cost of a decision into account?

In general, the courts are extremely unwilling *to tell public authorities how to spend money*, yet not unwilling at all *to make them spend money*. If a public authority has a discretionary power to decide how to spend money, the courts will be as restrained as they were in *Nottinghamshire* and *Hammersmith and Fulham*. And the expense of using a discretionary power one way rather than another may be a relevant consideration: in R (*Bancoult*) v *Foreign Secretary* (No 2) [2008] UKHL 61 (see p 240), the House of Lords held that in deciding whether to prohibit the Chagossians from returning to the Indian Ocean islands from which they had been removed in the 1970s, 'the advice that the cost of any permanent resettlement would be "prohibitive" was an entirely legitimate factor for the Government—which is responsible for the way that tax revenues are spent—to take into account' (Lord Rodger [113]; cf. Lord Hoffmann [55]).

But the fact that a public authority's legal duty requires it to spend money will not stop the court from enforcing the duty. First of all, the classic cases on due

---

[18]   As Lord Scarman said, 'There is a risk...that the judgment [in *Wednesbury*] may be treated as a complete, exhaustive, definitive statement of the law' (*Nottinghamshire*, 249).

process such as *Cooper v Wandsworth Board of Works* (1863) 14 CB (NS) 180 make the government spend money on administrative procedures, and the process costs that the law imposes in the 21st century are really serious. Secondly, in many cases on the exercise of discretionary power, the courts are prepared to tell public authorities that the impact on their resources is an *irrelevant* consideration.

The leading decision is R *v East Sussex County Council, ex p Tandy* [1998] AC 714 (HL). Beth Tandy could not go to school for medical reasons, so the local education authority provided her with tuition at home. After three years, the authority decided to cut the teaching from five hours a week to three hours per week, to save money. The education authority had a statutory duty to provide a 'suitable education'; that duty gave it a **resultant discretion** (see p 232) in deciding what was suitable for a particular student. But the House of Lords held that the decision had to be made without regard to the authority's financial resources. Similarly, in R *(Conville) v Richmond upon Thames LBC* [2006] EWCA Civ 718, the local authority had a statutory duty to provide accommodation that would give a homeless person 'a reasonable opportunity' of moving on to permanent accommodation. Without citing *Tandy*, the Court of Appeal took the same approach: 'While the authority can decide, subject to the supervision of the court under ordinary principles, what amounts to a reasonable opportunity, the expression does not permit them, in doing so, to have regard to considerations peculiar to them, such as the extent of their resources and other demands upon them. It is what is reasonable from the applicant's standpoint, having regard to his circumstances and in the context of the accommodation potentially available' [36].

Yet in other contexts, the courts sometimes show massive deference toward public authorities on decisions as to how to spend their money. In R *v Cambridge Health Authority, ex p B* [1995] 1 WLR 898 (CA), the health authority decided to deny lifesaving treatment to a nine-year-old girl. Sir Thomas Bingham MR said, 'Difficult and agonising judgments have to be made as to how a limited budget is best allocated to the maximum advantage of the maximum number of patients' (906),[19] and the Court deferred to the Health Authority on those judgments.

If we can reconcile *Tandy* and *Conville* with B, we will have a clear idea of the legally permissible role of financial considerations in administrative discretions. And in fact, the distinction between the two classes of case is clear and important: if a decision maker has a duty to abide by a standard that does not depend on its resources (such as a duty to provide a 'suitable education'), then it cannot get out of its legal duty on financial grounds. But if it has a wide discretion that includes the responsibility to decide how to distribute resources among competing needs (as health authorities often have in deciding what treatments to provide), then financial considerations become relevant: the public authority has a discretionary power to choose among different potential allocations of its resources. In the latter sort of case, the courts will give practically no protection against bad decisions. If the authority has to make a judgment as to how to allocate a limited budget among competing needs,

----

[19] Compare R *(Pfizer Ltd) v Secretary of State for Health* [2002] EWCA Civ 1566, in which a drug company unsuccessfully challenged restrictions on the circumstances in which the NHS would supply Viagra.

none of which the authority has a duty to meet, then 'That is not a judgment which a court can make', as Sir Thomas Bingham MR said in B (137).

This approach leaves the provision of some crucial social services up to the largely uncontrolled choice of administrative officials. If they make an overly stingy decision about whether to provide a crucial medical treatment, the courts will not put it right. That is justifiable, because of the court's limited capacity to decide how much expenditure on a service would be appropriate. Of course, administrative authorities may make bad decisions. If the difficult case of B had been decided the other way, the resulting turn toward more intrusive judicial review would have given judges the opportunity of righting wrongs; but this opportunity would have come at the risk of irresponsible judicial interference with public service provision. It is one of the drastic implications of comity, that the judges cannot right all wrongs.

So open-ended discretionary powers and duties to provide public services can be exercised on the basis of the administrative authority's judgment as to the best use of resources, with very little control. In R v Chief Constable of Sussex, ex p International Trader's Ferry Ltd [1999] 2 AC 418 (HL), Lord Slynn cited the B case and held that the police could take the impact on their resources into account in deciding how much police protection to give an animal exporter against animal rights demonstrators (430). The police had a duty to provide protection, but they also had a discretion as to how to carry it out, and the court was not prepared to tell them how much of their budget to commit to the claimant's problem.

7.3.3 Technical expertise

Don't even think of trying to get a court to change your grade in a university examination. The question of what grade you should receive is a non-justiciable question. Public universities are amenable to judicial review, and it is possible to imagine a professor giving your paper a grade that no reasonable professor would give, and still you have no hope of getting a court to quash it on that ground. This point is actually so obvious that it does not need authority, but you can find it stated by Lord Justice Sedley in Clark v University of Lincolnshire and Humberside [2000] 1 WLR 1988 [12]. It is something to keep in mind when we get to the remarkably intrusive forms of judicial review (developed, in part, by Lord Justice Sedley) that are considered in Chapter 8. A court may well quash a university grading decision on grounds of bad faith or improper process, but not on the ground that a grade was so low that no reasonable marker would give it.[20]

● Pop Quiz ●

Granted that judges should not review a grade in a chemistry exam because they lack the expertise that is needed to make the initial decision, should they be more willing to reconsider the mark given in a university law exam?

---

[20] But the first thing for a student to do would be to complain to the Office of the Independent Adjudicator for Higher Education—see p 495. She will not second-guess grade decisions, either.

Very many public authorities are organized (and their staff are appointed) in ways that will enable them to use special talents and training to draw conclusions from the facts of a situation better than judges could. The resulting forms of deference vary, and it is hard to generalize. The marking of exams is an extreme case, and there are less extreme forms of deference. An example is the deference shown to regulators. In *Great North Eastern Railway Ltd v Office of Rail Regulation* [2006] EWHC 1942, GNER argued that it was unfair that it paid a fixed charge to the rail regulator (ORR), while other operators on the same rail lines were able to pay a variable charge. The court decided that the complexities of the economic differences between the different operations were a reason for deference: 'Given the ORR's expertise in this highly technical field the Court would be very slow indeed to impugn the ORR's view...' [39].

A mistake in assessing the complexities in this area would leave GNER struggling to compete with rail operators who got a better deal for the rail lines. And the important point about that decision is that the issues at stake were *not* non-justiciable. The court would be 'very slow indeed' to impose its own view of the economic complexities on the rail regulator. But it is capable of forming a view, and so it is capable of quashing a patently unreasonable regulatory decision.

The deference to the regulator really does create a potential for the court to leave unjust decisions standing. And if the decision is unjust, it is unjust on a large scale: a few months after it lost its case, GNER forfeited its £1.3 billion London-to-Edinburgh franchise, because of the losses that had led it to challenge the regulator's decision.

7.3.4 Planning

In reviewing decisions to give or to refuse permission for new building projects, the courts will defer massively to the views of a local planning inspector (R (Springhall) v Richmond upon Thames [2006] EWCA Civ 19) or the Environment Secretary (Tesco Stores v Environment Secretary [1995] 1 WLR 759), as to what is in the public interest.

In *First Secretary of State v Hammersmatch Properties Ltd* [2005] EWCA Civ 1360, the judge in the Administrative Court had quashed a decision of a planning inspector to preserve a building in Welwyn Garden City rather than to allow a redevelopment. The Court of Appeal reversed the decision on the ground that the judge 'entered the arena of planning merits and has thereby exceeded his powers... Planning judgments are for planning authorities and not the courts' [32]–[33]. Pill LJ relied on the restatement of *Wednesbury* unreasonableness by Lord Bingham CJ in *Hindley's* case: 'To justify intervention by the court, the decision under challenge must fall outside the bounds of any decision open to a reasonable decision maker' (R v Home Secretary, ex p Hindley [1998] QB 751, 777).

Cynicism alert

Because the *Wednesbury* principles are so vague, you may start to think that the judges just quash whichever decisions they don't like, and say that no reasonable person could have made the decision. It is not surprising if that happens some-times, since it is easy for any of us to jump from thinking that a decision was wrong, to thinking that no reasonable person could agree with it.

But the *Hammersmatch Properties* case shows that the judges actually can refrain from interfering with decisions that they do not like. Lady Justice Smith plainly dis-agreed with the decision, but said that her 'personal view' was 'irrelevant in the present proceedings' [36]. Staughton LJ said, 'If I were the planning authority, I would stop preserving the Vospor building as a useless object...I suspect that it was what the people of Welwyn Garden City wanted, or some of them. However, I am not the planning authority, and neither is the judge' [40].[21]

Notice also that sometimes the courts expressly state that a decision on some point can lawfully be made *either way* by a public authority. *Boddington v British Transport Police* [1999] 2 AC 143 is an example: Lord Steyn stated that the railway company could permit some smoking or forbid all smoking on its trains, as it saw fit: either policy would be 'within the range of reasonable decisions open to a deci-sion maker' (175). *R v Monopolies and Mergers Commission, ex p South Yorkshire Transport* [1993] 1 WLR 23 (see p 334) is another classic example.

So the hands-off standards of control of discretionary powers make a differ-ence: although the judges *can* use the vague grounds of judicial review to step in and impose what they think the original decision maker ought to have done, they often succeed in leaving the public authority to do its own job.

7.3.5 Decisions approved in Parliament

Statutes often require that a particular kind of administrative decision (usually, administrative regulations) must be laid before Parliament for approval before becoming valid (or is subject to annulment by Parliament after being made). If the Houses of Parliament have approved a decision, it may seem that the courts should not review its substance at all, because of the **political responsibility** reason for deference (the third of the four basic reasons for deference). In fact, the situation is more complex.

When the Houses of Parliament approve a decision, or do not act on an oppor-tunity to invalidate it, that makes an impression on the judges. In *Hammersmith and Fulham* (see p 247), the fact that the rate-capping decisions could only take effect with the approval of the House of Commons seems to have made the House of Lords all the more reluctant to interfere with decisions about national financial policy: 'it is in the political forum of the House of Commons that they are properly to be debated and approved or disapproved on their merits' *R v Environment Secretary, ex p Hammersmith and Fulham LBC* [1991] 1 AC 521, 597 (Lord Bridge).

---

[21]   Cf. *Slattery v Naylor* (1888) 13 App Cas 446 (see p 220), in which Lord Hobhouse said that a more relaxed byelaw might have been wiser and more prudent, but added, 'supposing that to be so, it is quite a different question whether a bye-law like the present one is to be held unreasonable because such considerations have been overlooked or rejected by its framers' (452–3).

But there is no rule that any decision is unreviewable just because it has been approved by both Houses of Parliament. The constitutional difference between a statute and a ministerial order approved by both Houses is fundamental.[22] As Mustill LJ said in an unreported decision in 1985, the crucial question is whether a statute providing for an order to be laid before Parliament is to be interpreted 'to make the House of Commons the sole judge of whether the decision expressed in the draft order is too unreasonable to be allowed to stand' (R v Environment Secretary, ex p Greater London Council 3 April 1985, cited in R (Javed) v Home Secretary [2001] EWCA Civ 789 [47]). Lord Justice Mustill's answer was 'no': unless Parliament has said otherwise in the authorizing statute, the role of the House of Commons should be interpreted as an additional safeguard, with different purposes from the safeguard of judicial review on the Wednesbury principles. That approach reflects the different capacities of courts and of the House of Commons to secure responsible government (see p 53). And it is compatible with the very deferential approach in the Hammersmith and Fulham case: the House of Commons was well placed to pass judgment on the national finance issues at stake in Hammersmith and Fulham, and there was really no additional role for the courts to play in assessing the reasonableness of the public finance decisions.

Javed is an example of a case in which a regulation approved by both Houses of Parliament was quashed on the ground of 'irrationality': the Home Secretary had certified that there was in general no serious risk of persecution in Pakistan, so that the claims of asylum seekers from Pakistan could be dealt with on a fast track. The court decided that there was a serious risk of persecution to some women, and quashed the decision. The approval of the House of Commons did not stand in the way, because it is the court's special role to protect particular persons from an unreasonable attempt by the Home Secretary to streamline his processes in a way that would prejudice their claims to asylum. So the difference that approval in Parliament makes, if any, depends on the issues in the case.

7.3.6 Legal processes

Judges have totally unreviewable discretionary powers in making some procedural decisions. For example, a judge determining an application for permission to seek judicial review has an unfettered discretion as to whether it should be dealt with on the papers or after a hearing: R (Ewing) v Department for Constitutional Affairs [2006] EWHC 504. The courts have often stated that a High Court judge's various discretions under the Civil Procedure Rules are unfettered (e.g., Capital Bank PLC v Stickland [2004] EWCA Civ 1677). That does not mean that it is o.k. for the judge to act in an unprincipled way—far from it. But it does mean that the law does not tell the judge what would be a principled use of the power, and does not give a disappointed claimant any recourse against the judge's use of the power.

---

22   And has long been recognized: see R v Electricity Commissioners, ex p London Electricity Joint Committee Co [1924] 1 KB 171, 208.

For related reasons, other public authorities may have massive leeway in making decisions about the conduct of litigation, or the conduct of investigations into criminal allegations. So, 'absent dishonesty or mala fides or an exceptional circumstance', a decision of the Director of Public Prosecutions to consent to a criminal prosecution 'is not amenable to judicial review' (*R v DPP ex p Kebilene* [1999] 3 WLR 972, 985; cf. *Sharma v Antoine* [2006] UKPC 57 [14]). Similarly, it is almost impossible to get a court to stop the police from conducting an investigation into a suspected offence, even if the person being investigated can give good reason to think that they should not be a suspect, and even if the investigation (such as an investigation into possession of child pornography) is traumatic and damaging. The courts would only interfere if they found the investigation to be malicious or irrational (*R (C) v Chief Constable* [2006] EWHC 2352). As Lord Bingham has put it, 'only in highly exceptional cases will the court disturb the decisions of an independent prosecutor and investigator' (*R (Corner House Research) v Director of the Serious Fraud Office* [2008] UKHL 60 [30]).

The rationale for restrained review of decisions to investigate and to prosecute is that, for a defendant against whom an unreasonable investigation is conducted or an unreasonable prosecution is pursued, the criminal justice process itself provides a hearing. Judicial review is a last resort (see p 60), so it is not needed where the claimant has access to another judicial process.

But consider a decision *not* to investigate or to prosecute, and how dangerous such a decision could be if it concerned allegations against a public official or the investigation of wrongdoing in which the government has an interest. An independent and committed prosecution service is crucial to the rule of law. In England, this role is committed to the Crown Prosecution Service (CPS), and its independence is guarded by a politician, the Attorney General. He is traditionally meant to act independently from the government, but he is appointed on the advice of the Prime Minister, and attends Cabinet meetings. The Director of Public Prosecutions (the head of the CPS) has day-to-day responsibility, subject to his accountability to the Attorney General, and subject to the possibility that individuals may initiate a private prosecution. In making sensitive decisions not to prosecute, there is also a consistent practice of asking advice from senior Treasury counsel. Much of the decision turns on highly educated guesswork as to whether a jury will convict. The integrity of the system really depends on the independent attitude and the dedication of the Crown prosecutors who make particular decisions, and, ultimately, of the Attorney General. Is there any role for judges?

In *R v DPP, ex p Manning* [2001] QB 330, the Divisional Court ordered the DPP to reconsider the decision not to prosecute prison officers over the death of Alton Manning, after they restrained him in a violent struggle. A coroner's jury found that his death was an unlawful killing, but the CPS decided not to prosecute. The advising lawyer decided that there was no reasonable prospect of a conviction, because of the violence of the struggle, and because there was conflicting evidence as to how the prison officers had restrained Manning. The DPP's decision not to prosecute was quashed in judicial review, on the grounds that the Crown prosecutor had not taken relevant considerations into account, had applied a test higher than the Code, and had not given adequate explanation of the decision. So these limited judicial controls are added to the controls within the CPS. But in quashing the decision, the Lord Chief Justice, Lord Bingham, said, 'we must emphasise that the effect of this decision is not to require the Director to prosecute. It is to require reconsideration of the decision whether or not to prosecute. On the likely or proper outcome of that reconsideration we express no opinion at all' [42]. In fact, after reconsideration the CPS decided once more not to prosecute, and the Manning family's campaign was at an end.[23]

What of a decision not to investigate wrongdoing or not to prosecute, because doing so would not be in the public interest? No such decision had been quashed until the Divisional Court's decision in R (Corner House Research) v Director of the Serious Fraud Office [2008] EWHC 714, striking down a decision by the Director of the Serious Fraud Office (an investigator, who, like the DPP, makes independent decisions but is accountable to the Attorney General). The Director had called off the investigation of allegations that British Aerospace, a private company, had illegally given bribes to foreign officials in negotiating the sale of fighter aircraft to Saudi Arabia. The Divisional Court held that the Director had unlawfully surrendered to a threat from Saudi Arabia to withdraw from cooperation with the British Government in fighting terrorism, if the investigation continued:

> The rationale for the court's intervention is its responsibility to protect the rule of law. . . . The surrender of a public authority to threat or pressure undermines the rule of law. [60]

The House of Lords overturned the Divisional Court's decision, and restored the deferential approach to judicial review of independent investigations. The Law Lords all held that the Director could lawfully take into account an alleged risk to British lives if the Saudis withdrew from cooperation in fighting terrorism: R (Corner House Research) v Director of the SFO [2008] UKHL 60. They left it to the Director to assess the risks, and they also allowed him to defer to others (such as the British Ambassador to Saudi Arabia, the Prime Minister, the Foreign Secretary, and the Defence Secretary) who might know better what Saudi Arabia was likely to do, and what effect it might have in Britain. And they left it to him to weigh the supposed risk against other considerations, including the importance of upholding the rule of law.

The result of Corner House Research is a very hands-off form of review. The Saudis threatened not only to stop cooperating in fighting terrorism, but also to stop buying British aircraft. The Government and the arms manufacturer were urging the Director to stop the prosecution. A commercial threat would have been an irrelevant consideration. There was no evidence that the Director had based his decision on the commercial threat. But even though the Director had come under pressure to stop

[23] Compare the unsuccessful claim for judicial review by the family of Jean Charles de Menezes, who challenged the decision not to prosecute the police officers who shot and killed him in July 2005 when they mistook him for a suicide bomber: R (Da Silva) v DPP [2006] EWHC 3204 (applying the decision in Manning).

the investigation for patently irrelevant reasons, the Law Lords were not prepared to assess the issue (whether stopping the investigation might cost British lives) that mattered.

The Divisional Court thought that as judges, they had to quash a decision that was based on a threat because, 'At the heart of the obligations of the courts and of the judges lies the duty to protect the rule of law' [2008] EWHC 714 [63]. They quoted Lord Hope's remark in in R (Jackson) v Attorney General [2006] 1 AC 262, that 'the rule of law enforced by the courts is the ultimate controlling factor on which our constitution is based' [107]. The House of Lords' decision in *Corner House Research* underlines a harsh reality that the courts have to face: they do not always have the resources to enforce the rule of law. Protecting the rule of law is much more a responsibility of the executive, than it is the responsibility of the courts (see p 14), and the courts have a limited capacity to supervise the government's fulfilment of that responsibility.

Corner House Research leaves open a genuine danger that the government will pressure prosecutors into abandoning the rule of law on trumped up grounds of public safety, when they have other interests in mind; the Law Lords' justification for their decision was, in effect, that the courts could not guard against that risk, because they had to leave it to an independent investigator (and indirectly to government officials who were far from independent) to assess a risk to British lives. It may in some circumstances be a breach of comity for the courts to enforce the duty of the executive to protect the rule of law.

7.3.7 Decisions based on impressions

A court may be 'less qualified to make the decision under challenge than the decision maker' (*Higham v University of Plymouth* [2005] EWHC 1492) simply because the initial decision maker had a process by which he or she could see the people involved face to face. *Higham* was a case on a university's power (and duty) to remove a medical student from the register if the school cannot certify his fitness to practise medicine. The really crucial reason for deference was not expertise, but a **process reason**: Stanley Burton J held that 'the original decision maker, here the Committee, had the advantage of seeing and hearing the witnesses and, perhaps most importantly, Mr Higham himself, and were able to form a view of him and his personality that a consideration of the documents by this Court cannot approach' [29]. Then the court 'must approach that decision fairly made by those qualified to make it with the respect and deference due in such circumstances' [29].

Apart from any problems arising from the passage of time, you might think that this advantage of the initial decision maker could be solved through a hearing in the Administrative Court. But it is only in special circumstances (see p 331) that the court will repeat the fact-finding inquiry. The **presumption against interference** (see p 222) is also a presumption against starting from scratch on an assessment of the facts. Finding the facts all over again would be a way of solving mistakes in the first decision. But it would be a way of introducing new mistakes, too, and there is no reason for it unless the claimant can show *either* a lack of due process, or that the substance of a finding of fact was extremely unreasonable. That is why judicial review is not *generally* available against findings of fact, although a court will ask whether there is special reason to overturn a decision as to the facts (see section 9.2).

7.3.8 Policy in general

The instances of massive deference outlined here are some of the most dramatic, but they are only instances. The four basic reasons for deference play out in varying ways in diverse cases in which courts are very unwilling to interfere. R *v Ministry of Defence, ex p Walker* [2000] 1 WLR 806 (see section 2.1) is an instance of massive deference: if the military uses its inherent discretionary power to provide for soldiers by setting up a compensation scheme for injuries, and the scheme is not contrary to any statute, the courts will not want to strike down the eligibility criteria unless they really are extremely bad. So the House of Lords held in *Walker* that the criteria would have to be 'irrational' (812). The massive deference in the case is explained partly by the fact that Sergeant Walker was challenging a decision as to how to spend money. But deference was also due to the military's expertise in (and responsibility for) assessing the conditions of troops and the risks they faced in Bosnia and Northern Ireland.

Such decisions, it is often said, are policy decisions, and that explains the massive deference they attract in a variety of contexts. Apart from deference on matters of impression, can we say that all the instances of massive deference reflect the courts' unwillingness to pass judgment on policy matters? Yes, if you like, because the word 'policy' is so flexible. It can include *any* reason for a public decision (and in that sense of 'policy', there is no general deference on policy matters). Or it can mean any such reason that merits judicial deference to another decision maker. In the GCHQ case, Lord Diplock said that challenges to 'the application of Government policy ... do not normally involve questions to which ... the judicial process is adapted to provide the right answer' (*Council of Civil Service Unions v Minister for the Civil Service* [1985] AC 374, 411). But 'policy' in Lord Diplock's sense only gives an overall label to the considerations that reflect the four basic reasons for deference. To say that an issue is a matter of 'policy', in the sense that requires courts to defer to other public authorities, is just to say that the responsibility to decide it has been allocated to another public authority, and that authority's expertise, or political responsibility, or processes put it in a better position than the court to decide the issue.

7.4 Conclusion

Because judges have taken dramatic steps to control abuses of power, it is tempting to exaggerate the importance of judicial review in administrative law. To put it in perspective, consider the following summary of the ways in which the law controls the exercise of discretionary powers.

Summary: the law may control a discretionary power by:

(1) **allocating it to a particular person or agency;**
(2) **defining its extent:**
   - powers conferred by statutes and regulations are defined by the legislation that confers them;
(3) **imposing standards that the decision maker must apply, or identifying considerations on which a public authority must act;**
(4) **requiring a public authority to adhere to procedural requirements:**
   - openness and notice;
   - hearings;
   - lack of bias; and
   - reasons;
(5) **providing for review:**
   - internal review or appeal within an agency;
   - administrative justice (tribunals, ombudsmen, inquiries, etc.); and
   - judicial review and statutory appeals; and
(6) **imposing liabilities:**
   - for crimes and torts;
   - and in any other way Parliament sees fit to provide (e.g.: liability of councillors to make good any losses occasioned by the failure to make a rate (*Lloyd v McMahon* [1987] 1 AC 625)).

That summary is actually a summary of administrative law—this whole book is about legal conferral and legal control of discretionary powers. Judicial review plays an important but limited role; it is just one line in the summary. It is not even the primary technique for controlling the use of discretionary powers. Courts are only one of the institutions that review decisions. The tribunals system controls administrative decisions in much larger numbers than courts do (see p 431), and often with less deference.

It is also important not to *understate* the role of judicial review. While the judges have little control over the allocation of discretionary power,[24] they have played a leading role in the development of the law of due process, and they continue to take a dynamic approach to it. The Court of Appeal and the House of Lords will continue to play an important role in controlling the work of tribunals (see Chapter 12), and judges even control the work of ombudsmen. And the judges have played a central role in developing the liabilities of public authorities in tort and contract (see Chapters 14 and 15). To the overall structure of administrative law, the judges' law-making role is more important than their role in resolving particular disputes and preventing particular abuses of power. The common law rules of due process and of tort liability are

---

[24] They can, of course, decide under the Human Rights Act that an allocation of power is incompatible with a Convention right—see p 50. And they have had a very important incidental role, e.g., in deciding that Ministers could lawfully delegate many powers to civil servants (*Carltona Ltd v Commissioners of Works* [1943] 2 All ER 560 (CA)).

more important than the judges' ongoing power to supervise procedures in judicial review and to hear damages claims.

And the dramatic role of judges in reviewing the substance of administrative decisions is not as important as their role in imposing due process on the executive. That is because the judges' contribution to the law of due process brings a general change to the whole game; by contrast, the quashing of a decision on substantive grounds is always particular. Of course, a decision forcing a new interpretation of a particular statute on the government may have very far-reaching effect, but it does not affect administrative law in general. And consider also that the law of due process is capable of *guiding* the administration: officials can change their behaviour to respond to a requirement to give a hearing or to give reasons, but they cannot change their behaviour to respond to a requirement that they must not make extremely unreasonable decisions, or that they must interpret the law correctly. Public authorities do not need the courts to tell them that legislation should be interpreted correctly, or that they should not act irrationally. Regardless of judicial review, every public authority ought to use its power reasonably and on a correct interpretation of the law in every case.[25] And they more or less always (even in cases like *Roncarelli*) think that their interpretations are correct and their actions are reasonable. The effect of judicial review of the substance of decisions is to allocate power to the courts to decide what counts as a reasonable decision or a correct interpretation. *Ridge v Baldwin* [1964] AC 40 imposed a new obligation on a public authority; *A and X v Home Secretary* [2004] UKHL 56 merely replaced the view of the executive with the view of the judges on a particular question, creating a precedent for the future on that issue but not creating any new general rule of administrative law.

The real puzzle about judicial control of administrative discretion is that it seems on the one hand that the judges should not be interfering with a discretion that has been allocated to someone else—and on the other hand, that the judges should not leave a claimant to suffer the injustice of a bad decision. The mere fact that a power has been allocated to another body raises the presumption that judges should not interfere. But the presumption may be insurmountable or very easy to surmount, depending on the context. So the crucial element in resolving this apparent puzzle is the **principle of relativity** (see p 10). The reasons for deference to the initial decision maker vary widely; they may require the court to treat some issues as simply non-justiciable. It is the judges' responsibility not to turn a non-justiciability doctrine into something that the government can use to cloak abuses of power that the judges could identify. And even when non-justiciable issues really are at stake, it is still the courts' duty to protect a claimant's legal rights.

---

[25] The doctrine of legitimate expectations, discussed in section 8.4, includes a form of substantive control of discretionary power that *does* create a new obligation that public authorities can use to guide their decisions: it requires them to abide by certain sorts of expectation unless there is special reason to depart from what was expected.

> ### Injustice is not a general ground of judicial review!
> It would be a breach of comity if judges took it on themselves to right every injustice caused by administrative decisions. If this seems shocking, revisit the cases discussed in this chapter in which the courts were very deferential—such as R v Environment Secretary, ex p Nottinghamshire County Council [1986] AC 240—and ask yourself if the court ought to have decided those cases without deferring in any way to the initial decision maker. That is what it would require for the judges to review all decisions on the ground of injustice. No public decision should be unjust, but it is not always the judges' job to decide what is just.

TAKE-HOME MESSAGE • • •

- The control of discretion requires courts to examine the substance of the justification of executive action,
    - *but*: that does not mean that judges need to decide all questions as to the grounds on which the executive ought to act; the point of a 'reasonableness' standard is to find a way in which courts can control the executive without doing that;
    - *and*: the standard on which judges ought to intervene varies: it depends on the nature of the executive action under review.

- A discretionary power (such as a power to hire employees) is a power that gives some degree of choice as to how it is to be applied. A discretion is a choice. A public authority has no **discretion** to hire on racist or other abusive grounds, even though it has a **discretionary power** to hire employees.

- Judges **defer** when they leave it up to an administrative authority, to a greater or lesser extent, to make a decision. They defer completely on issues that they hold to be **non-justiciable**.

- Issues (not powers, or exercises of power) can be justiciable or non-justiciable. A *claim* is non-justiciable, if it could only succeed if the judges decided a non-justiciable issue.

- In imposing processes on the administration, judges can only breach comity by imposing wasteful or damaging processes; if the processes are appropriate for their purposes, the courts won't be interfering inappropriately. But in controlling the substance of administrative decisions, it can sometimes be damaging even to interfere with an unjust decision.

> *Critical reading*
>
> *Slattery v Naylor* (1888) 13 App Cas 446
> *Kruse v Johnson* [1898] 2 QB 91
> *Associated Provincial Picture Houses v Wednesbury Corporation* [1948] 1 KB 223

Roncarelli v Duplessis [1959] SCR 121

R v Home Secretary, ex p Khawaja [1984] AC 74

Council of Civil Service Unions v Minister for the Civil Service ('GCHQ') [1985] AC 374

R v Environment Secretary, ex p Nottinghamshire County Council [1986] AC 240

R v Environment Secretary, ex p Hammersmith and Fulham LBC [1991] 1 AC 521

R (Abbasi) v Foreign Secretary and Home Secretary [2002] EWCA Civ 1598

R (Corner House Research) v Director of the Serious Fraud Office [2008] UKHL 60

R (Bancoult) v Foreign Secretary (No 2) [2008] UKHL 61

CRITICAL QUESTIONS • • •

1 Administrative authorities always ought to make the best possible decision. So why isn't judicial review generally available on the ground that an authority didn't make the best possible decision?

2 Does the difference between inherent discretions, and discretions conferred expressly by statute, make any difference to judicial review?

3 Are there any unfettered discretionary powers?

4 Can you reconcile judicial control of discretionary power, with the principle that judges are only to strike down an action that the public authority had no power to take?

Further questions:

5 What is the relationship between the law of due process (Chapter 4), and the law of control of discretionary powers?

6 When a court questions the validity of a regulation approved in both Houses of Parliament, why isn't it contrary to Art 9 of the Bill of Rights ('…the freedom of speech and debates or proceedings in Parliament ought not to be impeached or questioned in any court or place out of Parliament')?

7 'It is well settled that a public body invested with statutory powers such as those conferred upon the corporation must take care not to exceed or abuse its powers. It must keep within the limits of the authority committed to it. It must act in good faith. And it must act reasonably. The last proposition is involved in the second, if not in the first' (*Mayor of Westminster v London and North Western Railway Company* [1905] AC 426, 430 (Lord Macnaghten). Does that mean there *is* (or was in 1905) a general rule that courts should strike down unreasonable exercises of statutory powers?

Visit the online resource centre to access the following resources which accompany this chapter: links to legislation and online reports of judicial decisions, summaries of key cases and legislation, updates in the law, suggestions for answering the pop quizzes and questions, and links to useful websites.

8 Substantive fairness

When there is reason for non-deferential judicial review, deference would actually mean abandoning the rule of law. The more interventionist grounds on which judges will control the substance of some decisions—**relevance**, **proportionality**, and **legitimate expectations**—may involve little deference, depending on the type of decision and the context in which it is made.

Each of the interventionist doctrines gives the judges the opportunity to do justice for a claimant and to improve public administration. For the very same reasons, each doctrine poses a danger that the judges will make themselves into surrogate administrators by overextending the reasons for the doctrines.

LOOK FOR • • •

- The issues on which judges will and will not defer to administrative authorities.

- Relevance.

- Proportionality.

- Legitimate expectations.

- Abuse of power.

> ❝ The differences in approach between the traditional grounds of review and the proportionality approach may . . . sometimes yield different results. . . . This does not mean that there has been a shift to merits review. On the contrary, . . . the respective roles of judges and administrators are fundamentally distinct and will remain so. ❞
>
> R (Daly) v Home Secretary [2001] UKHL 26 [28] (Lord Steyn)

8.1 Minimal deference and the principle of legality

Deference is not the default setting for judicial review; it depends on the issue. The **four basic reasons for deference** (see p 221) depend on the type of decision and the context in which it is made. In this chapter, we will see that the judges need to substitute their own judgment for that of an administrative authority on some issues, in order to give effect to the **principle of legality** (see p 19). That means examining the most non-deferential decisions in English judicial review: relevance (section 8.2), proportionality (section 8.3), and legitimate expectations (section 8.4).

The theme of this chapter is that none of these adventurous doctrines has led to a general rule that judges can review decisions without deferring to the judgment of the initial decision maker. Along the way we will see some hasty suggestions from the judges, that these doctrines have taken over judicial review, replacing the earlier, deferential approach of *Associated Provincial Picture Houses v Wednesbury Corporation* [1948] 1 KB 223. But they have not. There is no general rule authorizing judges to review administrative decisions without deference. On the other hand, there is no general rule requiring deference. It depends on the issue. Where judges can improve administrative decision making by passing judgment on the very questions of substance that the administrative authority had to decide, it is no breach of comity for them to do so. And where it is necessary to prevent arbitary government, the rule of law demands that they do so.

We can start with *zero* deference: the courts do not defer to administrative authorities on the question of whether they should carry out a legal duty.

8.1.1 Zero deference: no discretion to act unlawfully

The court will not leave it up to an administrative authority to choose whether to violate a legal rule. This simple point is a reminder of the difference between *discretionary power* and *discretion* (see p 233): even if a public authority has a very wide discretionary power, it has no discretion to use that power to do anything that is prohibited by law. As a result, the criminal law is part of administrative law, and in fact, part of our constitution: no one has any exemption from criminal liability on account of being a public official (see p 544).

8.1.2 Zero deference: the genuine exercise rule

An administrative authority also has no discretion to abdicate its powers. Every discretionary power carries with it a legal duty to consider whether and how to exercise it. Remember R (Abbasi) v Foreign Secretary [2002] EWCA Civ 1598, a case in which comity required the court not to interfere with the Foreign Secretary's judgment as to whether to demand the release of British prisoners in Guantánamo Bay (see p 4). The Court of Appeal deferred radically to the Foreign Secretary's judgment on the question of whether to make diplomatic representations on behalf of a subject whose fundamental rights were being violated by another country. But the Court made it plain that it would step in if the Foreign Secretary refused even to consider that question. If he did, the court would 'make a mandatory order to the Foreign Secretary to give due consideration to the applicant's case' [104]. On the issue of whether the Foreign Office should *consider* making representations, the judges will not defer to the Foreign Secretary's judgment at all.

Similarly, it is unlawful for an administrative authority to **fetter** its discretion by, for example, adopting rules that prevent it from considering particular cases on their merits. But that does not mean that administrative authorities cannot lawfully adopt rules or act on policies. In fact, we will see in this chapter that a claimant can be entitled to some form of judicial protection for expectations that are based on authorities' policies (section 8.4). It is sometimes unlawful to ignore arguments that a policy should not be applied in a particular case (British Oxygen Co Ltd v Board of Trade [1971] 1 AC 610). But even that depends on the nature of the decision: the government can decide the terms of a compensation scheme, for example, without being prepared to consider arguments that compensation should be awarded on different grounds in particular cases (Defence Secretary v Elias [2006] EWCA Civ 1293). The question is whether the purposes for which the authority has been given the power require it to be willing to consider special circumstances.

An administrative authority must not unlawfully **delegate** its decision-making power to anyone else. But that does not mean that all delegation is unlawful. For example, when the Home Secretary had statutory power to decide the tariff for life prisoners, the House of Lords held that it was lawful for him to delegate that decision to a junior minister (R v Home Secretary, ex p Doody [1994] 1 AC 531, 566). The question is whether delegation is incompatible with the reasons for which the power was given to the authority named in the statute.

These rules—against refusing to consider using a power, and against fettering or unlawfully delegating the exercise of a power—are, potentially, compatible with comity between judges and administrative authorities. Zero deference on the question of whether to exercise a discretion is compatible with due deference on the question of how to exercise it. The courts are not taking over the administrative officials' job, if they only make sure that the administrative officials actually make a genuine exercise of their own responsibility.

But the dangerous word in the doctrine is 'genuine'. There is a standing impulse for judges to say that a bad exercise of discretion was not an exercise of the authority's power at all. So this doctrine is only *potentially* compatible with comity between judges and administrative authorities. Depending on what they count as genuine, the judges may end up using the genuine exercise doctrine to replace other public authorities' judgment with their own. But as a technique for judicial innovation, it has been overtaken by the more openly non-deferential doctrines.

8.1.3 The principle of legality and the value of liberty

The most obvious instance of the principle of legality is the rule that there is no dis-cretion to use a power in a way that is prohibited by law. But the principle of legality has a wider application, because there are certain values that the courts will protect against the exercise of discretionary administrative powers, even where there is no legal rule prohibiting an action. The courts will not treat general powers as author-izing decisions that disregard those values. This reading-down of general powers is the most important general technique by which judges limit public authorities' lee-way in the use of discretionary powers. Which interests will be protected? There is no catalogue, and it is not the judges' job to codify the principle of legality. But it is their job to identify specific instances of it, and if there were a catalogue it would certainly include the following.

> **Examples of values protected by the principle of legality:**
>
> - liberty (*A and X v Home Secretary* [2004] UKHL 56, see p 6);
> - property (*Entick v Carrington* (1765) 19 Howell's State Trials 1029, see section 14.1);
> - access to courts (*R v Home Secretary, ex p Simms* [2000] 2 AC 115); and
> - administrative due process (*Cooper v Board of Works* (1863) 14 CB (NS) 180).
>
> Note the overlaps! Due process protects property and liberty.

Each is a value that the judges will protect against the exercise of general administra-tive powers, even when there are other relevant considerations at stake. In the rest of this chapter, watch for the ways in which the courts protect various values—not just liberty—against the exercise of discretionary powers.

> ● *Pop Quiz* ●
> Is conformity to obligations in international law a value protected by the principle of legality?

Liberty

In English law, 'every imprisonment is *prima facie* unlawful and . . . it is for a person directing imprisonment to justify his act' (*Liversidge v Anderson* [1942] AC 206, 245 (Lord Atkin)). Lord Atkin called that 'one of the pillars of liberty'. Liberty is the first and most famous of the values protected by the principle of legality.

   Habeas corpus is available as a process for challenging detention, if no other adequate process is available. But today, all the important forms of executive detention—by mental health authorities, or the police, or immigration officials—are regulated by statutory schemes. An application for *habeas corpus* will fail where a statute authorizes the detention. And *habeas corpus* is not available where a statutory scheme provides an adequate process for a court to determine whether the detention is lawful.[1] But it is an important feature of the law today, that the judges will take the

------

[1]   Extradition is governed by a statutory regime that retains *habeas corpus*: see the Extradition Act 1989. For a recent example of a grant of *habeas corpus* in the House of Lords in extradition pro-ceedings, see *Guisto: R v Governor of Brixton Prison* [2003] UKHL 19.

same creative approach to their task in controlling those statutory schemes, as they took centuries ago in developing *habeas corpus* (see p 5).

Instances of the special judicial concern for liberty: the prisoner cases

- In R v Home Secretary, ex p Doody [1994] 1 AC 531, R v Home Secretary, ex p Pierson [1997] 3 All ER 577 (HL), R v Home Secretary, ex p Venables and Thompson [1997] 3 WLR 23, the judges insisted on due process in the Home Secretary's decisions setting tariffs for life prisoners, and used the relevance doctrine to control the grounds on which the Home Secretary decided a tariff.
- Then under the Human Rights Act, the courts declared that the mere fact that the Home Secretary had power to decide the tariff was incompatible with the right to an independent tribunal in Art 6 of the Convention (R (Anderson) v Home Secretary [2002] UKHL 46 [3.5]). Parliament changed the legislation as a result, and tariff setting for life sentence prisoners is no longer a problem of administrative law.
- R v Home Secretary, ex p Simms [1999] 3 All ER 400, R (Daly) v Home Secretary [2001] UKHL 26: the courts protected a prisoner's freedom to communicate with lawyers and the media.

Judges have extended their scrutiny beyond the decision to detain, to impose intensive control on the treatment of a detained person. In R (Wilkinson) v Broadmoor Special Hospital [2001] EWCA Civ 1545, the doctors at a mental hospital decided that they needed to administer medical treatment under restraint to a patient who was detained because of a mental illness. The Court of Appeal held that in judicial review, the court's task was to make 'its own assessment of the relevant facts' [34], and to conduct 'a full merits review of the propriety of the treatment proposed' [36]. So instead of deferring to the mental health experts, the court has to decide whether it is right to impose the treatment on the patient, using evidence from the doctors, given under cross-examination. Because the treatment is forced, the courts treat the administrative decision as only provisional, and the treatment that ought to be given is an open question for the court to decide.

8.2 Relevance

It seems to be part of the genuine exercise rule: a public authority that does not act on relevant considerations is not *genuinely* doing what it was given power to do. Yet this ground of review can be dynamite. Lord Greene put it this way in *Wednesbury*:

> ❛ If, in the statute conferring the discretion, there is to be found expressly or by implication matters which the authority exercising the discretion ought to have regard to, then in exercising the discretion it must have regard to those matters. Conversely,…the authority must disregard…irrelevant collateral matters. ❜
> (228)

Twenty years after *Wednesbury*, the House of Lords made this doctrine into the basis of a highly political interference with the Minister of Agriculture's management of a milk marketing scheme, in *Padfield v Minister of Agriculture, Fisheries and Food* [1968] AC 997. The Minister had a discretionary power to refer complaints to a committee, and he refused to refer a complaint because he did not want to generate political pressure in favour of the opponents of the scheme. Lord Reid held,

> ❛Parliament must have conferred the discretion with the intention that it should be used to promote the policy and objects of the Act, the policy and objects of the Act must be determined by construing the Act as a whole and construction is always a matter of law for the court. ❜ (1030)

Public authorities always ought to act for proper purposes, and on the basis of the relevant considerations. But in a doctrine that courts are to decide which purposes are proper and which considerations are relevant, there is potential to abolish all deference to administrative authorities.

A *consideration* is simply something that a decision maker might take into account in a way that would affect the decision; it can be a **general** consideration as to how to use the decision-making power—a general ground of decision—or it can be one of the **facts** of a specific case on which the authority relies in applying the general grounds of decision to the case. A *relevant* consideration is one that the decision maker *ought to* take into account. Relevant considerations include legitimate general grounds for decision, and also those facts of the particular case on which the legitimate general grounds of decision depend.

In judicial review, should the judges decide what is relevant? The crucial point that will emerge from the following is that they must be prepared to *control* administrative judgments of relevance. Yet it is not generally the judges' job to do so by replacing the administrators' view of what is relevant, with their own view of what is relevant.

The remarkable thing about the decision in *Padfield* is not that the judges interfered in politics. They have been interfering in politics at least since the *Case of Proclamations* (1611) 12 Co Rep 74 and *Prohibitions del Roy* (1607) 77 ER 1342 decisions in the 17th century (see p 15). But those earlier decisions had only identified the actions that the Crown had power to undertake. In *Proclamations*, Lord Coke held that the King could not act like Parliament: he could not create new offences. In *Prohibitions*, Lord Coke held that the King could not sit as a judge. In *Padfield*, the House of Lords told the Government (some of) *the grounds on which it could and could not decide* whether to take actions that Parliament had authorized the Government to take. Is that approach compatible with the deferential approach that Lord Greene was outlining in *Wednesbury*? Or did the judges abolish deference in *Padfield*, by taking it on themselves to tell the government the grounds on which it could act? The answer has to be that *Padfield* did not abolish deference. But let's consider why it may seem to do so.

8.2.1 Relevance, deference: a contradiction?

Every abuse of power is the product of a decision made on irrelevant considerations. But then, whenever a different decision ought to have been taken, you can explain why by pointing out a consideration that the decision maker should have acted on, or failed to act on. So it seems that under *Wednesbury* itself, the judges must decide what decision ought to have been made, and then there is to be no deference to any administrative decision. But that is absurd. So you may think that administrative law contains a massive contradiction: judges are meant to defer (to some extent, on some issues), yet they are never to defer (since a decision is to be quashed if it was based on an irrelevant consideration). How can we resolve the contradiction?

There are two classes of relevant (and irrelevant) considerations:

(1) **grounds of decision that the law specifically requires the decision maker to attend to or to ignore (and the facts that relate to those grounds).** E.g.: **cost** is an irrelevant consideration in deciding what would count as meeting a local authority's duty to provide a 'suitable education': R v East Sussex County Council, ex p Tandy [1998] 2 All ER 769 (see p 249); and

(2) **grounds for a good decision that are not specified by law, but which no reasonable decision maker would ignore or which no reasonable decision maker would act on (and the facts that relate to those grounds).** E.g.: the statute in *Roncarelli* did not specify that **support for Jehovah's Witnesses** was irrelevant to the liquor licensing power, but it was an abuse of power for the Minister to pursue his vendetta by taking away Roncarelli's liquor licence because Roncarelli supported Jehovah's witnesses.

The *second* category of relevant and irrelevant considerations must be applied with deference. If the claimant cannot say that the law specifically demands or forbids consideration of a particular fact or ground of decision, but only that good reasoning requires attention to it, then the courts should hesitate to decide what counts as good reasoning. *Every* administrative decision ought to be made on the basis of good reasons, but it is not generally the task of judges to decide what counts as a good reason.

These two classes have not been stated very clearly in the cases. But the idea has entered English law from Cooke J's reasoning in a New Zealand case, CREEDNZ Inc v Governor General [1981] 1 NZLR 172. Cooke J started out by saying that a decision will only be quashed for failure to attend to relevant considerations 'when the statute expressly or impliedly identifies considerations required to be taken into account by the authority as a matter of legal obligation. . . . It is not enough that a consideration is one that may properly be taken into account, nor even that it is one which many people, including the court itself, would have taken into account if they had to make the decision' (183). Yet, later on the same page of his reasons, he added that 'there will be some matters so obviously material to a decision on a particular project that anything short of direct consideration of them by the ministers...would not be in accordance with the intention of the Act'.

The House of Lords adopted that reasoning in *Findlay* [1985] AC 318, 344. The result is that the relevance doctrine is really a rule that the court may quash a decision that was based on an unreasonable view as to what considerations are relevant. To see how far it can and should be applied so as to replace the judgment of an administrative authority with the judgment of the court, let's look at the one of the most remarkable examples of the use of the relevance doctrine: the Pergau Dam case.

8.2.2 The Pergau Dam

In 1993, the Foreign Secretary, Douglas Hurd, decided to spend £234 million to build a dam in Pergau, Malaysia. It was the largest single project that had been financed by the Overseas Development Administration ('ODA'), and it was a waste of money. The National Audit Office (see p 579) and even the ODA's own economists said it was a waste. The money was spent because Prime Minister Thatcher had promised financial assistance to Malaysia, while she was negotiating an arms deal in which Malaysia was to buy more than £1 billion worth of British fighter planes. So instead of using the development budget for development, the British government was using it as a sweetener to promote British arms sales.

In *R v Foreign Secretary, ex p World Development Movement* [1995] 1 WLR 386, the High Court held that the government had acted unlawfully in providing money for the dam from the Overseas Aid budget. The remarkable thing about the decision is that the judges were prepared to hold a spending decision unlawful, when the purposes of the decision were highly political and involved foreign relations. The minister argued that the judges should defer to his view as to what purposes were within the statute. The court disagreed:

> ' Whatever the Secretary of State's intention or purpose may have been, it is, as it seems to me, a matter for the courts and not for the Secretary of State to determine whether, on the evidence before the court, the particular conduct was, or was not, within the statutory purpose. ' (401)

This does *not* mean that the court will not defer on the relevant considerations. If there were no deference, then the minister would have no discretion in deciding which projects to find. It means that the court will not defer *on the question of what considerations the legislation rules out*. And that is so even where there is a reasonable argument in favour of the minister's view as to which considerations the legislation rules out.

But the minister does have discretion to choose among the purposes that the law does not prohibit. The Overseas Development and Co-operation Act 1980 s 1(1) gave the Secretary of State power to make grants, 'for the purpose of promoting the development or maintaining the economy of a country or territory outside the United Kingdom, or the welfare of its people' (390). He was certainly maintaining the economy of Malaysia by giving the government £400 million from the Overseas Development Fund. It is not implausible to argue that the Act authorized the action. But the court quite rightly rejected a plausible interpretation, in favour of an interpretation that better fulfilled the development purpose of the legislation.

● *Pop Quiz* ●

Can you distinguish R v *Foreign Secretary, ex p World Development Movement* [1995] 1 WLR 386 from R v *Environment Secretary, ex p Hammersmith and Fulham LBC* [1991] 1 AC 521? Both were challenges to Government funding decisions under statutory powers, but in *Hammersmith and Fulham*, the House of Lords refused to interfere with a funding decision unless it was 'so absurd that he must have taken leave of his senses'. Why wasn't the same hands-off standard applied in *World Development Movement*?

8.2.3 The *Balchin* litigation

The adventurous use of relevant considerations in *World Development Movement* pushes the doctrine as far as it ought to go. It has been pushed even further. In R v *Parliamentary Commissioner for Administration, ex p Balchin* [1997] JPL 917 (see p 488), Sedley J treated the relevance doctrine as conferring a general power on judges to decide what facts are relevant to an ombudsman's decision (and, presumably, to administrative decisions, too). That takes the relevance doctrine beyond its rationale.

Sedley J held that the test is 'whether a consideration has been omitted which, had account been taken of it, might have caused the decision-maker to reach a different conclusion' (929). It is easy to see the attraction in this view: if a claimant can establish that the decision maker ignored a consideration that might have made a difference to its own decision, then it seems that without any breach of comity, the court can require the decision maker to revisit the decision and come to its *own* conclusion, but on the basis of all the relevant considerations. But then the result would be that judges should quash any decision that they would have made differently. For whenever a judge would have decided differently, he or she will be able to identify a consideration which has been omitted, which might have caused the decision maker to reach a different conclusion. That fact points out the apparent contradiction in the relevance doctrine:

● acting on all and only the relevant considerations means making the best decision, and

● judges are meant to review decisions to decide whether they were made on relevant considerations, yet

● judges are not generally meant to quash a decision just because it was not the best decision.

8.2.4 The contradiction resolved: questions of relevance are *not* necessarily for courts

In fact, it is not the judges' job to decide all questions of relevance, just as it is not their job to decide what counts as a good decision. As Cooke J suggested in *CREEDNZ Inc*, the relevance doctrine only justifies interference with *unreasonable* decisions as to the relevance of a fact.

Several cases have emphasized this point: a decision maker may have discretion in deciding which considerations are relevant. In *Findlay* itself, the House of Lords held that the law neither required the Home Secretary to consider the Parole Board's view before making a policy change, nor prohibited him from doing so. Consider the following cases in which the judges have refused to decide what was relevant:

- R *v Panel on Take-overs and Mergers, ex p Guinness Plc* [1990] 1 QB 146: Lord Donaldson MR held that the Panel was 'a body which is itself charged with the duty of making a judgment on what is and what is not relevant, although clearly a theoretical scenario could be constructed in which the panel acted on the basis of considerations which on any view must have been irrelevant or ignored something which on any view must have been relevant' (159).

- In R *(Khatun) v Newham LBC* [2004] EWCA Civ 55, a local authority was making decisions as to where to house homeless people, without letting them see the property first. The claimant asked for the decision to be quashed on the ground that the potential tenant's view as to the suitability of the property was a relevant consideration that the local authority had ignored. The Court of Appeal refused; following *Findlay* and *CREEDNZ Inc*, Laws LJ held that, 'where a statute conferring discretionary power provides no lexicon of the matters to be treated as relevant by the decision-maker, then it is for the decision-maker and not the court to conclude what is relevant subject only to *Wednesbury* review' [35].

- R *(Al Rawi) v Foreign Secretary and Home Secretary* [2006] EWCA Civ 1279: 'what is and what is not a relevant consideration for a public decision-maker to have in mind is (absent a statutory code of compulsory considerations) for the decision-maker, not the court, to decide' (Laws LJ [131]).

- R *(Hurst) v London Northern District Coroner* [2007] UKHL 13: 'Some considerations are required to be taken into account by decision makers. Others are required not to be. But there is a third category: those considerations which the decision maker may choose for himself whether or not to take into account' (Lord Brown [57]).

- R *(Corner House Research) v Director of The Serious Fraud Office* [2008] UKHL 60: 'A discretionary decision is not in any event vitiated by a failure to take into account a consideration which the decision-maker is not obliged by the law or the facts to take into account, even if he may properly do so: *CREEDNZ Inc v Governor General* [1981] 1 NZLR 172, 183' (Lord Bingham [40]).

In none of these cases did the courts refuse to control the administrative decision as to what is relevant. In none of them did the courts treat judgments of relevance as judgments for the courts. That is the right approach, because *control* over judgments of relevance is essential if the courts are to prevent arbitrary government. But comity requires courts not to interfere with a reasonable judgment of relevance.

Relevance and the courts

Lord Greene did not treat questions of relevance generally as questions for the court. In *B Johnson & Co v Minister of Health* [1947] 2 All ER 395, decided less than four months before the *Wednesbury* hearing, he refused to substitute 'the opinion of the court as to what considerations should weigh with the Minister for the opinion of the Minister himself, which had been made by Parliament the decisive matter' (400). On Lord Greene's approach, it is not generally the task of the court to decide what considerations are relevant, but to ask whether the public authority has made reasonable judgments of relevance.

8.3 Proportionality and deference

It is unreasonable to use a sledgehammer to crack a nut, or to make a mountain out of a molehill. Proportionality is a requirement of reasonableness, and no public authority should ever act disproportionately. But that does not mean that judges should interfere when an administrative authority does so. The point of the *Wednesbury* doctrine was to recognize that comity generally requires judges not to decide what would be a reasonable decision, but only to interfere with a decision that no reasonable person *in the position of the administrative authority* would take. The *Wednesbury* principles apply quite broadly (though even they do not apply to all decisions by public authorities), because they offer ways in which judges can identify administrative decisions as *arbitrary*. But it is not necessarily arbitrary to do too much or too little. So proportionality calls for some rationale other than the judges' general responsibility to impose the rule of law on other public authorities. Proportionality should only be a ground of judicial review when there is good reason to empower judges to go beyond their ordinary role of imposing the rule of law by preventing arbitrary decisions. Proportionality reasoning empowers judges to require good decisions.

It sometimes seems that proportionality is poised to take over judicial review, with the result that judges are no longer to defer to other public authorities. To his version of The List of the grounds of judicial review (see p 339), Lord Diplock said that further grounds might be added in time, and mentioned 'the possible adoption in the future of the principle of "proportionality" which is recognised in the administrative law of several of our fellow members of the European Economic Community' *Council of Civil Service Unions v Minister for the Civil Service* [1985] AC 374, 410.

Then, after the enactment of the Human Rights Act, judges started to suggest that proportionality has become a general feature of English administrative law. For proportionality really has become a test of compatibility of administrative action with Convention rights (see section 3.6 for an account of the structure and the role of proportionality reasoning under the Convention). And it has come to seem to some, such as Lord Slynn, that proportionality cannot be restricted to Convention rights:

> ' I consider that even without reference to the Human Rights Act 1998 the time has come to recognise that this principle is part of English administrative law, not only when judges are dealing with Community acts but also when they are dealing with acts subject to domestic law. Trying to keep the *Wednesbury* principle and proportionality in separate compartments seems to me to be unnecessary and confusing. ' [2]

Separate compartments sound somehow artificial. But the simple fact is that proportionality has no place in judicial review unless there is some special reason *for judges to decide* just when government action goes too far, or not far enough.

Proportionality is *not* a general ground of judicial review, except in the sense in which proportionality is built into *Wednesbury* unreasonableness: it is generally unlawful for a public authority to act in a way that is *so* disproportionate that no reasonable public authority would act in that way. And even that aspect of *Wednesbury* is limited, because proportionality is a **relation** between two things, and it cannot arise as a ground of judicial review (even in the highly deferential *Wednesbury* form) until the law recognizes some interest that is to be protected by a judicial inquiry as to whether it has been damaged in a way that is out of proportion to the attainment of a public objective. Even in a deferential form, proportionality cannot take over the general judicial control of administrative action.

Proportionality has had a powerful effect on English public law, so that it is easy to forget that it is a ground of judicial review only when there is some special reason for judges to assess the proportionality of administrative action. If proportionality were a general ground of judicial review, think how a case like *World Development Movement* would be decided (see p 270). The judges would have to quash an overseas aid decision if it did not do *enough* to promote overseas development, or if the government was spending *too much* on a project. That really would turn the judges into the directors of the ODA. To see why proportionality reasoning can never take over administrative law, it is enough to remember the diversity of government conduct that is subject to judicial review. If proportionality were now a general standard of judicial review, then in a case like *R v Environment Secretary, ex p Hammersmith and Fulham LBC* [1991] 1 AC 521 (see p 247), the court would have to decide whether the government's decision to cap the spending of local authorities was proportionate (in its impact on their finances, presumably) to the pursuit of legitimate objectives. But that would put the judges in charge of central government spending. That would be absurd, and in spite of Lord Diplock's and Lord Slynn's suggestions, there is no reason to think that the judges are going to make proportionality into a general ground of judicial review.

To give a more dramatic example, if proportionality were a general ground of judicial review, the case of *Corner House Research* (see p 255) would have been decided

---

[2]   R (Alconbury) v Environment Secretary [2001] UKHL 23 [51].

very differently. Instead of holding that it was up to the prosecutor to decide whether 'the public interest in pursuing an important investigation into alleged bribery was outweighed by the public interest in protecting the lives of British citizens', (Lord Bingham [38]), the court would have to decide *how much* of a danger to the lives of British citizens is *enough* for the prosecutor to be legally justified in deciding not to pursue a prosecution. The House of Lords has established very clearly, in *Corner House Research* as well as in *Hammersmith and Fulham*, that it will not take that approach to judicial review of government action in general.

So proportionality reasoning cannot take over all of judicial review. But where the values protected by the principle of legality are at stake, proportionality reasoning will be applied: in R *(Daly) v Home Secretary* [2001] UKHL 26 [23], the courts really were prepared to decide *how much* interference with a prisoner's freedom to communicate with lawyers was *too much*. That is 'an orthodox application of common law principles derived from the authorities and an orthodox domestic approach to judicial review' (Lord Bingham [23]).

In Human Rights Act litigation, the role of proportionality is deeply entrenched and very wide-ranging. Within that compartment, is it abolishing judicial deference to the judgment of administrative authorities?

8.3.1 Deference and the Human Rights Act

The classic decisions on control of discretionary powers—*Slattery*, *Kruse*, and *Wednesbury*—would all be argued at least partly on Human Rights Act grounds, if they were argued today. Has that change abolished judicial deference?

In a Human Rights Act claim, the court is itself an original decision maker. The question before the court is whether a person's Convention rights have been violated, and *not* whether a public authority has used its power reasonably. So it may seem that the Human Rights Act imposes a legal limit on the exercise of discretionary powers, which involves no deference to the decisions of an administrative authority. A breach of a Convention right is simply unlawful (unless it was required by statute), whether or not it is so unreasonable that no reasonable public authority would act that way.

Yet deference actually plays a very important role in judicial decisions concerning Convention rights. Some of the most important judicial accounts of deference to administrative authorities come in decisions under the Human Rights Act, when the judges are rejecting a claimant's argument that the judges should impose the decision that they would have made, if they had the job of the initial decision maker. In R *v Director of Public Prosecutions, ex p Kebilene* [2000] 2 AC 326, Lord Hope said, 'In some circumstances it will be appropriate for the courts to recognise that there is an area of judgment within which the judiciary will defer, on democratic grounds, to the considered opinion of the elected body or person whose act or decision is said to be incompatible with the Convention' (381).

No case illustrates the role of deference in applying the Human Rights Act better than R *(Begum) v Denbigh High School* [2006] UKHL 15. Shabina Begum claimed that her school had violated her freedom of religion, by enforcing a uniform policy that banned the jilbab (see p 206). You might think that the House of Lords would simply decide whether the policy was 'necessary in a democratic society . . . for the protection of the rights and freedoms of others'—as it says in Art 9.2 of the Convention. But in fact, the House of Lords firmly refused to decide for itself what was necessary in Denbigh High School. Lord Bingham said, 'It would in my opinion be irresponsible of any court, lacking the experience, background and detailed knowledge of the head teacher, staff and governors, to overrule their judgment on a matter as sensitive as this. The power of decision has been given to them for the compelling reason that they are best placed to exercise it, and I see no reason to disturb their decision' [34]. And Lord Hoffmann agreed that 'an area of judgment, comparable to the margin of appreciation, must be allowed to the school' [64].

The issue in *Begum* was whether the impact of the school's uniform policy on Shabina Begum's freedom of religion was disproportionate to its value in protecting other girls' freedom. Do the **four basic reasons for deference** apply to the judges' decision on *that* issue? The first reason—the allocation of decision-making power to the administrative agency—is put in question by the passage of the Human Rights Act: Parliament may have allocated power to schools to determine uniform policies, but in the Human Rights Act, Parliament allocated power to *courts* to decide what counts as a breach of the freedom of religion under Art 9. So the **presumption of non-interference** (the principle that a court should not interfere with someone else's decision unless there is a special reason to do so—see p 222) does not apply.

Another basic reason for deference does apply, however, and it is very important: the familiarity of the school authorities with the needs of the pupils. On that issue, the school authorities are better informed than judges, in a way that cannot be remedied through the litigation process. An understanding of the social pressures faced by the girls is crucial to the decision whether it is legitimate to prohibit the jilbab, and people working in the school are better placed to reach the necessary understanding than people working in a court.

● *Pop Quiz* ●

Why did the House of Lords defer to the school's judgment as to what was needed to protect the girls' freedom in *Begum*, if they did not defer to the Home Secretary's judgment as to what was needed to protect the nation from terrorism in *A and X v Home Secretary* [2004] UKHL 56?

The House of Lords' deference to the school in *Begum* does not mean that the court will not control the school's decisions. The court will ask whether the school's choice was made responsibly, with due process, and on the relevant considerations. Their deference is limited; its extent is left rather vague by the decision in *Begum*, but can best be summed up by saying that the judges will not interfere with reasonable decisions of a school as to whether a school needs a uniform policy that limits religious expression. The law requires the school not to ban the jilbab, unless the ban is necessary for the protection of the freedom of others. But the judges will not pass judgment on that question; they will leave it to the school unless they can see—in spite of the advantages that the school authorities have—that there is no justification for the policy.

This approach is *less* deferential than the ordinary common law of control of discretionary powers, yet deference is essential to it. But notice that the judges did *not* defer on the question of what rights the Convention gave Shabina Begum. The Act requires the judges to answer that question of law without deferring to anyone else. The deference arises because *the application of the Convention Rights themselves* sometimes requires assessments that can best be made by public authorities other than courts.

As Lord Steyn said in the landmark proportionality case of *Daly*, the use of proportionality reasoning 'does not mean that there has been a shift to merits review. . . . the respective roles of judges and administrators are fundamentally distinct and will remain so' [28]. And Lord Brown explained, in *Tweed v Parades Commission for Northern Ireland* [2006] UKHL 53, that 'it is the court's recognition of what has been called variously the margin of discretion, or the discretionary area of judgment, or the deference or latitude due to administrative decision-makers, which stops the challenge from being a merits review' [55]. The result is a flexible, variable doctrine of deference in the application of proportionality reasoning, even in Human Rights Act claims.

8.3.2 Equality and non-discrimination

Like proportionality, equality is a relation. But it is a relation *between people*. Is there a general principle of judicial review that people should be treated as equals? Yes, according to the line of cases leading to *Wednesbury*. In *Slattery v Naylor* (1888) 13 App Cas 446 (see p 220), Lord Hobhouse suggested that the court might set aside some byelaws as unreasonable 'such, for instance, as a bye-law providing that the Roman Catholic cemetery should be closed to the Roman Catholic community, but remain available for others' (453). And Lord Russell said in *Kruse v Johnson* [1898] 2 QB 91 that byelaws would be unlawful 'If, for instance, they were found to be partial and **unequal** in their operation as between different classes' (99).

So there is an unspecific anti-discrimination principle in English public law that is more than a century old. It is simply *part* of the doctrine of relevance: passing a byelaw designed to treat the upper class better than the lower class would be acting on an irrelevant consideration.

In the 1970s, Parliament prohibited certain forms of discrimination (not only by public authorities, but also by private persons and companies) on the basis of race and sex, and the European Union (EU) has taken further measures that have effect in English law.[3] Those measures were designed to respond to traditional prejudices that caused particularly unfair disadvantages to people who had suffered discrimination. It took legislation to respond effectively to those grounds of discrimination.

---

3   Race Relations Act 1976; Sex Discrimination Act 1975 and Equal Pay Act 1970. Article 13 of the Treaty Establishing the European Community, as amended, provides that the EU 'may take appropriate action to combat discrimination based on sex, racial or ethnic origin, religion or belief, disability, age or sexual orientation'.

And the Human Rights Act gives effect to the general rule, in the European Convention on Human Rights Art 14:

> ‘ The enjoyment of the rights and freedoms set forth in this Convention shall be secured without discrimination on any ground such as sex, race, colour, language, religion, political or other opinion, national or social origin, association with a national minority, property, birth or other status. ’

Notice that Art 14 only bans discrimination that affects the way in which a Convention right is 'secured', and only bans discrimination on the specified 'proscribed grounds'. And the cases have held that a difference in treatment does not count as discrimination if it is objectively justifiable (see *Ghaidan v Godin-Mendoza* [2004] 2 AC 557 [133]–[134]).

In *R (Carson) v Work and Pensions Secretary* [2005] UKHL 37, a woman who had contributed to National Insurance for many years had moved to South Africa. She received her pension in South Africa, but the legislation denied her the annual cost-of-living increases received by pensioners living in Britain. She claimed that she was suffering discrimination. But the House of Lords rejected her appeal. Lord Hoffmann held that 'Discrimination means a failure to treat like cases alike' [14], and because there was a rational justification for basing pension benefits partly on where a pensioner lives, pensioners in Britain and pensioners abroad are not 'like cases', and the Government could treat them differently. He held that differential treatment based on grounds such as race or sex, by contrast, would *prima facie* reflect a denial of respect for persons. Because the differential treatment that Mrs Carson complained of was not based on one of those suspect grounds, Lord Hoffmann held that it could be justified on grounds of public interest. And he pointed out that 'decisions about the general public interest…are very much a matter for the democratically elected branches of government' [16]. So if a difference of treatment is not based on a ground that shows disrespect for the person, the courts will defer to the judgment of Parliament or of an administrative authority on the question of whether the difference of treatment is justifiable. As Lord Hoffmann held in another case, 'The fact that equality of treatment is a general principle of rational behaviour does not entail that it should necessarily be a justiciable principle—that it should always be the judges who have the last word on whether the principle has been observed' (*Matadeen v Pointu* [1999] 1 AC 98 (PC), 109).

8.4 Legitimate expectations

In *R (Bibi) v Newham LBC* [2001] EWCA Civ 607, a local authority promised to give permanent accommodation to Manik Bibi and his family within 18 months. The local authority thought that the family, who were homeless, had a legal right to it. Then the House of Lords held that local authorities had no obligation to give homeless people permanent accommodation, and should not be bumping homeless people up to the front of the housing queue (*R v Brent LBC, ex p Awua* [1996] AC 55). The council refused to provide the permanent accommodation it had promised, and the claimants sought judicial review. The Court of Appeal issued a declaration 'that the authority is under a duty to consider the applicants' applications for suitable housing on the basis that they have a legitimate expectation that they will be provided by the authority with suitable accommodation on a secure tenancy' [69].

That phrase 'legitimate expectation' is a technical term.[4] A legitimate expectation might better be called a 'legally protected expectation'. If a person has a legitimate expectation, it is not merely legitimate for them to expect something; the law will give the expectation some form of protection in judicial review. Bibi's case shows why this technique has been developed. On the one hand, Bibi had no legal right to permanent accommodation.[5] On the other hand, it would be hard on him and his family for the local authority to show no concern for what they had told him. It would be unfair to Bibi, and it would put the integrity of public services in doubt, if a public authority paid no attention to what it had said that it would do. As Lord Fraser put it in GCHQ, 'even where a person claiming some benefit or privilege has no legal right to it as a matter of private law, he may have a legitimate expectation of receiving the benefit or privilege, and, if so, the courts will protect his expectation by judicial review as a matter of public law' ([1985] AC 374, 401). Remember that word 'protect': the courts will *not* necessarily order a public authority to do what the claimant expected it to do.

The courts have been working—in a process that is still in flux—to find a way for the law to protect expectations that public authorities generate. In doing so, courts face a special and rather delicate problem of comity: how can they complete this development without taking over the judgments that a good administrator would make, in reconciling the protection of legitimate expectations with conflicting interests? In Bibi, Lord Justice Schiemann resolved the problem of comity in the following way:

> ʻ In an area such as the provision of housing at public expense where decisions are informed by social and political value judgments as to priorities of expenditure the court will start with a recognition that such invidious choices are essentially political rather than judicial. In our judgment the appropriate body to make that choice in the context of the present case is the authority. However, it must do so in the light of the legitimate expectations of the respondents. ʼ [64]

---

4   Lord Denning used it in a 1969 decision in which he held that if an alien's permission to stay in the UK is revoked early he should be given an opportunity of making representations even though he had no right to remain in the UK, 'for he would have a legitimate expectation of being allowed to stay for the permitted time' (*Schmidt v Home Secretary* [1969] 2 Ch 149, 171). The phrase had been used in a looser sense in the European Court of Justice (*Société commerciale Antoine Vloeberghs SA v European Coal and Steel Community* [1961] ECR 393 [8]). It was also used in a long line of English cases holding that when a statute authorizes the taking of property from mentally incompetent people, it is to be interpreted with the presumption 'that the Legislature did not intend to interfere with any legal rights or any legitimate expectations of any persons whatsoever' (*In re Barker* (1881) LR 17 ChD 241, 243).

5   The promise from the local authority gave them no rights in contract law, because it was a gratuitous promise (Bibi gave no consideration for it). On what a right is, see p 85.

So in a case like *Bibi*, the court:

- will defer very substantially on general questions as to priorities of expenditure;

- will not defer at all on the question of whether expectations induced by the public authority are relevant; and

- will defer to some extent on the question of whether the promise should be carried out, in a way that will vary substantially depending on the circumstances.

That last form of deference explains the difference between a legitimate expectation of housing, and a right to housing. If a person has a right to housing (conferred by statute or contract), the court will order housing (or compensation) to be provided. Courts do not defer to administrative authorities on the question of whether to respect someone's legal rights.

But if the claimant has a legitimate expectation, the court will defer to the public authority in a way that depends both on the authority's responsibility for setting funding priorities, and on the authority's capacity to identify the interests of third parties, such as people waiting in the queue for permanent housing, ahead of the Bibi family. Those third parties will not be treated fairly if their interests are simply subordinated to the expectations of the claimants. If the claimants had a legal right to housing, the authority's expenditure priorities would be irrelevant, and so would the interests of third parties.

As Schiemann LJ said, if a claimant has a legitimate expectation of a housing benefit, the court 'will not order the authority to honour its promise where to do so would be to assume the powers of the executive' [41]. He held that a local authority is 'abusing its powers' if it acts without even considering the fact that it is going back on a legitimate expectation [39]. The gist of the doctrine of legitimate expectation is that the court will quash a decision if the public authority's approach to the claimant's expectation was an abuse of power. There may or may not be 'only one lawful ultimate answer to the question whether the authority should honour its promise' [43].

8.4.1 What generates a legitimate expectation?

An expectation does not deserve legal protection merely because it was reasonable for a claimant to expect a particular action. There must have been a pattern of conduct, or a representation, or a promise, that makes it unfair for the public authority to disregard the expectation. Then, it becomes the business of the courts to protect the expectation in some way.

If the alleged legitimate expectation was generated by a promise, it must have been 'clear, unambiguous and devoid of relevant qualification' (R v Inland Revenue Commissioners, ex p MFK Underwriting Agents [1990] 1 WLR 1545, 1569 (Bingham LJ). See also R (Bancoult) v Foreign Secretary (No 2) [2008] UKHL 61 [60]). Ironically, it can be very unclear whether there has been a clear promise, and very controversial. In Bancoult (see p 240), the House of Lords was deeply divided 3–2 over whether the Foreign Secretary had clearly promised that the Chagossians would be allowed to return to the Chagos Islands.

An expectation can deserve judicial protection even if the public authority did not actually make a promise: a legitimate expectation may arise from 'the existence of a regular practice which the claimant can reasonably expect to continue', as Lord Fraser said in the GCHQ case ([1985] AC 374, 401). In that case, the practice of consulting unions had given the unions reason to believe that the practice would continue; the reason was that the practice created a relationship between the Government as employer and the union, in which the Government committed itself to recognizing the union's role in decision making. Similarly, the Revenue's 20-year-old practice of allowing late claims for a form of tax relief gave rise to a legitimate expectation in R v Inland Revenue Commissioners, ex p Unilever [1996] STC 681 (CA), so that it was an abuse of power for the Revenue to pull the rug out from under the claimants' feet by suddenly refusing late claims. It is implicit in Unilever that in order to generate a legitimate expectation, a practice, like a promise, must have given the claimant a clear, unambiguous, unqualified reason to expect an outcome.

And whether it arises from government practice or from a statement, the expectation must be one that the courts can legitimately protect. In R v Environment Secretary, ex p Hammersmith and Fulham LBC [1991] 1 AC 521, the Government had told the House of Commons that the Environment Secretary would not cap the spending of local authorities that set 'sensible' budgets. The authorities argued that they had set sensible budgets, and that it was therefore a breach of their legitimate expectation for the government to cap their spending. The argument failed so comprehensively that Lord Bridge only said that it was 'plainly misconceived', and did not even take the trouble to explain why. The reason was that, by promising not to interfere with 'sensible' budgets, the Government was not pinning itself down to any particular view of what counted as sensible. If the court had been willing to decide what was a sensible budget, it would have been taking over the Minister's job. There was nothing wrong with the local authorities expecting to be able to set a sensible budget without being capped; but they had no hope of getting a court to protect that expectation by deciding what would be a sensible local council budget.

The ratification of a treaty and legitimate expectations

In R v Home Secretary, ex p Ahmed and Patel [1998] INLR 570, the applicants claimed that because the UK had ratified an international convention on the rights of the child and the European Convention on Human Rights, they had a legitimate expectation that the government would act in accord with the two conventions. The Court of Appeal accepted the view of the High Court of Australia in Minister for Immigration v Teoh [1995] 183 CLR 273, 291, that the ratification of a convention is a 'positive statement' that the government will act in accordance with the convention, and that it 'is an adequate foundation for a legitimate expectation, absent statutory or executive indications to the contrary, that administrators will act in conformity with the Convention'. But there will be no such legitimate expectation if there is an 'executive indication to the contrary'.

8.4.2 Does reliance matter?

Yes. If a claimant acted to his or her detriment because of an expectation that a public authority induced, then that fact will most likely count in favour of an argument that it would be an abuse of power for the public authority to ignore the expectation. But reliance is not conclusive, because the requirements of public policy and the interests of third parties may mean that it is not an abuse of power to disappoint an expectation that a claimant has relied on. And reliance is not necessary, either. 'It is not essential that the applicant should have relied upon the promise to his detriment, although this is a relevant consideration in deciding whether the adoption of a policy in conflict with the promise would be an abuse of power' (*Bancoult (No 2)*, Lord Hoffmann [60]).

In *Bibi*, the Court of Appeal rejected an argument that a legitimate expectation as to a substantive benefit can only arise if the claimant has relied on the representation. It has been held that a claimant can have a 'legitimate expectation' that a public authority will act in accordance with a policy that the claimant does not even know about (so that the claimant did not expect anything at all). On these pseudo-legitimate expectations, see section 8.4.6.

But since it is relevant to the question of whether a court ought to protect an expectation, there are bound to be cases in which the very fact that a claimant did not rely on a representation or practice means that he or she has no legitimate expectation. *R v Education Secretary, ex p Begbie* [2000] 1 WLR 1115 is an example; Peter Gibson LJ said, 'It is very much the exception, rather than the rule, that detrimental reliance will not be present when the court finds unfairness in the defeating of a legitimate expectation' [48].

Estoppel and legitimate expectation: the land by the lake

Suppose I promise to give you my piece of land by the lake, and say that you can build a cabin there and move in. But I like the new cabin so much that I decide to keep the land, and try to have you ejected. I will be estopped (which is Norman French for 'stopped') from asserting my right in court. Does a legitimate expectation estop a public authority from asserting the lawfulness of an exercise of public power? No. I am estopped from asserting my right to the land by the lake because it would be unconscionable (i.e., selfish in a way that the law should not tolerate) for me to do so after I induced you to act to your detriment. In the case of a public authority, although there is 'an analogy between a private law estoppel and the public law concept of a legitimate expectation created by a public authority' (Lord Hoffmann in R (Reprotech) v East Sussex CC [2002] UKHL 8 [34]), the analogy is dangerous, because the rationale for protecting a legitimate expectation is not that the public authority is using private legal rights unconscionably. The rationale is abuse of public power. So 'remedies against public authorities also have to take into account the interests of the general public which the authority exists to promote' [34]. The court will insist that a legitimate expectation should be fulfilled only if it would be an abuse of power for the public authority not to do what the claimant expected. Both Lord Scarman and Lord Fraser made the same point in *Newbury District Council v Environment Secretary* [1981] AC 578, 616, 617.

And note that estoppel **always requires reliance**. No private person is estopped from retracting a gratuitous promise, if the promisee has not relied on it. But reliance is only one consideration in deciding whether the law ought to protect a claimant's expectation as to how a public authority will act.

● *Pop Quiz* ●
What if a public authority does the very things that would create an estoppel if they were done by a private person? Is the public authority estopped from asserting its right to the land by the lake? Or does the other party need to ask the court for protection of its legitimate expectation?

● *Another Pop Quiz* ●
If you pay money to someone by mistake, you can get a court to order it returned (that is 'restitution'). Can a public authority get restitution of money that it pays to someone by mistake? Or does the fact that it paid the money create a legitimate expectation, which entitles the recipient to keep the money?

8.4.3 What if a claimant expected that a public authority would do something unlawful?

A public authority's conduct or representation may lead a claimant to expect the authority to do something that is against the law. Even if the claimant's expectation is perfectly reasonable (if, for example, the claimant had no reason to think that the expected conduct was unlawful), it cannot count as a legitimate expectation. In order to generate a legitimate expectation, a public official's promise or undertaking 'must not conflict with his statutory duty or his duty, as here, in the exercise of a prerogative power' (*R v Home Secretary, ex p Ruddock* [1987] 1 WLR 1482, 1497 (Taylor J)). That means not only that no legitimate expectation arises from a representation that a public authority will do something that is specifically prohibited by law. It also means that no legitimate expectation arises, if it would stop the public authority from carrying out its duty to exercise a discretionary power on the basis of all the relevant considerations: 'the Secretary of State cannot fetter his discretion. By declaring a policy he does not preclude any possible need to change it' (*Ruddock*, 1497).

If a public authority cannot fetter its discretion, it may seem that a claimant cannot have a legitimate expectation that a public authority will use a discretion one way rather than another. But no; in *Ruddock* the decision simply means that the doctrine of legitimate expectation does not necessarily prevent a public authority from changing a policy that would have benefited a claimant. The courts have been working to find a way of protecting expectations as to how a discretion will be exercised, and to reconcile that protection with the need for public authorities to be able to change policies.

But Taylor J's decision *does* mean that a claimant cannot ordinarily have a legitimate expectation that a public authority will do something unlawful, even if the public authority's conduct has led the claimant to think that the public authority will act that way. It is a view that the House of Lords had adopted in *Re Findlay* [1985] 1 AC 318. Lord Scarman said that a prisoner had no legitimate expectation of being treated according to the parole policy that was in effect when he went to prison. 'The most that a convicted prisoner can legitimately expect is that his case will be examined individually in the light of whatever policy the Secretary of State sees fit to adopt provided always that the adopted policy is a lawful exercise of the discretion conferred upon him by the statute' (338). The House of Lords was concerned to ensure that the law should not protect an expectation, if doing so would prevent a public authority from exercising its responsibilities.

But there is one way to get legal protection for an expectation of unlawful conduct: under Art 1 of the First Protocol to the European Convention on Human Rights, 'No one shall be deprived of his possessions except in the public interest and subject to the conditions provided for by law and by the general principles of international law.' In *Rowland v Environment Agency* [2003] EWCA Civ 1885, the owner of property by a river quite reasonably expected the river authorities to protect her stretch of the river from entry by the public, since they had thought for more than 80 years that there were no public rights of navigation there. When they discovered that the public did have a right to use that stretch of the river, at common law she could not claim a legitimate expectation that the rivers authority would keep the public out [81]. But following decisions of the Strasbourg Court in *Pine Valley Developments v Ireland* (1991) 14 EHRR 319 and *Stretch v United Kingdom* (2003) 38 EHRR 196, the Court of Appeal held that her expectation was a 'possession' for the purposes of the Convention. That gave her a form of protection somewhat stronger than the protection that a legitimate expectation would give her at common law, because it required the Court to apply a proportionality test in asking what the rivers authority should do to reconcile the public interest with the claimant's expectation. The effect was to require judicial review of the substantive fairness of the conduct of the rivers authority; but Mrs Rowland still lost (except that the Court made it clear that the rivers authority would need to continue to take into account the fact that she had expected to have private use of her part of the river). All the authority had done was to take down signs indicating that the public had no right to enter her stretch of the river, and that was not disproportionate to the public interest. The Court of Appeal held that 'Courts should be slow to fix a public authority permanently with the consequences of a mistake, particularly when it would deprive the public of their rights' (Peter Gibson LJ [96]).

8.4.4 What protection does the law give to legitimate expectations?

In the 1980s and 1990s, there was much controversy over whether the doctrine gave substantive protection for legitimate expectations, or whether a public authority merely needed to provide special procedures before deciding to disappoint a legitimate expectation.[6] It seemed to some that an authority with a discretionary power had to be free to act regardless of the expectations of persons affected by the decision, or the courts would be taking away the discretion (and by the same token, they would be giving public authorities a technique for taking away *their own* discretion, by promising someone that they would use a power in one way rather than another). But as *Bibi* shows, that controversy is long over. The claimants in *Bibi* did not merely get a declaration that they were entitled to a hearing; by telling the local authority that the claimants' legitimate expectation had to be taken into account, the court spelled out considerations on which it had to decide. And that means determining part of the *substance* of the decision that it had to make. The authority could not deny Bibi what he had been promised unless there were overriding reasons not to give it to him.[7]

It should always have been obvious that the doctrine gave substantive protection. After all, it follows from the *Wednesbury* doctrine that if no reasonable public authority would disappoint an expectation, it is unlawful to do so. And that is unquestionably a matter of substance. Is substantive protection of expectations dangerous? Does it restrict a public authority's capacity to change its policy? And does it enable an authority to bind itself illegitimately, evading the law that requires it to make a genuine exercise of its discretion (see section 8.1.2)? Not necessarily. As Taylor J pointed out in *Ruddock*, substantive protection for legitimate expectations need not fetter the discretion of a public authority (1497). It can be a good *exercise* of discretion for a public authority to commit itself (after all, public authorities can enter binding contracts: see p 572). But the substantive impact of the doctrine ought to be limited, because no one can *legitimately* expect a public authority to be unable to change its policy under any conditions. The result in *Bibi* shows that the courts can protect legitimate expectations without taking away a public authority's discretion. In fact, in *Bibi*, the doctrine of legitimate expectation **simply acts as an instance of the relevance doctrine**, because the court held that the law required the authority to take its promise into account in exercising its discretion. That fact itself shows first of all that the doctrine of legitimate expectation is not a novelty, and secondly that it must provide some form of substantive protection. Like *Wednesbury* unreasonableness, the relevance doctrine unquestionably controls the substance of decisions. The strenuous

---

[6] In *GCHQ*, Lord Diplock had suggested that 'where the decision is one which does not alter rights or obligations enforceable in private law but only deprives a person of legitimate expectations, "procedural impropriety" will normally provide the only ground on which the decision is open to judicial review' ([1985] AC 374, 411). Cf. *O'Reilly v Mackman* [1983] 2 AC 237, 275 (Lord Diplock).

[7] There had been clear authority for this approach since *R v Home Secretary, ex p Khan* [1985] 1 All ER 40, and Taylor J unequivocally stated that the doctrine of legitimate expectation is 'not confined' to a right to be heard, in *R v Home Secretary, ex p Ruddock* [1987] 1 WLR 1482, 1497.

debates over the legitimate expectation doctrine have really concerned the extent of substantive protection. We will look at that problem in this section; it tests the limits of the judges' role.

In the idea that courts should prevent abuse of power, there is a rationale for some form of substantive protection for expectations that administrative authorities have induced. The courts must apply it with comity toward administrative authorities. You might think that it is no breach of comity for the judges to hold an administrative authority to a policy choice to which *the authority has committed itself*. Yet the courts still need to defer to some extent, because a public authority may have legitimate reasons to change a policy, or to create exceptions to it, and may need to reconcile it with competing interests. The deference the courts need to show may make it impossible for them to decide whether it is appropriate for a public authority to disappoint a legitimate expectation. The judges do not always keep hold of the principle of comity as clearly as they did in *Bibi*.

The leading case is *R v North and East Devon Health Authority, ex p Coughlan* [2001] QB 213 (CA). A car accident had left Miss Coughlan in need of constant nursing care. After she had been in a hospital for more than 20 years, the health authority promised her that, if she moved into a new nursing home called Mardon House, she could stay there for life. She agreed, but after five years the authority decided to close Mardon House and to move her again. The decision was made for financial reasons and because the facility was not clinically well suited for other health service functions that were located there [53]. The Court of Appeal held that the decision had been unlawful. The authority had deliberately considered the fact that Miss Coughlan had been promised a home for life, so the decision shows how legitimate expectation can move beyond the relevance doctrine.

Lord Woolf MR, for the Court of Appeal, pointed out that different expectations may deserve different forms of legal protection:

> (a) The court may decide that the public authority is only required to bear in mind its previous policy or other representation, giving it the weight it thinks right, but no more, before deciding whether to change course. Here the court is confined to reviewing the decision on Wednesbury grounds.... (b) On the other hand the court may decide that the promise or practice induces a legitimate expectation of, for example, being consulted before a particular decision is taken. Here it is uncontentious that the court itself will require the opportunity for consultation to be given unless there is an overriding reason to resile from it.... (c) Where the court considers that a lawful promise or practice has induced a legitimate expectation of a benefit which is substantive, not simply procedural, authority now establishes that here too the court will in a proper case decide whether to frustrate the expectation is so unfair that to take a new and different course will amount to an abuse of power. Here, once the legitimacy of the expectation is established, the court will have the task of weighing the requirements of fairness against any overriding interest relied upon for the change of policy. [57]

Of Lord Woolf's three categories of protection, the first is an application of the relevance doctrine,[8] and the second is an application of the law of due process.

If legitimate expectations can be protected in different ways, what determines the form of protection? The Court held that Miss Coughlan's case came within category (c), because the promise was so important to her, the number of persons affected by the promise was few, and the consequences of holding the authority to its promise were 'likely to be financial only' [60].

Lord Woolf's category (c) is a form of protection against substantive unfairness. But not just any unfairness. In order for a court to interfere, the claimant has to show that frustrating the expectation was unfair in a way that the judges can identify as an abuse of power. So Miss Coughlan did not win merely because the health authority had not given the right weight to her expectation. She won because their decision was *so unfair* as to be an abuse of their discretionary power. Understood in that way, the case is an orthodox application of principles that go back to *Kruse* and earlier; it is only remarkable because by deciding that the decision was an abuse of power, the judges took it on themselves to discount the financial consequences of keeping open an almost-redundant nursing home.

Yet, in their conclusion in *Coughlan*, the judges said, 'the Health Authority failed to weigh the conflicting interests correctly' [89]. That suggests that the Court decided what the correct balance is between the interests of a person with a legitimate expectation, and the interests that weigh against fulfilling the legitimate expectation. The Court also held that 'The propriety of such an exercise of power should be tested by asking whether the need which the Health Authority judged to exist to move Miss Coughlan to a local authority facility was such as to **outweigh** its promise that Mardon House would be her home for life' [83]. That is indeed the way for the health authority to decide whether to move Miss Coughlan; but the way *for the Court to decide whether it was lawful* is—according to the Court of Appeal in *Coughlan* itself—to ask whether it was *so* unfair as to amount to an abuse of power for the health authority to reach the conclusion that it reached. So there is an ambiguity in *Coughlan*: is it the judges' job to identify an abuse of power? Or to determine whether a public authority decided correctly?

In R v MAFF, *ex p Hamble Fisheries Ltd* [1995] 2 All ER 714, Sedley J had held that the court's duty was 'to protect the interests of those individuals whose expectation of different treatment has a legitimacy which in fairness **outtops** the policy choice which threatens to frustrate it' (731). Hamble Fisheries had refitted a boat to take advantage of the Ministry's way of counting fishing quotas; the Ministry changed its policy, and refused to make an exception to allow the company to take advantage of the old scheme. The word 'outtops' in Sedley J's reasons shows that he took it upon himself to decide whether the Ministry made the correct decision. In R v Home Secretary, *ex p Hargreaves* [1997] 1 All ER 397, Hirst LJ called Sedley J's approach 'heresy'. The heresy was that Sedley J made the decision that the Ministry had to make. He judged whether the policy change was important enough to justify the impact on Hamble

---

[8]   See *Coughlan* [73].

Fisheries, without deferring to the Ministry's view of the importance of the policy change. Hirst LJ said in *Hargreaves*, 'On matters of substance (as contrasted with procedure) *Wednesbury* provides the correct test.... while Sedley J's actual decision in the *Hamble* case stands, his ratio in so far as he propounds a balancing exercise to be undertaken by the court should in my judgment be overruled' (412).

Did *Coughlan* rescue *Hamble Fisheries* from *Hargreaves*? No, because *Coughlan* involved an abuse of power. Consider the fact that the Court of Appeal in *Coughlan* relied on *Kruse v Johnson* (*Coughlan* [72]). It would be completely foreign to Lord Russell's approach in *Kruse*, to say that the court must decide whether the policy objective was important *enough* to justify the impact on the defendants. His approach was not even to ask that question, but to ask instead, in anticipation of *Wednesbury*, if decisions were 'manifestly unjust; if they disclosed bad faith; if they involved such oppressive or gratuitous interference with the rights of those subject to them as could find no justification in the minds of reasonable men' (*Kruse v Johnson* [1898] 2 QB 91, 99–100; see p 220).

The Court of Appeal in *Coughlan* (which included Sedley LJ) certainly wanted to reject the *Hargreaves* view that *Wednesbury* provides the correct test for substantive protection of legitimate expectations. The Court in *Coughlan* held that in category (a) (where the public authority need only bear in mind its policy or representation), 'the court is confined to reviewing the decision on *Wednesbury* grounds'—implying that in category (c), the court is *not* confined to reviewing the decision on *Wednesbury* grounds. And the Court suggested that the right approach 'is to ask not whether the decision is ultra vires in the restricted *Wednesbury* sense but whether, for example through unfairness or arbitrariness, it amounts to an abuse of power' [67]. That presents *Wednesbury* as if it were restricted to irrationality (see *Coughlan* [62]). Then the Court pointed out that the decision of the health authority in *Coughlan* was perfectly rational, but could be quashed for unfairness amounting to abuse of process (using *Preston*, but also *Kruse* [72]). The Court presented the resulting doctrine of substantive protection for legitimate expectations as a progression beyond *Wednesbury*.

But the result in *Coughlan*, and the reasons for it, are perfectly compatible with Lord Greene's reasons in *Wednesbury*. Precisely because the Court held the decision in *Coughlan* to be an abuse of power, there is no arguable ground for the Court's suggestion that the decision requires a ground of review other than those that Lord Greene identified. No reasonable public authority would exercise its power in a way that is so unfair as to amount to an abuse of power. It would be deeply contrary to Lord Greene's approach in *Wednesbury*, to say that a decision may be so unfair as to amount to an abuse of power, and yet still be lawful because it is not irrational. The Court of Appeal in *Coughlan* had a convincing argument that a decision does not have to be irrational before it can be quashed as an abuse of power. But that convincing argument only shows that it has always been a mistake for the courts to describe *Wednesbury* unreasonableness as 'irrationality' (see p 228). The very fact that the Court of Appeal could rely on *Kruse* shows that *Coughlan* does not support the *Hamble Fisheries* rule that it is unlawful for a public authority to disappoint a substantive legitimate expectation whenever the court decides that the impact on the claimant outtops the public interest in a policy change. Their conclusion that the health authority had abused its power meant that *Coughlan* was simply too strong a case to give the Court an opportunity to rehabilitate *Hamble Fisheries*.

Yet in their conclusion on the legitimate expectation issue, the Court really did state the old heretical line from *Hamble Fisheries*—the line that the Court of Appeal had overruled in *Hargreaves*—by asking if the health authority had correctly weighed its reasons for wanting to close Mardon House against its promise not to. If *Coughlan* stands for the principle that the judges have that job, then it was revolutionary. But it is better to take the case as standing for the proposition asserted repeatedly through the decision—a proposition that is compatible with *Wednesbury* and (as the judges suggested by citing *Kruse*) goes back much further than *Wednesbury*. It is the proposition that an exercise of discretion can be quashed for 'unfairness amounting to an abuse of power' [89]. That sort of unfairness may, as in *Coughlan*, arise because of an expectation that the public authority has induced, but it need not. So legitimate expectation is indeed, as the judges suggested in *Coughlan*, an instance of a general doctrine of substantive unfairness. But substantive unfairness is a general ground of judicial review only when it amounts to abuse of power.

> **The relation between legitimate expectation and proportionality**
> What protection does the law give to legitimate expectations? It requires **proportionate process**: that is, forms of participation in public decision making as to whether to disappoint a legitimate expectation that give the claimant a role that is proportionate to the issues at stake.
>
> What about substantive proportionality? When a claimant has a legitimate expectation, the judges sometimes suggest that it is their job to decide whether the value of pursuing the public authority's purpose by disappointing the expectation is proportionate to the impact on the claimant of doing so. That was Sedley J's approach in *Hamble Fisheries*. But *Coughlan* itself shows that this view would give too much protection to legitimate expectations, because it would involve insufficient deference to the public authority's assessment of the value of a course of action that would disappoint the expectation.

8.4.5 Legitimate expectations: conclusion

What more does legitimate expectation give than the ordinary doctrines of due process and control of discretionary powers? Nothing: it is *part of* those doctrines. It can be procedurally unfair to disappoint an expectation without a hearing, and it can be substantively unfair to disappoint an expectation. And then, the decision is unlawful if it is procedurally unfair, or if it is so unfair in substance that it is an abuse of power.

The key concept that explains substantive protection for legitimate expectations is abuse of power. What is an abuse of power? The cases, of course, give no precise answer. 'Abuse' is vague. But the crucial point is that abusing power is *worse* than just making the wrong decision. An abuse of power is a departure from responsible government (see p 13). As Laws LJ said in R v *Education Secretary, ex p Begbie* [2000] 1 WLR 1115, to call someone's conduct an abuse of power is a 'condemnation' [81].

If the health authority in *Coughlan* moved Miss Coughlan when it did not need to do so, it made the wrong decision. If it abused its power, it did worse than that; it treated Miss Coughlan with contempt. Like the other vague terms that judges have used to explain their role (such as 'irrational', or 'perverse', or 'so unreasonable that no reasonable official could have done it'), the vagueness of the standard leads to a risk that judges will see a decision they don't like, and just call it an 'abuse of power'. But that only means that it is an idea that is open to misuse—not that it is meaningless. The special feature of abuse of power is that judges ought to be able to identify it without needing to second-guess the decision maker on matters that call for deference. *Wednesbury* unreasonableness was Lord Greene's attempt to articulate the basis of abuse of power: it is conduct that a court ought to condemn, because even from the court's detached point of view it can be seen that no one in the decision maker's position could seriously defend the decision.

Ordinarily, a decision is an abuse of power if it is abusive (not merely unfair or unjust) toward the claimant. That is only the *ordinary* case: consider R v *Foreign Secretary, ex p World Development Movement* [1995] 1 WLR 386, in which the Government took money that Parliament had allocated for overseas aid, and used it to give Malaysia a financial incentive to buy British military aircraft (see p 270). What made that decision an abuse of power—the thing that distinguishes it from making the wrong decision in general—is that it showed a flagrant disregard for the purposes for which a public authority has been given a power. The Government did not merely make a bad overseas aid decision; it didn't make an overseas aid decision at all. It decided to use the overseas aid fund for something else altogether.

8.4.6 Applying a policy: legitimate expectations without the expectations

In R *(Rashid)* v *Home Secretary* [2005] EWCA Civ 744, the claimant was a Kurd from Iraq whose application for asylum was turned down, on the basis that he could have escaped persecution within Iraq, by relocating to the Kurdish zone. Neither Rashid, nor his advisers, nor the caseworker who dealt with his claim knew that the Home Secretary had a policy that asylum claims were not to be refused on that ground. The Court of Appeal held that the rejection of the claim was an instance of unfairness amounting to an abuse of power.

The Court of Appeal described its decision in *Rashid* as an application of the doctrine of legitimate expectation. But Rashid had no expectations! He did not know about the Home Secretary's policy. The Court addressed this point, and said that he had a legitimate expectation *of being dealt with on the Home Office's policy, whatever it was*. It sounds as if Rashid ought to be able to expect that. Yet still, it is simply inescapable that what Rashid expected was irrelevant to the decision. In *Coughlan*, and even in *Bibi*, the public authority's conduct was substantively unfair *because the claimant expected a different course of conduct*. By contrast, it didn't matter what Rashid expected: a claimant in his position who had no expectation (or a claimant who had an expectation that the Home Office would act arbitrarily) would be in just the same position. The *reason for* preventing the Home Office from acting contrary to its own policy was not the fact that the claimant expected it to conform to its policies.

So the 'legitimate expectation' in *Rashid* was a pseudo-expectation. But *Rashid* is not the only case in which courts have found unfairness amounting to abuse of power, when a public authority fails to abide by the so-called 'legitimate expectation' created by a policy that the claimant did not know about (cf. R (S) v Home Secretary [2007] EWHC 51). What is the real rationale for these decisions, if it isn't the fact that the claimant expected something? The explanation is that the courts feel free to require some degree of consistency in adherence to policies. Lord Justice Laws put this as a requirement of good administration, in *Nadarajah v Home Secretary* [2005] EWCA Civ 1363:

> 'Where a public authority has issued a promise or adopted a practice which represents how it proposes to act in a given area, the law will require the promise or practice to be honoured unless there is good reason not to do so. What is the principle behind this proposition? It is not far to seek. It is said to be grounded in fairness, and no doubt in general terms that is so. I would prefer to express it rather more broadly as a requirement of good administration, by which public bodies ought to deal straightforwardly and consistently with the public.' [68]

Of course, it is not *generally* the job of judges to tell government departments what good administration requires. Courts should only do so if their view can be imposed on the department with no breach of comity. And if a department of government has a policy in favour of a claimant, and fails to apply it, the court can identify that as an arbitrary, irresponsible use of power (i.e., a use of power that does not respond to the considerations that it ought to respond to), even if it is not abusive. Since it is the defendant's own policy, there is no breach of comity in requiring the authority to conform to it. So there is a general rule that, as Laws LJ put it, a policy is 'to be honoured unless there is good reason not to do so'. The rule is *related* to the doctrine of legitimate expectations: both grounds of review are justified by the court's role in preventing acts of government that the court can identify as arbitrary.

And like the doctrine of legitimate expectation, the rule that policies are to be applied must be qualified, because public authorities need to be able to change their policies. Sometimes, it will be unclear whether a public authority has unlawfully neglected its policy, or has lawfully changed it. In *Nadarajah*, the court held against the claimant on the ground that the Home Office had changed its policy in a way that involved no abuse of power.

8.5 Substantive unfairness

The judges in *Coughlan* held that the ground for quashing the decision to move Miss Coughlan was 'an abuse of power or a failure of substantive fairness' [76]. Are they the same thing? Is substantive unfairness a ground of judicial review?

It is sometimes said, as Lord Diplock said in R v *Inland Revenue Commissioners, ex p National Federation of Self-Employed and Small Businesses* [1982] AC 617, that judicial review is not available 'for acts done lawfully in the exercise of an administrative discretion which are complained of only as being unfair or unwise' (637). Yet Lord Scarman said in R v *Inland Revenue Commissioners, ex p Preston* [1985] AC 835:

> ❛I must make clear my view that the principle of fairness has an important place in the law of judicial review: and that in an appropriate case it is a ground upon which the court can intervene to quash a decision made by a public officer or authority in purported exercise of a power conferred by law.❜ (851)

Who was right?

They were both right. If the claim is *only* that a decision was substantively unfair, that is not a ground of judicial review. But *certain forms* of unfairness can justify judicial review. In the ferment of judicial review in the 1980s (see section 2.6), this point became clear: the House of Lords held unequivocally and unanimously, in *Preston*, that the judges in judicial review can give relief against unfairness in the exercise of an administrative discretion, but *only if* the unfairness renders the decision an abuse of power by the commissioners (see Lord Templeman, 864).

So what more does it take, if unfairness is not enough by itself? It is not even enough that a decision is *very* unfair—after all, it did not matter how unfairly the Conservative Government was acting in capping the local authorities' rates in R v *Environmental Secretary, ex p Hammersmith and Fulham LBC* [1991] AC 521 and R v *Environmental Secretary, ex p Nottinghamshire County Council* [1986] AC 240 (see p 247); it still was not the judges' job to remedy the unfairness. The local byelaws in both *Wednesbury* and *Kruse* were substantively unfair if they were disproportionate (if the byelaw in *Wednesbury* restricted access to the cinema *too much*, or if the byelaw in *Kruse* did not give people *enough* freedom to sing hymns in public). But the judges in both cases insisted that it was not for them to decide those questions.

It is the principle of comity that distinguishes forms of unfairness that the court can and cannot remedy. Procedural unfairness *generally* justifies judicial review, because the judges can generally require another public authority to use a fair procedure, without interfering with that authority in a damaging way. But judges cannot generally decide whether the substance of an administrative decision was fair, without damaging the work of administrative authorities. If you think this is wrong— because unfair decisions shouldn't happen—go back to *Hammersmith and Fulham* and *Nottinghamshire*, and they will remind you that the courts cannot remedy all bad decisions. Substantive unfairness does *not* generally justify judicial review. The added something that is required is something that *the court is in a position to identify* as an abuse of power, something that is *manifestly* unfair—'conspicuous unfairness' (*Rashid* [19]). That is, judicial review requires something that is obvious *to a reviewing court.* That is the general standard today, for review of the substance of the exercise of discretionary power. It is vague, and offers courts the temptation just to quash any decision that they think should not have been made. But when they do that, they are stepping beyond the role of judges.

As Lord Scarman put it in *Nottinghamshire,* 'the courts may intervene to review a power conferred by statute on the ground of unfairness but only if the unfairness in the purported exercise of the power be such as to amount to an abuse of the power' (249–50).[9]

8.6 European Community law: legitimate expectations and proportionality

For generations, the European Union (EU) has been paying farmers to produce crops and livestock for which there is no adequate market. The Common Agricultural Policy ('CAP') has sustained the farmers' way of life.[10] It has also consumed vast resources and distorted international markets, hurting poorer farmers in third-world countries who are trying to compete with European farmers. The European Union has made fitful attempts to reform this massive administrative and financial programme. In 2003, the Council adopted Regulation 1782/2003, designed to replace payments for production with direct payments that would give farmers no incentive to overproduce cotton. To avoid a sudden upheaval in the cotton market, the regulation provided for 65% of the payments to be given as income support, rather than as a production subsidy. Not only that; the definition of 'production' was changed, so that farmers could collect the full payments without the cotton actually reaching harvest.

Spain's complaint was that the result would be such a reduction in production that the Spanish cotton processing industry would go out of business (which in turn would hurt those farmers who were still trying to harvest cotton, since they would have no one to process their crop). What recourse did Spain have in European law? The European Court of Justice (ECJ) can review the legality of certain acts of the European Parliament, the Council, and the Commission, under the EC Treaty Art 230. In just a few words, the statement of the grounds of review provides an interesting comparison with the English grounds of judicial review:

> 'lack of competence, infringement of an essential procedural requirement, infringement of this Treaty or of any rule of law relating to its application, or misuse of powers.'

---

9   Citing Lord Templeman's speech in *Preston,* 864–5.

10   The EC Treaty itself enshrines the extravagant aim of ensuring 'a fair standard of living for the agricultural community, in particular by increasing the individual earnings of persons engaged in agriculture' (Art 33).

You will recognize these grounds: the first three are roughly the same as lack of jurisdiction (see p 302), lack of due process (see Chapters 4 to 6), and failure to abide by a legal duty (see p 264). The fourth is something like abuse of power (see section 7.1).[11] Where do legitimate expectations come in? Just as they form part of the law of due process and abuse of power in English law, they can be a basis for identifying an 'essential procedural requirement' or a 'misuse of powers', in European law.

Legitimate expectations

In Spain's cotton case, Case C-310/04 *Spain v Council* [2006] ECR I-07285, the ECJ held that 'the principle of the protection of legitimate expectations is one of the fundamental principles of the Community' [81]. But no one has a legitimate expectation that institutions with power to change the CAP will not do so: 'if a prudent and circumspect operator could have foreseen that the adoption of a Community measure is likely to affect his interests', the principle is not violated if the measure is adopted. To rub it in, the Court added that 'economic operators are not justified in having a legitimate expectation that an existing situation which is capable of being altered by the Community institutions in the exercise of their discretionary power will be maintained, particularly in an area such as that of the common organisation of the markets, the objective of which involves constant adjustment to reflect changes in economic circumstances' [81]. As in English law, the doctrine of legitimate expectations is meant to support the capacity of public authorities to make appropriate changes to their policies; and the ECJ will defer to the legislative institutions, to some extent, on the question of which changes are appropriate.

The Court held that the Spanish had no legitimate expectation that the old production supports would be maintained, partly because fundamental reform had been under discussion for more than ten years. The only legitimate expectation they had was that no reform would be made in a way that *disproportionately* damaged their operations. So when it comes to the substance of a policy change, all that a claimant gets from the doctrine of legitimate expectation is something that can be stated as a distinct principle of Community law in any case: that the regulation should not interfere disproportionately with the farmers' operations.

Proportionality

The ECJ declared that the Council had infringed the principle of proportionality. But the form of review was very hands off, and it is important to see just what the Court meant; Spain actually won on the Community law equivalent of the requirement of genuine exercise of discretion, which the Court linked to its own relevance doctrine:

---

[11]   When the EC Treaty says 'misuse of powers', it must be understood to mean what English lawyers call 'abuse of power', or it would be the judges' job to quash any act that the Parliament or the Council or the Commission should not have adopted. That was patently not the intention of the parties to the Treaty.

> '...the Community institutions which have adopted the act in question must be able to show before the Court that in adopting the act they actually exercised their discretion, which presupposes the taking into consideration of all the relevant factors and circumstances of the situation the act was intended to regulate.' [122]

The principle of proportionality, 'one of the general principles of Community law', requires the following:

> 'that acts adopted by Community institutions do not exceed the limits of what is appropriate and necessary in order to attain the legitimate objectives pursued by the legislation in question; where there is a choice between several appropriate measures, recourse must be had to the least onerous, and the disadvantages caused must not be disproportionate to the aims pursued.' [97]

If proportionality is a general doctrine of European Community law (EC law), it may seem that it is the judges' job to decide *how much* disadvantage to a claimant is *too* much. But in *Spain v Council*, the ECJ did *not* decide 'the limits of what is appropriate and necessary in order to attain the legitimate objectives'—any more than Lord Russell decided what sort of byelaws would be reasonable in *Kruse v Johnson* [1898] 2 QB 91. Instead, the ECJ decided that, 'bearing in mind the wide discretion enjoyed by the Community legislature where the common agricultural policy is concerned, the lawfulness of a measure adopted in that sphere can be affected only if the measure is manifestly inappropriate in terms of the objective which the competent institution is seeking to pursue' [98].[12]

That word 'manifestly', repeated several times in *Spain v Council*, is the same word that Lord Russell used in *Kruse v Johnson*, and that Lord Bridge used in *R v Environment Secretary, ex p Hammersmith and Fulham LBC* [1991] 1 AC 521. And they all used it for the same purpose: to emphasize the court's limited role in passing judgment on the substance of a decision, when the decision maker has a broad discretionary power.

The considerations in *Spain v Council* depended on the especially political role that the treaties gave the EU legislative institutions in operating (and reforming) the Common Agricultural Policy. In other contexts, the ECJ will be less deferential. But remember: even though 'proportionality' is a general principle of Community law, there is no general doctrine of Community law that courts will quash measures that are disproportionate to their objectives. Where the institution responsible for the measure has a wide discretion, the Court will only interfere if the measure has

----

[12] The 'manifestly inappropriate' standard, and much of the rest of the Court's account of the law, can be found repeated verbatim in several cases reaching back to Case 265/87 *Schräder v Hauptzollamt Gronau* [1989] ECR 2237 [22]: 'in matters concerning the common agricultural policy, the Community legislator has a discretionary power which corresponds to the political responsibilities imposed by Articles 40 and 43. Consequently, the legality of a measure adopted in that sphere can be affected only if the measure is manifestly inappropriate having regard to the objective which the competent institution intends to pursue'.

a *manifestly* disproportionate impact. In *Spain v Council*, the ECJ did not decide that the measure had a manifestly disproportionate impact on the farmers; it decided that the Council 'has not shown before the Court that in adopting the new cotton support scheme established by that regulation it actually exercised its discretion, involving the taking into consideration of all the relevant factors and circumstances of the case' [133]. It is a European version of the **genuine exercise** rule (see p 264), and not a general rule that judges must decide how much is too much.

The role of deference in the EU proportionality doctrine shows why it would be a mistake to think that proportionality will oust the *Wednesbury* principles in English judicial review. The law of the European Convention has not brought a general standard of proportionality into English law, and EC law has not, either. The ECJ defers to the Council, to some extent, on the implementation of the Common Agricultural Policy. Notice that this does not mean that deference is the default position in ECJ review of the lawfulness of Community measures. As in English administrative law, whether and how a court should defer to another public authority is an open question, which depends on the type of decision, the nature of the decision maker, and the decision-making context. We cannot say that there is a general rule of deference, or a general rule of no deference.

> Deference means not minding, or not asking (to some extent), whether the initial decision was right or wrong! You can see why judges sometimes have difficulty deferring to administrative authorities.

8.7 Conclusion: abuse of power

Does abuse of power unify the grounds of judicial review? Lord Scarman thought so:

> ❝The ground upon which the courts will review the exercise of an administrative discretion by a public officer is abuse of power. Power can be abused in a number of ways: by a mistake of law in misconstruing the limits imposed by statute (or by common law in the case of a common law power) upon the scope of the power; by procedural irregularity; by unreasonableness in the *Wednesbury* sense; or by bad faith or an improper motive in its exercise. ❞ [13]

But that only stretches 'abuse of power', to make it into a catch-all phrase for the grounds of judicial review. It is no abuse of power for a public official to come to a different view of the law from a judge. To act in bad faith, on the other hand, really is an abuse of power. An abuse of power is an abandonment of responsible government.

---

[13] R *v Environment Secretary, ex p Nottinghamshire County Council* [1986] AC 240, 249.

Some of the ambiguity of the *Coughlan* decision results because it is not quite clear whether the judges were using 'abuse of power' to refer to something that really is abusive, or whether they were using it more broadly for a decision that ought to have been different.

This problem about the use of the term 'abuse' is only a difficulty of terminology; the important point to bear in mind is that judges should not invent for themselves the power to interfere with another public authority simply because it ought to have used its power differently. The courts have a very wide-ranging responsibility to interfere with official action that is unlawful because it does not conform to standards that Parliament has set for public authorities (in the Race Relations Act 1976, for example, or the Human Rights Act 1998, or the European Communities Act 1972). Judges should only impose standards of their own devising when doing so is justified by the **core rationale** for judicial review: that is, to promote responsible government by holding it unlawful for a public authority to act in a way that judges can identify as arbitrary (see p 65). It is the judges' duty of comity that distinguishes the decisions that should have been different (which may be none of the judges' business) from the decisions that ought to be quashed on judicial review.

This means that substantive unfairness is not in itself a ground of judicial review. But *some forms* of substantive unfairness justify interference by a court. The 19th-century law is still good on this point, and much of the 20th-and 21st-century progress has been to apply it more broadly, and with particular attention to special aspects of substantive unfairness: to the interests that may arise from expectations generated by officials, and to the potential for judges to protect people from abuse of power by asking (with a greater or lesser degree of deference where comity requires it) what burdens are disproportionate to the public interests that an authority is pursuing. The basic principles are more than a century old. Decisions 'such as reasonable men could not make in good faith' are one thing (and courts may quash them unless the issues at stake are non-justiciable): *Slattery v Naylor* (1888) 13 App Cas 446, 453. But decisions are not to be struck down as unreasonable (or disproportionate, or a breach of legitimate expectation) merely because they do not 'commend themselves to the minds of judges' (453).

Summary

Judges may control a discretionary power by:

- applying (and developing) the law of due process;
- applying any legal prohibition on the use of power (such as the prohibition in Human Rights Act 1998 s 6 on acting incompatibly with a Convention right, when primary legislation does not require it);
- deferential[14] review of fact finding (see section 9.2);
- non-deferential review of interpretations of the law (see section 9.1);
- protecting a legitimate expectation (by procedural or substantive means);

---

14   Depending on the type of decision—see p 331.

- deferential review for reasonableness (the extent of deference varies dramatically with the context).

Of course, you might say that the last point encompasses all the others: it is not the judges' job to tell another public authority how to use its power, or *even what would be reasonable*. But if the court can determine that a power has been exercised unreasonably without breaching its duty of comity to another public authority, there is ground for judicial review.

TAKE-HOME MESSAGE • • •

- The doctrines of **relevance, legitimate expectations,** and **proportionality** all require judges to pass judgment on the **substantive fairness** of administrative decisions.

- But there is still no general doctrine that an administrative decision should be struck down just because it is substantively unfair. The effect of that sort of general doctrine of substantive fairness would be to authorize judges to decide for themselves whether the initial decision maker ought to have done something different.

- Only certain forms of substantive unfairness justify judicial review. The vague general test for those sorts of unfairness is that the courts will interfere with an **abuse of power.**

- The application of that general test depends on the type of the decision and the context in which it is made. Judges really will substitute their own judgment for that of the initial decision maker on certain sorts of questions—in particular, on whether there are grounds for the use of a discretionary power to detain a person.

Critical reading

Re Findlay [1985] AC 318
R v Foreign Secretary, ex p World Development Movement [1995] 1 WLR 386
R v Inland Revenue Commissioners, ex p Unilever [1996] STC 681
R (Daly) v Home Secretary [2001] UKHL 26
R (Bibi) v Newham LBC [2001] EWCA Civ 607
R (Wilkinson) v Broadmoor Special Hospital [2001] EWCA Civ 1545
R v North and East Devon Health Authority, ex p Coughlan [2001] QB 213
R (Begum) v Denbigh High School [2006] UKHL 15
Case C-310/04 Spain v Council [2006] ECR I-07285
R (Corner House Research) v Director of the Serious Fraud Office [2008] UKHL 60

CRITICAL QUESTIONS • • •

1 **Are there any grounds *other than abuse of power*, on which judges may interfere with the substance of an exercise of a discretionary power?**

2 Can a public authority lawfully thwart a legitimate expectation?

3 Should the courts defer to a public authority on the question of what purposes the authority's powers can properly be used to pursue?

4 Should the courts defer to a public authority on the question of what considerations are relevant to the exercise of a discretionary power?

5 Why is proportionality a general principle of the law of due process, but not a general principle of the control of discretionary powers?

Further questions:

6 The courts have a doctrine of precedent (requiring them to abide by [some] previous decisions), and a doctrine of *res judicata* (giving conclusive effect to a decision once it is made and is not subject to any appeal). Is there a doctrine of precedent or a doctrine of *res judicata* for public authorities in general?

7 Your local council sends you a cheque for £1000 with a letter explaining that you paid too much council tax. You deposit the cheque (quite reasonably thinking that they must know what they are doing). Then the council accountants realize that because of a clerical error, they wrote the cheque and sent the letter to the wrong taxpayer. Can they demand the money back?

8 The government has a regular practice of responding to a declaration of incompatibility under the Human Rights Act by making an amending order. If a statute is declared incompatible, does a person affected by it have a legitimate expectation that the government will do so?

online resource centre

Visit the online resource centre to access the following resources which accompany this chapter: links to legislation and online reports of judicial decisions, summaries of key cases and legislation, updates in the law, suggestions for answering the pop quizzes and questions, and links to useful websites.

9 Errors of law and control of fact finding

Administrative authorities deciding someone's legal position must determine what the law is, and find the facts, and apply the law to the facts. This chapter asks how the courts control the exercise of power involved in those three elements of the application of the law.

LOOK FOR • • •

- Review for error of law.

- Deference on questions of law: is there any?

- Why a power to apply the law is a discretionary power.

- The fundamental union (downplayed and sometimes denied by the judges) between judicial review for error of law, and other forms of control of discretionary power.

> ❝We cannot correct an error in their proceedings, and ought to suppose what is done by a final jurisdiction, to be right.❞
>
> **Moses v Macferlan (1760) 2 Burr 1005, 97 ER 676 (KB), 679(Lord Mansfield CJ, on reviewing decisions of the Court of Conscience, a local small claims court set up by statute)**

> ❝...in general any error of law made by an administrative tribunal or inferior court in reaching its decision can be quashed for error of law.❞
>
> **R v Hull University Visitor, ex p Page [1993] AC 682 (HL), 702 (Lord Browne-Wilkinson)**

9.1 Errors of law

9.1.1 The discretionary power to determine the law

When Sergeant Walker applied to the Ministry of Defence for criminal injuries compensation in R v Ministry of Defence, ex p Walker [2000] 1 WLR 806 (see section 2.1), the Ministry of Defence had to answer three questions in order to decide whether he was entitled to compensation:

(1) What were the rules of the compensation scheme?

(2) What had happened to Sergeant Walker?

(3) How do the rules of the scheme apply to his case?

In a nutshell, English law controls these administrative decisions by:

(1) A rule that the court should correct any error of law (that is, any error the court finds in the administrative authority's answer to question 1): **section 9.1**;

(2) A more hands-off form of control of administrative fact-finding, in which the judges only interfere when for some special reason it is *obvious* (from their detached, judicial point of view) that the administrative authority got the facts wrong: **section 9.2**; and

(3) A rule that unless the administrative authority got question 1 wrong, the court will only interfere with question 3 if the administrative decision as to how the rules apply is so unreasonable that no reasonable decision maker could have reached it: **section 9.3**.

By creating a scheme of criminal injuries compensation for its soldiers, the Ministry of Defence took on responsibility for deciding whether a particular soldier's claim (such as Sergeant Walker's claim) fit the scheme's criteria for eligibility. The criteria would obviously be met in some cases, and in those cases it would be wrong for the Ministry to refuse compensation. But the operation of any such scheme will yield cases (such as Sergeant Walker's) in which it would be reasonable to decide that the claimant is eligible, and also reasonable to decide that the claimant is ineligible. Every uncertainty in the application of its terms in particular cases leaves a **resultant discretion** (see p 232) to the decision maker: a freedom to resolve the uncertainty as the decision maker sees fit, with no duty to decide one way rather than another. The scheme itself gives the choice to the body responsible for operating the scheme. The choice is to be made in light of the purposes of the scheme, but sometimes those purposes will be compatible with a decision either way. So, in Walker's case, the Ministry's power to apply the scheme was a discretionary power: it created a discretion whether to hold that the claimant was or was not eligible for compensation.

A legal power to decide a claim with legal effect is a **jurisdiction**. The Ministry had jurisdiction to decide Sergeant Walker's claim, and that power was subject to judicial review. You might think that this discretionary power would be controlled, like all discretionary powers, in the deferential style explained in Chapter 7, with attention to the principle of comity. But on one aspect of the exercise of an administrative jurisdiction the judges do not defer. Lord Slynn said, 'It is plainly open to the court on an application for judicial review to consider whether the Ministry of Defence has correctly interpreted the scheme... or whether its decision involves an error of law' (810). If the judges' role is to control the Ministry's exercise of its jurisdiction as it controls other discretionary powers, why did Lord Slynn claim that it was the judges' job to make sure it was exercised *correctly*?

The answer involves one of the most remarkable lines of cases in the history of English law. In the cases leading up to R v Hull University Visitor, ex p Page [1993] AC 682, the courts took upon themselves a power to review exercises of administrative jurisdiction for **error of law**. That development was grounded on mistaken arguments of precedent, and it cannot be justified on grounds of constitutional principle. The development of review for error of law made it seem confusing and irrelevant to think of administrative agencies as having any jurisdiction at all—when in fact, jurisdiction is a crucial tool for understanding the legal powers of public authorities. And along the way, the judges disregarded an act of Parliament. This chapter explains these remarkable developments leading up to *Page*, and also explains the substantial discretions that remain to administrative decision makers in identifying the facts, and in applying the law to the facts.

The phrase **'error of law'** is often used very broadly for any unlawful feature of a decision. That use of the phrase is attractive to courts hearing an appeal on a point of law, who have no jurisdiction to allow the appeal if there was no error of law. And it makes sense to use the phrase in that broad sense: if a public authority intends to act lawfully, then it makes an error of law whenever it does anything unlawful. 'Error of law' in this very broad sense includes, e.g., failure to give reasons where the law requires them (*Re Poyser and Mills' Arbitration* [1964] 2 QB 467, 478), and acting in a way that is *Wednesbury* unreasonable.[1] In this chapter we will use the term 'error of law' in

---

[1]   '...there is an error of law if a decision is one to which no reasonable decision-maker, properly instructing himself on the law, could have come on the evidence before him' (*Miftari v Home Secretary* [2005] EWCA Civ 481 [36] (Keene LJ)).

its narrower meaning, to refer to a mistaken conclusion as to the content of a legal standard that the public authority has to apply in a case.

The traditional doctrine was that a public authority acts unlawfully if it makes an error of law of a kind that leads it to act outside its jurisdiction. And that is what the House of Lords held in *Anisminic v Foreign Compensation Commission* [1969] 2 AC 147. Yet the Law Lords went on in later cases to invent a rule that it is unlawful for a public authority to make a decision based on *any* error of law. One remarkable feature of the novel doctrine is the way in which it arose from a myth about *Anisminic*.

9.1.2 *Anisminic*: the myth

The myth has taken on the aura of accepted doctrine in English administrative law. Lord Diplock said in *Racal* [1981] AC 374 (HL) that *Anisminic* was 'a legal landmark' that made the following 'break-through' in judicial control of administrative tribunals and authorities:

> '... the old distinction between errors of law that went to jurisdiction and errors of law that did not, was for practical purposes abolished. Any error of law that could be shown to have been made by them in the course of reaching their decision on matters of fact or of administrative policy would result in their having asked themselves the wrong question with the result that the decision they reached would be a nullity.' (383)

And in *O'Reilly v Mackman* [1983] 2 AC 237 (see p 350), Lord Diplock expanded on the 'break-through', in an account of the contributions that Lord Reid had made to judicial review:

> '*Anisminic*... liberated English public law from the fetters that the courts had theretofore imposed upon themselves so far as determinations of inferior courts and statutory tribunals were concerned, by drawing esoteric distinctions between errors of law committed by such tribunals that went to their jurisdiction, and errors of law committed by them within their jurisdiction. The break-through that the *Anisminic* case made was the recognition by the majority of this House that if a tribunal whose jurisdiction was limited by statute or subordinate legislation mistook the law applicable to the facts as it had found them, it must have asked itself the wrong question, i.e., one into which it was not empowered to inquire and so had no jurisdiction to determine.' (278)

In *Page*, Lord Browne-Wilkinson endorsed Lord Diplock's view as to the effect of *Anisminic* (702), and immediately added, 'Therefore, ... in general any error of law made by an administrative tribunal or inferior court in reaching its decision can be quashed for error of law'. Lord Browne-Wilkinson offered no authority for the rule, except Lord Diplock's account of *Anisminic*. And he offered no rationale for the rule;

in fact it seems to have appealed to him as providing *its own* rationale: an error of law is to be quashed *for error of law*. But all the Law Lords agreed with that view, and the consensus was repeated in *Boddington v British Transport Police* [1999] 2 AC 143 (HL).

9.1.3 Anisminic: the decision

What actually happened in the *Anisminic* case? Counsel for Anisminic did indeed ask the House of Lords to abolish the distinction between errors of law made within jurisdiction, and errors of law that deprive a decision maker of jurisdiction. But although the five Law Lords were deeply divided, *each* of them refused to do that—including the three in the majority:

> **Lord Wilberforce** approved a remark of Lord Denning that 'A tribunal may often decide a point of law wrongly whilst keeping well within its jurisdiction' (R v Northumberland Compensation Appeal Tribunal, ex p Shaw [1952] 1 KB 338, 346). He held that 'the commission has (admittedly) been given power, indeed required, to decide some questions of law', but that it did not have 'power to decide those questions which relate to the delimitation of its powers' (209).

> **Lord Reid** had said in R v Governor of Brixton Prison, ex p Armah [1968] AC 192, 234 that if 'a magistrate or any other tribunal' acts within jurisdiction, 'Neither an error in fact nor an error in law will destroy his jurisdiction.' In *Anisminic* he did not go back on that view; he added that a decision might still be a nullity if the tribunal 'decided some question which was not remitted to it' (171). And he said that a court can quash the decision of a tribunal 'not because the tribunal has made an error of law, but because as a result of making an error of law they have dealt with and based their decision on a matter with which, on a true construction of their powers, they had no right to deal' (174).

> **Lord Pearce** implied that there is a difference between 'excess of jurisdiction' and 'error of law', and held that the decision maker will 'step outside its jurisdiction' only if it asks itself the wrong question (195).

But those three judges *did* decide that the particular error of law that they found in the decision made the public authority's decision a nullity. Why did they hold that it was a nullity, rather than merely holding that the Commission had made an error of law that was within its jurisdiction? The key to all the confusion over *Anisminic* is the 'ouster clause'—a provision in the Act that set up the Foreign Compensation Commission:

> 'The determination by the Commission of any application made to them under this Act shall not be called in question in any court of law.'[2]

---

[2]   Foreign Compensation Act 1950 s 4(4).

Anisminic made an application to the Commission for compensation for the loss of a manganese mine, worth £4 million, that the Egyptian Government had confiscated in the 1956 Suez crisis. Anisminic was able to put enough commercial pressure on the Egyptian Government to induce it to 'buy' the mine the Egyptians had seized, for £500,000. Then, a reconciliation between Britain and Egypt led to a grant of £27.5 million from Egypt to compensate property owners.

The regulations on eligibility for compensation stated that the applicant had to be the owner of the property or the 'successor in title' of the owner, and that 'any person who became successor in title' of the applicant had to be British.[3] The Commission considered Anisminic's application, and decided that the Egyptian Government was Anisminic's successor in title. And since the Egyptian Government was not British, Anisminic was ineligible under the compensation scheme.

Anisminic claimed that the Commission had misinterpreted the obscure, badly drafted clause concerning the 'successor in title' of the applicant. But this is where the ouster clause kicks in: if the determination of the Commission could not be called in question in any court of law, how could Anisminic challenge the Commission's interpretation? The answer is that it could only do so if the 'determination' was not a determination at all. So its lawyers claimed that what the Commission had done was no determination: it was a 'nullity'.[4] They did not ask the court to question a determination, but to declare that there *was no* determination.

The majority in the House of Lords accepted this argument. Yet that meant denying the undeniable: that the Commission had determined the company's application. As Lord Morris put it, 'That which, they [the majority] say, should be disregarded as being null and void, is a determination explained in a carefully reasoned document nearly ten pages in length which is signed by the chairman of the commission. There is no question here of a sham or spurious or merely purported determination' (181). It may seem absurd that the majority could say that the Commission's determination was not a determination. In fact, although it was wrong, it was not absurd. The majority's decision takes a sound basic principle, and overextends it.

9.1.4 Anisminic: the kernel of good sense

Even if Parliament forbids the courts to interfere with a determination, the courts still have to decide whether a determination is genuine. After all, a legal rule that you must accept a £20 note as legal tender does not require you to accept a counterfeit £20 note. It was already 'well established' in the 19th century that the ouster clauses of the day—statutory provisions prohibiting *certiorari* (see p 374)—simply did not apply when a claimant challenged a decision on the ground that it was made without jurisdiction (Ex p Bradlaugh (1878) 3 QBD 509). As Lord Reid said, the word 'determination' in the statute does not include 'everything which purports to be a

---

3   See Anisminic (172).

4   On the role of nullity in judicial review, see section 10.4.7.

determination but which is in fact no determination at all' (170). Lord Reid gives the example of a forged 'determination'.

The kernel of good sense in the reasoning of the majority in *Anisminic* includes both this obvious point that a forged 'determination' is *not* a determination, *and* the sound insight that this reasoning can be taken further: there may be 'determinations' made by genuine public authorities that are not genuine determinations. But how far can the point be taken? What is the difference between a *bad* determination, and something that is *not* a determination? Lord Reid's answer is given in a list of things a tribunal might do or fail to do that are 'of such a nature that its decision is a nullity' (171).

The List of things that make an administrative decision a nullity: Lord Reid's version

1. 'It may have given its decision in bad faith.'
2. 'It may have made a decision which it had no power to make.'
3. 'It may have failed...to comply with the requirements of natural justice.'
4. 'It may in perfect good faith have misconstrued the provisions giving it power to act so that it failed to deal with the question remitted to it and decided some question which was not remitted to it.'
5. 'It may have refused to take into account something which it was required to take into account.
6. 'Or it may have based its decision on some matter which, under the provisions setting it up, it had no right to take into account' (171).[5]

The first two grounds are straightforward: If the Commission had acted in bad faith by, e.g., taking a bribe from Anisminic's enemies, it would make sense for a court to conclude that it had not made a real determination of Anisminic's application at all. And if the Commission issued a 'determination' in which it claimed to fine Anisminic for misconduct, the court would have jurisdiction to declare that the 'determination' has no effect; the Commission had no power to fine applicants, and Parliament only enacted that no determination *of an application for compensation* is to be questioned in a court. So bad faith and lack of the necessary power would be good grounds for holding that a 'determination' is not really a determination; they illustrate the kernel of good sense in the majority's reasoning.

What about failure to proceed in accordance with natural justice? Five years earlier, in *Ridge v Baldwin* [1964] AC 40, Lord Reid and the majority of the House of Lords had held that *any* procedural unfairness in an administrative decision is ground for holding that it was made without jurisdiction, so that it is a nullity. This radical

---

5   Compare this later remark by Lord Reid about what counts as a genuine use of a *discretion*, in *Dorset Yacht v Home Office* [1970] AC 1004, 1031: 'Then there may, and almost certainly will, be errors of judgment in exercising such a discretion and Parliament cannot have intended that members of the public should be entitled to sue in respect of such errors. But there must come a stage when the discretion is exercised so carelessly or unreasonably that there has been no real exercise of the discretion which Parliament has conferred. The person purporting to exercise his discretion has acted in abuse or excess of his power.'

approach to due process amounts to saying that a decision maker is not deciding at all, if it decides without due process. And perhaps that radical approach is justified by the courts' capacity to apply it with no breach of comity (as long as the courts remember their discretion over judicial review remedies; see p 381).

Now, what about the fourth, fifth, and sixth items on Lord Reid's list: misconstruction of 'the provisions giving it power', and not taking into account things the Commission was required to take into account (or taking into account things it had no right to take into account)? These grounds of nullity led to Lord Diplock's misinterpretation of the case. They are ambiguous, because they may be taken to mean either:

(1) that *some* misconstructions, or irrelevant considerations, or mistakes as to the basis of the decision can make a 'determination' null and void, or

(2) that a determination is null and void if it involves *any* misconstruction, or irrelevant consideration, or mistake as to the basis of its decision.

Lord Diplock assumes that Lord Reid took the second view. That is a misinterpretation of his speech, because Lord Reid relied on the distinction between mistakes of law that *are* and mistakes of law that *are not* 'of such a nature that its decision is a nullity' (171).[6]

So Lord Reid's judgment does not support Lord Diplock's rule. But the drawbacks in Lord Reid's explanation of his decision are both general (he did not explain how to distinguish between errors of law that do and do not make a decision a nullity), and particular (he gave no justification for the conclusion that the Commission had not determined Anisminic's application for compensation). Lord Morris's vehement dissent argued that Anisminic had to satisfy the Commissioners that it met the eligibility criteria, and that in deciding the meaning of the criteria, the Commissioners 'were at the very heart of their duty, their task and their jurisdiction. It cannot be that their necessary duty of deciding as to the meaning would be or could be followed by the result that if they took one view they would be within jurisdiction and if they took another view that they would be without' (189). The majority did not explain what it was about the commissioners' view that took them outside their jurisdiction; that is what led to Lord Diplock's misinterpretation of the case.

9.1.5 Lord Diplock's rule

It seems that the current, orthodox doctrine of judicial review for error of law is founded on *obiter dicta* by Lord Diplock,[7] which misinterpreted the judgment in a single case (*Anisminic*), which was wrongly decided by a badly divided House of Lords.

---

6   For this reason, it was a mistake for Lord Irvine to say in *Boddington v British Transport Police* [1999] 2 AC 143 (HL) that 'The *Anisminic* decision established, contrary to previous thinking that there might be error of law within jurisdiction, that there was a single category of errors of law, all of which rendered a decision ultra vires' (158).

7   In fact, all the House of Lords' assertions of the rule have been *obiter*, although there is no reason to doubt the authority of the consensus in favour of it. Lord Diplock's statements of his rule

Is it possible to say anything better than that for Lord Diplock's interpretation of *Anisminic*? How about this: the three Law Lords in the majority may have attempted to retain the distinction between errors of law that do and do not make the decision a nullity. But the distinction is so unstable that their decision must be construed as having the *effect* of abolishing it. Any error of law amounts to asking the wrong question. Any misinterpretation of the eligibility criteria would mean that the Commission *wrongly* asked itself the question, 'does Anisminic's application for compensation fit the criteria interpreted *in this way*?' Consider an example that Lord Reid gave, of an error that he thought would be *within* the Commission's jurisdiction:

> If the commission were entitled to enter on the inquiry whether the applicants had a successor in title, then their decision as to whether [the Egyptian government agency that bought the mine] was their successor in title would I think be unassailable whether it was right or wrong: it would be a decision on a matter remitted to them for their decision. The question I have to consider is not whether they made a wrong decision but whether they inquired into and decided a matter which they had no right to consider. (174)

That hypothetical erroneous decision could be stated like this: 'the Commission wrongly decided that a body is a successor in title *if it is a body of type X*'. And rather than being the wrong answer to the right question, that can be restated as an answer to the wrong question: 'was this a body of type X?' If it is a mistake to think that a body is a successor in title if it is of type X, then the question whether it is of type X is the wrong question. So any decision based on an error of law was reached by asking the wrong question, and on the authority of *Anisminic*, it is a nullity.

This construction of the decision in *Anisminic* will not wash, partly because only Lord Pearce expressed the majority conclusion by saying that a decision maker steps outside its jurisdiction if it asks itself the wrong question (195). Lord Wilberforce carefully rejected the idea:

> A tribunal may quite properly validly enter upon its task and in the course of carrying it out may make a decision which is invalid—not merely erroneous. This may be described as 'asking the wrong question' or 'applying the wrong test'—expressions not wholly satisfactory since they do not, in themselves, distinguish between doing something which is not in the tribunal's area and doing something wrong within that area—a crucial distinction which the court has to make. (210)

The problem with Lord Wilberforce's speech is that it faces the same general objection and particular objection as Lord Reid's speech: he did not explain how the

----

were *obiter* in *Racal* (because the rule does not apply to decisions of the High Court, like that in *Racal*) and in *O'Reilly* (in which he was only pointing out just how powerful judicial review is–see section 10.2). The Law Lords' endorsement of the rule was *obiter* in *Page* (because the rule does not apply to university visitors), and in *Boddington* (there was no error of law in that case).

court was to make the crucial distinction, and he did not justify his view that the Commission's decision in the case was 'invalid—not merely erroneous'.

9.1.6 Lord Diplock's presumption: law is for the judges

You may say that it is not particularly important that Lord Diplock's rule is based on a misinterpretation of *Anisminic*. If the rule is sound, it does not matter that the House of Lords invented it in mistaken *obiter dicta* in *O'Reilly* and *Page*, rather than in *Anisminic*.

And the rule may seem to be sound, because you may think that no determination based on a misconstruction of the law is a genuine determination *of the issues that Parliament established the Commission to determine*. Parliament must have established the Commission to allocate compensation on the basis of the *correct* interpretation of the criteria, and not on a misinterpretation. And then, if the Commission interprets the criteria incorrectly, it is not doing what Parliament created it to do.

This seductive line of reasoning completely misses a basic point: the mere fact that a public authority must do the right thing does not mean that a court has jurisdiction to decide what is right. Administrative authorities should certainly act on the correct view of the law. That does not actually require that courts should quash their decisions for error of law. All public authorities ought to make the best possible decisions (and Parliament can be presumed to intend that they should do so). But that does not mean that the judges have jurisdiction to hold that a decision was *ultra vires* on the ground that it was not the best decision that could have been made.

But of course, the discretionary power *to identify the law* seems to be the special preserve of the judges. So Lord Diplock held that *Anisminic* 'proceeds on the presumption that…Parliament intends to confine [an administrative agency's] power to answering the question as it has been so defined: and if there has been any doubt as to what that question is, this is a matter for courts of law to resolve in fulfilment of their constitutional role as interpreters of the written law and expounders of the common law and rules of equity' (383). Of course Parliament requires public authorities to answer the question that Parliament has set; but why presume that it is for courts to resolve any doubt as to what that question is? The presumption is new in English law—it only dates to the work of Lord Denning and Lord Diplock.[8] The novel presumption was foreign to Lord Mansfield.[9] It is not found in *Anisminic*, in which Lord Wilberforce said, 'I think that we have reached a stage in our administrative law when we can view this question quite objectively, without any necessary predisposition…that questions of law, or questions of construction, are necessarily for the courts' (209). Since *Page*, the judges have adopted that very predisposition.

---

[8] Lord Browne-Wilkinson endorsed it in *Page*, saying that there was 'a presumption that the statute conferring the power did not intend the administrative body to be the final arbiter of questions of law' Lord Browne-Wilkinson (703).

[9] See the quotation from *Moses v Macferlan* (1760) 2 Burr 1005, at the beginning of this chapter.

A presumption is a rule that an issue (such as whether Parliament intends an administrative tribunal to be the final arbiter of questions of law) is to be decided in a certain way, unless there is overriding reason to decide in a different way. One objection to the supposed presumption is that, applied to *Anisminic*, it would make nonsense out of Parliament's adoption of the ouster clause. The majority in *Anisminic* took the statutory provision,

> 'The determination by the Commission of any application...shall not be called in question in any court of law.'

and gave it the ambiguous effect that it would have if it said:

> 'The determination by the Commission of any application...shall not be called in question in any court of law, but a purported determination shall have no effect if the Commission arrives at it by doing something which was not in the tribunal's area.'

Lord Diplock's rule gives the statutory provision the *self-contradictory* effect that it would have if it said:

> 'The determination by the Commission of any application...shall not be called in question in any court of law, but the High Court may quash the determination by the Commission of any application for error of law.'

The majority disregarded the statute in *Anisminic*, because the Commission really had determined the company's application. Lord Diplock's rule commits the courts to disregard Parliament, whenever Parliament provides that an administrative decision is not to be questioned in a court.

Now let's forget the ouster clause that generated the confusion in *Anisminic*, and ask whether either the *Anisminic* approach, or Lord Diplock's rule, is generally the right approach to judicial review of the determinations of law made by another public authority (if there is no ouster of the court's jurisdiction).

There is still an objection to the presumption that Parliament intended all questions of law to be decided by courts. The crucial point is that the current rule—Lord Diplock's rule—is a rule against judicial deference to the public authority whose decision is under review. Lord Reid's approach did leave room (without explaining it) for deference. Even where there is no ouster clause, the judges should be prepared to defer to an interpretation of an administrative scheme by the public authority that is responsible for giving effect to the scheme. That deference ought to vary with the context. It is compatible with the rule of law, because the rule of law does not require that judges decide all questions of legal rights.

Is Lord Diplock's rule justified by constitutional principle?

Constitutional principles justify review for lack of due process, and for abuse of power, and for use of power in a way that is unreasonable in a justiciable respect, and for purported decisions made with no jurisdiction. Do those principles also justify review for error of law?

The rule of law, of course, requires all public authorities to apply the law faithfully, according to its terms. That may seem to justify Lord Diplock's rule. But that seemingly attractive view would be a mistake. It really is a failure in the rule of law when any public authority acts on a misguided view of the law. But why expect that the judge's view of the law will be better than the administrative authority's view? That might be the case **if the judges are more expert** at understanding and developing the standards of the law than the public authority in question. And it would be good for the judges to impose their view if that would achieve **consistency** among a variety of uncoordinated decision makers.[10] Note that these two reasons—superior expertise and coordination—lie behind the availability of appeals in the tribunals system and in the ordinary law courts: the Upper Tribunal, the Court of Appeal, and the House of Lords bring coordination to decisions, and the appellate tribunals and courts are designed to give responsibility for the development of the law to senior judges who are appointed on grounds of their expertise.

Those potential benefits do not justify Lord Diplock's rule. Judges are not *generally* more expert at the job of interpreting an administrative scheme than the very diverse administrative authorities are themselves. And whether the judges can bring consistency to administrative practice depends on whether there are a number of uncoordinated decision makers in the particular context.

But here is another potential justification for judicial review for error of law, which is quite distinct from the benefits that justify appeals within the courts: if the public authority has incentives to develop and elaborate its standards in the wrong way, then the judges' **independence** means that they can do a better job of it. Even the value of this important feature of judicial review depends on the context. The independence of administrative decision makers varies widely. And the *need* for independence varies widely too (see p 171).

The general rule of review for error of law is not justified by constitutional principle, because the benefits of imposing the judges' interpretation of the law do not apply generally; they depend on the type of decision and the context in which it is made.

---

[10]   Lord Denning mentioned this justification for judicial review for error of law in *Pearlman v Keepers and Governors of Harrow School* [1979] QB 56.

9.1.7 *Page* and the residual standard of review

It is more than ten years since a reported decision last departed from Lord Diplock's view of the law. In R v *Independent Television Commission, ex p TSW Broadcasting* [1996] EMLR 291 (HL), Lord Templeman said,

> ‘ Even if the ITC make mistakes of fact or mistakes of law, there is no appeal from their decision. The courts have invented the remedies of judicial review not to provide an appeal machinery but to ensure that the decision maker does not exceed or abuse his powers. ’ (304)

Counsel for the defendant university in *Page* relied on that case to show that not all errors of law give a ground for judicial review. But Lord Browne-Wilkinson brushed the precedent aside, claiming that Lord Templeman had meant that an error of law is only a ground of judicial review if it 'affected the decision itself' ([1993] AC 682 (701)). Nothing in the *TSW* case supports that view. Lord Browne-Wilkinson pointed out that Lord Templeman relied on Lord Greene's statement in *Wednesbury*, that 'a person entrusted with a discretion must, so to speak, direct himself properly in law' (*Associated Provincial Picture Houses v Wednesbury Corporation* [1948] 1 KB 223, 229). But Lord Greene's statement is consistent with the principle that interpreting the law (directing oneself in law) is a discretionary power, for all discretionary powers must be *exercised properly*. Ensuring that such powers are exercised properly does not mean dictating the outcome of their exercise. The court's job is to hold that discretionary powers have not been exercised properly when they have been exercised without due process (Chapter 4), or when the substance or outcome of their exercise is manifestly unreasonable (Chapter 7). Lord Browne-Wilkinson assumed without argument that proper exercise of a *power to identify the law* means exercising the power in the way that the judges think best. That is Lord Diplock's presumption, and it reflects the 'predisposition' that Lord Wilberforce had rejected: the predisposition to assume that law is for the judges.

That assumption is the only rationale on offer (in *Racal* or *O'Reilly* or *Page*) for Lord Diplock's rule. No constitutional principle supports the rule. The only thing that could support it would be an unsound principle that none of the judges has ever stated: that whenever a public authority is given responsibility for interpreting and elaborating a particular scheme of rules, the judges are better at that job than the people to whom it was assigned. Sometimes, that will actually be the case! But the judges cannot legitimately base a general standard of review of all other public authorities on the ground that they are better than other public authorities at understanding and elaborating administrative schemes.

Comity and errors of law

A rule that judges are to quash decisions based on **unreasonable** interpretations of the law will improve decision making, even if judges are no better than administrative authorities at deciding what meaning to give to the scheme that the administrative authority is responsible for. Judicial review for **error** of law will improve decision making *only if judges are better at understanding the standards that another public authority applies, than that public authority is.*

9.1.8 Is there any such thing as jurisdiction?

Is it even *possible* for someone other than a judge to have legal power to decide what the law is? Yes. English law still recognizes jurisdictions within which the courts will not interfere on the ground of an error in interpreting the law.

The Arbitration Act 1996 provides a scheme of arbitration of commercial disputes; the scheme allows the parties to agree that there will be no appeal on a question of law, and then an appeal can only be brought on the ground that the tribunal exceeded its powers. And an arbitrator does *not* exceed his or her powers by making an error of law. In *Lesotho Development v Impregilo SpA* [2005] UKHL 43, Lord Steyn held:

> ‘The reasoning of the lower courts, categorising an error of law as an excess of jurisdiction, has overtones of the doctrine in *Anisminic*…which is so well known to the public law field. It is, however, important to emphasise again that the powers of the court in public law and arbitration law are quite different.’ [25]

So an error of law does not *necessarily* take a decision maker outside a limited jurisdiction. And indeed, the courts used to treat public authorities like arbitrators, as we can see from *Board of Education v Rice* [1911] AC 179 (HL):

> ‘The Board is in the nature of the arbitral tribunal, and a Court of law has no jurisdiction to hear appeals from the determination either upon law or upon fact. But if the Court is satisfied either that the Board have not acted judicially…, or have not determined the question which they are required by the Act to determine, then there is a remedy by mandamus and certiorari.’ (Lord Loreburn LC, 182)

Lord Diplock's rule does not follow necessarily from the limited powers of public authorities, or it would have to apply to arbitrators, who have a limited power. It depends, as Lord Steyn said, on 'the powers of the court'. The rule is a novel technique of the English judges for controlling administration, by imposing their own understanding of the rules that other public authorities are responsible for applying. It is not required by the logic of the law, but only by the judges' novel view that it is their task alone—and not the task of other public officials—to decide what the law is in the field of public administration.

Another example of the possibility of error of law within jurisdiction is found, notably, in *Page* itself. In that case, the House of Lords would not interfere with a university visitor on the ground of error of law. While Lord Browne-Wilkinson's speech offers no reason in favour of the general rule that administrative authorities may be reviewed for error of law, we can learn something from the reasons he offers for not applying the doctrine to university visitors:

- a centuries-old common law doctrine that decisions of university visitors on fact and law were not to be reviewed,[11] and

- the fact that the visitors had a special, domestic jurisdiction: 'the visitor is applying not the general law of the land but a peculiar, domestic law of which he is the sole arbiter and of which the courts have no cognisance' (702).

Why not say that the Foreign Compensation Commission was applying not the general law of the land, but a peculiar law of which (given Parliament's decision that its determinations were not to be questioned in court) it was sole arbiter? The answer given in *Page* is only that the visitor's role is *domestic*—that is, it operates within a society (a university) that has its own rules. But that does not give any reason in itself for treating the visitor as special, once it is admitted (as Lord Browne-Wilkinson admits) that the university is not a private club, but a public authority that can be controlled in judicial review.

There is good reason for a court to defer to a university visitor in interpreting the university's rules, but the reason is not limited to domestic rules of a university. The rules of the university have a special context with which the visitor is familiar: that context gives a reason for anyone reviewing a decision from outside to defer to the visitor's expertise. The rules of foreign compensation, too, had a special context, and the Commission was familiar with it: this context gives a reason for anyone reviewing the Commission's work from outside to defer to the Commission's expertise. Consider that in *Anisminic*, Lord Pearce said that it is 'a matter of opinion' whether it would be unfair to treat someone who had already got partial compensation from the Egyptian Government in the same way as someone who had got none (206). That point, absolutely crucial to the interpretation of the confusing eligibility criteria in the case, is one on which the court ought to have deferred to the much better-informed opinion of the Commission, unless from the court's detached perspective, it was possible to identify the Commission's approach as unreasonable or abusive.

The rule of law is against *arbitrary* decision making. The rule of law is perfectly compatible with the deference that the House of Lords showed to university visitors in *Page*, and it would be compatible with deference to other public authorities on questions of interpretation of legal standards.

You may think, as many judges since Lord Denning have thought, that review for error of law is demanded by the rule of law, because of the following argument:

1. If a public authority does not correctly interpret the statutory provisions it has to apply correctly, then it is not acting in accordance with the law.

2. And although it is not the judges' job to do the public authority's job for it, it **is** the judges' job to intervene when a public authority acts unlawfully.

....

[11]   'If the judgment of the visitor be ever so erroneous, we cannot interfere in order to correct it.' R v Bishop of Ely (1794) 5 Durn & E 475, 477 (Lord Kenyon CJ).

3. Therefore, the judges **must** review administrative decisions for error of law, or they will not be doing their job of imposing the rule of law.

What's wrong with this argument? It falls for the idea that law is for judges. Step 1 in the argument is correct, but Step 2 is a mistake. Imposing the rule of law does not mean interfering every time a public authority acts contrary to law, or we would need a doctrine of error of fact, too (because a public authority does not act in accordance with the law when it misapplies the law to the facts). The mistake in Step 2 is to miss the point that a public authority may act lawfully, even when it does not apply the law correctly. The fact that the law requires every public authority to act in accordance with the law does not tell us who is to decide what is in accordance with the law. And while judges ought to exercise control over all such decisions, our constitution does not require that judges must make them.

Reasons for deference

There are two good reasons for the judges not to replace a university visitor's under-standing of the university's rules with their own understanding. The **first** is that the visitor can be expected to have a sensitivity to and familiarity with the needs of the university community and its members, which give the court reason to defer to his or her judgment on how to interpret and elaborate its rules. Lord Browne-Wilkinson accepted this point in the case of university visitors, adopting Lord Kenyon's view, expressed 200 years earlier, that 'any interference by us to control the judgment of the visitor, would be attended with the most mischievous consequences, since we must then decide on the statutes of the college, of which we are ignorant, and the construction of which has been confided to another forum' (R v Bishop of Ely (1794) 5 Durn & E 475, 477).

The judges may be as ignorant of the rules of a foreign compensation scheme as they are of the statutes of a university. In *both* cases, of course, they can learn (and hear argument as to) the rules. But as Lord Kenyon put it, there may still be reason for the judges to defer to another forum, to which the construction of the rules 'has been confided'. The point applies to university visitors and, for the same reasons, it applies to any administrative decision maker whose familiarity with a scheme of regulation (and its context) is helpful in deciding how to interpret and how to elaborate the rules of the scheme.

The **second** reason for deference to university visitors is a reason of process, which Lord Browne-Wilkinson pointed out in *Page*:

> 'The advantage of having an informal system which produces a speedy, cheap and final answer to internal disputes has been repeatedly emphasized in the authorities... If it were to be held that judicial review for error of law lay against the visitor I fear that, as in the present case, finality would be lost.... Although the visitor's position is anomalous, it provides a valuable machinery for resolving internal disputes which should not be lost.' (704)

Even though it is hard to generalize about administrative justice systems, these points about the process value of finality in decision making apply to many administrative decision-making institutions: they generally provide 'a valuable machinery', from which review for error of law may detract. The irony of *Page* is that Lord Browne-Wilkinson's good reasons for deference to university visitors count *against* Lord Diplock's rule.

> ### Summary of potential reasons for deference to administrative authorities on questions of law:
>
> (1) **the potentially better capacity of the administrative authority to form a good judgment as to how to interpret and elaborate the rules** (because of their experience in dealing with the scheme in question)
> (2) **process:** if the court starts all over again in interpreting the scheme in question in judicial review, it may detract from the work of a valuable machinery for resolving disputes.

These considerations can justify a form of judicial review that gives an authority some leeway in interpreting its scheme. Their importance varies with the context, and neither consideration would justify judicial refusal to control the way in which an administrative authority interprets its scheme. In a brief remark at the end of his reasons, Lord Browne-Wilkinson asserted a jurisdiction to review *visitors'* decisions:

> Judicial review does lie to the visitor in cases where he has acted outside his jurisdiction (in the narrow sense)[12] or abused his powers or acted in breach of the rules of natural justice. (704)

Just like that. No authority or rationale is offered for this assertion of judicial power over visitors.[13] Yet it does have a sound justification, in the **core rationale** for judicial review (see p 65): the Administrative Court's independence, its openness, its adversarial process and its effective power give it the opportunity to prevent abuses of power and to impose good process on other university visitors, in a way that will show no disrespect for the exercise of their jurisdiction. So Lord Browne-Wilkinson's residual standard of review for university visitors—as casually as he stated it—provides a sound template for judicial review in general. It is a form of judicial review that might have emerged from a good interpretation of the ambiguous decision in

---

[12] The phrase is borrowed from Lord Reid's speech in *Anisminic*; Lord Reid suggested that in a wide sense, a tribunal 'acts without jurisdiction' when its decision is a nullity. But he said that 'it is better not to use the term except in the narrow and original sense of the tribunal being entitled to enter on the inquiry in question' (171).

[13] But note that in *Thomas v University of Bradford* [1987] AC 795 Lord Griffiths had said: 'Although doubts have been expressed in the past as to the availability of certiorari, I have myself no doubt that in the light of the modern development of administrative law, the High Court would have power, upon an application for judicial review, to quash a decision of the visitor which amounted to an abuse of his powers' (825).

Anisminic. Judges will be preventing arbitrary use of power, without a breach of the comity they owe to a university visitor, if they quash a decision that was based on an interpretation of the university's rules that they can see to be unreasonable from their detached perspective.

● *Pop Quiz* ●

What do *you* think about the three questions addressed above:

1. Was *Anisminic* rightly decided?
2. Does *Anisminic* support Lord Browne-Wilkinson's conclusion in *Page*, that '. . . in general any error of law made by an administrative tribunal or inferior court in reaching its decision can be quashed for error of law.'?
3. Does *Page* set the right standard for judicial review?

9.1.9 Deference, North American style

Canada

Just before Lord Diplock took the law in a new direction, the Supreme Court of Canada had taken a decisive turn in the other direction, by clarifying the distinction (left obscure in *Anisminic*) between errors of law that do and do not make a decision a nullity. In *Canadian Union of Public Employees v New Brunswick Liquor Corporation* [1979] 2 SCR 227 ('CUPE'), the Liquor Corporation had been using managers to run its shops during a strike. The provincial Labour Relations Board—whose decisions were protected by an ouster clause like that in *Anisminic*—held that the policy was an unlawful interference with the strike. In judicial review, the Supreme Court of Canada rejected the idea that the Board's decision should be quashed if it was based on a misinterpretation of the law. Dickson J's reasons adopted the kernel of good sense in *Anisminic*: that if the Board misinterpreted the Act in such a way 'as to embark on an inquiry or answer a question not remitted to it', then it would have acted without jurisdiction. But he resolved the ambiguity in *Anisminic*, by holding that the decision maker would only be embarking on an inquiry not remitted to it, if its interpretation was 'so patently unreasonable that its construction cannot be rationally supported by the relevant legislation and demands intervention by the courts upon review' (237).

That reasoning neatly debunked the idea that *Anisminic* had the effect of abolishing the distinction between errors of law that do and do not make a decision a nullity. On the CUPE approach, the distinction is vague (just as any standard of review for reasonableness is vague), but perfectly coherent. If an interpretation is *patently* unreasonable, or 'cannot be rationally supported', then it makes sense to say that the decision maker has not made a decision within its jurisdiction at all. Its so-called 'determination' is not a determination. That is not because its interpretation was wrong, but because it was so clearly unreasonable that acting on that so-called 'interpretation' does not count as exercising the jurisdiction at all.

After the CUPE decision in 1979, the Canadian Supreme Court developed Dickson J's approach into a 'pragmatic and functional approach' aimed directly at giving effect to 'the role of the superior Courts in maintaining the rule of law' (*Union des employés de service v Bibeault* [1988] 2 SCR 1048 [123], [127] (Beetz J)). The courts applied three standards for review of administrative interpretations of the law (correctness, reasonableness, and the 'patently unreasonable' standard), with the choice depending on four factors:

- whether there is an ouster clause or a statutory right of appeal;

- the relative expertise of the tribunal and of the reviewing court;

- the purposes of the legislation; and

- the nature of the question.[14]

That approach adopted Lord Wilberforce's view that questions of law are not necessarily for courts, but that the courts must impose the rule of law on the exercise of an administrative jurisdiction to apply the law. It allows judges to ask just the right questions as to their role in controlling other public authorities. As we will see, its flexibility came at a cost.

> ● *Pop Quiz* ●
> How would *Anisminic* have been decided if the House of Lords had adopted the CUPE standard, that an interpretation of the law by an administrative tribunal will only be set aside if it was patently unreasonable?

The United States: the 'principle of deference to administrative interpretations'

In the 1980s, the U.S. Supreme Court, too, established a 'principle of deference' to an administration's interpretation of a statute, in *Chevron v Natural Resources Defense Counsel*, 467 US 837 (1984). That decision has been cited thousands of times, and is still good law; it has been called a 'quasi-constitutional text'.[15] As in many landmark decisions, the court claimed to be giving effect to long-established doctrine. And indeed the U.S. Supreme Court had held in 1827 that, 'In the construction of a doubtful and ambiguous law, the cotemporaneous construction of those who were called upon to act under the law, and were appointed to carry its provisions into effect, is entitled to very great respect' (*Edwards' Lessee v Darby* 25 US 206 (1827), 210).

Under the *Chevron* doctrine, the court is to ask:

1. whether Congress has 'directly spoken to the precise question at issue'.

If so, then the court must override any contrary interpretation by an agency. But if not, then 'the court does not simply impose its own construction on the statute', as if it were the initial decision maker. Instead, the court is to ask:

---

[14]   See the cases cited in *Zenner v Prince Edward Island College of Optometrists* [2005] 3 SCR 645 [28].

[15]   Cass Sunstein, '*Chevron* Step Zero' (2006) 92 Virginia L Rev 187, 187; cf. Antonin Scalia, 'Judicial Deference to Administrative Interpretations of Law' (1989) Duke LJ 511.

2. 'whether the agency's answer is based on a permissible construction of the statute' (843–4).

And an administrative agency has discretion, in construing the statute, 'to fill any gap left, implicitly or explicitly, by Congress'.

If Congress expressly gives the agency power to *make* rules, then those rules are subject to judicial review on the same ground as in English law: the court will overturn them if they are 'arbitrary, capricious, or manifestly contrary to the statute' (*Chevron* 844). But U.S. law treats administrative agencies as having discretion not only when they make rules, but also when they interpret statutes, if there is an 'interpretive gap created through an ambiguity in the language of a statute's provisions' (*National Cable & Telecommunications Association v Brand X Internet Services* 125 S Ct 2688 (2005), 2712 (Breyer J). When Congress delegates power implicitly, by authorizing an agency to give effect to legislation that does not resolve the precise question at issue in a dispute, the court will only overturn a decision if it is based on an unreasonable construction of the statute. The agency is 'the authoritative interpreter (within the limits of reason) of such statutes' (*Brand X*, 2701 (Thomas J)).

The Americans treat this as a two-step test: first, the court decides if Congress has answered the precise question in dispute, and *then*, if not, the court decides if the administrative agency has reasonably exercised its implicit power to resolve the question. We can think of it all as a single vague, flexible test of reasonableness, since it would be unreasonable to adopt an interpretation that is inconsistent with what Congress has enacted, if Congress has 'directly spoken to the precise question at issue'. So in U.S. law, any reasonable administrative interpretation of a statute will stand. A court may not substitute its own interpretation of a statute for the agency's interpretation; it must give 'considerable weight' to the agency's interpretation and uphold any 'reasonable' construction (844–5).

Like the Canadian approach, the *Chevron* doctrine gives effect to the resultant discretion that a legislature gives to an administrative agency when its legislation gives vague criteria. It does not presume that questions of law are for judges. That is not because the Americans underestimate the importance of judges in establishing the law. The courts' responsibility for the law is built into their Constitution, and the Supreme Court established more than two hundred years ago that it is 'emphatically the province and duty of the judicial department to say what the law is' (*Marbury v Madison*, 5 US 137, 177 (1803)(Marshall J)). The *Chevron* doctrine preserves the court's responsibility for the rule of law; it recognizes that the Congress can lawfully give discretion to an administrative agency to interpret the scheme for which it is responsible. The American judges assert control over that discretion, without eliminating it.

Like the Canadian approach, though, it creates deep controversy in the courts. The best example is the U.S. Supreme Court's first case on global warming: the Environmental Protection Agency under George W. Bush's administration decided that it could not regulate carbon dioxide emissions, because carbon dioxide did not count as 'air pollution'. On the question of whether the agency's interpretation was reasonable, a narrow 5–4 liberal majority quashed the agency's decision, with an energetic conservative dissent insisting that the Court should have deferred to the agency's decision under the *Chevron* doctrine (*Massachusetts v Environmental Protection Agency* 127 S Ct 1438 (2007)).

In the next section, we will see that although the American and Canadian approaches are better justified in constitutional principle, the difference in the effect of the English doctrine is not as great as you might think—except for the deep controversies that the more principled North American doctrines generate over the standard of review.

9.1.10 The limits of the error of law doctrine

The rule that all administrative decisions are subject to judicial review for error of law is novel. Its foundation in authority is a myth, and it unjustifiably presumes that judges will be better than the statutory decision maker at interpreting the rules of a statutory scheme.

But the effects of this excessive legalism are not always damaging. The first point to notice is that although it would be better for judges to defer to some extent on the interpretation of statutes or of rules made by the executive, there is no need for the categorical deference on these issues that the judges ought to adopt on issues that are non-justiciable. The deference that judges ought to show on some questions of law is only the qualified deference that they ought to show when the initial decision maker can do the job of interpretation as well, or better. So the only problem with the overly intrusive doctrine of review for error of law is that the judges impose their own view when they ought to be assessing the reasonableness of the initial decision maker's view.

The second point to note is that it would be worse for judges to abdicate their responsibility to quash arbitrary administrative decisions, than it is for them to exaggerate their responsibility.

Moreover, the doctrine is actually **less novel** than it might seem, and it has a **restricted scope**. The **alternatives create problems**, and it still **leaves discretion** to administrative authorities in applying the law.

Why the doctrine is not *entirely* novel

Long before *Anisminic*, the High Court had assumed power to correct errors of law 'on the face of the record'. As Lord Morris said in his dissent in *Anisminic*, 'the control which is exercised by the High Court over inferior tribunals ... is of a supervisory but not of an appellate nature. It enables the High Court to correct errors of law if they are revealed on the face of the record' (182). Review for such errors dates back at least to the 1500s.[16] The Court of King's Bench turned it into a very effective appeal mechanism from magistrates' decisions by the early 19th century (in spite of the

----

[16]   See *R v Northumberland Compensation Appeal Tribunal ex p Shaw* [1952] 1 KB 338, 350 (Denning LJ).

theory that it was only supervisory, rather than appellate). But from the mid-19th century until the 1950s the records of courts and tribunals were kept so sparse that review for errors manifest on the record became less effective. The record of decisions of tribunals and courts of specific jurisdiction (such as magistrates' courts) would often reveal nothing at all about the legal basis of the decision. This form of review came into brief prominence after Lord Denning took a very broad approach to deciding what counts as 'the record' (in *Shaw*). But even with that broad approach, an ouster clause really did exclude review for error of law on the face of the record. That is why the doctrine of review for error of law on the face of the record was not used in *Anisminic*.

So the judges, under Lord Denning's lead, were already developing a restricted form of review for error of law before *Anisminic*. Its prominence was brief because Lord Diplock's rule made it unnecessary.

The restrictions on the scope of the doctrine

In addition to the fact that it does not apply to visitors in 'educational, ecclesiastical and eleemosynary bodies' (*Page*, 704), Lord Diplock's rule is restricted in the following ways:

- it does not necessarily apply to courts of specific jurisdiction;[17]

- the error must be 'relevant' (*Page*, 702), or operative—a court will not quash a decision just because the tribunal made an error of law, if the error did not affect the outcome;

- even a decision that was reached on the basis of an error of law will not be quashed, if the decision did no substantive injustice;

- the error must be on a question of law—not on a question of fact (see section 9.2), and not on a question of the application of the law to the facts (see section 9.3).

The problems with the alternatives

In Canada, the law grew extremely complex, and the distinctions among standards of review grew tenuous. Some judges complained that the difference between the 'reasonableness' requirement and review for 'patent unreasonableness' was obscure (*Voice Construction Ltd v Construction & General Workers' Union* 2004 SCC 23, [2004] 1 SCR 609 [40]–[41], Lebel J), and there was enormous flexibility—and therefore, room for controversy—in the application of the four factors used to decide which of the three

---

[17]   In *Page*, Lord Browne-Wilkinson likened the university visitor to an 'inferior court', and suggested that Lord Diplock's rule applies only to administrative authorities and tribunals that are *not* inferior courts (703). But elsewhere, Lord Browne-Wilkinson said, 'the general rule is that decisions affected by errors of law made by tribunals or inferior courts can be quashed' (702). So the scope of the power to review decisions of courts of specific jurisdiction for error of law is up in the air. For errors of law by tribunals, see p 450.

standards (correctness, reasonableness, or patent unreasonableness) to apply. The question of the standard of review that applies to a particular administrative interpretation was a matter of huge controversy, going up to the Supreme Court again and again,[18] before the judges even got to the point of applying the standard.

So in *Dunsmuir v New Brunswick* [2008] SCC 9, the Supreme Court rewrote the law, abolishing the distinction between unreasonableness and patent unreasonableness, and requiring courts to apply either a standard of correctness, or a standard of reasonableness (with the extent of the court's deference under the reasonableness test depending on the same range of factors on which the choice between unreasonableness and patent unreasonableness had depended). *Dunsmuir* simplifies the law, and will end appeals on the question of whether the court should have applied an unreasonableness standard or a patent unreasonableness standard. But the Canadian approach still calls on the judges to pay attention to all the relevant circumstances in deciding what sort of deference they owe to an administrative interpretation of a statute. And for that very reason, it still invites appellate litigation over the approach that the court should take to its own role in particular circumstances.

Similarly, in the U.S., the *Chevron* approach generates huge controversy at each of its two steps: disagreement as to whether Congress has directly spoken to the issue in dispute, and over whether an administrative agency has exercised its interpretative discretion reasonably. *Chevron* deference has to vary in accordance with the same considerations that the Canadians have tied to different 'standards of review', including the relative expertise of the agency and the court, and the nature of the question. On these questions the American judges are deeply divided. The U.S. Supreme Court has divided angrily along political lines—not only in *Massachusetts v Environmental Protection Agency* (section 9.1.9), but in *Rapanos v US* 126 S Ct 2208 (2006) (over whether it was plausible to conclude that drains that dry up for part of the year count as part of the 'waters of the United States'). In another decision ten days after *Rapanos*, Justice Scalia referred to the dissenting judges in *Rapanos* as having reached the 'wildly implausible conclusion that a storm drain is a tributary of the waters of the United States' (*Hamdan v Rumsfeld* 126 S Ct 2749 (2006), 2839).

The remarkable fact about the *Chevron* doctrine is that it leaves room for bitter disagreement among the judges of the United States Supreme Court—not merely over how to interpret a statute, but over whether an agency's interpretation is even plausible, and over the degree of deference the judges owe to a particular agency in a particular situation. At present, there are no such disagreements in England over the standard of review. The standard is correctness. So disagreements work themselves out simply as disagreements over how best to interpret the legislation.

Here is the moral of the story: suppose that the English judges moderated Lord Diplock's rule, and adopted a form of deference to administrative decisions interpreting the law. That would bring the legal doctrine of English judicial review closer

---

[18]   See the 33 Supreme Court decisions since *CUPE* that are cited in *Dunsmuir v New Brunswick* [2008] SCC 9.

to the constitutional justification that it needs. The core rationale for judicial review requires judges to prevent arbitrary decision making, but does not require judges to replace other public authorities' judgment on all questions of law. But that change could generate the massive controversies that have been the focus of debate in dozens of decisions in the highest courts in Canada and the United States.

If judges really did ask the pertinent question (the question of what sort of deference they ought to accord to an administrative interpretation of the law, given the nature of the agency and the nature of the question), judicial review would be a battleground for competing understandings of the relative expertise and responsibility of courts and other public authorities. It is a battleground, as we saw in Chapter 8, when the judges decide how to control discretionary powers. But on questions of the interpretation of statutes, English judicial review gains a certain eerie calm from the fact that the barristers do not argue and the judges do not reflect on the rationale for interfering with an administrative authority's interpretations of the law. You may conclude that it is better to have review for error of law (and to trust the judges to apply it with an unstated respect for the initial decision maker's interpretation) than to have a complex doctrine of deference, because we would gain too little and pay too much if the judges addressed the real issues at stake in justifying judicial review. Lord Diplock did not offer that rationale for his rule, but no other is available.

The remaining discretion

Lord Diplock's rule of review for error of law requires no deference by courts to other public authorities on questions of the law that they administer. So in English law, administrative authorities have no discretion to act on a view of the law that is incompatible with the view that the court comes to. But since the power the judges have taken on themselves is itself a discretionary power, there is actually nothing to *stop them* from deferring to the public authority to which the decision was entrusted. That is, they can benefit from the reasons of the initial decision maker in deciding what to make of the law.

What's more, judicial review for error of law does *not* mean that administrative authorities have no discretion in applying the law, because the judges' view of the law may leave a range of lawful decisions to the administrative authority. If there is more than one correct way to apply the law, the court will not interfere.

We will see in section 9.3 that this is an important form of administrative discretion. To understand it, we first need to understand the ways in which judges control fact finding.

9.2 Control of fact finding

The result can be as unjust when an administrative body gets the facts wrong, as when it gets the law wrong. Perhaps that explains the emergence of a new myth that is even more remarkable than the error of law doctrine: the myth that a mere error of fact is ground for judicial review.

A claimant in judicial review can ask the court to determine the law, and then to quash the decision if the judge's view of the law is incompatible with the view of the administrative authority. That turns judicial review into a form of appeal. If there were judicial review for error of fact, then a claimant could ask the court to determine the facts, and then to quash the decision if its view of the facts is incompatible with the view of the defendant public authority. That would not turn judicial review into an appeal; it would turn judicial review into a rehearing of the original decision.[19]

This had better not be the state of the law, because there are two reasons why courts should often defer to the initial decision maker's judgment as to the facts:

Process: in judicial review, the court has neither the opportunity nor the techniques to find the facts.

Comity: it would show a massive disrespect for the good functioning of other authorities, if the judges were to take over the job of identifying the facts for administrative decisions in general.

9.2.1 Fact-finding processes

The courts act through a process that is not tailored to the particular situation in which a public authority finds the facts; it is tailored to the task of controlling a wide variety of decision-making processes, to restrain arbitrary decision making.

The processes for fact finding in ombudsman's reports and planning inquiries and parole board hearings and social security appeal tribunals (etc., etc.) are extremely diverse. The processes used by those decision makers are more or less investigative, inquisitorial, adversarial, depending on their particular purposes. Unlike judicial processes, many of them are quite appropriately designed to take advantage of information-gathering techniques that involve no rules of evidence except the rules that are necessary for due process—that the decision maker should give parties an opportunity to respond to adverse information where fairness demands it.

Unless those processes are badly designed, they will be much better for their purposes than the court's attempt to identify the facts by reading the parties' affidavits in a claim for judicial review, and ordering cross-examination where it seems necessary. For the court's process is summary (section 10.3)—that is, there is no trial. In a claim for judicial review, the judges have all the resources they need to decide what the law is (that is, they hear argument on points of law from each party to a dispute). But to have unrestricted judicial review for error of fact, they would need to have real hearings on the facts in dispute in the claim for judicial review. And even then, there

---

[19]   Unlike error of law, error of fact is not a general ground of appeal within the court system. So, for example, in appeals in family law cases, an appeal court must defer to the trial judge's decisions as to the facts (*Piglowska v Piglowski* [1999] 1 WLR 1360 (HL), 1372). Appeal courts do not defer to the trial judge's view of the law.

is no general reason to think that they will identify the facts more accurately than the initial decision maker. For example, in order to review an ombudsman's judgments as to the facts on a standard of *correctness*, the judges would need to conduct an ombudsman's investigation.

Finally, the courts will be at a comparative disadvantage in many situations simply because the initial decision maker made its inquiry into the facts *earlier*.

9.2.2 Fact finding and comity

The reasons of process and comity are connected: because judges do not have the processes needed for finding the facts, an attempt to do so would damage some of the administrative schemes whose operation is challenged in judicial review. Moreover, aside from their more effective processes, the people who make administrative decisions may have expertise or experience in their field that enables them to understand the facts of a case better than judges can (see section 12.4.3 on expert membership in tribunals).

But comity can be a reason for deference even where it would be possible for judges to do a good job of finding the facts. For judicial review *controls* other decision-making processes, and does not *replace* them. Even if another decision maker made a mistake, a claimant does not automatically have a right to a judicial rehearing of the decision. Judicial interference needs a rationale in constitutional principle. The fact that administrative decision makers can get the facts wrong does not mean that the legal system should give you a right to another fact-finding inquiry by a different agency.

Remember the four basic reasons for deference (see p 221):

- **legal allocation of power;**
- **expertise;**
- **political responsibility; and**
- **processes.**

The first two and the fourth are reasons for deference to administrative authorities on questions of fact. The mere fact that a statute has entrusted the fact-finding power to the administrative authority means that the court should not decide the facts afresh, but only supervise the work of that authority. And if the authority has relevant expertise, or has fact-finding processes that are better for the purpose than adversarial presentation of evidence in a courtroom, then those are reasons for greater deference to the authority's conclusions.

So judicial control of fact finding is limited by a variable but important requirement of judicial deference. The traditional role of the judges has been to decide whether a decision maker has 'acted without any evidence or upon a view of the facts which could not reasonably be entertained' (*Edwards v Bairstow* [1956] AC 14, 29 (Viscount

Simonds)). That applies the restrained, *Wednesbury* approach to the control of fact finding. As Lord Brightman put it in R *v Hillingdon LBC, ex p Puhlhofer* [1986] AC 484 (HL):

> ❛Where the existence or non-existence of a fact is left to the judgment and discretion of a public body and that fact involves a broad spectrum ranging from the obvious to the debatable to the just conceivable, it is the duty of the court to leave the decision of that fact to the public body to whom Parliament has entrusted the decision-making power save in a case where it is obvious that the public body, consciously or unconsciously, are acting perversely.❜ (518)

This restrained form of control would only deserve a brief note, except for two huge problems: first, we need to decide what to make of some revolutionary yet popular judicial assertions of a general power to review administrative decisions for error of fact. And then, we need to work out what sort of defect in fact finding makes a decision 'perverse' in Lord Brightman's sense.

9.2.3 An error of fact revolution?

When the Criminal Injuries Compensation Board decided against a claim without having seen a crucial police doctor's report, the claimant argued that 'there is jurisdiction to quash the board's decision because that decision was reached on a material error of fact' (R *v Criminal Injuries Compensation Board, ex p A* [1999] 2 AC 330, 344). Lord Slynn agreed. Citing Wade and Forsyth's view that 'Mere factual mistake has become a ground of judicial review...' (344), he said, 'I would accept that there is jurisdiction to quash on that ground in this case, but I prefer to decide the matter on the alternative basis argued, namely that what happened in these proceedings was a breach of the rules of natural justice and constituted unfairness' (345).[20]

Lord Slynn's apparent revolution had been anticipated by Sedley J in the *Balchin* case (section 14.10). In reviewing a report by the Parliamentary Ombudsman, he said that 'If there is [a reviewable error], ... it does not have to be classified as one of law or of fact (the latter too being reviewable if crucial to the decision' (928).[21] The views of both Lord Slynn and Lord Justice Sedley can be traced back through their reasons to *Education Secretary v Tameside BC* [1977] AC 1014—a remarkably intrusive House of Lords' decision controlling the Education Secretary's statutory power to reverse unreasonable decisions of local education authorities. Lord Wilberforce said that, in controlling a

----

[20] Cf. R *v Transport Secretary, ex p Alconbury* [2001] UKHL 23 [53] (see section 3.5), in which Lord Slynn said that the court has 'jurisdiction to quash for a misunderstanding or ignorance of an established and relevant fact'. His remarks in both *A* and *Alconbury* were obiter.

[21] This remark, too, was obiter. And contrast Sedley J's remark, in R *v Education Secretary, ex p Skitt* [1995] ELR 388, that striking down a decision for error of fact would be a 'novelty in English law' (398).

minister's discretionary powers, the courts 'cannot substitute their opinion for that of the minister: they can interfere on such grounds as that the minister has acted right outside his powers or outside the purpose of the Act, or unfairly, or upon an incorrect basis of fact' (1047).

If this remark seems to give authority for a general power of judges to find the facts and reverse administrative decisions that were based on an error of fact, the impression is very misleading. Lord Wilberforce *starts* from the principle that the court cannot substitute its opinion for that of the minister. The court must have a power to control the minister's fact finding, if is to carry out its role of preventing arbitrary uses of administrative power. But that purpose does not justify replacing the minister's opinion on the facts with that of the courts. It only justifies interfering when, from its detached vantage point and with the limited techniques available in the judicial review process, the court can see that the minister got the facts plain wrong. We have to interpret Lord Wilberforce's statement that courts can interfere if a minister has acted 'upon an incorrect basis of fact' in light of this duty of judicial deference. Judges have no general power to substitute their judgment for the judgment of an administrative decision maker on questions of fact—not even on crucial questions of fact.

Consider again *Begum v Tower Hamlets LBC* [2003] UKHL 5 (see p 169), a case that shows the courts' limited capacity to control fact finding. The decision depended on the reviewing officer's assessment of Mrs Begum's credibility, because she claimed to have been robbed in the area. What is the appropriate form of judicial control of that assessment? The local authority's housing officer was in a much better position than judges to assess Mrs Begum's credibility, partly because her familiarity with the area gave her an understanding of what Mrs Begum was talking about. And the reviewing officer had the advantage of meeting Mrs Begum and asking her questions in a different situation from the artificial setting of a court hearing, and of doing so earlier than the court could. These advantages have an important result: a good, honest judge in judicial review would not be able to do as good a job of deciding whether Mrs Begum was credible as a good, honest housing officer who talked to her.

The House of Lords concluded that the authority had discretion in reaching its conclusions on those questions (and that the discretion was not a breach of Art 6 of the European Convention): 'the decision as to whether the accommodation was suitable for Runa Begum was a classic exercise of administrative discretion, even though it involved preliminary findings of fact' [56] (Lord Hoffmann). Lord Millett held that 'A decision may be quashed if it is based on a finding of fact...which is perverse or irrational; or there was no evidence to support it.... The court cannot substitute its own findings of fact for those of the decision-making authority if there was evidence to support them; and questions as to the weight to be given to a particular piece of evidence and the credibility of witnesses are for the decision-making authority and not the court' [99].

Note the benefits *and* drawbacks of deferential review of fact finding:

If the housing officer has made an error of fact that is not glaringly obvious, the judges will not be able to put it right without finding the facts themselves. The reasons why the standard should still be deferential are that:

- judicial review for error of fact would address that risk of bad decisions ineffectively, by giving the decision to a decision maker that is not generally as good at finding the facts as the initial decision maker,
- the deferential standard **will** provide a form of protection against bad decision making (and no standard of review would provide perfect protection), and
- the fact that the standard will not guard against imperfect fact finding does **not** demand a second hearing on the facts by a decision maker that is not as well placed as the first decision maker to decide the facts.

Proportionate process requires the form of review that will provide a reasonable protection against bad decisions, without generating rehearings that are not equipped to yield better decisions.

Begum unequivocally establishes the limited approach to review of fact finding (and also that it is compatible with the European Convention). The decision can be reconciled with *Tameside*, if we pay attention to Lord Justice Scarman's point established in the Court of Appeal, that in order for the court to intervene, the actual state of the facts must be 'established' (or 'plainly established', as Lord Justice Scarman said later in his reasons). A finding of fact will not be set aside unless it is 'established' that the initial decision maker got the facts wrong, in the sense that it is plain to the court, in spite of its relative disadvantages as a tribunal of fact, that the finding of fact is untenable. A claimant in judicial review cannot ask the court to *establish* the facts by conducting the inquiry that it would take to do a better job than the initial decision maker. But in order to do what judges can do to guard against arbitrary decision making by the housing officer, the court should interfere if it is patently obvious, even from the judge's relatively disadvantageous position, that the officer has made a mistake.

Article 6 and fact finding

You might think that the right to an independent tribunal in Art 6 of the European Convention would require courts to find the facts afresh in judicial review of administrative bodies that are not independent. But in another example of the judicial construction of Art 6 as only requiring procedures that are fair and reasonable (see p 170), Lord Hoffmann said that he did not think that Art 6 'mandates a more intensive approach to judicial review of questions of fact' *Begum* [50]. A process for determining civil rights that is not independent of government does not infringe Article 6 if a court on judicial review has 'full jurisdiction to deal with the case as the nature of the decision requires' (Lord Hoffmann, *Alconbury* [87]). Deferential review of fact finding meets that requirement.

There is a difference between review on questions of fact and review on questions of law. Whether or not they were right to develop jurisdictional review into review for error of law, the English judges have not developed it into review for error of fact. They view questions of law as questions for the court, but they do not take the same attitude to questions of fact. Lord Slynn and Lord Justice Sedley may seem to be exceptions, except that it seems hard to imagine that they would actually consider that the administrative court should make its own finding as to (e.g.) whether a drug problem in a neighbourhood in Tower Hamlets is bad enough to make it an unsuitable place to house a homeless person.

In E v Home Secretary [2004] EWCA Civ 49, the Court of Appeal reviewed the law on errors of fact (though without citing Begum, which the House of Lords had decided a few months earlier), and held that at least in some contexts, 'the time has now come to accept that a mistake of fact giving rise to unfairness is a separate head of challenge in an appeal on a point of law' [66]. In spite of the suggestion that the doctrine was new, the carefully reasoned decision actually amounts to a new articulation of the traditional, limited approach. And it is a helpful new articulation: an error of fact is not enough, but the court can quash a decision if it can see that an error of fact gives rise to *unfairness*. The court gave the following 'ordinary requirements for a finding of unfairness':

> First, there must have been a mistake as to an existing fact, including a mistake as to the availability of evidence on a particular matter. Secondly, the fact or evidence must have been "established", in the sense that it was uncontentious and objectively verifiable. Thirdly, the appellant (or his advisers) must not been have been responsible for the mistake. Fourthly, the mistake must have played a material (not necessarily decisive) part in the tribunal's reasoning. [66]

That helpful articulation of the traditional approach confirms that, even if it is the judges' job to decide whether other public authorities have got the law right, it is not generally the judges' job to decide whether they have got the facts right.

9.2.4 What does it take for a finding of fact to be perverse?

Is *Puhlhofer* still good law? Yes, if we understand Lord Brightman's requirement of 'perversity' to be met where, as the Court of Appeal put it in E, a mistake of fact has given rise to unfairness.

'Perversity means what it says,' according to Laws J in CA v Home Secretary [2004] EWCA Civ 1165 [27]. But it doesn't, actually. Or to put it another way, perverse fact-finding decisions are not the only ones that will be quashed in judicial review. In order for judicial interference to be justified, an error of fact need not be outrageous or scandalous, and the decision maker need not have been at fault (as Lord Brightman made clear in *Puhlhofer*[22]). In order for a court to intervene, it must simply be obvious,

---

22   And see E [63], [65].

from the detached vantage point that the judge has in judicial review, that an injustice has arisen from an error of fact.

Asylum seekers often challenge fact-finding decisions, and their cases give examples of errors of fact that do and do not justify review. So Keene LJ held in R (Ahmed) v Home Secretary [2004] EWCA Civ 552,

> ❛while errors of fact often will not require a decision to be upset, these errors are so strange as to leave one wondering what was happening when the adjudicator wrote his determination. It is possible that he was confusing this appellant with another appellant or this case with another case.❜ [12]

In that sort of case, judicial review is justified whether the mistake was reasonable or not. The rationale for review is that the court is in a position to identify a mistake in spite of the initial decision maker's advantages. Perhaps we could say that the role of perversity is that the court will interfere not merely with a finding of fact that was *made* perversely, but also where it would be perverse to let the decision stand. So Lord Brightman was not quite right in *Puhlhofer*: it does not have to be 'obvious that the public body, consciously or unconsciously, are acting perversely'. It only needs to be obvious that an injustice has been caused by *an error that the judges can identify with no breach of comity.*

The court may therefore quash a decision that was made with **no evidence** (such a decision is 'perverse' in Lord Brightman's sense): R v Bedwellty Justices, ex p Williams [1997] AC 225. But the 'no evidence' rule has to be understood in light of the context. In B Johnson & Co v Minister of Health [1947] 2 All ER 395 (CA) (see p 115), Lord Greene said that it would be 'fallacious' to think that a minister's decision about a planning inquiry 'is in some sense a quasi-judicial decision which can be challenged on the ground of lack of evidence, for instance, in the courts in the same way as a judicial decision might be challenged' (400). Even though the antique 'quasi-judicial' terminology is dangerous (it was used in the early 20th century to restrict the law of due process (section 4.3)), there is an important point here: lack of evidence is not a ground on which planning decisions should be reviewed *in the same way* as convictions in magistrates' courts.

There is still a distinction between administrative and judicial decisions

Lord Hoffmann said in *Begum*:

'The concern of the [Strasbourg] court, as it has emphasised since *Golder's* case ((1975) 1 EHRR 524) is to uphold the rule of law and to insist that decisions which on generally accepted principles are appropriate only for judicial decision should be so decided. In the case of decisions appropriate for administrative decision, its concern, again founded on the rule of law, is that there should be the possibility of adequate judicial review' [57].

See p 117 on the change in the use of this distinction after *Ridge v Baldwin*. Lord Hoffmann's view is compatible with *Ridge*: the distinction between administrative and judicial decisions does not determine whether due process is required (as some decisions had suggested before *Ridge*); it determines, in part, what process is due.

Ministers' decisions concerning planning inquiries must be made with due process, but due process in planning inquiries does not demand the same sort of evidence as in criminal proceedings. So in *R v Bedwellty Justices, ex p Williams* [1997] AC 225 (HL), Lord Cooke held that 'To convict or commit for trial without any admissible evidence of guilt is to fall into an error of law' (233). That sort of decision requires evidence of the kind that courts expect in the criminal justice process. A minister's planning decision, by contrast, will only be set aside for error of fact if the court is able to decide that it was made without the sort of information that *ministers* ought to use in deciding whether a building project is in the public interest.

9.2.5 Radical fact finding

To understand the principle of relativity, it is essential to note that in some areas, the courts really have jumped in and decided the facts for themselves. Yet that does not support the myth of judicial review for mere error of fact, because you need special circumstances if you are to persuade judges to find the facts for themselves.

In *Khawaja v Home Secretary* [1984] AC 74 (HL) Lord Scarman pointed out that the form of review outlined by Lord Greene in *Wednesbury* 'excludes the court from substituting its own view of the facts for that of the authority. Such exclusion of the power and duty of the courts runs counter to the development of the safeguards which our law provides for the liberty of the subject' (109–10). That does not mean that there is anything wrong with what Lord Scarman called 'the *Wednesbury* principle'; it means that the common law does not apply the principle in the review of an executive decision to detain a person. When a man is detained as an illegal entrant, 'It is not enough that the immigration officer reasonably believes him to be an illegal entrant if the evidence does not justify his belief. Accordingly, the duty of the court must go beyond inquiring only whether he had reasonable grounds for his belief' (Lord Fraser, 97). So in that case, the court took over the job of deciding the facts that would determine whether Khawaja was an illegal immigrant.

The most striking instance of the principle of relativity (see p 10) in administrative law?

Even though it is *not* generally the job of the courts to determine the facts on which an executive decision ought to have been based, there is no deference to executive authorities' view of the facts that ground a decision to detain a person.

Why isn't this really extraordinary form of review (which amounts to a rehearing) a breach of comity? Part of the reason is that the judicial process is well equipped to identify the relevant facts, so that a rehearing would not damage the public interest that potentially required the detention. But more fundamentally, the reason is a justification of necessity in the interests of justice. When the decision is an extraordinary administrative decision to detain a person, it is not a breach of comity for judges to call it into question in a way that overrides the initial decision maker's fact finding. Far from supporting *general* review for error of fact, the *Khawaja* case shows the principle of relativity at work: the judges will not take over fact finding in planning cases, in the way that they did in the *Khawaja* case. It is important to note that in *Begum*, Lord Bingham rejected an argument that the fact finding in a housing case should be subjected to the sort of 'anxious scrutiny' or 'close and rigorous analysis' adopted in *Khawaja*, 'if by that is meant an analysis closer or more rigorous than would ordinarily and properly be conducted by a careful and competent judge determining an application for judicial review' [7].

To summarize, an administrative decision ought to be quashed in judicial review if it was based on a finding of fact that can be seen *from the court's detached and restricted vantage point* to result in an injustice. In special circumstances where the courts are capable of passing judgment on the facts in question, and justice demands it for the protection of essential interests such as liberty and security of the person, the courts can jump in and find the facts for themselves, quashing a decision merely on the basis that, in some relevant respect, the facts were not as the public authority had thought they were.[23] The purpose of the doctrine is to hold public authorities accountable, and it does *not* allow the courts to substitute their judgment for the judgment of other public authorities on questions of fact in general.

9.3 Applying the law to the facts: a 'permissible field of judgment'

Here is a puzzle about *R v Ministry of Defence, ex p Walker* [2000] 1 WLR 806 (see p 39). The criminal injuries compensation scheme included a provision that no compensation was available for injuries caused by 'military activity by warring factions'. The ministry decided that the restriction applied to the facts of Walker's case, so that he was not eligible for compensation. We have seen that the courts will review an interpretation of such a scheme on a standard of correctness: Lord Slynn said that the court had to decide whether the Ministry of Defence had interpreted the compensation scheme **correctly** (810). We have seen that they would review decisions as to the facts of a

---

23   On the processes for taking evidence in such a claim for judicial review see p 362 (discussing *R (Wilkinson) v Broadmoor Special Hospital Authority* [2001] EWCA Civ 1545, another landmark case in which the High Court substituted its judgment for an administrative authority's decision on questions of fact).

particular case on a standard of reasonableness.[24] What is the standard of review for a decision as to how to apply the scheme to the facts?

Lord Hoffmann thought that the court had to decide whether the Ministry had applied its rules **reasonably**:

> The next question is whether the injury to Sergeant Walker fell within the terms of the exclusion announced by the minister. I think it plainly did. He was fired upon by a Serbian tank. I do not see how it can be said that the ministry could not reasonably take the view that this was military activity by a warring faction. The fact that it was a criminal act under international law does not mean that it cannot have been a military activity within the meaning of the policy. It was a criminal military activity. (815)

If the court had to decide whether the Ministry interpreted the scheme *correctly*, then why was Lord Hoffmann concerned with whether it was *reasonable* to take the view that the exclusion applied to Walker?

The answer to the puzzle is that both Lord Slynn and Lord Hoffmann were right, because **interpreting** the scheme is different from **applying** it to a case. According to Lord Diplock's rule, the court will insist on its own interpretation of the scheme, and will quash a decision that is incompatible with its interpretation. But the court's interpretation may allow the administrative decision maker to apply the law for *or* against a claimant—and then, the court will not interfere.

There are two reasons why the courts do not apply a standard of correctness to decisions applying the law, in spite of the doctrine of judicial review for error of law:

1. **Deference on questions of fact:** The judges are at a disadvantage in applying the law to the facts, because they defer to other decision makers on questions of fact.

2. **The resultant discretion (see p 232) that vague standards give the initial decision maker:** The court's interpretation of the law may or may not require a particular outcome in a given case.

The second of these points is especially important: if the correct view of the law does not require one particular decision, then a public authority is free to decide one way or another.

That may seem impossible, because it may seem that there is no difference between **interpreting the law**, and **deciding how to apply the law**. In fact, the distinction between questions of interpretation and questions of application is simple, though vague. The distinction *seems* extremely confusing, because understanding it means working out two questions that seem mind-boggling: what interpretation is, and which questions are questions of law.

---

[24] There was no dispute as to the facts in *Walker*.

9.3.1 What is interpretation?

The interpretation and the application of the law are related, because an interpretation of the law is a rule for applying the law. If an administrative decision maker explains how, in its view, the law is to be applied, then it is giving its interpretation, and the court will decide whether it is mistaken or correct. If the court decides that the interpretation is mistaken, the court will correct the error. If the interpretation that the decision maker offers is correct, then the court will not interfere, unless the decision maker's application of the law to the facts is incompatible with that interpretation.

In a case like *Walker*, the correct interpretation may leave a wide discretion to the decision maker to decide in favour of an application *or* against it. The court will only interfere if the ministry's application of the scheme was incompatible with the best interpretation of the scheme. That is, the court will interfere either if the ministry's interpretation of the scheme was incorrect, or if the ministry's decision not to compensate, given the facts of Walker's case, was incompatible with the correct interpretation of the scheme. The power to apply the scheme is a discretionary power, because the best interpretation of the scheme may leave the administrative decision maker a choice to apply it in Walker's favour or not.

The classic case on judicial review of decisions applying the law was a statutory appeal on a question of law: *Edwards v Bairstow* [1956] AC 14. The leading recent authority is a decision on judicial review: *R v Monopolies and Mergers Commission, ex p South Yorkshire Transport* [1993] 1 WLR 23. Both cases show that administrative decision makers have discretion in applying the law, even though the courts will quash their decisions (either on a statutory appeal or in judicial review) for error of law.

In *South Yorkshire Transport*, The Transport Authority was buying up local bus services. The Conservative Trade and Industry Secretary wanted to break up this local government monopoly, so he referred the matter to Monopolies and Mergers Commission. The Commission had power to investigate acquisitions of companies that affected 'a substantial part of the United Kingdom' (and to unwind them, after investigation, if they were not in the public interest). The South Yorkshire bus companies had routes that affected an area between Leeds and Derby that covered 1.65% of the land area of the UK (with 3.2% of the population). South Yorkshire said that it was not a substantial part of the UK, so that the Commission should not have started an investigation.

South Yorkshire Transport was asking the court to decide whether the area between Leeds and Derby is a substantial part of the UK. They claimed that, 'If the commission has reached a different answer it is wrong, and the court can and must intervene' (32). But Lord Mustill did not altogether agree: he said that it *was* the court's job to identify 'the criterion for a judgment', even if 'opinions might legitimately differ' as to what the criterion ought to be. So he endorsed Lord Diplock's rule that the court should impose its understanding of the scheme on the authority responsible for operating the scheme, even if the authority's understanding was

Figure 9.1 A question of application: did South Yorkshire Transport's deal affect a substantial part of the United Kingdom?

reasonable. But, he added, if the 'criterion so established' is vague,

> '...the court is entitled to substitute its own opinion for that of the person to whom the decision has been entrusted only if the decision is so aberrant that it cannot be classed as rational: *Edwards v Bairstow* [1956] AC 14.' (32)

To identify the criterion for a judgment is to interpret the law. The criterion that Lord Mustill established in *South Yorkshire Transport* (his interpretation) was vague. He interpreted 'substantial part of the UK' to mean 'of such size, character and importance as to make it worth consideration for the purposes of the Act' (32), and he found that the Commission's decision was within the 'permissible field of judgment' (33) allowed by that criterion. Once the court has established its interpretation of the law, the court will interfere with decisions applying that interpretation only on the 'rationality' ground of review that is used in control of discretionary powers. Whether the rationality requirement leaves the administrative decision maker any leeway depends on how vague the 'criterion for a judgment' is. The standard that the court adopted in answering the question of law in *South Yorkshire Transport* left the Commission a very wide leeway.

That leeway is one example of the leeway that administrative authorities have in the exercise of discretionary powers. And in other cases, the judges have made it very clear that the general standard of review of decisions applying the law is *Wednesbury* unreasonableness. Lord Donaldson MR held in *O'Kelly v Trusthouse Forte plc* [1984] QB 90 that if a tribunal has stated the law correctly, an appellate court can interfere with the application of the law to the facts only if 'no reasonable tribunal, properly directing itself on the relevant questions of law, could have reached the conclusion under appeal' (123). And in *Moyna v Work and Pensions Secretary* [2003] UKHL 44, Lord Hoffmann held that the court cannot overturn a decision 'whether the facts as found or admitted fall one side or the other of some conceptual line drawn by the law... unless it falls outside the bounds of reasonable judgment' [25].

If it still seems odd that the doctrine of review for error of law can leave a wide 'permissible field of judgment' in applying the law, you should consider the decision that Lord Donaldson, Lord Mustill, and Lord Hoffmann all cited in *O'Kelly*, *South Yorkshire Transport*, and *Moyna*: Lord Radcliffe's classic speech in *Edwards v Bairstow*.

Harold Bairstow had bought a lot of spinning machinery for £12,000, and promptly sold it in bits at a profit of £18,000. The tax inspector claimed that the deal was an 'adventure or concern in the nature of trade', so that Bairstow had to pay income tax. Bairstow claimed that the deal did not count as trade because it was a one-off sale of an asset; the tax inspector thought it was still trade because Bairstow flipped it—that is, he bought it for the purpose of selling it at a profit. The tax commissioners (the tribunal for taxpayer complaints) decided that the deal did not count as trade. The tax inspector appealed on a question of law to the High Court. The High Court and the Court of Appeal held that there was no error of law, but the tax inspector won in the end: the House of Lords held that the only reasonable conclusion was that the sale of the machinery counted as trade.

But note that according to Lord Radcliffe, the court's role in deciding whether there was an error of law was *not* necessarily to decide whether a particular transaction counted as 'trade'. 'There are many combinations of circumstances in which it could not be said to be wrong to arrive at a conclusion one way or the other' (34). This statement takes the approach of *Slattery*, *Kruse*, and *Wednesbury* (see p 220), and uses it to control the discretion that administrative tribunals have in applying the law. Lord Radcliffe's speech has become the standard reference point for judges explaining the way in which they control the application of the law—though he rightly claimed to be stating old and well-established law.

9.3.2 What is a question of law?

You can see why the courts have struggled to decide whether a question of the application of a statute is a question of law, or a question of fact. In an appeal on a point of law (e.g., in *Edwards v Bairstow*), the appellant needs to persuade the court that the error that it alleges was an error on a question of law, or there is no jurisdiction to overturn the decision. And in judicial review (e.g., in *South Yorkshire Transport*), the claimant tries to persuade the court that the error it alleges was an error on a question of law, to get the court to substitute its judgment for the judgment of administrative tribunal.

Is a question of the application of a statute a question of law, or a question of fact? The key to this problem is that a question of the application of the law may be a question of law in one case, and not in another. It is a question of law if the law demands a particular answer to it. The law does not require one answer to it when it would be reasonable to decide it one way or another. A question of application is not a question of law if (as in *South Yorkshire Transport*) the law allows the tribunal to decide it in more than one way.

When it is reasonable to decide that the facts do or do not fall within the relevant legal category, the issue is *not* a question of law, which means that it is not a question on which the court needs to impose its own judgment (in an appeal on a point of law, or in judicial review under Lord Diplock's rule). As Lord Simon later said in explaining *Edwards v Bairstow*, if 'certain conduct must as a matter of law fall within the statutory language (as was the actual decision in *Edwards v Bairstow*)' or if it 'must as a matter of law fall outside the statutory language', then the question of application is a question of law (*Ransom (Inspector of Taxes) v Higgs* [1974] 1 WLR 1594 (HL), 1618).

9.4 Conclusion: the underlying unity of control of discretionary powers

Judicial control of administrative jurisdictions promotes the rule of law. The High Court's independence, its openness, its adversarial process, and its effectiveness give it the opportunity to prevent abuses of power and to impose good process on other decision makers. The remarkable doctrine of review for error of law gives the judges the more dramatic opportunity to improve administrative decision making, or to damage it by imposing the judges' misinterpretations on a decision maker that understands the purpose of the scheme in question better, and is responsible for applying it. *South Yorkshire Transport* shows the discretion that administrative authorities may have in applying the court's interpretation. The breadth of that discretion may be substantial: the courts will defer to a reasonable administrative decision as to how the law is to be applied.

It is popular to divide the law of judicial review into two compartments: control of discretionary powers (with *Wednesbury* as the leading case), and control of decisions applying the law (with *Anisminic*, as reinterpreted by Lord Diplock, as the leading case). It may seem to be an attractive division, because exercising a discretion is a matter for the body given the discretion, but applying the law seems to be a matter for judges. But that would be a basic mistake. It ought to have become clear in the course of this chapter that **a power to apply the law is a discretionary power**.

Consider the following puzzle about the relation between having a discretion, and applying the law: in R v Gaming Board for Great Britain, ex p Kingsley [1996] COD 178, the Gaming Board had to decide whether Kingsley was a 'fit and proper person' to operate casinos. Was the Board applying the law, or exercising a discretionary power? The answer is that it was doing **both**. The Board had to decide whether the legal category 'fit and proper person' applied to Kingsley. That category was so vague that the Board had a very wide resultant discretion in deciding whether to count Kingsley within the category. If the Board misinterpreted the term in the statute, it would *for that very reason* be acting on irrelevant considerations. So there is an underlying unity between the error of law doctrine (which concerns the interpretation of legal categories) and the control of discretionary power.

The Queen's Bench Division held in *Kingsley*, by the way, that it was for the Board to decide what considerations it would take into account in deciding whether a person is fit and proper, as long as it kept in mind the purpose of the legislation. That decision reflects both the discretion that a public authority still has in applying the law in spite of the error of law doctrine, and the rule that deciding which considerations are relevant is not generally a matter for the court (although the court has a general power to quash a decision based on an unreasonable view as to what is relevant; see p 272). So here is a template for the form of judicial review power that judges can legitimately take upon themselves. It is a model for ways in which they ought to give effect to the core rationale for judicial review.

The template for the judges' supervisory jurisdiction

Judicial review ought to be generally available to ask whether an administrative authority has:

- acted without jurisdiction; or
- acted without due process; or
- abused its powers; or

- used its discretionary powers (including any discretionary power to interpret or elaborate the rules that it is responsible for applying) in a way that judges can identify as unreasonable with no breach of comity; or
- acted contrary to any legal rule that the judges can identify with no breach of comity; or
- acted on a view of the facts that is, even from the judges' detached point of view, manifestly wrong.

Appendix: The List of grounds of judicial review— Lord Diplock's version

'Judicial review has I think developed to a stage today when without reiterating any analysis of the steps by which the development has come about, one can conveniently classify under three heads the grounds upon which administrative action is subject to control by judicial review. The first ground I would call "illegality," the second "irrationality" and the third "procedural impropriety" '.[25]

This seemingly neat list is very popular,[26] but it is incoherent. 'Procedural impropriety' makes sense—that means lack of due process. Lord Diplock meant 'irrationality' as a label for *Wednesbury* unreasonableness (410); but it is a misleading label—see p 339. And if 'illegality' means unlawfulness, it covers *all* the grounds of review.[27]

Lord Diplock tried to explain: 'By "illegality" as a ground for judicial review I mean that the decision-maker must understand correctly the law that regulates his decision-making power and must give effect to it' (410). But *all* the grounds of judicial review are part of the 'law that regulates' a decision-making power. Perhaps Lord Diplock thought of 'illegality' as a label for the doctrine of review for error of law, which he had been crafting in decisions just before the GCHQ case (*Racal* [1981] AC 374 (HL), *O'Reilly v Mackman* [1983] 2 AC 237 (HL)). Or perhaps illegality is meant to be a label for everything except procedural impropriety and irrationality, as Lord Bridge suggested in *R v Environment Secretary, ex p Hammersmith and Fulham LBC* [1991] 1 AC 521, 597. For judges who think that the *Wednesbury* principles (including the doctrine of judicial review for bad faith and, crucially, the doctrine of relevance) do not all fit into 'irrationality', it is a popular move to squish them into 'illegality' (along with the doctrine of legitimate expectations).

---

[25] *Council of Civil Service Unions v Minister for the Civil Service* [1985] AC 374, 410.

[26] Prominent House of Lords decisions adopting Lord Diplock's list include: *R v Environment Secretary, ex p Hammersmith and Fulham LBC* [1991] 1 AC 521, 594, *Boddington v British Transport Police* [1999] 2 AC 143 (HL), 152, *R v Lord Chancellor, ex p Page* [1993] AC 682, 701.

[27] So, e.g., in *R v Environment Secretary, ex p Nottinghamshire County Council* [1986] AC 240, Lord Scarman said that Lord Greene's speech in *Wednesbury* outlined 'the circumstances in which the courts will intervene to quash as being illegal the exercise of an administrative discretion' (249).

There is no particular reason to use 'illegality' as a label for bad faith and irrelevant considerations, if we don't use it as a label for procedural impropriety and irrationality (whatever may be meant by that) as well. And classifying relevance as a matter of 'illegality' would be dangerously misleading.[28] It would suggest that the standard for identifying the considerations on which a decision should be based is one of correctness (like the standard for determinations of law). But that is a mistake that generates excessive legalism in administrative decision making: judges ought to defer to public authorities, to some extent, on the question of what considerations are relevant to the public authority's decision (see p 272).

It is impossible—and unnecessary to encapsulate the grounds of review in three big words.

TAKE-HOME MESSAGE • • •

- It is not the judges' job to correct every **error of law**. But they should quash **unreasonable interpretations** of the standards that a public authority has responsibility for applying.

- It is not the judges' job to correct every **error of fact**. But they should quash decisions based on a conclusion as to the facts that they can see to be patently mistaken (from their detached perspective, and generally without having heard from the people from whom the initial decision maker heard, and without the benefit of any expertise that the decision maker may have in identifying the facts).

- A question of **how the law applies to a particular case** may or may not be a question of law. It is a question of law if the law requires it to be answered in a particular way, but it is not a question of law if the law allows it to be answered in different ways.

Critical reading

Edwards v Bairstow [1956] AC 14
Anisminic v Foreign Compensation Commission [1969] 2 AC 147 HL
Pearlman v Keepers and Governors of Harrow School [1979] QB 56 CA
Re Racal [1981] AC 374 (HL)
O'Reilly v Mackman [1983] 2 AC 237 (HL)
R v Lord Chancellor, ex p Page [1993] AC 682
R v Monopolies and Mergers Commission, ex p South Yorkshire Transport [1993] 1 WLR 23
Moyna v Work and Pensions Secretary [2003] UKHL 44
E v Home Secretary [2004] EWCA Civ 49

---

[28] And sometimes, judges have treated irrelevant considerations as part of the 'irrationality' ground of review: Lord Donaldson spoke of 'Irrationality,...in the sense of failing to take account of relevant factors or taking account of irrelevant factors...' (*R v Panel on Take-overs and Mergers, ex p Guinness Plc* [1990] 1 QB 146, 159).

CRITICAL QUESTIONS • • •

1   Is there any difference between judicial review for error of law, and a statutory appeal to the Upper Tribunal (see Chapter 12) on a question of law?

2   What is jurisdiction? Do administrative authorities have any?

3   Can you reconcile the decision in *Anisminic* with the statutory ouster clause? Would the approach of the majority in *Anisminic* have been the right approach, if there had been no ouster clause in the legislation setting up the Commission?

4   Is fact finding a discretionary power?

5   What is the relationship between The List of things that make an administrative decision a nullity in Lord Reid's speech in *Anisminic* (see p 306), and The List of substantive features of an exercise of power that make it unlawful in Lord Greene's reasons in *Wednesbury* (see p 226)?

6   How is the control of fact finding related to the requirement of due process?

Further questions:

7   If review for error of law is not supported by constitutional principle, and only arose from Lord Diplock's *obiter dicta* misinterpreting *Anisminic*, why do you think that there has been no judicial controversy over the doctrine in more than a decade since *Page*?

8   Every fact that is relevant to the exercise of a power is a relevant consideration. So if there is judicial review for failure to decide on the relevant considerations, doesn't that mean that there must be judicial review for error of fact?

9   Decisions of the High Court are not susceptible to judicial review. Does that mean that the High Court has unlimited jurisdiction?

online resource centre

Visit the online resource centre to access the following resources which accompany this chapter: links to legislation and online reports of judicial decisions, summaries of key cases and legislation, updates in the law, suggestions for answering the pop quizzes and questions, and links to useful websites.

Litigation

10 How to sue the government: judicial processes and judicial remedies

This chapter addresses the extraordinary process of judicial review, and the extraordinary remedies available to the court. The process and remedies are compared to the process and remedies in ordinary claims (which can also be used to challenge administrative action). In controlling these complex processes, the challenge for judges is to keep things in proportion: the attempt to achieve due process in judicial control of administrative action is essential to the administration of justice.

LOOK FOR • • •

- **Proportionality** as the key principle of judicial process (just as it is the key principle of administrative process).

- The courts' discretionary control over their own process (developed at common law, and preserved in modern reforms).

- **Process danger:** can the courts control their own process in a way that does justice and respects the public interest? Or does the process need to be controlled by rules that restrict the courts' discretion?

- The **irony of process** (see p 143) again: the courts need to provide forms of process that are excessive and wasteful in some cases, in order to protect the administration of justice.

> ❛A *mandamus*...ought to be used upon all occasions where the law has established no specific remedy, and where in justice and good government there ought to be one. Within the last century, it has been liberally interposed for the benefit of the subject and advancement of justice.❜
>
> R v *Barker* (1762) 3 Burr 1265, 1267 (Lord Mansfield)

10.1 The judicial process puzzle: why is this a problem?

The history of the common law has given the judges far-reaching discretionary power over their own jurisdiction to control administrative action. And in this century, the Civil Procedure Rules 1998 (CPR) have extended that judicial power. Due process is the goal for courts in controlling their own proceedings. That means affording claimants a way of challenging unlawful behaviour that is proportionate to the interests at stake—the claimant's interest in getting a hearing, and the potentially conflicting public interests in (1) finality in administrative decision making, and (2) the effective operation of a process that can impose the rule of law on administration.

If you are affected by an administrative action that you believe to be unlawful, what can you do? You might think this would be easy—that claimants could simply use any available court proceeding to get a court to apply the grounds of judicial review. Those grounds, introduced in Chapter 2 and unpacked in Chapters 3–9, are powerful techniques for judging administrative action to be unlawful. And there are *many* potentially useful judicial processes for deciding claims of unlawful administrative action.

- You may be able to bring an **appeal** (typically on a point of law, which will include error of law, unfair process, and unlawful exercise of discretion). The process for appeal to the courts from administrative tribunals has now been unified into an appeal from First-tier tribunals to the Upper Tribunal, within the tribunals system (with a further appeal to the Court of Appeal; see Chapter 12).[1]

- You may want to bring an **ordinary claim**. In an ordinary claim, the High Court can award damages or an injunction, and can issue a declaration that administrative action was unlawful. (CPR 40. 20)

- Best of all, the Civil Procedure Rules 1998 also provide an extraordinary process for judicial review. The **claim for judicial review** is a modern development of procedures that the court of King's Bench invented in the middle ages, to exercise the King's prerogative to inquire into the lawfulness of his officials' actions. Today,

---

[1]   In addition to such appeal processes, note that there are various special judicial processes such as statutory review under the Nationality, Immigration and Asylum Act 2002 s 101(2) (CPR 54.21 et seq.).

the Civil Procedure Rules define it as:

> ' a claim to review the lawfulness of—
>
> (i)   an enactment; or
>
> (ii) a decision, action or failure to act in relation to the exercise of a public function. ' [2]

The process offers special remedies (still called 'prerogative' remedies) available only in judicial review: a 'quashing order' to nullify a decision, a 'mandatory order' to require some official action, and a 'prohibiting order' to ban some official action. They were called 'certiorari', 'mandamus', and 'prohibition' until the Civil Procedure Rules 1998 came into effect. Declarations and the ordinary remedies of damages and injunctions are also available in a claim for judicial review. But a claim for damages alone cannot be brought by judicial review (CPR 54.3(2)).

- **Habeas corpus** is available to challenge unlawful detention in a very simple process that was invented in the middle ages and reformed in the Habeas Corpus Acts 1640 and 1679 (the process is now regulated by Rules of the Supreme Court (RSC) Order 54).

- **Proceedings under the Human Rights Act s 7** are available to a person who claims to be a victim of an action that is unlawful under s 6 of the Act. The proceedings may be brought either by ordinary claim or by a claim for judicial review, and the court can award 'such relief or remedy...within its powers as it considers just and appropriate' (s 8(1)). Damages for action that is unlawful under s 6 may be awarded if 'it is necessary to afford just satisfaction' (Human Rights Act 1998 s 8(3)(b)). If primary legislation necessitates the breach of a Convention right, the breach is not unlawful under s 6, but the High Court can declare that the legislation is incompatible with the Convention (see section 3.3).

- Finally, as a defendant in a civil claim or a criminal prosecution that depends on an administrative decision, you may be able to argue in your **defence to proceedings** that the decision was actually unlawful (if the decision was incompatible with the Convention, you may rely on the Convention right if you were a victim of the unlawful act: (Human Rights Act 1998 s 7(1)(b)).

The naming of parties

Before the changes to the Civil Procedure Rules,[3] a person seeking judicial review was called an **applicant**; the applicant sought **leave** to bring an **application for judicial review** of the conduct of a **respondent**. Now, a **claimant** seeks **permission**

---

[2]   CPR 54.1(1)(2)(a).

[3]   The Civil Procedure Rules were overhauled in 1998 on the basis of a report by Lord Woolf; but the judicial review procedure was left untouched until 2000; see CPR 54.

> to bring a **claim for judicial review** of the conduct of a **defendant**. In ordinary pro-
> ceedings before 2000, a **plaintiff** brought an **action** against a **defendant**; now
> a **claimant** brings a **claim** against a **defendant**. These are only changes of ter-
> minology. Since the procedural reforms in 1978, **'judicial review'** has often been
> used as a term for the process that used to be an application for judicial review
> and is now a claim for judicial review.[4] But of course, **judges review** the lawful-
> ness of governmental action in all sorts of proceedings, including tort claims (see
> Chapter 14) and criminal prosecutions (*Boddington v British Transport Police* [1999] 2
> AC 143 (HL)).

Of course, one problem of judicial process will concern the boundaries of administrative action: you cannot ask the judges to apply their supervisory techniques to control
a defendant's purely private decisions, and much litigation has concerned the twilight
zone between public decisions and private decisions (see section 15.5.1). You might
think that would be the only problem about judicial procedures in administrative law,
and that anyone who alleges unlawful administrative action would simply be able to
pick the most convenient judicial process from this extravagant array, in order to vindicate the rule of law by getting the public authority in front of the High Court.

But in fact, English law does *not* allow a judicial process for every complaint of
unlawful public action. You can only bring an ordinary claim if you assert a right of
action. You have no right to bring a claim for judicial review; at the beginning of the
process you must ask the court for permission to proceed. The process is restricted
by time limits (see section 10.3.1) and a requirement of standing (Chapter 11). And at
the end of the judicial review process, the remedies are discretionary (section 10.4.6).
Only *habeas corpus* is available as of right (*Jenke's case* (1676) 6 St Tr 1189, 1207–8)—and
that is only useful if you are being detained.

Why aren't the judicial processes freely available to anyone who alleges unlawful
administrative conduct? Because the rule of law does not actually demand that. In
fact, the rule of law requires a system that presumes that administrative decisions are
lawfully effective, and brings an end to disputes about their effect. As the European
Court of Human Rights put it, it is 'an important element of the rule of law . . . that the
verdicts of a tribunal should be final and binding unless set aside by a superior court
on the basis of irregularity or unfairness' (*Pullar v United Kingdom* (1996) 22 EHRR
391 [32]).[5]

So there is no general right to pursue a complaint against a public authority by a
judicial process. The jurisdiction of the courts over administrative action is 'supervisory', but the judges are not the sort of supervisors who can take it upon themselves to
inquire into just any complaint. They do not roam through government departments

---

4   Judicial review is sometimes called a 'remedy' (e.g., by Lord Diplock in *R v IRC, ex p Federation
of Self-Employed and Small Businesses Ltd* [1982] AC 617, 639, and by Lord Woolf in *M v Home Office*
[1994] 1 AC 377, 417) but it is not a remedy; it is a procedure for asking a court to give a remedy.
On remedies, see section 10.4.

5   The remark concerned a judicial tribunal, but the same principle applies for the same reasons to
administrative tribunals too.

imposing the rule of law; they resolve disputes brought by a party who has standing to make a claim, against a defendant. They have to wait for a claimant to bring proceedings, and they are restricted in the form of remedies they can give. And the courts will exercise their discretion not to hear a claim, if there is another remedy that will do justice. Judicial review is meant to be a last resort (see section 2.7).

Just as the judges have been creative in extending the grounds of judicial review, however, they have been creative in extending their processes. The judges' attitude in the 21st century is the same as Lord Mansfield's attitude in the 18th: they want to find a way of hearing serious claims of unlawful administrative action.

A very complex tension results, between the judges' urge to curb unlawful administrative conduct, and the need to adhere to the adversary system that gives judges their role *as judges* (and not as superintendents of administration). In this chapter, we will see the very real ways in which the courts' processes limit the role of judges in controlling administration. We will also see the ways in which the judges have expanded their opportunities to subject governmental conduct to the scrutiny of the courts.

The tension, incidentally, explains why you need to learn about judicial process to understand administrative law. You can learn contract law without learning very much about the judicial process. But in administrative law, the ways in which disputes come to court raise the fundamental problems of accountability and comity among public authorities.

The judicial process problem

It is not enough to allege that a public authority has acted unlawfully; you also need a further reason why you are entitled to initiate a *judicial process in response to the allegation*. There is no general right to litigate a complaint that a public authority has acted unlawfully. And, in particular, there is no general right to seek judicial review.

The judges' discretion over every stage of their process (from permission to remedies) enables the judges to achieve **proportionate process** (see p 119) in their own proceedings—at least, if they use their discretion responsibly. The Civil Procedure Rules have very deliberately retained and, in fact, enhanced the judges' control over their proceedings, by establishing 'the overriding objective of enabling the court to deal with cases justly' (CPR 1.1(1)). Dealing with cases justly requires judges to make judgments of proportionality, because it includes:

> dealing with the case in ways which are proportionate—
> (i)   to the amount of money involved;
> (ii) to the importance of the case;
> (iii) to the complexity of the issues; and
> (iv) to the financial position of each party. [6]

---

[6]   CPR 1.1(2)(c).

That provision extends to the judges' judicial review jurisdiction, and it gives them responsibility for their process. This chapter introduces some of the remarkable inventions of doctrine and practice, by which the courts have tried to take responsibility for a process that gives effect to the purposes of judicial control of administration.

10.2 Ordinary claims

It is a basic constitutional principle that an ordinary claim (or a criminal prosecution) can be brought against a public official in the same way as against a private defendant. Both the substance of the claim and the process are the same. The various opportunities for claimants are the same (such as the opportunity to get disclosure of information relevant to the claim from the defendant). And the protections for the defendant are the same—notably, limitation periods, and the opportunity to ask the court to strike out a claim that discloses no right of action. Applications to strike out are extremely important in litigation against public authorities (see p 520), but the process is the same as for private defendants. Whether the claim is against a public authority or a private defendant, the rationale for these features of an ordinary claim is the same: given the nature of (e.g.) a claim in tort, justice does not require that the claimant be able to proceed many years after the events, or without asserting a right of action.

But one important feature of ordinary claims has special implications for public authorities. The court may issue a declaration against a public authority, as against a private defendant. A claimant may seek a declaration without seeking any other remedy. So claimants have long used ordinary claims for a declaration to ask the court to declare that a public authority has acted unlawfully, and to declare the public authority's legal duties. Why hasn't the ordinary claim for a declaration become the universal judicial process in administrative law? The reasons are complex; they become apparent once we understand the creative things that people have tried to do with the claim for a declaration.

10.2.1 Claims for a declaration and O'Reilly's problem

The 20th-century classics of judicial review were not claims for prerogative remedies. *Associated Provincial Picture Houses Ltd v Wednesbury Corporation* [1948] 1 KB 223 was an action against the local authority, for a declaration that a restriction on the cinema's Sunday opening was *ultra vires*. *Ridge v Baldwin* [1964] AC 40 was an action against the members of the police authority for a declaration that Ridge's dismissal was *ultra vires*. *Anisminic v Foreign Compensation Commission* [1969] 2 AC 147 was an action against the Foreign Compensation Commission for declarations that the determination was a nullity and that Anisminic was entitled to compensation.

Cases like these were brought as actions for a declaration (rather than as applications for judicial review) because of the short time limits for applications for prerogative writs, and because of restrictions on the prerogative writ process, imposed by the judges on the ground that the process did not involve a trial. In *Anisminic*, the plaintiff needed disclosure of the Commission's reasons, and the courts at that time did not order disclosure in applications for judicial review.[7] Given the advantages of bringing an action in those cases, should a claimant simply be able to choose the proceeding that is better suited to his or her claim? The courts allowed the actions in *Wednesbury*, *Ridge*, and *Anisminic* to proceed, without really thinking about it. But the House of Lords expressly endorsed a flexible approach in *Pyx Granite Co Ltd v Ministry of Housing and Local Government* [1960] AC 260, a case in which the Ministry claimed that the plaintiff ought to have proceeded by judicial review. Lord Goddard said, 'I know of no authority for saying that if an order or decision can be attacked by certiorari the court is debarred from granting a declaration in an appropriate case. The remedies are not mutually exclusive, though no doubt there are some orders, notably convictions before justices, where the only appropriate remedy is certiorari' (290).

In the report that led to reforms in 1978, the Law Commission said that ordinary actions should remain available, and that the reformed judicial review procedure 'should not be exclusive in the sense that it would become the only way by which issues relating to the acts or omissions of public authorities should come before the courts'.[8] The new rules of the Supreme Court in 1978 said nothing about the choice of procedure.

But the Law Lords set out to resolve the question, in *O'Reilly v Mackman* [1983] 2 AC 237. Lord Diplock attempted to bring 'speedy certainty' to administrative law. Instead of certainty, the decision generated litigation: eight other claims have been argued all the way to the House of Lords, on the issue of whether judicial review should have been used to bring the act or omission of a public authority before the courts.[9] This fiasco of judicial process has largely been resolved, by clever back-pedalling in a succession of House of Lords cases. But the injustice of *O'Reilly*'s case itself has never been put right. We will see why the House of Lords would be justified in reversing itself, if faced with a case on all fours with *O'Reilly*.

Christopher O'Reilly was serving fifteen years for robbery in Hull Prison. In 1976, there was an extremely violent four-day riot in the prison. The prisoners ransacked the canteen, assaulted prison officers, and camped out on the roof, throwing slates at the police. After the dust settled, the Prison Board of Visitors held an inquiry. They sentenced O'Reilly to a heavy penalty: 196 days in solitary confinement, and the

---

7   See *O'Reilly v Mackman* [1983] 2 AC 237 (280); in *Ridge*, Lord Morris said that 'considerations of convenience [presumably the need for disclosure] would probably have pointed against' seeking *certiorari* ([1964] AC 40, 126). The reasons for seeking a declaration are not mentioned in *Wednesbury*.

8   *Report on Administrative Law Remedies*, Law Com No 73, Cmnd 6407 [34].

9   *Cocks v Thanet DC* [1983] 2 AC 286 (decided on the same day as *O'Reilly*), *Davy v Spelthorne* [1984] 1 AC 262, *Wandsworth LBC v Winder* [1985] AC 461, *Roy v Kensington & Chelsea FPC* [1992] 1 AC 624, *Mercury Communications v Director General of Telecommunications* [1996] 1 WLR 48, *Boddington v British Transport Police* [1998] 2 All ER 203, *Steed v Home Secretary* [2000] 1 WLR 1169 and *Kay v Lambeth LBC* [2006] UKHL 10 [30].

loss of 510 days' early release. O'Reilly said he had an alibi. But the Board of Visitors would not listen to O'Reilly's witnesses. He wanted the court to declare that the decision was *ultra vires*, because he had not had a fair hearing.

● *Pop Quiz* ●

Imagine that O'Reilly had been allowed to go ahead with his action for a declaration, and that he proved that the Board of Visitors had refused to listen to witnesses who would support his claim that he had an alibi. How should such a case be decided?

How was O'Reilly to get the Board of Visitors into court? Like the plaintiffs in *Wednesbury*, *Ridge*, and *Anisminic*, he commenced an action for a declaration that the Board of Visitors' decision was *ultra vires*. But the House of Lords struck out his pleading, using the High Court's common law power to prevent an abuse of its process. O'Reilly was left to spend more than six months in solitary confinement, and an extra year-and-a-half in prison, without his claim of procedural injustice being heard.

Why did the Law Lords think that it would be an abuse of process for O'Reilly to commence an action against the Board of Visitors? For centuries, it had been possible to apply for a prerogative writ, instead of bringing an action. Now that the 1978 reform had improved the application process, it seemed unnecessary to allow the kind of ordinary action for a declaration that had proceeded in *Wednesbury*, *Ridge*, and *Anisminic*. There had been a short, six-month limit on applications for prerogative writs; the new improved judicial review procedure had an *even shorter* three-month deadline for applications for judicial review. If people like O'Reilly could choose between an ordinary action and an application for judicial review, then the three-month deadline would be a bit pointless: it would only mean that after three months, he would have to bring an action for a declaration rather than an application for judicial review. Lord Diplock decided that the short time limit and the **summary** process of an application for judicial review had a purpose of bringing 'speedy certainty' to the administration, which O'Reilly's action would thwart. A 'summary' process is a judicial process designed to resolve a dispute without a trial.

That was the gist of the House of Lords' reasoning in *O'Reilly*. Lord Diplock paid tribute to the ways in which Lord Reid had advanced judicial review in *Padfield*,[10] *Ridge*, and *Anisminic*. And he decided that now that Lord Reid had made judicial review into a *powerful* technique for control of public authorities, the judges needed to *protect* public authorities from it. He reckoned that it was fair to insist on that protection, now that the rules committee of the Supreme Court had improved the process on an application for judicial review. So he viewed it as an abuse of process, after the 1978 reforms, for the court to allow the sort of action that had proceeded in *Wednesbury*, *Ridge*, and *Anisminic*.

Here are the main differences between the process in an ordinary claim, and a claim for judicial review.

---

[10]   *Padfield v Minister of Agriculture, Fisheries and Food* [1968] AC 997.

	Time limit	Permission	Discovery	Cross-examination	Remedies
Ordinary claim	None fixed."	Not required.	By right.	By right.	Ordinary remedies (damages, declaration, injunction).
Judicial review proceedings pre-1978	six months.	Required.	None in practice (the judges could have allowed it).	None in practice (the judges could have allowed it).	Prerogative orders only: *Certiorari* (quashing orders), prohibition (prohibiting orders) and *mandamus* (mandatory orders).
Judicial review proceedings post-1978 (Order 53[12])	Three months.	Required.	Available by order.	Available by order.	Prerogative orders and ordinary remedies.

Figure 10.1

Of these changes, Lord Diplock treated the changes to discovery, cross-examination and remedies as the removal of *disadvantages* of the old process. He treated the leave (permission) requirement and the time limit as *protections for public authorities*. His conclusion was that given the removal of disadvantages, it had become unacceptable for a complainant to evade the protections for public authorities:

> '...it would in my view as a general rule be contrary to public policy, and as such an abuse of the process of the court, to permit a person seeking to establish that a decision of a public authority infringed rights to which he was entitled to protection under public law to proceed by way of an ordinary action and by this means to evade the provisions of Order 53 for the protection of such authorities.' (285)

The 'protection' of the time limit is the key to the *O'Reilly* problem, because it is the short three-month time limit that makes Lord Diplock's general rule *harsh*, and yet it is the time limit that seems to make the general rule *necessary*. There would be nothing wrong with a rule that a claimant cannot bring an ordinary claim if permission to seek judicial review was refused (or would have been refused).[13] But what about someone like O'Reilly, who simply wants to go to court long after the three-month limit on judicial review (in fact, four years later in O'Reilly's case)? If it is allowed, it seems to

---

11   There are limitation periods on rights of action, but no time limit on the process; a court could in principle strike out a claim as an abuse of process on ground of delay, if the delay were unfair to the defendant.

12   The 1978 reforms were made by the Rules Committee of the Supreme Court, in Order 53; the reforms were then given statutory force in the Supreme Court Act 1981 s 31.

13   Lord Denning made this point in the Court of Appeal in *O'Reilly* [1982] 3 WLR 604, 622.

make the time limit pointless, and the judges hate to treat a provision of the rules of court—let alone the Supreme Court Act—as pointless.

Speedy certainty and proportionate process

But is it an abuse of a process that has no time limit, to allow a claimant to proceed with it after the time limit has run out for a different process? Here's how to decide: ask whether the time limit is necessary for good public administration, so that it is fair to tell a claimant that he can no longer drag a public authority into court, three months after the claim arose. The crucial failing in Lord Diplock's reasoning is his overly general assumption that the time limit has that kind of importance to administration in all decision-making contexts. Counsel for O'Reilly argued that the action should go ahead, because the court could use its discretion to refuse a remedy if the delay amounted to 'tardy harassment' of the public authority (284). Lord Diplock's response was, in effect, that there would be a **process danger** even in letting the litigation proceed that far: it 'would defeat the public policy that underlies the grant of those protections: *viz.*, the need, in the interests of good administration and of third parties who may be indirectly affected by the decision, for speedy certainty as to whether it has the effect of a decision that is valid in public law' (284).

There is something to it, because *sometimes* it is crucially important to the public interest (and to the private interests of third parties) to know with speedy certainty whether a public decision will stand up. The best examples come from the law of planning and compulsory purchase: speedy certainty as to the lawfulness of a decision as to how land may be used is often essential, either in the public interest (in order for a public authority to proceed with a public building project), or for the good of private parties given planning permission (to enable them to proceed with their own projects), or third parties. Where an applicant for planning permission appeals to the Secretary of State against the decision of a Local Planning Authority, the Town and Country Planning Act 1990 provides that the validity of the Secretary of State's decision must be challenged within six weeks (s 288(3)), and the Acquisition of Land Act 1981 imposes the same very short time limit for challenging compulsory purchase decisions (s 23(4)). But the shortest time limits are in the law of asylum—in 2004, Parliament accepted the Government's view that the pressure of claims demanded urgent action, and imposed a five-day limit on the application to challenge a decision of the Asylum and Immigration Tribunal.[14] Those short limits are imposed because of the ways in which planning, compulsory purchase and asylum decisions affect the community and the persons subject to them. Public decisions are incredibly diverse, and they do not *generally* affect public or private interests in the same ways. So there is

---

[14] Nationality, Immigration and Asylum Act 2002 s 103A, as amended by the Asylum and Immigration (Treatment of Claimants, etc.) Act 2004 s 26; the court can accept an application outside the time limit when it could not 'reasonably practicably' have been made in five days.

no *general* need for speedy certainty. In cases where speedy certainty is unnecessary, Lord Diplock's rule represents a failure of proportionate process.

O'Reilly itself shows up this failing in the House of Lords' reasoning because, iron-ically, the case is *a model example of a case in which speedy certainty has no value.* Imagine that the House of Lords had allowed O'Reilly to proceed with his action. The result would have been that, four years after the Prison Board of Visitors' decision, the Board would face litigation over whether it gave O'Reilly a fair hearing. If he won, he might walk out of prison earlier, on the ground that he had been unfairly deprived of time off his sentence.[15] If a man walks out of prison early because an unfair punishment has been nullified, there is no detriment of any kind to the public interest or to the private interests of third parties. Compare a criminal conviction in the High Court: the Court of Appeal will overturn it decades later, if the prisoner comes up with new evidence that exposes the conviction as a miscarriage of justice. The fact that the conviction happened years ago does not generate any public interest in keeping the prisoner in prison. In this context, speedy certainty is just not an issue. The adminis-trative justice process by which O'Reilly was disciplined is similar to a criminal trial in this way: the public interest will not be damaged, if either process is challenged years after the events in question. There is simply no general need for the speedy cer-tainty of a three-month time limit on challenging administrative decisions.

> **Overly general assumptions about the public interest violate the principle of relativity (see p 10)**
>
> In *O'Reilly*, Lord Diplock said, 'The public interest in good administration requires that public authorities and third parties should not be kept in suspense as to the legal validity of a decision the authority has reached in purported exercise of decision-making powers for any longer period than is absolutely necessary in fair-ness to the person affected by the decision' (280–1). But that is true only in particu-lar contexts; and the contexts in which the public interest demands a three-month limit are few.

Even though speedy certainty is not needed in O'Reilly's particular situation, it *would be* necessary to apply the rule generally, if (1) it were impossible for courts to distin-guish justly between cases where speedy certainty is and is not needed, and (2) the need for speedy certainty were so great in *some* cases, that it would be fair to extend the rule to the cases in which it is not needed. But the courts can handle this distinc-tion. In fact, the Supreme Court Act 1981 presupposes it: the court may refuse to grant permission to proceed with a claim on the ground of delay *within* the three months' time limit, 'if it considers that the granting of the relief sought would be likely to

---

[15]   It would be an abuse of process to bring a proceeding after a delay that is prejudicial to the other party; it may seem that the delay in O'Reilly's case would be unfair to the prison authority because four years' delay might make it hard for the officials to substantiate their response to his claim. But that problem is partly met by the fact that O'Reilly would have the burden of prov-ing his case, and it can be completely met by the court's discretion over remedies.

cause substantial hardship to, or substantially prejudice the rights of, any person or would be detrimental to good administration' (s 31(6)).

The final possible argument for refusing O'Reilly's action is that the court should not turn the time limit into a dead letter even if it is over-general (especially since the Supreme Court Act 1981 gave it statutory force). But note that before 1978, the courts had allowed plaintiffs to evade the more generous six-month time limit on applications for prerogative orders, by bringing a claim for a declaration. And Parliament's purpose in the Supreme Court Act was only to give effect to a scheme that had been worked out as a reform of the court's own rules.

If you think three months is short...

The European Court of Justice has a wide jurisdiction to review the legality of many acts of the institutions of the EU (see p 293), but proceedings must 'be instituted within two months of the publication of the measure, or of its notification to the plaintiff, or, in the absence thereof, of the day on which it came to the knowledge of the latter, as the case may be' (EC Treaty Art 230).

Exceptions and 'exceptions'

General rules may allow exceptions; rules that are *overly* general cry out for exceptions. Lord Diplock said that 'There may be exceptions, particularly where the invalidity of the decision arises as a collateral issue in a claim for infringement of a right of the plaintiff arising under private law' (285). And the courts immediately started crafting exceptions, because the three-month time limit makes Lord Diplock's general rule harsh.

One important exception is that you can wait for legal proceedings to be taken against you, and then argue in your defence that a public authority's decision was unlawful. The defence is called a **'collateral'** (i.e., indirect) **challenge** to the public authority's decision. Arguments that the defendant ought to have brought a direct challenge to the decision by judicial review have consistently failed. So it is not an abuse of process for a tenant to argue that a public authority's rent increase was unlawful, in defence to an action for the rent, even if he could have challenged it by an application for judicial review (*Wandsworth LBC v Winder* [1985] AC 461). And the validity of a public authority's decision can be challenged in a defence to a criminal prosecution (*Boddington v British Transport Police* [1999] 2 AC 143 (HL)) or a civil claim by a private party (*Dwr Cymru Cyfyndgedig v Corus UK Ltd* [2006] EWHC 1183). And European Convention arguments, which could be made in a claim for judicial review, can be used as a defence to a landlord's proceedings for possession of property (*Kay v Lambeth LBC* [2006] UKHL 10 [30]). It is unfair to expect potential defendants to take on the burden of litigating the validity of a decision. That is why the rule about defences is an exception to Lord Diplock's rule.[16]

---

[16]   There is a similar exception in European Community law: after the two-month time limit for challenging the legality of a Community act has passed, a person may still argue that a

> ### What is an exception?
> If a rule does not apply in a class of cases, that class represents an exception to the
> rule if the rule *would* apply except for a special reason for not applying it in those
> particular circumstances; if the special reason is not compatible with the ration-
> ale for the rule itself, then the rule is, to some extent, undermined. The old saying
> that 'the exception proves the rule' is a confusing way of saying that you can tell
> that people are following a rule if they depart from its general requirements only
> when there are special considerations that are compatible with the rationale for
> the rule.

But in the ensuing line of decisions, the House of Lords crafted 'exceptions' that put
the rule itself in question. It has come to be established that **any claim with a private
law element** can be litigated in an action, even where the validity of the public authority's decision was not *collateral* to a claim of right in private law, but actually *determined
the extent* of the claimant's private law rights.

In *Roy v Kensington & Chelsea FPC* [1992] 1 AC 624, a health authority had reduced a
doctor's pay by 20% because he had been away from his NHS practice for one-third to
one-half of each year; the NHS regulations required him to be paid the regular salary
as long as he was 'devoting a substantial amount of time to general practice under the
National Health Service' (631). Dr Roy wanted to argue that the regulation had been
misapplied, and his pay improperly reduced. He could undoubtedly have challenged
the decision in an application for judicial review; instead, he brought an action (long
after the three-month limit for applications for judicial review). The House of Lords
allowed his action to proceed. Lord Lowry insisted that *Roy's* case was different from
O'Reilly's, because *Roy* had 'individual private law rights against the committee, arising from the statute and regulations and including the very important private law
right to be paid for the work that he has done' (649–50). Lord Bridge said it didn't
matter if the claim 'may incidentally involve the examination of a public law issue'
(628). But the public law issue in *Roy* was not incidental (or collateral). The public law
issue determined his private law entitlement to salary. It is true that Roy could bring
an ordinary action, without asserting any proposition of public law, if the NHS had
simply refused to pay his salary. But that would be irrelevant to Lord Diplock's rule
in *O'Reilly*: in order to make his argument, Roy had to assert that the decision of the
committee was unlawful. His reasons for arguing that it was unlawful were grounds
of judicial review. Roy was doing just what Lord Diplock said was an abuse of process:
in an ordinary action, he was 'seeking to establish that a decision of a public authority infringed rights to which he was entitled to protection under public law' (285).

Lord Lowry said in *Roy* that he preferred a 'broad approach' to *O'Reilly*, in which
Lord Diplock's rule did not even apply to cases that involved private rights. But he said
that he was 'content for the purpose of this appeal to adopt the narrow approach', on

---

regulation is unlawful 'in order to invoke before the Court of Justice the inapplicability of that
regulation' (EC Treaty Art 230).

which Lord Diplock's rule had exceptions in some cases 'when private rights were involved' (653).

So *Roy* set a course toward restricting the effect of *O'Reilly*, but left it unclear whether there were to be substantial (and unspecified) exceptions to the rule, or whether the rule itself was being confined to cases like O'Reilly's, in which the claimant has no relation with the public authority in private law. In *Mercury Communications v Director General of Telecommunications* [1996] 1 WLR 48, the House of Lords continued to characterize the restrictions as exceptions, and yet, in effect, abandoned the general rule against ordinary actions being used to get 'protection under public law' for the plaintiff's rights. Mercury needed to use British Telecom's telephone lines to provide long-distance services. The defendant public authority regulated Mercury's dealings with BT; Mercury challenged its determination as to how much Mercury had to pay BT. Mercury was not defending any private law right against the regulator, but the House of Lords allowed the action to proceed because it affected Mercury's contract with BT. Lord Slynn pointed out that there were exceptions to Lord Diplock's rule, and said that flexibility was essential because 'the precise limits of what is called "public law" and what is called "private law" are by no means worked out' (57). That statement is true, but it is irrelevant to the application of Lord Diplock's rule. There was no problem of the limits between public law and private law in *Mercury*: the public law issue (whether the public authority had set Mercury's charges lawfully) determined Mercury's rights in private law against BT. As in *Roy*, the public law issue was not collateral to a claim in private law. The important effect of the decision in *Mercury* lay in Lord Slynn's conclusion that 'It has to be borne in mind that the overriding question is whether the proceedings constitute an abuse of the process of the court' (57). *O'Reilly* held that ordinary actions seeking 'protection under public law' for the plaintiff's rights *were* an abuse of process unless there was some exceptional reason for allowing it. If the question of abuse is itself 'overriding', then the courts are no longer using Lord Diplock's rule to decide it.[17]

Does the flexible approach change the rule in *O'Reilly*? While emphasizing the fact that Lord Diplock's rule was only a *general* rule, Lord Slynn's speech in *Mercury* suggests an unwillingness to treat it as a rule at all. If ordinary claims seeking the protections of public law are not exceptional, then Lord Diplock's rule is no longer in effect. The rule has been distinguished away.

How to distinguish a precedent

Cases on relevantly similar facts are to be decided in the same way as previous cases, and a court that is bound by precedent (such as the High Court) is bound to treat the *ratio* of a decision as a reason for reaching the same decision on the same facts in a future case. The *ratio* is the reasoning that the court gives for its conclusion. If the facts of a new case are relevantly different from an earlier case, and if

---

17   Lord Slynn reiterated the flexible approach in *Steed v Home Secretary* [2000] 1 WLR 1169 (HL), still citing Lord Diplock's general rule, and treating his flexible approach as an approach to *exceptions*.

the *ratio* in the earlier case does not apply, then the earlier decision does not apply. In that situation, the earlier case *doesn't need* to be distinguished; it is not a precedent for a decision either way in the later case (though lawyers and judges often talk of 'distinguishing' an earlier case as if 'distinguishing' meant 'explaining why the earlier case is irrelevant').

If the facts of the new case are the same, then the earlier case cannot be distinguished.[18] If the facts of the new case are relevantly different, but the *ratio* (i.e., the court's reasoning) in the earlier case applies to the new case, then the later court **can distinguish** the earlier decision. The later court does this by deciding that the difference in the facts justifies restricting the *ratio* of the earlier case so that it still applies to the earlier case, but is inapplicable to the new case.

Roy is a textbook case of distinguishing: Lord Diplock's general rule applied to the facts in *Roy*, but the House of Lords restricted the rule (by excluding cases in which the claimant argues that a private law right was defeated by an unlawful decision of a public authority). That **did not overrule** *O'Reilly*, since the ruling in *Roy* is consistent with the result in *O'Reilly* (and, incidentally, the difference in result is supported by Lord Diplock's statement that exceptions were to be developed case-by-case). *Mercury* distinguished *O'Reilly* more fundamentally, by departing from Lord Diplock's ruling that there was a general rule against seeking the protection of public law in an ordinary action.

Yet even if the House of Lords has now overturned the general rule on which *O'Reilly* was decided, the decision in *O'Reilly* has still not been overruled, since Lord Slynn's ruling in *Mercury* is consistent with the outcome in *O'Reilly*. The decision in *O'Reilly* will only be overruled, if the House of Lords expressly overrules it, or implicitly overrules it by deciding a case with the same facts differently from *O'Reilly*.

What is the effect of the 21st-century Civil Procedure Rules on these developments? Lord Woolf, who led the reforms, has supported Lord Diplock's idea that public authorities generally need the protection of the time limit (*Dennis Rye Pension Fund Trustees v Sheffield City Council* [1998] 1 WLR 840, 848).[19] Yet he has also diverged from the rule in *O'Reilly* in a more far-reaching way than Lord Slynn did. In *Dennis Rye*, he said, 'If the choice [of proceeding] has no significant disadvantage for the parties, the public or the court, then it should not normally be regarded as constituting an abuse.' (849) That view does not merely adopt Lord Slynn's 'flexible' approach; it is a rejection of Lord Diplock's general rule. According to Lord Woolf, abuse of process is the exception that only applies if particular circumstances exist.

But the most radical departure from the rule in *O'Reilly* to date was in another Lord Woolf decision, *Clark v University of Lincolnshire & Humberside* [2000] 1 WLR 1988. A student brought an action for breach of contract against her University on grounds

[18]   It can be overruled by a higher court.

[19]   See 'Public Law–Private Law: Why the Divide? A Personal View' [1986] PL 220.

that could have been pursued in an application for judicial review. The University decided that she could not receive a higher result than a Third in her degree, as a penalty for plagiarism; she claimed that the University breached its own regulations in making the decision [9]. The Court of Appeal rejected the University's application to strike out her claim. Following *Roy* would have been enough to decide the case;[20] like Dr Roy, Joanne Clark had a contract with the public authority. But Lord Justice Sedley and Lord Justice Woolf MR changed the law in a way that took Lord Slynn's flexible approach substantially further. They focused squarely on the crucial issue of the time limit, acknowledging that the ability to bring an action rather than an application for judicial review would enable a claimant to evade the judicial review time limit. But they held that the new Civil Procedure Rules allowed the court to prevent exploitation of the procedures 'without resorting to a rigid exclusionary rule capable of doing equal and opposite injustice' (Lord Justice Sedley [17]). Lord Woolf insisted that the new Part 24 of the CPR enabled the court to take delay into account in giving summary judgment in an ordinary claim, so that if a claimant brought an ordinary action after an 'unjustified delay' [35], the court could strike it out. The effect is that there is no general rule that an action after the three-month time limit for an application for judicial review is an abuse of process if the claimant is seeking the protection of public law. Like Lord Slynn in *Mercury*, the Court of Appeal in *Clark* decided that it is an open question whether it is an abuse of process to bring an ordinary claim after the time limit for judicial review has expired—at least, where the claimant has a contract with the public authority [38]. More clearly than Lord Slynn had done, they held that no general rule governs the issue.

The importance of the Civil Procedure Rules in *Clark* is that they seemed to offer the Court of Appeal a legal basis for departing from the effect of the House of Lords ruling in *O'Reilly*. 'The emphasis can therefore be said to have changed since *O'Reilly v Mackman*', Lord Justice Woolf said: the question now is whether allowing an ordinary claim would be 'inconsistent with the proceedings being able to be conducted justly in accordance with the general principles contained in Part 1' of the Civil Procedure Rules. Those principles are 'central to determining what is due process' [39]. The basic principle is 'the overriding objective of enabling the court to deal with cases justly' (CPR 1.1(1)) and, crucially, at the centre of Part 1 is the principle of proportionate process. That is just the principle that was missing in *O'Reilly*.

But the courts were already equipped to take delay into account in applications to strike out claims before the new Civil Procedure Rules, as Lord Justice Woolf pointed out [33]. So the courts in the 1980s had every opportunity to give effect to proportionality. *O'Reilly* was implicitly based on a judgment that proportionality did not demand a hearing in that type of case. If Lord Diplock's general 'speedy certainty' argument were sound in 1983, it would be sound in the 21st century, even after the Civil Procedure Rules. The Court of Appeal would still have to follow *O'Reilly* today, in a case with the same facts. The *Clark* case is distinguishable from *O'Reilly* in the same

---

20   As Lord Justice Sedley shows at [16].

way as *Roy*, because a contract was involved. The rule in *O'Reilly* has been abandoned, but the decision has not been overruled.

After *Roy*, *Mercury*, and *Clark*, the law on the availability of ordinary claims is fairly relaxed. The spate of House of Lords' cases on the choice of proceeding has abated. Yet the law is topsy-turvy. In a case like *Roy*, delay really does create administrative problems: the availability of an ordinary claim leaves the public authority uncertain as to its budget for years, because it cannot know whether its administrative decision will be challenged.[21] In a case like *Winder*, a defence that a public law decision was invalid will 'affect many third parties', and upset 'the basis of [the public authority's] financial administration' *Wandsworth LBC v Winder* [1985] AC 461, 509 (Lord Fraser). In a case like *Mercury*, the availability of an ordinary claim leaves third parties unable to rely on the administrative decision for years. In all such cases, an ordinary claim is available even though speedy certainty would be valuable.[22]

Yet, in a case like *O'Reilly*, where there is no need for speedy certainty (either in the public interest, or for the good of third parties), the law still forbids an ordinary claim (because no private law right was affected by the decision in that case[23]).

So the House of Lords ought to overrule itself, if a case arises that is on all fours with *O'Reilly*. It would be unjust to send the claimant away without hearing his complaint of breach of procedural unfairness, because (1) hearing his complaint in a claim for a declaration would not damage the administration of the prison, and (2) the courts are able to distinguish between ordinary claims after the expiry of the time limit that would damage the administration, and claims that would not. The flexible approach is fundamentally inconsistent with the decision in *O'Reilly* itself. Because the flexible approach is a good approach, the House of Lords should overrule *O'Reilly*, and not merely distinguish it.

A proposal

It would be best to amend the Supreme Court Act to provide that if a claim depends on the unlawfulness of the action of a public authority, it will be heard in the Administrative Court, and that the Administrative Court will proceed by the judicial review procedure under CPR Part 54, unless the Court orders a trial.

Then the only serious problem is the time limit; as a general limit, a return from three to six months would not damage public administration. To solve O'Reilly's problem, the courts already have the appropriate power under CPR 3.1(2) (a) to 'extend or shorten the time for compliance with any rule, practice direction or

---

[21] This problem does *not* mean that the claimant should not be able to proceed by an ordinary claim in a case like *Roy*: that depends on whether the damage to the public interest is so great that it would be fair to refuse to listen to Dr Roy after three months.

[22] Note, too, that the public interest or the interests of third parties may be damaged by the delay involved in ordinary claims in tort or contract that do not raise any question of the public law powers of a public authority, e.g., contracts of sale between public authorities and stationery suppliers (see section 15.3). Those claims are available without any special protection for the public authority.

[23] O'Reilly had no private right to liberty, because he was in the middle of a prison sentence.

court order (even if an application for extension is made after the time for compliance has expired)'. But the law needs to change, to make it clear that judges can allow a claim for judicial review to proceed, even after the time limit, where there is no material public or private interest in speedy certainty as to the validity of a public authority's decision. In such a case, the claimant would still need permission. Claimants would no longer try to bring an ordinary claim to get around the time limit; the court could make the decision as to whether there should be a trial without reference to the time limit, on the grounds that actually matter (i.e., whether a trial is the best way to resolve the issues in dispute).

This reform could be accomplished by amendment of the Supreme Court Act and Part 54 of the Civil Procedure Rules, or by the judges themselves through use of 'the overriding objective of enabling the court to deal with cases justly' (CPR 1.1(1)). But the Civil Procedure Rules can only be used in that way if the House of Lords overrules its decision in O'Reilly (because the rule that it is an abuse of process to allow a claimant in O'Reilly's position to proceed must be rejected before the courts can use CPR 1.1(1)).

Time limits could be provided by legislation (as they have been in many areas) in contexts where Parliament decides not to leave it to the Administrative Court to decide whether speedy certainty is needed.

Note that:
(1) We would still need different forms of proceeding (because summary process is reasonable for some disputes, while a trial is needed for others).
(2) We would still need to distinguish public law proceedings (because of the problem of which defendants ought to be subject to judicial supervision, for which sorts of decisions—see p 585).

10.3 Summary process in judicial review

A claim for judicial review is something out of the ordinary: the court decides the dispute without a trial. The point of a trial in an ordinary claim is to resolve the issues of fact on which a claim is based. The summary process in a claim for judicial review is designed on the assumption that resolving issues of fact is not the point of the litigation. The point is for the court to review the lawfulness of a public authority's conduct, and while the issue of lawfulness is likely to be very controversial, there is often no dispute as to what the public authority has done or proposes to do.

The facts that do need to be put before the court are asserted in sworn witness statements ('affidavits') by the claimant and representatives of the public authority; the court can order cross-examination on the affidavits, but it is unusual. It needs to be ordered, though, if there is contentious evidence on which the court needs to pass judgment in order to decide the claim. In R (Wilkinson) v Broadmoor Special Hospital Authority [2001] EWCA Civ 1545, a patient detained in a secure hospital challenged his doctors' decision to give him anti-psychotic medication against his will (see p 267).

The Court of Appeal ordered that the doctors should be cross-examined. Since their evidence was contested, and the judges decided that they needed to pass judgment on the issues that the affidavits addressed, it became obvious that cross-examination should be ordered. This follows from the often-unstated principle of our adversary system of litigation: that the court should act only on evidence presented by a party, and only after giving the other party an opportunity to test it.

If a claim against a public authority involves a substantial dispute as to the facts, how should the court deal with it? One way is for the claim to proceed as a claim for judicial review, with cross-examination of the witnesses who swore the affidavits. And under CPR 8.6, the court can permit oral evidence at the hearing.

But another possibility is for the court to allow the claim to proceed as an ordinary claim. In *Dennis Rye*, Lord Woolf suggested that a claimant should be able to bring an ordinary claim, in spite of the rule in *O'Reilly*, if the facts are in dispute (850–1). The Administrative Court can transfer a claim for judicial review to the ordinary claim process, and vice versa (CPR 54.20, 30). So, if a claimant brings an ordinary claim against a public authority that could be dealt with summarily, the Court should require it to proceed as a claim for judicial review. And a claim for judicial review that requires a trial of the issues can be required to proceed as an ordinary claim.

10.3.1 Time

The **bad news** is that the general time limit of three months for a claim for judicial review (CPR 54.5(1)(b)) is short! The **other bad news** is that even within the three months, the claim must be brought 'promptly' (CPR 54.5(1)(a)), which means the court can refuse permission to bring a claim for judicial review on the ground of delay *within* the time limit. **And** even if permission is given, the court can later refuse the claim because of undue delay (Supreme Court Act 1981 s 31(6)).[24] But the claim can only be refused on that ground if it would damage the interests of third parties (*R v North West Leicestershire DC, ex p Moses* [2000] Env LR 443), or 'would be detrimental to good administration' (s 31(6)).[25]

The **good news** is that the Civil Procedure Rules give the Court an undefined discretion to extend the three-month time limit ('the court may extend or shorten the time for compliance with any rule' CPR 3.1(2)(a)).[26] But the courts will not extend the

---

[24] When this happens, it makes you wonder why the court ever gave permission in the first place. An example is *R (Corbett) v Restormel Borough Council* [2001] EWCA Civ 330 (relief denied at the judicial review hearing, partly because of the claimant's delay of three years). But this way of proceeding can be quite appropriate if the court cannot tell, at the permission stage, whether there is some good reason to listen to the claim in spite of the delay.

[25] Lord Goff sensibly decided that any delay beyond the three months in the Civil Procedure Rules counts as 'undue delay' for s 31(6): *R v Dairy Produce Quota Tribunal for England and Wales, ex p Caswell* [1990] 2 AC 738, 747 (HL). His speech explains the farcical legislative mix-ups by which two different and hard-to-reconcile delay provisions ended up in the rules of the Supreme Court (R S C, Ord 53, r 4) and the Supreme Court Act (s 31) (745–7).

[26] Note, though, that the time limit 'may not be extended by agreement between the parties'—an innovation in the 2000 reform to the Civil Procedure Rules (CPR 54.5(2)). But the consent of

time limit just because it is hard on the claimant. In R (M) v Oxford County Council [2001] EWHC Admin 245, a group of families asked for permission to seek judicial review, three months and one day after the Council decided to close Oxford's middle schools. Jackson J refused permission, following a line of cases taking 'the firm approach' [20], especially in challenges to school reorganization. The firm approach is justified if the claim for judicial review would interfere with a public project that needs to proceed quickly. As Lord Justice Schiemann put it, 'Applicants in these school cases must realise that it is important to give early warning as to what is going on so that people can endeavour to conclude matters soon, so that the whole education system in the city is not kept in suspense while legal proceedings drag on' (R v Leeds City Council, ex p N [1999] ELR 324, 334 (CA)). And under s 31(6) of the Supreme Court Act 1981, the court will not give parents permission to challenge allocation of secondary school places for their children unless the claim can be determined before the school year starts—even if that means seeking permission well before the three months' time limit runs out (R v Rochdale MBC, ex p B [2000] Ed CR 117 (QBD)).

Yet conversely, the House of Lords has sometimes been generous in deciding when the clock starts running, even in cases where there is a public interest in speed. In R (Burkett) v Hammersmith and Fulham London Borough Council [2002] UKHL 23, a local planning authority passed a resolution authorizing the grant of planning permission for a major development. Six months later, Mrs Burkett applied for leave to seek judicial review of that decision. The actual grant of planning permission was issued the month *after* she applied. The House of Lords gave permission for her to seek judicial review of the grant of planning permission.[27] CPR 54.5(1) provides that the three months start running when 'the grounds to make the claim first arose'. Mrs Burkett's claim challenged the resolution, and it seems obvious that the grounds for a challenge to a resolution arise when the resolution was made. That shows how generous the House of Lords is prepared to be toward the time limit. Lord Steyn said: '. . . the context is a rule of court which by operation of a time limit may deprive a citizen of the right to challenge an undoubted abuse of power. And such a challenge may involve not only individual rights but also community interests, as in environmental cases' [45].

So how do you square these varying tendencies to be firm and to be generous? They result from the judges' attempt to achieve proportionality in the exercise of their discretion over time limits. It seems that the really essential issue (both in counting the time, and in the discretion to allow a late application) is how to reconcile the need for speedy certainty—where there is one—with the reasons in favour of hearing the claim. Those reasons may include protecting private interests from an injustice, as well as protecting the public interest in the rule of law. So Laws J had a point, in R v Trade and Industry Secretary, ex p Greenpeace Limited [1998] Env LR 415, when he said that

---

the defendant would, no doubt, be relevant to the court's discretion to extend the time limit (CPR 3.1(2)).

[27] Sedley J had actually accomplished the same result five years earlier, in R v Somerset CC, ex p Dixon [1998] Env LR 111.

'the rule of law is not threatened, but strengthened' by 'a strict discipline' (424) in controlling judicial proceedings in a way that brings finality to administrative decision making. The rule of law can demand finality or judicial review, depending on the circumstances. This does not mean that the rule of law is incoherent; it does not demand both at once. It requires a reasonable opportunity for people affected by an unlawful decision to get the problem before an independent review. That is compatible with time limits, but not with an arbitrary requirement of speed. The requirement is arbitrary if there is no public interest in speed, and especially if there is a public interest in relaxing the requirement.

R v Home Secretary, ex p Ruddock [1987] 1 WLR 1482 also demonstrates this role of the public interest in dealing with the time limit discretion. Permission was given after the three months, even though Taylor J was 'unimpressed' by the reasons for the delay, because of the general importance of the issues (a claim that the Home Secretary was unlawfully tapping phones).[28]

The fact that the House of Lords sometimes adopts a generous approach does not mean that the courts will allow a late application whenever there would be no detriment to administration; for one thing, the courts will not be able to do that until they abandon the O'Reilly v Mackman idea that public authorities generally need speedy certainty. After the three months, the onus remains on the claimant to give special reasons why judicial review should proceed.

A floodgates argument that works!

Public authorities often argue that a claim should be rejected, to prevent a flood of similar claims. A floodgates argument may be (i) that the courts cannot cope with the flood, or (ii) that the potential defendants (or third parties) ought to be protected from the flood. Sometimes a floodgates argument is a bad argument because there will be no flood: the new liability may lead the potential defendants to change the behaviour that generates the claims. Even if there really will be a flood, a floodgates argument is ordinarily a bad argument. If the claims are just, the flood ought to flow. If the claims are frivolous or groundless, the floodgates problem only makes it more important to refuse claims that should be refused anyway.[29]

So floodgates arguments are typically bad arguments.[30] But here is a good one, which Lord Goff used in interpreting the phrase 'detrimental to good administration' in the Supreme Court Act 1981 s 31(6). In R v Dairy Produce Quota Tribunal for England

---

[28] See also R v Secretary of State for Foreign and Commonwealth Affairs, ex p World Development [1995] 1 WLR 386, 402.

[29] For an argument that standing should be used to prevent a flood of 'irresponsible applications' see R v IRC, ex p Federation of Self-Employed and Small Businesses Ltd [1982] AC 617, 630 (Lord Wilberforce).

[30] As, e.g., in R v Home Secretary, ex p Doody [1994] 1 AC 531 (HL) and R (Javed) v Home Secretary [2001] EWCA Civ 789, in which the courts brushed off the Home Secretary's argument that thousands of life prisoners and asylum seekers might bring claims if the courts imposed due process.

and Wales, ex p Caswell [1990] 2 AC 738 (HL), a group of farmers wanted to challenge the milk production quota that the tribunal had assigned them. The tribunal had to share out 'a finite amount of quota' among farmers, and the judge found on the leave application that allowing a claim 'would lead to re-opening the allocation of quota over a number of years'. So Lord Goff held that allowing the delayed claim would have a retrospective effect on a quota scheme that needed to operate pro-spectively, which would be detrimental to good administration (750).

Floodgates arguments are bad arguments, unless there is a serious process danger (see p 111).

In working out the requirements of proportionate process, the courts now have to consider whether the CPR and their own practice are compatible with the require-ments of the European Convention on Human Rights. In *Burkett*, Lord Steyn not only took a generous approach to counting the three months; he also questioned whether CPR 54.5(1)(a), requiring the claim to be brought 'promptly' even within the three months, is compatible with Article 6 of the Convention: 'there is at the very least

For:	The time limit is:
A claim for judicial review	—three months (*and even within that time, you must act promptly, but there is a discretion to extend the time for special reason*).
Ordinary claims for damages	—six years for most claims in tort and contract; three years for personal injury claims (Limitation Act 1980 ss 2, 5, 11).
A claim that a public authority has acted unlawfully under the Human Rights Act s 6	—one year, subject to an equitable jurisdiction to extend the time (Human Rights Act 1998 s 7(5)).
Complaints to an ombudsman	—12 months (*but the ombudsmen can decide to accept a late claim[31]*).
Statutory appeals	—it depends on the statute, e.g.: <ul><li>to appeal a refusal of Tax Credit, 30 days;[32]</li><li>to appeal from an Employment Tribunal to the Employment Appeals Tribunal: six weeks.[33]</li></ul>
Planning appeals against adverse planning permission decision	— six months.[34]

Figure 10.2 Time limits

---

[31] Parliamentary Commissioner for Administration Act 1967 s 6(3); Local Government Act 1974 s 26(4).

[32] Tax Credits Act 2002 s 39(1).

[33] Employment Appeals Tribunal Rules 1993 SI 1993/2854 (as amended) rule 3(3), created under Employment Tribunals Act 1996 s 30(2)(a).

[34] Town and Country Planning (General Development Procedure) (Amendment) (England) Order 2004 SI 2004/3340 s 2.

doubt whether the obligation to apply "promptly" is sufficiently certain to comply with…the Convention' [53]. It remains to be seen how the doubt will work out; the answer to it ought to be that the courts can deal with the uncertainty (as to some extent they have already), by developing a doctrine that within the three-month time limit, a claimant will be held to have proceeded promptly unless there is an urgent public or third-party interest in speed that ought to have been evident to the claimant.

● *Pop Quiz* ●

Is the three-month time limit on claims for judicial review compatible with the right to a fair hearing in Art 6 of the Convention?

10.3.2 Permission to proceed

The application for permission to proceed with a claim for judicial review is ordinarily made without a hearing. The claimant submits written evidence along with the claim form. But, in a small revolution in the Civil Procedure Rules in 2000, the permission procedure became *inter partes* rather than *ex parte*. That is, the defendant public authority is given notice of the application for permission, and may briefly outline its grounds for resisting the claim in its acknowledgement of service. A judge of the Administrative Court then decides whether to give permission on the basis of the papers (CPR PD 54.8.4). This provision creates a risk of arbitrary refusals of permission, because oral advocacy can show the seriousness of an application (if it is serious), and also serve to answer the judge's doubts about the proceeding. The only way the danger can be avoided is if the judges allow permission unless the papers themselves show a reason not to do so, that could not be countered by oral representations. The 'paper hearing' has survived a claim that it was *ultra vires* and incompatible with Art 6 and 8 of the Convention in R (Ewing) v Department for Constitutional Affairs [2006] EWHC 504. One reason is that the judge has a discretion to direct an oral hearing (CPR 54.12), and a claimant who is refused permission on the papers can ask for reconsideration in an oral hearing (CPR 54.12(3)). If there is an oral hearing, the defendant may (but need not) take part, as long as it filed an acknowledgement of service (CPR 54.9(1)(a)).

The decision on the papers was one of two 21st-century innovations designed to deal with a massive volume of applications for permission (the other being the 'Pre-Action Protocol'). The problem was caused by the fact that claimants pressed by the three-month deadline seek permission for judicial review before there is time to negotiate with the public authority. The majority of cases that receive permission are then settled before the judicial review hearing. Without a change to the deadline, it became necessary to streamline the permission process.

Push-me-pull-you

The courts are trying to encourage alternative dispute resolution, but the time limit damages the prospects! It forces claimants to start legal proceedings right

> away, rather than negotiating another way forward with the prospective defend-
> ant. The **Pre-Action Protocol for Judicial Review**[35] encourages the parties to use
> ombudsmen, mediation, and early neutral evaluation (see p 455), and states, 'The
> Courts take the view that litigation should be a last resort, and that claims should
> not be issued prematurely when a settlement is still actively being explored.' But
> the Protocol also warns that the action it requires for trying to resolve the dispute
> before seeking judicial review 'does not affect the time limit' for bringing a claim.
>
> In R v Hammersmith & Fulham London Borough Council, ex p Burkett [2002] UKHL 23,
> Lord Steyn agreed with Paul Craig's view that 'The short time limits may, in a para-
> doxical sense, increase the amount of litigation against the administration' [53].

The requirement of permission reflects the extraordinary process; no one needs permission to bring an ordinary claim, because an ordinary claim asserts a right to a
remedy. Since no one has a right to a prerogative remedy,[36] the centuries-old practice
of the courts was to allow proceedings for a prerogative writ to commence only after
a judge had decided to give permission. The reforms of the judicial review procedure
in 1978 and 2000 have sustained that ancient practice by giving the court discretion
to decide the test for permission. But the discretion is constrained: the court should
deny permission if it is evident from the papers that:

- undue delay in the application will cause undue detriment to administration;

- the claimant does not have a sufficient interest in the matter of the claim (Supreme
  Court Act 1981 s 31(3)); or

- an alternative remedy should have been pursued, instead of judicial review.

Each issue remains relevant at the hearing of the claim itself, where delay, lack of sufficient interest, or the existence of an alternative remedy may be grounds for denying
a remedy.

As for any further test for permission, there is not a peep in the Civil Procedure
Rules, which only say that 'The court's permission to proceed is required in a claim
for judicial review' (CPR 54.4). Lord Diplock said that the purpose of the requirement
of permission 'is to prevent the time of the court being wasted by busybodies with
misguided or trivial complaints of administrative error', and to remove uncertainty
(R v IRC, ex p Federation of Self-Employed and Small Businesses Ltd [1982] AC 617, 643). But
people who are not busybodies may still be wasting the court's time. The crucial
question seems to be whether the court can see, at the permission stage, that the proceedings are doomed to failure. So the most common way of describing the test for
permission is to say that the claimant must have an 'arguable case' (R v Home Secretary,
ex p Swati [1986] 1 WLR 477: 'an applicant must show more than that it is not impossible that grounds for judicial review exist.... he must at least show that it is a real, as

---

[35] http://www.justice.gov.uk/civil/procrules_fin/contents/protocols/prot_jrv.htm.

[36] With the exception of habeas corpus; see p 5.

opposed to a theoretical, possibility. In other words, he must have an arguable case'
Sir John Donaldson MR, 485).

Perhaps the best way for the Administrative Court to use this flexible power is to
apply the same test that the High Court applies in an ordinary claim, when a defendant applies to have the claim struck out. In that situation, the Court assumes that all
the facts in the claim will be proved (this has to be assumed, since there has been no
trial); then on that assumption, the Court decides whether the claimant would have
a case.

That is *almost* right (and note that the House of Lords has emphasized that the
power to strike out a claim should be used sparingly[37]). But the Administrative Court
needs to apply the test with a painful awareness of how limited its resources are in
the permission application. Unless the judge directs an oral hearing, he or she will
not have the benefit of argument from each side (a striking-out application in an
ordinary claim, by contrast, involves legal argument from both parties). The defendant's acknowledgement of service will give the court a 'summary' of the defendant's
grounds for contesting the claim (CPR 54.8(4)), but the claimant won't have had an
opportunity to respond to those grounds, and the summary itself may be misleading
when the court deals with it on paper without argument. So it seems that permission should not be denied merely on the ground that the judge thinks it will most
likely fail. The judge should allow the claim to proceed to judicial review, rather
than refusing permission on speculation. But there is a third alternative: the court
can require an oral hearing between the parties just on the question of permission
(*R v Home Secretary, ex p Rukshanda Begum* [1990] Imm AR 1). In the early 1990s, Lord
Donaldson MR decided that it is only when there is clearly an arguable case that leave
should be granted on the papers (*R v Legal Aid Board, ex p Hughes* (1992) 24 HLR 698).
But if it is unclear *whether* there is an arguable case, oral argument should be heard
from both sides. Lord Donaldson's approach is proportionate, because it allows an
oral hearing on permission where it would actually be useful. But it is important to
remember that even after an oral hearing on the issue of permission, it may remain
unclear whether there is any prospect of success if permission is granted. Then the
only appropriate course is to give permission.

The permission process is flexible in another way: where a claim ought to proceed, the judge needn't give the claimant permission to pursue all of it. The courts'
new case management role under the CPR has encouraged them to do something they
already had the discretion to do: to give permission only on a tightly defined issue
(a good example is *R (Thompson) v Law Society* [2004] EWCA Civ 167). Since diligent
counsel with a good case may put in all sorts of arguments that are only potentially
attractive, this technique is an important control on the judicial review hearing itself.
It does something to achieve **proportionate process**, by giving the claimant a hearing

---

[37]   As Lord Browne-Wilkinson said in *X v Bedfordshire County Council* [1995] 2 AC 633, 740–1: 'if, on
the facts alleged in the statement of claim, it is not possible to give a certain answer whether in
law the claim is maintainable then it is not appropriate to strike out the claim at a preliminary
stage but the matter must go to trial when the relevant facts will be discovered.' See p 520.

in judicial review only on points that justify a hearing. But the courts are liable to find (as in the *Thompson* case) that counsel keep on trying to press other avenues, once they have their foot in the door.

Permission should only be denied outright if the papers disclose that the case is *unarguable*, since the point is to prevent pointless litigation, and not to demand that the claimant make the argument at the permission stage.

A barrier to justice?

Substantially fewer than half of the claimants who apply for permission actually proceed to a judicial review hearing.[38] Many of them withdraw their claims for a variety of reasons; but a substantial proportion (perhaps 30%) of applications are refused permission to proceed.[39] That starts to sound as if the courts are seriously restricting access to judicial review, rather than preventing abuse of process by busybodies. Yet we could not pass judgment on whether that proportion is too high, without assessing each of the cases to see whether 30% of applications are pointless. That is not as implausible as it may sound. Reasonable people often seek permission for claims that are in fact doomed, because (1) the three-month time limit forces some people to seek permission in a hurry, and (2) the very existence of the permission process encourages people to seek permission for judicial review as part of negotiations with a public authority, and (3) even doomed litigation can generate very gratifying publicity in a campaign against the government.

So it is not easy to generalize about how strict the judges are at the permission stage. As for the approach they ought to take, the judges' duty at the permission stage is only to prevent pointless proceedings, and *not* to try to decide whether the claimant ought to succeed. That is a matter for the hearing of the claim. If the court refuses permission when it is not possible to determine justly that the proceedings are pointless, it abdicates its responsibility for the rule of law.

And believe it or not, the courts sometimes grant permission where they consider the claim to be of great public interest, *even where the claimant has no arguable case*. In *CND v Prime Minister* [2002] EWHC 2777, the Administrative Court gave permission for the Campaign for Nuclear Disarmament to make a claim that the court simultaneously held to be non-justiciable and therefore, categorically unarguable: that the Prime Minister would be violating international law if he ordered the invasion of Iraq without waiting for a specific UN resolution authorizing it (see [47], [49]). And in *R (Gentle) v Prime Minister* [2006] EWCA Civ 1078, the Court of Appeal gave permission to seek judicial review of the Government's refusal to hold an independent public inquiry into the circumstances leading up to the Iraq war. The Court did not find an arguable case that the refusal was unlawful, but only that 'if it is otherwise appropriate to hold an inquiry, it is at least arguable that the question whether the invasion was lawful (or

---

[38] http://www.judiciary.gov.uk/keyfacts/statistics/index.htm.

[39] L Bridges, G Meszaros, M Sunkin, 'Regulating the Judicial Review Caseload' [2000] PL 651, 668.

reasonably thought to have been lawful) as a matter of international law is worthy of investigation' [15]. So the Court allowed judicial review to proceed 'not on the basis that we have concluded that the application for judicial review has a real prospect of success ... but on the basis that because of the importance of the issues and the uncertainty of the present position there is a compelling reason' [22] to hold a full hearing of the claim for judicial review. Other important examples of doomed claims that were permitted to proceed are the *Abbasi* case (see p 4), and *R v Foreign Secretary, ex p Rees-Mogg* [1994] QB 552 (see p 406).

In such cases the grant of permission sometimes amounts to a symbolic gesture of openness, because the court is able to dismiss the substantive claim for judicial review at the same time that it grants permission, without further procedural steps. But sometimes, as in *Gentle*, it leads to a fuller hearing and a media victory for opponents of government policy who have no case.

Permission to appeal

The Administrative Court can give permission to appeal to the Court of Appeal; if it is refused, the claimant can ask the Court of Appeal for permission (both decisions are discretionary). If there is no prospect of success in an appeal, the general importance of the issues may not in itself justify an appeal, even if permission for judicial review was granted. Simon Brown LJ refused permission in the CND case, saying, 'there comes a point in litigation when however momentous the issues raised, it cannot sensibly be permitted to continue'. But in *Gentle*, the Court of Appeal reached the opposite conclusion, and granted leave to appeal for the same reason (a public interest in a full hearing) as the reason for giving permission for judicial review.

Even where the court refuses permission, it is often done with long argument and deliberation by the judges, which allows the claimant to benefit from the publicity and notoriety they get by taking the government to court. That is what happened when the editor of the *Guardian* brought a doomed claim for a declaration that the Attorney General should promise not to prosecute him under the Treason Act 1848 for advocating republicanism (*R v Attorney-General, ex p Rusbridger* [2003] UKHL 38). It was 'unnecessary litigation ... commenced in order to obtain obvious results' (Lord Scott [47]), and permission was refused, but it got the Guardian a hearing all the way to the House of Lords, on the issue of permission. It is a classic case of the **irony of process** (see p 143) at work: *just on the issue of permission*, the courts had to give Rusbridger a complex set of hearings that was out of all proportion to his complaint. It had to be done in order to sustain a system capable of giving litigants a fair hearing.

Costs warning!

One damper on speculative applications for permission is that a successful defendant can ask the court to order the would-be claimant to pay part of its legal costs— not only after judicial review, but also **after a failed application for permission**

> (R (Mount Cook Land Ltd) v Westminster City Council [2004] 2 P&CR 405). The practice
> of ordering costs has developed since the permission stage became *inter partes* in
> the 2000 reform. If there is an oral hearing as to permission, the costs can be sub-
> stantial. According to the Court of Appeal, the doctrine 'must not be applied in a
> way which seriously impedes the right of citizens to access to justice, particularly
> when seeking to protect their environment' (R (Ewing) v Office of the Deputy Prime
> Minister [2005] EWCA Civ 1583 [41]). So costs awards on failed applications for per-
> mission are modest; as Collins J said in R (Gentle) v Prime Minister [2005] EWHC 3119,
> 'This may seem thoroughly unfair to the public body which is on the receiving end
> of a claim', but it is 'a price that must be paid to ensure that there is no unreason-
> able fetter on the right to come to court and seek redress for a supposed breach of
> rights, or an unlawful decision made, or an unlawful administrative action taken,
> against an individual' [108].
>
> The Court of Appeal has expressed particular concern that the government
> should find a way of funding environmental litigation, which can be deterred by
> the costs regime (R (Burkett) v Hammersmith and Fulham LBC (Costs) [2004] EWCA Civ
> 1342). On the role of costs in public interest litigation, see p 413.

10.3.3 Vexatious claims

The Supreme Court Act 1981 provides a process for the 'restriction of vexatious
legal proceedings' (s 42). The point is that the court's powers to strike out vexatious
claims, and even the requirement of permission in judicial review, are not enough to
prevent some claimants from harassing defendants with pointless claims. One vexatious litigant, Terence Ewing, has pushed the courts to elaborate the law. The power
is not only used to protect private defendants from harassment; the court can use it
to prevent a claimant from making ordinary claims against public authorities, and
from seeking judicial review (Re Ewing (No 2) [1994] 1 WLR 1553 (CA)). The Attorney
General can apply to the High Court for a 'civil proceedings order' against a person
who has brought vexatious proceedings (Bhamjee v Forsdick [2003] EWCA Civ 1113). An
order prevents a claimant from starting a claim without permission from the High
Court (and an application for permission to seek judicial review is a 'proceeding' for
that purpose: Ex p Ewing [1991] 1 WLR 388).

This process might seem to have no real effect in judicial review, since a claim
for judicial review cannot be commenced without permission in any case. So Lord
Donaldson held that if a vexatious litigant wants to seek judicial review, a judge who
thinks permission should be granted for judicial review 'will of course have no difficulty in deciding' that the claimant should be allowed to proceed in spite of the civil
proceedings order (Ex p Ewing, 393).

But Mr Ewing kept at it, and in this century the Court of Appeal decided that the
two kinds of permission might be 'staged' (R (Ewing and another) v Office of the Deputy
Prime Minister [2005] EWCA Civ 1583 [35]). The suggestion is that there might be cases
in which the vexatious litigant has to give two different grounds for permission (one
ground for permission to bring proceedings at all, and another for permission to

seek judicial review). Moreover, the Court of Appeal suggested that a vexatious litigant has a *special* problem with standing: 'The section 42 permission procedure is designed to ensure that a vexatious litigant is not denied his right of access to the court to pursue his own genuine legal grievances, not to set himself up as a public champion' [37] (Carnwath LJ).

10.4 Judicial remedies

The court's powers in judicial review proceedings are extremely flexible. From the 12th to the 20th centuries, claimants went to court seeking a particular remedy, and there were different forms of proceeding for different remedies. For all its foibles, the 1978 reform nicely harmonized the procedures for different remedies. Declarations and injunctions and (most importantly) damages were added to the judicial review toolkit, and it no longer matters which remedy the claimant seeks. It used to be possible for a claimant lose as a result of seeking the wrong remedy.[40] Now, instead of bringing proceedings for a particular remedy, a claimant simply brings judicial review proceedings, and the remedies for unlawful administrative action can be worked out as the court sees fit. And as a result, there is a good deal of redundancy: the judges' toolkit is full of devices that can be used together or interchangeably. Some of them are very, very old, and very useful.

10.4.1 Prerogative remedies

The naming of prerogative remedies

Until 2004, a **quashing order** was called an **order of *certiorari***, a **mandatory order** was called an **order of *mandamus***, a **prohibiting order** was called an **order of prohibition**.[41] Until 1938, they were all called **'prerogative writs'**.[42] But *habeas corpus* is still a writ.[43]

The double importance of the prerogative origins of the ancient common law writs is (1) that the **process** for seeking them has always been by summary application rather than the ordinary trial process, and (2) that they are issued in the **discretion** of the

---

[40]   E.g. *Re HK (an infant)* [1967] 2 WLR 962: the administrative decision was fairly made, so it couldn't be unwound by *certiorari* or *habeas corpus*; *mandamus* might have worked to make the officer consider new information, but it was not given, because the applicant hadn't sought it.

[41]   Civil Procedure (Modification of Supreme Court Act 1981) Order 2004 SI 2004/1033 Art 3.

[42]   The Administration of Justice Act 1938 s 7 abolished the prerogative writs of *mandamus*, prohibition, and *certiorari* (which the courts had developed at common law), and replaced them with 'orders' of the same names. The point was to signal a simplification in procedure, and *habeas corpus* was left untouched for symbolic reasons.

[43]   See Rules of the Supreme Court Order 54, which is in the Civil Procedure Rules Sch 1 (not to be confused with the Civil Procedure Rules Part 54, which governs all claims for judicial review other than a claim for a writ of *habeas corpus*).

Crown (a discretion that the judges exercise for the Crown), as an instance of the Queen's prerogative to hold her officials to account. The orders have a statutory basis now under the Supreme Court Act 1981, but the same discretion remains under the Act and the Civil Procedure Rules.

FROM THE MISTS OF TIME

Although the prerogative features of the writs were ancient, it seems that the first time they were grouped together and called 'prerogative' was in R v Cowle (1759) 2 Burr 834, 855–6; Lord Mansfield called *mandamus*, prohibition, *habeas corpus*, and *certiorari* 'Writs not ministerially directed', because they were not automatically issued by the court office at the request of a claimant to commence proceedings. He said that they were 'sometimes called prerogative writs, because they are supposed to issue on the part of the King'. Lord Mansfield was a royalist judge who wanted to emphasize the King's prerogative to do justice according to law by bringing complaints of unlawful administration before his Court of King's Bench.

At common law,[44] the prerogative remedies largely developed as techniques by which the judges could control the jurisdiction of **inferior courts** (courts of specific jurisdiction). **Prohibition** stopped a public authority from doing something unlawful—traditionally, it was a way of stopping proceedings in progress before lower courts that were acting outside their limited jurisdiction.[45]

Certiorari also started as a way of controlling courts of specific jurisdiction after they had made a decision. It was actually a direction to a public authority to bring the record of its decision to the court (i.e., to certify its record); the judges would then decide whether to quash the decision (see, e.g., Ex p Stott [1916] 1 KB 7). But it was natural to translate the name as 'quashing order' in the Civil Procedure Rules, because 'certiorari' had come to be used as a term for the whole business of ordering a decision to be brought up to the court and then quashing it. A **mandamus** required a public authority to use a legal power in a particular way; it was generally harder to get than *certiorari* (and the procedure was more difficult for the claimant), because the court had to decide that the law gave the public authority no choice but to act in the required fashion. *Certiorari* only quashed a decision; by *mandamus* the court actually told the public authority what to do (though it was often simply an order to a lower court to carry out its legal duty to hear a matter). In R v Barker (1762) 3 Burr 1265, 1267 (see p 346), Lord Mansfield said that *mandamus* 'was introduced, to prevent disorder

---

44   But the prerogative writs were also available under the equitable jurisdiction of the Court of Chancery.

45   E.g., R v Horseferry Road Justices, ex p Independent Broadcasting Authority [1987] QB 54. It was not until R v Greater London Council, ex p Blackburn [1976] 1 WLR 550 that it became clear that the order was not restricted to judicial tribunals deciding people's rights: Lord Denning said, 'the prerogative writ of prohibition has, in the past, usually been exercised so as to prohibit judicial tribunals from exceeding their jurisdiction. But just as the scope of certiorari has been extended to administrative authorities, so also with prohibition. It is available to prohibit administrative authorities from exceeding their powers, or misusing them' (559).

from a failure of justice, and defect of police.' By 'police', he meant, roughly, public policy. Lord Mansfield viewed it as a potentially wide-ranging remedy that ought to be issued where justice and good government required it, 'from analogy and the reason of the thing' (1267).

10.4.2 Declarations

A declaration states the law on the issues in dispute. A claimant with no entitlement to any other remedy can ask the court simply to say that an action of a public authority was (or would be) unlawful. It is unlike a mere statement of the law given in reasons for judgment, because it *is* a judgment. So a declaration puts an end to the proceedings; and conversely if the claimant is unsuccessful, the court will dismiss the claim and issue no declaration.

A declaration is not exactly a remedy (it is often described as 'relief' rather than as a remedy). It does not order the public authority to do this or that. Yet it changes the legal position, by making it impossible for the defendant to dispute the claimant's legal position. And it has an extremely useful remedial effect, because of the governmental practice of adhering to the law as stated in a declaration (backed, in many contexts, by the remedies that a claimant would have if the public authority acted in a way that, according to the declaration, is unlawful). This extremely flexible judicial technique is the youngest, dating from as late as the nineteenth century. The judges had not been willing to issue declarations (except incidentally when making another order); they wanted to keep a tight rein on their process by ordering what was to be done, rather than merely saying what the law was.

The Court of Chancery Procedure Act 1852 s 50, authorized courts to issue declarations without any court order being sought or made. But the judges still wouldn't do it—until in *Dyson v Attorney-General* [1911] 1 KB 410, the Court of Appeal suddenly saw its potential, and decided that a declaration was a good way to impose the rule of law on the Inland Revenue Commissioners. Dyson asked for a declaration that a demand for tax returns was unlawful, so that he wouldn't face the choice between complying, or waiting to be prosecuted. The Attorney General made a floodgates argument (see p 365): listening to Dyson's claim would be inconvenient, because there would be 'innumerable other actions for declarations as to the meaning of numerous other Acts of Parliament which impose a penalty, thus adding greatly to the labours of the law officers' (413). The Court of Appeal had no sympathy for that argument. Farwell LJ pointed out that the courts had a discretion to refuse to listen to unnecessary claims (and to 'punish with costs'). But he added, 'if inconvenience is a legitimate consideration at all, the convenience in the public interest is all in favour of providing a speedy and easy access to the Courts for any of His Majesty's subjects who have any real cause of complaint against the exercise of statutory powers by Government departments and Government officials' (423).

After *Dyson*, why didn't the declaration become the all-purpose judicial technique for dealing with unlawful conduct of public bodies? It nearly did, through the 20th century judicial adventure (see p 56): think of *Ridge v Baldwin*, *Anisminic*, and

Wednesbury. Through declarations in an ordinary action, Anisminic and Charles Ridge got everything that they could have got through *certiorari* in judicial review. In *Anisminic*, counsel for the Foreign Compensation Commission claimed that the court had no jurisdiction to issue a declaration, partly because of the ouster clause (see p 63), and partly because, if a declaration is available in such a case, 'there is no reason why declarations should not take the place of certiorari and mandamus. If a declaration can be granted here, it is hard to see why certiorari and mandamus should even be used at all' (167). The Law Lords brushed this argument aside (Lord Reid, 169; Lord Pearce, 196), and allowed declarations to coexist with the prerogative remedies.

Then the 1978 reform made declarations available in judicial review proceedings. Since then, a declaration can accomplish anything that the prerogative remedies can. So, for example, if O'Reilly (section 10.2.1) had been allowed to proceed with an action for a declaration, he would have got the same result that he could have achieved in an application for *certiorari*. The prison authority could have been expected to comply with a declaration that the decision to discipline him was a nullity.

And declarations even work against the Crown. By Crown Proceedings Act 1947 s 17 and s 21, the court can give a declaration in an ordinary claim (in form, the claim is against the relevant department or the Attorney General). It has to be done by such a claim, because although the Supreme Court Act 1981 s 31(2) gives the court power to issue a declaration in a claim for judicial review, it does not give the court power to give judicial review of the Crown.

No prerogative remedies against the Crown

There are no claims for judicial review called *R v R ex p* ___. In *R v Powell* (1841) 1 QB 352, Lord Denman CJ said that the court could not issue the prerogative writs if there was no one against whom they could be enforced, and also that 'there would be an incongruity in the Queen commanding herself to do an act' (361).

But don't worry: you can seek judicial review of the conduct of the minister or other person or agency that decided on the action that was taken in the name of the Crown. It seems never to have been done until the 19th century, and even then, only concerning exercise of statutory powers. Today, 'a distinction probably no longer has to be drawn between duties which have a statutory and those which have a prerogative source' (*M v Home Office* [1994] 1 AC 377, 417 (Lord Woolf)), and all conduct of ministers is amenable to judicial review if the issues at stake are justiciable. Examples of judicial review of the conduct of ministers on behalf of the Crown include *GCHQ* [1985] AC 374, *Padfield v Minister of Agriculture, Fisheries and Food* [1968] AC 997, etc., etc.).

CPR 54.6(1) and 25.1(1)(b) even provide for interim declarations. These seemed impossible at common law, because a declaration was meant to lay down the law, and the court did not want to do that before a hearing. But there is actually no problem: before the hearing, the court can declare the legal duties that the public authority has at that time, in light of the fact that the court has yet to resolve the issue (e.g., it can declare that the law requires the public authority to maintain the status quo until the hearing is complete).

There are, however, at least four reasons why the declaration has not become the universal remedy:

(1)   **A declaration is partly redundant, since prerogative remedies are easily available in a claim for judicial review.** Most often a claimant challenging the act of a public authority asks for 'a declaration that the act was unlawful and/or a quashing order' (*ID v Home Office* [2005] EWCA Civ 38 [59]).[46] A claimant who can ask for a compulsory order will always do so. It may seem like more of a triumph over the public authority, if the court actually *quashes* its decision, or orders the authority to do this or that. Which leads to the second reason why declarations have not taken over entirely.

(2)   **A declaration binds a public authority only in the way that any legal duty binds it, and not in the way that a compulsory order of a court binds.** So contempt of court is only available to back up the mandatory and prohibiting orders and injunctions.

(3)   **When the claimant is challenging an administrative determination of his or her legal status, a quashing order will sometimes be a complete solution in itself.** This is especially the case in judicial review of the sort of decision that the Civil Procedure Rules call a 'judgment, order or conviction' (CPR Practice Direction 54.5). In such a case (let's call it a 'determination case'), declaratory relief (typically requested along with a quashing order) will be refused as unnecessary. *R v Home Secretary, ex p Venables and Thompson* [1998] AC 407 is an example.

(4)   **The court uses a quashing order to nullify an unlawful determination of the claimant's position, even if a declaration would establish that such a determination is a nullity.**

Yet the declaration is very common, and very important. Often in determination cases, a declaration will be added to the quashing order, to settle the basis on which any new determination would have to proceed.[47] Several of the great Home Secretary cases have been resolved in this way: *R v Home Secretary, ex p Khawaja* [1984] AC 74 (HL), *R v Home Secretary, ex p Doody* [1994] 1 AC 531 (HL), *R (Javed) v Home Secretary* [2001] EWCA Civ 789.

And the declaration really has taken over in cases where the court decides that the public authority has acted unlawfully, otherwise than in making a legal determination of the claimant's position. In the past decade, a pattern has emerged in several of these important cases: the claimant asks for a quashing order and a declaration, and the court upholds the claim, but issues a declaration alone, as sufficient to accomplish the court's purpose (*R v Foreign Secretary, ex p World Development Movement* [1995] 1 WLR 386). Even in a determination case, if it is too late for a quashing order

----

[46]   Examples are very common: see, e.g., *R v DPP, ex p Kebilene* [1999] 3 WLR 175.

[47]   Even though the court can accompany a quashing order 'with a direction to reconsider it and reach a decision in accordance with the findings of the High Court' (Supreme Court Act s 31(5)).

or a mandatory order to do any good, a declaration is standard. So in R *(Begum) v Denbigh High School* [2005] EWCA Civ 199, the claimant abandoned the claim for a mandatory order, and the Court of Appeal issued declarations (which were overturned when the House of Lords held that the school's conduct had been lawful; see p 206).

> ### Advisory declarations
>
> The courts are in principle willing to advise the government as to its legal responsibilities by declaring them in a claim for judicial review, even where the government has not acted unlawfully and is not proposing to do so. The 'essential purposes' of advisory declarations are, 'first, to reduce the danger of administrative activities being declared illegal retrospectively, and, secondly, to assist public authorities by giving advice on legal questions which is then binding on all' (CND *v Prime Minister* [2002] EWHC 2777 [46] (Schiemann LJ)). But the courts are very reluctant to do so even where the issues are justiciable (and the issues were not justiciable in the CND case).

10.4.3 Injunctions

Injunctions require someone to do or to refrain from doing something that the court describes—just like mandatory and prohibiting orders. But their history is entirely separate from the prerogative writs. Injunctions developed in equity as a judicial order in private law, to restrain a tort or other unlawful action. Common law damages were, in effect, the best the court could do to remedy a situation in which an injunction was impossible (because the damage had already been done, or because some equitable consideration prevented the issue of an injunction).

Injunctions should be unnecessary in administrative law, given the jurisdiction to issue mandatory orders. The use of injunctions in public law reflects the haphazard history of procedural drawbacks in the judicial review procedure. So before the 1978 reforms, actions for an injunction were used to obtain disclosure and cross-examination. But they had their own drawbacks; a special requirement of standing prevented them from playing a major role in the development of public law. Since 1978 they have been available in claims for judicial review, with the same relaxed standing requirement as all judicial review remedies. They can be useful because the court can grant an interim mandatory injunction (in exceptional circumstances) but, it seems, not an interim mandatory order.[48] And since R *v Transport Secretary, ex p Factortame (No 2)* [1991] 1 AC 603 and M *v Home Office* [1994] 1 AC 377, it has been possible to get an interim injunction against the Crown (i.e., an injunction issued before

---

[48] R *v Kensington and Chelsea Royal LBC, ex p Hammell* [1989] QB 518: to get an interlocutory mandatory injunction, the claimant must have permission to proceed with judicial review, and a very strong *prima facie* case.

the dispute is resolved, to prevent the irreparable damage to the parties' interests that might otherwise be caused in the meanwhile).

10.4.4 Damages

The most important improvement in the 1978 procedural reform was the provision for the award of damages in judicial review. But crucially, the court must be satisfied 'that such an award would have been made if the claim had been made in an action begun by the applicant at the time of making the application' (Supreme Court Act 1981 s 31(4)(b)). So the change did not impose any new liabilities on public authorities; the claimant must show 'a cause of action sounding in damages' (*R v Deputy Governor of Parkhurst Prison, ex p Hague* [1992] 1 AC 58, 155), just as if the proceeding were an ordinary claim.

> #### Public debt
> In 1981 the Supreme Court Act only provided for **damages** in judicial review, and not for an order for payment of **money owed** by a public authority, so that debts of public authorities could only be pursued by an ordinary claim (*Dennis Rye Pension Fund Trustees v Sheffield City Council* [1998] 1 WLR 840, 849–51). But now s 31 of the Act has been further improved to allow 'restitution or the recovery of a sum due'.[49]
>
> ● *Pop Quiz* ●
> Does that change affect the approach to the *O'Reilly* problem that Lord Woolf took in the *Dennis Rye Pension Fund* case?

There is no jurisdiction to hear a claim for damages in judicial review if the claimant is not seeking any other remedy (CPR 54.3(2)).[50] So simple claims in tort or contract, in which the claimant does not allege any wrong on the part of the public authority other than the tort or breach of contract, must still be conducted through an ordinary claim. Note that many tort claims—especially in misfeasance in public office, and breach of statutory duty—presuppose that a decision of a public authority was unlawful in ways that would give grounds for judicial review. In such a case, the claimant can proceed with an ordinary claim in tort without asking the court for a quashing order or declaration.

For the grounds on which damages will be awarded against public authorities, see Chapter 14.

> #### Substitutionary remedies
> In 2000, a far-reaching provision for a 'substitutionary remedy' was added to the Civil Procedure Rules (CPR 54.19(3)), authorizing the Administrative Court to step

---

[49] Civil Procedure (Modification of Supreme Court Act 1981) Order 2004 SI 2004/1033 Art 4(4).

[50] See discussion in *ID & Others v Home Office* [2005] EWCA Civ 38 [58].

> in and make the decision that the public authority should have made if 'there is no purpose to be served in remitting the matter to the decision-maker'. The court does not have to require a new and wasteful administrative justice process if it is unnecessary, but can resolve the dispute straightaway at the point where it decides that the initial administrative decision cannot stand.

10.4.5 Contempt of court

Contempt of court is either an interference with court process, or a refusal to abide by the requirements of a court order. When it is done by a public authority, it shows what you might call a criminal lack of comity toward the court.

In 1922, the High Court imprisoned thirty Labour councillors from Poplar (a very poor borough in what is now part of Tower Hamlets in east London) for contempt (R v Poplar Borough Council, ex p London County Council (No 2) [1922] 1 KB 95). They had refused to obey a mandamus issued by the High Court to force the borough to pay contributions to London County Council expenses (R v Poplar Borough Council, ex p London County Council (No 1) [1922] 1 KB 72). The Poplar Council had withheld the contributions on the ground that structural injustices in the rates system left them unable to help the poor in their borough, while requiring them to make disproportionate contributions to the costs of services for London, in a scheme that favoured rich boroughs. The Poplar councillors wanted to spend the money fighting tuberculosis, distributing free milk, and paying the Council's own employees (both men and women) a minimum wage of £4 per week.

The Councillors spent six weeks in prison, before the Government backed down and reformed the contribution system. The fiasco shows (1) that court orders in public law can be backed by coercion, and (2) that the prerogative remedies can get extremely personal (it was a public authority—the Council—that failed to levy the necessary rates and pay the contributions, but the mandamus was addressed personally to the human beings on the Council), and (3) that even a conviction for contempt and imprisonment itself may form valuable tools in a political campaign.

Action that is incompatible with a quashing order (e.g., carrying on as if the quashed order were valid), or with the legal position as stated in a declaration, is not contempt of court; it is only unlawful conduct. But failure to comply with a mandatory order, a prohibiting order, or an injunction[51] is a contempt of court. The court can punish a contempt with a fine or imprisonment.

Contempt and the Crown:

The courts exercise the judicial power of the Crown, and the Crown cannot be held in contempt of court. But a minister exercising a power on behalf of the Crown can be held in contempt in his capacity as a minister. After many centuries of English

---

51   See M v Home Office [1994] 1 AC 377.

legal history, it was done for the first time in *M v Home Office* [1994] 1 AC 377. But a minister still cannot be imprisoned for contempt (M).

10.4.6 Judicial discretion over remedies

In an ordinary claim, a claimant who establishes a cause of action has a right to a remedy (whether the defendant is a public authority or a private person). But the remedies available in judicial review are discretionary.[52] So, for example, if a university unfairly refuses to reinstate a student, the court will not issue a mandatory order requiring her to be reinstated, if reinstatement would serve no useful purpose: *R v University of Cambridge, ex p Persaud* [2001] EWCA Civ 534 [44]. Likewise, the court has discretion whether to grant a declaration in an ordinary claim, as Lord Diplock pointed out in O'Reilly: '...the remedy by way of declaration of nullity of the decisions of the board was discretionary—as are all the remedies available upon judicial review' (*O'Reilly v Mackman* [1983] 2 AC 237, 284).

To understand the discretionary nature of the remedies, you need to consider the reasons for it, and the constraints the law imposes on it.

Reasons for discretion in remedies

1. It **reflects the standards** to which the process is designed to give effect. An ordinary claim vindicates claims of right; the remedies in judicial review vindicate claims that a public authority has acted unlawfully. That sort of claim can be well-founded even where the claimant has no entitlement to anything at all. How, and even *whether* the public authority should answer for its unlawful conduct partly depends on the public interest. The **public interest litigation** cases (see p 406) are the best reminder of this fact. Incidentally, the discretion over remedies compounds the discretion that the vagueness of the grounds of judicial review gives to the judges.

2. It is closely associated with the **nature of the process**: judicial review is (and has been since the middle ages) a technique for the state to control itself. By contrast, the process and the remedies in an ordinary claim are a state process designed to vindicate the claimant's claim of right. But note that by virtue of controlling the state, the process and the remedies may incidentally vindicate the rights of claimants: so Charles Ridge had a right to a fair hearing before being dismissed, and it could be pursued either in an application for a prerogative remedy or in an action for a declaration (*Ridge v Baldwin* [1964] AC 40).

3. It is **in harmony with the courts' discretion over *access* to judicial review**— that is, the court's discretion over remedies is justified by the same considerations that justify its discretion over permission, and over standing.

---

[52] It is a discretion *of the court*, and not of the Administrative Court judges. So the Court of Appeal and the House of Lords will not defer to the decision of the Administrative Court, but will 'exercise the discretion which ought to have been exercised in the first instance' by the Administrative Court. *R v IRC ex p Federation of Self-Employed and Small Businesses Ltd* [1982] AC 617, 664 (Lord Roskill).

4. It is **reproduced** by many modern statutes providing judicial remedies, which typically say that the court 'may' give a remedy (the Human Rights Act is an example, even though its purpose is to vindicate rights).

Constraints on discretion in remedies:

The judges' discretion over remedies is a discretion over the administration of justice. Like other public authorities' administrative discretions, it is:

- **limited** (the court has no discretion to interfere with a decision where there is no ground of judicial review);

- **supervised** (by the availability of appeals to the Court of Appeal and House of Lords); and

- **regulated** (by the law on the particular point in issue).

Discretion is the same thing when judges have it, as when other public authorities have it: a power to choose one way or another with legal effect, with no legal duty to make one choice rather than another. A power may be discretionary even though the law controls its exercise, as long as the law does not require a particular outcome. The court's discretion may be taken away by any rule of law that requires a particular result: so, for example, the Town and Country Planning Act 1990 s 288(5)(b), gave the court a discretion to quash an *ultra vires* planning decision. But Lord Hoffmann said, 'I doubt whether, consistently with its obligations under European law, the court may exercise that discretion to uphold a planning permission which has been granted contrary to [an EC] Directive [Council Directive 85/337/EEC]' (*Berkeley v Environment Secretary* [2001] 2 AC 603, 616).

But is it really discretion?

Concerning the decision whether to quash a planning permission, Lord Justice Sedley has said, 'I am hesitant to treat a decision so fraught with basic principles as one simply of discretion. It seems to me...to be better described and regarded as a matter of judgment' (*R (Corbett) v Restormel Borough Council* [2001] EWCA Civ 330 [29]).

The important truths are that legal principle will in all cases forbid *some* conceivable remedial decisions (and the court has no discretion to choose those decisions), and may in some circumstances demand a particular remedial decision (and then the court has no discretion in that particular case). The *power* is discretionary because the legal principles at stake often allow the judge to decide either way, without acting unlawfully. And the fact that it is a matter of judgment does not mean that it is not a matter of discretion; it is both, if the law leaves a choice to the judge that must be exercised with judgment. All discretionary powers are like this—including administrative discretions (see p 233), and other judicial discretions (as to sentence, for example, or as to costs).

Discretion and remedies under the Human Rights Act

Declarations of incompatibility under the Human Rights Act are discretionary (*Lancashire County Council v Taylor* [2005] EWCA Civ 284 [42] (Lord Woolf for the Court)). Section 6 (making the conduct of a public authority 'unlawful' if it is contrary to a Convention right, unless a statute requires it; see p 73) confers no discretion.[53] But if a claimant establishes that a decision was unlawful under s 6, the remedies for the unlawfulness remain in the discretion of the court (s 8—the court 'may grant such relief or remedy, or make such order, within its powers as it considers just and appropriate').

Section 3 says that legislation 'must' be given effect in a way that is compatible with Convention rights, so far as possible. That provision gives no express discretion, but by leaving the court to decide what is possible, it gives a far-reaching resultant discretion (see section 3.3.1). Section 4(4) gives an implied discretion; it states that 'If the court is satisfied . . . it may make a declaration of that incompatibility.' In R v A (No 2) [2002] 1 AC 45, Lord Steyn, explaining his preference for using s 3 rather than s 4 to solve the problem when legislation is arguably incompatible with Convention rights (see p 76), said 'A declaration of incompatibility is a measure of last resort. It must be avoided unless it is plainly impossible to do so' (68).

> ### Collateral effect
> Although the power to give a remedy under the Human Rights Act 1998 s 8 is a discretionary power, the court does not have discretion over the effects of unlaw-fulness under the Act. So if, e.g., a byelaw is contrary to a Convention right, the Court has no discretion to allow a conviction under that byelaw to stand. But this is true of the general standards of judicial review as well: if a byelaw were unlawful according to the rule in *Kruse v Johnson* (see p 220), the court would have no dis-cretion to uphold a conviction under it. And remember *Cooper v Wandsworth Board of Works* (see p 108): once it was decided that the decision to tear down Cooper's house was unlawful, the court had no discretion to decide that the Board of Works had a defence to the tort of trespass.

How can remedies under the Human Rights Act be discretionary, if their whole point is to vindicate rights? Part of the answer is that the Act was never meant to guarantee the Convention rights, or to incorporate the Convention into English law, but only to give certain legal effects to the Convention rights. Those effects were left subject to Acts of Parliament, and to the processes and techniques of the English legal system.

The other part of the answer is that the Convention itself delegates the remedial responsibility to contracting states, and allows a discretion in carrying it out.[54]

---

[53] Except the discretion that results (see p 232) from the vagueness of the Convention rights.

[54] *Vilvarajah v UK* (1992) 14 EHRR 248 [122]: '. . . Article 13 does not go so far as to require any par-ticular form of remedy, Contracting States being afforded a margin of discretion in conforming to their obligations under this provision'.

10.4.7 Quashing and the nullity paradox

A quashing order quashes a decision, and a declaration that a decision of a public authority was invalid is the court's statement that there never was a valid decision. And subject to the *O'Reilly v Mackman* problem, the two are interchangeable. Yet, if there was never any valid decision, there is nothing to quash! So what are the judges doing when they hold a decision unlawful in a case like *Ridge v Baldwin*? Are they taking away the legal effect of the decision, or are they deciding that there never was any legally effective decision in the first place?

Here is another aspect of the same puzzle: if some action of a public authority is unlawful (like the decision to sack Ridge), how can the judges have any discretion over remedies? It seems contrary to the rule of law for anyone to have a discretion to let an unlawful decision stand. Lord Hobhouse said that this puzzle about nullity is a paradox, because it presents the possibility of 'the illegal act which the court nevertheless does not restrain, the ultra vires act which is nevertheless effective'(*Attorney-General's Reference (No 2 of 2001)* [2003] UKHL 68 [122], and see his speech in *Crédit Suisse v Allerdale Borough Council* [1997] QB 306, 350).

A paradox is a chain of reasoning that seems to be sound, but seems to lead to a contradiction. Here, the premise that a decision was unlawful, plus the premise that a court has discretion over remedies, seems to lead to contradiction: that a court of law can give effect to something unlawful. As in all paradoxes, the contradiction in this one is only apparent.

If there is ground for judicial review of a decision, then the decision is unlawful— that is, the process by which it is made, or its substance, does not meet the standards that the law imposes. But that does not determine what is to be done about it. The paradox seems to arise, only because it seems that if a decision was unlawful, the court just *must* hold that it has no legal effect.

The appearance of paradox is heightened by the fallout from *Anisminic v Foreign Compensation Commission* [1969] 2 AC 147. Lord Reid held that the Commission's decision was a nullity, because the error that he found in the Commission's interpretation of the Egypt Order meant that it had reached its decision without jurisdiction. And Lord Diplock[55] transformed that holding into a doctrine that any administrative decision is a nullity if it is based on an error of law. And in *R v Lord President of the Privy Council, ex p Page* [1993] AC 682, (701), Lord Browne-Wilkinson extended this doctrine into a uniform view that administrative action in general is *ultra vires* if it is based on an error of law, or made 'in a manner which is procedurally irregular or is *Wednesbury* unreasonable' (701). Then, it seems, wherever there is ground for judicial review of an administrative decision, the decision is a nullity (and not a decision at all).[56] It is like a counterfeit £20 note.

[55] In *Re Racal* [1981] AC 374 and *O'Reilly v Mackman*; see p 303.

[56] Lord Browne-Wilkinson cited *In re Daws* (1838) 8 Ad & E 936. In fact, the idea may be as old as the 17th century: Lord Coke said in the *Case of Proclamations* (1611) 12 Co Rep 74, 'we do find divers precedents of proclamations which are utterly against law and reason, and for that void.'

But the nullity paradox is not just a result of *Anisminic*. It had already created massive confusion in *Ridge v Baldwin*. Lord Evershed, dissenting, said that *certiorari* was not available if a decision was taken outside jurisdiction (74), because in such a case there would be nothing to quash. Lord Morris insisted that the police authority's decision *was* outside jurisdiction, yet he thought that Ridge could have applied for *certiorari*. As in *Anisminic*, Lord Reid held that the decision was a nullity, to evade the effect of a statute that, according to the dissenters in both cases, insulated the decision from judicial control. Lord Devlin pointed out in *Ridge* that the majority conclusion meant that 'during the whole time taken up in the elucidation of this difficult point of law, the appellant has legally been in office and entitled to the appropriate emoluments [i.e., payments]'.[57] Blaming the situation on the statute, he concluded with feeling, 'It can be said with much force that all this is the result of ousting the ordinary jurisdiction of the courts' (140).

The artificial reasoning generated by ouster clauses in *Ridge* and *Anisminic* has become the general orthodoxy of administrative law today: that any ground of judicial review makes an administrative decision a nullity. But the decision does not count as a nullity in law unless a court determines that it was a nullity. And judges have discretion not to issue a declaration or a quashing order, even if a decision *was* a nullity. Except as regards ouster clauses, the orthodoxy is no different in effect from a doctrine that decisions are valid unless a court decides to invalidate them. The orthodoxy supports Lord Reid's technique for evading ouster clauses (see p 305).

The orthodoxy seems to suggest that there is nothing to be done about an unlawful decision but to declare it a nullity. But in fact, the judges have held on to the principle that in the interests of the rule of law itself, they need to control their process by retaining discretion in remedies. In R (Corbett) v Restormel Borough Council [2001] EWCA Civ 330, a council was held to have given planning permission unlawfully. The Environment Secretary modified the permission—which stopped the development, but potentially entitled the landowner to compensation. A councillor asked the court to decide that 'the permission which had been unlawfully granted should be treated as though it had never had any legal existence' [15]—so that the council would not be on the hook for compensation. Schiemann LJ saw 'a certain elegance' [15] in the argument, but pointed out that it had to be qualified to account for the court's remedial discretion, and for the potential that justice might demand protection of reliance induced by unlawful decisions. He said that the **principle of legal certainty** and the **principle of legality** may clash [16]; the elegance of the principle of legality led him to conclude that an unlawful decision is to be quashed on judicial review 'unless the person resisting the quashing can show at least that he would be harmed by the quashing or some other reason is shown for not striking down' [17]. Sedley LJ, likewise, held that quashing is 'the usual consequence of illegality in public law' [34] but that it should not be done in *Corbett* (chiefly because of the landowner's reliance on the unlawful planning permission).

----

57 Lord Reid's disposition of the case was to 'declare that the dismissal of the appellant is null and void and remit the case to the Queen's Bench Division for further procedure' (81).

Corbett shows the complex orthodoxy at work:

(1) if any of the grounds of judicial review apply to a public authority's decision, the decision is a nullity,[58] but

(2) no public authority's decision is to count as a nullity unless a court decides (in a proceeding that is brought properly) to treat it as a nullity (i.e., there is a presumption of validity),[59] and

(3) there is a further presumption that the court will treat such a decision as a nullity, although

(4) the court has discretion not to do so where there is special reason.

This orthodox set of doctrines achieves the right approach to remedies in *spite* of the confusing language of nullity generated in *Ridge* and *Anisminic*. The same results (except for the Lord Reid treatment of ouster clauses) could be achieved without using nullity as a part of the courts' technical equipment at all, in the following way:

(1) if any of the grounds of judicial review apply to a public authority's decision, then it was unlawful for the public authority to make the decision that it made.

(2) the court has discretion to deal with the unlawfulness in a way that is just and in the public interest, taking into account the legitimate interests of the claimant, and any effect on parties who reasonably relied on the decision, and considerations of good administration.

Presumptions

The courts' presumptions (that an administrative decision is valid unless a court decides otherwise, and that a decision that is shown to have been unlawful will be treated as a nullity unless there is reason for the court to use its discretion otherwise) are not requirements of logic; they are the judges' attempt to give effect to the rule of law in their response to unlawful official conduct.

The case of the horrible ASBO

Corbett shows why the law gives the courts the power to treat an unlawful decision as valid. But it can be a dangerous thing to do. Consider the case of the horrible ASBO.

---

[58] Cf. Lord Justice Sedley's view in *R v Higher Education Funding Council, ex p Institute of Dental Surgery* [1994] 1 WLR 242 that a public authority's legal obligation, such as an obligation to give reasons, is 'a ground of nullity where it is violated' (259).

[59] It is called 'the presumption omnia praesumuntur rite esse acta' [everything is presumed to have been done properly] —*Inland Revenue Commissioners v Rossminster* [1980] AC 952, 1013 (Lord Diplock). The presumption is that the public authority subject to judicial review acted *intra vires*. It can be displaced by showing any ground of judicial review, but that can only be shown if the claimant has standing, and proceeds in time, etc.

Michael T was 13 when Manchester City Council applied for an anti-social behaviour order (ASBO) against him. A District Judge granted the order for two years; among other things, it required Michael not to 'act in an anti-social manner in the City of Manchester' (*Crown Prosecution Service v Michael T* [2006] EWHC 728 [5]). Of course, no one ought to act in an anti-social manner. But an order not to do so, backed by the threat of imprisonment for breaching the order, creates a serious, personal criminal offence that is roughly as wide as bad behaviour. It is both too vague, and overbroad. It is not decent penal law. So the ASBO was a breakdown in the rule of law: it amounted to telling Michael T that he could be imprisoned if the officials decided that he misbehaved.

The order was, therefore, unlawful. But when Michael T was convicted of trying to steal a scooter 21 months later, he was also prosecuted for breaching the ASBO. The District Judge held that the ASBO was 'unenforceable and void' [15]. On an appeal by the prosecution, the Administrative Court reversed that decision. It was not that the court thought the ASBO was all right: Richards LJ held that 'such a wide provision...should never again be included in an ASBO' [45], and said that its vagueness and breadth would be ground for an appeal. Yet the court held that the ASBO remained valid: although it could be set aside on appeal, the magistrates' court had no jurisdiction to rule that the ASBO was invalid, when a defendant was charged with breaching the ASBO.[60]

There is an attraction in treating court orders as valid unless set aside on appeal. After all, in the great case of *M v Home Office* [1994] 1 AC 377, the House of Lords held that it was contempt of court for the Home Secretary to ignore a court order, *even if the court order was made without jurisdiction*. Contrast M with *Boddington v British Transport Police* [1999] 2 AC 143, in which the House of Lords held that a defendant could argue that an administrative byelaw was unlawful in his defence to a charge of breaching it. T is, in a way, intermediate between M and *Boddington*. The ASBO, unlike the order in M, was not an order of the High Court, but of a court of specific jurisdiction. On the other hand, the ASBO was a court order, unlike the administrative byelaw in *Boddington*. And Michael T had a right of appeal against the ASBO, whereas Boddington would have had to seek judicial review of the smoking byelaw in order to challenge it before smoking on the train.

One remarkable thing about T is that the Administrative Court departed from an earlier Administrative Court decision that the magistrates *can* decline to enforce an ASBO that is 'plainly invalid' (R (W) v DPP [2005] EWHC 1333, Brooke LJ [12][61]). The ASBO in that case was not as extreme as Michael T's ASBO (it required the youth not

....

[60] Michael T had in fact appealed; the appeal was struck out on the ground that his mother had agreed to the ASBO; the Administrative Court quashed that decision ([2005] EWHC 1396), which left him free to pursue the appeal, and yet the appeal was never completed (see [2006] EWHC 728 [8]).

[61] The W case was referred to and, apparently, endorsed by the Court of Appeal in R v English [2005] EWCA Crim 2690 [11].

	The first decision:	The second decision maker:
M v Home Office	—an injunction issued by a High Court Judge.	The Home Secretary **may not** treat the unlawful decision as ineffective.
Boddington	—British Railways Board byelaw, under a statutory power to regulate railways.	Magistrates **may** treat the unlawful decision as ineffective.
CPS v T	—an ASBO issued by a District Judge.	The very same District Judge who issued the ASBO may **not** treat the decision as ineffective (T [2]).

Figure 10.3 Who can treat whose unlawful decision as ineffective?

to commit any criminal offence) yet the Court held it invalid, because it was 'plainly too wide'.[62]

As the court in T pointed out, there are also cases, such as B v B [2004] EWCA Civ 681, in which the Court of Appeal has held that orders made without jurisdiction in the County Court 'remain in force until such time as they are discharged' [68]. So the law on the legal effect of decisions of courts of specific jurisdiction is a mess that needs sorting.

What are the principles on which the mess should be sorted out?

The essential question is whether allowing the second decision maker to decide the validity of the first decision will lead to arbitrary government. The risks can be seen from Figure 10.3. The danger in M was a danger to the rule of law: that a politician might (in fact, he did) take it on himself to decide—on a politically charged issue—whether an injunction was valid. There was no such danger in *Boddington*, because (as the House of Lords thought) the magistrates were capable of asking whether the anti-smoking byelaw was lawful, without arbitrarily interfering with regulation of train services by the Railway Board (which would in any case be protected by the prosecution's ability to appeal). And there was no such danger in T, because (1) the law already prohibited the behaviour for which T was prosecuted (the ASBO only aggravated the penalty), and (2) the situation does not lend itself to abuse, because allowing the second decision maker to treat the first as ineffective only means giving control over the effect of a District Judge's order to a District Judge.

The court in T concluded that it was improper for a District Judge to have that control. Yet ironically, the Administrative Court did deprive the ASBO of its legal effect in the end: the Court exercised its own discretion not to quash the District Judge's decision, because 'it would have been wrong in principle to impose any penalty additional to that imposed in respect of the underlying offence' [47]–[48]. The effect, then was the same as if the ASBO had indeed been quashed by the District Judge, and this result was required by principle.

---

[62] The court in T did not follow W, on the ground that the prosecution in W had conceded that the Magistrates could treat an unlawful ASBO as invalid. That prosecution concession in W had no legal effect, so the decision in T amounts to a judgment that the Administrative Court had made a mistake by not hearing argument.

The better course for the law is the course that Brooke LJ had adopted in *R(W) v DPP* [2005] EWHC 1333: if an ASBO is patently unlawful, in a way that makes it an abuse of process to hold the defendant liable for its breach (as it would have been in Michael T's case), then it is appropriate for one District Judge to give no effect to the ASBO made by another District Judge (or, of course, by the same District Judge). The difference between this case and *M v Home Office* is that there is a danger of arbitrariness in leaving a Home Secretary to decide whether a judicial order against him is unlawful, but there is no serious danger of arbitrariness in leaving it to a District Judge to make the judgment that an ASBO is patently unlawful.

Is there a danger that offenders can abuse the process by waiting to challenge their ASBO until they are prosecuted for breaching it? None at all, if the District Judge hearing the prosecution uses the 'plainly invalid' requirement set out in *W*.

Invalidity follows from the law's response to unlawful conduct

The core question that the courts need to ask is **whether the decision under review was unlawful**. The only other question they need to ask, is **what response the rule of law requires** to unlawful conduct, in the circumstances. The courts do not need to ask whether the decision was void, or invalid, and the idea of invalidity *is not a helpful piece of technical equipment for their purpose.* A justifiable holding of invalidity follows from the first two steps: that the decision under review was unlawful, and that the rule of law requires that the court respond to the unlawfulness, at the time of review, by treating the decision as ineffective.

As Lord Radcliffe said in *Smith v East Elloe Rural District Council* [1956] AC 739 (769):

'An order, even if not made in good faith, is still an act capable of legal consequences. It bears no brand of invalidity upon its forehead. Unless the necessary proceedings are taken at law to establish the cause of invalidity and to get it quashed or otherwise upset, it will remain as effective for its ostensible purpose as the most impeccable of orders.' But the courts have a remarkable breadth of discretion to determine what counts as 'the necessary proceedings'.

10.5 Conclusion

Why do the names of judicial review cases begin with 'R'? It leads judges to make quite divergent remarks about what is going on in judicial review:

> ❛In judicial review proceedings there is no true *lis inter partes* or suit by one person against another.❜ [63]

---

[63] *R v Stratford-on-Avon District Council, ex p Jackson* [1985] 1 WLR 1319, 1323 (May LJ). So issue estoppel (the rule that a party may not raise an issue in litigation that has been decided in previous litigation between the same two parties) does not operate in judicial review: R v Environment

> ❝ In reality, such proceedings represent a contest between the applicant, who both initiates and pursues the proceedings, and the authority against which the proceedings are brought. Judicial review proceedings are brought neither by nor at the instigation of the Crown. ❞ [64]

The judges in these cases were saying something important about judicial review, but both are wrong, in a sense: there really is a dispute between parties in a claim for judicial review. But it isn't merely old-fashioned to say that the Crown brings the proceedings on behalf of the claimant; it reflects the nature of judicial review in the 21st century. It is an extraordinary process, which in the public interest is made available at the discretion of the court to someone who doesn't have a right of action. And the remedies—even where a public authority is shown to have acted unlawfully—are in the discretion of the court. The law on judicial process is *much* more complex than in Lord Mansfield's day, but the principle is still as he put it: that the courts ought to use their remedial powers 'upon reasons of justice... and upon reasons of public policy, to preserve peace, order, and good government' (R v Barker (1762) 3 Burr 1265, 1267). When the courts have an overly-general concern not to interfere with the administration (as in O'Reilly v Mackman [1983] 2 AC 237), the result is injustice. When they forget that not every unlawful action demands a judicial process, the result is a lack of comity toward other public authorities.

The extraordinary discretionary power of the judges over the process has a principled basis: the rule of law does not generally demand *or* forbid the provision of a judicial process for remedying unlawful official conduct. The rule of law *does* demand a judicial process, where that is what it takes to prevent arbitrary government (and it demands the form of process that is best for that purpose). And so the various judicial discretions are dangerous, unless the judges are prepared to use them for the purpose of preventing arbitrary government. That means, for example, never refusing permission for judicial review, and never refusing a remedy, merely because it would be better that way for the state. So the legitimacy of the processes depends not only on the judges' independence from government interference. It also depends on the independent attitude of the judges, and their willingness to take responsibility for the administration of justice, and to act with comity toward other public authorities.

Proportionate process

Remember that the judges' job is not only to achieve proportionality between the claimant's interest in a procedure, and the public interest in restricting

---

Secretary, ex p Hackney LBC [1984] 1 WLR 592 (CA). But 'the court has an inherent jurisdiction as a matter of discretion in the interests of finality not to allow a particular issue which has already been litigated to be re-opened' (Dunn LJ, 602).

[64] R (Ben-Abdelaziz) v Haringey LBC [2001] 1 WLR 1485 [29] (Brooke LJ). The issue was whether judicial review proceedings counted as 'proceedings brought by or at the instigation of a public authority' under Human Rights Act s 22(4), which enabled people to rely on Convention rights under s 7(1)(b) before the Act came into effect. The court's answer was 'no'.

proceedings. The public *may* have a more or less vital interest in the procedure going ahead, to impose the rule of law on administration.

TAKE-HOME MESSAGE • • •

- The **rule of law** does not require an unlimited opportunity to challenge the lawfulness official action. It requires (1) proportionate processes for the vindication of the legal rights of claimants, and (2) proportionate processes for the review of official action where a review is in the public interest.

- The Civil Procedure Rules give the judges a flexible, discretionary power to hear claims for judicial review with proportionate process.

- The **discretionary power** of judges to control their own process extends to the remedies they give.

- A claimant has a right to a remedy against an infringement of his or her **legal rights** by administrative action. But a claimant has no right to a remedy against **unlawful government action** in general.

- **Comity** among public authorities requires judges not to impose processes on administrative agencies that are disproportionate to the nature of the claim. And it requires other public authorities to comply with orders of the court, and to act in accord with declarations as to their legal position.

> *Critical reading*
>
> *Ridge v Baldwin* [1964] AC 40
> *O'Reilly v Mackman* [1983] 2 AC 237
> *M v Home Office* [1994] AC 377
> *Clark v University of Lincolnshire & Humberside* [2000] 1 WLR 1988
> *R (Corbett) v Restormel Borough Council* [2001] EWCA Civ 330

CRITICAL QUESTIONS • • •

1 ❝ How, one wonders, is good administration ever assisted by upholding an unlawful decision? ❞ R (Corbett) v Restormel Borough Council [2001] EWCA Civ 330 [32] (Sedley LJ)
   Can you answer Lord Justice Sedley's question?

2 ❝ ... the judicial review court, being primarily concerned with the maintenance of the rule of law by the imposition of objective legal standards upon the conduct of public bodies, has to adopt a flexible but principled approach to its own jurisdiction. ❞
   (R v Trade and Industry Secretary, ex p Greenpeace Limited [1998] Env LR 415, 424 (Laws J)
   Is it possible for the law on access to judicial review to be both flexible and principled?

3   Do the judicial processes measure up to the requirements of due process (see Chapter 4) that judges impose on *other* public authorities?

4   Even after *O'Reilly v Mackman* had led to a lot of pointless litigation, the Law Commission reported in 1994 that 'the need for speed and certainty in adminis-trative decision-making' is a good policy reason for forbidding the use of an action (what is now called an 'ordinary claim') in 'purely public law cases' (Law Com No 226 [3.13]. Is that true?

5   What is the purpose of the requirement of permission to apply for judicial review? Is it to control the workload of the Administrative Court? Is it to protect defend-ants from litigation?

Further questions:

6   Why is it contempt of court for a public authority to decide that a court order is invalid (*M v Home Office* [1994] 1 AC 377), but it is not contemptuous for a court to decide that a decision of another public authority is invalid?

7   The prosecution made a floodgates argument in the case of the horrible ASBO—they said that if the defendant has a defence that the ASBO was invalid, floods of defendants would challenge their ASBOs when they were prosecuted for breaching them. Is that a good argument?

online
resource
centre

Visit the online resource centre to access the following resources which accompany this chapter: links to legislation and online reports of judicial decisions, summaries of key cases and legislation, updates in the law, suggestions for answering the pop quizzes and questions, and links to useful websites.

11 Standing: litigation and the public interest

The law determines who can seek judicial review, in which matters, and who can bring an ordinary claim against whom. The law is very generous to claimants, because the judges want to find a way to hear genuine complaints of unlawful administrative conduct. But the courts' doors are not open to everyone who wants to complain: the requirement of standing reflects the basic principle that judicial process requires a genuine legal issue between interested parties.

LOOK FOR • • •

- The purpose of judicial review: is it to police the lawfulness of administrative action? To right injustices to claimants?

- The relation between standing (the entitlement to be heard by a court) and the purposes of judicial review.

- The increasing potential for political campaigners to use judicial review as a platform to hold the government to account.

- The role of intervenors in litigation against public authorities (and the very relaxed approach to intervention in the English courts).

> ‘I regard it as a matter of high constitutional principle that if there is good ground for supposing that a government department or a public authority is transgressing the law, or is about to transgress it, in a way which offends or injures thousands of Her Majesty's subjects, then any one of those offended or injured can draw it to the attention of the courts of law and seek to have the law enforced, and the courts in their discretion can grant whatever remedy is appropriate. ’
>
> **R v Greater London Council, ex p Blackburn [1976] 1 WLR 550, 559**
>
> **(Lord Denning MR)**

> ‘ not every applicant is entitled to judicial review as of right ’
>
> **R v Inland Revenue Commissioners, ex p Federation of Self-Employed and**
>
> **Small Businesses Ltd [1982] AC 617, 645 (Lord Fraser)**

11.1 The butcher, the baker, and the grave lacuna

In R v Home Secretary, ex p Ruddock [1987] 1 WLR 1482, Taylor J advanced the judicial review of the prerogative, and the doctrine of legitimate expectations. Only there was no such case as R v Home Secretary, ex p Ruddock. Joan Ruddock was the chair of the Campaign for Nuclear Disarmament. Ruddock and the vice-president, John Cox, sought judicial review, claiming that MI5 had breached the Government's guidelines by tapping Cox's phone. Taylor J held that Ruddock did not have 'a sufficient interest to apply for any relief' (1485). Ruddock's complaint was that the Home Office had tapped Cox's phone, and judicial review was not available to everyone Cox spoke to. 'Otherwise,' Taylor J said, the Home Secretary 'would be open to judicial review at the instance of his butcher, his baker and whichever other innocents were intercepted on his line.' So the case is really R v Home Secretary, ex p Cox; it is in the law reports as 'ex p Ruddock' only because it had commenced with Ruddock's name on the application. She had no standing to seek judicial review.

11.1.1 What is standing?

Standing is the entitlement to be heard. No judicial process of any kind may proceed without it. In an ordinary claim, the claimant's standing is based on his assertion of grounds for his claim to a remedy (the old-fashioned name for those grounds is 'a cause of action'). You needn't establish that there are *good* grounds for a claim in order to have standing—that is the question to be decided at trial. So, for example, in an action for damages for breach of contract, the claimant has standing because he asserts that he has a contract with the defendant, and that the defendant is in breach of it. But if a statement of case 'discloses no reasonable grounds for bringing...the claim' (Civil Procedure Rules (CPR) 3.4(2)), the claimant has no standing to proceed to a trial. The Court may strike out the claim, on its own initiative or on the application of the defendant (CPR Practice Direction 3.4).[1] No one has standing to proceed with an ordinary claim, if their statement of case does not state grounds on which a right to a remedy can be claimed.

In a claim for judicial review, the claimant does not assert a right to a remedy. An allegation of a tort or a breach of contract gives the victim standing, but an allegation of unlawful administrative conduct does not by itself give anyone standing. So how can a claimant have standing for judicial review? The answer lies in the medieval constitutional roots of the remedies given in judicial review—a heritage that suited the 20th-century judicial adventure (see p 36) very well. In the origins of the common law, the judges were not only commissioned to give effect to legal rights in an ordinary action, but also to hear pleas that the King should exercise his prerogative to do justice. The judges had discretion to do so, when a claimant alleged an unlawful action, but could assert no legal right to a remedy. Lord Mansfield took the jurisdiction to new frontiers in *R v Barker* (1762) 3 Burr 1265. Yet he claimed to be following ancient doctrine when he said the following of *mandamus* (the prerogative remedy that evolved into what the Civil Procedure Rules now call a 'mandatory order'):

> ' A mandamus is a prerogative writ; to the aid of which the subject is intitled, upon a proper case previously shewn, to the satisfaction of the Court. The original nature of the writ, and the end for which it was framed, direct upon what occasions it should be used. Therefore it ought to be used upon all occasions where the law has established no specific remedy, and where in justice and good government there ought to be one. ' (1267)

Pentecost Barker was one of the trustees of a Presbyterian meeting house in Plymouth; after a disputed election for a new pastor, the dissidents sought *mandamus* to compel the trustees to acknowledge the election of their candidate. Lord Mansfield decided that the dispute was 'of a nature to inflame men's passions' (1269), and could lead to a breach of the peace, and that was enough to persuade him to hear the case. Whether the case should be heard was a matter for the satisfaction of the court, and the court would be satisfied if 'justice and good government' required the dispute to be heard.

Discretion and jurisdiction

Standing determines the court's *jurisdiction* (i.e., whether the court can lawfully decide the claim),[2] and yet standing is subject to the *discretion* of the court (that

---

[1] On standing to bring an ordinary claim for a declaration, without asserting a right to a remedy, see p 414.

[2] See *R v Social Security Secretary, ex p Child Poverty Action Group* [1990] 2 QB 540, 556, *R v Foreign Secretary, ex p World Development Movement* [1995] 1 WLR 386, 395.

> is, to some extent the court gets to choose whether to grant standing). This may seem bizarre, but it simply reflects the High Court's remarkable discretionary control over its own process: the court's jurisdiction is, to some extent, up to the court. This discretion was a feature of the court's inherent jurisdiction over the administration of justice at common law, and is preserved by the Supreme Court Act 1981 and the Civil Procedure Rules.

By the 20th century, standing requirements were more complex, and varied for different prerogative writs, and it was less clear that the judges had such a wide discretion; but it was a fair generalization when Lord Wilberforce said, in *Gouriet v Union of Post Office Workers* [1978] AC 435, 482, that 'the courts have allowed . . . liberal access [to judicial review] under a generous conception of *locus standi*' (*locus standi* meaning standing—'a place to stand').

When the judges and Parliament reformed the judicial review process in the 1978 rules of the Supreme Court, and the Supreme Court Act 1981, they provided that an applicant for judicial review needed to have a 'sufficient interest in the matter', in order to proceed.[3]

11.1.2 Standing to seek judicial review: 'sufficient interest'

There are three crucial points to note about the statutory requirement of a 'sufficient interest':

1. **Although it is often described as a vague test of standing, it is actually not a test at all. It is a shorthand way of saying that the court is to decide the test.**

Imagine that your mom asks you to bring home eggs from the market. You ask how many, and she says 'sufficient'. She has left it to your judgment. Likewise, the Supreme Court Act does not say what kind or degree of interest is sufficient; it leaves that question to the court. The evident purpose of the provision was to preserve the court's control over (and responsibility for) its own process.

The phrase 'sufficient interest' was, in fact, borrowed from judicial decisions, in which the judges had said that they would exercise their discretion to allow an application for *certiorari* (today, a quashing order) only if the applicant had a 'sufficient interest' (*Ex p Stott* [1916] 1 KB 7, 9). The point of that wording in the judgments was to emphasize that although an applicant could not seek judicial review without any interest in the matter, there was no need to allege an infringement of a legal right (such as a taking of property). Not just any interest would do, but the courts were prepared to work out what was sufficient case by case.

---

3   Rules of the Supreme Court Order 53 r 3(5); Supreme Court Act 1981 s 31(3). The Rules have been superseded by the Civil Procedure Rules; the Supreme Court Act is still in force.

> ## Rights and interests
>
> Your **interest** is what's in it for you. Your interest is legally protected if the law requires someone deciding the matter to take into account what would be good for you. You have a **right** if your interest ought to be protected or promoted regardless of (some) contrary considerations. You have a **legal right** if the law requires someone to protect or promote your interest regardless of (some) contrary considerations.
>
> **Example:** I have an interest in whether planning permission will be granted for a development on my land, but I have no right to be given permission. But I have a right not to have my land trespassed upon by strangers.

But 'a sufficient interest' was not an agreed, general formulation of what the judges were looking for; in some cases, it had been held that an applicant for *certiorari* must be a person 'aggrieved', and an applicant for *mandamus* must have 'a specific legal right' at stake (R *v Russell, ex p Beaverbrook Newspapers Ltd* [1969] 1 QB 342, 348).[4] So although the new rules borrowed the language from the judges, the 1978 rules of the Supreme Court and the Supreme Court Act 1981 did change the law, and simplified it. The Supreme Court Act preserved the discretion the judges had (in their inherent jurisdiction over prerogative proceedings) to decide what was required for standing, at the same time limiting it by preventing them from hearing a case in which the claimant has no interest at all. Though the remaining discretion is very wide, that does not mean that the judges can treat just any interest they like as sufficient. As Lord Wilberforce said in R *v Inland Revenue Commissioners, ex p National Federation of Self-Employed and Small Businesses Ltd* ('Fleet Street Casuals') [1982] AC 617, 'the court must decide on legal principles' (631). What are those principles? That depends on the second crucial thing to note about 'sufficient interest'.

2. **'Sufficient ...' implies '... for some purpose'.**

The relevant purpose is the purpose of bringing a claim for judicial review. So the Supreme Court Act 1981 s 31(3) should be read as requiring enough of an interest in the matter *to justify allowing this claimant to pursue this claim against this defendant*. The question is not, 'is the claimant seriously affected by the decision?', but, 'does the claimant have an interest that gives the court a reason to hear their claim (and, incidentally, to make the defendant respond to it)?'

So for which reasons should the court allow a claimant to pursue a claim? In order to redress an injustice to the claimant? Or to stamp out unlawful conduct in general? If the former were the only reason, then no one should have standing unless they claim to be the victim of an injustice. If the latter is enough, then anyone who alleges unlawful behaviour should be allowed to proceed. The judges' vision of the purpose

---

4   And in *Ex p Stott*, the court suggested that an applicant for *certiorari* had to be aggrieved by the decision in order to have a sufficient interest ([1916] 1 KB 7, 9).

of the judicial review procedure is not entirely clear, although it has some perfectly clear aspects. They will not give standing just because the claimant alleges unlawful conduct by a public authority. But they will listen to claimants who have suffered no injustice.

3. Sufficiency is a question of proportionality.

The court faces the question of what kind of interest is needed, and also how much of an interest is enough. So the test of standing is a proportionality test. As a requirement of proportionate *process*, it is part of the general law of due process, which applies generally across the vast variety of administrative and judicial decision making (see Chapter 4). Proportionality in this case is a relation between the process value of hearing a claim of judicial review, and the process cost and any process danger that may result. Like any proportionality standard it is rather favourable to the claimant in some ways, because the court will ask the open-ended question of whether the claimant is getting *enough* access to judicial review. Yet it also limits judicial review: no one is to be allowed to bring a public authority into court if they do not have enough of an interest in the matter.

The result of these three points is that the court has wide-ranging discretion to give proportionate process in a way that supports the purposes of judicial review (which the judges have not stated very clearly). There is nothing more definite than that in the '*Fleet Street Casuals*' case—the only House of Lords decision on what counts as a sufficient interest. Thousands of casual newspaper workers had been cheating on their income tax, by giving the newspapers false names. The Inland Revenue worked out a deal to end the frauds and to create a new reporting system, while seeking repayment of only part of the back taxes. A Federation of angry businessmen wanted to challenge the deal as a breach of the Inland Revenue's statutory duty to assess and collect tax; the Federation claimed that it should be given standing because its members, like all taxpayers, were adversely affected by the frauds. In the High Court, the Federation was given permission to apply for judicial review, but at the hearing of the application, the Inland Revenue persuaded the court to hold that the Federation had no sufficient interest to bring the application. The Court of Appeal overruled that decision. Lord Denning held that the Federation's allegation gave it a sufficient interest. He said that the federation and its members 'are not mere busybodies', but 'have a genuine grievance' ([1980] QB 407, 425).

The House of Lords overruled the Court of Appeal. The crucial point in the decision was the Law Lords' conclusion that although the Revenue owed a duty of fairness to taxpayers in general, that duty allowed for the sound management of taxes, which gave them a discretion to decide whether it was better tax policy to go after all the tax that the casuals owed, or to cut a deal with them that would improve tax collection. The House of Lords concluded that Federation did not have standing to challenge the lawfulness of the Revenue's approach, although it *would* have had standing, if it had alleged something outrageous: 'some exceptionally grave or widespread illegality' (Lord Fraser, 647), 'a case of sufficient gravity' (Lord Wilberforce, 633), or a breach of statutory duty due to 'some grossly improper pressure or motive' (Lord Roskill, 662). Although Lord Diplock similarly said the Federation would have standing if it alleged 'flagrant and serious breaches of the law' (641), he also suggested (unlike the other Law Lords) that the Federation would have standing to seek judicial review of any *ultra vires* conduct (644).[5]

It may seem that the House of Lords decided that the Federation's allegation of unlawful conduct had no merit, and *then* decided that the Federation had no standing. That would put the cart before the horse, because the question of whether the claimant has standing 'has to be answered affirmatively before any question on the merits arises' (Lord Fraser, 645). Yet the Law Lords decided that the conduct was not unlawful, and *on that basis*, it seems, they decided that the Federation had no sufficient interest. Does that mean that the court needs to decide the merits (i.e., how good the claimant's case is), in order to decide standing? Yes and no, unfortunately. It is wrong to say that no question of the merits arises until standing is decided. But it is also a serious (but popular) mistake to think that 'in reality the issue of standing collapses into the wider question of substantive merit'.[6] Questions of merits are not *generally* relevant to standing; instead, they are relevant in two particular ways:

- **No one has standing to proceed with a claim that patently has no merit.**

This isn't something special about judicial review; at any point in any proceeding, if the court can determine through a fair process that the claim has no merit, the right thing to do is to dismiss it. So in any proceedings, including judicial review, the court may give summary judgment (i.e., decide the dispute without a trial) if the claimant 'has no real prospect of succeeding on the claim' (CPR 24.2(a)(i)). And in an ordinary claim, the court may strike out a statement of case if it 'discloses no reasonable grounds' for a claim (CPR 3.4) or if it is 'totally without merit' (CPR 3.3(7)). In judicial review, the claimant has to ask for permission before proceeding. The requirement of an arguable case at the permission stage *is a standing requirement*. If the court can see that the claim cannot possibly succeed, the claimant has no standing to proceed to a judicial review hearing.

- **In order to decide whether the claimant's 'interest in the matter' is sufficient to justify a hearing, the court needs to decide *what the 'matter'* is.**

In the *Fleet Street Casuals* case, the Federation would have had standing if 'the matter' it was alleging was something outrageous (*unless* the court could tell at the permission stage that the claim was not arguable). The court could only reach that view of the situation after the Inland Revenue had explained the role of the impugned decision

---

5   Note that all the important cases on standing, including the *Fleet Street Casuals* case, were decided when the permission decision was made *ex parte* (i.e., without hearing from the defendant at all). The Civil Procedure Rules now allow the defendant to respond to the application for permission on paper, which enables the defendant to argue that the claimant has no sufficient interest.

6   As was said by counsel for the applicant seeking standing in R v Employment Secretary, ex p Equal Opportunities Commission [1995] 1 AC 1, 19.

in tax management—which persuaded the House of Lords that another taxpayer had no sufficient interest to challenge the decision on the grounds the Federation offered, given the discretion of the Inland Revenue in deciding what was required for the sound management of taxes. The more serious the alleged conduct (so long as the allegation is arguable), the less individual involvement the applicant needs in order to have a sufficient interest in it. Very often, as in the *Fleet Street Casuals* case, the court will only be able to decide that the claimant has no right to a hearing, after having given a hearing. That is not because the court needs to decide *the merits* of the claim in order to decide standing, but because the court needs to decide what *the matter* (i.e., the claim) is, in order to decide whether the claimant has a sufficient interest in it to justify a hearing.

> ### The irony of process (see p 143)
>
> The fact that standing plays a role in the substantive hearing of a claim for judicial review is an instance of the irony that parties often need to be given *more* process than is actually due to them. A claimant without a sufficient interest in a matter is not entitled to be heard, but it is often necessary to hear the whole story from the claimant *and* the defendant, in order to decide whether the claimant has a sufficient interest. So the court must often give a process that turns out to be more than what is due to the claimant—and that is what happened in the *Fleet Street Casuals* case.

Once a court decides the merits of a claim, of course, the claimant's standing is exhausted (although an unsuccessful claimant may then have standing to bring an appeal).

So merits are relevant to standing in those two ways, and yet Lord Fraser in the *Fleet Street Casuals* case was right in a sense when he said that the standing question was prior to that of the merits: a claim may have no merit whatsoever, and yet the claimant may have standing to proceed to a hearing, if the court cannot yet see that the claim has no merit.

It is a popular idea, drawn from the *Fleet Street Casuals* case, that 'standing should not be treated as a preliminary issue' (R v Foreign Secretary, ex p World Development Movement [1995] 1 WLR 386, 395). But it is a mistaken idea. Standing *is* a preliminary matter, because the Administrative Court is not allowed to give permission to proceed, if it is apparent at that point that the claimant has no standing (Supreme Court Act 1981 s 31). But the court often has to allow a claim to proceed past the permission stage without having been able to determine *whether* the claimant should be given standing or not.

11.1.3 Standing and the purpose of judicial review

Does *Fleet Street Casuals* give us any picture of the purpose of judicial review? There are suggestions that the purpose is ordinarily to right an injustice to the claimant. All the Law Lords (except Lord Diplock) indicated that a taxpayer might only have standing to pursue an allegation of illegality in the treatment of another taxpayer where it is exceptionally grave.[7] And since the decision, it has been held that a claimant has standing to challenge the Inland Revenue's treatment of another taxpayer *if* that treatment unfairly makes it cheaper for that other taxpayer to produce the same product that the claimant is producing (*R v The Attorney-General, ex p Imperial Chemical Industries* [1987] 1 CMLR 72 (CA), 107). Why does standing normally require some impact on the claimant? Why isn't it enough that the claimant is alleging that the public authority acted unlawfully? Lord Diplock, alone, suggested in the *Fleet Street Casuals* case that a mere allegation of unlawful conduct is enough for standing:

> It would, in my view, be a **grave lacuna** in our system of public law if a pressure group, like the federation, or even a single public-spirited taxpayer, were prevented by outdated technical rules of locus standi from bringing the matter to the attention of the court to vindicate the rule of law and get the unlawful conduct stopped. (644)

This grave lacuna is a bit of a mystery. Lord Diplock's talk of 'bringing the matter to the attention of the court' suggests that the courts have a general responsibility to listen to anyone, in order to vindicate the rule of law whenever a public authority has acted unlawfully. Was he saying that anyone can bring any allegation of unlawful conduct in front of a court? Let's call that an 'open doors' policy on standing. The rest of this section aims to explain why it would be a mistake to think that the law has or ought to have an open doors policy.

If all unlawful official conduct just must come before a court to get quashed, then we really do need an open doors policy. But what is the point in making something unlawful? Doing so has all sorts of particular purposes; generally, the point is simply to guide and to constrain public authorities to act justly and for the public good. The point is *not* to turn the judges into a general government complaints department. If it seems pointless to make something unlawful without automatically providing a process to 'get the unlawful conduct stopped', remember that processes need a justification of their own. They can be absolutely crucial (so that the law can become pointless if the process fails). But they need some justification other than the mere fact that a public authority has allegedly done something unlawful.

---

[7] A taxpayer can even challenge the legality of a governmental expenditure decision (at least, if the issue is of general importance): *R v HM Treasury, ex p Smedley* [1985] 1 QB 657, 670 (Slade LJ). But it will ordinarily be difficult to show the arguable case that is required for permission to seek judicial review, because of judicial deference to government on spending decisions—see p 248.

The rule of law may not require a legal response to unlawful conduct!

It may sound surprising, but there is no general public interest in having a court hear a complaint that a public authority has acted unlawfully. The rule of law *does* require that officials (and people in general) abide by the law. But when they don't, the rule of law requires the operation of a process for interfering only when that process itself will improve conformity to the law—either by changing official conduct for the future, or by remedying the unlawful results of a particular action. Just as the rule of law does not require the police to seek a prosecution every time they have information that someone has committed an offence, the rule of law does not demand that every instance of unlawful action by a public authority should be brought before a court. Similarly, although the rule of law requires a process enabling one private person to seek a remedy against a tort by another person, it does not require that every tort should result in a claim in the High Court. There is no lapse in the role of law, if the victim of a tort decides not to sue.

So there is no grave lacuna just because some unlawful conduct does not come before a court, any more than there is a grave lacuna if some criminal or tortious activity is not brought 'to the attention of the court to vindicate the rule of law and get the unlawful conduct stopped'.

Remember the butcher and the baker. If they phone someone whose phone is being unlawfully tapped by MI5, they have no standing to seek judicial review. What if the person whose phone was tapped does not want to seek judicial review (or has left the country, or has died)? Then, it seems, the rules of standing mean that no one[8] can bring the matter to the attention of the court—even a person with an arguable claim that a public authority has acted (or is acting) unlawfully. And that is not because the standing requirements are 'outdated technical rules' (*Fleet Street Casuals*, 644); they reflect a judgment (first of the courts, and then of Parliament (Supreme Court Act 1981 s 31(3)), that it is not the role of the courts to vindicate the rule of law by listening to all plausible allegations of unlawful official conduct. Judicial review is to be a procedure in which the claimant must have an interest in the matter that gives the court some reason to listen to them. The opportunity to stamp out unlawful administrative conduct in general does not justify a judicial review proceeding. It is not enough for the claimant to assert a general interest in getting unlawful conduct stopped. And yet, as we will see, if the claimant can persuade the court that a hearing would be in the public interest, *that* may be enough.

---

8   Except the Attorney General, who has standing on behalf of the public, and has a general responsibility for safeguarding the rule of law—see p 420. And the Attorney General has no general duty to bring proceedings whenever something unlawful has occurred; he has a discretionary power.

Representative standing

Notice that even if the Inland Revenue's decision had been unfair to the angry businessmen, it wouldn't have been unfair to the Federation itself as an organisation. So the Federation had no stake in the litigation! But in fact associations of all kinds are regularly given standing for judicial review in a very relaxed fashion (the question of whether the Federation had standing to represent its members in court was not even argued in the Fleet Street Casuals case; the only issue there was whether the members had a sufficient interest). Standing of associations actually is a problem in ordinary claims, because the association can only be a claimant if it can assert a cause of action. But there is no such problem in judicial review. For the purpose of litigating matters in which the people they represent have a sufficient interest, the courts have given standing to trade unions, the Association of British Civilian Internees Far East Region, the British Parachute Association, and the president of a Jewish Burial Society.[9]

The courts have consistently been willing to assume that pressure groups work in the interest of the people they claim to represent. No doubt, a failure to do so would be a ground to refuse standing, but the defendant would need to press the matter. The courts prefer to presume that a famous organization like Greenpeace is acting responsibly, instead of scrutinizing its structures and behaviour.

11.2 Campaign litigation: a special standing problem

Making an allegation of unlawful conduct is not enough to give a claimant a sufficient interest; but can a claimant without a personal interest nevertheless have a sufficient interest in the matter *because the litigation is in the public interest?* All judicial process is public interest litigation in a sense: the people of the community share an interest in a system of justice. The reason for the proceeding (even if it is an action for breach of contract between two private persons) is the public interest in the administration of justice. And all judicial review cases are public interest litigation in a further sense: the people of the community share an interest in a system that prevents arbitrary government, so that the government acts responsibly on their behalf.

Can some more particular public interest give a claimant a sufficient interest for the purpose of standing? Advocacy groups often want to turn from politics to litigation, to pursue a campaign for a purpose that they argue is in the public interest. Win or lose, judicial review gives them a voice in a prestigious forum, and forces the government to defend itself before a neutral authority. The courts have to decide whether, as the claimant says, the community's *interest in the outcome* provides a reason

---

[9]   R v Trade and Industry Secretary, ex p Unison [1996] ICR 1003, R (British Civilian Internees—Far Eastern Region) v Defence Secretary [2003] EWCA Civ 473, R v Shrewsbury Coroners Court, ex p British Parachute Association (1988) 152 JP 123, R v Greater Manchester North District Coroner, ex p Worch and Brunner [1987] 2 WLR 1141.

for allowing the claim to proceed. The question is whether campaign litigation is in the public interest.

The Federation in the *Fleet Street Casuals* case[10] asked for standing on the ground of their members' own private interest. Their grievance was that it was unfair *to them* for the Inland Revenue to make a special deal for the casual workers. They claimed that they had been adversely affected by the deal (see Lord Roskill's speech, 660). But counsel for the Inland Revenue said that the Federation 'are seeking to represent the public interest and this they cannot do. A fortiori, ... they can have no "sufficient interest" to bring these proceedings' (621). This argument was not addressed explicitly in the speeches in the case. Imagine that the Federation were alleging some grossly improper conduct (in which case they would have standing to proceed). It is not clear whether the Law Lords decided that in such a case the Federation would have a *private* interest sufficient to justify their proceeding, or whether they would be treated as having a sufficient interest on the ground that the proceeding would be in the *public* interest. But Lord Diplock's grave lacuna is certainly a matter of the public interest, and he proposed that the lacuna might be filled by giving standing to 'a single public-spirited taxpayer'. But why a taxpayer? If the Inland Revenue is behaving grossly improperly, why not let just anybody fill the grave lacuna? Can public spirit give a claimant standing, if the law requires that the claimant must have an interest in the matter?

In *World Development Movement*, the High Court held that the Government had used the foreign aid budget unlawfully to support an uneconomical dam project in Malaysia. It was a remarkable instance of judicial control of discretionary power (on the substance of the decision, see p 270); it was also remarkable that the court listened to the application at all. The Movement was a 'non-partisan pressure group' (393). The interests of the Movement as an organization were not at stake; the whole point of the Movement was to promote *other people's* interests. So how could the Movement have a sufficient interest in the matter? The idea of an interest is ambiguous: in one sense, you have an interest in a matter if it affects you for good or ill. In another sense, you have an interest in a matter if you find it interesting. By requiring a 'sufficient interest' in the matter, the Supreme Court Act cannot have meant that the claimant must find the matter sufficiently interesting. But the courts have treated persons who are *involved with a matter* as having a potentially sufficient interest, even if the resolution of a dispute does not affect them for good or ill. What more does it take then, than just finding the matter interesting?

11.2.1 Factors in the standing of a campaign litigant

Rose LJ set out the following factors in the *World Development Movement* case:

- 'the importance of vindicating the rule of law' (citing Lord Diplock's comment on the grave lacuna in the *Fleet Street Casuals* case (644))

---

[10] *R v Inland Revenue Commissioners, ex p National Federation of Self-employed and Small Businesses Ltd* [1982] AC 617.

- 'the importance of the issue'

- 'the likely absence of any other responsible challenger'

- 'the nature of the breach of duty' (but of course, this is part of 'the importance of the issue')

- 'the prominent role of these applicants' in the field of foreign aid (395).

The first factor only begs the question: even though the rule of law requires official conformity to the law, it does not *generally* demand judicial process for interfering with unlawful conduct. It is important to vindicate the rule of law *by judicial process* only if the proceeding is in the public interest. So we can generally say that a litigant seeking to promote the public interest will be given standing for judicial review if the following criteria are met.

The three requirements in *World Development Movement*
A campaign litigant has standing if:

(1)   the issue is important to the public,
(2)   no one else could make a responsible challenge, and
(3)   the claimant has a 'prominent role' in the field.

Only the last of these factors has anything at all to do with the claimant's interest in the matter. The importance of the case and the 'no one else' factor are considerations that can make it a good idea to allow campaign litigation; the role of those considerations is to lead the court to treat a claimant such as the World Development Movement as *having an interest* in the matter that is sufficient to justify judicial review, even though *the group's interests are not at stake* in the decision.

Representation by campaign groups
Campaign litigation involves an element of representation, when it is conducted by a pressure group that has members or supporters. The representative role of the group plays no important role in *World Development Movement*. It had standing *not* because its members were affected by the decision, but because its membership and organization made it an effective body to make a case that the government had acted unlawfully.

In *R v Inspectorate of Pollution, ex p Greenpeace (No 2)* [1994] 2 CMLR 548 (discussed below), Otton J suggested that the most important reason for giving standing to Greenpeace was that they had 2500 members in Cumbria, who 'are inevitably concerned about…a danger to their health and safety from any additional discharge of radioactive waste even from testing' [81]. But the Cumbrian members seem to be a red herring, given the nature of Greenpeace: it is a global environmental campaign organization, and not a Cumbrian residents' health and safety association. That is, the representative role of the pressure group should have been no more relevant in that case, than it was in *World Development Movement*.

11.2.2 The advantages of campaign litigation

Even though no one has a right to litigate issues that do not affect their rights, it can be a really good idea to let them do so: think of a case like R v Ministry of Defence, ex p Walker [2000] 1 WLR 806 (see section 2.1), in which Sergeant Walker claimed that the Ministry had unlawfully denied his criminal injuries compensation claim. Walker obviously did have a sufficient interest in the matter, but the public interest also favoured allowing his claim for judicial review to be heard. He had no right to compensation, and yet it was in the public interest to let him proceed both because of the public interest in the administration of justice, and also because of the public interest in ensuring that public authorities do not use their power arbitrarily. Aside from the importance of giving a fair process for him to seek to promote his own interest in the outcome of the case, there was also an important public interest in hearing Walker's case.

Likewise, pure campaign litigation can be a good idea—even if the claimant is promoting some special interest, rather than the public interest. In World Development Movement, the court did not assess the pressure group's agenda to decide whether their agenda was in the public interest—and that has been a common feature of litigation by pressure groups. Groups such as the World Development Movement and Greenpeace think that it is in the public interest that their special causes should succeed. Did the court need to decide whether they were right about that? Not in order to give them standing. A special interest group can engage in litigation that is in the public interest, because any danger that the group's special interest is contrary to the public interest can be met by the participation of the public authority in the adversary process of judicial review. The standing question is not whether the claimant is promoting the public interest; it is whether the claimant has enough of an interest to proceed, given the public interest in hearing the claim.

Of course, campaign litigation creates a real danger that argument in court will become a phoney substitute for the political debates that ought to be conducted in Parliament or in local councils or in the media. And that is often precisely what a claimant is seeking to achieve by bringing a claim for judicial review. The examples include challenges to the signing of treaties: Blackburn v Attorney-General [1971] 1 WLR 1037 (seeking a declaration that it would be unlawful for the government to sign the Treaty of Rome to bring Britain into the European Community) and R v Foreign Secretary, ex p Rees-Mogg [1994] QB 552, in which a member of the House of Lords sought to litigate issues (concerning the signing of the Maastricht Treaty on the European Union) on which he had lost the debate in Parliament. In these cases, the claimant's lawyers will be explaining to them from the start that there is no chance of success; the claimant goes ahead anyway for publicity purposes, and for the symbolic value of forcing the government to justify its actions before a judge. Even where there is no chance of success, there can be publicity value in getting a court to question the lawfulness of government action.

It would be entirely reasonable to deny standing in these cases. But the courts prefer to deal with them by means of (1) the requirement of an arguable case, and (2) the grounds of judicial review, with the limits that they impose on the judicial role. If the judges are self-disciplined and do not extend their reach beyond the lawful grounds of judicial review, then generous standing for campaign litigants does not raise a danger of illegitimate judicial interference with government—just a risk of wasted court time and costs in proceedings that will generate publicity for the campaign group, but cannot succeed. So in *Blackburn* and *Rees-Mogg*, the court gave no serious consideration to the question of standing. Blackburn's claim was struck out on the ground that he had no arguable case. The *Rees-Mogg* litigation involved four days of hearings at substantial public expense on an application that was, all along, plainly unarguable.

In *Rees-Mogg*, there was 'no dispute as to the applicant's locus standi' (561). But the fact that a defendant does not dispute standing does not mean that a claimant has standing, and it would have been quite legitimate for the court to refuse permission for judicial review on the ground that the applicant had no standing. Yet even in a case like *Rees-Mogg*, there may be a certain sort of value in a careful judicial explanation of why there are no grounds for judicial review. The proceeding becomes the court's way of reminding the community of how limited the court's responsibility is for good government. And generous standing is justified because it actually will promote the rule of law, where (1) there is a significant public interest at stake, and (2) the public authority's behaviour actually was a flagrant abuse of a legal power. Then (as in the *World Development Movement* case) the litigation will be justified.

FROM THE MISTS OF TIME

Public interest standing is nothing new. At common law, the courts in principle actually did have an open doors policy, because of their responsibility for 'public order in administration of law' (*Worthington v Jeffries* (1875) LR 10 CP 379, 383). So the judges might listen to a claim, 'by whomsoever brought before them, that an inferior Court is acting without jurisdiction, or is exceeding its jurisdiction' (ib., and see *Wadsworth v Queen of Spain* (1851–2) LR 17 QB 215). In *The King v Speyer* [1916] 1 KB 595, a mere 'stranger' challenged the validity of the appointment of two Privy Councilors, and the Chief Justice said that the applicant 'appears to have brought this matter before the Court on purely public grounds without any private interest to serve, and it is to the public advantage that the law should be declared by judicial authority' (613). The judges in the late 20th century saw themselves as developing a new, more liberal approach to standing, but it is not nearly as liberal as the older common law. In those earlier cases, though, the courts did not have to deal with pressure groups like Greenpeace or the World Development Movement.

In more recent times, Lord Denning advocated an open doors policy: he held that 'the discretion of the court extends to permitting an application to be made by any member of the public' (*R v Greater London Council, ex p Blackburn* [1976] 1 WLR 550, 559). But Lord Denning's open door policy was restricted to claimants who allege that a public authority is breaking the law 'in a way which offends or injures thousands of Her Majesty's subjects' (*Attorney-General, ex rel McWhirter v Independent Broadcasting Authority* [1973] QB 629, 649), and did not apply to 'busybodies'.

Decision	Standing given	The claimant	The matter
R v IRC, ex p National Federation of Self-Employed [1982] AC 617	✗	Businessmen's pressure group.	Whether the Inland Revenue could lawfully overlook some of the tax owed by other taxpayers.
R v HM Treasury, ex p Smedley [1985] 1 QB 657	✓	A 'man of many parts' who 'seeks the assistance of the court in his capacity as Mr. Smedley, British taxpayer and elector' (Sir John Donaldson MR, 664).	Whether the Government could lawfully contribute to a supplementary budget of the EC, without a new act of Parliament.
R v Environment Secretary, ex p Rose Theatre Trust [1990] 1 QB 504	✗	A company formed by local residents, the local MP, and distinguished archeologists, to campaign to preserve the remains of the Rose Theatre.	Whether the Environment Secretary had unlawfully refused to list a Shakespearean theatre as a monument protected from development.
R v Social Security Secretary, ex p Child Poverty Action Group [1990] 2 QB 540	✓*	Two national associations that 'play a prominent role in giving advice, guidance and assistance' to claimants for social security benefits (Woolf LJ, 546).	Whether the Minister had misinterpreted his statutory duties in deciding claims for supplementary benefit.
R v Foreign Secretary, ex p Rees-Mogg [1994] QB 552	✓*	A member of the House of Lords with 'sincere concern for constitutional issues' (Lloyd LJ, 562).	The lawfulness of signing the Maastricht Treaty.
R v Inspectorate of Pollution, ex p Greenpeace (No 2) [1994] 2 CMLR 548	✓	'a well-known campaigning organisation which has as its prime object the protection of the natural environment' (Otton J, 551).	Whether new operations at a nuclear power plant could lawfully be carried out by a variation of old licences.
R v Foreign Secretary, ex p World Development Movement [1996] 1 WLR 386	✓	Non-partisan pressure group promoting interests of the poor in the third world.	Whether it was unlawful for the Foreign Secretary to use the overseas development fund for non-development purposes.
R v Somerset CC, ex p Dixon [1998] Env LR 111	✓	Local resident, parish councillor, environmentalist, election candidate in the area affected.	Whether a grant of planning permission was lawful.
R (Hasan) v Trade and Industry Secretary [2007] EWHC 2630	✓	A Palestinian living in territory occupied by Israel.	Transparency in the award of arms export licences.

Notes: all of these decisions except *Dixon* were made after the permission stage, at the judicial review hearing. In none of them did the court hold that permission to seek judicial review ought to have been refused on the ground of a lack of standing.
✓ : the claimant was given standing
✗ : the claimant was not given standing
* : Standing was not disputed

Figure 11.1 Standing in campaign litigation

Has the law now reached an open doors policy for campaign litigants? Schiemann J denied it in R v Environment Secretary, ex p Rose Theatre Trust [1990] 1 QB 504. A trust company was formed to campaign for the preservation of the remains of a Shakespearian theatre, and it sought judicial review of a Minister's refusal to list the remains as a monument. Schiemann J pointed out that 'the law does not see it as the function of the courts to be there for every individual who is interested in having the legality of an administrative action litigated' (522). That is quite true: the law requires something extra. But he went on to say that the extra is that an individual claimant, or the individuals represented by a pressure group, must have 'a greater right or expectation than any other citizen of this country to have that decision taken lawfully' (522). The other cases on campaign litigation have made no such requirement—almost the reverse. Instead of requiring any special private interest, they have welcomed pressure group litigation where, as in R v Foreign Secretary, ex p World Development Movement [1995] 1 WLR 386, it is unlikely that someone else could make a responsible challenge.

So that remark of Schiemann J no longer represents the law.[11] But that does not mean that the outcome in Rose Theatre Trust was wrong. In fact, it is remarkably similar to the Fleet Street Casuals case, and can be reconciled with the other decisions as a case in which the claimants would only have had a sufficient interest in seeking judicial review if they had been alleging a grossly improper use of the Minister's discretion; Schiemann J concluded that the Minister had the same sort of managerial discretion over negotiations with landowners who discover ancient remains on their property, as the Inland Revenue has over tax collection.

11.2.3 An applicant with a 'prominent role'

Moreover, it seems that Schiemann J may not have had the same confidence in the Rose Theatre Trust, that the judges have expressed concerning pressure groups in other cases. In Greenpeace (No 2), Otton J pointed out that the group's experience and access to experts meant that it was 'able to mount a carefully selected, focused, relevant and well-argued challenge' (571). Here is the last real block to open standing in public interest cases: the claimant must be a person or group that can be expected to make a case that is worth listening to. The final criterion for standing in the World Development Movement case was the group's 'prominent role' in the field of overseas development.

There is a double danger in this criterion: (1) that the judges may not really be able to make good decisions as to how sound or how dodgy a pressure group is, and (2) that their application of the criterion may discriminate in favour of the famous and against the underprivileged. But there is no particular reason to think that these dangers have come to pass, because the courts have been so generous in granting standing.

---

[11] In R v Somerset CC, ex p Dixon [1998] Env LR 111 (117), Sedley J said 'I would decline to follow the decision' in Rose Theatre Trust (a case in which he had successfully opposed standing, as counsel for the intervening landlord).

In fact, standing has become quite freely available—with the surprising result that there have been no contested cases on 'sufficient interest' in campaign litigation in the 21st century (partly, perhaps, because it is not generally politically attractive for the defendant public authority to try to portray the pressure group as irresponsible).[12] So the last word, for now, goes to Sedley J, who held in R v Somerset CC, ex p Dixon [1998] Env LR 111 that 'there will be, in public life, a certain number of cases of apparent abuse of power in which any individual, simply as a citizen, has a sufficient interest to bring the matter before the court' (117). That is not an open doors policy. For one thing, it is consistent (as Sedley J pointed out) with Rose Theatre Trust, because it does not apply to all cases; Sedley J agreed with Schiemann J's view that 'not every member of the public can complain of every breach of statutory duty' ([1990] 1 QB 504, 520). The cases in which 'any individual, simply as a citizen, has a sufficient interest' will include claims of grossly improper conduct, and may include any claim of 'general public importance' (as it was put in World Development Movement), in which the claim has enough merit to meet the test of an arguable case.

While adopting the reasoning of World Development Movement, Sedley J did not insist that Mr Dixon must have a 'prominent role' in order to have standing. The result is a return to the view of the old common law, and of Lord Denning, that a good citizen ought to be able to bring some complaints of abuse of power to the court. Perhaps the prominent role criterion from World Development Movement applies to campaign groups; citizens bringing a claim in their own name need only show that they have no 'ill motive' (Dixon, 121).

So the doors are just about open in campaign litigation cases, with the following provisos:

(1) campaign groups still need to show a prominent role in the issues involved in the claim (this point distinguishes, e.g., Greenpeace from Rose Theatre Trust).

(2) if there is some **particular potential claimant** who is specially affected, the court will not be prepared to hear a claim from anyone else. So if Cox's phone has been tapped, the court will not hear a claim for judicial review from people who phoned him up;[13] and

(3) Dixon, like many other cases, emphasized that **busybodies** do not have a sufficient interest (117).

No one likes a busybody: in Fleet Street Casuals, Lord Fraser said 'a mere busybody does not have a sufficient interest. The difficulty is...to distinguish between the

---

[12] With the exception of R (Feakins) v Environment Secretary [2003] EWCA Civ 1546, in which the government claimed that the applicant did not have standing to seek judicial review over the disposal of thousands of carcasses of cattle on her land after the foot-and-mouth epidemic, because she was only trying to pressure them into giving her more compensation. The Court of Appeal gave permission for judicial review, holding that she would only be deprived of standing if she had been acting in bad faith.

[13] As in R v Home Secretary, ex p Ruddock [1987] 1 WLR 1482—see p 394.

desire of the busybody to interfere in other people's affairs and the interest of the person affected by or having a reasonable concern with the matter to which the application relates' (Lord Fraser, 646).[14]

It seems that a busybody is a person with no reasonable concern for the issues. It cannot be merely a person who does not have an arguable case, or the process would only need a requirement of permission, and not a requirement of sufficient interest. Counsel for the Ministry in the *Greenpeace* case argued unsuccessfully that Greenpeace was a busybody. The court rejected that argument because of the group's fame, its commitment to advocacy on environmental issues, and its resources. To be a busybody, it is not enough to be a member of the House of Lords who wants to continue a debate in court after losing in Parliament—or standing would have been denied in *R v Foreign Secretary, ex p Rees-Mogg* [1994] QB 552. In fact, that case makes it hard to imagine who does count as a busybody. The court in *Rees-Mogg* said, 'we accept without question that Lord Rees-Mogg brings the proceedings because of his sincere concern for constitutional issues' (562). So perhaps a busybody is a person with an *insincere* interest in the issues—a timewaster. Or perhaps a busybody is someone who tries to interfere in a decision about some other particular person's rights or interests, as Lord Denning suggested when he said that the courts will not give standing to 'a mere busybody who is interfering in things which do not concern him' (*R v Greater London Council, ex p Blackburn* [1976] 1 WLR 550, 559). Where the three requirements from *World Development Movement* are met, it seems that no one is a busybody unless they are acting in bad faith. If the claim raises any serious issue of the public interest, and no one else is in a better position to bring the claim, the court will grant standing if it considers the claimant to be worth listening to.

We have not quite arrived at an open doors policy. We have, though, reached a point where anyone who, in good faith, looks set to put a responsible case on a matter of general public importance will be given standing (unless perhaps some other litigant is in a better position to do it). And in the only important case on standing in the ten years since *Dixon*, a High Court judge has extended to a non-citizen the standing that Sedley J gave to 'any citizen' to challenge abuses of power. In *R (Hasan) v Trade and Industry Secretary* [2007] EWHC 2630, Collins J held that a Palestinian living in territories occupied by Israel had standing to seek judicial review of decisions granting licences for arms manufacturers to export arms to Israel. The claimant asked the court to order the Secretary of State to give an explanation of the decisions that would go beyond the requirements of a statutory scheme of disclosure in Parliament, and beyond the additional voluntary disclosure that the government had given. The Government did not oppose standing at the hearing, and Collins J granted it on the ground that the claimant was 'indirectly affected by any trade in military equipment to Israel' [8]. It is true that people living in Israeli occupied territory (and, in fact, anywhere that Israel can exert military power) are indirectly affected by trade in military equipment to Israel. But the case offers no explanation as to why being indirectly affected by trade to a foreign country gives standing to seek judicial review of a trade

---

[14]   See also Lord Scarman (653) and Lord Diplock (642–3), and *R v Monopolies and Mergers Commission, ex p Argyll Group* [1986] 1 WLR 763, 773 (Sir John Donaldson MR).

decision in the English court. Perhaps this is one aspect of the liberal approach to standing: the courts do not address hard questions as to why they should listen to a claimant.

The case was decided in a 'rolled up' hearing [7], in which permission and the merits of the claim were decided at once. That enabled a foreign citizen to challenge British arms exports in court, in a case that had no prospect of success at all. If you are alarmed at the extraordinary prospect of access to judicial review for the billions of people around the world who may be indirectly affected by British arms exports (or other forms of trade?), bear in mind that this case is only really an application of the rule in *World Development Movement*: it is campaign litigation in which it was useful for purposes of public advocacy for a claim to be made in the name of an individual. Nevertheless, the Court ought to have denied standing in *Hasan*, on the ground that the claimant was not alleging any abuse of power, but was only seeking transparency from the government. A refusal of standing would have been entirely compatible with the liberal approach of *World Development Movement* and *Dixon*.

Note that it is not only pressure groups and campaigning individuals that can be given standing in the public interest. Journalists have standing to challenge decisions of public authorities prohibiting publication of information, apparently in the public interest rather than for the journalists' own sake.[15] But the family of a murder victim does not have standing to challenge the tariff of imprisonment set for a person convicted of the murder. Because the Crown is a party to the criminal proceedings, including the tariff-setting decision, 'there is no need for a third party to seek to intervene to uphold the rule of law'—that is the role of the Crown (*R (Bulger) v Home Secretary* [2001] EWHC Admin 119 [21], Rose LJ).

Campaign litigation and the time limit

Lord Steyn cast doubt on a suggestion of Laws J that 'delay will be tolerated much less readily in public interest litigation' (*R v Trade and Industry Secretary, ex p Greenpeace Limited* [1998] Env LR 415, 425). Laws J had said that public interest litigation 'is now an accepted and greatly valued dimension of the judicial review jurisdiction, but it has to be controlled with particular strictness' (425). He thought that if a claimant had no private interest in the litigation, the court should assert the public interest in speedy certainty. But on Lord Steyn's approach, that public interest has to be reconciled with the public interest in hearing a claim of 'abuse of power which in the interests of good administration should be exposed' (*R (Burkett) v Hammersmith and Fulham LBC (No 1)* [2002] UKHL 23 [44]). There isn't *necessarily* any public interest in speedy certainty (see p 355), although there was such a public interest in the *Greenpeace* case. It depends on the context.

---

[15]   *R v Felixstowe Justices, ex p Leigh* [1987] QB 582, *R v Home Secretary, ex p Brind* [1991] 2 WLR 588.

11.3 Costs in campaign litigation: the bad news and the good news

Campaign litigation doesn't just a raise a problem of standing; there are special implications for costs.

The bad news is that the ordinary rule is the starting point—the court will order an unsuccessful litigant to pay a substantial part of the winner's costs, unless there is some special reason not to. In public law claims in general, the courts have long been prepared in principle to 'punish with costs persons who might bring unnecessary actions' (*Dyson v Attorney-General* [1911] 1 KB 410, 423, Farwell LJ). And you cannot create a company to serve as claimant, just to avoid the effect of an order of costs.[16]

And although a public interest case may just succeed (as in the *World Development Movement* case), it is a risky business. Public interest claims tend to be more speculative than other claims (the *Greenpeace* and *Rees-Mogg* cases are examples). Claimants bring such chancy claims partly because of one of the really salient features of campaign litigation: it offers **good publicity**, and a form of **accountability**, even if the prospects for a favourable outcome are slim or non-existent. Whatever the outcome, the process itself is a way of bringing public authorities to account by forcing them to explain themselves to a court. And **even losing** may have benefits to the pressure group, as the litigation itself still shows the group's supporters how serious the group is. Losing may have a symbolic value in showing that the establishment is against them.

But a public interest litigant needs to think about the financial implications of losing: 'an unprotected claimant... if unsuccessful in a public interest challenge, may have to pay very heavy legal costs to the successful defendant, and... this may be a potent factor in deterring litigation directed towards protecting the environment from harm' R (*Burkett*) v *Hammersmith, Fulham LBC (Costs)* [2004] EWCA Civ 1342 [80] (Brooke LJ for the Court).

The good news is, you can apply for a **protective costs order** (Supreme Court Act 1981 s 51, CPR 44.3). That is, you can ask the court to order that you are not to be required to pay the defendant's costs if you lose (and failing that, you can ask the court to put a cap on your exposure). The courts have always had a discretion to do this, but they used to be extremely wary, and treated it as something to be done 'only in the most exceptional circumstances' (R v *Lord Chancellor, ex p Child Poverty Action Group* [1999] 1 WLR 347, 355 (Dyson J)). Things have changed in the 21st century. The first reported case of such an order was in R v *The Prime Minister, ex p Campaign for Nuclear Disarmament* [2002] EWHC 2712. CND asked the court to declare that United Nations resolutions did not authorize the use of force against Iraq. The Administrative Court capped CND's costs exposure at £25,000.

------

[16]   If you try it, the company may be refused standing, or the court may order the company to give security for costs before proceeding. See R v *Environment Secretary, ex p Kirkstall Valley Campaign Ltd* [1996] 3 All ER 304, 309; the company in that case was allowed to proceed because it was not formed as a way of avoiding costs.

If it really is in the public interest that the litigation should proceed, then it may be better for the public to bear the costs, than for the private claimant to be deterred by the risk. But it is remarkable that judges should take it on themselves to decide that public authorities are to fund litigation against themselves. Judges are generally wary of deciding how public authorities should spend their money (see p 248); they have felt able to do so in this context because of their very wide discretion over litigation costs under the Civil Procedure Rules.

When will the courts use that discretion to make a protective costs order? The Court of Appeal set out the considerations in R (Corner House Research) v Trade and Industry Secretary [2005] EWCA Civ 192. Protective costs orders will be made if:

> (i)   the issues raised are of general public importance;
> (ii) the public interest requires that those issues should be resolved;
> (iii) the applicant has no private interest in the outcome of the case;
> (iv) having regard to the financial resources of the applicant and the respondent(s) and to the amount of costs that are likely to be involved, it is fair and just to make the order; and
> (v)   if the order is not made the applicant will probably discontinue the proceedings and will be acting reasonably in so doing. [74]

The orders are meant to be exceptional, but the test has been substantially relaxed: Corner House Research removed an earlier requirement that the court must be able to see that the case has sufficient merit (Child Poverty Action Group, 358). As a result, as long as the issues you raise are of general public importance, you can apply for a protective costs order without showing that your case is any stronger than it needs to be to get past the permission stage. This change is important, because it potentially removes an important deterrent against claims that will probably not succeed. The permission requirement is not a perfect way of meeting this problem, because of the irony of process (see p 371): given the imperfect information available at the permission stage, a court that uses a decent standard for permission will need to let many claims proceed that will turn out to be unarguable at the hearing stage.

While endorsing the Corner House Research principles, recent decisions have emphasized the 'fair and just' part of the test, and have suggested that the orders may not be as exceptional as the Court of Appeal in Corner House Research indicated (R (British Union for the Abolition of Vivisection) v Home Secretary [2006] EWHC 250), and have cast doubt on the requirement that the claimant should have no private interest (Wilkinson v Kitzinger [2006] EWHC 835).

The whole thing is potentially revolutionary: a judicially invented ad hoc public fund for campaign litigants.

11.4 Standing in an ordinary claim for a declaration

You can ask for a declaration in an ordinary claim, and unlawful administrative action is grounds for a declaration. So if you do not have an interest in the matter that is sufficient for judicial review, can you seek a declaration instead? No: an action for a declaration has its own special standing requirement.[17] *Because* you can seek a declaration without having a cause of action (*Dyson v Attorney-General*), the courts developed a standing requirement to decide whether to hear claims for a declaration, and this common law requirement is in fact much stricter than the standing requirement for judicial review.

A claimant must allege 'either an interference with some private right of his or an interference with a public right from which he has suffered damage peculiar to himself': *Barrs v Bethell* [1982] Ch 294, 306 (Warner J). Warner J limited this holding to claims by ratepayers against local authorities, and said that 'local authorities and their members are particularly vulnerable to actions by busybodies and cranks' (313). But aside from *obiter* comments of Lord Denning (which were discounted in *Barrs* (311)), the rule is consistent with other cases on declarations, and can be regarded as a general rule of standing to bring an ordinary claim for a declaration.

It may seem strange to impose one standing requirement on a claimant seeking a declaration in a claim for judicial review, and a different requirement on a claimant seeking a declaration in an ordinary claim. But it makes sense for a reason emphasized in the *Barrs* case: the permission requirement gives a reason for the liberal standing doctrine in a claim for judicial review. If a claimant who would not be given permission to seek judicial review could seek a declaration in an ordinary claim instead as a matter of right, it would allow vexatious litigants to circumvent the permission requirement. This really *would* be an instance of the abuse of process that Lord Diplock had in mind in *O'Reilly v Mackman* [1982] 2 AC 237, 285 (see p 352).

Note that the 1978 judicial review reforms[18] liberalized proceedings for a declaration by providing that a declaration could be sought in judicial review, and by hinting that it could be done when the applicant did not have the standing to bring an action for a declaration (because the 'sufficient interest' provision applied to all applications for judicial review, without regard to the remedy). It was only a hint, because the courts might have decided that a person seeking a declaration does not have a sufficient interest unless the matter adversely affected his private interests. But in the *Fleet Street Casuals* case, the majority held that the issue of standing was the same regardless of the remedy.

> ### Standing is not more restricted in judicial review
> The standing requirements for judicial review are **not special obstructions restricting judicial review:** standing in judicial review is actually *more generous* to litigants than the requirement in an ordinary claim, for which the claimant must either have a right of action (see *Ewing v Office of the Deputy Prime Minister* [2005]

---

[17]   The same is true of an ordinary claim for an injunction.

[18]   Rules of the Supreme Court Order 53, given statutory force in the Supreme Court Act 1981 s 31.

EWCA Civ 1583 [35]), or else must fulfil the strict test of standing to bring an ordinary action for a declaration.

11.5 Standing in Human Rights Act proceedings

By the Human Rights Act s 6, an action of a public authority that is incompatible with
a Convention right is for that reason unlawful (unless the public authority could not
have acted differently because of primary legislation). So you might think that any
campaign litigant would be able to bring the unlawful conduct before a court. But
no: s 7(1) provides that a claimant can only bring proceedings based on s 6 'if he is
(or would be) a victim of the unlawful act'. If the proceeding is a claim for judicial
review, the claimant only has a sufficient interest to raise a Convention right issue if
he is or would be a victim (s 7(3)). That reflects the Convention itself, which provides
that claims may be brought in the Strasbourg Court by 'any person, non-governmental organisation or group of individuals claiming to be the victim of a violation by one
of the High Contracting Parties of the rights …' (European Convention on Human
Rights (ECHR) Art 34). The Strasbourg court has held that the 'victim' requirement
'does not permit individuals to complain against a law in abstract simply because they
feel that it contravenes the convention' (Klass v Germany (1978) 2 EHRR 214 [33]. The
claimant must be 'directly affected' [33]).

A very important exception!

The Equality Act 2006 creates an express exception to Human Rights Act s 7(1) and
s 7(3), giving the Equality and Human Rights Commission (see section 13.12) standing
to bring Human Rights Act proceedings. It only needs to show that there is or would
be some actual victim (Equality Act 2006 s 30(3)). This provision creates a technique
for litigation in the English courts by an independent advocacy commission.

Subject to the special statutory role of the Equality and Human Rights Commission,
it is 'doubtful in the extreme' that a court would use its discretion to declare that
a statute is incompatible with a Convention right, if the person seeking the declaration was not a victim of the incompatibility (Lancashire County Council v Taylor [2005]
EWCA Civ 284 [42] (Lord Woolf for the Court)). The defendant in that case was a tenant of a public authority, and argued that the legislation on termination of tenancies
was incompatible with the anti-discrimination provision in Art 14 of the Convention.
The Court of Appeal refused to consider a declaration of incompatibility, because the
alleged discrimination would not have affected the defendant.

The distinction between standing in general judicial review and standing under
the Human Rights Act reflects the different responsibilities of the court in applying
the Convention rights, on the one hand, and engaging in judicial review on the common law grounds, on the other. In applying the Convention rights, the court is given
no general responsibility for overseeing government; its job is only to hear a claim of
right. Under traditional judicial review, the courts have a more general responsibility

for reviewing allegations of unlawful administrative action, so that the focus of the court's attention is not simply to protect someone whose rights have been violated, but to control administrative action.

So the restriction on standing under the Human Rights Act does not leave a grave lacuna in our public law. It goes to show that the rule of law does not require an open doors policy; the processes for giving effect to the law are absolutely crucial, but they do not need to be engaged in every case of unlawful conduct. In the case of the Human Rights Act, the purpose of s 6 is to give legal effect to the Convention rights. Limiting standing strictly to victims is compatible with that concern for those rights; the purpose of making official conduct unlawful (giving effect to the Convention rights) can be met if standing is restricted to the victims of unlawful conduct.

So is there no room for campaign litigation over Human Rights Act issues? There is plenty of room, actually, but the proceedings need to be fronted by a representative claimant who is a victim of the alleged violation of a Convention right. An advocacy group can support the litigant (in fact, it can persuade the litigant to start proceedings in the first place), or can apply to intervene in the proceedings. Moreover, an intervenor need not be a victim, and the courts are generous in allowing intervention in Human Rights Act proceedings (*R (MH) v Health Secretary (Application for Permission to Intervene)* [2004] EWCA Civ 1321).

The possibility of public interest Human Rights Act litigation does not mean that the 'victim' requirement is meaningless. It not only means that the pressure group needs to persuade such a person to put their name to the proceedings; it also means that the argument and the reasoning of the judges are focused on the effect of an incompatibility on that party. As Lord Woolf has put it for the Court of Appeal, 'The primary objective of the Convention is to secure for individuals the rights and freedoms set out in the Convention', and Human Rights Act proceedings are designed to focus on that objective (*Lancashire County Council v Taylor* [2005] EWCA Civ 284 [37]).

11.6 Standing before the European Court of Justice

Article 230 of the EC Treaty allows any person to bring proceedings in the Court of Justice to challenge a decision, if it was 'addressed to that person' *or* 'is of direct and individual concern' to them. So, as with the Human Rights Act, standing cannot be given in the public interest, in the way that standing can be given for judicial review in English law. But the claimant does not need to be the victim of an adverse decision. The provision concerning 'direct and individual concern' suggests a half-way house, but the Court of Justice has treated it restrictively. 'Individual concern' is treated as requiring that the act in question concerns the claimant just as specifically as it concerns a person to whom it is addressed. As the Court of Justice has put it, the act must concern the claimant 'by reason of certain attributes peculiar to them, or by reason of a factual situation which differentiates them from all other persons and distinguishes them individually in the same way as the addressee' (Case C-50/00 P *Unión de Pequeños Agricultores v Council of the European Union* [2002] ECR II-6677

[36]).[19] It must be the case that the lawmaker actually took the applicant into account (or ought to have) in making the decision.

The Court of Justice insisted that its strict approach to standing did not abandon the rule of law:

> The European Community is...a community based on the rule of law in which its institutions are subject to judicial review of the compatibility of their acts with the Treaty and with the general principles of law which include fundamental rights. Individuals are therefore entitled to effective judicial protection of the rights they derive from the Community legal order ... [37]–[38]

Notice the emphasis on rights, which is the common thread in the doctrine of standing before British courts under the Human Rights Act, and before the European Court of Justice under EC law. Effective judicial protection of rights does not require campaign litigation; it requires a process adapted to the purpose of the law. So this strict doctrine does not create a grave lacuna in European law, either; the purpose of judicial proceedings need not be to open the doors to all complaints of illegality.

Finally, note that the system of European law relies on the national courts of member states. Those courts do not have jurisdiction to declare European Community measures invalid (Case 314/85 *Foto Frost* [1987] ECR 4199). But any person who wishes to rely on the invalidity of a Community measure can ask the national courts to make a reference to the European Court of Justice for a ruling on validity. And it is up to the national courts to operate procedural rules for people who want the court to give effect to European law. A campaign litigant in judicial review proceedings could ask the English courts to make a reference to the Court of Justice for a preliminary ruling on the validity of a Community measure, under the EC Treaty Art 234.

And if a claimant wants to argue that the action of a public authority in England is contrary to a directly effective provision of EC law, the national court must provide a process for the claim. The process may be subject to the same procedural restrictions (such as a requirement of standing) as in domestic law, *except* that if the restrictions make it practically impossible to enforce the right claimed under EC law, the national court must remove them. So a claimant will be given standing in judicial review, even if standing would ordinarily be refused, if denying standing would make 'the enforcement of a directly effective provision of the Treaty practically impossible' (R v *The Attorney-General, ex p ICI* [1987] 1 CMLR 72 (CA) [92]).

Greenpeace in the ECJ

Greenpeace has pushed unsuccessfully for campaign litigation before the European Court of Justice. It had no hope, as a campaign litigant, of convincing the ECJ (1) that it was representing its members, and (2) that the EC's decision to give millions of Euros to Spain for a nuclear power plant (a project that allegedly violated an

---

[19]   It is an ancient case law doctrine, dating back to Case 25/62 *Plaumann v Commission* [1963] ECR 95.

EC environmental directive) was of individual concern to its members. For while representative standing is allowed, the case was doomed by the strictness of the 'individual concern' doctrine. The Court of Justice held that the financing was only indirectly of concern to Greenpeace's members, so that Greenpeace did not have standing (Case 321/95 P *Stichting Greenpeace Council (Greenpeace International) v Commission* [1998] ECR I-1651). In any case, as the Court pointed out, Greenpeace's members had redress for any breach of the Directive in administrative proceedings in the national courts.

In order to:	You must:
Bring a claim for judicial review	have a sufficient interest in the matter.
Seek a declaration or injunction in an ordinary claim	assert a private right, or be subject to special damage.
Bring a claim in contract or tort	assert a right of action (see Chapter 14).
Bring a statutory appeal	be a party to the decision under appeal; i.e., a person whose legal position was determined by the decision (but this may depend on the statute).[20]
Bring proceedings under the Human Rights Act	be the victim of an alleged breach of a Convention right.
Bring proceedings in the European Court of Justice	be the addressee of the measure that is being attacked, or be directly and individually concerned by the measure.[21]
Bring a complaint to an ombudsman	complain that you have suffered injustice as a result of maladministration)[22] and, in the case of the Parliamentary ombudsman, find an MP willing to refer the complaint.[23]
Seek information under the Freedom of Information Act 2000	(**standing is open**: 'Any person' can request information: s 1(1)).
Get involved in statutory consultation exercises	(it depends on the statute; some, such as consultation over listing monuments, are open[24]).

Figure 11.2 Summary of standing requirements

[20]   The courts have been very relaxed in deciding who meets the common formula, 'person aggrieved': *Cook v Southend Borough Council* [1990] 2 QB 1. But if you are refused planning permission, the Planning Inspectorate will hear an appeal from you, but not from a third party who thinks you ought to have been given permission (Town and Country Planning Act 1990 s 78). And see *R v Medicines Commission, ex p Organon Laboratories* [1989] COD 479, aff'd [1990] 2 CMLR 49 (CA).

[21]   Art 230 EC Treaty. Note that the European Parliament, Council, Commission, and Member States are 'privileged' applicants with special standing; the Court of Auditors and the European Central Bank are 'quasi-privileged' applicants—Art 230.

[22]   Parliamentary Commissioner Act 1967 s 5(1); Local Government Act 1974 s 26(1). Representative standing is only expressly allowed if the person represented has died. But the Acts allow complaints by 'any body of persons whether incorporated or not' (PCA 1967 s 5(1); LGA 1974 s 27(1)), and the ombudsmen investigate complaints brought by campaign groups representing aggrieved persons.

[23]   Parliamentary Commissioner Act 1967 s 5(1). A complainant before the European Ombudsman need not have suffered injustice as a result of maladministration (and the European Ombudsman can initiate his own investigations—The European Ombudsman Statute—see p 498.

[24]   See *R v Environment Secretary, ex p Rose Theatre Trust Co* [1990] 1 QB 504, 520.

11.7 Standing for public authorities

The **Attorney General**, the Cabinet minister responsible for government legal services, has standing on behalf of the Crown to seek prerogative writs, and can also bring ordinary claims for an injunction or declaration. These special privileges in litigation reflect the fact that the government has a general responsibility for the rule of law. Not that the Attorney General must use these powers whenever he hears of unlawful conduct; it is up to him to decide when the public interest requires it. He can commence litigation at the request of (or 'at the relation of') any person; his discretion whether to conduct such 'relator' proceedings is (more or less) unreviewable (*Gouriet v Union of Post Office Workers* [1978] AC 435). A relator claim (brought as an ordinary claim for an injunction or declaration, or by the judicial review procedure) may be brought against a public authority on the same grounds as in a claim for judicial review. It may also be brought against any private person committing a public nuisance or otherwise violating what used to be called 'public rights'. Lord Wilberforce in *Gouriet* called the distinction between private rights and public rights one of the 'pillars' of the law (482); if it seems quaint today, that is because increasingly sophisticated regulatory regimes since the 1970s have generally accomplished the protection of certain public interests (particularly in pollution control) without the need for the Attorney General to initiate judicial proceedings. It seems that a public right arises where the law imposes a duty on a person for the public good, without giving anyone else a corresponding right to a remedy for breach of the duty.

FROM THE MISTS OF TIME

In *R v Inhabitants of Clace* (1769) 4 Burr 2456, Lord Mansfield said: 'I remember a case from Bristol, where the Attorney General, on behalf of the Crown, moved for a certiorari to remove some orders of two justices made for the relief of glassmakers from an over-charge upon them by the officers of Excise: and it was holden "that the King had a right in every case where the Crown is concerned, to demand a certiorari; and that the Court are bound to grant it, unless the King's right to it is restrained by some Act of Parliament"' (2458). Lord Mansfield remembered the case from Bristol because he was the Attorney General who made the argument (see *R v Amendt* [1915] 2 KB 276).

Largely because of the courts' generous approach to standing in judicial review, relator proceedings are now obsolete for practical purposes. They are still available, and it would be possible to imagine circumstances in which they would be useful; but there have been no relator claims in England in the 21st century. Yet in principle, in *any* public interest claim, the Attorney General could have brought proceedings to uphold the rule of law. But although officials of the Crown ought to be good at upholding the rule of law in criminal prosecutions (where the problem is how the criminal justice system should respond to crimes by private persons), they are systematically ineffective at bringing each other to account for unlawful conduct. So, for example, in the *World Development Movement* case, the Attorney General could have brought proceedings for a declaration that the Foreign Secretary had unlawfully plundered the overseas development budget. But in spite of a constitutional convention that the Attorney General is meant to give advice to the government on the law as he sees it, without political bias, he does not have the independence that it would take to make him a watchdog over unlawful administrative action.

● Pop Quiz ●

Why hasn't Supreme Court Act 1981 s 31(3) removed the prerogative to bring relator proceedings? It says 'no application for judicial review shall be made unless the leave of the High Court has been obtained in accordance with the rules of court; and the court shall not grant leave to make such an application unless it considers that the applicant has a sufficient interest in the matter'.

Only the Attorney General has this special, open standing at common law. But standing can be conferred by statute; a very important example concerns **local authorities**. Judicial review has long been used by and against local authorities,[25] but it took an act of Parliament to establish their general access to the courts. They can 'appear in any legal proceedings and, in the case of civil proceedings, may institute them in their own name', if they 'consider it expedient for the promotion or protection of the interests of the inhabitants of their area' (Local Government Act 1972 s 222).[26] They would not be given standing if they unreasonably considered the proceedings expedient (*Stoke-on-Trent City Council v B&Q* [1984] AC 754). But their standing is ordinarily taken for granted.

Public authorities very commonly seek judicial review, and standing is seldom argued. But without the sort of legislative authorization provided by s 222, a public authority, like any other claimant, needs to have a sufficient interest under Supreme Court Act 1981 s 31(3).

In *R v Environment Secretary, ex p Hammersmith and Fulham LBC* [1991] 1 AC 521, Lord Bridge suggested that public authorities may have standing for the same reason as private persons. He held that due process protects private parties who may be affected by decisions of public authorities 'in their person, their property or their reputation', and he concluded that '(t)he principle equally applies to public bodies or public authorities affected by an administrative decision [of another public body] which is based upon . . . [the other public body] . . . having acted, or which necessarily implies that they have acted, unlawfully or discreditably' (598). But protecting the person, property, or reputation of public officials cannot be the main reason for giving one public authority standing to seek judicial review of the conduct of another.

....

[25] E.g., the London County Council used *mandamus* to enforce a borough's legal obligations in R v Poplar Borough Council, ex p London County Council (No 1) [1922] 1 KB 72 (see p 380).

[26] A classic instance is R v Environment Secretary, ex p Hammersmith and Fullham LBC [1991] 1 AC 521 (see p 247), in which 20 local authorities unsuccessfully challenged the Government's funding policies (their standing is not discussed in the case). And on a more local scale, the ability to seek injunctions has proven useful in enforcing such local decisions as tree preservation orders: Kent County Council v Batchelor (No 2) [1979] 1 WLR 213. Note that s 222 even allows local authorities to seek injunctions to enforce the criminal law: Kirklees Metropolitan Borough Council v Wickes Building Supplies [1993] AC 227.

The central justification, implicit in most claims brought by public authorities, is a form of public interest standing: the public purposes for which the public authority exists may sometimes be legitimately pursued through judicial review of the lawfulness of another public body's conduct. That implicit rationale for local authority standing is essentially the same as the rationale spelt out in the Local Government Act (i.e., standing 'for the promotion or protection of the interests of the inhabitants of their area').

Strange standing

Occasionally, local councillors have been given standing on behalf of a local council to challenge the council's own planning decisions. The Court of Appeal has endorsed this arrangement as 'convenient and appropriate' if it 'is not abused' (R v Bassetlaw District Council, ex p Oxby [1998] PLCR 283, 293).[27] It gives the council a way of referring its own decision to the court to be quashed. The only way it can be done while maintaining an adversarial proceeding is if (as in Oxby's case) there is a party adverse in interest to the councillor and the council, who can intervene.

This public interest rationale for litigation by public authorities has been recognized in R v Employment Secretary, ex p Equal Opportunities Commission [1995] 1 AC 1. The Employment Secretary argued that the EOC had no standing to seek judicial review of compliance with EC law on equal pay for men and women. The EOC was an independent Commission established by Parliament (see section 13.13). The Employment Secretary's argument was that the EOC had no right, interest, or legitimate expectation at stake, and had suffered no damage. That was all irrelevant in the view of the majority: the question of whether the EOC had a sufficient interest in the matter depended on its public role. Lord Keith pointed out that the Sex Discrimination Act 1975 gave the EOC responsibility 'to work towards the elimination of discrimination' (s 53(1)). That was enough to support the conclusion that 'the statutory duties and public law role of the EOC' gave it a sufficient interest in the matter (Lord Keith, 26). This result may seem comparable to the standing of local authorities: that is, it is a standing conferred by statute. But the better view is that the capacity to have standing without having anything to gain or lose from the decision follows from the Commission's role in promoting the public interest. It has standing because of the purpose for which Parliament set it up, and not because Parliament decided to give it standing.

There is one aspect of litigation by public authorities that creates a special problem of comity for the courts: some public authorities have tried to use judicial review to escape the consequences (or merely the disappointment) of being criticized by government agencies such as Local Government Ombudsmen (e.g., R v LCA, ex p Croydon LBC [1989] 1 All ER 1033) and the Audit Commission (R (Ealing LBC) v Audit Commission [2005] EWCA Civ 556). In those cases, the courts have to be especially careful to

---

27   See also R (Corbett) v Restormel Borough Council [2001] EWCA Civ 330.

avoid pointless and expensive interference with another independent decision maker (see p 492).

(see p 492).

● *Pop Quiz* ●

The Parliamentary Commissioner Act 1967 prohibits the Parliamentary ombuds-man from investigating complaints by local authorities, and by public authorities whose members are appointed by the Crown or whose funds are mainly granted by Parliament (s 6(1)). Why would that be?

11.8 Standing to intervene

A claimant in judicial review proceedings must 'state the name and address of any person he considers to be an interested party' (CPR 54.6(1)). The court will ordinarily allow those parties to 'take part' in the proceedings. So there is very easy access for private parties who are adverse in interest to claimant.[28] What's more, anyone who wishes can apply to intervene, and the court has an undefined discretion to allow them to file evidence or make representations at the hearing (CPR 54.17(1)).

The courts also allow public interest intervention, and the test is really quite relaxed. The matters the intervenor raises must be of 'of some general importance', and there must be 'a real possibility that the court would be assisted by its inter-vention' (*R (MH) v Health Secretary (Application for Permission to Intervene)* [2004] EWCA Civ 1321 [8]—allowing Mind, a national mental health advocacy organization, to intervene in a claim that the Mental Health Act 1983 was incompatible with the Convention). Public authorities do not generally have an incentive to oppose inter-vention; although intervention will slightly increase the public authority's costs, it may be politically unattractive to stand in the way of advocacy groups having an input in the litigation.

Perhaps the most extravagant example of public interest intervention yet was *R v Bow Street Metropolitan Stipendiary Magistrate, ex p Pinochet Ugarte (No 3)* [1999] 2 WLR 827, in which Amnesty International, the Medical Foundation for the Care of Victims of Torture, the Redress Trust, the Association of the Relatives of the Disappeared Detainees, and three individuals were given leave to intervene, and Human Rights Watch was permitted to present written submissions.

Life and death

The Court of Appeal accepted written submissions from the Archbishop of Westminster in *A (Children) (Conjoined Twins: Medical Treatment) (No 1)* [2000] 4 All ER 961. The Court did not explain why the submissions were accepted, though Ward LJ stated that doing so was exceptional (966). And the House of Lords accepted

---

[28] *R (Corbett) v Restormel Borough Council and Land and Property Limited* [2001] EWCA Civ 330 is an example. And British Nuclear Fuels Plc intervened in *R v Inspectorate of Pollution, ex p Greenpeace (No 2)* [1994] 2 CMLR 548.

written submissions from the Archbishop of Cardiff (again without giving reasons) in R (Pretty) v Director of Public Prosecutions [2001] UKHL 61, in which Mrs. Pretty unsuccessfully challenged the DPP's refusal to grant immunity to her husband should he help her to commit suicide. The courts' acceptance of the submissions reflects an openness to contributions from campaigners on the basis of the same sort of grounds as in R v Foreign Secretary, ex p World Development Movement [1995] 1 WLR 386: the intervenor's serious concern with the issues, experience in advocacy work, and resources for providing information or making an argument. The question of whether a person has wisdom to offer on ending human life because he is an Archbishop is not justiciable. But this is true of the question of the wisdom of any public interest intervenor. Any help the court gets from the submissions will depend purely on the content of the submissions.

In the European Court of Human Rights, contracting states other than the defendant, and other persons, can ask for leave to submit written comments or take part in a hearing,[29] and it will be granted if it is 'in the interest of the proper administration of justice' (ECHR Art 36).

But the European Court of Justice takes a tougher stance, which matches its approach to standing: intervention will only be allowed if the party's legal position would be directly changed by the ruling in the case; it is not enough that the intervenor might have something to say that would assist the court (see Case T-201/04 R 5 Microsoft Corp v Commission [2006] 4 CMLR 9, denying leave to 'think tanks' advocating policies that related to the issues in the case).

11.8.1 Intervention by public authorities

The courts are very liberal in allowing public authorities to intervene in proceedings started by private claimants: see R (Pretty) v Director of Public Prosecutions (Home Secretary intervening) [2001] UKHL 61. And note the important case of R v North and East Devon Health Authority, ex p Coughlan [2001] QB 213, in which the Secretary of State for Health was given leave to intervene and was treated as a party. The Royal College of Nursing also made written submissions [5]. As is common in intervenor decisions, no reasons were given; but it is evidently enough that the intervenors have an interest in the matter that makes it potentially useful for the court to hear them in order to decide the issues raised by the claimant and defendant.

11.9 Conclusion: the limits of administrative law

The point of administrative law is to facilitate and to control decision making in the public interest. The rule of law requires official action in accordance with law. But if

---

[29] A contracting state has a right to intervene, if one of its nationals is seeking a remedy against another contracting state.

an official has engaged in unlawful conduct, there may or may not be a public interest in taking any response to it. The rule of law only demands judicial processes that are needed for the purpose of preventing arbitrary government. So **proportionate process** is a principle that ought to govern judicial processes as well as administrative processes. The public interest in imposing the rule of law on the administration does not demand unrestricted access to judicial process. Requirements of standing that restrict access to judicial review are *potentially* justifiable. For the purposes that justify administrative law, access to justice is crucial. But the doors of the courts do not need to be open to everyone who complains that the government has acted unlawfully.

There is not a grave lacuna in our system of public law just because some unlawful conduct cannot be brought before the court. But there will be a grave lacuna, if there is no process for a person with sufficient interest to seek a remedy when the public interest demands a remedy. The purposes of administrative law do not demand a judicial process or remedy, however, if there is another satisfactory way of resolving a dispute.

TAKE-HOME MESSAGE • • •

- The requirement of **'sufficient interest'** for standing to seek judicial review gives the court a discretionary power to decide who should be given standing—that is, whom the courts should listen to.

- The courts' doors are not open to everyone who alleges that a public authority has acted unlawfully. For example, judges will not ordinarily give standing to an individual to argue in judicial review that another individual has been treated unlawfully.

- Standing will be given to **campaign groups** to seek judicial review, if they have an arguable case on an issue of public importance, and there is no particular claimant who would be better placed to seek judicial review, and the group has a prominent role in the field in question.

- Standing to seek remedies under the ECHR in the Strasbourg Court, and under the Human Rights Act in the English courts, is more limited: the claimant must be a victim of an alleged violation of a Convention right.

- Standing for private parties to seek invalidation of European Community measures in the European Court of Justice, too, is limited to persons who are themselves directly affected.

···· *Critical reading* ···
R v Inland Revenue Commissioners, ex p National Federation of Self-employed and Small Businesses Ltd ('Fleet Street Casuals') [1982] AC 617
R v Home Secretary, ex p Ruddock [1987] 1 WLR 1482
R v Social Security Secretary, ex p Child Poverty Action Group [1990] 2 QB 540
R v Inspectorate of Pollution, ex p Greenpeace (No 2) [1994] 2 CMLR 548

R v Foreign Secretary, ex p World Development Movement Ltd [1995] 1 WLR 386

R v Somerset CC, ex p Dixon [1998] Env LR 111

CRITICAL QUESTIONS • • •

1 In enforcing the criminal law, it is the task of the police to investigate any serious allegation of criminal conduct, from anyone who has information to offer. Is the task of the courts in administrative law similar, i.e., to investigate any allegation of unlawful conduct from anyone who has information to offer?

2 How would an open doors policy on standing to seek judicial review (giving standing to anyone with an arguable case that a public authority has acted unlawfully) differ from the standing rules we have?

3 Was the Fleet Street Casuals case an example of public interest litigation?

Further questions:

4 Should leave to apply for judicial review be refused in a case where the applicant could have gone to an ombudsman?

5 Would it be right for a court to give a government of a middle eastern country standing to challenge arms exports to Israel in judicial review in the English High Court? If not, was R (Hasan) v Trade and Industry Secretary [2007] EWHC 2630 rightly decided?

online resource centre

Visit the online resource centre to access the following resources which accompany this chapter: links to legislation and online reports of judicial decisions, summaries of key cases and legislation, updates in the law, suggestions for answering the pop quizzes and questions, and links to useful websites.

Administrative justice

12 The reconstruction of tribunals

Panels, committees, tribunals, referees, adjudicators, commissioners, and other public authorities decide many thousands of disputes each year over (for example) entitlement to benefits, or tax liability, or political asylum, or the detention of a patient in a secure hospital. The massive array of agencies reflects the great variety of benefits and burdens that 21st-century government assigns to people. The array had no overall organization until 2007, when Parliament transformed it into a complex system. Integrating these decision-making agencies brings advantages, but the law needs to tailor their structure, processes, and decision-making techniques to the variety of purposes they serve. And the law needs to achieve proportionate process, by reconciling the competing interests in legalism and informality in tribunal processes.

LOOK FOR • • •

- The reconstruction of tribunals in the Tribunals, Courts and Enforcement Act 2007 (TCE Act 2007), creating a new administrative justice system.

- The tensions that the reconstruction of tribunals creates between legalism and informality.

- Proportionate dispute resolution.

- The irony of process: in order to accomplish 'administrative justice', tribunals need to give processes that will be *more than* proportionate in some cases.

> ' Excise: a hateful tax adjudged not by the common judges of property, but by wretches hired by those to whom excise is paid. '
>
> **Samuel Johnson's *Dictionary*, 1755 (in 1643, Parliament had given Commissioners jurisdiction to apply excise taxes and to impose penalties)**

12.1 Introduction: proportionate process in administrative justice

Every programme of government generates grievances. Those that especially affect particular individuals generate disputes that need a legally binding resolution. **'Administrative justice'** is a term for administrative processes that are designed to resolve disputes over the implementation and operation of those projects. It is a recent term—in Samuel Johnson's day and, in fact, until the late 20th century, it was generally presumed that the common law courts ought to be resolving disputes between government and subject.

Government schemes give social security benefits, and impose taxes, and keep people locked in hospitals on the ground that they are dangerously mentally ill. But the projects are much more diverse than that. They have been launched (most of them over the past hundred years) with *ad hoc* legislation resulting in an extravagant variety of techniques for redress of grievances caused by the schemes' operation. The variety reflects the diversity of the projects.

No one knows how many government institutions there are for resolving disputes.[1] Among the most important bodies dealing with grievances about government services are the Social Security and Child Support Appeals Tribunal, the Criminal Injuries Compensation Appeals Panel, the Commissioners of Income Tax, the Asylum and Immigration Tribunal (AIT), the Mental Health Review Tribunal, the Land Tribunal (which decides rating appeals and disputes over compensation for the compulsory acquisition of land), and the School Admissions and Exclusion Appeal Panels. There are dozens more, such as the National Parking Adjudication Service, the National Lottery Commission, the Sea Fish Licence Tribunal, and the Antarctic Act Tribunal.

And those are only the 'person-and-state'[2] tribunals: they hear appeals against decisions made by or on behalf of the government. Others are 'party-and-party' tribunals, government agencies designed to resolve disputes between private persons. These include the Employment Tribunals, the Copyright Tribunal (which controls

---

[1]   Approximately 97 are overseen by the Administrative Justice and Tribunals Council (see p 435). Tribunals and Inquiries Act 1992 Sch 1.

[2]   They are often called 'citizen-and-state' tribunals, but one of the largest—the Asylum and Immigration Tribunal—does not involve citizens.

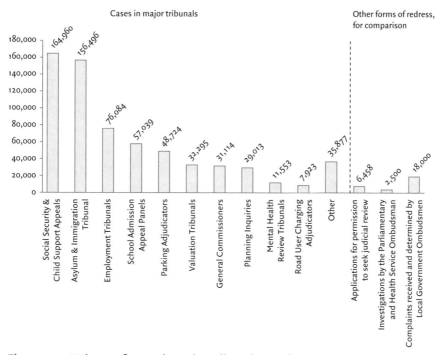

Cases in major tribunals

Other forms of redress,
for comparison

Figure 12.1 Volume of cases in major tribunals, 2006[3,4]

collective licensing of copyright material), and the Residential Property Tribunal
Service (which decides disputes between landlords and tenants).

Are party-and-party tribunals a concern of administrative law?

The Employment Tribunals hear complaints against private employers by private
individuals. So what does this tribunal have to do with administrative law, when
it decides relations between two private parties? The tribunals are governed by
administrative law, because they are public authorities. They are 'public authorities' for the purposes of the Human Rights Act. The power that such public
authorities wield over private parties needs to be controlled by law. And that is
particularly the case where the authority has been established not merely as a service for resolving disputes between private parties, but with a remit of promoting
the public interest (as in the case of the Copyright Tribunal).

3   The figures are for tribunals under the oversight of the Council on Tribunals, from its Forty-
    Eighth Annual Report, 2006/2007; House of Commons 18 July 2007, 72 (http://www.council-on-
    tribunals.gov.uk/docs/ar_07.pdf).

4   Figures for Ombudsmen are from Parliamentary and Health Service Ombudsman Annual Report
    2007/2008, House of Commons, 18 July 2007, 59 (http://www.ombudsman.org.uk/pdfs/ar_07.
    pdf), and the Local Government Ombudsman Annual Review 2006/2007 (http:www.lgo.org.
    uk/publications/annual-report). For judical review see http://www.judiciary.gov.uk/keyfacts/
    statistics/.

But person-and-state tribunals raise one crucial public law problem that does not arise with party-and-party tribunals. It is a problem of separating powers. In a hearing before a person-and-state tribunal, the tribunal is part of the apparatus of the state, *and* it decides a dispute between the person and the state. The reconstruction of tribunals has dealt with this problem by taking tribunals out of the departments of government, and creating a Tribunals Service with oversight by the independent Administrative Justice and Tribunals Council, and by the Ministry of Justice.

A party-and-party tribunal (such as an Employment Tribunal, where the employer is a private company) is independent of the parties. Most of the discussion in this chapter will deal with person-and-state tribunals.

The diversity of tribunals is reflected in their names, but only imperfectly: the names have been thought up (and often changed) in a series of historical accidents reflecting decisions about how best to present new decision-making authorities to the public. So the Social Security and Child Support Appeals (SSCSA) Tribunal is actually a first-level tribunal hearing complaints against social security decisions; the Social Security and Child Support Commissioners are judges who sit as an appeal tribunal against decisions of the SSCSA Tribunal. But the body performing the same appellate function for first-level Employment Tribunals is the Employment Appeals Tribunal. The terms are used in various ways, and only some very general pointers as to their use are possible.

What's in a name?

- **'Commissioner'** and 'Commission' are ancient terms[5] and imply appointment by the Crown with a commission that is more-or-less akin to the commission of a judge. From the introduction of the income tax in 1799, the Tax Commissioners were appointed to serve both as tax collectors and as an appeal body; their work became purely adjudicative in 1946, and they are becoming a first-tier chamber under the reconstruction. In the 21st century, the term 'commissioner' is used for some important bodies that have oversight responsibilities for particular areas of government (the Audit Commission for local government, and the Care Quality Commission for health care), and for combating discrimination (the Equality and Human Rights Commission).[6]
- The more common term **'tribunal'** can simply mean 'decision-making body' (that is its meaning in the European Convention on Human Rights Art 6). But since the aftermath of World War I, when the first major tribunal system was created to deal with complaints about war pension decisions, the term

---

[5] The Commissioners of Sewers date back to the Middle Ages—see p 9.

[6] It is also used for one important tribunal, the Special Immigration and Appeals Commission—see p 459.

'tribunal' has been used in English administrative law to refer to a body outside the ordinary courts that has legal power to decide disputes between parties.[7]

- **'Adjudicator'** is sometimes used for a person who resolves a dispute (**'referee'** is sometimes used that way too). But 'adjudicator' is sometimes used for an ombudsman.
- **'Ombudsman'** means an officer who receives and investigates a complaint and reports on the result of the investigation (see Chapter 13).
- **'Service'** means the same as 'agency' but is meant to sound more consumer-friendly.
- **'Authority'**, **'Board'**, **'Agency'**, and **'Panel'** are neutral terms for public authorities, some of which are tribunals, that may have a variety of functions and powers.
- **'Appeal'** can mean a challenge to the decision of a government body (e.g., over social security or tax), or a challenge to the decision of the First-tier Tribunal.

The principle of **proportionate process** (see p 119) means that these different bodies need different decision-making techniques. Some tribunals reconsider the denial of a benefit, such as disability living allowance or compensation for criminal injuries. Others, such as the AIT and the Mental Health Review Tribunal, determine personal freedom. These differences have crucial implications for the personnel of tribunals (i.e., whether the members should be lawyers, or experts in some relevant profession, or lay people, or some combination). Special technical issues (such as mental health) may affect not only the membership of the tribunal itself, but also the use of assessors to advise the tribunal, or the taking of expert evidence. The same particularities determine whether an oral hearing is essential, whether complainants need legal representation or special advice, what form of appeal is necessary, if any, and what form of independence is needed.

Yet, there are common features among all tribunals:

- they hear a dispute between parties (in a person-and-state tribunal, one of the parties is a government agency),

- they determine a resolution to the dispute with binding effect,

- they determine the case according to the law,

- their jurisdiction is restricted to a specified subject matter, and

- they are not courts.

---

[7]   Warning: the term 'tribunal' has sometimes been used for an inquiry, ever since the Tribunals of Inquiry (Evidence) Act 1921. 'Tribunals of inquiry', or just 'inquiries' are public investigations. They are often chaired by a judge, and involve testimony under oath. But since they are investigations rather than an adversarial process for resolving a dispute between parties, they are dealt with in Chapter 13.

Or more precisely, they are not courts like the High Court. They are established by statute, they have no inherent jurisdiction, and they are subject to the oversight of the Administrative Justice and Tribunals Council. Until the reconstruction of tribunals, they were ordinarily subject to the supervisory jurisdiction of the High Court in judicial review.[8] The Lands Tribunal is chaired by a judge or barrister appointed by the Lord Chancellor, and an appeal from its decisions lies to the Court of Appeal, which gives its decisions a similar effect to decisions of the High Court (Lands Tribunal Act 1949 s 3(4)). But members of the Lands Tribunal other than the President can be either lawyers or 'persons who have had experience in the valuation of land appointed after consultation with the president of the Royal Institution of Chartered Surveyors' (Lands Tribunal Act 1949 s 2(2)). And unlike the High Court, the Lands Tribunal only hears disputes defined by statute (chiefly concerning compensation for compulsory acquisition of land for public projects), and has no jurisdiction to determine its own jurisdiction.

Superior courts, inferior courts, and tribunals

An inferior court is subject to the supervision of the High Court by judicial review. Magistrates' courts and coroners' courts are examples of inferior courts. The Crown Court, the High Court, the Court of Appeal and the House of Lords are not subject to that supervision; they are superior courts (Re Racal Communications [1981] AC 374 (HL)). The Special Immigration and Appeals Commission was made a 'superior court of record' so that its decisions would not be subject to judicial review, but only subject to appeal to the Court of Appeal (like judgments of the High Court) (Anti-terrorism, Crime and Security Act 2001 s 35—see p 459).

But there is no general legal distinction between courts and tribunals; as Lord Edmund-Davies said, 'it has unfortunately to be said that there emerges no sure guide, no unmistakable hallmark by which a "court" or "inferior court" may unerringly be identified' (A-G v BBC [1981] AC 303, 351). The word 'court' has no fixed legal meaning, although it is very commonly used (including in this book) as a shorthand for 'superior court'. Any tribunal that applies the law is a 'court' in a sense. The distinction between courts and tribunals is not as important as the distinction between bodies that are and bodies that are not covered by contempt of court, or bound by rules of evidence, or required to give an oral hearing, and so on. The blur between courts and bodies that are not courts reflects the principle of proportionate process, because the reasons for resolving different disputes in different ways do not create a sharp divide between the types of dispute-resolution institutions that we need.

---

[8]   See sections 12.4.8 and 12.4.9 on the way in which judicial supervision of tribunals has been reconstructed.

12.2 The reconstruction of tribunals

The TCE Act 2007 has brought some unity to tribunals.[9] From November 2008, they have operated in a system of First-tier Tribunals with a unified system of appeals to the Upper Tribunal.

Given the diversity of the bodies, is it valuable to unify tribunals? The unification creates new tensions between legalism and informality, and between uniformity and flexibility. But we will see that the reconstruction has distinct advantages, and is worthwhile in spite of the risks and drawbacks.

The system is supported by a new Tribunals Service, for which the Secretary of State for Justice is responsible to Parliament. The Ministry of Justice has overall responsibility for the whole of the new system of which the Tribunals Service forms the administrative branch. As in the courts, judges now run the judicial work of tribunals (e.g., assigning judges to particular cases).

The Administrative Justice and Tribunals Council (AJTC) oversees the Tribunals Service, to 'keep the administrative justice system under review' (TCE Act 2007 Sch 7 para 13(1)). The AJTC advises the Lord Chancellor and the Tribunals judiciary on how to improve the system. The Act defines the term 'the administrative justice system' to mean:

> the overall system by which decisions of an administrative or executive nature are made in relation to particular persons, including—
>
> (a) the procedures for making such decisions,
> (b) the law under which such decisions are made, and
> (c) the systems for resolving disputes and airing grievances in relation to such decisions. (Sch 7 para 13(4))

The AJTC has replaced the Council on Tribunals, which had performed a similar role since the 1950s. The change of name reflects the government's determination to look at administrative techniques for dealing with grievances across the board, making tribunal processes flexible and open to alternative dispute resolution ('ADR')—that is, to negotiation or mediation that may enable the parties to reach a resolution without a hearing. But a claim will still be lodged with the department that made the original decision, in the hope that the department will be able to sort it out without a tribunal hearing (White Paper 7.13).

The diversity of the tribunals themselves remains. Tribunals do not merely apply different statutory schemes within their different jurisdictions; they also have different procedures. But the diversity now operates within a system.

---

9 Part One of the Act (the part dealing with the reconstruction of tribunals) is based on a White Paper (i.e., a government policy proposal) of 2004 called 'Transforming Public Services: Complaints, Redress and Tribunals', Secretary of State for Constitutional Affairs, July 2004 (Cm 6243). I will call it 'the White Paper'.

Not included

Local government tribunals are excluded from the reconstruction. And two of the largest tribunal schemes have not had their jurisdictions transferred to the new system under the TCE Act 2007: the AIT and the Employment Tribunals and the Employment Appeal Tribunal. They will be served by the Tribunal Service, and overseen by the Senior President of Tribunals, but will continue to exercise their old jurisdictions. The AIT has been kept separate to maintain its single-tier structure, introduced in 2004 in an attempt to reduce appeals in asylum cases (Asylum and Immigration (Treatment of Claimants etc) Act 2004). The employment tribunals and the Employment Appeal Tribunal are party-and-party tribunals with an existing appellate structure, and the government decided to leave it alone.

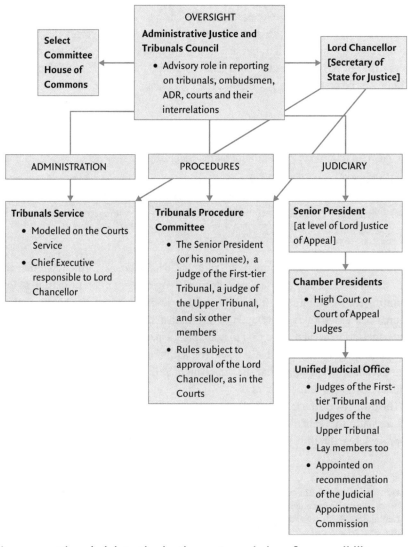

Figure 12.2 **The administrative justice system: chains of responsibility**

The Tribunals Service[10] has responsibility for the management of cases and the allocation of tribunal resources. It will share building space with the Courts Service, allowing more economical use of resources and at the same time contributing to the integration of tribunals with courts. The Tribunals Service also looks after the crucial business of communicating with complainants.

The judicial branch of the administrative justice system has a Senior President, appointed by the Queen on the recommendation of the Lord Chancellor (TCE Act 2007 s 2), who has standing and experience equivalent to a Court of Appeal judge, and has overall responsibility for running and developing the judicial part of the service. Below the Senior President are the presidents for the various 'chambers'. The chambers bring together jurisdictions of the old tribunals. For example, the new Social Entitlement Chamber deals with Asylum Support, Social Security and Child Support, and Criminal Injuries Compensation.[11] The Chambers allow for more flexible judicial appointments (as the Senior President can assign the same judge to more than one chamber). Chamber presidents are judges who are responsible for running the judicial work for their particular tribunal jurisdictions (including the issuing of guidance on changes in law and practice as they relate to their chambers).

The unified judicial office has two tiers, with the titles of 'Judge of the First-tier Tribunal'[12] and 'Judge of the Upper Tribunal' (TCE Act 2007 s 4). There is a core of salaried judicial officers and part-time ('fee paid') judges. Both will tend to specialize; they can work in more than one chamber, but they need to be assigned by the Senior President (TCE Act 2007 Sch 4 para 9) to each chamber in which they work. Lay members are retained, but their role is under review (see section 12.4.3).

The most significant form of unification is the new appeals system. Appeals in the old days were specific to each tribunal. From some, there was a right of appeal to another tribunal, from others there was a right of appeal on a point of law to the High Court, or no appeal at all. Under the unified system, the first general rule is that the First-tier Tribunal can review its own decisions, either on its own initiative or on an application from a complainant (s 9). And then there is an appeal on a point of law from a First-tier Tribunal to a unified appellate tier (the Upper Tribunal, TCE Act s 11), made up of the Senior President, Chamber Presidents, judges of the ordinary courts, and the current appellate members of the tribunal system (s 5). The Upper Tribunal, too, can review its own decisions (s 10), and there is an appeal from the Upper Tribunal on a point of law to the Court of Appeal (s 13), but only if the Upper Tribunal or the Court of Appeal gives permission to appeal.[13] The power of both levels of tribunals to review their own decisions is designed to avoid

---

[10] The Tribunals Service was created by the Government (it did not require legislation) and launched in April 2006.

[11] http://www.tribunals.gov.uk/Tribunals/Firsttier/socialentitlement.htm.

[12] A tribunal member who is not legally qualified is simply called 'member of the First-tier Tribunal'.

[13] TCE Act 2007 s 13(6) allows the Lord Chancellor to make rules restricting these appeals to cases that 'would raise some important point of principle or practice', or in which 'there is some other compelling reason' for hearing an appeal.

unnecessary appeals: it provides for a form of ADR within the tribunal system, and it distinguishes them from courts.[14] It is quite likely that the tribunals will only set aside their own decisions where there has been an obvious mistake: particularly in a challenge to a First-tier decision, a really controversial challenge will deserve to be heard as an appeal in the Upper Tribunal.

One final aspect of the integration of tribunals with the courts is very important: **the Upper Tribunal has a judicial review jurisdiction** (ss 15–21). It will serve the same role as the Administrative Court, in judicial review cases delegated to it by the High Court under rules made by the Lord Chief Justice and approved by the Lord Chancellor. From its inauguration, the Lord Chief Justice gave the Upper Tribunal responsibility for judicial review of the Criminal Injuries Compensation Scheme, and of First-tier Tribunal decisions where there is no right of appeal to the Upper Tribunal.[15] Section 19 of the TCE Act 2007 amends the Supreme Court Act 1981 to require the High Court to transfer claims for judicial review covered by those rules to the Upper Tribunal, and empowers the High Court to transfer other claims where the High Court judge decides that it would be just and convenient to do so.

12.3 The judicialization of tribunals

These are major changes to the organization of tribunals. They have created a new system of administrative justice alongside, and similar to, the system of ordinary courts. Many of the changes are similar to changes made earlier for social security appeals by the Social Security Act 1998. That legislation led to a unification of tribunals in its field (particularly in appeals), and it judicialized social security disputes.

The features of judicialization in social security included the unification of appeal tribunals under a judicial President, division of the social security tribunal service into judicial and administrative branches (with a full-time social security judiciary), the effective abolition of lay membership on panels,[16] and the gradual removal of inquisitorial decision-making techniques.[17] The last of these changes was partly brought about by a change in the considerations that an appeal tribunal was to take into account. The Social Security Act 1998 provided that an appeal tribunal:

---

[14] The High Court cannot review its own decisions. But the House of Lords has 'power to correct any injustice caused by an earlier order of this House' (R v Bow Street Metropolitan Stipendiary Magistrate, ex p Pinochet Ugarte (No 2) [2000] 1 AC 119, 132 (Lord Browne-Wilkinson)).

[15] http://www.tribunals.gov.uk/Tribunals/Upper/upper.htm#q6.

[16] In the Social Security Act 1998, and through decisions under regulations.

[17] For a discussion see Nick Wikeley, 'Burying Bell: Managing the Judicialisation of Social Security Tribunals' (2000) 63 MLR 475.

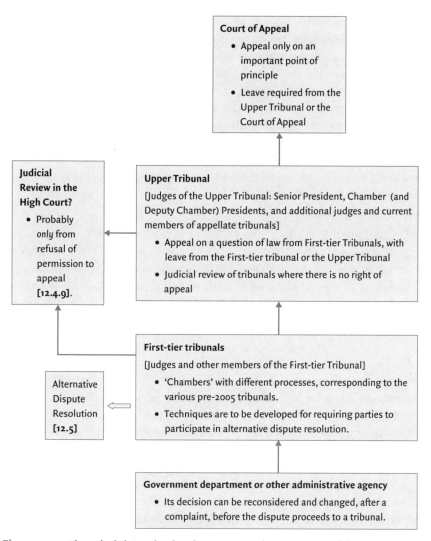

Court of Appeal

- Appeal only on an important point of principle
- Leave required from the Upper Tribunal or the Court of Appeal

Judicial Review in the High Court?

- Probably *only* from refusal of permission to appeal [12.4.9].

Upper Tribunal

[Judges of the Upper Tribunal: Senior President, Chamber (and Deputy Chamber) Presidents, and additional judges and current members of appellate tribunals]

- Appeal on a question of law from First-tier Tribunals, with leave from the First-tier tribunal or the Upper Tribunal
- Judicial review of tribunals where there is no right of appeal

First-tier tribunals

[Judges and other members of the First-tier Tribunal]

- 'Chambers' with different processes, corresponding to the various pre-2005 tribunals.
- Techniques are to be developed for requiring parties to participate in alternative dispute resolution.

Alternative Dispute Resolution [12.5]

Government department or other administrative agency

- Its decision can be reconsidered and changed, after a complaint, before the dispute proceeds to a tribunal.

Figure 12.3 **The administrative justice system: the progress of disputes**

> (a) need not consider any issue that is not raised by the appeal; and
> (b) shall not take into account any circumstances not obtaining at the time when the decision appealed against was made. (s 12(8))

Think for a moment about these two features of the new way of resolving a complaint over the refusal of a social security benefit. They regulate the process in a way that gives the government new, tighter control over a massive and expensive welfare bene-fit programme. The **first rule** gives the tribunal no general responsibility for *good administration*, but only a responsibility to hear issues raised by a party. It makes the process more adversarial, and less of an investigation into whether the scheme is achieving its purposes. The **second rule** prevents the tribunal from assuming general responsibility for *good social security provision*, by reducing the range of considerations on which a tribunal may act. The question for the tribunal is not, *whether a good social security system would give the benefit to the complainant*, but *whether the decision of the department conformed to the rules when it was made*. By making the job of the tribunal more like that of a court, these changes constrain the tribunal's power, and tighten the government's control over social security. The judges' independence actually *serves* the government's purpose of controlling decision making, because judicial independence goes along with the application of rules in a way that is not directed to the judge's own view of good social policy.

> ### Ombudsmen, tribunals, courts
>
> Judicialization of tribunals strengthens the basic distinction between tribunals and ombudsmen: a tribunal hears a dispute between parties; an ombudsman investigates a complaint. Making tribunals more like courts makes them less like ombudsmen, by focusing the tribunals' work on resolving a dispute as to the application of rules, and turning it away from any general inquiry into good administration (see Chapter 13).

Judicialization brings with it the promise of impartiality, and the trained scrutiny of decisions that can be expected from lawyers, and good process. Those features may seem to reduce the government's control over decisions. Yet the judicialization of the tribunal process also brought with it features that *enhance* the government's control over social security. By restricting tribunals to the sort of considerations that judges typically handle, the reforms reduce the discretionary element in dispute resolution.

At the same time, the reconstruction is firmly committed to *avoiding* or reducing certain forms of judicialization, especially legal representation before tribunals. The new system will, as a result, need to resolve inbuilt tensions between legalism and informality. In the following discussion of the reconstruction of tribunals in general, we will need to keep in mind the ways in which judicialization will promote good administration and due process, and the ways in which it can potentially—ironically—detract from both.

12.4 Testing the reconstruction: eleven elements of administrative justice

Is the reconstruction an improvement? The administrative justice system needs to get each of these elements right, in order for the system to be just overall:

12.4.1 Appointments	12.4.3 Role of non-lawyer members
12.4.2 Judicial offices	12.4.4 Evidence

12.4.1 Appointments

Appointment of Tribunal Judges is now done on the recommendation of the same Judicial Appointments Commission that appoints High Court judges (TCE Act 2007 s 48(1)). Appointment of non-legal members is also on the recommendation of the Judicial Appointments Commission, with the difference that the Commission takes advice from professional bodies on qualifications of professional experts. This change is a dramatic feature of the reconstruction. Under the Tribunals and Inquiries Act 1992, the Council on Tribunals could give advice on appointment, but the tribunal chairman was usually appointed by a departmental minister from a panel selected by the Lord Chancellor (s 6). The Lord Chancellor appointed most tribunal members, but others were simply appointed by the minister responsible for the department that made the original decision. And the departmental minister paid them (and could remove them: Tribunals and Inquiries Act 1992 s 7[18]), and ran the tribunal.

The change to court-style appointments reflects the legalization tension: it makes tribunal members more independent, and it makes them more like judges of the High Court, complementing the titles (Judge of the First-tier Tribunal, Judge of the Upper Tribunal). But it downplays the differences between their work and the work of the courts.

Appointment as a Tribunal Judge does not mean that a person can hear just any dispute; the assignment of judges to a particular Chamber is done by the managing judges (the Senior President, with the concurrence of the Chamber Presidents and the judge who is to be assigned: TCE Act 2007 s 7(8)).

12.4.2 Judicial offices

One of the biggest symbolic changes in the reconstruction is the creation of a 'single judicial office': legal members on First-tier Tribunals are called 'Judges of the First-tier Tribunal', and on Upper Tribunals they are called 'Judges of the Upper Tribunal'. A Senior President is the head of the entire 'tribunal judiciary', which potentially gives tribunal judges a collective voice that they have never had before. The status of the Senior President as a Lord Justice of Appeal will add both to the prestige and to the sense of judicial hierarchy in the tribunals: the presidents of particular chambers are High Court judges or Court of Appeal judges. Judges have served on some

---

[18]   In some cases the minister needed the consent of his or her colleague in the government, the Lord Chancellor.

tribunals for generations; now it will be a full-time job with a similar title and the same forms of career progression and self-government that they have in the courts.

12.4.3 Role of non-lawyer members

As for the non-lawyers serving on tribunals (including the doctors, accountants, surveyors, and others who bring expertise to the making of decisions), the TCE Act 2007 does not change their position, but the White Paper called for a review. They are part of a unified 'judiciary', yet their role is put in question: the White Paper asks what the function of non-lawyer members should be: 'is it to add balance to the panel? Or to ensure particular interests are represented?' (White Paper 6.67). Moreover, the White Paper cast doubt on the fairness of tribunals with expert members:

> for expert members a further area that needs to be developed is whether in fact it is desirable for a tribunal to have a particular expert on the panel as opposed to being available as a witness for the tribunal. Where an expert member carries out his or her own examination or investigations the parties are unable to question that member or rebut his or her conclusions. Indeed it may even give the impression that the tribunal will favour the views of that expert over the case findings of witnesses who are equally expert. (White Paper 6.67)

This attitude to tribunals applies the model of courts. Judges in the law courts must decide a dispute on the basis of the evidence put before the court by the parties, and not on the basis of the judge's own views, or on information the judge receives from any other source. But the point of expert membership on tribunals is that tribunals are different from courts: the purpose of a member's expertise is not to enable him or her to compete with the witnesses, but to help the tribunal to understand the witnesses and the complainant. The point is to bring perspective to the deliberations of the lawyers and lay members on a panel. And it is not necessarily unfair, because of the ways in which the issues before tribunals differ in various ways from the issues in (say) a murder trial.

It has long been recognized that the members of some tribunals may properly rely on their own knowledge and experience, while still abiding by the rules of natural justice.[19] The open questions in the White Paper take a step toward converting tribunals into courts. They suggest that it is generally improper for a tribunal member to bring any perspective to a dispute other than the perspective of a High Court judge.[20]

---

[19]   See, e.g., A-G v BBC [1981] AC 303, 351 (Lord Edmund Davies).

[20]   Yet elsewhere, the White Paper endorses the value of 'the expertise of Surveyor Members of the Lands Tribunal', and states that the new appellate tribunals might use the same expertise in deciding tax cases as well (White Paper 7.17). The result is an unresolved tension in the Government's attitude to non-lawyer members.

The role of non-lawyers varies, even on a single tribunal. Panels of the Mental Health Review Tribunal consist of a lawyer (who chairs the panel), a consultant psychiatrist, and a lay member who is neither a doctor nor a lawyer. If the psychiatrist member disagrees with an expert witness, he or she must say so at the oral hearing to give the parties a chance to respond. The lay member 'provides balance to the Tribunal as a representative of the community outside the legal and medical professions'.[21] 'Balance' is a good term for the perspective that a layperson brings. But it is dangerous to call him or her a 'representative', because that might make it seem that the layperson's job is to act *for* the community and *against* the complainant.

On the Mental Health Review Tribunal, the three members of a panel decide cases by majority vote. So here the non-lawyers perform both expert and purportedly representative roles. Risk of injustice arises from the possibility that the panel will mistakenly trust the psychiatrist member's opinion over that of other medical experts, or that the 'representative' role of the lay member will introduce a biased agenda into the deliberations. Those risks could be met by the legalistic model that the White Paper hints at. But the legalistic model has risks too: it would leave resolution of an adversarial battle between the parties' expert witnesses to a non-expert, and it would choose the lawyer's perspective on the situation, over the commonsense perspective that the lay member (potentially) offers.

Experts on tribunals

Unlike the White Paper, the judges have no doubts about the fairness—and the value—of having non-lawyer expert membership on tribunals: 'One of the strengths of the tribunal system as it has been developed in this country is the breadth of relevant experience that can be built into it by the use of lay members to sit with members who are legally qualified... its integrity is not compromised by the use of specialist knowledge or experience when the judge or tribunal member is examining the evidence' (*Gillies v Work and Pensions Secretary (Scotland)* [2006] UKHL 2 [22] (Lord Hope)).

12.4.4 Evidence

Closely allied to the role of lay members is the use of evidence.[22] Tribunals are not generally bound by the law of evidence that restricts the information that the High Court can consider (e.g., the prohibition on hearsay, and the prohibition on a judge using his or her knowledge of facts that cannot be 'judicially noticed'[23]). The point

---

[21]   http://www.mhrt.org.uk/AboutUs/membersRoles.htm.

[22]   The TCE Act 2007 enables the Tribunal Procedure Committee to make rules about evidence (s 22(3), Sch 5 para 10).

[23]   Judges in the High Court will take notice of facts without proof, if they are so obviously true that it is not unfair to the disadvantaged party for the court to accept it without making the other party prove it. E.g., the court will accept without proof that there are many men in southeast London who fit the description, 'a tall black man wearing a black hood' (*R v Irvin* [2007] EWCA Crim 2701 [11]).

of an expert tribunal is that it should be able to rely on its own expert knowledge. As Edmund Davies LJ said in *Metropolitan Properties Ltd v Lannon* [1969] 1 QB 577, 'members [of tribunals] are not restricted to the evidence adduced before them; they are free to draw upon their cumulative knowledge and experience of the matter in hand' (603).

This difference in evidence rules between tribunals and courts cannot be justified on the ground that courts decide more important disputes. A tribunal decision can win you back your job, or lead to your deportation, or uphold your detention in a secure hospital. The justification has to be that there are different risks of prejudice from unrestricted information in courts, and that tribunals can do a fair job of handling a less restricted range of information on the specific range of issues that they decide.

The law of evidence in the High Court is deeply tied to the common law adversarial system of dispute resolution. First, the information before the court in criminal proceedings is restricted because those proceedings subject one party to charges of wrongdoing against the community. The common law has always held that in those proceedings, the court should not consider any information that the defendant cannot effectively challenge during the hearing. And even civil proceedings in courts are generally *more adversarial* than proceedings in tribunals: the model of the common law courts involves two parties putting their case in such a way that information comes before the court only from the parties. Tribunals do not need to hold as strictly to that adversarial model as the High Court does. Since the question in a person-and-state tribunal is always a question as to the lawfulness and justice of administration, the tribunal can take a more inquisitorial role than a High Court judge takes in a claim for breach of contract.

In practice, particular tribunals have developed their own techniques of dealing with information. Behind those techniques, there is one general principle: that all information on which the decision is to be based (including views of tribunal members on technical issues) should be put to both parties for their response.

12.4.5 Hearings

The new system borrows case management from the law courts. Some tribunals already had it, but there was no uniformity. Case management means that the tribunal controls the progress of a dispute; the tribunal can require the parties to meet to discuss settlement, and can expedite the process when one party is delaying.[24]

But case management will only happen once the dispute reaches the tribunal. And tribunals are different from courts: in social security and tax in particular, appeals against the government department's decision have always been filed with the department in question. That allows the department to reconsider and to defuse some disputes by changing its mind before a tribunal hearing. The new system is

---

[24] The Tribunal Procedure Committee can make case management rules: see TCE Act 2007 Sch 5 Part I.

committed to alternative dispute resolution, so complainants will still file appeals with departments in most cases.

The earlier reform of social security tribunal processes had involved a reduction in oral hearings—from a presumption that a hearing was to be given, to a requirement of permission for an oral hearing. The White Paper took the same approach, aiming in general to avoid unnecessary oral hearings (though promising that 'No appellant will lose their right to a hearing' (White Paper 6.31)). The reasoning was that oral hearings are not only expensive, but stressful and painful for complainants. The TCE Act 2007 empowers the Tribunal Procedure Committee to make rules for dealing with a matter without a hearing (s 22(3), Sch 5 para 7).

Even if oral hearings are stressful, there is no doubt that they tend to benefit complainants. In a major study of Disability Living Allowance in 2003, the Auditor General found as follows:

> Of 34,000 [social security benefit] appeals cleared at oral hearing between April and June 2002, 52 per cent were decided in favour of the customer, compared with 23 per cent of the 11,000 paper hearings. For Disability Living Allowance, 61 per cent of oral hearings were decided in favour of the customer, compared with 34 per cent of paper hearings, and the President of Appeal Tribunals has indicated that the presence of the appellant has a significant impact on the outcome. [25]

The writers of the White Paper knew that complainants succeed better in oral hearings; but they had an answer:

> In many cases appellants succeed before tribunals because they bring new evidence, possibly as a result of advice, or because they are more articulate orally than on paper and the tribunal is the first opportunity they have had to explain their case.... it is possible to imagine ways in which the same benefit could be achieved without the stress and formality of a hearing. (White Paper 6.20)

The Government's tribunals policy is averse to oral hearings, and as a result, the continued availability of oral hearings where they really are useful is under doubt. It will be decided by:

- the ways in which the Tribunals Service carries out its responsibility for alternative dispute resolution,

- the work of the Administrative Justice and Tribunals Council in overseeing tribunals,

----

[25] Comptroller and Auditor General, 'Getting it right, putting it right: improving decision-making and appeals in social security benefits' (Report to the House of Commons, HC 1142, 7 November 2003) [4.17–4.18].

- government efforts to offer alternatives to oral hearings at departmental level, and eventually, no doubt,

- further legislation.

Perhaps it would be best to have no presumption for or against oral hearings. Their value and importance depend on whether they are necessary in order for the claimant to have an effective way of participating in the process, and that depends on the context in which a decision is made.

12.4.6 Reasons for decisions

The TCE Act 2007 says nothing about whether tribunals will give reasons; perhaps that reflects the degree to which reason-giving has come to be taken for granted as a requirement of due process for any body that determines a claim to legal rights (see section 6.2). Not that tribunals in the new system will always give reasons. The social security tribunals do not give reasons as a matter of course, because it would cause too much expense and delay. But a complainant who wants to appeal can request a statement of reasons.

The Tribunals and Inquiries Act 1958 had made a huge step forward by imposing a general duty on the tribunals it covered, to give reasons for decision (s 12).[26] As Lord Diplock put it, the Act filled a 'lacuna' in the law, because tribunals had been able to avoid effective judicial review before that by declining to give reasons (*O'Reilly v Mackman* [1983] 2 AC 237, 277).

Reasons become all the more important under the reconstruction, because decisions of the Upper Tribunal will become binding precedents. Reasons are needed for the development of precedent, as well as for fair communication with the parties to the decision. So tribunals must generally give reasons, or be prepared to do so on request. What must the reasons include? The requirement of reasons in the Tribunals and Inquiries Act 1958 was given teeth in *Re Poyser and Mills' Arbitration* [1964] 2 QB 467, when Megaw J held that Parliament's requirement of reasons 'must be read as meaning that proper, adequate reasons must be given. The reasons that are set out must be reasons which will not only be intelligible, but which deal with the substantial points that have been raised...' (478). Yet reasons that would fail to explain a decision to an outsider do not necessarily make a tribunal's decision unlawful, as long as they are sufficiently clear to enable an aggrieved party to establish whether there was an error of law (*S v Special Educational Needs Tribunal* [1996] 1 All ER 171). 'A reasons challenge will only succeed if the party aggrieved can satisfy the court that he has genuinely been substantially prejudiced by the failure to provide an adequately reasoned decision' (*South Buckinghamshire District Council v Porter No 2* [2004] UKHL 33 [36] (Lord Brown)). Like other duties to give reasons (see Chapter 6), the reasons requirement for tribunals needs to be tailored to its purpose.

---

[26] The provision was retained in the Tribunals and Inquiries Act 1992 (s 10(6)).

12.4.7 Representation and advice

The government favours a policy of reducing legal representation in tribunal hearings. The White Paper pointed out that there is no absolute right to publicly funded legal advice in the tribunal process, and that 'full-scale legal representation at the taxpayer's expense in every administrative dispute or tribunal case would be disproportionate and unreasonable' (White Paper 10.3). But that sensible principle is turned into a general purpose of avoiding legal representation, which itself risks a failure of proportionality in process:

> we aim to create a situation where individuals in dispute with the State or who might be taking a case to a tribunal, or defending one, will be able to have their case resolved with little or no support or assistance. (White Paper 10.1)

That aim is at odds with the judicialization of tribunals under the reconstruction. And for years, free legal representation has been available before many tribunals, including asylum tribunals, the Mental Health Review Tribunal, and the Employment Appeal Tribunal (though not in the Employment Tribunals). It may become inevitable that that legal representation, and legal aid, will have to extend to the Upper Tribunal, on the model of the Employment Appeals Tribunal.

The TCE Act 2007 adds nothing to the law on legal representation, and takes nothing away. But legal representation is going to be hard to avoid in many tribunal hearings, for various reasons:

- the complexity of the legal issues and of the presentation of relevant facts;

- the need for skilled advocacy in a court-like tribunal;

- disabilities or lack of relevant skills on the part of complainants; and

- the use of expert witnesses, which will make it more valuable to have a lawyer as advocate.

The White Paper allows only the last of these as an ongoing reason for assistance before tribunals; it aims to fix the first problem by simplifying the law, and the second by making it easier for claimants themselves to participate in hearings. But it is highly unlikely that the law of tax, or asylum, or even disability living allowance will ever be simplified to the point that complainants will be able to challenge all official decisions effectively without representation by a lawyer or a specialist advocate. And representation not only gives help with complex legal problems; it helps complainants who (apart from any disability) simply don't have the self-confidence or the skills to challenge an official decision. Representation also helps complainants by making their complaint look more serious from the point of view of the tribunal. Although it is certainly not necessary to have a lawyer speaking for you at every tribunal hearing, the reconstruction itself, with the increased judicialization of tribunals it ushers in, has made it harder for complainants to put their case without representation.

Unlike in the law courts, the need for representation can be met without a barrister or a solicitor, and a variety of voluntary or private independent advisors and representatives can potentially help with tribunal proceedings. Even though it was not seriously dealt with in the White Paper, lay representation is important in practice (especially representation by welfare rights workers). Nevertheless, it will be very useful to have a lawyer at certain stages, since appeals to the Upper Tribunal are to be on a point of law. And the judicial nature of the hearing and the mystique of the legal profession make it look even more useful than it is.

In 1989, Hazel and Yvonne Genn wrote a report for the (then) Lord Chancellors' Department on 'The Effectiveness of Representation at Tribunals', which reached the unambiguous conclusion that complainants with representation were more successful in the four tribunals they studied: 'in all four tribunals, the presence of a skilled representative significantly and independently increased the probability that a case would succeed'.[27]

Advocacy helps even in an informal tribunal. Representation is not needed merely because of legal technicalities. In a disability living allowance case, even if the issue is simply whether you can cook for yourself, it will be useful for you to have an advocate stand up and put the case, and to rebut arguments from the department's representatives.

Nothing in the White Paper addresses these points; the White Paper makes the same generalizations that policy makers used to make in the 1980s, without any empirical support:

> 'Tribunals bear many similarities to courts but the hearings are intended to be less formal and adversarial in nature which ought in time to reduce the need for representation. The relevant law may also be simpler than in many court cases and even where it is not in many tribunals there will rarely be a need for a party to concern themselves with technical evidential issues or to deploy the traditional lawyer skill of cross-examination of witnesses.' (White Paper 10.11)

That may be true in some cases, such as a hearing before a Parking Adjudicator in which the complainant wants to argue that the traffic warden made a mistake. But advocacy will be useful in most tribunal hearings, including social security benefit appeals. Legal representation is not always in the interest of the claimants themselves; but we need a system that will make it available when it is needed. Unfortunately, as with so many procedural steps, there is no fair way of allowing representation when it is needed, and *only* when it is needed. Perhaps the solution to this dilemma is partly that many complainants do not need a *lawyer*, although they do

---

[27] Hazell Genn, 'Tribunals and Informal Justice' (1993) 56 MLR 393, 400. See also the 2003 report of the Auditor General into Disability Living Allowance, which showed that complainants who were represented were significantly more successful (Comptroller and Auditor General, 'Getting it right, putting it right: improving decision-making and appeals in social security benefits' Report to the House of Commons, HC 1142, 7 November 2003) [4.17].

need an advocate: someone with experience of the tribunal in question, knowledge of the regime it applies, and the skills needed to represent the complainant.

The Law Society (the professional body of solicitors, who often act as advocates in tribunals) has argued that legal aid ought to be *extended* to hearings before Employment Tribunals and the social security tribunals, because of the increasing complexity of tribunal procedures (White Paper 10.13). The Government rejected that out of hand, and is actually aiming to reduce representation. To do so, they have in mind an 'Enhanced Advice Project' (White Paper 10.10), which is an open-ended scheme to improve the information that tribunals provide to claimants, and the advice and support available to them from independent advice agencies such as charities.

There is an important difference between courts and tribunals in this respect: advice about the opportunity to go to a tribunal can be more important than representation. On this point the White Paper is straightforward and persuasive: 'There are indications from a number of studies that there may well be significant numbers of individuals who, for a variety of reasons, do not seek redress when they could' (White Paper 3.26).[28] Access to courts can be difficult in many ways, but at least people generally know that courts exist. They may simply not know that there is a tribunal waiting to hear a challenge to a public authority's decision. Advice to potential complainants, and clear provision of information by initial administrative decision makers, is one important area in which the Administrative Justice and Tribunals Council and the Ministry of Justice can potentially make an improvement.

12.4.8 Appeals within the Tribunals Service

In the old days, some tribunal schemes had appeals tribunals and some did not. One dramatic unifying feature of the reconstruction is the appellate system. Any party can appeal on a point of law to the new Upper Tribunal, if permission is given by the First-tier Tribunal or by the Upper Tribunal. The Upper Tribunal includes non-lawyer members, and assignment of Judges of the Upper Tribunal to its chambers is done by the Senior President on the basis of expertise (as in the First-tier Tribunals).[29] But otherwise, the Upper Tribunal functions much like the High Court in hearing an appeal on a question of law. And the membership of the Upper Tribunal includes Court of Appeal and High Court judges seconded to the Tribunals Service (TCE Act 2007 s 6).

Statutory appeals from tribunals to the courts on a question of law have long been standard practice. Appeals could be brought to the High Court from 12 types of tribunals under the Tribunals and Inquiries Act 1992 by a party 'dissatisfied in point of law' (s 11 and Sch 1), and there were dozens of other statutes providing for an appeal

---

[28] The White Paper relies on *Tribunal Users Experiences, Perceptions and Expectations: A Literature Review*, available at www.council-on-tribunals.gov.uk/publications/577.htm.

[29] TCE Act 2007 s 7(8), giving effect to Sch 4 para 9(1)(b).

on a question of law.[30] That work will now be done by the Upper Tribunal, rather than by the High Court. It represents a large volume of litigation. By taking it over, the Upper Tribunal is also taking over the role of developing the law for tribunals. It is this step that creates a new kind of judicial institution in our legal system: the Upper Tribunal is an administrative appeals court.

Appeals on a question of law

In *Woodhouse v Peter Ltd* [1972] QB 520, Lord Denning stated that the correct meaning of a statutory term was a question of law, *and* that if a tribunal drew the wrong conclusion from the primary facts it was wrong in law.[31] The more orthodox approach was that of Lord Radcliffe, who said in *Edwards v Bairstow* [1956] AC 14 (HL) that an appeal would not be granted on a question of law unless 'the true and only reasonable conclusion contradicts the determination' (36).[32] He seemed to introduce a reasonableness test for the answers that tribunals gave to questions of law: if a decision either way is reasonable, the court will not interfere, but if only one decision is reasonable, the court will hold the tribunal to it.

Moyna v Work and Pensions Secretary [2003] UKHL 44 confirms the *Edwards v Bairstow* approach. Mrs Moyna suffered angina attacks which meant that for one to three days in a week, she could not cook for herself. She applied for the lowest form of Disability Living Allowance, which is available to a person who 'cannot prepare a cooked main meal for himself if he has the ingredients' (Social Security Contributions and Benefits Act 1992 s 72(1)(a)(ii)). She was turned down; she appealed to the tribunal and lost on the ground that she could 'on most days, prepare a cooked main meal for herself, and that it is not unreasonable to expect her to do so' [13]; she appealed to the Commissioner (an appeal tribunal) on a question of law, and lost again; then she appealed to the Court of Appeal, and won on the ground that the Commissioner and the tribunal had erred in law. The Secretary of State appealed to the House of Lords, and Mrs Moyna finally lost.

In a matter worth £15 pounds per week (for a year-and-a-half until her condition worsened), on the issue of whether she could cook for herself, these five tiers of decision making cannot be called proportionate dispute resolution. The expense of the first tribunal hearing must have been greater than the cost of the claim. Lord Hoffmann, though, made a general holding that (if it is followed) will reduce the number of cases that go through a series of decisions up to the highest court in the land: he overturned the Court of Appeal decision on the ground that the initial tribunal's decision was 'within the bounds of reasonable judgment' [28].

---

[30]   One important example was the Social Security Administration Act 1992 s 24 (appeal from Commissioners to the Court of Appeal on a question of law).

[31]   Cf. *Pearlman v Keepers and Governors of Harrow School* [1979] QB 56 (Lord Denning).

[32]   Lord Radcliffe borrowed the phrase 'true and only reasonable conclusion' from Lord Cooper's speech in *IRC v Toll Property Co Ltd* [1952] SC 387 (HL), 393.

Under the reconstruction of tribunals, Mrs Moyna would have four potential hearings (First-tier Tribunal, Upper Tribunal, Court of Appeal, House of Lords) rather than five. But she would be refused appeal from the Upper Tribunal to the Court of Appeal unless she could persuade one or the other that her case raised a matter of principle of general importance. And Lord Hoffmann's decision itself binds the new Upper Tribunal. So an appeal to the Upper Tribunal should not be a rehearing of the matter, but an appeal on the *Edwards v Bairstow* standard, which recognizes that it may be lawful for the First-tier Tribunal to decide either way (within the bounds of reasonable judgment) in the application of imprecise standards.

12.4.9 Appeals to the courts and judicial review

Since there is an appeal on a question of law, decided by judges, within the Tribunals Service, it may seem that there should be no supervisory jurisdiction left for the Administrative Court in reviewing tribunal decisions. One of Lord Denning's rationales for aggressive judicial review of tribunals before the reconstruction was the fact that the High Court could impose consistency on a variety of tribunals (*Pearlman v Keepers and Governors of Harrow School* [1979] QB 56). The new Upper Tribunal can apply a doctrine of precedent and will be able to impose uniformity *within* the Tribunals system.

The reconstruction has indeed been geared to reducing judicial review and appeals to the Administrative Court. Although it is not at all easy for Parliament to control judicial review, it can be expected that the creation of the Upper Tribunal will largely take the place of judicial review. The Administrative Court (a division of the High Court) will not be prepared to accept applications for judicial review from an applicant who has not taken advantage of the appeal provided within the administrative justice system.

But the reconstruction itself allows the losing party in the Upper Tribunal to bring an appeal to the Court of Appeal on a question of law (if permission is given either by the Upper Tribunal itself or by the Court of Appeal: s 13(4)). That provision enhances the prestige of the Upper Tribunal in a way, by treating its decisions as important enough that they should be reviewed by the Court of Appeal, rather than by a High Court judge. And it was the obvious strategy for the government to take, because losing parties in the Upper Tribunal would certainly have applied to the Administrative Court for judicial review, if the TCE Act 2007 had provided no appeal from the Upper Tribunal. The appeal provision neatly leaves out the Administrative Court, while accepting that the Court of Appeal and the House of Lords must have control over the Upper Tribunal. An attempt to oust judicial review would have been politically costly, or ineffective, or both.

Does the reconstruction *eliminate* judicial review of tribunal decisions? Not necessarily. Any solicitor whose client is refused permission to appeal from the First-tier Tribunal to the Upper Tribunal will think of seeking judicial review. The TCE Act

2007 s 13(8)(c) provides that the right to appeal to the Court of Appeal from the Upper Tribunal does *not* apply to decisions on permission to appeal from the First-tier Tribunal to the Upper Tribunal. So, if both the First-tier Tribunal and the Upper Tribunal refuse permission to appeal a First-tier decision, the complainant could presumably seek judicial review in the Administrative Court of the refusal of permission. Or perhaps the complainant could ask for judicial review of the substantive decision of the First-tier Tribunal.

Remember that *Anisminic v Foreign Compensation Commission* [1969] 2 AC 147 (HL) (see section 9.1) was a claim for a declaration against a tribunal with an ouster clause. In the TCE Act 2007, the Government quite reasonably despaired of trying to oust the judicial review power of the High Court altogether. The Government set out to side-line it, instead. The residual role for judicial review is very limited: the Administrative Court will not be in a hurry to hold that the First-tier Tribunal and the Upper Tribunal have both acted unlawfully in refusing permission to appeal. That is all the more the case, because the TCE Act 2007 confers a judicial review jurisdiction on the Upper Tribunal itself (see p 438). So by and large, appeals within the administrative justice system (with a final appeal to the Court of Appeal) will replace judicial review under the TCE Act 2007.

But there will still be an appeal from the Upper Tribunal to the Court of Appeal on a question of law. Will the increased judicialization of tribunals affect the standard applied in those new appeals? It will make some appeals more like an appeal from the High Court to the Court of Appeal. But there is no general doctrine of restraint in such appeals: the Court of Appeal simply grants an appeal if the decision of the High Court was based on an error of law. Similarly, in appeals from an appeal tribunal to the Court of Appeal on a question of law, the question has previously been simply whether the appeal tribunal was right or wrong in its decision that there was or was not an error of law in the first-tier tribunal's decision.[33] There is potentially a strong argument that since the Upper Tribunal forms a court of appeal within the administrative justice system, the Court of Appeal should defer to some extent to the Upper Tribunal's judgment on the law of tribunals. As Baroness Hale said in *Hinchy v Work and Pensions Secretary* [2005] UKHL 16 [49], 'if the specialist judiciary who do understand the system and the people it serves have established consistent principles, the generalist courts should respect those principles unless they can clearly be shown to be wrong in law'.

12.4.10 Administration and independence

In the old days, tribunals were operated by the government department that had made the decision being challenged. The minister in charge of the department appointed the members, the department paid them and administered their work, and the department provided information about the tribunal to complainants. The

---

[33] See, e.g., *CA v Home Secretary* [2004] EWCA Civ 1165: 'was the Immigration Appeal Tribunal right to find such an error of law?' [24] (Laws LJ).

tribunal members might still have an independent attitude, but they looked as if they were dependent on the department. By the 1990s, some tribunals had already changed in this respect (social security is an example). But one important feature of the reconstruction is the general end of sponsorship of tribunals by the department whose decision was being questioned. That is a radical change in the administration of tribunals. There is one unified Tribunals Service (just like the Courts Service, the administrative arm of the courts), run by the Ministry of Justice.

It is also of symbolic importance that s 1 of the TCE Act 2007 amends the Constitutional Reform Act 2005 s 3, to extend the guarantee of continued judicial independence to tribunal members. So, like other judges, they are covered by the duty of the Lord Chancellor and ministers to uphold their independence. The other increase in the independence of tribunals lies in appointments: the new Judicial Appointments Commission that advises the Lord Chancellor on appointment of judges will also advise him on appointment of tribunal members (TCE Act 2007 Sch 8 para 66).

The guarantee of independence and the use of the Judicial Appointments Commission will not only make tribunal membership more independent; they will also make tribunals more like courts. Along with the administration of the unified tribunal system in the Ministry of Justice, the new appointments technique will change the appearance (if not the ethos) of tribunals into an independent system.

12.4.11 Oversight

The Administrative Justice and Tribunals Council (AJTC) serves as an advisory body to government, and has a general duty to review the functioning of the administrative justice system and to oversee relationships among courts, tribunals, ombudsmen, etc. So it has the wider role that the Council on Tribunals recommended for itself in a report in 1980.[34] The Council, set up by the Tribunals and Inquiries Act 1958, had an ongoing responsibility to review and report on the constitution and working of tribunals. So its role was purely advisory, and its only legal role was that ministers could not make procedural rules for tribunals without consulting the Council. A long list of tribunals was stated to be under the 'supervision' of the Council,[35] but the Council did not supervise tribunals. It watched what they did and reported. The Franks Committee, which proposed the Council on Tribunals in 1957, had recommended that it should be a governing body with genuine supervisory powers, including appointment of tribunal members, and regulation of pay and procedures.[36] But Parliament did not give the Council on Tribunals regulatory power. Its main role was to be consulted on procedural changes and membership appointments.

The reconstruction has not made the new Council into a governing body as Franks wanted; the AJTC will not appoint members, or decide procedures, or administer the

---

[34] 'The Functions of the Council on Tribunals' (Cmnd 7805, 1980).

[35] See Tribunals and Inquiries Act 1992 Sch 1. 'Report of the Committee on Administrative Tribunals and Enquiries' (Cmnd 218, 1957).

[36] 'Report of the Committee on Administrative Tribunals and Enquiries' (Cmnd 218, 1957).

tribunals, or even regulate them. It will advise the Ministry of Justice. Yet the AJTC does have a wider responsibility than the Council on Tribunals had. The enhancement in the role reflects the scope of the reconstruction: first of all, the Council is now reviewing and reporting on the whole administrative justice system (and also on the tribunals that are still outside the system). Secondly, it reviews the relation between tribunals, first-instance decision making, alternative dispute resolution mechanisms, other forms of redress such as public sector ombudsmen, and the courts. It will actually be overseeing a system. The enhanced role will reduce departmental control over tribunals.

12.5 Alternatives to tribunal hearings: proportionate dispute resolution

The TCE Act 2007 requires the Senior President to attend to 'the need to develop innovative methods of resolving disputes that are of a type that may be brought before tribunals' (s 2(3)(d)). Alternative dispute resolution ('ADR') involves a tension between the value of providing quicker, cheaper, less confrontational resolutions on the one hand, and on the other hand, the danger of railroading disadvantaged complainants into shortcut processes that do not give them a real hearing, and outcomes that violate their rights or disregard their interests. Those dangers sound awful, and the results of ADR really can be awful. There is a risk of process failure, because the very reasons for having an independent and impartial tribunal may be reasons not to leave the parties to the outcome of a process that avoids a hearing before a tribunal. But it is still a good idea for the administrative justice system to work at alternatives to tribunal hearings, because sometimes the complainant really does not need a hearing.

And the system can already provide useful alternatives. Section 24 of the TCE Act 2007 provides for a tribunal member to serve as a **mediator**—that is, as someone who discusses the complaint with the two parties, to help them to reach an outcome that both agree to. Section 24(1) restricts mediation:

> (a) mediation of matters in dispute between parties to proceedings is to take place only by agreement between those parties;
> (b) where parties to proceedings fail to mediate, or where mediation between parties to proceedings fails to resolve disputed matters, the failure is not to affect the outcome of the proceedings.

The restrictions are meant to prevent mediation from interfering with the complainant's right to a hearing.

The tribunals' case management powers under the Act would enable the Tribunal Rules Committee to encourage the use of ADR before a tribunal hearing, but s 24 makes it clear that the rules cannot impose compulsory mediation. The rules could, however, empower a tribunal to postpone formal proceedings during a case to carry out ADR through the s 24 mediation process, or to allow the parties to pursue other options. The options all depend on some sort of agreement between the parties. **Negotiation** is simply a discussion between the parties aimed at settlement; **mediation** is negotiation with an intermediary as a facilitator; **arbitration** is dispute resolution that is binding because the parties agree in advance to accept whatever the arbitrator decides. But there are other possibilities, too, such as **early neutral evaluation**, which gives the parties an independent opinion on their case, in order to help them decide whether to reach an agreement without a hearing.

In the ordinary courts, pre-action protocols encourage the use of ADR before proceeding to a trial (see p 368). Similar protocols could be used before tribunal hearings. But in the courts, this aspect of case management works because the court can award very substantial legal costs against a party that does not cooperate. There have generally been no costs awards in tribunals. The TCE Act 2007 s 29 provides that the Tribunal has discretion over costs, subject to Tribunal Procedure Rules (Sch 5 Pt 1 para 12 includes a power to make rules concerning costs). Control over costs may allow greater scope for tribunals to press complainants to try ADR. The Tribunal Rules Committee, composed of the senior tribunal judges and other tribunal members, will need to work out whether that would conflict with the evident commitment in the TCE Act 2007 to voluntary ADR processes. The rule against compulsory mediation suggests that ADR ought to be voluntary, which calls into question the use of cost penalties to back up case management powers.

How can the new system deal with these challenges? The rules, which are under development, will have to vary to some degree with the needs of individual First-tier jurisdictions. Proportionate dispute resolution is meant to be the harmonizing principle,[37] but that is only a way of posing the difficult question: the question of how much pressure to settle a dispute is compatible with fair process and good decision making. That question of proportionality depends on the reconciliation of various potential advantages and disadvantages of ADR as shown in Figure 12.4.

The **Social Security and Child Support Appeals Tribunal** is trying out early neutral evaluation for disability living allowance appeals. A tribunal chairman will give the complainant and the department an early assessment of the case, in an attempt to identify opportunities for resolution without a hearing. The scheme will be voluntary: if the complainant refuses, that is not meant to affect the hearing, and if the complaint goes to a hearing after an early neutral evaluation, the hearing is to be unaffected by the evaluation.[38]

Proportionality is the basic principle. A good resolution to an administrative dispute should follow a process that is no more expensive, time-consuming, legalistic, and formal than it needs to be for its purposes. Those purposes are:

- to give the complainant a decent voice in the proceedings,

....

[37] 'Tribunals Court and Enforcement Bill: Detailed Policy Statement on Delegated Power' December 2006, Ministry of Justice, http://www.justice.gov.uk/docs/TCEbill-policy-statement-delegated-powers.pdf.

[38] Tribunals Service Annual Report and Accounts 2006–7 (22) http://www.tribunals.gov.uk/Tribunals/Documents/Publications/annualreportaccounts0607.pdf.

Alternative Dispute Resolution	
Pros	Cons
Compared with a tribunal hearing, the alternative may: • be quicker, • be less expensive to the parties and to the administrative justice system, • give the complainant a form of involvement in a consensual resolution that enhances his or her control over the process and the outcome, • cause **less stress**, • **reconcile parties** who may need to be able to cooperate in future. And ADR may lead to a resolution that the court could not have ordered, since the parties can be **more flexible** in reaching an agreement, than the court could be in applying the law to the issues raised in a complaint.	If the parties have **unequal bargaining power**, then a mediated agreement may not be fair (unless the mediator abandons his or her neutrality). **The impartiality of the tribunal itself may come into question**, since it is common practice for a mediator to have discussions with each party separately. Any steps that a tribunal takes to encourage mediation may put pressure on the parties, and it will be difficult to guard against **undue pressure**. A good outcome **cannot influence other cases** in the way that a precedent influences other cases after a tribunal decision.

Figure 12.4

- to reach an outcome that gives effect to the complainant's legal rights, while showing respect for the complainant's private interests and responding to them in a way that is in the public interest,

- to hold a public authority accountable for its conduct, and

- to shape the law in a way that (so far as the law is able to do it) promotes good administration.

Doing all that may require a process that is expensive, time-consuming, legalistic, and formal. And the irony of process means that the system may have to overdo the process, in order to make sure that the rights and interests at stake do not get trampled in the rush to a resolution.

> ### The Australian experience
> Australia has entrenched mediation and conciliation processes in the work of administrative tribunals at state and federal level. The federal Administrative Appeals Tribunal uses pre-hearing mediation and conciliation processes. The legislation requires tribunals to 'pursue the objective of providing a mechanism of review that is fair, just, economical, informal and quick', and empowers them to call a conference between the parties, or to refer the dispute for mediation, neutral evaluation, case appraisal, or conciliation (Administrative Appeals Tribunal Amendment Act 2005).[39]

---

[39] http://www.austlii.edu.au/au/legis/cth/num_act/aataa2005403/sch1.html. See also http://www.dca.gov.uk/research/2005/8_2005_full.pdf.

12.6 Justice between parties, or service to customers?

The tensions in the reconstruction of tribunals are reflected in the White Paper's approach to complainants. They are not called complainants; they are sometimes called 'users', and sometimes 'customers'.[40] The White Paper started out by considering 'the types of problems and disputes people face, and what outcomes they want to achieve' (White Paper 2.5). But the outcome that complainants want is a decision in their favour. And they are fundamentally different from customers, because an independent tribunal gives no services to the parties before it (except purely ancillary services such as a decent waiting room and helpful information about times of hearings). A tribunal decision is not a service to the complainant, but a judgment between the arguments of the complainant and the arguments of the government. The service that tribunals provide, like the service that the courts provide, is a public service and not a service to customers. But the Courts Service uses the same lingo. It is just patronizing to call a defendant charged with murder a 'customer' of the justice system. And if I have been refused disability living allowance, and I want to complain, it is patronizing to call me a 'customer'. Doing so disguises the fact that courts and tribunals are there to do justice after an independent and impartial hearing of a claim.

The White Paper raises the prospect of applying to tribunals the same strategy for improving public services that the government applies to services such as schools and hospitals, through the monitoring of performance against targets:

> The key performance indicators for the new service will be focussed on the needs of users. We have taken as a starting point what we think users are entitled to from the service... (White Paper 6.89)

'Key performance indicator' is management-speak for a measurable test of success for a business organization. The needs identified in the White Paper include independence, and consistent and comprehensible decisions, and for these objectives, 'customer satisfaction' is listed under 'scope of potential measurement', and 'Sample Potential KPIs' include '% of users satisfied with independence of outcome or process...' and 'Number of appeals raised against first tier decisions' (White Paper 6.89).

But the point of a tribunal is to decide a dispute, and if it is part of a system of administrative justice, then customer satisfaction cannot serve as an indicator of success. It is a tribunal's duty to leave a 'customer' dissatisfied if he or she does not have a good complaint. Any decent form of resolution of person-and-state disputes

---

[40] Note that the Asylum and Immigration Tribunal already has a 'customer service centre': See http://www.ait.gov.uk/glossary.htm. The Tribunals Service's website calls complainants 'customers', as does its 2007–8 Strategic Business Plan.

will generate a great deal of 'customer' satisfaction (when it decides in favour of the complainant), and a great deal of dissatisfaction (when it decides against the complainant). Customer satisfaction is beside the point, except in keeping down delay, providing useful information, and maintaining convenient hearing centres.

12.7 Tribunal engineering: flux in the immigration and asylum tribunals

The reconstructed tribunal system needs to meet the challenge of the diversity of tribunals. And it will need to respond to the variation over time that has arisen and will continue to arise from political pressures to respond to real or perceived problems by tampering with tribunal processes. The asylum and immigration system provides the best example of flux.

Since signing the Geneva Convention on the Status of Refugees in 1951, Britain has been committed to giving asylum to refugees (persons seeking safety in a foreign country for fear of persecution at home). And under a varying set of entry criteria, Britain has also been prepared to accept immigrants who are not refugees. Since 1969, there has been a tribunal system for deciding appeals over whether would-be entrants fit the immigration criteria, or qualify for refugee status. The First-tier Tribunal was an adjudicator (appointed by the Home Secretary), who heard an appeal on the merits of the decisions of the immigration officers or the Home Secretary. From the adjudicator's decision, there was an appeal to the Immigration Appeal Tribunal (whose members were appointed by the Lord Chancellor) (Immigration Appeals Act 1969).

The Immigration and Asylum Act 1999 allowed any dissatisfied party to bring a further appeal to the Immigration Appeal Tribunal (IAT), after an adjudicator's decision on the first appeal (Sch para 22). The Court of Appeal held that the IAT could overturn the adjudicator's decision for error of fact or error of law, but that the IAT did have to identify an error, and could not overturn merely on the ground that the IAT would have reached a different decision (*Subesh v Home Secretary* [2004] EWCA Civ 56).

The radical changes to this system began after September 11, 2001, when fear of terrorism coincided with a media frenzy about large numbers of bogus asylum seekers who were supposedly abusing the IAT process to stay in Britain. The Nationality, Immigration and Asylum Act 2002 changed the appeals provisions to provide an appeal to the adjudicator on facts or law, but no appeal to the IAT on the facts or the merits.[41] Appeals to the IAT required permission of the IAT. The government became badly vexed by large volumes of judicial review decisions overturning refusals of permission to appeal.

---

[41] 'A party to an appeal to an adjudicator...may...appeal to the Tribunal against the adjudicator's determination on a point of law.' Nationality, Immigration and Asylum Act 2002 s 101. See *CA v Home Secretary* [2004] EWCA Civ 1165 [10], [30] (Laws LJ).

So in 2004, Parliament replaced the two tiers with one Asylum and Immigration Tribunal (Asylum and Immigration (Treatment of Claimants, etc) Act 2004). The Adjudicators and the members of the Immigration Appeal Tribunal all became members of the new AIT. Most initial AIT decisions are made by a single immigration judge. A written request for reconsideration of the judge's decision can be made to the High Court, but there is a very short (five-day) time limit. The request is filtered by an AIT judge, who decides whether to send the request to the High Court; if the judge decides not to send it, the complainant can still ask the High Court to consider the request. If that request is successful, a three-member panel of the AIT will reconsider the decision; after reconsideration, its decision can be challenged on appeal to the Court of Appeal (with permission either from the AIT or from the Court of Appeal).

Meanwhile, if the Home Secretary wants to remove a person from the country for reasons of national security or international relations, or the appeal requires disclosure of sensitive information, there is no appeal under the Nationality, Immigration and Asylum Act 2002 from the Home Secretary's decision (Nationality, Immigration and Asylum Act 2002 s 97). The only recourse is to the Special Immigration Appeals Commission, under the Special Immigration Appeals Commission Act 1997. The word 'special' reflects its unusual secrecy, and 'commission' marks the Government's purpose of keeping it out of the ordinary appeal processes of tribunals. SIAC makes decisions by a panel of three members, one of whom has held high judicial office and another of whom has been an immigration judge. There is an appeal from SIAC to the Court of Appeal on a question of law (Anti-terrorism, Crime and Security Act 2001 s 35).[42]

Does all this legislation[43] amount to a progression toward proportionate dispute resolution? Proportionality is under constant political pressure from public anxiety both about immigration and about terrorism, and from government anxiety to be seen to be doing something. The steps in the progression have been dictated by crises such as the September 11 attacks on the U.S. Panic measures are dangerous ways of dealing with problems of due process. A community committed to the rule of law has to face the cost involved: the irony of process (see p 143) is that we have to allow procedures that will be disproportionate in particular cases (procedures that allow some people to go on challenging a decision farther than is warranted, and give them more of a role in the process than some people can justly demand), in order to ensure proportional process for people who need it.

Parliamentary process

Parliament has stood in the way of the progressive reduction of procedural protections for asylum seekers and terrorism suspects, in spite of the Government's

---

[42] The Act makes SIAC a superior court of record and prevents judicial review of decisions of the SIAC.

[43] And there is more: the UK Borders Act 2007 created new powers of detention at airports and required the Home Secretary to deport foreigners convicted of serious crimes with no appeal, unless it would breach their Convention rights.

haste. The Asylum and Immigration Bill 2004 would have ousted judicial review of Asylum and Immigration Tribunal decisions, but after the House of Commons approved it, the Government dropped the ouster clause before the Bill passed in the House of Lords. And in October 2008, the Government suffered its heaviest defeat in ten years in the House of Lords (309 votes to 118) on a bill to allow detention of terrorism suspects for 42 days without charge. The Government removed that provision from its Counter-Terrorism Bill, saying that it would bring it back to Parliament in case of emergency.

12.8 Conclusion: the irony of process

The reconstruction of tribunals is just beginning. Its most striking feature is the Upper Tribunal, which will play the role of a new administrative appeals court. The new appeal process unifies tribunal appeals, and the Upper Tribunal will have the opportunity to play a major role in the development of administrative law.

Its focal challenges will be to promote the two purposes of tribunals: administrative justice and proportionate dispute resolution. A cynic might say that 'administrative justice' means 'you don't get your day in court', and 'proportionate dispute resolution' means 'you get as little process as possible'. An optimist might say that the reconstruction promises the administration of justice in a way that is tailored to the needs of the people who are seeking justice, without imposing alienating (and, incidentally, expensive) formal procedures. The cynic and the optimist would both be overemphasizing aspects of a complex situation; the same governmental impulses have led to a really impressive reconstruction of tribunals, and *have also* created new risks of process failure.

The reconstruction has created an administrative justice system for the first time. It is a system that will affect all areas of tribunal decision making, but its main features reflect an evolution of the welfare state. In the earliest schemes for national insurance and soldiers' pensions before and after World War I, decision making was non-judicial, relatively informal, geared to reflect expertise and the purpose of the benefit in question. The massive development after World War II created a chaotic and expensive system. Under Prime Minister Thatcher and then Prime Minister Blair, the trend has been to increase control of the costs both of benefits, and of the decision-making process. But it is a complex trend, involving substantial judicialization of processes but also countervailing moves toward alternative dispute resolution and decision making without oral hearings and without representation.

Are Tribunals the exception to a rule that disputes ought to be resolved by courts?

The Franks Committee in 1957 held on to a general principle that 'a decision should be entrusted to a court rather than to a tribunal in the absence of special considerations which make a tribunal more suitable'.[44] Yet Franks saw benefits that can often make tribunals more suitable: 'openness, fairness and impartiality'.[45] And the Franks Committee's recommendations, including the first Tribunals and Inquiries Act and the Council on Tribunals, contributed to making tribunal decision making a standard feature of the legal system, rather than a special exception to judicial decision making.

Now the Government has abandoned the principle that courts are the standard way of deciding entitlements under government schemes, and the idea that tribunals are an exception needing special considerations. Instead, the reconstruction of tribunals accepts the principle of proportionate decision making as the general principle (White Paper 3.23). The presumption that disputes as to legal rights are to be determined by the courts has been abandoned; meanwhile, the tribunals are to become more like courts. The reconstruction will undoubtedly enhance the impartiality of tribunals; its impact on their openness and fairness will be much more complex.

But it is so much easier to apply this crucial principle of proportionality in judicial review, than to give effect to it in a *system* that will provide a structure of process rights. In a judicial review case like *Ridge v Baldwin* [1964] AC 40 (see p 116), the judges can look at the particular context in which the decision was made, and learn what was at stake, and decide whether, all things considered, the process was proportionate to the issues at stake. In reconstructing tribunals into a system, however, it is impossible to consider all things. So the principle of proportionality has to be applied with a healthy awareness of the irony of process: all process is imperfect, so that it is necessary to create processes that will be *disproportionate* in some cases, in order to guarantee the protections that will be necessary in other cases. This irony means that processes will not be sufficient to do justice (that is, they will not be proportionate), if they do not allow scope for waste and even abuse (by, e.g., bogus asylum seekers, or murderers).

The White Paper was written with little sense of the irony of process, because it holds out the promise of giving customers what they want. But customer satisfaction is an incoherent goal for a system of justice. Complainants cannot generally be given what they want. But they cannot *merely* be given what they have a right to, either: they have to be given procedures that are sometimes more than they have a right to, in order to protect the right to a fair hearing.

There is no good way of deciding which hearings are pointless, without a hearing! Consider what proportionality requires in the most politically contentious tribunal scheme, asylum and immigration:

- *enough* procedural protection to asylum seekers and would-be immigrants to secure just decisions with fair participation by the people affected,

---

44   *Report of the Committee on Administrative Tribunals and Enquiries* (Cmnd 218, 1957) [38].

45   Ib. [41].

- *without* furnishing illegal immigrants and fake refugees with a way of staying in the country or delaying their removal.

The irony of process is that it is impossible to accomplish both. Without serious reconsideration on an appeal to an independent decision maker, there is no good way of sorting the refugees from the many people who seek refugee status without meeting the requirements of the Geneva Convention. There is no way of setting up such a process without giving people who have no right to asylum a technique to delay, or even to deceive, a tribunal or court that cannot assess the situation perfectly. So a commitment to justice in asylum and immigration requires a commitment to provide processes that can be abused. That is actually true of *all* tribunals, and of courts, too.

Governmental instincts (to cut the costs of waste in the tribunals, and to streamline decision making) risk misjudgments of proportionality. But the increased independence and the unification in the reconstruction of tribunals are impressive. The crucial features of the reconstruction are the removal of tribunal sponsorship from departments, the appointment of tribunal judges on the recommendation of the Judicial Appointments Commission, and the creation of a unified appeals tribunal. Those major reforms bring their own costs, through the increased judicialization of tribunals. The costs will be worth paying if they help people to get a fair hearing in, e.g., a claim for disability living allowance.

It will be a constant challenge for government to operate genuinely fair and sensible processes for the exercise of new decision-making powers. The work of tribunals is going to be permanently in flux, as government creates new bodies and reorganizes the work of the old bodies. One advantage of the reconstruction is that the new unity of the administrative justice system will bring some stability to tribunals, and put a drag on dangerous innovations made in public emergencies.

FROM THE MISTS OF TIME

Albert Venn Dicey is famous for arguing that in England, the rule of law is secured by making the lawfulness of administrative action a matter for the ordinary courts (*Introduction to the Study of the Law of the Constitution*, 1885). The reconstruction of tribunals creates, in the Upper Tribunal, an administrative appeals court that is not part of the ordinary courts. Today, if a tribunal has decided your complaint unlawfully, you cannot go to the High Court. So is the reconstruction anathema to the traditions of the British constitution?

In his Preface to the 8th edition in 1914, Dicey wrote, 'France has with undoubted wisdom more or less judicialised her highest administrative tribunal, and made it to a great extent independent of the Government of the day. It is at least conceivable that modern England would be benefited by the extension of official law. Nor is it quite certain that the ordinary law Courts are in all cases the best body for adjudicating upon the offences or the errors of civil servants. It may require consideration whether some body of men who combined official experience with legal knowledge and who were entirely independent of the Government of the day, might not enforce official law with more effectiveness than any Division of the High Court.' Today in England, the reconstruction of tribunals has judicialized administrative tribunals, and they have the independence that Dicey considered essential to the rule of law. Even on Dicey's view, the reconstruction represents a new way of imposing the rule of law on administration, and not a departure from the rule of law.

TAKE-HOME MESSAGE • • •

- The most important features of the reconstruction of tribunals in the **Tribunals, Courts and Enforcement Act 2007** are:

  - the new **appeal process in the Upper Tribunal** (along with its judicial review jurisdiction over some tribunal matters), with a further appeal to the Court of Appeal;

  - **the Upper Tribunal's opportunity to develop case law** that will govern the work of tribunals;

  - support and oversight for the administrative justice system from:
    - a unified **Tribunal Service**,
    - a **Tribunal Procedure Committee**, and
    - the **Administrative Justice and Tribunals Council**; and

  - a move toward encouraging **ADR** in matters brought before tribunals.

- The Upper Tribunal is an innovation of constitutional significance: it is the closest thing that Britain has ever had to an **administrative court** distinct from the High Court.

- The reconstruction creates new tensions in the system between **informality** and **legality**:
  - it makes tribunals more like courts in some ways (in the method of appointment of tribunal judges, and their independence, and the Government aims to move away from expert and lay membership on tribunals); and yet
  - the Government aims to keep proceedings informal, and to restrict legal representation before tribunals.

Critical reading

Edwards v Bairstow [1956] AC 14 (HL)
Moyna v Work and Pensions Secretary [2003] UKHL 44
The White Paper, 'Transforming Public Services: Complaints, Redress and Tribunals', Secretary of State for Constitutional Affairs, July 2004 (Cm 6243)
Tribunals, Courts and Enforcement Act 2007, Part 1

CRITICAL QUESTIONS • • •

1   What can courts do that tribunals cannot do?

2   What can tribunals do that courts cannot do?

3   Why do tribunals form part of our administrative justice system? What is their purpose and why is it best served by a tribunal as opposed to a court or some other
dispute resolution system?

4   If a tribunal fails to give a fair hearing, is the possibility of an appeal on a question
of law enough to remedy the unfairness?

Further Questions:

5   Is there any good reason for the Asylum and Immigration Tribunal to have a different structure and process from other tribunals?

6   Is there any general difference between a person-and-state tribunal decision, and
the decision of a court in a tort action against a public authority? Why couldn't tribunals take over the complaints that are currently pursued in the tort actions discussed below in Chapter 14?

7   What is the difference between the principle of proportionate decision making, and
the principle (from the 1958 Franks Committee) that a dispute should be resolved
by a court unless special considerations make a tribunal preferable?

8   If the order provided for in TCE Act 2007 s 13(6) is passed, appeals from a decision
of the Upper Tribunal to the Court of Appeal will only be allowed on a question of
law, with the added limitation that the appeal must raise some important point
of principle or practice, or that there is some other compelling reason to hear the
appeal. Will it be possible to apply for judicial review of an Upper Tribunal decision
that does not satisfy the criteria for appeal?

9   In the new appeals *within the tribunals judiciary*, should the Upper Tribunal be more
willing or less willing to overturn decisions, than the High Court was in statutory
appeals from tribunals before the reconstruction?

Exercise: Try going to the Ministry of Justice website, www.justice.gov.uk, and typ-
ing 'customers' in the homepage search engine.

online
resource
centre

Visit the online resource centre to access the following resources which
accompany this chapter: links to legislation and online reports of judicial
decisions, summaries of key cases and legislation, updates in the law,
suggestions for answering the pop quizzes and questions, and links to useful
websites.

13 Ombudsmen and other investigators

Instead of adversarial litigation in a court or tribunal, an independent investigation of a complaint may be the best process for securing administrative justice. Here we look at ombudsmen and other forms of investigation of the working of government, and the ways in which they can resolve disputes and improve administration.

LOOK FOR • • •

- The ombudsmen's four keys:
    (1) they are **independent**;
    (2) they **investigate** a complaint;
    (3) they look for **injustice** caused by **maladministration**; and
    (4) they make a **report**.
    —that's all they do!

- The way(s) in which the government ought to respond to reports by ombudsmen.

- The European Ombudsman, and the ways in which it differs from the UK ombudsmen.

- Differences and similarities between local and Parliamentary Ombudsmen.

- The increasingly diverse techniques available for investigation of complaints.

- The role of courts in controlling investigation processes.

> ❛ Access to justice is achievable as often through institutions other than the
> courts of law. ❜
>
> *R v Lambeth LBC, ex p Crookes* [1997] 29 HLR 28 (QBD),
> 39 (Sir Louis Blom-Cooper)

13.1 Introduction: the 'Debt of Honour' investigation

In 2000, years of lobbying paid off for people who had been interned by the Japanese in World War II. After half a decade of campaigns, political pressure in the House of Commons pushed the Government into a sudden announcement of a scheme of payments. Administrators from various departments were quickly assembled for a working party which met on a Friday, and had to make proposals to ministers the following Monday. Just eight days later, on November 7th, a minister announced in the House of Commons that the Government would make payments of £10,000 each to former detainees, not as compensation, but to recognize the country's 'debt of honour' to those who endured captivity in the Far East during the Second World War. He said that the payments would go to 'British civilians who were interned'.

Thousands of payments were made, starting in January 2001.[1] But the Government never adopted any view on what 'British civilians' meant until March 2001, when an interdepartmental working group decided that payments would be made only to civilian internees who were born in the United Kingdom or who had a parent or grandparent born in the United Kingdom. This 'bloodlink' test was not announced until July 2001. The bloodlink test ruled out hundreds who had been British subjects during World War II. It not only denied those British subjects the £10,000, it also antagonized them, because it suggested that the country did not owe them a debt of honour. The Japanese had interned them because they were British, and they were 'British civilians' in the sense that they were British subjects at the time of their internment, but under the bloodlink test they were not British enough.

Jack Hayward complained to the Parliamentary Commissioner for Administration (the 'Parliamentary Ombudsman'). His father was a British subject born in India, and his mother was born in Iraq; after the war, he came to Britain to live with an aunt, went to school and university and did National Service in England, and eventually became a professor of politics. He had been interned as a Briton with his family, and he thought he would qualify when the Government announced payments to 'British civilians'. But his application was rejected in June 2001, because he did not satisfy the bloodlink criterion. The Parliamentary Ombudsman investigated Hayward's complaint as a representative of many other complaints, and reported that

---

[1] By 2004, more than 23,000 payments of £10,000 were made.

maladministration in the development of the scheme had caused him an injustice. It was a 'significant departure from standards of good administration' to announce the scheme in a way that raised the hopes of all British detainees, without clearly saying who would be eligible.[2]

In July 2005, the Ombudsman's report recommended that the Ministry of Defence review the operation of the scheme, and reconsider the position of Hayward and those in a similar position. She also recommended an apology, and that the Ministry should consider expressing regret 'tangibly'.[3]

The Ministry of Defence accepted the finding of maladministration, and the last two recommendations. But it refused to review the operation of the scheme, or to reconsider Hayward's eligibility for the payment. So the Parliamentary Ombudsman used her power under the Parliamentary Commissioner Act 1967 s 10(3) to issue a special report to Parliament, indicating that she had found injustice caused by maladministration, which the Government did not propose to remedy. After that report, and the intervention of the Public Administration Select Committee, the government finally revised the eligibility criteria in March 2006, to include people like Jack Hayward.

Four findings of maladministration—the Ombudsman's summary:

- the scheme was devised too quickly and in a way that made eligibility unclear;
- the Ministerial statement was confusing;
- the Government should have reviewed the bloodlink criterion to ensure that it did not lead to unequal treatment; and
- the Government failed to inform complainants that the criteria had been clarified when they were sent a questionnaire to establish their eligibility.[4]

The Debt of Honour case demonstrates the strengths and the limitations of an investigation by the ombudsman. The ombudsman *investigates* a complaint, and that provides a form of scrutiny of administration that neither Members of Parliament nor judges can offer. What the complainant does not get is a legal remedy. But on the other hand, the ability to place a special report before Parliament when injustice is not remedied provides a form of response to a complaint that no court can give. As a technique for controlling administration, ombudsmen are distinctly different from courts and they can be more valuable to people with a complaint.

---

[2]   Parliamentary Ombudsman, '"A debt of honour": the ex gratia scheme for British groups interned by the Japanese during the Second World War', 4th Report—Session 2005–2006, HC 324 (2005–2006) [155–9].

[3]   Ib. [212–18].

[4]   Ib. [199].

13.2 The ombudsman process: four keys

Ombudsmen share these traits:

The keys of the ombudsmen process:

- **their independence:** they are free of control by the bodies they scrutinize;
- **their investigative process:** their scrutiny takes the form of investigation of a complaint;
- **their task:** they look for injustice caused by bad administration; and
- **their reporting function:** the result of their investigation is simply a report that concludes with recommendations, if an ombudsman finds that injustice has been caused by bad administration.

Already you can start to see how different their role is from, on the one hand, the role of a public authority in considering a complaint about its own conduct, and on the other, the role of a tribunal, or of a court in judicial review. To unpack these key features of ombudsmen, we will start with the central government ombudsman, who is a *parliamentary* ombudsman because of a uniquely British effort to squeeze the Scandinavian ombudsman principle into our constitution.

Thank you, Sweden!

When Sweden lost Finland to Russia in 1809, the Swedish nobles deposed the king and appointed a new one. They retained the constitutional allocation of executive power to the king, and legislative power to Parliament. But they took the opportunity to invent a 'iustitie-ombudsman': a representative appointed by Parliament for people with a complaint, whose job was to protect individual rights against the executive. There was no legal technique for the ombudsman to invalidate executive action; he simply investigated and made a report. It worked.

Modern ombudsmen are impartial investigators, not representatives. Otherwise, though, the first ombudsman's office nearly 200 years ago has been the model for the modern public sector ombudsman: an independent public official appointed to investigate complaints against administrative acts of government. Since the 1960s, the model has spread throughout the common law world.

The Parliamentary Ombudsman was the first ombudsman in Britain. Local Government Ombudsmen were set up by statute in 1974, and today they carry a greater caseload than the Parliamentary Ombudsman. Their powers and their role are different, in ways that reflect differences between central and local government.

The role of ombudsmen's investigations in both local government and central government *overlaps* with the role of judicial review. Moreover, courts have taken upon themselves the task of reviewing the work of the local and Parliamentary Ombudsmen. Judicial review of the work of ombudsmen raises a difficult question about the purpose of judicial review itself: why should courts interfere at all in the work of another independent institution set up to do justice for complainants? The judges have given judicial review of ombudsmen's reports, but they have not answered this question.

13.3 The Parliamentary Ombudsman

The idea of the Parliamentary Commissioner Act 1967 was to take advantage of the Scandinavian model to create an informal investigator. But we ended up with a special British version of the institution, because of a British problem. The office of ombudsman seemed to be at odds with the tradition that complaints against the administration of government are to be resolved by writing to one's Member of Parliament (MP). An MP can pursue a complaint by contacting the department in question. By convention, the department must respond to inquiries from MPs, and an MP who is not satisfied with the response can raise the matter in the House of Commons. The role of an ombudsman as an informal investigator of central government administration seemed to clash with that role of MPs as the people's representatives. And it may have seemed to the politicians that it was not quite right for the British Government to face investigation by any authority outside Parliament.

The solution to the clash was to make the ombudsman *parliamentary* in three respects: the ombudsman was to investigate a complaint only on referral from an MP, and would make reports to the House of Commons (an annual report (s 10(4), and a special report on any failure by a public authority to comply with a report on an investigation), and would be supported by a Select Committee of the House of Commons (it is not mentioned in the Act, but the Public Administration Select Committee considers ombudsmen's reports on behalf of the House of Commons). The reporting role, together with the connection to the Committee, provides a resolution to the tricky question of the effect of ombudsmen's reports.

Before drawing general conclusions about the value of the office in the control of administration, we will need to look in detail at the scheme of the 1967 Act, and at the ways in which the Parliamentary Ombudsmen have developed their role.

13.3.1 The Parliamentary Commissioner Act 1967

(1) **Who** is the Parliamentary Commissioner for Administration (the 'Parliamentary Ombudsman')?

She is appointed by the Crown (Parliamentary Commissioner Act 1967, s 1(2)), i.e., by the government. But after appointment, she is independent of the Government. Like a judge, she holds office 'during good behaviour' (s 1(2)), which means that she can only be removed by addresses from both Houses of Parliament (s 1(3)).[5] And her salary is fixed by a resolution of the House of Commons, not by the Government.

(2) **Whom** can the Ombudsman investigate?

---

[5]   But she can be removed by the Crown on grounds of medical incapacity: Parliamentary and Health Commissioners Act 1987 s 2.

The major government departments[6] and over 200 agencies are open to investigation. The 1967 Act gave a list (Sch 2); the Government can extend it, but only to governmental bodies exercising functions on behalf of the Crown, or set up by the Government and receiving at least half their revenue from Parliament (s 4). Educational institutions, bodies that regulate the professions, complaints investigators, and commercial bodies are excluded.[7]

(3) **How** does a complaint get to the Ombudsman?

The Ombudsman does not act on her own initiative. She can only investigate matters raised by a complaint. And the 'MP filter' in the 1967 Act provides that she can only act on a complaint after an MP refers it to her (s 5(1); see p 471).

(4) What can the Ombudsman **not** investigate?

The legislation rules out:

- Complaints by a public body (e.g., a local authority, s 6).
- Complaints about 'any action in respect of which the person aggrieved has or had' a remedy before a tribunal or a court. But the Ombudsman may investigate even if there is such an alternative, if 'it is not reasonable to expect him to resort or have resorted to it' (s 5(2)) (see p 479).
- Complaints about excluded subject matters listed in Sch 3 to the 1967 Act, including international relations, crime, and security investigation, contracts, or other commercial transactions (but the compulsory acquisition of land is fair game), and personnel (pay, appointments, etc.).

(5) **When** must a complaint be brought?

Complaints must have reached an MP within 12 months after the complainant had notice of the problem (although the ombudsman has a discretion to take complaints out of time, if there are special circumstances (s 6(3)). (Remember, this is more generous than the three-month *prima facie* time limit on judicial review (see p 363).)

(6) How does the Ombudsman **proceed**?

- First, she decides whether a complaint is duly made (s 5(9)).
- Then, the Ombudsman decides whether to investigate, over which she has discretion (s 5(5)).
- She gives the public authority an opportunity to comment on the complaint (s 7(1)).
- She conducts her investigation in private, in the manner she considers appropriate (s 7(2)).
- She can require a department or a public body to furnish information and documents relevant to the investigation, and can summon witnesses. For these purposes, the Ombudsman has the same powers as the Courts (s 8).

---

[6]   But not the Law Officers' Department, the Offices of the Leader of the House of Commons or the Privy Council. The Parliamentary Commissioner Act 1994 extended the Ombudsman's role to investigating the administration of tribunals.

[7]   Parliamentary and Health Service Commissioners Act 1987 s 1, amending s 4 of the 1967 Act. On higher education, see p 495 on the Office of the Independent Adjudicator.

- Public interest immunity (see p 30) does not apply to Ombudsman investigations (s 8(3)), but Cabinet proceedings cannot be disclosed to her (s 8(4)).
- Obstruction of an investigation will be treated like a contempt of court (s 9).

(7) **What** *does the Ombudsman look for?*

The Ombudsman reports on whether 'injustice has been caused to the person aggrieved in consequence of maladministration' (s 10(3)). 'Mal-' just means 'bad'. That is an extremely broad, undefined remit.

(8) **What outcome** *does the Ombudsman give?*
- If she decides not to conduct an investigation, she must send a statement of her reasons to the referring MP (s 10(1)).
- A report of the results of an investigation must be sent to the complainant, to the MP, and to the investigated department/body (s 10(2)).
- After conducting an investigation, if it appears to the Ombudsman that the Government is not going to remedy an injustice caused by maladministration, she may lay a special report before each House of Parliament (s 10(3)), as she did in the Debt of Honour case.

So the Ombudsman is different from courts in her process, and in the substance of her inquiry. Her process is investigative rather adjudicative. And she looks for bad administration, not unlawful administration. Those essentials apply to all ombudsmen. But before delving further into those essentials, we need to see why the Parliamentary Ombudsman is *parliamentary*, and how the Local Government Ombudsmen are different.

13.3.2 The Parliamentary Ombudsman and Parliament

The most important feature of the Ombudsman's relationship with Parliament is her ability to lay reports before each House, and her link with the Public Administration Select Committee. These features defuse the potential for crisis when a public body wants to reject a recommendation of the Ombudsman, making the issue a matter for Parliament, and giving the Ombudsman a special technique for bringing it to the attention of Parliament (see section 13.7.2).

The more controversial feature of the Ombudsman's parliamentary role has been the MP filter. Its rationale was to preserve the role of MPs (and in fact, to enhance it by giving them an investigative facility to invoke when they receive a complaint). But it has faced widespread criticism outside Parliament, and a survey by the Parliamentary Ombudsman in 2004 found that of the 207 MPs who replied, 66% thought the MP filter should be removed.[8] After a review in 2000, the Government actually accepted the view that the filter should be removed. But this reform is unlikely to find its way into the Government's crowded legislative timetable anytime soon.

---

[8] http://www.ombudsman.org.uk/improving_services/special_reports/pca/test_of_time/part_2.html.

In practice, the MP filter is a minor issue. Since the 1970s, the Ombudsman has been forwarding direct complaints to the constituency MP of the person complaining, rather than rejecting them.[9] Today, you can find your MP and e-mail him or her directly from the Ombudsman's website. If your MP does not want to ask the Ombudsman to investigate, you can find another MP. Upheld by the courts,[10] and not likely to be removed soon by legislation, the MP filter has become a technicality with some symbolic value in asserting the responsibility of MPs for involvement in complaints against government. It is potentially a nuisance, but not a serious obstruction to justice.

Timing

The Ombudsman's process was designed to provide informal and easy redress for grievances, but the investigations can take a long time. The Debt of Honour investigation took two years; the investigation did not even start for 18 months after the complaint was made, as the Ombudsman waited for the related ABCIFER[11] litigation to end. That was extraordinary; the Ombudsman apologized for the delay, but of course much of it was not caused by her office. The information that the Ombudsman requests from government departments is likely to take months to emerge, especially when the issues are complex, several departments or agencies are involved, the files are massive, and the civil servants are both busy with other crises, and anxious to put the best face they can on the administration. In 2007–8, 87% of Parliamentary Ombudsman reports were completed within 12 months.[12]

13.4 Local Government Ombudsmen

The Local Government Act 1974 provided for Commissioners for Local Administration ('Local Government Ombudsmen') to investigate complaints of maladministration by local government. The difference between local and central government makes for some important differences from the role of the Parliamentary Ombudsman:

- People can **complain directly** to the Local Government Ombudsmen. There was initially a filter through councillors, like the Parliamentary Ombudsman's MP filter, but it was removed in 1988, and investigations jumped by 44% in one year.[13]

---

9   See C Harlow, 'Ombudsmen in Search of a Role' (1978) 41 MLR 446, 451.

10   The court will not make any order inviting or requiring an MP to submit a complaint, or inviting or requiring the Ombudsman to investigate: R (Murray) v PCA [2002] EWCA Civ 1472.

11   R (Association of British Civilian Internees—Far Eastern Region) v Defence Secretary [2003] EWCA Civ 473.

12   http://www.ombudsman.org.uk/improving_services/annual_reports/aro8/fig_17.html.

13   The 1974 Act required a complaint to be 'made through a member of the authority concerned' (s 26(2)); the Local Government Ombudsman could dispense with that requirement 'if he thinks

- Unlike central government departments and agencies, the local authority **must be given an opportunity to consider the complaint** before the Ombudsman can investigate (s 26(5)).

- The local authority investigated **must respond** to an adverse report. Failing to do so can result in a further Local Government Ombudsman report, and continued inaction can result in the local authority being required to publish the Ombudsman's recommendations in local newspapers (with their reasons for non-compliance, if they wish).[14]

- The Local Government Act 1974 s 31(3) gave local authorities an **express power to pay compensation** to a person suffering injustice in consequence of maladministration.

These differences are explained by the difference between the role of Parliament, and the more limited role of local democracy. First of all, local councillors do not have the special constitutional role that MPs have in holding the government to account. Secondly, whereas the Parliamentary Ombudsman reports to Parliament, it was felt necessary to give some independent clout to Local Government Ombudsman reports by requiring the local authority to reply. The Local Government Ombudsmen actually conform more closely to the Scandinavian model of ombudsmen, because their role is not complicated by the special place of Parliament in the British constitution. But by the same token, the Local Government Ombudsmen lack the support that the Parliamentary Ombudsman gets from the Public Administration Select Committee. And the Local Government Ombudsmen are subject to a special limitation that the Parliamentary Ombudsman does not face: they cannot investigate matters that concern most or all of the inhabitants of an area.[15] That prevents them from investigating any general complaint about local council spending (a role that is performed by the Audit Commission).

There are three Local Government Ombudsmen (based in London, Coventry, and York), and they are partly integrated with the Parliamentary Ombudsman; together they make up the Commission for Local Administration in England (CLAE). The Local Government Ombudsmen have express power to issue advice and guidance; the Government is proposing a similar provision for the Parliamentary Ombudsman.

The range of subject matter for Local Government Ombudsmen is vast; it includes education (including the contentious business of school choice and provision for special educational needs), social services, housing, council tax, and planning. They handle more than five times as many complaints in a year as the Parliamentary Ombudsman.

---

fit' (s 26(3)). Direct access was provided in the Local Government Act 1988, s 29. See The Local Ombudsman Annual Report, 1988–9 (9).

[14] Local Government Act 1974 s 31, as amended by Local Government and Housing Act 1989 s 26.

[15] Local Government Act 1974 s 26(7).

Like the Parliamentary Ombudsman, they can ordinarily take on an investigation only if the complaint is made within 12 months of the matter coming to the attention of the complainant. But they can give themselves a wide latitude where there are special considerations: in the Balchin investigation (see p 490), the Local Government Ombudsman considered a complaint made 12 years after the events that were investigated.

The Standards Board for England

The Local Government Act 2000 set up a 'Standards Board' to oversee local authorities' codes of conduct for council members. The Board investigates complaints of breaches of those codes. Investigators can refer a matter to an Adjudication Panel, which can impose sanctions (up to a five-year disqualification from office). There is no requirement that the complainant must have suffered injustice, because the Standards Board does not provide or recommend a remedy for complainants.

The Standards Boards play a role in local democracy that is similar to the role of the Parliamentary Commissioner for Standards in Parliament. But the executive and legislative roles of local councils are integrated, whereas Members of Parliament have a historical independence from government. The work of the Standards Boards and the Local Government Ombudsmen can overlap, and they have reached a memorandum of understanding providing for cooperation (with the consent of a complainant) when they both receive the same complaint, or when one receives a complaint that the other could also investigate. So the Local Government Ombudsmen and the Standards Boards can cooperate, whereas the work of the Parliamentary Ombudsman and the Parliamentary Commissioner for Standards never overlaps.

An example: neighbourhood nuisance[16]

Mr Akbar lived in a council flat with his wife and children. He complained about racial harassment by their neighbours over a five-year period.

The Local Government Ombudsman found the Council's response to Mr Akbar's harassment complaint to be 'ineffectual, confused and entirely inadequate'. The council agreed to pay £1,000 for failing to remedy damage and disrepair at Mr Akbar's former home, and £3,500 for failing to investigate and to act properly in response to the racial harassment complaint, and committed itself to improve its procedures for dealing with harassment complaints.

The Local Government Ombudsman published a special report on this issue ('Neighbourhood Nuisances and Anti-Social Behaviour'), in an effort to provide advice and guidance to local authorities in order to minimize future maladministration.[17] The outcome shows the remedial advantages of the ombudsmen over the courts—not only did Mr Akbar receive some financial redress for his past distress

---

[16]   Housing Digest 2004–5, http://www.lgo.org-uk/publications/digest-of-cases.

[17]   http://www.lgo.org.uk/publications/special-reports.

caused by maladministration on the council's behalf, but the council also planned to improve its procedures and the Local Government Ombudsman published a special report advocating a better response to harassment complaints by local authorities in the future.

13.5 Bad administration and unlawfulness, ombudsmen and courts

13.5.1 What is maladministration?

Here is how the Parliamentary Ombudsman explains maladministration in her press releases:

> Maladministration covers a range of shortcomings. These include: failure to follow rules and procedures; knowingly giving advice which is misleading or inaccurate; faulty procedures; ignoring valid advice or overruling considerations which would produce an uncomfortable result for the overruler; cavalier disregard of guidance which is intended to be followed in the interest of equitable treatment of those who use a service. This list is not exhaustive. [18]

That open-ended list is very different from the grounds of judicial review that courts have developed, but the two overlap. There are many ways in which public bodies may engage in bad administration, and the legislation does not lay down the grounds on which the ombudsman may make an adverse report. The Local Government Ombudsmen's guide for advisers says that the question is, 'has the council done something wrong?'[19]

Judicial attempts to tell the ombudsmen what counts as maladministration have not been helpful. The first attempt was in R v Local Commissioner for Administration, ex p Eastleigh Borough Council [1988] QB 855, in which Lord Donaldson MR suggested (but did not define) a narrow scope for maladministration: 'Administration and maladministration have nothing to do with the nature, quality or reasonableness of the decision itself...' (863). But Parker LJ recognized that the terms of the Local Government Ombudsman legislation 'do not preclude the ombudsman from questioning the merits of all discretionary policy decisions, but only those taken without maladministration' (868).

Perhaps the most important judicial decision on maladministration established that maladministration is not to be approached using standards of lawfulness developed in judicial review. When Liverpool City Council gave planning permission for Liverpool Football Club to build a new stand at Anfield, the Local Government Ombudsman made an adverse report after investigating complaints that Council members should

---

[18] www.ombudsman.org.uk/news/press_releases/pr06–04.html.

[19] www.lgo.org.uk/guide-for-advisor/maladministration-service-failure/.

have revealed that they were season ticket holders or regularly attended matches. The Council sought judicial review of that report, partly on the ground that instead of applying the standard of disclosure of interests in the Councillors' Code of Conduct, the Ombudsman ought to have used the less stringent test for bias developed in judicial review. The Court of Appeal held that although there is a substantial overlap between maladministration and unlawfulness, there is no reason why the considerations determining maladministration should be the same as those determining unlawfulness. In investigating complaints of maladministration, the Ombudsman need not be 'constrained by the legal principles which would be applicable if he were carrying out the different task (for which he has no mandate) of determining whether conduct has been unlawful' (R v LCA, ex p Liverpool City Council [2001] 1 All ER 462 (CA) [47] (Chadwick LJ)).

13.5.2 Maladministration, merits, and unlawfulness

There is no closed set of criteria of maladministration. Yet there are still three constraints on both the subject matter of investigations, and the content of reports:

(1) the problem has to be bad *administration*;

(2) the Ombudsmen may not investigate maladministration that could have been remedied in judicial review, unless it is unreasonable to expect the complainant to go to court (s 5(2) of the 1967 Act, s 26(6) of the 1974 Act; see p 479).

(3) The Ombudsmen are not authorized to 'question the merits of a decision taken without maladministration' (s 12(3) of the 1967 Act, s 34(3) of the 1974 Act).

The Act does not say that the Ombudsman cannot question the merits of a decision taken *with* maladministration. This statutory conundrum leaves it to the Ombudsman to resolve the tension between telling the administration what policies or programmes to pursue (which is not meant to be the Ombudsman's job), and telling the administration how to administer them (which is her job).

In the Debt of Honour investigation (see section 13.1), the Parliamentary Ombudsman complimented the Government on a scheme that 'was, after all, a highly commendable attempt to recognise "a debt of honour" ', but she could not resist saying what she thought of the merits of the bloodlink criterion for payments:

> ‘ In the circumstances, it is not for me to address the aspect of the complaints I have received which relates to the fairness of the specific criterion. I will go no further than to say that it is perhaps surprising that this particular criterion was chosen as being the means to repay 'a debt of honour' to those interned as British civilians by the Japanese. ’ [20]

In straying into the merits, the Ombudsman still showed restraint: she did not recommend a change in the criterion (even though she recommended a review of the

---

[20]   'A debt of honour' (above n 2) [229], [163].

'operation of the scheme'). The decision to adopt the criterion was taken with maladministration, but the Ombudsman resisted the temptation to base any recommendation on the merits of the bloodlink criterion.

● *Pop Quiz* ●

Since it is impossible to investigate maladministration without criticizing government policy, does the work of the Parliamentary Ombudsman clash with the political responsibility of the House of Commons?

What is the relation between maladministration and unlawful administration? Consider the litigation in the Debt of Honour case. Before they complained to the Ombudsman, the internees had sought judicial review of the bloodlink criterion, in the ABCIFER case.[21] In a complex decision, the Administrative Court rejected the argument that British civilians in general who had been interned by the Japanese had a legitimate expectation (see section 8.4) of a payment. The Minister's initial announcement of the scheme had been too woolly to count as the 'clear and unequivocal representation' that would give rise to a legitimate expectation. The Ombudsman picked up where the Court left off, referring to that decision and saying, 'in my view, it is precisely that lack of clarity which represents such a significant departure from standards of good administration to the extent that it constitutes maladministration.'[22]

Finally, *after* the Ombudsman's report, in R (Elias) v Defence Secretary [2006] EWCA Civ 1293, the Court of Appeal held that the bloodlink criterion was a form of indirect race discrimination, and therefore unlawful under s 1(1)(b) of the Race Relations Act 1976. If a statute makes it unlawful to adopt a policy that indirectly discriminates, then you need a court rather than the Ombudsman: the Ombudsman cannot say that indirect racial discrimination is maladministration. But the pattern of litigation and investigation in the Debt of Honour case shows one way in which the ombudsman's remit is much more far-reaching than judicial review: bad administration is *not necessarily unlawful*. Since the early days of the ombudsmen, it has been clear that maladministration and unlawfulness are different, as the Court of Appeal pointed out in *Congreve v Home Office* [1976] QB 629:

> ❛ No criticism of a government department could be more devastating than that contained in the Parliamentary Commissioner's Report. It is no part of our duty in this court to condemn the conduct of the Home Office. If their various actions vis-à-vis the plaintiff after March 26 were lawful, they do not become unlawful because the Home Office conducted the whole matter both before and after that date with lamentable incompetence. If their actions were at any time unlawful, they cannot be made lawful merely because the Home Office had acted, if they had, with extreme administrative efficiency and the most laudable of motives in serving what they believed to be the true public interest. ❜ (Roskill LJ 654–5)

---

[21] R (Association of British Civilian Internees—Far Eastern Region) v Secretary of State for Defence [2003] EWCA Civ 473.

[22] 'A debt of honour' (above n 2) [155].

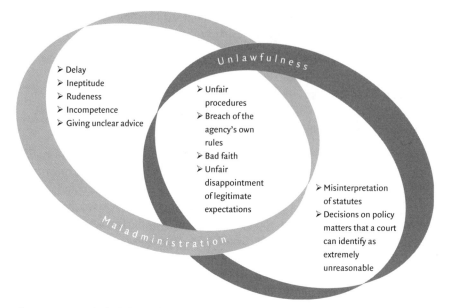

Figure 13.1 **Maladministration and unlawfulness: the overlap**

Note, however, that much bad administration *is* unlawful! Consider the open-ended list of forms of maladministration given to the House of Commons by Richard Crossman, the Minister proposing the Parliamentary Commissioner Bill in 1967: 'bias, neglect, inattention, delay, incompetence, ineptitude, perversity, turpitude and so on'.[23] Bias affecting a decision is unlawful. Perversity is unlawful. Turpitude implies bad faith, and that is unlawful. Of course, 'bias', 'perversity', and 'bad faith' have special senses for judicial purposes, and their content is determined by tests that the judges have developed to control their own interference with other public authorities, and can only be understood in particular contexts of administration. But bias and perversity and bad faith in those special judicial senses are unlawful and are also maladministration. Moreover, as has been pointed out by the High Court, 'Every procedural irregularity is likely to exhibit maladministration' (*R v Lambeth London Borough Council, ex p Crookes* (1997) 29 HLR 28 (QBD), 36 (Sir Louis Blom-Cooper)).

But then, much maladministration is *not* in itself unlawful—such as delay and ineptitude. Note also that much unlawful conduct is not maladministration: a *Wednesbury*-unreasonable policy decision may be unlawful,[24] but does not count as

23   Note the 'and so on', which reflects the open-ended nature of the Ombudsman's remit. Crossman's list of forms of maladministration is cited in *R v Local Commissioner for Administration for the North and East Area of England, ex p Bradford Metropolitan City Council* [1979] QB 287 (CA), 311 (Lord Denning MR), and *R v Parliamentary Commissioner for Administration, ex p Balchin* [1997] JPL 917, 925.

24   Remember that the courts will not apply the *Wednesbury* unreasonableness to all decisions, so that an extremely unreasonable policy decision may not be unlawful—see p 247.

maladministration for the Ombudsman's purposes. So the Ombudsman can address both more and less than judicial review addresses.

13.5.3 The ombudsmen or judicial review?

The ombudsmen legislation excludes investigation if the complainant 'has or had a remedy' in a court, unless 'in the particular circumstances it is not reasonable to expect him to resort or have resorted to it' (s 5(2)(b) of the 1967 Act, s 26 (6) of the 1974 Act). Because much maladministration is also unlawful, this exclusion of matters that could be remedied in court means that an ombudsman cannot investigate *all* complaints of maladministration. A complainant must take a complaint of unlawful administration to a court, unless he or she cannot reasonably be expected to do so. Does the reasonableness proviso mean that the ombudsman cannot investigate unless for some reason it would be especially difficult for the complainant to go to court? Or can the ombudsman investigate whenever an investigation would be a better way for the complainant to get his or her problem solved (so that it would be unreasonable to expect the complainant to engage in litigation that would be more expensive or slower or more complex)? Given the ombudsman's mandate to report on injustice caused by maladministration, there is every reason for her to take a generous approach to access. The nature of the ombudsman's office is at stake. Narrowly interpreted, s 5(2) of the 1967 Act can scarcely ever bar a complaint, because it is generally unreasonable to expect a person to engage in stressful and expensive litigation rather than take advantage of the free ombudsman process with its investigative access to government information. Widely interpreted, s 5(2) forbids an ombudsman investigation whenever the same conduct could have been brought into question on judicial review.

In the 'Debt of Honour' investigation, the Ombudsman postponed the decision whether to investigate, until the ABCIFER litigation was completed, and then asked herself whether Hayward (the complainant) had exercised a judicial remedy or could reasonably be expected to do so. She concluded that Hayward *had not* exercised an alternative remedy because he had not been party to the ABCIFER litigation [23]. But even if he had already sought judicial review, he would not have had an alternative remedy if he was complaining of maladministration that was not unlawful. And the Ombudsman made this crucial point in deciding that it would not be reasonable to expect Hayward to seek another remedy: if the complaint is that lawful actions amounted to maladministration, then the complainant *has no* remedy in judicial review. After the ABCIFER litigation, it was clear to the Ombudsman that the very conduct that she considered to be maladministration (the unclear announcement, and the lack of certainty that the bloodlink criterion was consistently applied) was not unlawful.

Note that the Ombudsman also held that the emotional and financial costs of the potentially distressing adversarial process of judicial review were relevant: 'court proceedings are adversarial in nature and . . . I did not consider it reasonable to expect [Professor Hayward] to have to resort to such a process when that could have been distressing and as he had firmly indicated that instead he wished me to investigate his complaint' [26–27].

The Ombudsman also pointed out that her fact-finding powers made an investigation very attractive to Hayward, who did not have the Ombudsman's access to the files and to the civil servants of the various departments involved in the payment scheme. The Ombudsman concluded that an investigation was 'more appropriate than expecting Professor Hayward to initiate legal proceedings'[28]. That approach is lenient toward complainants; it is more than Hayward needed (since it was evident after the ABCIFER case that he had no alternative remedy), and it turns the proviso in s 5(2)(b) into a way of allowing any complaint to go to the Ombudsman when investigation would be more appropriate than litigation. That generous interpretation of the proviso is a good interpretation: it helps the complainant in a way that cannot be detrimental to the administration (unless the ombudsman wastes a public body's time by investigating a bad complaint on behalf of a vexatious complainant who could never have afforded litigation). The generous approach to access to the Ombudsman improves access to justice.

Meanwhile, the courts have also had to consider when a complaint ought to be brought to an ombudsman, and when it ought to go to judicial review. Remember that courts have a discretion whether to give permission to a claimant to seek judicial review (see section 10.3.2), they can refuse permission on the ground that another remedy was available. The trend has been toward encouraging or even requiring complainants to use ombudsmen rather than courts where possible. In R v Lambeth, ex p Crookes [1997] 29 HLR 28, Sir Louis Blom-Cooper held that complaints of delays and procedural failings in paying housing benefit were 'incomparably better conducted through the informal procedure of the local government ombudsman than in the restrictively forensic forum of the courts', and concluded that 'any complaint of injustice resulting from maladministration, dressed up in the language of procedural irregularity for the purposes of judicial review, ought initially to be directed to the local government ombudsman' (39).

The law on this point is in flux, and we certainly cannot say in general that the High Court will exercise the discretion over relief in judicial review to send away anyone who could have taken a complaint of poor procedures to an ombudsman. But at least we can say that the ombudsmen should feel encouraged to take a relaxed approach to their capacity to start an investigation even when the complainant might have been entitled to some form of relief in judicial review.

And the relaxed approach of the Parliamentary Ombudsman in the Debt of Honour case was endorsed in the leading judicial decision on the point, R v LCA, ex p Liverpool City Council [2001] 1 All ER 462 (CA) (see p 476). Liverpool argued that the Ombudsman should not have started an investigation, because the complainants could have sought judicial review. The Court of Appeal held that it was a clear case in which the proviso in s 26(6) of the 1974 Act applied: even though the complainants could seek judicial review, it was not reasonable to expect them to, because they were unlikely to have the means to fund judicial review, and because the investigative role of the ombudsman could uncover what really went on (whereas they would not have been able to get the evidence they needed for judicial review). Henry LJ said, 'the commissioner's investigation and report can provide the just remedy when judicial review might fail to do so' (472). This result supports the Parliamentary Ombudsman's approach in the Debt of Honour investigation. It means that an investigation can be started whenever it would provide a better way for the complainant to seek justice.

So there is every reason for a relaxed approach to the scope of ombudsmen's investigations. In one respect, though, the courts and ombudsmen have taken a strict approach: an applicant who succeeds in judicial review cannot go on to an ombudsman afterward, and seek a recommendation of compensation for loss caused before the judicial review decision put an end to unlawful conduct.[25] That rule means that a person with a complaint should consider going to an ombudsman *first*. An ombudsman can recommend compensation for the effects of past maladministration, as well as a change for the future.

13.6 Injustice

The ombudsman cannot investigate just any maladministration. For an investigation to begin, the complainant must claim 'to have sustained injustice in consequence of maladministration' (s 5(1)(a)).

This restriction has the effect of a requirement of standing for complaints to the ombudsman, because the ombudsman will not investigate maladministration that could not have caused you injustice. This is a *more restrictive* requirement than the requirement of standing to seek judicial review (see section 11.2). Yet it can be met as long as you were affected by the maladministration in some way. In the 'Debt of Honour'[26] investigation, Hayward had suffered no material loss from the maladministration that the Ombudsman found; he had no right to a payment, and he would not necessarily have received a payment if the scheme had been administered well. But the Ombudsman decided that he and the others in his position 'suffered outrage at the way in which the scheme has been operated and distress at being told that they were not "British enough" to qualify for payment under the scheme. That outrage and distress constitutes an injustice' [207].

This broad understanding of 'injustice' will eliminate the statutory requirement, if ombudsmen find that the complainant has suffered injustice whenever he or she is angry about the maladministration. But it is an approach that the courts have been willing to accept in judicial review of the ombudsmen. And as in the case of maladministration, the judges have used Richard Crossman's remarks in the House of

---

[25] R v Commissioner for Local Administration, ex p H [1999] ELR 314 (CA).

[26] 'A debt of honour' (above n 2).

Commons as a starting point. Proposing the Parliamentary Commissioner Bill, he said that injustice was meant to include 'the sense of outrage aroused by unfair or incompetent administration, even where the complainant has suffered no actual loss'. So in the *Balchin* litigation (discussed in detail below, section 13.8.1), Sedley J said that 'injustice' can include a sense of outrage at maladministration (*R v Parliamentary Commissioner for Administration, ex p Balchin* [1997] JPL 917, 926 (*Balchin* (No 1)); see below). If some stranger were genuinely outraged at the treatment that Hayward or Balchin received, their sense of outrage would count as injustice on Crossman's formulation or Sedley J's formulation.

Crossman, the ombudsman, and the courts have actually departed from the requirement of injustice. Outrage is not injustice. Outrage is a person's *response* to a decision; injustice is an outrageous feature or an outrageous effect of the decision. The ombudsman should be willing to investigate even when the victim of maladministration has suffered no material loss, but the requirement of injustice in the act should be construed as requiring that the complainant was a victim of unjust treatment by the administration. So it has been held in one judicial review of a Local Government Ombudsman that some 'some prejudice' to the complainant had to be shown for a finding of injustice to be justified *R v Commissioner for Local Administration, ex p S* (1999) 1 LGLR 633. The outrage felt by someone like Hayward is their response to an injustice or perceived injustice; if there is an injustice, it is that officials have treated him contemptuously (even if it does not cause him loss).

Of course, the injustice requirement is not only a restriction on standing; it has an effect on the outcome of the investigation too, because the ombudsman's report will not recommend any action in the complainant's favour if the maladministration did not cause the complainant injustice.

13.7 What is an ombudsman's report actually worth to the complainant?

The outcome of an investigation for the complainant depends both on what the ombudsman is willing to recommend, and on whether the government will comply. The Debt of Honour investigation got Hayward an apology and, eventually, payment of £500 as a tangible indication of the Government's regret at the maladministration that the Ombudsman had identified. He did *not* immediately get the payment of £10,000 that the Government gave to some British internees. But then, he had no legal entitlement to the £10,000 (as the ABCIFER[27] litigation shows), because the Government refused to reconsider his case. In the end, though, intervention by the Public Administration Select Committee put pressure on the Government, and

---

[27]   R *(Association of British Civilian Internees—Far Eastern Region) v Secretary of State for Defence* [2003] EWCA Civ 473. The decision in R *(Elias) v Secretary of State for Defence* [2006] EWCA Civ 1293 that the bloodlink criterion was unlawful under the Race Relations Act 1976 did not give the persons affected a right to the £10,000 either, as the decision left it open for the government to impose new, non-discriminatory criteria.

the criteria were changed to include Hayward. Sometimes, the ombudsman gets a really valuable result for a complainant.

13.7.1 Recommended outcomes

One example will show how far-reaching an ombudsman's recommendation can be: in 2003, the Child Support Agency (CSA) delayed for two months in sending out an enquiry form to the father of Mrs R's children; the delay meant that the father's child support obligation was calculated under a new system of calculation that was less favourable to Mrs R. The CSA awarded her £50 for the delay; the Independent Case Examiner (a specific ombudsman—see section 13.9) upheld her complaint and the CSA awarded her £500, pointing out that they did not know how much she had lost through the delay, and could not legally require the father to provide them with the information to calculate the loss. Then the Parliamentary Ombudsman recommended that they ask the father for the information, even though they could not require it. The father provided the information, and the CSA agreed to compensate Mrs R for the loss, annually until the children are beyond the age for child support.[28]

The result fulfils the ombudsmen's policy, where maladministration has caused financial loss, of recommending payments that will put the complainant in the same position as if the maladministration had not occurred. This policy is extremely valuable to complainants: it gives the same outcome as tort law. And it does so where no tort has been committed, and where internal complaints and even investigation by a specific ombudsman for complaints about the CSA (the Independent Case Examiner) had not resulted in recovery.

So the outcome of an investigation can be very rewarding for a complainant (the report in the *Balchin* case[29] (see section 13.8.1) yielded recommendations of payments of £100,000 by both the local authority and the department). And in large programmes such as Child Support or Tax Credits, a recommendation can be valuable for thousands of people.

13.7.2 Compliance: a crisis?

Public authorities *almost* always carry out ombudsmen's recommendations. Over ten years, the Local Government Ombudsmen have found maladministration causing injustice 1,531 times, and the authority's response has been 'unsatisfactory' only 12 times.[30] The Parliamentary Ombudsman has had to use the s 10(3) power to report the Government to Parliament for non-compliance only six times.[31]

---

[28] See the account of Mrs R's case in the Parliamentary Ombudsman's Annual Report 2004–5, at p 23: www.ombudsman.org.uk/pdfs/ar_05.pdf.

[29] www.ombudsman.org.uk/improving_services/special_reports/pca/redress05/index.html.

[30] With 55 cases awaiting remedy. See Local Government Ombudsman Annual Report 2006–7, Appendix 3: www.lgo.org.uk/publications/annual-report/.

[31] See http://www.ombudsman.org.uk/about_us/our_history/timeline.html.

So the Government's rejection of part of the Debt of Honour report was exceptional. But it may have started a trend: in March 2006, the Parliamentary Ombudsman found maladministration in the role played by the Department of Work and Pensions in explaining private occupational pension schemes to the public. After massive shortfalls left some pensioners without the benefits they expected, the Ombudsman reported that the Department had not adequately explained the risks, and had published leaflets that were 'sometimes inaccurate, often incomplete, largely inconsistent and therefore potentially misleading'.[32] She recommended that the department consider restoring part of the pension funding to provide the benefits that had been expected in some cases (and that the department consider consolation payments to members). The costs would have been in the billions—perhaps £15 billion over 60 years.

For the first time ever, the Department both decided not to take the steps the Ombudsman had recommended, and comprehensively rejected her findings of maladministration.[33] The Department's view was that the leaflets had not been misleading, and that the scheme members would not have saved themselves billions by making different investments if the information provided by Government had been more complete. So the Department thought it had good reason to dispute the report. How should such a dispute be resolved?

The 1967 Act makes Parliament the appropriate forum. The Act says nothing about any duties of government agencies that are subject to an adverse report by the ombudsman; it authorizes the ombudsman to lay before each House of Parliament an adverse report if it appears to her that 'the injustice has not been, or will not be, remedied' (s 10(3)). The Ombudsman must lay before each House of Parliament an annual general report, and may lay other reports before Parliament as she sees fit (s 10(4)). Since 1967, the Public Administration Select Committee has become the House of Commons' way of scrutinizing her reports, and the Government's responses.

The Ombudsman laid her adverse report on the Pensions investigation before Parliament under s 10(3); in testimony to the Committee, she said that she was 'disappointed to see the Government picking over and reinterpreting my findings of maladministration and injustice, re-arranging the evidence, re-doing the analysis and acting as judge on its own behalf'.[34] The Committee felt the same: 'We are disappointed that the Government has chosen to act as judge on its own behalf by rejecting and qualifying a number of the Ombudsman's findings'.[35]

So the Pensions report created a crisis in relations between the Government and the Ombudsman. The power to report to both Houses of Parliament (and then to attend

---

[32] Parliamentary Ombudsman, 'Trusting in the pensions promise: government bodies and the security of final salary occupational pensions' 6th Report—Session 2005–2006, (HC984).

[33] www.dwp.gov.uk/publications/dwp/2006/pensions/response-ombudsman.pdf [59]–[64].

[34] http://www.publications.parliament.uk/pa/cm200809/cmselect/cmpubadm/219/219.pdf, Evl.

[35] http://www.publications.parliament.uk/pa/cm200809/cmselect/cmpubadm/219/219.pdf, 3.

the Public Administration Select Committee for discussion) is all that the ombudsman has, and according to Cecil Clothier, Parliamentary Ombudsman from 1979 to 1984, it is 'as good an enforcing power as any reasonable Ombudsman could wish for'.[36] Clothier thought that the power to make a mandatory order would be a 'despotic power', which could only be controlled by an appeals system which would rob the ombudsmen of their speed and finality.

Meanwhile, of course, the dispute was not just between the Ombudsman and the Government. There were also the people who had complained to the Ombudsman in the first place. In *Bradley v Work and Pensions Secretary* [2007] EWHC 242, dissatisfied pensioners brought the first judicial review challenge to a governmental decision to reject a Parliamentary Ombudsman's report. The Administrative Court judge held that the Minister was not legally bound to do what the Ombudsman recommended, but *was* legally bound to accept the Ombudsman's findings of maladministration, unless they were 'objectively shown to be flawed or irrational, or peripheral, or there is genuine fresh evidence to be considered' [58].

In the Court of Appeal, counsel appeared for the Parliamentary Ombudsman, and presented argument that 'the Secretary of State must proceed on the basis that the ombudsman's findings of injustice caused by maladministration are correct unless they are quashed in judicial review proceedings' (*Bradley v Work and Pensions Secretary* [2008] EWCA Civ 36 [135]). That was in accord with the Administrative Court's decision, and it would have meant a remarkable judicialization of the Ombudsman's office. But the Court of Appeal unanimously overruled that approach, holding that it is not necessarily unlawful for a public authority to reject the Ombudsman's conclusions even if those conclusions were rational. The judges held that it would be 'wholly foreign to the purpose' of the 1967 Act [41], to require a minister to seek judicial review to quash an ombudsman's report, instead of defending his or her rejection of its conclusions in Parliament:

> The minister whose department had, on investigation, been found by the commissioner to have been guilty of maladministration must expect to have to justify, in the parliamentary arena, why his department has not put in hand arrangements to provide a remedy in respect of the citizen's complaint. But there is, as it seems to me, no reason to think that it was any part of the Government's intentions, in introducing the legislation, to preclude a minister who was called to account before Parliament from explaining, as part of his justification for the decision to provide no remedy in respect of the complaint, his reasons for rejecting the commissioner's finding of maladministration. [41] (Sir John Chadwick)

Yet the Court of Appeal upheld the conclusion that the minister had acted unlawfully. '[T]he focus of the court must be on [the minister's] decision to reject' [71], and the Minister's decision to reject an ombudsman's report must be 'based on cogent

---

Cecil Clothier, 'The Value of an Ombudsman' [1986] PL 204, 209.

reasons' [72]. According to *Bradley*, the court should quash the minister's response as unlawful, 'if no reasonable Secretary of State could rationally disagree' with the ombudsman's findings [73]. The Court of Appeal considered the Minister's view to be irrational, and quashed his decision. That did not require the Minister to do as the Ombudsman recommended, but it required him to make a fresh decision on the basis that she was right that the leaflets were misleading.

Granted that a department must have cogent reasons for rejecting a finding of maladministration (and granted that the Secretary of State should accept the ombudsman's findings if no reasonable Secretary of State could rationally disagree), why is judicial review available? *Bradley* gives no explanation. It appears to have seemed obvious to the judges: the Minister had a discretionary power to act on the Ombudsman's report, and the Court was only applying the ordinary *Wednesbury* principles to control that discretionary power.

And it may seem that this residual role for the court must enhance the role of the Ombudsman, since *Bradley* only supports judicial review for an irrational response to an Ombudsman's report. But as we have learned (see p 228), the application of the so-called 'irrationality' standard in English law requires the judge to enter into the substance of a decision, in order to decide whether it was *so bad* that it amounts to an abuse of power. And that is what happened in *Bradley*. The Court of Appeal had to engage in a long and sophisticated analysis of the Government's leaflets about pensions [73]–[94], in order to come to the judgment that the leaflets were *so clearly misleading* that it was irrational for the Minister to reject the Ombudsman's finding that they were misleading.

The result of *Bradley* is that as far as the law is concerned, a department can reject a Parliamentary Ombudsman's report and face the music in Parliament. A department need not seek judicial review, if it disagrees either with a finding of maladministration or with a recommendation in a report. The Court of Appeal made the crucial point that the House of Commons is the right arena for consideration of a department's response to recommendations. Yet according to *Bradley*, the complainants can drag the matter out of the parliamentary arena into the judicial arena—and get a new inquiry, by judges, into the facts of the case. That inquiry itself may interfere with the parliamentary process, as the Public Administration Select Committee and the House of Commons will need to suspend consideration of a department's response, while legal proceedings are under way to determine whether the government's response was unlawful.

The missing element in the Court's reasoning in *Bradley* is an explanation of the rationale for judicial review. When the Home Secretary makes a *Wednesbury*-unreasonable decision to deport an asylum seeker (see p 229), the **core rationale** for judicial review (see p 65) applies. The rationale for judicial review goes without saying: it is necessary in the interests of justice for the court to impose the rule of law, to stop the deportation. No other suitable remedy is available against the abuse of power. But if a minister makes a *Wednesbury*-unreasonable decision that the ombudsman was wrong to find maladministration, there is an alternative process, established by statute. She can report to Parliament. And by the practice of the House of

Commons, the Public Administration Select Committee provides an arena in which the ombudsman's findings of fact and the department's response can be scrutinized. The interference with the process in *Bradley* would only be justified if the parliamentary process (so carefully explained by the Court of Appeal in *Bradley*) were inadequate for remedying an unreasonable refusal by a department to accept the findings of the ombudsman. And although it is easy to imagine the Public Administration Select Committee or the House of Commons going along with an unreasonable conclusion of a department after such a dispute, the judges are in no position to reach the conclusion that the process is inadequate. After *Bradley*, the courts have taken on responsibility for reviewing matters that can be reviewed in Parliament. Judicial review is supposed to be a last resort (see p 60), and it should not have been made available when there is another resort.

Meanwhile, in December 2007, before the *Bradley* case reached the Court of Appeal, the Government announced enhanced compensation for pensioners that amounted to compliance with the Ombudsman's main recommendation. The litigation may well have served as an instrument in the pensioners' political campaign for a spending decision in their favour. If judicial review is a last resort, though, there was no reason for the litigation to proceed.

Interventions

It should be obvious that something went wrong in the *Bradley* litigation, just from the fact that the Speaker of the House of Commons intervened in the claim for judicial review (on the question of whether the Court should take into account the Ombudsman's evidence to the Public Administration Select Committee), and the Parliamentary Ombudsman intervened in the appeal (to argue that the judge had misunderstood the content of her report, and that the Secretary of State had misrepresented her report in the litigation, and to respond to the 'collateral attack' that she saw the minister as making against her report [127]. It should all have been fought out in the House of Commons, and in the Public Administration Select Committee of the House. There is a good argument—if the matter ever reaches the House of Lords—that *Bradley* should be overruled, and that the Administrative Court ought to refuse permission to seek judicial review of a governmental response to a report of the Parliamentary Ombudsman.

13.8 Judicial review of ombudsmen

Ombudsmen have legal powers to compel testimony and production of documents, and it would be unlawful for them to try to use those powers for some purpose other than the purpose for which Parliament enacted the powers. A person could lawfully refuse to cooperate with an unlawful demand, or could seek judicial review of a direction from the Ombudsman to give evidence (s 8 of the 1967 Act). To resist disclosure successfully, a claimant would have to show bad faith on the part of the ombudsman, or a very strong case that an ombudsman was asking for information that could not possibly help in a legitimate investigation. The High Court will uphold a subpoena (a witness summons) by an ombudsman as long as it is 'bona fide required for the purpose of the investigation', and the Ombudsman is willing and able to keep confidential information secure.[37]

Those powers to compel evidence are the ombudsmen's only legal powers. In writing a report they do not exercise legal power. They do not change the legal position of the complainant or the public body. Ombudsmen are not part of the administration of government, either. They are independent investigators of the administration. There ought to be at least one appeal or other form of review from any judicial decision and from many administrative decisions, but an ombudsman is an *investigator* rather than administrator or an adjudicator. So you might think that the courts would have no role in controlling the ombudsmen's investigations or reports. But in fact, people who are disappointed by ombudsmen's decisions have persuaded the courts to assume the role of supervising the work of ombudsmen.

13.8.1 Judicial review of the Parliamentary Ombudsman

Sedley J extended the frontiers of judicial review in *R v Parliamentary Commissioner for Administration, ex p Balchin* [1997] JPL 917, the first judgment to overturn a report of the Parliamentary Ombudsman.[38] The irony of the *Balchin* decision is that it takes the impressive tools that judges developed to oppose unlawful administration, and uses them to control an independent officer who *investigates* complaints of bad administration. It seems that the Ombudsman is now subject to all the forms of judicial review that courts exercise in respect of administrative bodies. The problem with that approach is the **principle of relativity** (see p 10): the reasons for judicial interference with other public authorities depend on the functions of the authorities subject to review, and on the capacity of courts to ensure that those functions are better fulfilled than they would be without judicial review. The rule of law does not require the same judicial scrutiny of the Ombudsman's reports that it requires of, for example, decisions of a minister of the Crown to close a school, or to deport an asylum seeker.

Norfolk County Council decided to build a bypass a few metres from Maurice and Audrey Balchin's house, 'Swans Harbour'. The bypass was not even built, but before the plan was abandoned, Maurice had lost the equity in the house that he needed to secure his business debts. The county council had no legal obligation to help out the Balchins by buying their house, although it had a discretion to do so.[39] Norfolk decided not to help the Balchins.

---

[37] *In re a subpoena issued by LCA, The Times* 4 April 1996 (QBD).

[38] See also *R (Cavanagh) v Health Service Commissioner for England* [2005] EWCA Civ 1578 (Sedley, Latham and Wall LJJ), the first judgment to overturn a report of the Health Services Commissioner (a post held by the Parliamentary Ombudsman). The case marked a significant increment in judicialization of ombudsmen, as the judges held that it is their job to decide what issues are raised by the complaint.

[39] Highways Act 1980 s 246(2A), as amended by the Planning and Compensation Act 1991.

The Department of Transport (DoT) entered the picture because Norfolk's road order had to be confirmed by the Secretary of State. The decision letter accompanying the confirmation from the DoT mentioned an inspector's hopes that Norfolk would look sympathetically on the Balchins' plight. But the letter also pointed out that it was a matter for Norfolk. In response, the Chief Executive of Norfolk wrote to a minister in the DoT to say that Norfolk knew that it had a legal duty to *consider* buying the blighted property, but that it had no legal duty to buy property out of sympathy, and added, 'I do not wish to sound harsh or bureaucratic but local government is frequently told to act within its powers and to curtail unnecessary expenditure...' (924). Norfolk's approach *was* harsh and bureaucratic, and Sedley J made it clear that in his view, the Council could have been held on judicial review to have fettered its discretion unlawfully (929). But how could the Balchins complain to the Parliamentary Ombudsman that the DoT engaged in maladministration that caused them injustice? Their case was that the DoT, if it had engaged in good administration, would not have confirmed the road order without first seeking assurances from Norfolk that the Balchins would be adequately compensated. The Ombudsman found no maladministration; the Secretary of State could not have made the confirmation order conditional on a sympathetic approach to the Balchins, and whatever the DoT said to Norfolk, 'the council... would have refused such a purchase' (923).

Sedley J held that the Ombudsman's report unlawfully omitted to evaluate a relevant consideration, 'the role and impact of Norfolk County Council's stance' (929). The conclusion seems to be that if the Ombudsman had considered Norfolk's hostility, he might have found that the Balchins suffered injustice in consequence of the DoT's maladministration in omitting to point out to Norfolk a power that Norfolk knew it had, and was determined not to use. The effect of the decision was not only to apply to the Ombudsman the same techniques that were developed to prevent arbitrary government; it was also to extend those techniques, by treating it as the task of the judge to decide what facts of a case are relevant to another public authority's decision. That was a departure from the law of judicial review, which only authorizes courts to control another public authority's decision making by quashing *unreasonable* decisions as to the relevance of facts (see p 272).

After the decision in *Balchin (No 1)*, a new Ombudsman reconsidered the complaint in the light of Sedley J's judgment, and like his predecessor he found that the DoT had not engaged in maladministration. In a second application for judicial review, Dyson J quashed the Ombudsman's report on the ground that the Ombudsman had failed to give reasons for finding that the DoT did not overlook Norfolk's power. The case is authority for the proposition that ombudsmen must give reasons that 'address the principal important controversial issues, but not every single point raised by the parties...' (R v PCA, ex p Balchin (No 2) (2000) 79 P&CR 157, 167). A third Ombudsman's report found maladministration in respect of part but not all of the complaint, and the Ombudsman concluded that the injustice had found sufficient redress in an apology from the DoT. In a third application for judicial review, the judge once more overruled the Ombudsman on the ground of insufficient reasons (R v PCA, ex p Balchin (No 3) [2002] EWHC 1876). The reasons challenges in *Balchin*

(No 2) and (No 3) reflect the intrusive control that Sedley J had imposed in *Balchin* (No 1); once it is the court's job to decide the relevance of the facts of the case, the Ombudsman acquires a legal duty to give reasons that enable the court to do that job. In a *fourth* investigation, the Ombudsman broke new ground by collaborating on a joint report with the Local Government Ombudsman. Finally in October 2005, 13 years after the DoT had written to the County Council to express the hope that it would consider the Balchins' plight 'with the utmost sympathy not to mention urgency', the Ombudsmen reported maladministration by both the Council and the DoT, and recommended a payment of £100,000 from each level of government. The DoT's supposed maladministration was a failure 'to ensure that they did not knowingly allow Councils to mislead themselves as to the intention of any legislation (for which the DoT was responsible) to which the Council were obliged to have regard, and to step in to offer a correct interpretation of the current legislative position if the Council clearly misrepresented that'.[40] But the Council had had regard to the legislation. It is hard to see any ground for the Ombudsman's finding of maladministration, except a desire to bring a halt to the extravagant sequence of judicial review decisions. The saga is outlined in Figure 13.2.

Is this level of control of the Ombudsman's work justified? It gives the judge the job of deciding the relevance of facts to the Ombudsman's task of identifying maladministration. Public administration has nothing to gain from the general principle that judges, rather than the Ombudsman, should decide the considerations on which the Ombudsman should base her reports. The doctrine of relevance is a crucial part of the law's opposition to arbitrary government, and the **core rationale** (see p 65) for judicial review supports the judges' role in deciding what considerations are relevant to the exercise of a discretionary power, when doing so can prevent arbitrary government. The following chain of reasoning seems very attractive:

(1) the ombudsman is a public official with a discretionary power;

(2) the discretionary powers of public officials must be supervised by judges in the interests of the rule of law; and therefore

(3) the reports of an ombudsman should be controlled by judges to impose the rule of law.

But the doctrine of relevance in a case like *Padfield v Minister of Agriculture* [1968] AC 997 is based on the danger that the holder of a discretionary governmental power might use it arbitrarily for his or her improper private or political purposes. Like judges, and unlike government ministers, the Ombudsman is independent. And her task is not to govern; it is to decide whether to make a public criticism of the government. As a result, Sedley J's enhanced doctrine of judicial control over relevance is not necessary to impose the rule of law on government. It may incidentally improve

---

[40] Forward to 'Redress in the Round: remedying maladministration in central and local government', 11 October 2005, 5th Report, Session 2005–2006 (HC 475 [2005–2006]), available at www. ombudsman.org.uk/improving_services/special_reports/pca/redress05/redress_foreword. html.

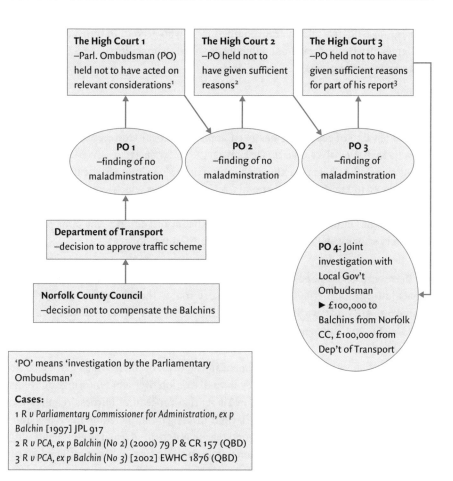

Figure 13.2 **The *Balchin* saga: oversight overkill**

the ombudsman process, whenever judges happen to make better decisions than she does as to what is relevant to her work. But it would only be justified as a standard of judicial review, if judges were generally better at an ombudsman's work than ombudsmen are.

Judicial decisions quashing ombudsmen's reports are still not likely to be common, though: the three in the *Balchin* saga have been the only ones in the Parliamentary Ombudsman's 41 years. Even on the intrusive relevance test, it will ordinarily be difficult to persuade a court to second-guess the ombudsman.[41] Judicial review should not even happen, if it cannot improve the work of the ombudsmen. The only argument in favour of any form of judicial review of the ombudsmen is the prospect that it may prevent feeble ombudsmen from unreasonably withholding a

----

[41]   And the court will not supervise correspondence by the Parliament Ombudsman with potential complainants: *R (Murray) v PCA* [2002] EWCA Civ 1472. *Balchin* does not cite *Re Fletcher's Application* [1970] 2 All ER 527 (CA), in which the Court of Appeal held that there is no judicial jurisdiction to order the Parliamentary Commissioner to investigate a complaint.

valuable investigative facility from complainants who need it. In the *Balchin* case, the Parliamentary Ombudsman undoubtedly provided that facility to the Balchins at the first step in the long saga.

13.8.2 Judicial review of the Local Government Ombudsmen

The *Balchin* line of reasoning has been applied to Local Government Ombudsmen as well. In R *v Local Government Ombudsman, ex p Turpin* [2001] EWHC Admin 503, Mr. Justice Collins held that 'there is nothing in the legislation to exclude the court's usual power to consider whether a discretion, however widely conferred, has been exercised in accordance with law'. But he also emphasized that it is not the court's role to tell the Ombudsman what counts as maladministration.[42] The same point was made very strongly in R *(Doy) v LCA* [2001] EWHC Admin 361:

> ' In essence, the Ombudsman and not the court is the arbiter of what constitutes maladministration. The court's supervisory role is there to ensure that he has acted properly and lawfully. However much the court may disagree with the ultimate conclusion, it must not usurp the Ombudsman's statutory function. '   [16]

Perhaps one single general improvement in the work of ombudsmen can be attributed to judicial review: although they have discretion over what information to disclose to a complainant, it was held in *Turpin* that procedural fairness requires that they disclose information gathered in their investigation, including interview notes with officials, unless there is some good reason not to do so (such as confidentiality). They cannot withhold any information purely on the basis that it was gathered for the purpose of their investigation.

13.8.3 Judicial review on behalf of a public authority

Can a public authority use judicial review to challenge a report of the *Parliamentary Ombudsman*? It follows directly from the reasoning in *Balchin* that a report adversely criticizing a department must be quashed on judicial review if the judges disagree with the ombudsman as to what counts as maladministration, or if the judges take a different view from the ombudsman on the relevance of one of the facts of the case. But allowing judicial review on those grounds at the request of a department would distort the process, and no government agency has ever sought judicial review of a report. Even if an ombudsman made a *Wednesbury*-unreasonable report, the appropriate process is that used by the government in the Debt of Honour case and in the crisis over the Pensions report: the department in question should simply reply to the report. Then the Ombudsman can make a special report to Parliament, and the crisis becomes Parliamentary business (conducted in the first instance through the Public Administration Select Committee). There is no role for the court to play; the

---

[42]   Cf also R *v Commissioner for Local Administration, ex p S* (1999) 1 LGLR 633.

Ombudsman is Parliamentary not just in name (and not just in having an 'MP filter'), but in her capacity both to bring out the facts by her investigation, and to put pressure on the department by reporting her assessment of the facts to Parliament. So it seems that if a public body ever sought judicial review of a report of the Parliamentary Ombudsman, *Balchin* ought to be distinguished, and permission for judicial review ought to be refused. The only justification for judicial interference on behalf of a complainant such as Maurice Balchin is to ensure that the ombudsman does not improperly fail to provide the investigative function that Parliament instituted; that rationale does not require any judicial interference at all on behalf of a public body.

By contrast with the Parliamentary Ombudsman, Local Government Ombudsmen have several times been subjected to judicial review on the application of a public authority. In R *v Local Commissioner for Administration, ex p Eastleigh* (1987) 86 LGR 145, Nolan J found that there were defects in the Ombudsman's report, but viewed it as pointless to give a declaration against a report that the local authority simply had to consider, and publicize, and respond to. In the Court of Appeal (R *v Local Commissioner for Administration, ex p Eastleigh* [1988] QB 855) Lord Donaldson rejected that approach: 'The Parliamentary intention was that reports by ombudsmen should be loyally accepted by the local authorities concerned.... in the absence of a successful application for judicial review and the giving of relief by the court, local authorities should not dispute an ombudsman's report and should carry out their statutory duties in relation to it' (867). But there is no support for the alleged intention of Parliament. Lord Donaldson found it in local authorities' statutory duties to publicize ombudsman's reports, and to respond. But a local authority has no statutory duty *to implement* a Local Ombudsman's report, or even to act on the basis of the findings in a report; the crucial provision in the 1974 Act is that 'it shall be the duty of that authority to consider the report' (s 31(2)). Lord Donaldson's approach reflects an unwillingness to accept the ombudsman principle: that is, the principle that an independent complaints investigator can improve administration without making a legally binding report.

In *Bradley v Work and Pensions Secretary* [2008] EWCA Civ 36, the Court of Appeal backed up Lord Donaldson's approach, but qualified it to make only the finding of maladministration binding. Sir John Chadwick said,

> It is clear to me that Lord Donaldson of Lymington MR, in saying that local authorities should "loyally accept" an LGO's report, only intended to refer to findings that maladministration and injustice have occurred and not to recommendations. The 1974 Act, like the 1967 Act, gives the ombudsman no power to make mandatory orders. It would be extraordinary if an LGO could do so by the back door in the form of recommendations. Suppose, for example, that the LGO made a recommendation which the local authority declined to carry out for the reason that it was too expensive. It is difficult to see on what established ground for judicial review the court could intervene to quash the recommendation: yet the allocation of budgets and the establishment of spending priorities are classic issues for the elected body's discretion. [50]

After *Bradley*, a local authority can lawfully decide not to act on a recommendation in an ombudsman's report, without seeking judicial review. But a report has the effect of a mandatory order (which the local authority can challenge in judicial review) to act on the basis of the ombudsman's finding of maladministration. That judicialization of the ombudsman process was misguided in *Eastleigh*, and the discussion in *Bradley* was *obiter*, as the Court of Appeal in *Bradley* took pains to explain that the Parliamentary Ombudsman differs from the Local Government Ombudsmen because the role of Parliament has no parallel in the local government context.

Ironically, because there is no Parliamentary process for resolving disputes between local authorities and Local Government Ombudsmen, there is good ground for applying to local government the rule that *Bradley* applies to central government: that is, a decision by a local authority to reject an ombudsman's report is an exercise of discretionary power that ought to be open to challenge by a dissatisfied complainant on the *Wednesbury* grounds. But there is no basis for judicializing the process by requiring a local authority to go to court to challenge a finding of maladministration. There is good ground to argue that the 1974 Act imposes precisely the obligations on local authorities that it states: i.e., to consider an ombudsman's report, and to publicize the report and its response. And then permission for judicial review should be refused if any public authority seeks to challenge the report of an ombudsman—local or parliamentary—in court. But after *Eastleigh* and *Bradley*, that argument could only be pursued in the House of Lords.

Learning from Europe?

The decisions of the European Ombudsman (see section 13.10) whether to investigate a complaint (and, it seems, his reports) simply cannot be challenged in court. In Case T 103/99 *Associazione delle Cantine Sociali Venete v Ombudsman and Parliament* [2000], ECR II-4165), the applicant argued that 'an action for failure to act against the Ombudsman would be admissible in order not to deprive his extra-judicial function of all effect' [35]. The Court held, curtly, that the application was inadmissible because 'the Ombudsman is not a Community institution within the meaning of Article 175 [now Art 232] of the Treaty' [46]. An ombudsman's report does not 'produce legal effects' and is not binding on the European Parliament [50]. It seems unlikely that we will adopt this sensible separation between courts and ombudsmen, because of the English judges' deeply ingrained idea that they are responsible for supervising every other public authority except Parliament.

13.9 Specific ombudsmen

Ombudsmen schemes have become increasingly popular techniques for dealing with complaints in specific subject areas: examples include the **Prisons and Probation Ombudsman**,[43] who reports to the Home Secretary, the **Adjudicator's**

---

[43]　http://www.ppo.gov.uk/.

Office,[44] which investigates complaints about HM Revenue and Customs, the **Independent Case Examiner**,[45] who investigates complaints about several government programmes including the Child Support Agency, and the **Independent Review Service**,[46] which responds to complaints about the discretionary social fund (a scheme created in 1988 to enable Jobcentres to give crisis grants and loans to the very poor). They have varying roles that differ from those of the Parliamentary and Local Government Ombudsmen because of their specializations. They sometimes review the merits of decisions, and sometimes have a conciliation or mediation function. Here we will look at one particularly interesting specific ombudsman scheme.

13.9.1 The Office of the Independent Adjudicator for Higher Education

For centuries, complaints against universities and colleges were within the jurisdiction of the institution's Visitor—a bishop or other dignitary who would delegate the hearing of a complaint to a judge or lawyer.[47] In 2004, Parliament abolished the jurisdiction of the Visitors over student complaints, and created the Office of the Independent Adjudicator (OIA), a compulsory ombudsman scheme for complaints against higher education institutions.[48]

In spite of the name, the OIA is not an adjudicator, but an ombudsman service. The Adjudicator does not hold a hearing, but writes a report on the basis of written submissions and her investigation. The recommendations in a report are not legally binding, but the institution is expected to go along with whatever is recommended, and is required to report on steps taken as a result of a report. The OIA deals with examinations, disciplinary decisions, decisions about a student's capacity to engage in studies, etc.—every kind of institutional decision affecting a particular student except admissions. In all these areas, the OIA is not supposed to second-guess academic judgment, but to assess an institution's processes and its adherence to those processes in a particular case. But it can make an adverse report based on a generalized sense that something has gone wrong and that something should be done about it.

In its first year, the OIA received 120 complaints, 86 of which were eligible, and found that at least part of the complaint was justified in 50% of cases. The emerging pattern is that the OIA is serious about deferring to a university on questions involving academic judgment (for example, it will not recommend a change in degree classification even where an examination process has gone wrong, but will only recommend reconsideration). But the OIA will recommend a remedy where the university has used

---

44 www.adjudicatorsoffice.gov.uk.

45 http://www.ind-case-exam.org.uk/.

46 http://www.irs-review.org.uk/.

47 At least, in institutions founded before 1992. The Visitor's jurisdiction was well insulated from judicial review; see p 313–14.

48 Higher Education Act 2004: www.oiahe.org.uk.

an unfair procedure, or has broken its own rules. The OIA will recommend small sums in compensation for technical failures of an institution to follow its procedures (e.g., the OIA has awarded £50 to a student who admitted plagiarism, on the ground that the university had not followed its disciplinary proceedings in the initial hand-ling of the allegation). And substantial sums will be recommended in compensation where studies have to be repeated; one report recommended £9,000 in compensation for each student in a course for which the university failed to arrange professional accreditation promptly; the sum included £2,000 for curriculum failings, £2,000 for 'distress and inconvenience', and £5,000 for loss of opportunity for earnings, caused by the late accreditation. Awards on the latter sort of ground in particular are poten-tially substantial.

The OIA is already having a significant impact on internal complaints. Higher education institutions have no general duty to get a decision maker from outside the institution to make discipline or academic exclusion decisions. But they need to do what they can within a collegiate community to give an impartial decision on issues that affect a student; including an appeal on disciplinary decisions to a decision-making body that has not been involved in earlier decisions, and that adheres strictly to procedural steps announced to students.

13.9.2 The OIA and the courts

The OIA will not investigate a complaint if the student has already gone to court. And the courts may be unwilling to allow litigation against a higher education insti-tution to proceed when the OIA offers a cheaper and simpler alternative.[49] But various forms of litigation could follow an investigation. The OIA is amenable to judicial review (R (Siborurema) v Office of the Independent Adjudicator [2007] EWCA Civ 1365). Rejecting the argument of the Adjudicator that judicial review would damage the scheme by mak-ing it more formal and legalistic, the Court of Appeal held that 'For it to become a law unto itself would not achieve the statutory intention' [50]. Even if that is right, there is as little room for judges to improve the operation of the scheme as there is for them to improve the operation of the Parliamentary Ombudsman, and it will be difficult for any claimant to persuade a court to hold that the OIA has acted unlawfully. The courts should not give permission for judicial review unless the claimant has a serious allegation of bad faith or discrimination. But if they follow the *Balchin* reasoning (see p 490), the judges will quash an OIA decision wherever it is based on an interpretation of the legislation that is different from the judges' interpretation.

Aside from seeking judicial review of the OIA decision, a student dissatisfied after an investigation could still sue the institution in contract, or apply for judicial review of an institution's own conduct. As with any ombudsman scheme, the Higher Education Act 2004 provides no legal remedy if an institution fails to carry out a

---

[49]   That applies both to applications for judicial review, for which permission to proceed might be refused on the ground that an alternative recourse has not been pursued, and to actions for tort or breach of contract (see *Anufrijeva v Southwark LBC* [2003] EWCA Civ 1406: an action can be stayed pending alternative forms of recourse, including the OIA).

recommendation of the OIA. But in an application for judicial review of the institution's conduct it might be very useful for a student to be able to point it out. An adverse recommendation of the OIA might be relevant to a claim in judicial review that the institution had abused its power or failed to provide fair procedures, and would be relevant in a claim in breach of contract insofar as it might indicate a breach of terms that are to be implied from the context of the relationship between the institution and the student.[50] But the remedy would be the ordinary remedy on judicial review or for breach of contract, rather than an order enforcing the OIA's recommendation.

How is an investigation by the OIA different from judicial review? Like the OIA, a court in judicial review will not second-guess the academic judgment of the institution,[51] and cannot order the institution to award a degree (R v Liverpool John Moores University, ex p Hayes [1998] ELR 261 (QBD)). Ordinary grounds of judicial review apply to universities and colleges, such as bias (R v Leeds Metropolitan University, ex p Manders [1988] ELR 502 (QBD)), and unfair procedures. But the courts have deferred to universities in applying them (even where the university did not have a Visitor), at least so long as the university has followed its own procedures:

> ‘Only the clearest and most obvious unfairness or departure from the university's own regulations would justify an attempt by judicial review to impugn an academic decision of this character [to require a student to retake exams she had failed]....If, as here, the academic registrar and the independent member of academic council, having considered the student's detailed written appeal and listened to her for over an hour, conclude that there is frankly nothing in her grievance, this court will not readily hold such a decision to be erroneous in point of law. ’[52]

13.10 The European Ombudsman[53]

The European Ombudsman (EO) was introduced by the Maastricht Treaty 1992 (TEU). The office was designed to promote the project of closer European integration, by improving direct links between the European institutions and the citizens.

The EO interacts with national ombudsmen, and provides an interesting comparison with the British ombudsmen. Like them, the EO has the task of promoting good standards of administration in general by investigating particular complaints of maladministration. Maladministration is as open-ended in the EU as in Britain,

---

[50] On claims in contract, see Clark v University of Lincolnshire and Humberside [2000] ELR 345 (CA), holding that an action may proceed even if a remedy could have been sought in judicial review.

[51] Including on the question of whether examiners are suitably qualified: R v Cranfield University, ex p Bashir [1999] ELR 317 (CA).

[52] R v University of Portsmouth, ex p Lakareber [1999] ELR 135, (CA), 140 (Simon Brown LJ).

[53] http://www.euro-ombudsman.eu.int/home/en/default.htm.

and overlaps with unlawfulness. In Europe as in the U.K., recommendations of the European Ombudsman are not legally binding. And like the Parliamentary Ombudsman, the European Ombudsman's weapon of last resort is a special report laid before the European Parliament.[54]

(1) **Who** is the European Ombudsman?

He is an independent official (Art 9) appointed by the European Parliament (Art 6(1)) (usually after having served as a national ombudsman) and removable by the European Court of Justice on request of the European Parliament (Art 8).

(2) **Whom** can the EO investigate?

- The EO investigates 'community institutions and bodies, with the exception of the Court of Justice and the Court of First Instance in their judicial role' (Art 2(1)).
- 'The European Ombudsman...cannot investigate complaints against national, regional or local authorities, even when the complaints are about Community law.'[55]

(3) **How** does a complaint get to the EO?

- The complainant can make a complaint either directly or through an MEP (Art 2(2)).
- The Ombudsman can conduct investigations on his own initiative, as well as following a complaint (Art 3(1)).

(4) **What** can the EO **not** investigate?

- If the complaint concerns an employment relationship between a Community body and a member of staff, the internal complaints procedure of the body must be exhausted by the complainant before he complains to the Ombudsman (Art 2(8)).
- The EO cannot investigate cases before the courts, or question the soundness of a court's ruling (Art 1(3)). Note that the similar restrictions are simply taken for granted in the UK legislation! They are spelled out in the EU statute because the Finnish and Swedish Ombudsmen have responsibility for investigating complaints about judicial decisions.

(5) **When** must a complaint be brought?

The complainant must refer his complaint within two years from the date when the facts on which the complaint is based came to his attention (Art 2(4)) (twice as long as the 12-month restriction in ordinary circumstances for the British ombudsmen).

....

[54]   The community law provisions relating to the EO were introduced by the Maastricht Treaty, and have since been incorporated into the European Ombudsman's statute. Decision 94/262 of the European Parliament on the Regulations and General Conditions governing the performance of the Ombudsman's duties (9th March 1994, as amended by Decision 14 March 2002) available at www.euro-ombudsman.eu.int/lbasis/en/statute.htm or OJ 1994 L 113 p 15.

[55]   'What can the European Ombudsman do for you?— A Guide for Citizens' at p 8 www.euro-ombudsman. eu.int/guide/pdf/en/guide_en.pdf.

(6) How does the EO **proceed**?
- Institutions and member state authorities must give EO the information he requests, subject to legally regulated secrecy restrictions.
- Officials must testify at EO's request (while remaining bound by their duty of professional secrecy) (Art 3(2)).

(7) **What** does the EO look for?

The EO investigates 'instances of maladministration' (Art 2(2)). There is no requirement of injustice to the claimant.

(8) **What outcome** does the EO give?
- If maladministration is found after an investigation, the EO seeks a 'friendly solution' with the institution to eliminate the maladministration and satisfy the complainant.
- Failing that, the EO may close the file and note a 'critical mark' against the institution. This may be the outcome where the maladministration did not have any serious implications, or where the maladministration cannot be put right.
- Otherwise, the EO will inform the institution of the finding of maladministration and make 'draft recommendations' to which the institution has three months to respond.
- If the institution does not adequately respond or does not accept the draft recommendations, the EO may report to the European Parliament with recommendations.
- The EO also submits annual reports to the European Parliament (Art 3(8)).

There are some important ways in which the EO's remit is more far-reaching than that of ombudsmen in Britain:

Initiation of Investigations: Access of complainants to the EO is direct, and the EO can initiate his own investigations.

Exclusions and limitations to jurisdiction
- There is no exclusive list of bodies to which the European Ombudsman's jurisdiction applies. He can investigate all 'Community institutions and bodies'.
- There is no list of matters excluded from the ombudsman's jurisdiction like that in the British legislation. So, for example, the EO can investigate complaints about commercial and personnel decisions.

There is no 'injustice' requirement: 'A Guide for Citizens' states 'You do not have to show that you are directly concerned by the alleged maladministration to lodge a complaint' (7).

13.11 Administrative audit

In her Special Report to Parliament on the Debt of Honour investigation, the Ombudsman did not simply recommend that Hayward should have an apology. She made three general recommendations about the administration of *ex gratia* schemes: that they should never be announced before eligibility had been worked out, that any change in eligibility should be communicated clearly, and that it is good administrative practice to review a scheme that generates widespread complaints.[56]

Do those general recommendations reflect an appropriate role for an ombudsman, or should she stick to recommending a response to a particular complaint? And if she has a more general role to play in promoting good administration, shouldn't she be able to perform administrative inspections on her own initiative (like the European Ombudsman; see section 13.10), rather than merely investigating particular complaints? And shouldn't she have some more general supervisory technique for improving administrative practice in general? Does the requirement of injustice to a complainant, in particular, prevent the ombudsman from playing a general role?

In fact, the ombudsmen have a very important general role to play in improving administration, but the investigation of particular complaints actually promotes that general function. The Select Committee in 1993 suggested that the Parliamentary Ombudsman should be able to carry out administrative *audits*: general inspections of the administrative practice of departments and agencies. The Government rejected the suggestion, on the basis that an audit that approves of a department's administration could prejudice the Ombudsman against those who later complain of maladministration in that department. That point reflects a value of the ombudsmen's role as investigators of particular complaints: the existence of the complaint itself gives a focus and legitimacy to the ombudsman's investigation. The reason for the initiation of an administrative audit would have to be the auditor's own agenda. An ombudsman's investigation has a rationale that arises from the complaint. A general role as an inspector of administration would have some advantages, but it would distort the ombudsman's role in responding to complaints.

Note that the Public Administration Select Committee not only oversees the work of the Ombudsman and examines her reports; it has a general remit to inquire into the quality and standards of administration provided by civil service departments. So the Committee *does* have a general role. The general effect of the ombudsmen's work arises out of their role as investigators of particular complaints. But there are already several major ways in which the ombudsmen have a general effect on administration:

(1) the Parliamentary Ombudsman **gives general advice** in her reports on particular complaints. There is at present no legislative requirement for the Government to respond to such advice, but it has the force of the handwriting on the wall: a complainant (and the Ombudsman herself) will be able to refer to the general advice in future investigations;

(2) there is already provision for **annual reports** to Parliament (s 10(4) of the 1967 Act), which give her the opportunity to bring general administrative problems to the attention of the Select Committee;

----

[56] 'A debt of honour' (above n 2) [223]–[226].

(3) the Local Government Ombudsmen have the **Commission for Local Administration**, which serves both as a forum for the three Local Government Ombudsmen and the Parliamentary Ombudsman to achieve general consistency, and also gives advice on good administrative practice;

(4) moves toward **coordination** of Local and Parliamentary Ombudsmen's investigations (see the fourth *Balchin* report[57]) and coordination with other complaints resolution agencies (such as the Adjudicator's Office in the Tax Credit investigation, see below) are giving a more general effect to investigations; and

(5) the investigation of a single complaint can have **ramifications** for many more people affected by a large-scale administrative scheme. The report on pensions and the Ombudsman's 2005 Special Report on Tax Credits[58] are the most striking examples.

The ombudsmen's role in responding to complaints gives focus to their work and actually enables them to make general contributions to good administration. Unlike the European Ombudsman, the British ombudsmen are not likely to develop a role of initiating their own general investigations of success and failure in the administration of public authorities, because the Government has found other ways of instituting administrative audits for a wide range of government services (some of which the ombudsmen do not investigate). These new techniques suit the target-based, incentive-led, 'customer'-focused approach to public administration described in Chapter 15.

Four educational inspectorates were unified in **Ofsted** (the Office for Standards in Education, Children's Services and Skills[59]) in 2007. It sets administrative standards and sends inspectors to hundreds of schools every week, publishing its reports on particular schools and reporting to Parliament. The **Quality Assurance Agency** is an independent inspectorate that performs a similar role for nearly 200 universities and colleges, carrying out 'institutional audits' of academic standards and administrative processes in particular institutions.[60] The Health And Social Care Act 2008 has unified the Commission for Social Care Inspection, the Healthcare Commission, and the Mental Health Act Commission into a single **Care Quality Commission**.[61] Police, prisons, and the probation service are regulated by independent inspectorates.[62] These bodies share certain features in regulating very different services: they

---

[57] www.ombudsman.org.uk/improving_services/special_reports/pca/redress05/redress_foreword.html

[58] 'Tax Credits: Putting Things Right' 3rd Report, Session 2005–2006, HC 124 (2005–2006), available at www.ombudsman.org.uk/improving_services/special_reports/pca/taxcredits05/index.html.

[59] http://www.ofsted.gov.uk/.

[60] www.qaa.ac.uk.

[61] http://www.cqc.org.uk/.

[62] http://inspectorates.homeoffice.gov.uk/.

are independent, they undertake inspections at their own instigation, they have associated roles in setting standards of good administration, and reporting on performance to the Government or to Parliament. Finally, and perhaps most importantly, they all publicize their findings in forms that allow the public to compare the performance of different schools, universities, hospitals, prisons, and police forces.

In local government, the Audit Commission carries out general inspections of the performance of authorities under the Government's 'Best Value' scheme (see p 575) (Local Government and Public Involvement in Health Act 2007 s 152). From 2009, local authorities face a new scheme of 'Comprehensive Area Assessment' by the Audit Commission, designed not only to assess public services in delivered by a council, but to assess cooperation among local authorities, other government agencies (including health, education, and police authorities), and charities.[63] The **Standards Board**[64] monitors the performance of local authority standards committees in hearing complaints about the conduct of council members, and can take over the investigation of serious complaints.

In central government administration, the approach to administrative audit is different. The Labour Government initiated **'Capability Reviews'** in 2006. A team of civil servants from the Cabinet Office investigates practice and structures in departments and makes public assessments of their capacity to meet future challenges.[65] The team uses independent experts—mostly drawn from the business world—but the scheme is not independent. It is a government scheme, without the independence of the commissions that oversee local government administration and the health, education, police, prison, and probation services. And it is not aimed to identify maladministration, but to propose strategic improvements in administration.

13.12 The Equality and Human Rights Commission

In October 2007, the new Equality and Human Rights Commission began its work. A project that might have started nine years earlier when the Human Rights Act was enacted, the Commission was created by the Equality Act 2006, and has taken over the work of the Commission for Racial Equality, the Equal Opportunities Commission (which dealt with gender discrimination), and the Disability Rights Commission. Like its predecessors, the Equality and Human Rights Commission is an independent agency established by Parliament to fight discrimination. In addition to dealing with race, gender, and disability, the new Commission is meant to combat discrimination on the basis of age, sexual orientation, and religion or belief, as well as discrimination that is unlawful under the Human Rights Act.

---

[63] http://www.audit-commission.gov.uk/caa/.

[64] www.standardsboard.co.uk.

[65] http://www.civilservice.gov.uk/about/accountability/capability.

The Commission has a general responsibility for monitoring and campaigning and producing anti-discrimination publicity. And that general information and publicity role is backed by legal powers: the Commission can:

- issue codes of practice—s 14 (a code takes legal effect if the Secretary of State approves and lays it before Parliament: s 14(7));

- conduct inquiries (into general discrimination questions, such as the causes of inequality)—s 16;

- conduct assessments (of compliance of public bodies with duties not to discriminate)—s 31;

- issue a compliance notice requiring a public body to comply with its legal duties—s 32;

- provide conciliation services to resolve disputes involving complaints of discrimination—s 27; and

- conduct investigations into allegations of unlawful discrimination by particular persons.

If an investigation leads to the conclusion that a person has acted unlawfully, the Commission can make an 'unlawful act notice' (against which the person may appeal to a court or tribunal) (s 21). The Commission can enter into a legally binding agreement with the person as to a remedy for the problem, or can require the person to make an action plan.

The Commission's role in litigation is important: it supports the investigation and assessment processes, but goes further, too. The Commission can:

- apply to a court for an injunction, if it 'thinks that a person is likely to commit an unlawful act'—s 24;

- apply to a court for an order requiring the person to comply with an action plan—s 22;

- apply to a court for an order requiring a public body to comply with a compliance notice—s 32;

- provide advice and legal representation to private litigants—s 28;

- bring judicial review proceedings on grounds of discrimination, in its own name, or intervene in proceedings brought by someone else—s 30; and

- bring Human Rights Act proceedings, even though it does not meet the 'victim' test for standing (see p 416) in the Human Rights Act—s 30.

The litigation role is inherited from the predecessor discrimination commissions; it was the Equal Opportunities Commission that pioneered this role in dealing with gender discrimination. In R v Employment Secretary, ex p Equal Opportunities Commission [1995] 1 AC 1, the House of Lords held that the Commission had standing to seek judicial review, and then went on to demonstrate the potential of such litigation by striking down British legislation restricting part-time workers' rights as incompatible with the EU Equal Treatment Directive.

The Commission's power to intervene will enable it to support claimants who allege discrimination. A notable example of intervention by the Commission for Racial Equality arose in the Debt of Honour saga. The CRE intervened in *R (Elias) v Defence Secretary* [2006] EWCA Civ 1293 (see p 477). All three commissions have appeared as intervenors; they all did so in the same case in *Igen et al v Webster; Equal Opportunities Commission, Commission for Racial Equality, and Disability Rights Commission, Intervenors* [2005] EWCA Civ 142.

In its developing role, the Equality and Human Rights Commission will be serving as an investigator. But its investigative role is very different from that of ombudsmen, because it has a general duty to take action on its own initiative to fight a range of forms of discrimination (by private persons as well as by public authorities). It is a hybrid between an ombudsman, a prosecutor, and an advocacy organization.

13.13 The Inquiries Act 2005

Ad hoc public investigations are often set up by the government, as a response to a disaster or a public embarrassment. Important examples include the 1999 inquiry into the racist murder of Stephen Lawrence, the BSE Inquiry in 1997, and the Hutton Inquiry concerning the death of the government weapons expert David Kelly in 2003, in the controversy over the Iraq war. The purpose of such an inquiry is to find out what went wrong, and to make a report recommending changes for the better in public policy or public administration.

Setting up an inquiry is a way of saying that a situation needs a serious independent look. That can give the Government something to do in response to a scandal, without admitting mistakes or taking unpopular decisions. But then the onus is on the Government to take the report seriously.

> ### Will a court order the Government to hold an inquiry?
> The right to life in Art 2 of the Convention has been held to require an inquiry into any death that may have been the result of the state's failure to carry out its obligation to protect people's lives (*R (Middleton) v West Somerset Coroner* [2004] UKHL 10). That duty of the Government is generally carried out through the system of coroners' inquiries that we have had since the middle ages.
>
> But in *R (Gentle) v Prime Minister* [2006] EWCA Civ 1689, the claimant sought judicial review of the Government's refusal to hold an independent inquiry into whether its decision to invade Iraq violated international law. The Court of Appeal dismissed the claim, because there was no arguable case that the Government had breached Convention obligations; even if what it did was contrary to international law (which the Court would not decide), the Convention does not incorporate international law.

The Government can always just ask someone to investigate something. But it has proved useful to create statutory schemes conferring powers on inquiries to compel testimony and production of evidence, and regulating their procedures.[66] As with tribunals, provisions for inquiries had been added to various legislative schemes over decades,[67] with no system. The Inquiries Act 2005 has done the same thing for inquiries (but on a much smaller scale) that the Tribunals Courts and Enforcement Act 2007 has done for tribunals. It replaces dozens of pieces of legislation governing inquiries commissioned by ministers, and creates a new framework regulating their establishment, the appointment of people to conduct them, their procedures, and their powers, and the submission and publication of reports. The difference between the Labour Government's inquiries legislation and the tribunals legislation is that inquiries will remain a flexible tool under control of the government, while the reconstruction of tribunals will dilute government control over them.

Uniformity is elusive: the Act leaves it to the minister to state the questions the inquiry is to address, to appoint the panel members, to decide the terms of reference (and to change them during an inquiry), to decide whether the inquiry is to make recommendations, and to suspend an inquiry or (after consulting the chairman and giving reasons) to end it. The Government will still be able to set up a non-statutory inquiry if it wishes, and specialized schemes will remain for certain areas such as financial services.

The biggest ever inquiry was the Scott Inquiry into the British Government's support for the export of high-tech military machine tools to Iraq.[68] Customs officers had prosecuted Matrix Churchill Ltd for violating export restrictions, but the prosecutions broke down when it emerged that the Government had encouraged the company to violate the export restrictions. During the prosecutions, Ministers signed certificates asking the courts to keep documents immune from disclosure in the prosecution, on the ground of public interest. In fact, the documents showed that the prosecutions were improper: without telling the Customs officers, the Government had secretly encouraged Matrix Churchill's exports. Disclosure of the documents was not at all against the public interest; it was against the Ministers' personal political interests.

The Scott Inquiry uncovered all this, and yet obscured its revelations in a massive process and an 1,800-page report, written with such extremely judicious care that the Ministers in question could keep their jobs and the Prime Minister could escape the embarrassment of resignations. But the Inquiry at least gave the opposition material to portray the Government as sleazy, and it played a role in the death throes of the Conservative Government. The Hutton Inquiry, by contrast, very largely exonerated

----

[66] The first such legislation was the Tribunals of Inquiry (Evidence) Act 1921.

[67] E.g., the Childrens Act 1989 s 81 (repealed by the Inquiries Act 2005), which was used in the inquiry into the death of a young girl, Victoria Climbié. See www.victoria-climbie-inquiry.org.uk.

[68] Scott R, 'Report of the inquiry into the export of defence equipment and dual-use goods to Iraq and related prosecutions' (London: HMSO, 1996).

the Blair Government on the limited issues that were before it. Yet it, too, made secret and embarrassing information available to the public.[69]

Inquiries into governmental scandals are so careful, and they elicit such a volume of complex information, that they are unlikely to inflict the simple political damage that will bring down a government. They are not rapid or decisive; they tend to defuse a crisis and to dissipate political forces by generating mountains of information that can be interpreted in different ways. And even though the decision maker is often a judge, there is a *crucial* difference between inquiries and adjudication: the decision maker does not have to find anyone liable or not liable, and need not decide whether anyone acted lawfully or unlawfully. So the conclusions tend to be complex and qualified, rather than decisive. But regardless of their conclusions, they can give the opposition some very useful material to work with. Inquiries of this kind play a political role in the management of scandals, rather than a legal role in the regulation of government.

Inquiries American style

UK parliamentary committees scrutinize policy and the regular operations of government, but the tradition of using *parliamentary* inquiries to respond to scandals and crises largely broke down nearly a century ago.[70] By contrast, the U.S. tradition of Congressional inquiries grew stronger through the 20th century, and was used to deal with the attack on Pearl Harbour in 1941[71] and the attacks of September 11, 2001.[72]

Conversely, the Americans view it as constitutionally inappropriate for the judges to conduct crisis inquiries:

> 'The legitimacy of the Judicial Branch ultimately depends upon a reputation for impartiality and non-partisanship. That reputation may not be borrowed by the political Branches to cloak their work in the neutral colors of judicial action.'[73]

The separation of the Presidency from Congress makes it easier for the legislature to call the Executive to give evidence to an inquiry, even though Congress is partisan. So Condoleezza Rice, the National Security Adviser, was an important witness

---

[69] The report, running to only 328 pages, is available at www.the-hutton-inquiry.org.uk/. The Hutton Inquiry broke new ground in the volume of information it made freely available on the internet during the process. For other examples see: www.bloody-sunday-inquiry.org/, or the Stephen Lawrence Inquiry report at www.archive.official-documents.co.uk/document/cm42/4262/sli-00.htm.

[70] A turning point came when a committee of the House of Commons split on party lines after its inquiry into allegations of ministerial corruption in the Marconi affair, 1912. But inquiries by parliamentary committees still play an important part in overseeing administration.

[71] www.ibiblio.org/pha/pha/congress/part_0.html.

[72] www.9-11commission.gov/.

[73] *Mistretta v United States* 488 US 362 (1989), 407.

before the 9/11 Congressional Commission. But committee investigations can play part of partisan politics in the legislature, as they did most flagrantly when Joseph McCarthy used his chairmanship of the Senate Permanent Subcommittee on Investigations to hunt for communists in the Government in 1953–4. Opportunities for partisan politics are always available, as committees need majority voting even to subpoena witnesses. When the 9/11 Commission report was issued unanimously by five Democrats and five Republicans, it was a sign of bipartisan solidarity.

13.14 Conclusion: the limits of administrative law

The Parliamentary and Local Government Ombudsmen have become valuable institutions both for securing redress for claimants who have no legal entitlement to a remedy, and also for improving public administration in general. Their investigative function is in some ways better tailored to promoting just public administration than the application of standards of administrative legality in judicial processes. It is important to remember just how non-legal the ombudsman schemes are: the law that establishes them gives no legal effect to their reports (except by imposing a duty on local authorities to consider and to reply[74]), and the only legal powers they have are the powers of access to the information they need in their informal investigations. Ombudsmen ask, in an open-ended fashion, whether something went wrong and what could be improved.

Then what role do the ombudsmen play in the constitution? It may seem that the answer is, 'none': they are a response to the complexity of modern government, rather than a constitutional essential. We tend to think of the rule of law as a constitutional ideal that is imposed by courts and other legal authorities, such as tribunals (see Chapter 12), and which must be respected by the agencies that exercise the executive power of the state. Since ombudsmen's reports have no legal authority, and ombudsmen exercise no executive power, it may seem that they contribute to good administrative practice but not to the rule of law. And in a sense that is right: the whole point of the ombudsman institution is that we should expect more of the administration of government than just legality. So it may seem that the task of ombudsmen is to promote aspects of good administration that the rule of law (and the constitution) cannot promote.

But remember the unclear announcement of payments to 'British civilians', which was ground for the Ombudsman's recommendations in the Debt of Honour report (see p 466). Its lack of clarity had no legal consequences; a more definite announcement, by contrast, would have given rise to a legitimate expectation. In criticizing the unclear announcement, the Ombudsman *promoted* (in a way that the law could not do) the same values that the rule of law promotes. The ombudsman process offers an obstacle to arbitrary government, because it can expose and criticize a way of

---
[74]   Local Government Act 1974 s 31, as amended by Local Government and Housing Act 1989 s 26.

administering the scheme that suits a government's political imperative at the cost of ignoring the interests of people affected by the scheme. It is an obstacle to arbitrary government first because it enhances accountability: the ombudsman exposes bad government to criticism and requires a response even though the recommendations are not binding. Secondly, it enhances the representative function of the House of Commons (at national level), and it enhances local democracy. So the ombudsmen actually promote the ideal of controlled government that lies *behind* the rule of law. The rule of law is valuable because it is opposed to arbitrary government (above, Chapter 2). The work of the ombudsmen, too, is opposed to arbitrary government.

So ombudsmen represent a step forward from 40 years ago, both in good administration and in access to justice; it is an expensive step forward that causes aggravation to public officials, and can lead to the extravagant excess of process that we saw in the *Balchin* case (section 13.8.1). The process creates a risk of recommendations that are themselves arbitrary, in the sense that they reflect the ombudsman's whims, or hasty and over-burdensome judgments swayed by the difficult situation of a complainant. But that risk is minor because of the informal effect of reports, and the risk is worthwhile because the ombudsmen offer an effective way to hold government accountable for botched programmes like the tax credit scheme and the Debt of Honour scheme—even when nothing unlawful has been done. And it is a process that allows an investigation that neither judges nor MPs are suitable for, or entitled to conduct. So the ombudsmen promote the constitutional ideal of responsible government.

TAKE-HOME MESSAGE • • •

- Both ombudsmen and courts are independent from the administration. Their process and remedies are fundamentally different.

- The ombudsman **investigates**; the judge **adjudicates** between two adversaries. The judge makes an order with legal effect. The ombudsman does not give a *remedy* at all; she makes a report that is not legally binding, and the public agency makes decisions (and may give recompense) in response.

- Equally importantly, the judge cannot interfere with lawful acts of administration. The ombudsman can deal with anything bad in the administration. And because of the investigative role, the ombudsman may provide the very useful outcome of discovering what really happened, where a court could not. Note that tribunals share the limitations and powers of courts, except that their process is meant to be (and *sometimes* is) less formal than that of a court; see Chapter 12.

- Ombudsmen can make recommendations that extend **beyond the complaint**; the courts must make an order that is limited to disposing of the specific dispute.

- The British ombudsmen have no general role of initiating **audits of administration** to identify shortcomings or successes, or to advise on how to improve services. But that auditing role is filled for a variety of government services by a plethora of specific investigation and scrutiny commissions and, in respect of discrimination, by the Equality and Human Rights Commission.

Critical reading

R v LCA, ex p Bradford City Council [1979] QB 287

R v LCA, ex p Eastleigh BC [1988] QB 855

R v LCA, ex p Croydon LBC [1989] 1 All ER 1033

R v PCA, ex p Balchin [1997] JPL 917

Bradley v Work and Pensions Secretary [2008] EWCA Civ 36

The Ombudsman's fourth report on the *Balchin* case: 'Redress in the Round' 11 October 2005, HC 475

http://www.ombudsman.org.uk/improving_services/special_reports/pca/redress05/index.html

The Debt of Honour report: http://www.ombudsman.org.uk/improving_services/special_reports/pca/internees05/index.html

The Public Administration Select Committee's views on the Government's rejection of the Ombudsman's report on pensions:

http://www.publications.parliament.uk/pa/cm200809/cmselect/cmpubadm/219/219.pdf

CRITICAL QUESTIONS • • •

1 **What can the ombudsmen do that the courts cannot do?**

2 **What can the courts do that the ombudsmen cannot do?**

3 **Why is the Parliamentary Ombudsman *parliamentary*? Would it be better to have a central government ombudsman, independent of Parliament?**

4 **Can you explain the relations among:**
   (i) **maladministration,**
   (ii) **the lawfulness of a decision, and**
   (iii) **the merits of a decision?**

5 **If an action is unlawful, does that mean that it should not be identified as maladministration in a report of the Parliamentary Ombudsman?**

6 **Who should decide what constitutes maladministration—the ombudsmen, or the judges?**

Further Questions:

7 **In *Bradley v Work and Pensions Secretary* [2008] EWCA Civ 36, the Court of Appeal quite deliberately set out to act on 'the principle of mutual respect' (Sir John Chadwick [63])—that is, on the constitutional principle of comity (see p 17). Did the decision adhere to that principle?**

8 In *R v LCA, ex p Liverpool City Council* [2001] 1 All ER 462 (CA), Henry LJ said the following about the overlap between judicial review and investigation by the Local Government Ombudsman: 'What may not have been recognised in 1974 was the emergence of judicial review to the point where most if not all matters which could form the basis for a complaint of maladministration are matters for which the elastic quality of judicial review might provide a remedy' (471). So the overlap is greater now, than in 1974. Does that mean that ombudsmen should leave more complaints to be pursued in judicial review?

9 Why is the Parliamentary Commissioner for Administration subject to judicial review, if the Parliamentary Commissioner for Standards is not?

10 The European Ombudsman can investigate complaints of maladministration with no requirement that the complainant has suffered injustice as a result. Would a similar regime be an improvement in the role of the British ombudsmen?

11 The Finnish Parliamentary Ombudsman oversees the legality of actions of the armed forces and government ministers, and oversees the courts. The Swedish Parliamentary Ombudsmen also oversee courts, as they have done since 1809 (but not ministers). Both can initiate investigations without having received a complaint. Is there any good reason why our Parliamentary Ombudsman is more limited in scope?

**online
resource
centre**

Visit the online resource centre to access the following resources which accompany this chapter: links to legislation and online reports of judicial decisions, summaries of key cases and legislation, updates in the law, suggestions for answering the pop quizzes and questions, and links to useful websites.

Private law and public authorities

14 Torts

A claim for damages for loss caused by a public authority may give a court two opportunities: to do justice for the claimant, and also to impose the rule of law on the administration. The challenge is to do both without interfering inappropriately in the administrative pursuit of public goods, and without creating public compensation funds that only a legislature can legitimately create.

LOOK FOR • • •

- The special justification that tort law needs: even if a public authority has acted unlawfully, why should a claimant receive compensation for loss caused by the unlawful action?

- Ways in which rights to compensation can affect public authorities' use of their discretionary powers.

- What makes an unlawful administrative action a tort, if it is a tort.

- Special compensation schemes under the European Convention on Human Rights (given effect by the Human Rights Act 1998), and European Community Law (given effect by the European Communities Act 1972).

> ❛It is one thing to provide a service at the public expense. It is another to require the public to pay compensation when a failure to provide the service has resulted in loss.❜
>
> *Stovin v Wise* [1996] AC 923, 954 (Lord Hoffmann)

14.1 Introduction: trespass to property

The common law has rewarded the lawyers who, as Lord Reid put it in a tort case, 'struggled and fought through the centuries to establish the rights of the subject to be protected from arbitrary acts of the King's servants' (*Attorney-General v Nissan* [1970] AC 179, 208). One way for judges to control arbitrary government is by quashing decisions in judicial review; another way is by holding the act to be a tort, and awarding an injunction or damages.

The law of tort has been especially jealous of property rights.[1] On November 11, 1762, Nathan Carrington and three other men broke into John Entick's house in Stepney. They spent four hours rummaging through papers and breaking open chests, and they carried away hundreds of pamphlets that Entick had printed. So he sued them in trespass. Trespass to property is a tort—that is, unlawful conduct that gives the victim a legal right to a remedy. Not just any unlawful action counts as a tort. A tort gives the victim a right to claim compensation for loss caused by the action, or to claim an injunction to require the defendant not to continue the tort. When Entick sued the four men in tort, they claimed that their actions were lawful (and therefore not tortious) because the Earl of Halifax, one of the King's principal secretaries of state, had given them a warrant to search Entick's house and to take his papers. Entick published pamphlets for the radical John Wilkes, who had been criticizing the Prime Minister. The defendants in Entick's case claimed that the Secretary of State had 'a jurisdiction' to seize Entick's papers, because the Government had to be able to control sedition. In *Entick v Carrington* (1765) 19 Howell's State Trials 1029, the Chief Justice, Lord Camden, rejected this 'argument of state necessity':

> ❛...the common law does not understand that kind of reasoning, nor do our books take notice of any such distinctions....If the king himself has no power to declare when the law ought to be violated for reason of state, I am sure we his judges have no such prerogative.❜ (1073)

---

[1] It needn't be ownership: 'The common law protects possession as well as title. A person who is in actual possession of land is entitled to remain in peaceful enjoyment of the property without disturbance by anyone except a person with a better right to possession. It does not matter that he has no title. A squatter can maintain a claim of trespass.' *Harrow v Qazi* [2003] UKHL 43 [87] (Lord Millett).

Lord Camden was able to present his decision as an act of judicial *modesty*, but it was the *judge-made* law of his time that protected people from arbitrary governmental invasions of property, by treating them as trespasses.

The constitutional importance of Entick's case is that the court used the law of tort to control the administration. The case shows both the opportunity the law gives the court to do justice, *and*, by the same token, the opportunity to restrain the abuse of state power. The court carried out two of its responsibilities: to do justice between two persons in private law, and to impose the rule of law on the Government. The courts have faced difficulties reconciling the principles of public law with those of private law, but it is important to see how deeply private law and public law supported each other in Entick: the private law of tort demands compensation for loss caused by a trespass to property, and the public law of the constitution demands that the Government should not be able to claim a special dispensation from private law on grounds of state necessity.

Entick v Carrington in the United States

Twenty-five years after Entick was decided, the United States adopted a bill of rights guaranteeing that 'the right of the people to be secure in their persons, houses, papers, and effects, against unreasonable searches and seizures, shall not be violated' (U.S. Constitution, Fourth Amendment). In *Boyd v United States* 116 US 616, (1886) 626, the U.S. Supreme Court called Lord Camden's decision in Entick a 'great judgement', 'one of the permanent monuments of the British Constitution', and a guide to understanding the Fourth Amendment.

'The principles laid down in this opinion affect the very essence of constitutional liberty and security. They reach farther than the concrete form of the case then before the court, with its adventitious circumstances; they apply to all invasions on the part of the government and its employees of the sanctity of a man's home and the privacies of life' (630).

A government minister cannot give anyone a defence against tort law, but Parliament can do so. A tort is an unlawful act, and if Parliament has authorized an act of a public authority (or of a private person for that matter) that would otherwise be a tort, it is not a tort. The defendant has a defence of statutory authority. But a simple lack of procedural fairness in performing such an act may deprive the public authority of the defence. So *Cooper v Board of Works* (1863) 14 CB (NS) 180 (one of the landmarks of the law of due process—see section 4.1) was, like Entick's case, an action in the tort of trespass to property. The alleged trespass was the demolition of Cooper's house by the Board of Works, and the Board's defence was that, because Cooper had not given the required seven days' notice before the beginning of construction, the Metropolis Local Management Act, 1855 gave them a statutory power to demolish the house. The defence failed, because even though the Act did not require a hearing, 'the justice of the common law will supply the omission of the legislature' (Byles J, 194). In spite of the statutory power, a demolition is an unlawful interference with property (and therefore a trespass), if a public authority does it without due process.

● *Pop Quiz* ●

The trespass in *Cooper* was a tort. Was it also a crime? Can you think of a tort that is not a crime? A crime that is not a tort? An unlawful action that is neither a tort nor a crime? See p 544 on criminal liabilities of public officials.

To do justice in a case like *Cooper* or *Entick*, the law needs to award the claimant compensation for the injury caused by the wrong. A court in judicial review could declare such abuses of power unlawful, and if the claimant got to a judge in time, the court could issue a mandatory order to a public authority not to search Entick's house, or not to demolish Cooper's house without giving him a hearing. But it is easy to see why the law needs liabilities to compensate, and not just a process for quashing decisions. Cooper and Entick could not get to a judge in time. So they suffered harm that could not be put right with the quashing of a decision, or with a declaration that the public authority had acted unlawfully. 'The justice of the common law' demands not only judicial power to quash unlawful decisions, but also *compensation* to make people in the position of Cooper or Entick as well off (to the extent that an award of damages can do so) as if the wrong had not been done. How does the law decide which unlawful decisions lead to a right to compensation? It is an important rule of public law that the answer to that question is *generally* the same whether the defendant is a public authority or not. But we will see that by contrast with the law of trespass, it is very difficult to work out how to apply the ordinary law of negligence. It is difficult because of the unique relationships of power and dependency between public authorities and the people they ought to care for.

Beyond the general rule that public authorities face the same tort liabilities as other defendants, there is one special public tort (misfeasance in a public office (see section 14.5), and Parliament has imposed special duties of compensation on public authorities (see section 14.3). Moreover, the Human Rights Act gives courts a discretion to award damages in compensation for certain losses caused by infringements of Convention rights (see section 14.6), and we will need to understand how different that power is from the court's duty in tort law to award compensatory damages. And finally in respect of European Community law, public authorities face something that they do not face in domestic law: a pure duty to compensate for loss caused by action that is unlawful (see section 14.7).

14.2 Tort liability of public authorities: the basic principles

The two classic cases in the tort of trespass, *Entick* and *Cooper*, show the two basic principles of tort liability of public authorities.

1. **Administrative authorities have no immunity from liability for their torts.**[2]

---

[2]   See p 517–18 on the immunity of the Crown at common law, before the Crown Proceedings Act 1947.

2. **If Parliament authorizes a public authority to do what would otherwise be a tort, it is not a tort.**

Public authorities are liable in tort. Government ministers and other administrative authorities (unlike judges and members of Parliament) have no immunity from liability for torts. If a truck runs you down in the street because the driver was not paying attention, it *makes no difference* whether the truck was being driven on behalf of your city council, or on behalf of Tesco. Administrative authorities are liable for torts in the same way as any private person, and are vicariously liable for the torts of their employees in the same way as any employer (*Mersey Docks & Harbour Board Trustees v Gibbs* (1866) LR 1 HL 93).

To the first two basic principles, we should add two principles that restrict tort liability, which you might miss if you only read *Entick* and *Cooper*:

3. **Acting unlawfully is not in itself a tort. Even acting in a *Wednesbury*-unreasonable way is not a tort in itself.[3] There is no general legal right to compensation for loss caused by unlawful administrative action.**

For a public authority to have committed a tort, there must be reason for the law to give a private person a right to a remedy. The reason may be that the ordinary principles of the common law of tort require a remedy. But the fact that the public authority acted unlawfully is not, by itself, a reason for a private person to have a right to a remedy.

4. **There is no tort where the court would have to pass judgment on unjusticiable questions in order to find the public authority liable.**

The third and fourth basic principles show why tort law faces a special set of challenges in dealing with losses caused by the conduct of public authorities.

> ## The special position of the Crown
> 'The King can do no wrong' is an old slogan of the common law. And a tort is a wrong. So at common law the Crown was not liable in tort. Of course, 'the King can do no wrong' can mean either 'it is not unlawful if the King did it', or 'if it's unlawful, it wasn't the King who did it'.[4] So ministers of the Crown were sometimes held liable in tort even when they had the King's authorization (*Earl of Danby's Case* (1679) 11 St Tr 599), and if the defendants in *Entick* had been told by the King himself to ransack Entick's house, they would still have been liable in trespass. There were other techniques, too, for avoiding the injustice that resulted from the rule that the

---

3   There is much authority: e.g., *Jones v Swansea City Council* [1990] 1 WLR 54.

4   In *The King v Speyer* [1916] 1 KB 595, Avory J said that the maxim 'only means that His Majesty individually and personally and in his natural capacity is independent of, and not amenable to, any other earthly power or jurisdiction . . . . It is a fundamental general rule that the King cannot sanction any act forbidden by law' (619).

Crown was not liable in tort.[5] But the Crown Proceedings Act 1947 abolished the immunity. For most purposes, the Crown is liable in tort and breach of contract in the same way as a private individual. Acts of the Crown include many acts of ministers and government departments, but not acts of other public authorities such as local authorities, police authorities, or bodies created by statute. Such authorities never benefited from the immunity of the Crown in tort.

14.3 Statutory liabilities

Parliament can authorize what would otherwise be a tort, and can also impose a liability that a defendant wouldn't otherwise have. Judges and legal scholars say that there is a 'tort of breach of statutory duty'. But the name is misleading, because breaching a statutory duty is not a tort in itself. This so-called tort is a way of talking about a liability to compensate a claimant for loss caused by a breach of statutory duty *for which an act of Parliament requires a remedy*.

Breaching a statutory duty is not a tort

Lord Denning tried to change this: '... if the public authority flies in the face of the statute, by doing something which the statute expressly prohibits, or otherwise so conducts itself—by omission or commission—as to frustrate or hinder the policy and objects of the Act, then it is doing what it ought not to do—it is going outside its jurisdiction—it is acting *ultra vires*. Any person who is particularly damnified thereby can bring an action in the courts for damages or an injunction, whichever be the most appropriate' (*Meade v Haringey LBC* [1979] 1 WLR 637, 647. This view has never been made the ratio of an award of damages, and it was disapproved in *X v Bedfordshire* [1995] 2 AC 633 by Sir Thomas Bingham MR (699) and Lord Browne-Wilkinson (768).

So for example, the Road Traffic Act 1988 s 39 imposes a duty on local authorities to 'carry out a programme of measures designed to promote road safety'. But a local authority is not liable in tort to a claimant who suffers injury because the authority failed to carry out a programme of measures (*Gorringe v Calderdale MBC* [2004] UKHL 15). The tort that people call 'breach of statutory duty' only arises if:

- the duty was imposed for the benefit of the claimant, and

- the statute gives a right to compensation.

It is obvious that if Parliament confers a right to compensation, that right can be asserted in a claim. So why are statutory liabilities interesting? The answer is that the

---

5   The 'Petition of Right' was a way of asking for a remedy for loss caused by conduct that would have been a tort or breach of contract if the defendant were not the Crown. It was a plea to the King for justice, which in practice became a form of judicial remedy.

question of whether a statute confers such a right can be surprisingly controversial. The controversies concern the foundation of the relationship between people and the state.

Yet there is nothing distinctly administrative, or public, about this tort; the classic cases concern the liability of private factory owners to workers injured as a result of failure to follow statutory safety rules, or the liability of drivers who breached traffic regulations to people who were injured as a result.[6] The specially administrative feature of the tort is that claimants have made creative attempts to persuade the judges that liability arises out of the statutory duties of public authorities, even where Parliament does not expressly create a right of action. Those attempts have largely failed. In fact, it may seem that the House of Lords has carefully developed more restricted liability for breach of statutory duty by public authorities than by private persons. In the private defendant cases, liability was said to arise, *prima facie*, when the statute imposed a duty for the benefit or protection of a class of persons, and a member of that class suffered injury as a result of a failure to perform the duty. Lord Wright held that the right of action was 'a specific common law right.... The statutory right has its origin in the statute, but the particular remedy of an action for damages is given by the common law in order to make effective, for the benefit of the injured plaintiff, his right to the performance by the defendant of the defendant's statutory duty' (*London Transport Board v Upson* 168).

It seems that another requirement has been added in public authority cases. It was first stated clearly by Lord Jauncey, when a prisoner sued the prison governors for damages for breach of the prison rules: 'The fact that a particular provision was intended to protect certain individuals is not of itself sufficient to confer private law rights of action upon them, something more is required to show that the legislature intended such conferment' (*R v Deputy Governor of Parkhurst Prison, ex p Hague* [1992] 1 AC 58, 170–1). Not only does that approach add an additional requirement, it suggests that the 'tort' is a right of action that Parliament confers, contrary to Lord Wright's claim that the tort is a common law right of action.

Have the courts been imposing common law liability on private defendants to abide by statutes, and protecting public authorities from liability? No. A public authority operating a factory would have the same liabilities as a private company, as would a public authority whose employees operate motor vehicles. The requirements imposed in the public authority cases are sometimes explained by pointing out that the intention of Parliament and the nature of the duties was always the basis of the tort (as Lord Jauncey said in *Hague* (170)), or by saying that the cases in which liability had been found involved statutes that aimed to protect people against dangers of personal injury (as Lord Bridge said in *Hague* (159)). They have been explained by saying that an action for damages arises only where a statutory duty is 'very limited and specific as opposed to general administrative functions imposed on public bodies' (*X v Bedfordshire County Council* [1995] 2 AC 633, 731–2 (Lord Browne-Wilkinson). But the key is that the point of the factory safety rules and the traffic regulations was not to enable factory owners

6   See *Groves v Lord Wimborne* [1898] 2 QB 402, *London Transport Board v Upson* [1949] AC 155.

and drivers to operate schemes for the public good; it was to control the special harms that arise from the operation of factories and vehicles, in a way that would protect the potential victims. In that context, a right to compensation may promote that statutory purpose of imposing a duty. It is one thing to make factory owners liable to compensate injured workers for breach of statutory duty, when a statute requires them to protect workers from the factory's dangerous machines. It is another thing to make government inspectors of factories compensate injured workers for breach of statutory duty, when a statute requires them to help the workers by inspecting factories.

In *O'Rourke v Camden* [1998] AC 188, the plaintiff sought compensation for breach of a statutory duty to provide accommodation; his action was struck out because the court was not prepared to supplement the duty to provide accommodation with a duty to provide compensation for a failure to provide accommodation. Provision of a social welfare scheme by Parliament does not mean provision of compensation to those who do not receive the benefits they should have received.

From the claimant's point of view, you may think that the social welfare scheme is frustrated if there is no remedy for a failure to provide the benefit. But the point of the benefit is *not* to confer a right on the claimant that calls for compensation if it is not delivered. In *Cocks v Thanet DC* [1983] 2 AC 286, Lord Bridge had suggested that once a housing authority decided to exercise its discretion in favour of giving a person housing, that created a private law right enforceable in an ordinary claim: 'Once a decision has been reached by the housing authority which gives rise to [a duty to provide housing], rights and obligations are immediately created in the field of private law. Each of the duties referred to, once established, is capable of being enforced by injunction and the breach of it will give rise to a liability in damages' (292–3). But the House of Lords has departed from that view: Lord Hoffmann decided in *O'Rourke* that 'the breach of statutory duty of which the plaintiff complains gives rise to no cause of action in private law', whether the housing authority had decided to give temporary housing or not (197).

Striking out

Public authority defendants in tort claims often argue that they have no liability to the claimant *even if* all the allegations of fact in the claim are proven to be true. The civil procedure rules allow a defendant to ask the court before trial to strike out the claim, if the statement of case 'discloses no reasonable grounds' for bringing the claim (Rule 3.4(2)). Like *O'Rourke*, many of the cases in this chapter were decided before trial on a motion to strike a claim (see also *X v Bedfordshire* [1995] 2 AC 633). The court will only strike out a claim if there is no realistic chance that liability will be established if all the facts alleged in the claim are proven; it has long been established that a claim will not be struck out unless there is no 'real point of difficulty that requires judicial decision' (Lord Abinger CB in *Deare v Attorney-General* (1835) 1 Y & C Ex 197, 208), and the judges are especially hesitant to strike out a claim in negligence against a public authority, because it is especially important to understand the facts: see *Barrett v Enfield* [2001] 2 AC 550, 557.

14.4 Negligence

The 'tort of negligence' is the lawyer's way of referring to a liability that the common law imposes on you to compensate someone who suffers loss because you wrongly failed to look out for their interests. But you have no legal responsibility to look out for all the interests that everyone has. A 'duty of care' is a responsibility to take reasonable steps to look out for someone else's interest; failure to do so supports a negligence claim, if loss results from the failure. Identifying the duties of care owed by public authorities may be the most difficult and complex problem in public law.

The easy part is that public authorities are liable for their negligence just like anyone else. If you are run down by a careless driver, or injured by a surgeon's carelessness, it does not matter at all whether the driver or the surgeon was acting in a private capacity or on behalf of a public authority. Either way, you have the very same right of compensation (from the person whose carelessness caused your injury, and from their employer). '. . . [T]he owners of a National Health Service Hospital owe precisely the same duty of care to their patients as do the owners of a private hospital and they owe it because of the common law of negligence and not because they happen to be operating under statutory provisions' (Lord Jauncey in *X v Bedfordshire County Council*, 729).

The difficulties arise with the public authorities whose purpose is to care for people (the best examples are the emergency services, education authorities, the National Health Service, and social services). When a claimant suffers from violent crime, or from a failed education, or from abuse by parents or foster parents, he or she may look for redress from the public authorities that were set up to combat that very harm. The claim will be based on an allegation that the harm would not have been suffered if the authority had taken reasonable care in performing its statutory function.

That allegation by itself, even if it is substantiated, does not support a right of action. This is an important rule that arises from our third basic principle above (the principle that acting unlawfully is *not* in itself a tort):

> **Even if a public authority has failed to carry out a legal duty to care for a person, the public authority has no general liability to compensate a person who would have been better off if the authority had carried out its duty.**

What more does it take, than that the claimant would not have suffered a loss if the public authority had acted with reasonable care? Claims of this kind face two general problems: one is that there may be no reason for liability *to compensate*, even if a public authority carelessly fails to perform its public function. The second is that the courts have been wary of imposing a duty of care in a way that will distort the authority's approach to its public function.

14.4.1 The two problems: *East Suffolk Rivers*

In 1936, a spring tide and a gale broke a sea wall in East Suffolk, flooding a pasture. The rivers authority sent two men to repair the breach. It was an exercise in futility:

they did it so badly that the flood went on for 178 days, when it could have been repaired in two weeks if they had used reasonable skill. 'Studd, upon the instructions of Clark, started a quite ridiculous attempt to fill up the breach by throwing into it bags of clay...' (*East Suffolk Rivers Catchment Board v Kent* [1941] AC 74, 99 (Lord Romer)). The farmer sued the authority in negligence to recover losses that he would not have suffered if the authority had taken reasonable care.

The authority's men had behaved in a way that would come to be described as *Wednesbury* unreasonable (see p 44) just a few years later: they 'selected a method of repairing the respondents' wall...that no reasonable man would have adopted' (97). Yet the plaintiff lost. As Lord Romer put it, 'they cannot be made liable (if honest) for any damage that would have been avoided had they executed their discretion in a more reasonable way' (102). (Note that the parenthesis about honesty leaves room for the tort of **misfeasance in public office** (section 14.6).)

● *Pop Quiz* ●
Was the rivers authority's conduct unlawful in *East Suffolk Rivers*?

When *East Suffolk Rivers* was decided, it was already a well-settled legal principle that 'statutory powers must be exercised with reasonable care' (85), and that the claimant could recover damages for injury caused by the defendant's negligence. So how could the claimant lose?

One reason is that the judges were wary of imposing a duty of care that would interfere with the public authority's decision making. Lord Justice du Parcq in the Court of Appeal had warned of the 'inconvenience' of a court deciding a question 'involving consideration of matters of policy and striking a just balance between rival claims of efficiency and thrift' (102). Lord Porter pointed out that, faced with the liability the plaintiff was arguing for, a public authority would need to refuse to help, unless it was prepared to spend sufficient resources of money and management time to make sure that the job would be done carefully: 'no prudent authority could safely act at all except in a case where certainty of success at a limited cost could be guaranteed' (106). Taking reasonable care is only good sense, but in any organization, it is not necessarily good sense to *make sure* that reasonable care is taken by all the people involved in the organization. It is expensive. The House of Lords was not willing to make the public authority choose between facing that expense, and refusing to help landowners. The House of Lords' unwillingness to interfere with the public authority's decisions as to funding is a form of deference (see pp 235–6), and puts what I will call a '**deference limit**' on negligence liability.

But the deference limit is really secondary to another, more basic reason for the decision in *East Suffolk Rivers*. Negligence is not simply careless conduct that leaves the claimant worse off than if the defendant had been careful. A defendant will only be held liable in negligence if loss has been caused by the breach of a *duty of care to the claimant*. The House of Lords in *East Suffolk Rivers* held that the rivers authority had no legal duty to the plaintiff to improve his situation by preventing further flood damage. The authority had a duty to the public to use its statutory powers to fight floods, but its only legal duty to the plaintiff was to take care not to make things worse. Even though the authority's workers were at fault, and the loss would not have been suffered if they had not been at fault, the House of Lords was not prepared to hold the authority responsible for compensating the plaintiff. Parliament had created an agency to help people like the plaintiff; imposing liability for failing to prevent flood damage would have added *another* support: a compensation scheme. 'The justice of the common law', as Justice Byles called it in *Cooper*, does not require such compensation (although of course Parliament could create such a scheme). If a helpful neighbour had tried to help and made a ridiculous failure of it, the neighbour would not be liable for the loss caused by the failure. Even though the rivers authority was created to prevent flood damage, it was no more liable to compensate than a neighbour would have been.

The crucial point to keep in mind is that even though it was wrong for the rivers authority to act as it did, justice may not require compensation for the wrong. When negligence liability does arise, the rationale for it is that justice demands not only that a defendant should look out for a person's interests, but also that a defendant should give compensation for a failure to do so. The House of Lords held in *East Suffolk Rivers* that justice required compensation for carelessly injuring the plaintiff, but not compensation for carelessly failing to help the plaintiff. That requirement limits the impact of negligence liability on public authorities. I will call it the '**justice ingredient**' in negligence liability.

We can state the justice ingredient and the deference limit in this way:

- **The justice ingredient:** Public authorities are only liable in negligence to the extent that the ordinary tort law principles of compensatory justice require it.

- **The deference limit:** The courts will avoid imposing a duty of care in a way that interferes with a public authority's exercise of its public functions.

Both the deference limit on negligence liability and the justice ingredient were controversial in *East Suffolk Rivers*; the following two sections address the ways in which the law on both issues has developed since. For now, notice why the deference limit is of secondary importance to the justice ingredient. The rivers authority *would* have been liable to compensate the plaintiff if the workers had made the flooding worse by carelessly breaking a wall. In that case, it would have been no answer for the authority to say that negligence liability would interfere with the way in which the authority carried out its public function. The concern not to interfere with the authority's function simply vanishes if a public authority carelessly injures someone; the deference limit is a reason for the courts to be cautious in imposing liability when a public authority carelessly misses an opportunity to help someone.

The justice ingredient and the deference limit in other torts

The justice ingredient and the deference limit are features of tort liability *in general*. Negligence law is challenging because it poses special difficulties in working out what those criteria require. *Entick* and *Cooper* were good decisions (i) because justice demanded compensation for the loss caused, *and* (ii) because the defendants' arguments in *both* cases that the courts should defer to a government official were bad arguments.

In claims based on statutory liability, the justice ingredient is that the claimant has a right to compensation because Parliament conferred it. So *O'Rourke v Camden* (see p 520) was a decision that the justice ingredient *for compensation* is lacking, when a public authority fails to give a person housing that a statute required. Justice requires that the benefit be provided,[7] but does not demand compensation for a failure to provide it in the past. The deference limit operates in these claims, to the extent that the courts should defer to other public authorities in assessing what counts as proper fulfilment of the duty imposed by the statute.

We will see that in the tort of misfeasance in public office, the defendant's bad faith provides the justice ingredient. And the court does not need to defer to the judgment of a defendant public authority that was acting in bad faith.

14.4.2 The justice ingredient in negligence

It may seem odd that a public authority with a statutory duty to care for people has no 'duty of care' to use its powers to benefit the people in question—as if it were o.k. for a public authority to be careless in performing its functions. Of course, that is not o.k. If an applicant for a housing benefit is entitled to it under a statute, and someone in the office carelessly drops the application behind a radiator, the local authority will be in breach of its statutory duties to consider the application, and to award the benefit. But a breach of those duties is not the same as the breach of a duty of care to a potential victim that gives rise to liability in negligence. A duty in public law is a reason for a public authority to do something regardless of the reasons of policy the authority may have for wanting to do otherwise. A duty of care is not *simply* a reason for someone to take care for someone else's interests, but also a reason for compensating that person for loss caused by a failure to take care. So:

- a duty of care is *owed to* a particular person or persons. A duty in public law is not owed to particular persons; and[8]

- the breach of a duty of care gives rise to a right to damages, if the breach causes loss. Even when it is unlawful for a public authority to exercise its powers in a way that is *Wednesbury* unreasonable, a person injured does not necessarily have any right to compensation.

Donoghue v Stevenson [1932] AC 562 was the first attempt by an English judge to state the justice ingredient in negligence liability. Lord Atkin offered a 'general conception

---

7 Remember that in a case like *O'Rourke*, judicial review is available to seek an order requiring the public authority to provide the benefit.

8 It is 'owed to the Crown' as Lord Reid and Lord Diplock put it in *Home Office v Dorset Yacht* [1970] AC 1004, 1030.

of relations giving rise to a duty of care':

> ❛ You must take reasonable care to avoid acts or omissions which you can rea-
> sonably foresee would be likely to injure your neighbour. Who, then, in law is
> my neighbour? The answer seems to be—persons who are so closely and directly
> affected by my act that I ought reasonably to have them in contemplation as being
> so affected when I am directing my mind to the acts or omissions which are called
> in question. ❜ (581)

Lord Atkin warned against making a general rule of liability out of his famous
attempt to explain the justice ingredient,[9] and it is easy to see why. Applied to decisions of public authorities, that 'neighbour principle' seems to require compensation whenever a public authority carelessly fails to use a statutory power to benefit
a claimant who is so directly affected that a reasonable public authority would have
them in mind. Although he was cautious about the generality of his principle, Lord
Atkin certainly meant to create a wide-ranging basis for the duty of care. And in *East
Suffolk Rivers* itself, Lord Atkin in his dissent suggested that the decision in *Donoghue v
Stevenson* required that the public authority should be liable for its careless failure to
help the plaintiff (*East Suffolk Rivers*, 92).

Since *Donoghue v Stevenson*, English courts have made progressive (though
uneven) attempts to control and to restrict the reach of Lord Atkin's principle. It
does not provide a general guide to negligence liability. Landmark cases on liability of public authorities have helped to shape the development. Lord Atkin's defeat
in *East Suffolk Rivers* was the first such case; the second was *Home Office v Dorset Yacht*.
The plaintiff brought an action in negligence, alleging that officers from a Borstal
(a young offenders institution) had carelessly failed to keep custody of seven boys
who damaged the plaintiff's yacht. The House of Lords held that if the officers' custody of the boys caused a manifest risk that the boys would damage the plaintiff's
property, the officers owed the plaintiff a duty to take reasonable care to prevent the
boys from doing so. Lord Diplock held that Lord Atkin's statement of the neighbour
principle in *Donoghue v Stevenson* could not apply generally to all allegations of negligence: 'misused as a universal it is manifestly false' (1060). But there was no agreement in the House of Lords as to how to contain the principle: Lord Reid held that
the neighbour principle ought to be applied unless there is some reason to exclude
liability.

The House of Lords took Lord Reid's approach in the next public authority landmark, *Anns v Merton* [1978] AC 728. A homeowner brought a claim in negligence to
recover a loss in the value of a house, after the defendant local authority's building
inspectors had carelessly failed to spot a mistake by the builder. Lord Wilberforce

---

[9]   '... it is of particular importance to guard against the danger of stating propositions of law in
wider terms than is necessary. . . . it is very necessary in considering reported cases in the law of
torts that the actual decision alone should carry authority' (*Donoghue v Stevenson*, 583–4).

offered a two-stage test based on *Donoghue v Stevenson*:

> ' First one has to ask whether, as between the alleged wrongdoer and the person who has suffered damage there is a sufficient relationship of proximity or neighbourhood such that, in the reasonable contemplation of the former, carelessness on his part may be likely to cause damage to the latter—in which case a prima facie duty of care arises. Secondly, . . . it is necessary to consider whether there are any considerations which ought to negative, or to reduce or limit the scope of the duty or the class of person to whom it is owed or the damages to which a breach of it may give rise. ' (751–2)

As the House of Lords found no special reason *not* to award damages, the *prima facie* liability under Lord Atkin's principle led to an award of damages against the local authority.

That remarkable decision changed the shape of the negligence liability of public authorities for some time. It amounted to a decision that the justice ingredient can be satisfied simply by foreseeability of damage, and proximity between defendant and claimant (and Lord Wilberforce suggested that proximity arose from foreseeability). The defendant in *Anns* was held liable for failing to help the plaintiff, and that is impossible to reconcile with the ruling with *East Suffolk Rivers*. In *Anns*, Lord Wilberforce suggested that the House of Lords in *East Suffolk Rivers* had not yet fully digested the implications of *Donoghue v Stevenson*, so that they had not yet recognized 'the conception of a general duty of care, not limited to particular accepted situations, but extending generally over all relations of sufficient proximity, and even pervading the sphere of statutory functions of public bodies' (757).

That 'general duty of care' has not survived: even if the requirements of foreseeability and proximity are met, there needs to be additional reason to impose liability. Lord Keith began the change in approach in two Privy Council cases on negligence of public authorities, *Rowling v Takaro* [1988] AC 473 ('a too literal application' of Lord Wilberforce's two-stage test was not the right way to decide 'whether it is appropriate that a duty of care should be imposed' (501)), and *Yuen Kun Yeu v Attorney-General of Hong Kong* [1988] 1 AC 175 ('the two-stage test in *Anns v Merton* is not to be regarded as in all circumstances a suitable guide to the existence of a duty of care' (194)). But the idea that foreseeability and proximity create a *prima facie* duty of care was really laid to rest in a case on the liability of auditors, *Caparo v Dickman* [1990] 2 AC 605. Since 1990, the House of Lords has consistently stood by Lord Bridge's conclusion in *Caparo* that another ingredient was required besides foreseeability of loss and proximity between the claimant and defendant. Even if those requirements are met, no duty of care arises *unless* it is 'fair, just and reasonable that the law should impose a duty of a given scope upon the one party for the benefit of the other' (*Caparo*, 618). Lord Bridge also insisted on identifying duties of care incrementally, by reference to established situations in which they have been imposed, rather than by applying a general principle.

For our purposes, *Caparo* raises a simple question (which has no simple answer). Is it fair, just, and reasonable to impose a common law duty on a public authority to carry out its statutory role in a way that will benefit a claimant? *Caparo* does not answer the question. The House of Lords departed from *Anns* in *Murphy v Brentwood* [1991] 1 AC 398, but they decided *Murphy* on the issue of liability for economic loss. They expressed no view as to whether the local authority owed a duty of care. The impact of *Anns* was narrowed by *Murphy* and *Caparo*, but the possibility survived that a public authority might be liable in negligence for a careless failure to help the claimant.

In *Stovin v Wise* [1996] AC 923, though, Lord Hoffmann cast doubt on Lord Wilberforce's reasoning in *Anns*. In *Stovin*, a county council had decided to use its statutory power to cut away a bank from a roadside to improve visibility at a dangerous junction in a highway. But the council had done nothing to pursue the plan, when the plaintiff was injured in an accident on the highway. The defendant driver claimed that the council breached a duty of care to the plaintiff by failing to follow through on its plan to remove the bank. For the majority, Lord Hoffmann concluded that Lord Wilberforce had offered no rationale for imposing a duty of care, except his argument that the deference limit does not *forbid* liability. So Lord Hoffmann concluded that *Anns* offered no way of meeting the requirement of a justice ingredient:

> ' Upon what principles can one say of a public authority that not only did it have a duty in public law to consider the exercise of the power but that it would thereupon have been under a duty in private law to act, giving rise to a claim in compensation against public funds for its failure to do so? ' (950)

Perhaps Lord Wilberforce thought that proximity itself is the justice ingredient, and that the power to inspect in *Anns* generated a duty of care because it put the inspectors in that relationship of proximity to the homeowners (by giving the inspectors a responsibility to help the homeowners). That is the approach that *Caparo* abandoned. But *Caparo* did not concern public authorities, and *Stovin* represents Lord Hoffmann's solution to the question of the justice ingredient in public authority cases: before a public authority can be liable for carelessly failing to use its statutory power to benefit the claimant, there must be 'exceptional grounds for holding that the policy of the statute requires compensation to be paid to persons who suffer loss because the power was not exercised'. In *East Suffolk Rivers*, the House of Lords was never so explicit, and Lord Hoffmann pushes the reasoning of that case further in *Stovin*:

> ' It is one thing to provide a service at the public expense. It is another to require the public to pay compensation when a failure to provide the service has resulted in loss.... Before imposing such an additional burden, the courts should be satisfied that this is what Parliament intended. ' (954)

The logic is that because it was Parliament that created the service (to fight floods, or to remove dangers from roads), the courts should leave it to Parliament to decide whether to create a right to compensation, too.

Lord Hoffmann still distinguished between the tort of breach of statutory duty, and a cause of action in negligence for failure to use a statutory power. The distinction is unclear: unlike the former, the latter is 'not exactly a question of construction [of the statute], because the cause of action does not arise out of the statute itself. But the policy of the statute is nevertheless a crucial factor in the decision' (952). Yet the policy of the statute can only be identified by construction of the statute. Lord Hoffmann, though, does not apologize for the apparent lack of a distinction between the tort of breach of statutory duty, and liability for a careless failure to use a statutory power to benefit a claimant: 'If the policy of the Act is not to create a statutory liability to pay compensation, the same policy should ordinarily exclude the existence of a common law duty of care' (953). The view that emerges is that it is *not* fair, just, and reasonable (in the terms of *Caparo*) to hold a public authority liable to compensate a claimant for carelessly failing to use its powers to benefit the claimant.

In spite of his radical disagreement with Lord Wilberforce's reasoning, Lord Hoffmann did not actually depart from the result in *Anns*. He said that the main ground of that decision was 'general reliance'—a widespread assumption in a community that a power will be exercised with reasonable care. So an assumption that a statutory power of safety inspection will be exercised with reasonable care may ground a duty of care (*Stovin v Wise*, 954). General reliance is *not* reliance—as least, the claimant need not have relied on the public authority taking care. 'General reliance' is best understood as a label for the judges' conclusion that the justice ingredient is supplied by some special responsibility of the public authority to take care in a particular context.

Failing such a special responsibility (and it is not clear what is required for a special responsibility), the inexorable logic of *Stovin* suggests that there is no negligence liability for a failure to help the claimant. But there is still a catch. Think about the liability of a doctor employed by a public authority. There is no doubt that a doctor who carelessly injures a patient is liable in negligence (and the public authority is vicariously liable). That is consistent with *East Suffolk Rivers*. But suppose a doctor attends an emergency, and carelessly fails to provide successful treatment, when any reasonable doctor would have healed the patient. It seems that the doctor is in the same position as the authority in *East Suffolk Rivers*: the doctor has carelessly failed to help the claimant, but has not harmed the claimant. Yet the judges want to say that there was a breach of the duty of care that a doctor owes to a patient. In *Phelps v Hillingdon* [2001] 2 AC 619, the House of Lords held that doctors had such a duty to take care, and the Law Lords extended it to educational psychologists, and even to teachers. Lord Slynn stated that the *Caparo* 'fair, just and reasonable' criterion was met in *Phelps* because:

> ❛ it is long and well-established, now elementary, that persons exercising a particular skill or profession may owe a duty of care in the performance to people who it can be foreseen will be injured if due skill and care are not exercised...A doctor, an accountant and an engineer are plainly such a person. So in my view is an educational psychologist or psychiatrist and a teacher including a teacher in a specialised area, such as a teacher concerned with children having special educational needs. ❜ (654)

Can that well-established form of liability be reconciled with the basic principle of *East Suffolk Rivers*, as extended by Lord Hoffmann in *Stovin*? Perhaps the special professional responsibility of a doctor or psychologist provides the justice ingredient. And conversely, perhaps the dependence and vulnerability of the claimant provide the justice ingredient in a way that distinguishes a patient in a medical emergency, or the schoolgirl in *Phelps*, from the plaintiffs in *East Suffolk Rivers* and *Stovin*.[10] In any case, the special liability of professionals such as doctors meets Lord Bridge's constraint in *Caparo*, that duties of care should be extended incrementally from established situations of duty. But that approach means that the courts have given up on Lord Atkin's impulse to generalize: the ways of meeting the justice requirement are various and are not explained by a single principle.

> ### Examples of the justice ingredient for negligence liability:
>
> **Making things worse:** in *East Suffolk Rivers* justice *would* have required compensation if the authority had carelessly made the flooding worse (but not if the authority carelessly fails to improve the situation). In *Dorset Yacht* justice might require compensation if the borstal officers created the danger to the yacht by bringing the boys to the island.
>
> **The 'normal professional duty of care'** (as Lord Browne-Wilkinson called it in *X v Bedfordshire County Council* [1995] 2 AC 633, 771). *Phelps*, too, held that justice may require compensation if professionals fail to carry out a special responsibility to provide help to the people they serve.
>
> **Reliance:** justice may require compensation if the plaintiffs relied on the public authority to help them. There was no reliance in *East Suffolk Rivers* or *Anns v Merton*. Suppose that the plaintiffs in those cases could have taken measures of their own, but decided not to because they reasonably believed that there was no need, as the authority was dealing with the problem (by setting out to end the flooding, or to prevent bad construction work). Then the plaintiff's case in *East Suffolk Rivers* would presumably have had the justice ingredient, and *Anns* would not have been a controversial case.[11]
>
> **General reliance:** justice may require compensation if there is a general pattern of reliance on a public authority's role in protecting people from some harm (even if *the claimant* does not rely): *Stovin v Wise*, Lord Hoffmann at 954).

14.4.3 The deference limit

In *X v Bedfordshire County Council*, the House of Lords faced a series of unprecedented negligence claims. Several children sought damages in negligence (1) against child

---

[10]   See Lord Nicholls in *Phelps* at 666.

[11]   For a case of reliance, see *Swinney v Chief Constable of Northumbria Police Force* [1997] QB 464: if the police take evidence from a witness, they owe a duty of care to keep the witness's identity safe from criminals, because in communicating with the police, the witness has relied on their taking responsibility for the confidentiality of information (486).

protection authorities for carelessly taking a child into care in one case, and for carelessly failing to take children into care in five other cases, and (2) against education authorities for failing to assess special education needs carefully. The question was whether the child protection authorities and the education authorities could owe a duty of care to the children. Lord Browne-Wilkinson approached it by pointing out that they could not be liable for doing what Parliament had authorized. If Parliament has given a discretion—that is, lawful authorization to act one way or another (see p 233)—neither way of acting can be a tort. Since the statutes in X gave the authorities discretion as to how their duties were to be performed, Lord Browne-Wilkinson held that the authorities could not be liable in negligence unless 'the decision complained of is so unreasonable that it falls outside the ambit of the discretion conferred upon the local authority' ([1995] 2 AC 736, relying on Lord Reid's speech in *Dorset Yacht*, 1031). He added that if the issues relevant to the exercise of the discretion included 'matters of policy' that are not justiciable, the court would not be able to reach the conclusion that the action was outside the ambit of the discretion (738). Finally, he held that even if there is no defence that an action was within a statutory discretion, the court will not impose a duty of care in the exercise of a statutory duty or power if it would inappropriately interfere with the authority's functions.

Following Lord Browne-Wilkinson's influential speech in X, we can say that the courts have three ways of limiting claims that a public authority has negligently exercised a statutory power:

- the rule that discretion gives a defence of statutory authorization;

- the rule that the court will not be able hold that there is no defence of statutory authorization if the issues are non-justiciable; and

- the rule that the court will not impose a duty of care that improperly interferes with the authority's performance of its functions (X 748–9).

All three rules require the courts defer to public authorities in identifying a duty of care.

Discretion

Lord Browne-Wilkinson's idea that a lawful exercise of discretion cannot be a breach of a duty of care was not new. In *Dorset Yacht*, the House of Lords had made it clear that that there could be no negligence liability if a boy escaped as a result of 'a system of relaxed control intentionally adopted by the Home Office as conducive to the reformation of trainees' (Lord Diplock, 1068). Similarly, for all the controversies over *Anns*, it is uncontroversial that the local authority would not have been liable if the faulty foundations had gone undetected because the local authority reduced the number of inspections for reasons of cost. The court would defer to the local authority's decision as to how many inspections it could carry out, rather than being prepared to hold that an insufficient number of inspections was a breach of a duty of care. So the defence of statutory authorization includes deference to a public authority's discretionary decisions.

Yet cases since X have cast doubt on the idea. In *Barrett v Enfield LBC* (2001) 2 AC 550, both Lord Slynn and Lord Hutton said that the fact that an action is taken in the exercise of a discretion does not mean that no duty of care can arise. They suggested that it is only when non-justiciable considerations are at stake (see below) that a duty of care is excluded. Lord Hutton said that X did not preclude 'a ruling in the present case that although the decisions of the defendant were within the ambit of its statutory discretion, nevertheless those decisions did not involve the balancing of the type of policy considerations which renders the decisions non-justiciable' (585). And in *Phelps*, Lord Slynn said that he could not accept Lord Browne-Wilkinson's statement that 'an educational authority owes no common law duty of care in the exercise of the powers and discretions relating to children with special educational needs' (657–8).

After *Phelps* and *Barrett*, X can no longer be relied on for the proposition that educational and social services professionals have no private law duty to take care in making decisions as to children's special education needs, or in making child welfare decisions. And in *D v East Berkshire NHS Trust* [2005] UKHL 23, the Law Lords were clearly of the view that there can be such a duty of care (though they held that there is no duty of care to the parents). But it is possible to explain the cases after X simply as extending what Lord Browne-Wilkinson called the 'normal professional duty of care' (X, 771). He had held that that duty only applied if the public authority was providing the service of the professional to the claimant, and not if the professional was advising the public authority on the exercise of its powers. That distinction has not survived the later cases.[12] But the cases do not abolish the rule that a public authority cannot be held liable in tort for doing what Parliament gave it discretion to do.

Having a discretionary power, and having a discretion (see p 233):

The fact that a power is discretionary does not mean that there can be no negligence liability for using it carelessly (though the justiciability rule and the rule against inappropriately interfering with public functions (below) protect some exercises of discretionary powers from negligence liability). A local authority deciding whether to take a child into care exercises a *discretionary power* (that is, a power to make choices that are not entirely determined by law). But it has no *discretion* to make the decision on the basis of a bribe, or on racist grounds, or on the basis of careless professional advice... If a public authority has a discretion to do A or B, there can be no negligence liability for doing either A or B (see *Barrett v Enfield*, 571). The distinction is hard to remember, because judges often use the word 'discretion' to mean 'discretionary power'.

Justiciability

Lord Wilberforce in *Anns* distinguished between policy decisions and operational decisions, concluding that 'It can safely be said that the more "operational" a power

---

[12] See *Phelps*, 654 (Lord Slynn).

or duty may be, the easier it is to superimpose upon it a common law duty of care' (754). Lord Wilberforce said that the courts call questions of 'policy' questions of 'discretion', but Lord Browne-Wilkinson treated 'policy' questions as non-justiciable questions in X (737). Similarly, in *Rowling v Takaro* [1988] AC 473, Lord Keith said that Lord Wilberforce's distinction between policy and operation, while not a 'touchstone of liability', was a reminder that the courts should not impose a duty of care in 'cases in which the decision under attack is of such a kind that a question whether it has been made negligently is unsuitable for judicial resolution' (501).

> **Jargon alert**
>
> 'Non-justiciable' means, as Lord Keith put it, 'unsuitable for judicial resolution'. But a question can be more or less suitable for judicial resolution (see p 241). The issues that Lord Wilberforce called 'policy' issues are issues on which judges ought to defer to an administrative authority's judgment to some degree. They are not necessarily issues that judges simply must not consider.

The distinction between policy and operation has often been criticized.[13] Sometimes the criticism has been that it is a vague distinction, but the law needs to draw many vague distinctions, and we cannot expect any sharp distinction between acts on which courts should and should not superimpose a duty of care. The more potent criticism, voiced by Lord Hoffmann in *Stovin v Wise*, is that even when a public authority's action is clearly operational, that fact gives no reason in itself to superimpose a duty of care. But in spite of various notes of caution, and Lord Hoffmann's withering attack, the judges have not quite abandoned Lord Wilberforce's distinction as a way of describing acts of public authorities that are challenged in a negligence action.[14] Perhaps the best sense we can make both of *Anns* and of the continuing use of the distinction is simply this: there is reason for judges *not* to impose liability on a public authority for carelessly making a bad decision, when judges cannot assess the relevant considerations. That is, the policy/operation distinction is best understood as a way of describing the justiciability rule in X. Lord Browne-Wilkinson made something useful of the distinction in X by turning it into a way of stating the rule that a duty of care cannot be imposed if doing so would demand judicial assessment of non-justiciable considerations.

Which considerations are non-justiciable? As in *Council of Civil Service Unions v Ministers for the Civil Service* [1985] Ac 374 on control of discretion (see p 238), the judges have given some suggestive examples, but no full explanation. The examples include those of Lord Browne-Wilkinson in X: 'social policy, the allocation of finite financial resources between the different calls made upon them or (as in *Dorset Yacht*) the balance between pursuing desirable social aims as against the risk to the public inherent in so doing' (737). Perhaps the nearest thing to an explanation of the idea

---

[13]   See, e.g., Lord Nicholls' speeches in *Stovin v Wise* (938), and in *Phelps* (666).

[14]   Lord Slynn said in *Phelps* that there was 'some validity' in the distinction (658).

of justiciability is Lord Diplock's attempt to say why a court should not hold that it is a breach of a duty of care to decide to adopt a system of relaxed control of young offenders in a Borstal:

> The material relevant to the assessment of the reformative effect upon train-ees of release under supervision or of any relaxation of control while still under detention is not of a kind which can be satisfactorily elicited by the adversary pro-cedure and rules of evidence adopted in English courts of law or of which judges (and juries) are suited by their training and experience to assess the probative value. (1067)

Justicability is complex. It is not only a matter of the expertise or knowledge of judges; it is also a matter of the suitability of the 'adversary procedure and rules of evidence' for deciding an issue. And most important of all is a problem that Lord Diplock hints at but does not state: the problem of political responsibility. By requiring due pro-cess, and giving effect to legal entitlements to benefits, and being prepared to quash corrupt decisions, the courts affect the implementation of social policy, spending policy, and national security policy. But they can do so with no breach of **comity** (see p 17), because those forms of interference do not prevent the public authority in ques-tion from doing its job. But when the judges impose a duty to take reasonable care, they will breach the requirement of comity if they do not defer to the public author-ity's view as to what is reasonable. The judges should not assume the task of decid-ing which policies would be reasonable—and they should not take away other public authorities' political responsibility for those decisions.

Interfering with the functions of public authorities

Neither the discretion rule nor the justiciability rule has any application in *East Suffolk Rivers*. The plaintiff's complaint was against sheer incompetence, of a kind that was obvious even to judges. Even so, the court will not impose a duty of care, if it would inappropriately interfere with the work of the public authority.

The problem is nicely illustrated by *Alexandrou v Oxford* [1993] 4 All ER 328. The police had invited businesses to connect their burglar alarm to the police station to make it easier for the police to investigate break-ins. When the burglar alarm went off at Alexandrou's computer warehouse the police investigated, but Alexandrou alleged that they carelessly failed to find the burglars (who finished their burglary after the police left). The claim was struck out. For the striking out decision, it had to be assumed that the police officers acted carelessly in what Lord Wilberforce would have called a purely operational task. Even then, the courts would not impose a duty of care: if the police became liable to provide compensation for the consequences of a failure to respond carefully to an alarm, they would have to abandon the scheme of connecting burglar alarms to the police station unless they could afford to pro-vide crime victims with insurance against carelessness by police officers. An initia-tive that improves policing might have to be dropped, if the courts added a duty to operate the scheme carefully. The same problem affected the decision in *East Suffolk Rivers Catchment Board v Kent* [1941] AC 74:

> ❛ A local authority faced by such a series of disasters as occurred in the present case might consider that the flooded land was not very valuable, but that they were justified in making an attempt to clear it of water provided the expense was not serious, and think that the expenditure of some small sum would not be too great in an attempt to prevent the damage.... If the respondents be right such a decision could never be made safely. ❜ (Lord Porter, 106)

It is expensive even to take steps to avoid purely operational carelessness. So to avoid interfering with good decision making about flood control, the court had to find no liability even for incompetence.

We can put X itself in the same category as *East Suffolk Rivers* and *Alexandrou*, because the House of Lords did not strike out any of the claims on the grounds that non-justiciable issues arose, or that it was clear that the plaintiffs would not be able to prove that the public authorities acted outside the ambit of their discretion. The claims[15] were struck out because it was not reasonable to impose a duty of care. It would distort the authorities' performance of their statutory functions, and imposing a duty of care would depart from the 'incremental' approach of *Caparo* (X, 751). Since X, the law has moved forward incrementally, and the 'normal professional duty of care' has been extended in *Phelps* and *Barrett*. But the House of Lords has not abandoned the principle that a duty of care should not be imposed if it will interfere with a public authority's service to the public interest: in *D v East Berkshire NHS Trust* [2005] UKHL 23, in decisions whether to take a child into care, the House of Lords refused to impose on social workers a duty of care *to parents*, on the ground that it would interfere with the critical need for the social workers to attend to the interests of children, where there was reason to think that they might need to be taken into care.[16]

14.4.4 Good interference? Turning the deference limit on its head

By not helping the plaintiff in *East Suffolk Rivers*, the rivers authority was by the same token failing to accomplish its public purpose. If the public purpose was to protect flood victims, and a duty of care in negligence is only a duty to meet the standard of care that can reasonably be expected of flood control workers, wouldn't the imposition of a duty of care *improve* the public authority's conformity to its public purpose? It may seem that this is like *Entick*: the private law of tort can support the public law requirement that the public authority should not perform its role in a way that is *Wednesbury* unreasonable.

---

[15]   That is, all the claims in negligence except the claims in the special education cases based on the 'normal professional duty of care'.

[16]   See also *Jain v Trent Strategic Health Authority* [2007] EWCA Civ 1186.

Lord Reid in *Dorset Yacht* rejected the idea that duties of care would induce public authorities to make bad decisions: 'Her Majesty's servants are made of sterner stuff' (1032).[17] In *Phelps*, Lord Slynn held that it would only be in exceptional circumstances that 'liability on the part of the authority may so interfere with the performance of the local education authority's duties that it would be wrong to recognise any liability' (653).

And occasionally, judges have taken the more positive view that imposing duties of care may *improve* the performance of a public function. So Lord Nicholls, in a vigorous dissent in *Stovin v Wise*, said, 'if the existence of a duty of care..., in the shape of a duty to act as a reasonable authority, has a salutary effect on tightening administrative procedures and avoiding another needless road tragedy, this must be in the public interest' (941). And in *X* itself, Lord Bingham MR in the Court of Appeal had said, 'I cannot accept, as a general proposition, that the imposition of a duty of care makes no contribution to the maintenance of high standards' (662). Lord Browne-Wilkinson rejected that approach, but Lord Slynn in *Barrett* approved Lord Bingham's remark, and also the view of Lord Justice Evans in the Court of Appeal in *Barrett*, that there was no reason 'why the law in the public interest should not require these standards to be observed' (*Barrett*, 568).

So the judges are divided over whether they should try to use duties of care to improve public services. No uniform, general approach emerges from the cases. That is not just a reflection of judicial disagreement. It also reflects the fact that the ways in which duties of care may affect administrative decisions will vary widely depending on the nature of the duty of care, and the context in which it operates. There is certainly good reason to doubt that duties of care are generally an appropriate way of improving administrative effectiveness: as Lord Hoffmann said in *Stovin*, 'there must be better ways of doing this than by compensating insurance companies out of public funds' (955). In the cases of *Alexandrou* and *East Suffolk Rivers*, since public authorities cannot guarantee that their employees will act carefully, liability for carelessness may make it too costly for them to take on the risk of making a reasonable attempt to help someone. It may be very important, if their public function is to be carried out effectively, for them to be able to take that risk without being prevented by a duty to act carefully. But cases like *Phelps* and *Barrett* are different: in those cases, a public authority could not avoid a liability by deciding not to provide a service, and then (as long as the courts remember the discretion rule, and do not impose misconceived standards of care) there is little danger of disrupting good administration by imposing a duty to make decisions with reasonable care.

Emergency services

The police, in criminal investigations, have no duty of care in negligence law to people who might be injured by a criminal who is still at large: in *Hill v Chief Constable*

---

[17] But Lord Reid did not abandon the discretion rule: if a body was exercising a discretion, he said, there would be no liability unless the discretion was 'exercised so carelessly or unreasonably that there has been no real exercise of the discretion' (1031).

of *West Yorkshire* [1989] AC 53, the House of Lords struck out a claim against the police for negligence in failing to stop the Yorkshire Ripper after they had evidence as to his identity. But the police have no immunity from negligence liability (*Swinney v Chief Constable of Northumbria Police Force* [1997] QB 464).

Fire Brigades have a statutory duty to provide efficient fire-fighting services (Fire Services Act 1947), but 'are not under a common law duty to answer the call for help, and are not under a duty to take care to do so. If, therefore, they fail to turn up, or fail to turn up in time, because they have carelessly misunderstood the message, got lost on the way or run into a tree, they are not liable' (*Capital & Counties v Hampshire CC* [1997] QB 1004 (CA), 1030 (Stuart-Smith LJ), approved by Lord Hoffmann in *Gorringe v Calderdale MBC* [2004] UKHL 15 [32]).

● *Pop Quiz* ●

Can you reconcile *Hill* and *Capital & Counties* with *Kent v Griffiths* [1999] Lloyd's Rep Med 42, in which it was held that an **ambulance service** owes a duty of care to a person for whom an ambulance has been called?

14.4.5 Conclusion on negligence

In the Court of Appeal in the X case, Lord Bingham MR said that the first policy consideration in developing the law of negligence is that wrongs should be remedied. The House of Lords approved that view in X (Lord Browne-Wilkinson, 749). But Lord Bingham's comment can only apply to *legal* wrongs; a wrong is not to be righted by courts if the law does not recognize it as wrong (if, for example, Parliament has authorized it expressly or by giving a public authority discretion to do it, or if the court would need to pass judgment on non-justiciable issues in order to identify it as wrong). Most controversially, the judges disagree on whether it is their role to right a wrong, if doing so might distort the way in which a public authority exercises its functions. That is the point on which Lord Browne-Wilkinson departed from Lord Bingham's decision in the Court of Appeal in X. Since X, the House of Lords has come around to Lord Bingham's view on the particular question of social services' duties of care to children. But there is no general duty to use public powers with care.

Here we should return to the easy part of negligence liability: if you are run down because a truck driver for a public authority was not watching the road, it will do the authority no good at all to argue that negligence liability will create a drain on public funds, or that liability will distort the way in which it carries out its statutory powers. One way of explaining the difference between those easy cases and the controversial cases such as *East Suffolk Rivers* or *Stovin* is that a careless driver acting on behalf of a public authority causes harm, whereas the authorities in *East Suffolk Rivers* and *Stovin* only failed to provide to a private person a benefit that the authority was responsible for providing to the public. But that distinction (between carelessly causing harm, and carelessly failing to help) does not give a rigid division between situations in which public authorities do and do not have a duty of care, because of the 'normal professional duty of care' recognized in X and extended in *Phelps* and *Barrett*. In the professional duty of care cases, a public authority really is liable for loss caused by a careless failure to help the claimant. And in deciding whether to take a child from its parents, a public authority has no duty to the parents to take care before making a decision that harms them.

The complexity of the law can best be understood if we remember the basic principle of *Caparo*: that negligence liability does not arise unless it is reasonable to impose a duty of care. As Lord Blackburn said in *Geddis v Bann Reservoir Proprietors* (1878) 3 App Cas 430, 455–6, an action lies 'for doing that which the legislature has authorised, if it be done negligently'. That statement still holds good, but we need to remember that 'if it be done negligently' does not mean 'if it be done carelessly'. It means 'if it be done in breach of a duty of care'.

There is no more definite guide to identifying a duty of care than the following.

Summary on public authorities' duties of care:

- a duty of care cannot require a public authority not to act in a way in which it has been given **discretion** to act;
- a duty of care cannot arise if identifying it would require a court to pass judgment on **non-justiciable considerations**;
- a duty of care cannot arise unless there is a relation of **proximity**, and it is **foreseeable** that the loss in question will result if reasonable care is not taken;
- even if there is proximity and the loss is foreseeable, a duty of care cannot arise unless there is a further **justice ingredient**: it must be fair, just, and reasonable to impose the duty of care (the justice ingredient is to be identified 'incrementally' by analogy with previous cases);
- the judges will avoid imposing a duty of care if doing so would inappropriately **interfere with the functions of a public authority** (but imposing ordinary duties of care—e.g., to drive carefully and to perform surgery with reasonable care—is never an inappropriate interference;
- public authorities may be vicariously liable for failures by doctors and certain other professions to meet the **'normal professional duty of care'**;
- there may be circumstances in which a court will find that imposing a duty of care would **improve the public authority's exercise of its functions**.

Because of these principles,

- if a public authority had power to help the claimant, but carelessly failed to help the claimant, that is not enough for it to have breached a duty of care;
- but a public authority may breach a duty of care by carelessly failing to use its power to benefit a claimant, if it has a relation with the claimant that involves an **assumption of responsibility** toward the claimant, or if it has induced **reliance by the claimant**, or if there is **general reliance** on the public authority's reasonably careful performance of its functions.

● *Pop Quiz* ●

Can you find the authority for these propositions?

14.5 Misfeasance in public office: the administrative tort

Abuse of power is a ground of judicial review (see p 223). It also forms the basis of the one tort that is specifically public. It may be a tort (a tort of 'misfeasance', sometimes called 'malfeasance') for a public officer to act in a way that causes loss to the claimant, if the conduct is an abuse of the office. But abuse of power is not enough. A power may be abused by a very unreasonable decision, and that is not enough to count as a tort. There is a further requirement, which narrowly restricts the tort of misfeasance. The abuse of power must be done in bad faith.

If loss is caused by official abuse in bad faith, the claim has the justice ingredient, and can get past the deference limit. No deference is owed to the public officer if the court can identify an abuse (that is why abuse of power is a ground of judicial review of discretionary powers). And for centuries, the courts have held that justice requires compensation for a malicious abuse of power. In other torts it really does not matter whether the defendant is exercising public power. But a defendant can only be liable in the tort of misfeasance if the alleged misconduct was *in public office*.

So the tortious conduct must be conduct as a public officer. Suppose that a private person deliberately decides not to come forward with evidence that would convict an offender, and does so in the hope that the offender will injure you, and the offender is acquitted and does injure you. You have no right of action. But if the defendant is a public officer, the requirements of the tort would be satisfied by such an improper motive unless the alleged tortious conduct was completely independent of the public role of the officer in question (*Racz v Home Office* [1994] 2 AC 45, 53 (Lord Jauncey). The misfeasance need not be an exercise of a public law power (or even a legal power). The essential thing is that the defendant abused his or her position as a public officer (*Cornelius v Hackney LBC* [2002] EWCA Civ 1073).

Note that although misfeasance is a public tort, it is also a very *personal* tort. It is committed by particular human beings holding public office, not by public authorities. Yet the public authority is vicariously liable, as the result of a landmark decision of the House of Lords in *Racz*. The decision in *Racz* rejected an *obiter dictum* of Lord Bridge in *R v Deputy Governor of Parkhurst Prison, ex p Hague* [1992] 1 AC 58, that the prison governor and the Home Office cannot be vicariously liable for the tort of a prison officer who 'deliberately acts outside the scope of his authority' (*Hague*, 164). That statement would have ruled out vicarious liability for misfeasance altogether, since in every instance of misfeasance, the public officer deliberately acts outside the scope of authority. Since *Racz*, it is clear that the public authority is vicarious liable for 'a misguided and unauthorised method of performing [its officers'] authorised duties', though not for 'an unlawful frolic of their own' (*Racz*, 53).

You can see that this tort based on abuse of public office presents a tempting alternative for claimants who cannot succeed in negligence: if only they can persuade the court that the conduct that caused their loss was a malicious abuse of power, they have a right to compensation for loss caused. The claimant does not have to establish that the defendant owed a duty of care. The tort of misfeasance has come under heavy pressure from such claims. A public officer who has acted in bad faith deserves no deference, but the advance of this tort has created difficult questions of what counts as bad faith. So far, however, bad faith (which is, roughly, a legally bad attitude toward the claimant) remains as a restrictive requirement of the tort.

14.5.1 Malice and bad faith

The House of Lords identified two forms of the tort in *Three Rivers District Council v Bank of England* [2003] 2 AC 1, a landmark case based on the collapse of the Bank of Credit and Commerce International (BCCI) in 1991. Investors who had lost billions of pounds wanted compensation from the Bank of England. They claimed that the Bank of England, as the regulatory agency for banks, ought to have closed down BCCI before their money disappeared in massive frauds by BCCI officers. The investors had no claim in negligence: the Bank of England owed them no duty of care, but only a public law duty to use its regulatory powers lawfully. But the amounts at stake made it worth pursuing a difficult and groundbreaking claim in misfeasance in a public office.

The two forms of the tort identified by Lord Steyn in *Three Rivers* have two different 'mental elements'.[18] He calls the first 'targeted malice' (191); the second is bad faith in the sense of knowledge that the conduct in question is unlawful (or recklessness as to whether it is unlawful), plus knowledge that it will probably harm people in the position of the claimant (or recklessness as to whether it will harm such people). The unifying element in the two forms of the tort is, Lord Steyn said, 'abuse of power accompanied by subjective bad faith' (191). As Lord Millett and Lord Bingham have pointed out, the two forms of the tort can be unified by saying that the tort of misfeasance requires that 'the public officer was at least reckless whether such damage would be caused or not' (*Watkins v Home Office* [2006] UKHL 17 [22] (Lord Bingham). That recklessness is a form of bad faith.

What is subjective and what is objective?

A subjective test depends on the subject of the test (that is, the person whose conduct is being tested), and an objective test depends on the object (that is, on what the subject did). The standard of care in negligence law is objective (it is a question of whether the object (what the subject did) was reasonable). The standard of bad faith in misfeasance is subjective (it is a question of whether the subject whose conduct is being tested had a bad attitude). These confusing labels can be left out, by the way: it adds nothing to a mental element in a legal standard to call

---

[18] The two forms were suggested by Lord Diplock in *Dunlop v Woollahra* [1982] AC 158: 'in the absence of malice, passing without knowledge of its invalidity a resolution which is devoid of any legal effect is not conduct that of itself is capable of amounting to such "misfeasance" as is a necessary element in this tort' (172). The suggestion is that *either* malice *or* knowledge of unlawfulness would satisfy the mental element of the tort.

it 'subjective', because any mental element must be subjective (if an act is done with malice, for example, the malice is a feature of the subject).

So in Lord Steyn's phrase, 'subjective bad faith', the word 'subjective' should be read as just a reminder that when he says that the tort requires bad faith, he means that it is not enough for the claimant to show that the defendant did something unreasonable (even extremely unreasonable). The defendant is not liable unless he or she had a bad attitude as well.

There was no precedent for recklessness as a sufficient mental element for the tort, Lord Steyn said in *Three Rivers*, but he held that this 'organic development' in the law was appropriate because 'reckless indifference to consequences is as blameworthy as deliberately seeking such consequences' (192). That statement is too broad, because some acts, such as murder, are especially blameworthy just because they are deliberate. Yet within it lies a good support for the decision. Recklessness of the kind Lord Steyn mentions meets the justice ingredient for tort liability: there is a special injustice in the use of a public office with deliberate disregard for the interests that the law protects. And the deference limit is no objection to liability based on recklessness as to the lawfulness of an action, because the judges will not be interfering with discretions inappropriately if they hold a public officer liable when he or she sets out to *disregard* the proper use of the discretion. Even after *Three Rivers*, the tort requires more than just unlawful action causing harm; it also requires contempt for the people affected. Misfeasance in a public office is *not* a tort of ultra-negligence.

● *Pop Quiz* ●
Would the conduct in *Roncarelli v Duplessis* [1959] SCR 121—cancelling a restaurant's liquor licence to punish the owner for providing bail money for Jehovah's Witnesses (see p 216)—be a tort in England today?

14.5.2 The scope of the tort: proximity and causation

Suppose that a public officer has engaged in misfeasance (that is, he or she has acted unlawfully with the intention or the reckless attitude that Lord Steyn describes). Which persons qualify as claimants, and which losses will be compensated? In addition to its importance for understanding the mental element of the tort, *Three Rivers* is important for the House of Lords' approach to these questions as to its scope.

The Court of Appeal had held that the tort was limited by a requirement of proximity between defendant and claimant. The House of Lords overturned that holding. As a result, the only limits on the availability of damages (if a public officer has engaged in misfeasance) are:

● that the defendant knew that it was probable that loss of the kind suffered would result, or was reckless as to whether it would result (192), and

● that the claimant's loss was caused by the misfeasance (194).

The causation question is a 'matter of fact' to be decided at trial.

After *Three Rivers*, the Court of Appeal clarified the scope of the tort in *Akenzua v Home Office* [2002] EWCA Civ 1470. Delroy Denton had been arrested in 1994 for possession of drugs and an offensive weapon. He turned out to have entered Britain on a false passport from Jamaica, where he had a record of violent crime. In order to use him as an informer on Yardie gangsters, police and immigration officers decided to let him remain in Britain. His drugs charges and, later, a rape charge were dropped. Then in 1995, he raped a woman and stabbed her to death. When her family sued the Home Office and the police for misfeasance, the High Court struck out their claim. But the Court of Appeal reversed that decision, and allowed the case to go to trial. The point in dispute was as to the scope of the tort, not as to the nature of the mental element. That is, the defendants claimed that under the law as stated in *Three Rivers*, before the second form of the tort could arise, the claimant needed to be a member of an identifiable class of persons toward whose interests the defendant was knowingly or recklessly indifferent. But the Court of Appeal in *Akenzua* decided that the existence of an identifiable class was not essential. Harm to a person arising from Denton's known tendencies would be enough, if the other elements of the tort were made out [20]. That result follows naturally from *Three Rivers*.

New law made in *Three Rivers*:

- an abusive failure to exercise a power can count as misfeasance (but the failure must be deliberate rather than neglectful? Or only reckless?);
- a defendant who did not know that the conduct in question was unlawful may be liable in misfeasance as long as he or she acted with bad faith—a requirement that is satisfied by recklessness as to whether the conduct is unlawful;
- the tort can be committed without any intention that the loss in question should be caused; it is not enough that the loss is foreseeable, but it *is* enough that the defendant was reckless as to a probable loss; and
- there is no requirement of proximity between the claimant and the defendant (confirmed, in the face of some uncertainty about the necessity of an identifiable class of claimants, in *Akenzua*).

14.5.3 Has the tort expanded?

If you read *Three Rivers* and *Akenzua* quickly, it may seem that the tort has been opened up in a way that exposes public authorities to a vast range of new claims in tort. Now a public officer can commit the tort without setting out to hurt anyone, without knowing that the conduct is unlawful, and without even knowing that it will hurt anyone.

Yet, for the present, the tort remains narrowly limited. The House of Lords' decision in *Three Rivers* left the claimants needing to prove not merely that the Bank of England had acted unlawfully, or even that its conduct was *Wednesbury* unreasonable. That would not nearly be enough: in order to succeed, the claimants would have had to prove that the officers of the Bank did not care whether their conduct was lawful, and did not care whether their conduct would harm investors. Even a grossly careless decision isn't enough. The test is so demanding that the House of Lords was divided in the decision, not over the ingredients of the tort, but over whether it was an abuse of the process of the court for the case to proceed to a trial, because it was so implausible that the claimants would be able to establish those ingredients. Lord Hobhouse wrote that 'the real grievance of the actual plaintiffs is that they believe that the law ought to allow actions in negligence against regulators but they accept through their counsel that it does not' (289). And Lord Millett thought that there was simply no prospect of success, as the Bank of England would have a defence if their officers honestly believed that there was a reasonable prospect that BCCI would be rescued (294).

The only really significant opening up of misfeasance in public office as a result of *Three Rivers* is that claims will be more likely to proceed to trial. They are not very much more likely to succeed. Speculative allegations of misfeasance will not fail on the question of scope, or on the distinction between intention and recklessness (where *Three Rivers* does change the law, at least by stating what the House of Lords had not determined before). The real hurdle is like the hurdle in sustaining an allegation of fraud in a commercial dispute: without some evidence of corruption or a vendetta, it is very hard to prove an allegation of bad faith in a trial.

Think of the situation in *Akenzua*. If the defendants were reckless in the sense required by *Three Rivers*, they were reckless as to whether the risk of releasing Denton was bad enough that they had a public law duty to keep him in custody—that is, they were reckless as to whether it was so unreasonable to release him because of the risk, that no reasonable police authority would do so. Even if it *was Wednesbury* unreasonable, they would have a defence if they honestly believed that it was not *Wednesbury* unreasonable. And to succeed, the claimants would have to prove that they had no honest belief of that kind.

If the police and immigration officers arranged for Delroy Denton to be at large for any of the following reasons, they would commit the tort of misfeasance:

- they wanted him to kill a particular person;

- they wanted to see him kill someone, but they didn't care who it was;

- they took a bribe to release him, hoping that he would not hurt anyone but knowing that he probably would;

- they did not care whether they were creating a risk so bad (so out of proportion to the protection of the public that they might achieve by using him as an informer) that no reasonable authority would do so.

But they would not commit the tort if they honestly believed the risk was worthwhile, even if the belief was *Wednesbury* unreasonable (because it was extremely unreasonable to assess the risk as they did, or because they were absurdly optimistic about the benefits of using him as an informer). Even a *Wednesbury*-unreasonable decision is not misfeasance, if it is honest. The House of Lords in *Three Rivers* itself insisted that the recklessness required for the tort must be 'advertent',[19] rather than a mere

---

[19]   See the important discussion of forms of recklessness by Lord Steyn (192–3).

failure to pay attention to a relevant consideration. We might put it that it would not be tortious if the public officers simply failed to give any thought to the interests of people whom Delroy Denton might attack. The relevant form of recklessness arises only if the officers (1) were aware of those interests and (2) deliberately chose to set Denton at large regardless. It would not be enough if they made a horrendously bad misjudgment as to the whether the risk was worth running in order to prevent other crimes, or even if it never occurred to them for a moment that there might be a risk.

Since the courts will not strike out the claim in a case like *Three Rivers*, a claimant can try to persuade the trial judge that bad faith can be inferred from the failure of a public authority to meet a reasonable standard. But that will be difficult to do, as *Three Rivers* itself demonstrates: after years of seeking to prove that the Bank of England had acted in bad faith, the claimants' case collapsed and they had to pay 'indemnity costs' (that is, costs that cover a greater than usual proportion of the defendant's legal expenses) on the ground that they had made scandalous allegations that they could not substantiate.

So liability in misfeasance has not expanded dramatically, though it has been clarified. An abuse of power is not a tort if the public authority did not act in bad faith. As it stands, the law is committed to retaining, as Lord Steyn said in *Three Rivers*, 'a meaningful requirement of bad faith in the exercise of public powers which is the raison d'être of the tort' (193). No case has abandoned that requirement. But after *Three Rivers*, it is much easier for a claimant to force a defendant into a pointless trial. And at trial, it will be a challenge for the courts to hold onto the bad faith requirement in such cases, if it is shown that a *Wednesbury*-unreasonable use of discretion harmed the claimants. After all, the difference between an abuse of power, and an abuse of power accompanied by bad faith may seem a strange one: how can a public officer abuse his or her power in good faith? If you are considering whether to release a violent offender, it is blameworthy to do so without weighing up the risks carefully. Suppose that in a case like *Akenzua*, the police and immigration officers took no thought whatever to the risk that Denton might kill someone. Then a claimant might try to argue that even without bad faith, their conduct should be held to be tortious because of the disregard it showed for the interests of persons affected by their use of power. If the courts accepted that a culpable failure to act reasonably is actionable without bad faith, it would mark a real change in the law that would be much more far-reaching than *Three Rivers* or *Akenzua*. It would replace the requirement of bad faith with an objective test. Public authorities would be liable in tort for abuse of power in general.

Striking out misfeasance claims

Remember that it is hard to get a court to strike out a tort claim. In misfeasance in particular, it has been held that whether public officers have abused their position is 'a question of fact', so that it is not appropriate to strike out a misfeasance claim on the ground that an official's conduct did not amount to an abuse: *Cornelius v Hackney LBC* [2002] EWCA Civ 1073.

> The developments in *Three Rivers* have made it a lot harder for a defendant to succeed in striking out a claim, without making it much easier for a claimant to succeed at trial. Given the choice, of course, claimants would prefer to proceed to trial and take their chances, than to have their claim struck out. Proceeding to trial may give them some kind of leverage in negotiating with the public authority, even when the prospect of success is slender.

14.5.4 Criminal liability

The rule of law is protected by the rule that it is no defence to criminal charges for the defendant to say that he was acting on behalf of a public authority. Criminal law controls the actions of public authorities even though, for example, if a police officer commits an assault while on duty, it is the officer in his own personal capacity who can be prosecuted, rather than the police authority.

In *East Suffolk Rivers*, Lord Atkin mentioned that in the case of a statutory duty, 'speaking generally, in the absence of special sanctions imposed by the statute the breach of duty amounts to a common law misdemeanour' (88). Lord Atkin was speaking *too* generally. Not all unlawful acts of public authorities are torts, and they are not all crimes either. Not even a breach of a Convention right is a crime.

What more does it take for an unlawful act to be a crime? It is enough if the conduct would be a crime if a private person committed it. And just as misfeasance in a public office is a specifically public tort, **misconduct in a public office** is a specifically public offence. It has a very broad reach, but the misconduct in question has to be the sort that justifies a criminal sanction. Corruption is the obvious example: in R v Bowden [1996] I WLR 98 (CA), the chief building maintenance officer of Stoke City Council was convicted of the offence for sending council employees to do plumbing and electrical work on the home of 'the defendant's lady friend'. But the offence does not require corruption, and it does not even require that the official take any action; a wilful and culpable neglect of a duty is enough. 'Errant' prison officers 'might well be indictable for the common law offence of misconduct in public office' (*Watkins* [26] (Lord Bingham)). In R v Dytham [1979] QB 722, a police officer was convicted of misconduct for having done nothing to intervene or to get help as a man was beaten to death outside a club. The same behaviour by a private person would not have been a crime.

In addition to ordinary criminal liabilities, some important offences have been created by statute to control the actions of public officials. Torture, in particular, is a crime if it is done by 'a public official or person acting in an official capacity' (Criminal Justice Act 1988 s 134).

14.6 Just satisfaction: damages under the Human Rights Act

Suppose a man is detained unlawfully and tortured by a public official. If a court merely declared that there had been an infringement of his Convention right not to be tortured, that wouldn't be enough to vindicate his right. The state won't really be treating him as a person who has a right not to be tortured, unless he gets some sort of remedy for the harm done, as well. In case the state does not give a proper remedy, the Convention provides that the Strasbourg Court 'shall, if necessary, afford just satisfaction to the injured party' (Art 41).

To enable English courts to give the satisfaction that a claimant can obtain in Strasbourg, the Human Rights Act 1998 s 8 gives the court power to 'grant such relief or remedy, or make such order, within its powers as it considers just and appropriate' (if an act of a public authority is held to be unlawful under s 6(1) of the Act because it violates a Convention right). Courts that have power to award damages may do so, though only if 'the court is satisfied that the award is necessary to afford just satisfaction to the person in whose favour it is made' (s 8(3)). Many ways of infringing a Convention right would be torts. If a claimant had suffered torture at the hands of a public official, an award of damages under the Human Rights Act would most probably not be necessary, because the remedy in the tort of assault will count as 'just satisfaction'. But in addition to tort damages, the claimant would be entitled to a declaration under the Human Rights Act that the Art 3 right not to be subject to torture had been violated. Where an infringement of a Convention right is a tort, separate Human Rights Act damages will only be available if the remedy in tort is insufficient to vindicate the Convention right (see *Dobson v Thames Water* [2007] EWHC 2021).

Human Rights Act damages had the potential to revolutionize the law of compensation for unlawful executive action. Misfeasance in a public office requires bad faith, and negligence requires special reasons for identifying a duty of care. Infringing Convention rights does not require bad faith, and even if there is no common law duty of care, a failure to help someone may be an infringement of a Convention right: Art 2 imposes a positive duty to protect life, Art 3 imposes duties to prevent degrading treatment, and the Art 8 right to respect for private and family life imposes duties to provide certain forms of support to persons and families (see p 89). Any bad administrative decision that affects a claimant (for example, any failure to provide a social security benefit that a person is entitled to) has the potential to affect their private and family life. And mere bad administration—not otherwise unlawful in English administrative law—may affect people's private and family life severely.

What's more, damages are not available at common law for loss caused by a failure of due process, but since Art 6 of the Convention guarantees many of the same process rights as the common law, the Human Rights Act gives courts power to award damages for failures of due process. The Human Rights Act gave judges tools that they might have used to order compensation for more or less any unlawful action that causes substantial loss to a claimant.

But there has been no such revolution. The English courts have carefully restricted the availability of damages, following certain strands in the decisions of the Strasbourg Court.[20] Human Rights Act damages have an important but surprisingly

----

[20] The Human Rights Act requires the courts to 'take into account the principles applied by the European Court of Human Rights in relation to the award of compensation under Article 41 of the Convention' (s 8(4)). But the Strasbourg Court's decisions on compensation awards are not

limited role in the vindication of Convention rights and in the control of administration. Public authorities now need to make good certain losses caused by infringements of Convention rights, but the courts have decided that victims of Convention rights infringements can generally get 'just satisfaction'—which simply means something that ought to satisfy the victim—without an award of damages, or with the payment of such a modest sum that it would be dwarfed by the cost of the litigation. The reasons for the restrained approach reflect the purpose of the European Convention and of the Human Rights Act; yet we will see that those reasons turn out to be related to the restrictions on compensation in the law of tort.

14.6.1 Article 8: private and family life

Anufrijeva v Southwark LBC (see p 90) was the turning point in the restrained approach to Human Rights Act damages. Several asylum seekers claimed that local authorities had infringed their rights under Art 8 of the Convention. The authorities failed to provide special needs accommodation required by statute for a family member, and maladministration led to delay in deciding two successful asylum applications and in allowing family members to join a refugee in the UK.

The allegations in *Anufrijeva* would not support a claim for damages in tort. Failing to provide a housing benefit or financial support required by statute is unlawful, and a court could order the benefit to be paid, but the unlawful failure gives a claimant no right to compensation for any resulting loss.[21] Maladministration causing delay is not even unlawful.[22] So the claimants in *Anufrijeva* needed something beyond the law of tort. They argued that unlawful conduct and maladministration by the public authorities had had a detrimental impact on their private and family life, infringing Art 8. The Court of Appeal held that maladministration causing delay and unlawful withholding of benefits do not generally infringe Art 8, even though they do affect private and family life detrimentally. Article 8 is not infringed unless a public authority shows a culpable lack of respect for the claimant's private and family life (which requires, in particular, that the officials involved know that the claimant's private and family life are at risk), and the impact on the claimant is severe [45], [48], [143]. Carelessness is not enough in itself. So claimants cannot bypass the restrictions on liability in misfeasance and in negligence, by pointing out that administrative failings affect their private and family life.

The law remains uncertain because of the unlimited variety of ways in which administrative failures may affect people, and because of the Strasbourg Court's

---

very consistent (see *Anufrijeva v Southwark LBC* [2003] EWCA Civ 1406 [57]), and are not explained very fully.

[21] Except that depriving someone of a benefit in bad faith would be misfeasance (in *Anufrijeva*, the court rejected an allegation that one local authority had acted in bad faith, and there was no claim in misfeasance).

[22] Unless the public authority has acted in a way that is *Wednesbury* unreasonable by delaying. Even then, the delay would not support a claim in tort unless it was malicious.

unpredictable decisions.[23] In English law, it seems that an unlawful failure to provide social security benefits *may* amount to an infringement of Art 8, if it is bad enough, and in *Bernard v Enfield* [2002] EWHC 2282 the High Court awarded damages of £10,000 for infringement of Art 8, where a local authority had shown 'a singular lack of respect for the claimants' private and family life' [34] by housing a family (contrary to their statutory duty under the National Assistance Act 1948 s 21) in a flat that left the severely disabled mother 'lacking privacy in the most undignified of circumstances' [32], so that the claimants had to 'endure deplorable conditions, wholly inimical to private and family life' [61]. As Sullivan J held in *Bernard*, 'Whether the breach of statutory duty has also resulted in an infringement of the claimants' Article 8 rights will depend upon all the circumstances of the case. Just what was the effect of the breach in practical terms on the claimants' family and private life?' [32]. The Court of Appeal in *Anufrijeva* discussed the award in *Bernard* and evidently approved of it. Yet *Anufrijeva* reflects the judges' decision not to use the Human Rights Act to impose any general liability on public authorities to compensate people whom they unlawfully fail to help.[24] A claim that Art 8 has been infringed by a merely careless failure to help is bound to fail. Compensation for maladministration or even for unlawful delay in providing a benefit will only be available in the case of grave violations causing severe loss (*Anufrijeva* [67]).

The Court of Appeal found no infringement of Art 8 in *Anufrijeva*, so there was no question of whether an award of damages was necessary for just satisfaction. But the judges took the opportunity to write a guide to the award of damages under the Human Rights Act at [49] to [56], which the House of Lords has approved (*R (Greenfield) v Home Secretary* [2005] UKHL 14 [9], [30]). Here are the highlights:

- the victim of a tort has a right to compensation for loss caused by the tort,[25] but under the Human Rights Act there is no right to compensation, even if a Convention right has been infringed [50];

- the point of litigation in the Strasbourg Court or the English courts, is 'to bring the infringement to an end and the question of compensation will be secondary' [53];

- 'there is a balance to be drawn between the interests of the victim and those of the public as a whole' [55];

---

[23] So, e.g., for unlawful telephone surveillance the European Court of Human Rights awarded £10,000 damages with no proof of harm caused by the breach in *Halford v UK* (1997) 24 EHRR 523, but the declaration of a violation of Art 8 was considered enough for just satisfaction for rather similar tapping of a home phone in *Kopp v Switzerland* (1998) 27 EHRR 93.

[24] And Sullivan J held in *Bernard* that 'not every breach of duty under section 21 of the 1948 Act [empowering a local authority to provide support to the disabled] will result in a breach of Article 8' [32].

[25] Sometimes damages are nominal, when no real loss has resulted from the tort; courts never need to award nominal damages for an infringement of a Convention right. If there is no real loss, no damages are necessary for just satisfaction.

- exemplary damages are not awarded (*Anufrijeva* [55]);[26] and

- in fact, damages are only awarded as a 'last resort' [56] (though it is a last resort that the court ought to take in the exercise of its discretion, whenever it decides that damages are necessary for just satisfaction).

If a court finds that a Convention right has been infringed, it then asks a further question: whether it is necessary to award compensation for any loss caused by the infringement, in order to vindicate the claimant's Convention right. In a case like *Bernard*, the question will really be whether sending the claimant away with no damages would represent a failure *by the court*, on behalf of the United Kingdom, to show respect for the claimant's right to private and family life.

There is a final important point to note about *Anufrijeva*: the judges said that the costs of the litigation (funded on both sides by the public) were 'truly horrendous' [79] and 'out of all proportion to the issues at stake' [117]. The Court of Appeal gave a very explicit warning that 'courts should look critically at any attempt to recover damages under the Human Rights Act for maladministration by any procedure other than judicial review in the Administrative Court' [81]. That warning applies the principle of **proportionate process** (see p 119) to claims for compensation under the Human Rights Act. It does not mean that someone like the claimant in *Bernard* can no longer ask for damages of the kind awarded in that case: they simply have to seek them in a less expensive claim for judicial review (which must involve other claims—such as a declaration that the public authority's conduct was unlawful, or a quashing order). The warning in *Anufrijeva* only prevents a claimant from demanding a disproportionate commitment of resources to supporting litigation that cannot result in more than a modest award of compensation.

14.6.2 Article 2: the right to life

'Everyone's right to life shall be protected by law', and the Strasbourg Court has concluded that a state may fail in that duty of protection, if the police do not take measures to prevent crimes. So claimants have sought Human Rights Act damages in English courts and in Strasbourg, as a way of getting around the rule that the police owe no duty of care in the investigation of crime to people who might be injured by a potential suspect (see p 535). But the potential is limited by the Strasbourg Court's approach. It has held that the police only infringe Art 2 through careless investigation in a limited set of cases:

> '... it must be established to [the court's] satisfaction that the authorities knew or ought to have known at the time of the existence of a real and immediate risk to the life of an identified individual or individuals from the criminal acts of a third

---

[26] The European Court of Human Rights rejected a claim for exemplary damages in *Selçuk and Asker v Turkey* (1998) 26 EHRR 477.

> party and that they failed to take measures within the scope of their powers which, judged reasonably, might have been expected to avoid that risk. '[27]

Interpreted in this way, the right in Art 2 is not a very promising way of getting around the rule in Hill v Chief Constable of West Yorkshire [1989] AC 53, that when investigating crime, the police owe no duty of care to members of the public who might be injured or killed by a suspect or potential suspect. The claimant in Hill itself would not have succeeded under Art 2, for example. And in Van Colle v Chief Constable of Hertfordshire [2005] UKHL 14, the House of Lords unanimously held that Art 2 had not been infringed in a case in which the police knew that a suspect had made threats to a witness to a crime, and the suspect then murdered the witness. Even though a disciplinary tribunal had found the police officer involved guilty of failing to perform his duties conscientiously in investigating the suspect's attempts to intimidate witnesses, the police had not had reason to perceive a real and immediate risk to the witness's life. It is worth noting that even in the Osman case, in which the 'warning signs' were clearer than in Van Colle (see Van Colle [39]), the Strasbourg Court found no infringement of Art 2 for a similar reason: although the police knew that the eventual murderer had made threats and was harassing the victim, they never had reason to suspect a real and imminent risk to the victim, of a kind that would have justified using their powers of arrest or their power to seek detention on mental health grounds [121].[28]

Perhaps the crucial point, demonstrated by Van Colle, is that Art 2 is not infringed merely because a person is murdered after the police culpably fail to take steps that might well have prevented the murder. But the Strasbourg Court in Osman rejected the United Kingdom's argument that a failure of policing only infringes Art 2 if it is 'tantamount to gross negligence or wilful disregard of the duty to protect life' (Osman [116]). If the police do know (or ought to know) that there is a real and imminent threat to someone's life, Lord Bingham held in Van Colle that they would infringe the right to life if they 'did not do all that could reasonably be expected of them' to avoid the risk [30].

14.6.3 Article 6: due process

It is very, very hard to get damages for infringement of the right in Art 6 to a fair hearing within a reasonable time. In R (Greenfield) v Secretary of State for the Home Department [2005] UKHL 14, a prisoner was given 21 additional days of imprisonment after a hearing that infringed Art 6 (the decision maker was not independent, and the prisoner was wrongly denied legal representation). Lord Bingham, with whom all the Law Lords agreed, held that no damages should be awarded. He approved the view of the Court of Appeal in Anufrijeva that in Human Rights Act cases, 'the concern will

---

[27] Osman v UK (1998) 29 EHRR 245 [116].

[28] In Kilic v Turkey (2001) 33 EHRR 58, by contrast, the security forces were held to have infringed Art 2 by failing to respond to specific death threats.

usually be to bring the infringement to an end and any question of compensation will be of secondary, if any, importance' [9]. He said that 'the pursuit of damages should rarely, if ever, be an end in itself in an Article 6 case', and approved the *Anufrijeva* warning that claimants should not seek damages that are bound to be much smaller than the cost of pursuing them [30]. The difference between damages in tort and under the Human Rights Act started to emerge in *Anufrijeva*. But Lord Bingham went further. The Court of Appeal in *Anufrijeva* had held that, although 'the discretionary exercise' of awarding Human Rights Act damages is different from the remedial decision in tort law, 'the levels of damages awarded in respect of torts' may 'provide some rough guidance' in exercising the s 8 discretion [74]. Lord Bingham said in *Greenfield* that 'this approach should not be followed' and held that the Human Rights Act 'is not a tort statute', and that its purpose 'was not to give victims better remedies at home than they could recover in Strasbourg' [19], so that the English courts should not award damages by analogy to tort damages.

The two grounds on which claimants seek damages for infringement of Art 6 are that the infringement cost them an opportunity to get a better outcome, and that it caused them distress. In refusing to award damages, Lord Bingham very candidly pointed out that a legal representative might have persuaded the decision maker 'to take a different view' of the case against him; but that was not enough to justify an award of damages: 'It is inappropriate to speculate' about the outcome of a fair hearing that never happened [28]. In order to receive damages for loss of an opportunity, a claimant would have to persuade the judges that they can tell, without speculation, that things would have gone differently if the hearing had conformed to Art 6.[29]

In *Osman v UK* (1998) 29 EHRR 245, the Strasbourg Court awarded damages for infringement of Art 6 'on an equitable basis' of £10,000, holding (like Lord Bingham) that 'the Court cannot speculate as to the outcome' that would result from proceedings conforming to Art 6 [164]. 'On an equitable basis' means that the damages are meant to treat the claimant fairly without actually reflecting the magnitude of the loss that was suffered; in *Osman*, the Court was in no position to put a figure on the value of the loss of an opportunity to pursue a claim.

The 'equitable' approach

The court sometimes presumes that a loss has occurred and awards equitable damages, and has made awards without even taking evidence on what the actual loss is.[30] This approach adds to the inconsistency of the court's compensation decisions. Yet there can be good reasons for taking the equitable approach when a

---

[29] In *R (KB) v Mental Health Review Tribunal* [2003] EWHC 193, Stanley Burnton J held that damages would only be awarded for loss of an opportunity if it could be proved on a balance of probabilities that the outcome of a Convention-compliant hearing would have been favourable to the claimant.

[30] See, e.g., *Öneryildiz v Turkey* (2005) 41 EHRR 20 [159].

> loss is not readily quantifiable: the Strasbourg Court is not well equipped to assess losses, its compensatory role is really not central, and its awards are modest. A wild guess at a modest figure is its way of vindicating a victim whose Convention right has been infringed.
>
> Lord Bingham held in *Greenfield* that the English courts should follow the Strasbourg Court's equitable approach: 'The court routinely describes its awards as equitable, which I take to mean that they are not precisely calculated but are judged by the court to be fair in the individual case. Judges in England and Wales must also make a similar judgment in the case before them' [19].

As for the anxiety and frustration caused by being subject to a process that infringed Art 6, the Strasbourg cases are not consistent, but Lord Bingham said that the Strasbourg Court has been 'very sparing' ([16], citing *Saunders v UK* (1996) 23 EHRR 313 and *Robins v UK* (1997) 26 EHRR 527), and that 'the sums awarded have been noteworthy for their modesty' [17]. He felt no need to remit the matter in *Greenfield* itself to a judge to assess the seriousness of the impact of the infringement of Art 6 on the victim. The remedy of a declaration itself gave just satisfaction. It has been accepted in the Strasbourg Court that financial compensation is not generally necessary to give just satisfaction for an infringement of Art 6 (*Kingsley v UK* (2002) 35 EHRR 177). But it has not been uncontroversial: two dissenting judges in *Kingsley* said, 'a mere finding of a violation cannot constitute in itself adequate just satisfaction. Applicants are entitled to something more than a mere moral victory or the satisfaction of having contributed to enriching the Court's case law' [O-III2].

14.6.4 The puzzle about Human Rights Act damages: what are they for?

In tort, the question of whether compensation should be awarded is packed into the question of liability. Once liability in tort is established, the defendant must compensate the claimant for loss caused by the tort. Under the Convention, however, the court (in Strasbourg or in England) finds an infringement and *then* asks whether a remedy in damages is needed to do justice. As Lord Hoffmann put it in *R (Wilkinson) v Inland Revenue Commissioners* [2005] UKHL 30, the Human Rights Act 'did not create a statutory duty for which damages could be recovered as if the breach of Convention rights was a tort in English law. And the jurisprudence of the Strasbourg court shows that it is more concerned with upholding human rights in member States than with awarding damages' [25]. If Human Rights Act damages, and compensation awarded by the Strasbourg Court, are not like tort damages, and are not the courts' central concern, what are they for?

They are evidently not meant to punish the state, since exemplary damages are not awarded. Strasbourg decisions regularly say that the point is to put the claimant in the same position as if the right had not been infringed: *Piersack v Belgium* (1984) 7 EHRR 251 [12] 'the applicant should as far as possible be put in the position he would have been in had the requirements of Art. 6 not been disregarded'.[31] This principle was adopted by the Court of Appeal in *Anufrijeva* [59] and by the House of Lords in *Greenfield* [10] and *Wilkinson* [26]. But that is puzzling, because putting a claimant in the same position as if a wrong had not been committed is the underlying principle of tort damages (*Livingstone v Rawyards Coal Co* (1880) 5 App Cas 25, 39 (Lord Blackburn)). Another puzzle is that the courts' practice, both in Strasbourg and England, defies the supposed principle.

First of all, the Strasbourg Court's 'equitable' approach is a rejection of the attempt to put the claimant in the same position as if the right had not been infringed. Instead of trying to put a value on the loss and award that amount, it offers a token amount, instead, that is meant to be a fair response to the infringement of a right.

Secondly—but this is really a part of the equitable approach, too—the claimant's own conduct is relevant to awards of just satisfaction in Strasbourg, so that their purpose is not really compensatory at all. In *McCann v United Kingdom* (1996) 21 EHRR 97, three IRA members went to Gibraltar to carry out a terrorist attack. SAS soldiers who planned to arrest them shot them dead, thinking that they were about to set off car bombs. By a narrow 10–9 majority the European Court of Human Rights held that the bombers' right to life had been infringed because the soldiers' instructions gave them a misguided impression that the bombers had to be shot to prevent explosions. If the court really set out to put the victims in the same position as if their Art 2 right had not been infringed, they would presumably have awarded the damages that the victims' families sought. But the Court dismissed the claim: 'having regard to the fact that the three terrorist suspects who were killed had been intending to plant a bomb in Gibraltar, the Court does not consider it appropriate to make an award under this head' [219].

Here is the secret to this puzzle: the damages are the state's response to the *breach of Convention right*. They are quite different from tort damages, which are a remedy for loss caused by a breach of a duty to the claimant. The purpose of Human Rights Act damages (and of damages ordered by the Strasbourg Court) is really to vindicate the claimant's Convention right, and they are not to be awarded at all unless they are *necessary* for that purpose. Providing financial redress for loss caused by a violation of a right *can* be an essential step in vindicating the right; it depends on the nature of the violation. For example, English law would fail to respect the right not to be tortured, if torture were not a tort, and tort compensation is the only adequate way of responding to the fact that the victim's right not to be tortured has been violated. But in other cases (such as *McCann*, or *Greenfield*), damages that aim to put the claimant in the position he would have been in if the infringement had not happened are not necessary for the purpose of treating the victim as a person whose Convention rights are respected. The question is whether, *after the court's decision*, he is in a position to complain that the U.K. is not treating him as someone who holds the rights guaranteed in the Convention.

---

[31]   Cf *Hobbs v UK* (2007) 44 EHRR 54 [67] ('the principle underlying the provision of just satisfaction is that the applicant should as far as possible be put in the position he would have enjoyed had the violation found by the Court not occurred').

> **Awards of Human Rights Act damages are rare**
> Perhaps the only examples in English courts until 2008 were *Bernard v Enfield* [2002]
> EWHC 2282 (£10,000 for infringement of Art 8); and *R (KB) v Mental Health Review*
> *Tribunal* [2003] EWHC 193 (amounts ranging from £750 to £4,000 were awarded to
> six claimants for delays in tribunal hearings).

14.7 Conclusion: tort and the rule of law

There is *one* context in which public authorities are liable to compensate a claimant for
loss caused by unlawful government conduct. In Case C-6/90 *Francovich v Italy* [1991]
ECR I-5357, the European Court of Justice (ECJ) held that a claimant could get compensation in the court of a member state, for loss caused by a failure to implement EC
law. Italy had failed to implement an EC directive to protect workers from losing back
pay when their employer went bankrupt. The ECJ awarded compensation against
the Italian state to workers affected by a bankruptcy. The ECJ set requirements for
liability for failure to implement a directive: the directive must have been intended to
require the state to create identifiable rights for individuals, and the particular claimant's loss must have been caused by the failure to implement. The liability extends to
any state action that violates EC law; it applies to state decisions that infringe directly
effective rights. Later cases have required that the breach of European law must be
serious; 'the decisive test for finding that a breach of Community law is sufficiently
serious is whether the member state or the Community institution concerned manifestly and gravely disregarded the limits on its discretion' (Case C-46/93 *Brasserie du*
Pêcheur [1996] ECR I-1029 [55]).

   That requirement of seriousness indicates what is going on in these EC cases: they
are concerned with the relation between the European Union and its member states.
Francovich compensation is targeted against disregard by member states toward their
legal obligations under EC (including directives). Even in Europe, the point is not
that all loss caused by unlawful government action ought to be compensated. The
decision in *Francovich* was one of the ECJ's very inventive exercises in giving effect to
EC law within the legal systems of member states, by giving 400,000,000 people the
opportunity to sue their government for damages if the state was refusing or failing
to comply with EC law. The ECJ was trying to take a unique international agreement
and make it into a 'legal order'. State liability for loss caused by unlawful government
action is an extraordinary technique for making EC law effective.

   Why has no such imperative been felt to make *English* law effective, by awarding compensation for loss caused by unlawful action? The common law judges have
not been less inventive than the ECJ judges. Since the 1200s, they have been more or
less actively intent on subjecting public authorities to the rule of law. But the simple
point is that, although the rule of law requires that public officials abide by the law,
it does not require that loss caused by unlawful conduct of officials should always be
compensated.

And then the principles on which compensation *should* be awarded in tort against a public authority defendant are generally the same as against a private defendant. There must be a *reason for compensation*. It is an important constitutional principle that reasons for compensation for wrongs by a private defendant are also reasons for compensation against wrongs by a public authority. That rule creates an important control on the exercise of discretionary powers, just by compensating a claimant for loss caused when the executive branch of government violates the respect for property and persons that we are entitled to from each other. Apart from that, compensation for wrongs requires some special legislative basis, such as the European Communities Act 1972 (giving effect in English law to *Francovich* compensation for breaches of EC law) or the Human Rights Act 1998.

But we should remember the one exception. A malicious abuse of public power leads to compensation (and may be a crime), where malicious abuses of power by private persons give no right to compensation (and are not in themselves criminal). The common law does not just declare abuses of power unlawful; it remedies the harm done, where justice between persons and government demands it.

Administrative action contrary to European Law: liability to compensate, and fines too

In Case C-64/88 *Commission v France (Fisheries)* [1991] ECR I-2727, the ECJ held that France was not enforcing fishing quotas adequately. After giving France warnings, the Commission went back to the ECJ. In Case C-304/02 *Commission v France* [2005] ECR I-6263, the ECJ held that the sale of undersized fish, which France was failing to control, was enough 'to prejudice seriously…the Community system for conservation'. The ECJ imposed a lump sum fine of €20 million, plus a €58 million penalty payment for each six months of continued infringement. This liability for an administrative failure to implement EC law is part of the general liability of member states for violation of EC law. In domestic administrative law, there is nothing like this direct, legal control of administration with a view to requiring compliance with the law. That is partly because there is no equivalent in domestic law to the Commission (a body committed on behalf of the EU to seeing that EU decisions have effect).

The decision invented a power in the ECJ to impose *both* a lump sum fine and a penalty payment (and to do so when the Commission had not asked for a lump sum fine). Like the liability to compensate in *Francovich*, it is another in the long line of creative ECJ moves to increase its own powers in order to enhance the uniform effectiveness of EC law.

TAKE-HOME MESSAGE • • •

- There is **no general right to compensation** for a person who was harmed by unlawful administrative action, or even for a person whose Convention rights have been violated.

- But there is **no general immunity** from liability in tort for public authorities (some public officials have immunities, such as the immunity of judges from liability for harming someone by carelessly making a bad decision).

- The **Human Rights Act** authorizes compensation for an unlawful violation of a Convention right, if it is necessary to give the victim **just satisfaction**.

- The courts have refused to use common law **duties of care** to impose liability on a public authority that could and should have used its power to benefit a member of the public.

- Public authorities can be vicariously liable for a breach of the special duty of care that certain **professionals**, including doctors, educational psychologists, and teachers, owe to the persons they care for.

- A claimant is entitled to compensation from the British Government for loss caused by a serious failure to implement **EC directives** that were designed to lead to the conferment of identifiable rights on the claimant.

Critical reading

Entick v Carrington (1765) 19 Howell's State Trials 1029
East Suffolk Rivers Catchment Board v Kent [1941] AC 74
Home Office v Dorset Yacht [1970] AC 1004 (HL)
Caparo v Dickman [1990] 2 AC 605
Case C-6/90 Francovich v Italy [1991] ECR I-5357
X v Bedfordshire [1995] 2 AC 633
Case C-46/93 Brasserie du Pêcheur [1996] ECR I-1029
Stovin v Wise [1996] AC 923
O'Rourke v Camden [1998] AC 188
Barrett v Enfield [2001] 2 AC 550
Phelps v Hillingdon [2001] 2 AC 619
Three Rivers District Council v Bank of England [2003] 2 AC 1
Anufrijeva v Southwark LBC [2003] EWCA Civ 1406
Gorringe v Calderdale MBC [2004] UKHL 15
D v East Berkshire NHS Trust [2005] UKHL 23

CRITICAL QUESTIONS ● ● ●

1   **Should there be compensation for all loss caused by unlawful acts of public authorities?**

2   **Should compensation at common law depend on the wrongfulness of the official action? Why not on a principle that the public should pay for losses that are incurred in achieving benefits for the public?**

3   If it is not a tort for a public authority to cause you harm by acting unlawfully, why is misfeasance in public office a tort?

4   Do Human Rights Act damages make any real difference to the availability of compensation for unlawful administrative conduct?

Further questions:

5   Can a public authority be liable in negligence for carelessly misinterpreting a statute?

6   A police officer lies in testimony at my trial, to try to get me convicted when he knows I'm innocent. Do I have a right of action against him or the police authority?

7   Could the applicants for judicial review in R v Minister of Agriculture, ex p Padfield [1968] AC 997 (see p 45) have succeeded in a claim for the tort of misfeasance in public office?

8   The claimant in R (Greenfield) v Secretary of State for the Home Department [2005] UKHL 14 was sentenced to an additional 21 days for a drugs offence. He claimed that the proceedings infringed Art 6 of the Convention. What if the prisoner had brought a claim in the tort of false imprisonment—claiming that his imprisonment during those days was unlawful—instead of seeking Human Rights Act damages?

9   The claimants in Three Rivers District Council v Bank of England [2003] 2 AC 1 thought that they had lost their money because the regulator, the Bank of England, had not shut down the Bank of Credit and Commerce International when it should have. Why couldn't they just claim that the Bank of England had been negligent?

online resource centre

Visit the online resource centre to access the following resources which accompany this chapter: links to legislation and online reports of judicial decisions, summaries of key cases and legislation, updates in the law, suggestions for answering the pop quizzes and questions, and links to useful websites.

15 Contract

Contracts are used to structure the legal relationship between government and private service providers. And contract forms a new model both for relationships among public agencies, and for the relationship between government and the people it serves. For the government, the challenge is to deliver services with integrity, equity, and efficiency. For administrative law, the challenge is to provide forms of accountability that do what the law can do to promote those goals.

LOOK FOR • • •

- Jargon and acronyms: PPP, PFI, NDPB, Executive Agencies, contracting out, internal contracting, New Public Management, Best Value.

- The ways in which, for the purpose of contracting, public bodies are the same as *and* different from private parties.

- The role of courts in supervising contracting decisions of public authorities.

- The scope of judicial review: what role should the judges have in supervising private bodies that ought to be accountable for acting in the public interest?

> ' To meet these challenges [from 'globalization'] the State must provide the same level of customer service as the public have come to expect in every other aspect of their lives. To achieve this, the role of the State is not to control, but to enable. Making modern public services the cornerstone of the enabling state—where the State provides strategic direction not micro-management—requires a transformation of how we deliver our services. '
>
> **Tony Blair, 'Foreword' to Capability Reviews: The Findings of the First Four Reviews, Cabinet Office, July 2006.[1]**

15.1 Government by contract and proportionate administration

Contracts have been an important technique of government for centuries. Modern England was shaped by the move from the medieval feudal system, to a system in which the government got things done through contracts. The importance of contracts grew, evolved, and was then eclipsed after World War II, when Britain's welfare system and state industries were built on direct administration of government projects by government departments. The role of contracts as an instrument of government has massively increased since the 1980s, as they have become the basis for new kinds of partnership between government and private companies. And the really new development since the 1980s is that contracts have become the model for agreements *within* government, between departments and the wide range of new agencies created to provide services.

Just as dispute resolution is not just a job for judges (see pp 460–1), administration is not just a job for government departments. The move toward **proportionate process** (see p 430) means that there is no presumption that a legal dispute is to be resolved in a court (though courts have very far-reaching supervisory jurisdiction over institutions that resolve legal disputes).

This chapter explains the parallel development of a principle of **proportionate administration**: that is, delivery of public services through techniques of service provision and techniques of accountability that are in proportion to the public interests at stake. There is now no presumption that public administration is to be conducted by a government department (though departments have a very far-reaching role in making and overseeing arrangements with private companies and a variety of public agencies).

So we have undergone a third constitutional shift in public administration, which is more recent than the shift to proportionate process, or the judicial adventure of the 20th century (see p 56), and which is still under way. Like those shifts, the move to proportionate administration has ancient roots.

It was presumed in the mid-20th century that administration of public projects and programmes was a job for government officials. The idea was that public

---

[1]   http://www.civilservice.gov.uk/reform/capability_reviews/publications/pdf/summary.pdf.

administration was to be done by servants of the Crown, exercising powers and carrying out duties imposed by Parliament (with funding appropriated by Parliament). They would act under direction by ministers of the Crown. The ministers and the civil servants were accountable to the courts for the lawfulness of their conduct. The civil servants were accountable to their ministers for all aspects of their conduct. A management hierarchy gave the ministers control over the civil servants, and the ministers were accountable to Parliament for all aspects of their departments' work. That was the **command model**—a pattern of administration by public servants carrying out the commands of the ministers of the Crown, to give effect to Parliament's decisions as to the provision of public services.

Since the 1980s, the United Kingdom has been shaking off the command model, in favour of the provision of services by organizations that are meant to be especially good at service delivery (such as agencies that are partly independent from government departments, and private companies that provide services for profit). Government departments retain very far-reaching control—in a variety of forms— over the delivery of public services. Civil servants have a new role of advising ministers on how to secure value for money from private service providers. The Government is committed to deliver services through techniques tailored for efficiency, and tailored to provide accountability in forms that are **proportionate** to the need for accountability.

It seems that the potential benefit is an enhancement of public services, and the potential danger is loss of accountability in the push for efficient service provision. But we should not take it for granted that government by contract will either enhance services, or destroy accountability.

Robocop (1987): An American administrative law classic

In a world where crime and disorder are rampant, Omni Consumer Products runs the Detroit police force. The corporation abuses the police officers and plans to replace them with robots. After Model ED-209 goes on a killing spree, a young executive introduces Robocop as a safer alternative: a robot built from the remains of a police officer killed on duty. A crooked rival has Robocop's inventor killed by drug traffickers, and orders ED-209 to destroy RoboCop. The moral is, don't sell the police force to a crooked multinational corporation.

Robocop is the story of a failure of **proportionality** in public administration. Detroit outsourced the police to achieve effective public service delivery—and lost the rule of law (and, therefore, responsible government—see p 13) because of the loss of accountability.

The challenge for public administration is to achieve accountability techniques that are proportionate to the needs of the particular form of service.

Robocop is a satire on government by contract. Britain has not sold off the police. But much of the business of government (the postal service, the health service, schools, nursing homes, the prison service…) has been transformed by the impulse that went out of control in Robocop.

15.1.1 Privatization

Since the 1970s, these great government projects have all been privatized:

- coal mining (nationalized 1946, privatized 1994);
- railways (nationalized 1948, privatized 1982–1993);
- telephone service (largely nationalized 1912, privatized 1984);
- utilities:
  - water (nationalized from local authorities in 1973, privatized 1989),
  - gas (nationalized 1948, privatized 1986), and
  - electricity (nationalized 1947, privatized 1991).

Privatization means that the Government has got out of administering the enterprise altogether, having sold its coal mines and railways and utilities to private enterprise, subject to regulation by government agencies. Privatization reflects a decision that an industry should not be administered by the Government at all. So it actually eliminates problems of administrative law. It generates whole new legal regimes of regulation.

Regulatory agencies

Privatization of the government's monopoly industries changed accountability problems within the public sector into problems of how to regulate parts of the private sector. A whole range of new non-departmental public bodies, independent of government, were created to prevent abuses of market position, and to protect the public from other sorts of service failure. Others have been created to regulate industries that had never been nationalized (such as food), and the Competition Commission investigates concerns referred from the regulators or from government, with powers to stop companies from merging, or to require a company to sell off part of its business. The major agencies are:

Care Quality Commission
Charity Commission for England and Wales
FSA (Food Standards Agency)
National Lottery Commission
Ofcom (Office of Communications)
Ofsted (Office for Standards in Education)
OFT (Office of Fair Trading)
Ofgem (Office of Gas and Electricity Markets)
Ofqual (Office of the qualifications and examinations regulator)
ORR (Office of Rail Regulation)
Oftenant (Office for Tenants and Social Landlords)

Ofwat (Water Services Regulation Authority)

Postcomm (Postal Services Commission)[2]

Independent regulation of industries by these bodies is a new development since the 1980s. They reflect a trust in technical expertise and in the capacity of regulators with job security and independence from government to pursue the public good. Those features of independence and expertise mean that people with complaints will have difficulty persuading the court to overturn their decisions in judicial review. The license-and-regulate agencies are undoubtedly subject to judicial review, but their independence tends to protect them from due process claims, and their expertise is a reason for judicial deference on issues of substance. The legislation setting them up gives them very open-ended roles in setting standards that are generally very technical, which means that the judges will not substitute their judgment for that of the regulator on the substance of the standards.[3]

The industries they regulate (especially communications, utilities, and food) are so vast that these regulators have substantial power over the nation's economy. Are they accountable for their exercise of that power?

Deferential judicial review is only a guard against extraordinary failings. The regulators have transparent processes and decisions, which subject them to a form of accountability (see section 15.2). But no one regulates the regulators. Regulators, like judges, ombudsmen, and auditors, are not chiefly controlled by processes to resolve disputes about their decisions. Instead, the system relies on the openness of their work, on good appointments, and on the independence of the regulators.

15.1.2 Public–private partnerships

Many aspects of the business of government that have not been privatized have been contracted out. For any organization, contracting out means taking a function that has been done in-house, and hiring someone else to do it (and ideally, to do it better and/or at lower cost). It was invented by large companies in the 1980s, and applied to government by the Conservatives and then Labour. When the resulting deal involves an ongoing relationship, the Government calls it a **'Public–Private Partnership'** or

---

2 http://www.competition-commission.org.uk/our_role/what_investigate/index.htm, www.food.gov.uk, http://www.natlotcomm.gov.uk/CLIENT/index.asp, www.ofcom.gov.uk, www.ofsted.gov.uk, www.oft.gov.uk, www.ofgem.gov.uk, www.ofqual.gov.uk, www.rail-reg.gov.uk, www.communities.gov.uk/news/corporate/799522, www.ofwat.gov.uk, www.psc.gov.uk.

3 See, e.g., *ScottishPower Energy Management Ltd v Gas and Electricity Markets Authority* [2005] EWHC 2324; *R (Friends of the Earth) v Food Standards Agency* [2007] EWHC 558. See also *R v National Lottery Commission, ex p Camelot Group Plc* [2001] EMLR 3, a remarkable case in which the Commission had decided that neither Camelot's bid to operate the National Lottery nor Sir Richard Branson's bid was acceptable. The Commission then negotiated with Branson alone, and the court held that that decision was 'so unfair as to amount to an abuse of power' [82]. Yet it is evident that if the Commission had simply chosen Branson's bid, the court would not have second-guessed its judgment.

PPP. New public enterprises such as the National Lottery have been constructed from the start on the basis that:

- the Government decides what service is to be provided (and typically presents legislation to Parliament to structure the scheme, and to authorize expenditure);

- companies bid for the contract to provide the service;

- a '**non-departmental public body**' (NDPB[4]) awards a licence or licences to one or more providers; and

- the NDPB regulates the work of the provider.

The idea is that government should choose what public goods need to be secured, but can best achieve 'delivery' by involving private companies that are seeking profits. It will work, if the incentives of a marketplace can be brought to bear so that the profit seeker will avoid waste in supplying the service, and at the same time address the requirements of the people who receive the service (the 'consumers'). It remains the role of the public authority in the partnership to set standards, and to assure itself that they are met.

Delegation of powers and contracting out

In *Carltona v Commissioners of Works* [1943] 2 All ER 560 (CA), Lord Greene said that the act of an official in a department can count as the act of the minister. The functions given to ministers are 'so multifarious that no minister could ever attend to them ... Constitutionally, the decision of such an official is, of course, the decision of the Minister. The Minister is responsible. It is he who must answer before Parliament for anything that his officials have done under his authority ...' (563). As a result, if officials in a department make a decision on behalf of a minister, it is not an *ultra vires* delegation of a statutory power that Parliament conferred on the minister, and it is not a violation of the **genuine exercise** rule (see p 264).

The Deregulation and Contracting Out Act 1994 allows a minister to delegate discretions to a **private body** in the same way as discretions can be delegated to civil servants under Carltona. It does that in one of the most remarkable pieces of opaque drafting in the statute books:

's 69(2): If a Minister by order so provides, a function to which this section applies may be exercised by, or by employees of, such person (if any) as may be authorised in that behalf by the office-holder or Minister whose function it is.'

---

4 An NDPB is a 'body which has a role in the processes of national Government, but is not a Government Department or part of one, and which accordingly operates to a greater or lesser extent at arm's length from Ministers'. Cabinet Office, 'Public Bodies 2007' (3). See http://www.archive.official-documents.co.uk/document/caboff/bodies97/intro-1.htm. In 2007, there were 203 Executive NDPBs (ib.).

Under this provision, the difference between private companies and departmental officials is that the acts of departmental officials can count as acts of the minister without the minister having issued an order.

The provision applies to any function of a minister conferred by 'any enactment' (s 69(1)(a)), but with exclusions: functions that interfere with the liberty of an individual, powers of search or seizure and entry to property, and powers to make subordinate legislation must still be exercised by the minister or civil servants.

15.1.3 Internal contracting

PPP techniques, combined with privatization of some industries, have served as a model for new ways of regulating relations *within* government through techniques that mimic the market-based, incentive-driven, target-led operations of private companies. **Internal contracting** is the practice of regulating public administration through agreements between government agencies. The New Labour term for public agencies set up to provide services is '**Executive Agency**'. They operate under arrangements with government departments that are like contracts with private bodies. There are hundreds of these agencies,[5] and three-quarters of central government employees work in them. The traditional accountability to the minister (with the minister in turn accountable to Parliament for oversight of the agency) was kept in principle. To oversee the agency, the department formulates a 'Framework Agreement' which sets out the agency's budget, and procedures for the department to set and monitor performance targets. It is a strange sort of agreement: it is not a contract, because the agency has no separate legal personality from the department. And it is not really a deal negotiated between two parties who could each take their business elsewhere. But the 'agreement' is symbolically important as a government-by-contract technique that aims at the businesslike creation of incentives and setting of targets.

Executive agencies can be investigated (and their chief executives can be grilled) by parliamentary select committees. But since the theory was that an agency would operate within a policy framework set by the department, the government has wanted to think that accountability would be secured through the agreement. With the agency restricted to delivering a service, and with the department setting targets and regulating the agency through the framework agreement, what could go wrong?

In fact, executive agencies have been faced with some of the most massive administrative challenges in the country, with the Child Support Agency, the Rural Payments Agency, and the Prisons Service, for example, operating controversial and difficult schemes in which the policy formation and administration aspects of 'service provision' cannot be picked apart. And then the question is whether their programmes can be carried out with better attention to the public interest by an organization that

---

[5] See an index organized by department at http://www.cabinetoffice.gov.uk/ministerial_responsibilities/executive_agencies.aspx.

has a form of independence and distance from the parent department, or whether the independence and distance destroy an important form of accountability.

15.1.4 Citizens as customers

Finally, the relationship between all these organizations and the people they serve has been reconceived on the contract model: the citizen has become a **'customer'**, whose choices are meant to drive public service delivery in the way that customer choices drive pizza delivery.

> #### Choose and Book: patients as customers in the NHS
> On the 'NHS Choices' webpage[6]—which serves as the front page for the whole National Health Service—you can find facilities and services offered at different hospitals, performance ratings, patient feedback, waiting times, MRSA blood infection rate, and even patient survival rates for some operations. Then, if you need a hip replacement, you can go to 'Choose and Book'.[7] You can get advice from your GP, but you can make your own choice of a hospital for your operation with a location that suits you, a convenient time slot, good facilities, and an attractive survival rate. 'You can choose any hospital in England funded by the NHS (this includes NHS hospitals and some independent hospitals). You can choose the date and time of your appointment. You experience greater convenience and certainty. With Choose and Book, the choice is yours.'[8]
>
> The point is both to give patients a new form of control over their own lives, and to improve service delivery by subjecting NHS service providers to an economic imperative to compete with each other for funding that flows from patient choices. The scheme moves beyond target setting for competitive processes between service providers, to create a market driven by customer choices. The dangers include the potential market failures that may arise from faulty information in any market: inefficient choices will distort service delivery if the customer has limited information, or is misled by it. And the service providers only indirectly face incentives to improve services; their direct incentives are to improve customer perceptions through advertising, public relations, and finding ways to raise the ratings on the NHS Choices site. The dangers also include the risk of damaging the public service ethos of the health service.

15.1.5 New public management

These things go together: privatization, PPPs, new executive agencies with arrangements modelled on PPPs, and a wide-ranging commitment to 'customer' choice. The

[6] http://www.nhs.uk.

[7] http://www.chooseandbook.nhs.uk/.

[8] http://www.chooseandbook.nhs.uk/patients/whatiscab.

whole array of businesslike attitudes to public service provision has been called '**New Public Management**' for so long that it really isn't new any more.[9] Introduced by the Conservatives, it became standard practice in this country when New Labour came into power in 1997 and took the agenda forward in new, more sophisticated ways. Today, the major political parties only disagree about how to implement it. The New Public Management agenda involves:

> '...a focus on management, performance appraisal and efficiency; the use of agencies which deal with each other on a user-pay basis; the use of quasi-markets and contracting out to foster competition; cost-cutting; and a style of management which emphasises, among other things, output targets, limited term contracts, monetary incentives and freedom to manage.'[10]

Consider the following flowchart for administrative structuring. In 1998, the Cabinet Office under New Labour directed public bodies to ask these questions every five years, regarding every activity they do:

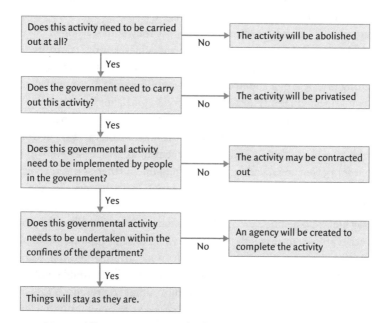

Figure 15.1 New public management: the flowchart

Proportionality (see p 24) provides the pattern for the reasoning: the first question is what is needed, and then the government's involvement in the relevant activity

9 See, e.g., Christopher Pollitt, *Managerialism and the Public Services* (2nd edn, 1993).

10 'Public Service', Report of the House of Lords Select Committee on the Public Service (chaired by Lord Slynn), 19 January 1998: http://www.publications.parliament.uk/pa/ld199798/ldselect/ldpubsrv/055/psrep01.htm.

should be proportionate to the need. It seems to be the right approach in principle: why would we want more government activity than is required for accomplishing something worthwhile?[11] But the right approach in principle can lead in practice to decisions that damage the public interest—either by abandoning valuable governmental functions, or by damaging accountability for their performance. Those two results will come about if economy and efficiency come to be seen as the purposes of government action, when in fact they are only crucial requirements in carrying out functions whose purpose is public service.

So the basic model for achieving proportionality in 21st-century British public administration—accepted by both major political parties—is to privatize services that can be privatized, to contract out what cannot be privatized, and to create internal analogues of contracts for provision of services that cannot be contracted out. The common strand in all these aspects of government by contract needs to be appreciated: they divide the public decision as to what public services should be provided, from the provision of the service. Contract is the central device in the still-evolving management of public services. The core management technique is a deal between the policy maker and the service provider (between government and a private service provider, or between government agencies).

Government by contract may seem to support Tony Blair's vision of an 'enabling state', which does not control people's lives, but achieves proportionality in public service by empowering them to make choices as consumers. Or it may seem to raise a frightening prospect of a country losing its public service ethos, and abandoning administrative accountability in favour of service provision by companies seeking to profit by taking public money and cutting corners. This chapter will focus on the challenges that the political choices raise for the law, and on the ways in which legal accountability can be secured under government by contract. But we will see that the search for proportionate administration requires further political choices to be made—by the courts, and by the Government, and by Parliament—in the development of legal accountability measures.

Robocop blows up genuine proportionality dangers into a thriller. But now think of every other police movie you have seen, in which the bad cops are public servants. The accountability disaster in *Robocop* arises from privatization, but accountability can be fragile in traditional public administration, too. It would be simplistic to think that the new model, which is still in flux, simply represents a loss of public accountability for the sake of efficient public services. Accountability and efficiency are both more complicated than that.

┌─ FROM THE MISTS OF TIME ─────────────────────────────

If only by hiring private persons to do jobs, governments have always used contracts (*except* those governments that have not accepted that anything is private).

---

[11] Here is a potential answer to the question: to achieve social justice by using public employment —regardless of whether the workers are doing something worthwhile—to redistribute wealth or to provide social security. That purpose was abandoned even in the Labour Party by the 1990s.

In England, government by contract emerged in the 14th century, when the feudal techniques for raising armies broke down. To pay soldiers for extended campaigns, the King needed to make deals with the nobles who were in theory obliged to provide troops. Parliament was a forum for working out the deals between King and country that were needed for fighting the French: Parliament started as a PPP and evolved into a general political accountability mechanism.

In early modern times, Britain's imperial policy emerged through deals between the Crown and private companies of investors and adventurers in North America (the Hudson's Bay Company) and India. The East India Company was given a charter by the King, which allowed the government to use licensing-and-regulation techniques similar to those used in 21st-century privatized industries (though the relationship was coloured by the commercial success of the Company, which endangered the House of Commons' capacity to make decisions without corruption in the public interest). With a massive private army and a huge bureaucracy, ruling a fifth of the world's population, the Company had wider powers than Omni Consumer Products had in the fictional Detroit of *Robocop*.

15.2 Accountability and efficiency

In any public project, there are various ways in which different actors may be held accountable **through** different processes, **for** different aspects of their conduct, **to** different institutions or to the public.

In principle, the media and voters in an election and the people's representatives in the House of Commons can hold the government to account to the public for any aspect of public service provision. But those general forms of accountability are not effective at achieving good administration in particular cases. Particular cases come to the attention of the media and Parliament only when there is a scandal. Even when a scandal leads to questions in the House of Commons, Parliament is likely to be an ineffective forum for achieving justice.

Legal accountability techniques should hold government accountable in ways that cannot be secured through parliamentary politics or the force of public opinion. Legal accountability is essential for providing good public services with integrity; the challenge in this chapter is to work out how accountability for particular decisions can best be secured through law, when the government uses contract as a technique of administration.

A contract itself is an accountability structure, that identifies what a party is accountable **for**, and identifies (or takes for granted) processes **through** which the party may be held accountable **to** the other party. Here is the promise for achieving economy and efficiency through contractual techniques: competition for business can stimulate higher quality in the provision of public services, with less waste. Several companies competing for customers can provide telephone services much better and more cheaply than a government department can. The profit pressure motivates the company both to provide what the customers really want, and to do so

		TO	THROUGH	FOR
Ministers		Parliament	—questions in the House of Commons[12]	—their department's work.
MPs		electors	—an election	—their conduct in office.[13]
A private company in a PPP	may be accountable	the partner department or agency	—an action in the High Court[14]	—compliance with the contract.
Civil servants		ministers	—managerial control	—implementing government policy.
Courts		the parties, and the public	—openness in their process, and the giving of reasons	—just and lawful decisions.
All of the above		the public	—the media	—anything that interests the media and cannot be kept secret.

Figure 15.2 Examples of accountability

without wasting money. If the company faces competition from other companies, it will be under pressure to provide the service at a low cost to the user. It is really difficult to organize government departments so that they provide services at low cost.

Also, and equally importantly, the career advancement pressure on individual employees will operate differently in a private organization, where it will be tied to the profit pressure on the company. Private companies can be wasteful, but they tend to be better at tying the criteria for rewards and advancement to success in delivering valued services at low cost.

15.2.1 An example: care for the disabled

In Britain, as part of the creation of a welfare state after World War II, the National Assistance Act 1948 required local authorities to provide housing for elderly or

[12]   There are other accountability mechanisms in Parliament, including the National Audit Office, select and standing committees, and investigations by the Parliamentary Ombudsman. All of these techniques are backed by the Government's need for the confidence of the House of Commons.

[13]   Of course, the role of elections in holding an MP or a whole government accountable for what they have done is incidental to their role in choosing a member for the new Parliament, and choosing a new government.

[14]   An action for breach of contract is *not* the main accountability mechanism for contracting out, though it forms a backstop that gives force to the department's ability to hold a contractor to targets set out in the agreement, and to demand a remedy. The commercial pressure on contractors to perform well in order to secure further government contracts can also enhance the effectiveness of the contract as an accountability technique.

disabled people who needed care that was not otherwise available to them. The local authorities could operate nursing homes of their own or provide housing by arrangement with a charity. As part of the shift to government by contract, the Conservatives' National Health Service and Community Care Act 1990 (s 42) amended the 1948 Act to allow local authorities to contract out to bodies providing housing 'professionally or by way of trade or business'. What role should accountability play in that scheme, and how can it be secured if provision of care in nursing homes is contracted out?

Accountability should help to secure the delivery of public services in a way that pursues a good public purpose without waste, and with integrity (that is, honest, faithful application of a scheme) and equity (that is, substantive fairness). In the provision of housing for disabled people in nursing homes, do those purposes require accountability to the nursing home? Or accountability to Parliament? Or accountability to the taxpayer? Or to a court or tribunal? It's obvious: those purposes require all these forms of accountability, and more. Accountability to Parliament will help to ensure the accomplishment of Parliament's purposes in creating the scheme. Accountability to the taxpayer will put pressure on the government to achieve those purposes without waste. Accountability to the resident in the nursing home will protect the integrity of the scheme by helping to ensure that it is not operated in a way that abuses anyone or withholds benefits from anyone arbitrarily. And accountability to the resident will also help to ensure that the purpose of the scheme is accomplished; if the scheme itself is a good one, that result will promote equity.

Legal accountability may offer ways of backing up accountability to the resident, e.g., through a claim by the resident for breach of contract (if she has a contract with the nursing home). Judicial review of the conduct of the nursing home (as in *R v North and East Devon Health Authority, ex p Coughlan* [2001] QB 213; see p 286) backs up the nursing home's accountability to the resident, with the authority of an independent court with a supervisory jurisdiction to impose the rule of law on the administration. And accountability of staff in the nursing home to a court through a criminal prosecution for murder or assault is essential for the protection of vulnerable people.

Accountability danger and accountability cost

Accountability techniques carry dangers and costs. Accountability to the taxpayer may put pressure on the government not only to avoid waste, but also to favour the wealthy by leaving the destitute without support. Accountability to the patient through a court will subject the scheme's operators to expensive litigation that can be pursued by people with no legitimate complaint (**process cost**—see p 111), and may lead to distorted decision making that privileges the particular complaint in a way that damages the ability of a home to benefit other residents or potential residents (**process danger**—see p 111). Process danger and process cost are instances of accountability danger and accountability cost.

Accountability is **not necessarily a good thing**: it depends on the form of accountability, and whether it promotes good government without creating disproportionate costs or dangers. Judges, for example, are accountable to the public and the parties because they have to hear cases in open court and give reasons for many of their decisions. But it would be an abandonment of the rule of law if courts could be held to account **to** any other institution for the justice or lawfulness of their decisions **through** any technique for interfering with the judges' decision. And Parliament must not be held to account **to** courts **through** judicial review **for** the wisdom of its enactments.

The government could build and operate nursing homes, or contract the work out to a private nursing home operator, or privatize and give vouchers for the disabled to buy services from private homes. The potential benefit from privatizing or contracting out public services is that private companies may be able to provide them more efficiently, with less waste than a government department. Efficiency will mean better services, or lower cost to the public, or both. The potential drawback is loss of accountability for integrity and equity and quality of service. But the challenge is not to choose whether to have unaccountable but efficient private delivery, or inefficient but accountable public delivery. The choices are extremely complex because private agencies are not necessarily more efficient or less accountable than public agencies, and accountability and efficiency are not always opposed to each other. Accountability is necessary for securing efficiency.

Any scheme of social provision of nursing homes will require legal accountability techniques that promote the responsible application of the scheme, without unduly impairing its efficiency. Accountability in public administration (in all its forms) is a way of securing some public good; here are three public goods:

1. the social provision of places in good nursing homes, and

2. efficiency in provision, and

3. faithful application of the scheme.

It is the third public good that legal accountability can help to secure. That good is based on the first and second goods. The first good requires sound decisions as to whether a particular person needs care, and whether he or she is able to pay for it. And (since the first good is the provision of good **homes**) it requires that residents be treated with respect, as people who should be involved in decisions about their home.

Market mechanisms may help to secure the second good, but they may put pressure on the application of the scheme, so that legal accountability becomes more important. And, conversely, legal accountability techniques should be developed in a way that does not damage efficiency in provision (by subjecting the scheme to overly expensive processes, or by requiring the provision of services that will not promote the first good, e.g., by privileging a complainant over other residents).

What about equity? We shouldn't put it fourth on our list of public goods that social housing can promote, because it is the form of social justice that justifies the whole scheme. It can only be achieved through the political construction of a scheme that sets out to provide homes to meet real needs, and efficient implementation, and application that not only has integrity, but also involves the exercise of discretions with concern to meet the needs that justify the scheme.

The question of how, if at all, legal accountability techniques can help to secure equity in nursing home provision is one of the most challenging in public law, and we will come to grips with it **(section 15.5)** after dealing with the capacity of public authorities to enter into contracts **(section 15.3)**, and surveying legal techniques for controlling public authorities' decisions whether to enter into contracts **(section 15.4)**.

15.3 Capacity to contract

15.3.1 The Crown

The Crown has an inherent (see pp 231–2) general power to contract, exercised on its behalf by departments. The capacity to contract is not a prerogative of the Crown, because the Crown has it in the same way as most public authorities. It is not exactly the same as private persons' legal power to contract, because the law gives them that power for the purpose of enabling them to exercise the autonomy that an individual or a private commercial association ought to have in a civil society. Public authorities have power to contract because it is useful for the fulfilment of their roles, and there is nothing unjust or contrary to constitutional principle in their capacity to contract.

Yet the law finds something awkward about the Crown's liability in contract. Before the Crown Proceedings Act 1947, the only remedy for breach of contract was a 'petition of right'. In legal terms it was merely a request. It worked because the government found it useful to be bound by its agreements. Even today, injunctions and orders for specific performance cannot be made against the Crown (Crown Proceedings Act 1947 s 21[15]). And damages awards cannot be enforced against the Crown by ordinary processes of execution.

It may seem that being bound by contract would limit the freedom of decision that the Crown needs to have in the public interest. In fact, the truth is almost the reverse: being capable of entering into a binding agreement is extremely valuable. If you cannot bind yourself, it is hard to get people to deal with you. The Crown Proceedings Act 1947 overturned a legal immunity of the Crown for good constitutional reason: it is in the public interest for the Crown to be able to bind itself in the same effective, transparent manner as other contracting parties, and persons who contract with the Government ought to have the same recourse as they have against other contracting parties.

But ministers cannot bind the Crown in a way that will obstruct the future use of the prerogative. During the First World War, the Government gave an undertaking to a Swedish shipowning company not to detain their ship in Britain. But once it arrived, the government refused to let the ship leave. The company sought damages

---

[15] Except that the Public Contracts Regulations 2006, implementing the EU procurement rules (see p 581), give the court power to grant an injunction (s 47(10)).

for breach of contract (by a petition of right against the Crown). The judge advising on the petition held that there was no contract: *The Amphitrite* [1921] 3 KB 500.

How can that be reconciled with the Crown's general capacity to contract? In *The Amphitrite*, Rowlatt J held that the government can bind itself by a **commercial** contract, and if it does so it must perform it or pay damages for breach like any other contracting party. But this was not a commercial contract; it was an arrangement as to future 'executive action':

> ' ...it is not competent for the Government to fetter its future executive action, which must necessarily be determined by the needs of the community when the question arises. It cannot by contract hamper its freedom of action in matters which concern the welfare of the State. ' (503)

Of course, commercial transactions are executive, too. So we have to read Rowlatt J's phrase 'executive action' as a technical term for, roughly, 'executive action that must, in the public interest, be unhindered by commitments that the government has purported to make'. The interesting thing about *The Amphitrite* doctrine is that it is a court that must decide when the public interest requires the Government to have that freedom.

In principle, a contractor may find that an agreement with the Government is unenforceable. And the government's freedom means that the Government lacks the power that comes with contractual competence: as in other areas of contract law, the inability to enter a contract can be very inconvenient. That potential inconvenience has not seriously hampered the Government—or it would have put legislation before Parliament in the many decades since *The Amphitrite* was decided.

15.3.2 Statutory bodies

Should all public authorities have power to contract? Their functions are more specific than those of the Crown; but their specific functions may require it—and then, if the power to contract does not create a special risk of abuse, they ought to have it.

But the traditional common law rule is that they have no general power to contract. Whether they can make contracts depends on whether the statute establishing the body empowers them to do so. And if the statute gives a limited power, a contract will be invalid if it is outside the power.

Take a body with very specific powers—a railway company. Lord Blackburn held in *Attorney General v Great Eastern Railway* (1880) 5 App Cas 473 that, 'where there is an Act of Parliament creating a corporation for a particular purpose, and giving it powers for that particular purpose, what it does not expressly or impliedly authorize is to be taken to be prohibited' (481). Local authorities have much wider functions, but Lord Templeman applied the traditional approach in *Hazell v Hammersmith LBC* [1992] 2 AC 1, 22: 'A local authority, although democratically elected and representative of the area, is not a sovereign body and can only do such things as are expressly or impliedly authorized by Parliament.'

The rule would be damaging, except that the courts are prepared to hold that the power to contract is impliedly authorized where the statutory body needs it. As Lord Selborne LC said in the Great Eastern Railway case, 'whatever may fairly be regarded as incidental to, or consequential upon, those things which the legislature has authorized, ought not (unless expressly prohibited) to be held, by judicial construction, to be ultra vires' (478). The result (although the courts have not put it this way) is the same as if there were a general doctrine that public authorities have inherent power to make contracts that they need to be able to make if they are to carry out their responsibilities well. Of course, it is not generally the judges' job to decide what public authorities need to do their job well. Parliament can always specify the powers of a public body if it sees fit, but if it does not do so, the courts have to decide what specification of those powers is necessary to accomplish what Parliament set the body up to do. The courts must decide the public interest here, just as they must decide when the public interest requires that the Crown should not be bound by an agreement.

Although their ability to raise money is very tightly controlled, local authorities are the best example of a public authority with an unspecific statutory grant of power to contract:

> a local authority shall have power to do any thing (whether or not involving the expenditure, borrowing or lending of money or the acquisition or disposal of any property or rights) which is calculated to facilitate, or is conducive or incidental to, the discharge of any of their functions. [16]

The uncertainty as to what sort of contracts are authorized by these broad provisions makes it harder for local authorities to contract, where it is unclear whether a particular sort of contract is within an authority's power. If the contract is in the end held to be outside the authority's powers, one party or the other will be able to escape from a bargain that it made with the intention of binding itself.

In *Crédit Suisse v Allerdale BC* [1997] QB 306, a local council added a time share complex to a recreation centre, to help pay for the swimming pool. The time share operation was set up as a company, whose directors were council members and officers. The time share units did not sell well and the company went bankrupt. The bank tried to cash in on a guarantee that the council had given for the company's debts, but the Court of Appeal held that the guarantee was *ultra vires*, because the council lacked statutory authority to set up the company and enter into the guarantee. As Neill LJ put it, far from being necessary to its functions, the setting up of the company and the giving of the guarantee were actually designed to *escape* the controls placed on borrowing by local authorities in the 1972 Act.

The *Crédit Suisse* case created a serious problem for local authorities, since banks had to expect that if any clever financing arrangement ran into difficulty, the council's

---

[16] Local Government Act 1972 s 111.

agreement with the bank might be held to be *ultra vires*. And it wouldn't even matter if the council wanted to honour its agreement, because the council's auditors can take issue (as in *Crédit Suisse*) with payments under a contract that may be *ultra vires*. Parliament addressed the problem in the Local Government (Contracts) Act 1997, which allows a local authority to enter into a 'certified' contract, which will have effect *as if* the local authority had power to enter into it, even if it was actually *ultra vires* (s 2). So a local authority will not be able to get out of a certified contract, and that enables local authorities to deal with banks in spite of *Crédit Suisse*. A certified contract can still be challenged in judicial review (s 5); if the contract is held to be unlawful, the Act gives the court wide discretionary power (which the court would in any case have had under the ordinary law of judicial review remedies; see p 381) to do justice to anyone who entered into the 'contract'.

● *Pop Quiz* ●
A breach of contract is unlawful. Does that mean that a breach of contract is a ground of judicial review?

15.4 How does the law control government contracts?

From the late 1980s, the Conservative Government introduced contracting out as standard practice in central government, and imposed it on local authorities as compulsory competitive tendering (CCT).[17] The goal was to get better value for money by bringing competition into public projects. CCT did not merely require local authorities to seek competitive bids when they contracted out; it required them to put internal operations up for tender—to contract the services out if a private company made the best bid, and to contract the services *in* if the best bid came from within the public body.

In competitive tendering, if a bid from a private contractor is successful, the private contractor carries out the project and the resulting PPP is governed by a real contract. If the in-house department wins the competitive tendering, the work is carried out under a so-called 'contract' between the local authority and one of its own departments. That forced the works departments and education departments of local authorities to compete (as 'Direct Service Organizations' (DSOs)) with private contractors for, e.g., provision of housing maintenance and school meals.

The courts gave little help to council workers who resented the contracting out of housing services through CCT. For example, the Court of Appeal held that a resolution of a council to accept an internal tender gave the workers no legitimate expectation that the council would continue to provide them with work (*R v Walsall, ex p Yapp* [1994] ICR 528). The council accepted an internal tender for housing maintenance and repair, and then decided to seek new tenders for the work, using its power to vary its resolutions. Nolan LJ held that 'The only legitimate expectation of the applicants and their fellow employees under public law, as it seems to me, was that the council

---

[17] Local Government, Planning and Land Act 1980, Local Government Acts 1988 and 1992.

would not vary the resolutions...save on rational grounds, and after due consultation with those affected' (537). The courts will not superimpose a requirement of substantive fairness on the council's tendering decisions.

On the other hand, the courts upheld the council's ability to choose its own internal works department over the bids of private contractors: councils have no general duty to choose the cheapest private bid over an internal bid (R v Portsmouth City Council [1997] CLC 407 (CA)).

Local authorities resented the compulsory programme, and after 1997 the Labour Government set out to achieve the same benefits in a less rigid scheme called '**Best Value**'. The Local Government Act 1999 designated English local authorities (and other bodies such as police authorities) as 'best value authorities' (s 1), and required that 'A best value authority must make arrangements to secure continuous improvement in the way which its functions are exercised, having regard to a combination of economy, efficiency, and effectiveness' (s 3(1)). That duty is backed by duties to consult council tax payers and service users, and to publish 'Best Value Performance Plans'. The Secretary of State has a very wide power to require an authority to exercise its functions with economy, efficiency and effectiveness, and can even take over a function of the authority (s 15).

The new regime gives central government a flexible power to impose on local authorities the same compulsion that CCT involved. The powerful language of the Local Government Act 1999 s 15 means that the courts are likely to be as deferential toward ministers in their use of those powers, as the Court of Appeal was (in the Leicester case) toward the minister's role in enforcing CCT. 'Best value' authorities will not be able to satisfy central government that they have pursued 'economy, efficiency and effectiveness' without testing the open market for provision of a service. So Labour's Best Value regime provides just as important a role for competition and contracting out, while adding more flexible ministerial control than the Conservative CCT regime.

Contracting out under CCT or the Best Value regime creates a PPP between a public authority and private companies that provide services. And when a local authority decides that 'economy, efficiency and effectiveness' are best served by choosing to have the service provided by an internal department after competitive tendering, it makes the organization of government more businesslike through internal contracting. Either way, the government moves away from the command model toward a deals model of administration.

Beyond 'Best value'

The Audit Commission runs the Government's 'Comprehensive Performance Assessment' scheme, a programme of periodic ratings of the work of local councils designed to provide 'the basis for a proportionate and risk-based approach to regulation'.[18] That scheme in turn is morphing into 'Comprehensive Area

---

[18]   http://www.audit-commission.gov.uk/cpa/guide/guidesummary.asp.

Assessment', which is to provide overall evaluation and rating of public services in localities, in a collaboration between the Audit Commission and the commissions that regulate social care, health care, education, police, probation, and prisons.[19] Each of those various regulatory commissions is responsible for overseeing the work of private companies providing services through PPPs (even the police contract out some services, such as detention after arrest).

CCT is a form of contracting out in which the finance is provided by the Government. In 1992, John Major's Conservative government developed a model in which funding for public infrastructure projects would come from private investors. In opposition in the 1990s, Labour opposed the resulting **Private Finance Initiative** ('PFI'), but since 1997 successive Labour governments have expanded it.

15.4.1 The Private Finance Initiative[20]

The PFI is a variety of PPP in which the private partner brings a financial investment to the partnership. The private partner or partners ordinarily design, build, finance, and operate an 'asset' such as a hospital, a bridge, a prison, or a school, under a contract that gives the private partner a return over the lifetime of the project. It is different from privatizing (e.g.) a hospital, because even though the private partner owns the hospital, a public authority, rather than the market, decides what service is to be provided, and funding to the private partner is determined through a contract with the public authority. And the private partner has a stake in the success of the initiative, too.

The PFI is now the main source of funding for new projects such as prisons and hospitals, and has delivered more than 200 new schools and dozens of major transport projects, including the Channel Tunnel Rail Link.[21] So, for example, without needing to raise taxes or borrow £15,000,000,000 to renew the London Tube, the Department for Transport and Transport for London are getting the work done through a PFI.[22]

A PFI deal is meant to transfer to private companies some of the risks associated with the project, and enables the government to set performance standards in the contract, backed up with financial penalties. So the prospect is more efficient delivery of, e.g., the Tube renewal, with the public paying only for the services actually received, when it receives them.

But it isn't magic: it all has to be paid for eventually, through a substantial stream of revenue to the private partner over many years (from the government or from users of the service, or both). The risk spreading and the government's ability to penalize

---

[19] http://www.audit-commission.gov.uk/caa/.

[20] http://www.hm-treasury.gov.uk/ppp_index.htm.

[21] For the list of current PFI Projects, see http://www.hm-treasury.gov.uk/ppp_pfi_stats.html/.

[22] http://www.tfl.gov.uk/assets/downloads/transforming-the-tube-brochure.pdf.

poor performance only work if the private partner stays solvent (and one of the private consortia working on the Tube has gone into administration). Which, of course, means that the risk isn't altogether transferred: the public authority will have to cope with the service need, if the private partner goes bankrupt.

And the transaction costs of a good PFI are substantial: the government will be fleeced by the private partners if it does not invest skill and resources in forecasting the risks and costs and benefits of the project, when it enters into the initial agreement. The cost of the work that needs to be done before entering into a PFI (and of monitoring work as the project proceeds) means that PFI is only feasible for large projects; for smaller projects, direct administration by a department or Executive Agency will be cheaper even if the department or agency is inefficient.

The partners in a PFI deal may agree that the government will take a share in the ownership of the asset, or the asset may belong to the private partner. In the contract, the government will insist that the private partner take at least some of the risk of cost overruns, but the private partner will insist that the government take at least some of the risk that public demand for the project will dry up. The private partner gets the promise of a stream of revenue either in payments from government for provision of services, or through payments made directly by the public (such as tolls on the Skye bridge).

The public benefit of getting projects built sooner, at reduced risk, comes at a cost. Along with the accountability risks of other PPPs, the PFI imposes a financial burden: the burden of promising the private partner a stream of income. So the government is committed to entering into PFIs only when the benefit (through accelerated, economical investment, or through sharing of risk) makes it worthwhile for a public authority to take on the commitment.

The 'factors' the Treasury looks for to decide whether a PFI project would give value for money ('VfM'):

- 'a major capital investment programme, requiring effective management of risks...;
- 'the structure of the service is appropriate, allowing the public sector to define its needs as service outputs that can be adequately contracted for in a way that ensures effective, equitable, and accountable delivery of public services...;
- 'the nature of the assets and services..., as well as the associated risks, are capable of being costed on a whole-of-life, long-term basis;
- 'the value of the project is sufficiently large to ensure that procurement costs are not disproportionate;
- 'the technology and other aspects of the sector are stable...;
- '...confidence that the assets and services provided are intended to be used over long periods into the future; and
- 'the private sector has the expertise to deliver, there is good reason to think it will offer VfM and robust performance incentives can be put in place.'[23]

---

[23]   'Value for Money Assessment Guidance' (2006) HM Treasury.

Notice that **accountability** is in that list of factors, and so is **equity**. The list shows how those two fundamental principles of any good public service can get lost in a welter of other considerations of risk, demand, cost, and return on investment, which involve financial guesswork. The accountability risk is that the fragile link between policy formation and policy execution will be disrupted altogether. A school or a prison or a hospital can only be run well by people who are committed to the good of the community and of the individuals at school or in prison or in hospital. And their commitment needs to be supported by the management of the operation.

So one of the risks of pursuing efficiency through various forms of PPP, including PFI, arises from the fact that work is done by employees of a private service provider, rather than by public employees. That can be very attractive to the public partner, as it offers a way of operating a project with low wages, without the public authority having to pay a political price for paying low wages. It is politically easier for a private employer than a public employer to treat employees poorly. The Government is committed to PFI decisions that 'deliver clear value for money without sacrificing the terms and conditions of staff'.[24] But it does not treat equity and accountability as requirements of justice or constitutional principle. It treats them as factors to be considered alongside value for money and financial risk management. And it puts a distance between government and the people who guard prisoners and make school meals, giving those people an indirect, commercial relationship with the community they serve.

15.4.2 Parliamentary control and the National Audit Office

Parliamentary control is available in principle over all governmental contracting (including the PFI), because the government has *no inherent power to raise money, or to spend it.*

FROM THE MISTS OF TIME

In the late middle ages, the King could spend his own private wealth as he saw fit, but the wealth of the country was not his to deal with except with the consent of those in the country (the wealthy barons) from whom he wanted it. This principle should have been obvious right from the Norman Conquest in 1066, but the barons had to force the King to admit it in Magna Carta, and to assemble a council—a precursor of Parliament—to negotiate taxes (Magna Carta 1215 cl 12, 14). Magna Carta was only a decree of successive kings, and the principle was not securely established until the Bill of Rights 1689 enacted 'That levying Money for or to the Use of the Crowne by pretence of Prerogative without Grant of Parlyament for longer time or in other manner then the same is or shall be granted is Illegall' (Art 4). That is the law today.

---

[24] http://www.hm-treasury.gov.uk/ppp_index.html/.

The control of Parliament over government by contract should not be underestimated, but it operates at a very abstract level, and in a way that is only a part of parliamentary politics in general. Whenever the government MPs in The House of Commons think that the government's policies on government by contract are harming their chances at re-election, that will generate political pressure on the government. Since that accountability mechanism is so abstract and tenuous, Parliament needs a much better focused technique in order to do its job of scrutinizing expenditure. The National Audit Office (NAO) is the technique.

The Comptroller and Auditor General (the head of the NAO) is an independent officer of the House of Commons; he has to confirm to Parliament that government spending transactions have parliamentary authority. And the constitutionally important provisions of the Exchequer and Audit Departments Act 1866 are still in effect:

> ‘ s 14. When any sum or sums of moneys shall have been granted to Her Majesty by a resolution of the House of Commons, or by an Act of Parliament, to defray expenses for any specified public services, it shall be lawful for Her Majesty from time to time, by her royal order under the Royal Sign Manual, countersigned by the Treasury, to authorize and require the Treasury to issue, out of the credits to be granted to them on the Exchequer account as herein-after provided, the sums which may be required from time to time to defray such expenses, not exceeding the amount of the sums so voted or granted. ’

It is conceivable that the government might make a contract and then have no lawful power to pay a price stipulated in the contract, if Parliament has not appropriated any moneys that could be used for that purpose. Then under the Crown Proceedings Act 1947, a claimant could get a judgment for damages for breach of contract (though not an order of specific performance) against the department in question or the Attorney General, but neither the department nor the Attorney General would be able to pay the damages, and no one would be in contempt of court as a result. This is not a practical problem: if the House of Commons were prepared to block government spending by refusing to appropriate funds, it would already have lost confidence in the Government. So the Commons spending control does not itself put a damper on government contracting.

But meanwhile, the Comptroller and Auditor General has taken on a much wider role since 1866; the NAO audits the accounts of all government departments and most non-departmental public bodies. And the NAO carries out Value for Money audits designed to pursue 'three Es': **Economy** ('spending less'), **Efficiency** ('spending well'); and **Effectiveness** ('spending wisely').[25] That role is *far* more intrusive than judicial review. As creative as the judges have been, lack of efficiency or wisdom is

[25]   http://www.nao.org.uk/what_we_do/value_for_money_audit.aspx. The National Audit Act 1983 authorizes the NAO to 'carry out examinations into the economy, efficiency and effectiveness with which any department...has used its resources in discharging its functions' (s 6).

not a ground of judicial review. So, for example, the NAO's report on 'Widening participation in higher education' really did set out to tell universities what they can do 'through outreach and other widening participation activities to raise the aspirations and attainment of people'.[26] And the NAO's report on the Iraq war passed judgment on the military success of the campaign (favourably) and on the Government's planning for reconstruction after the war (unfavourably).[27]

That role in providing accountability *for efficiency* is crucial to the government-by-contract agenda. The NAO is the watchdog, and serves as the chief technique for efficiency-accountability in central government. The Audit Commission fulfils the same watchdog role for local authorities, health, and fire services, as part of the Best Value scheme.[28] The role of auditors today is not simply to check the accounts; it is very similar to the role of management consultants in private industry; they are prepared to take an overall view of how an organization can pursue its purposes better. While it is not their job to identify the purposes,[29] they *do* pass judgment as to what counts as success in the organization's work, and not just on how to cut costs.

But a value for money audit report makes no legally binding decision. The role of the NAO is simply to make a criticism of government's workings after an independent investigation. Its role is like that of an **ombudsman** (see Chapter 13), because it is to investigate and report. But there are at least three important differences between the NAO and ombudsmen:

- the NAO does not resolve particular complaints about administration;[30]

- conversely, unlike an ombudsman, it can start its own investigation of general issues; and

- unlike the ombudsmen, its role has not been judicialized (see p 488).

It is simply clearer in the case of the NAO than in the case of ombudsmen, that the role is purely to make a report on an investigation. The reports of the Auditor General have never been judicially reviewed.[31] If anyone ever sought judicial review, there

---

[26] HC 725 Session 2007–2008, 25 June 2008 [4].

[27] 'Operation TELIC—United Kingdom Military Operations in Iraq' HC 60 Session 2003–2004: 11 December 2003 [6.4]–[6.4].

[28] http://www.audit-commission.gov.uk/. The European Court of Auditors has the same role in the European Union; it has an auditing function and a general mandate to improve financial management: http://eca.europa.eu.

[29] The NAO cannot 'question the merits of the policy objectives of any department, authority or body in respect of which an examination is carried out' (National Audit Act 1983 s 6).

[30] The NAO invites complaints directly from citizens about central government spending, and for complaints from government workers, it has a whistleblowers' hotline (see http://www.nao.org.uk/whistle.htm). But the role of the complaint is to bring to light a matter needing investigation in the public interest; the role of the NAO is not to give an individual redress for an injustice that he or she has suffered.

[31] The Audit Commission, though, has been subject to judicial review, in a claim by a local authority. The Court of Appeal took the availability of judicial review for granted, and did not need

would be a strong argument that permission (see p 367) should be refused. Anyone with a complaint about a value for money report from the NAO (whether a government department, or a member of the public) ought to look to Parliament and not to a court for a remedy, if any remedy is needed.

The work of the Office is overseen by the Public Accounts Commission, which is really a committee of MPs (consisting of the Chairman of the Committee of Public Accounts, the Leader of the House, and seven other MPs appointed by the House who are not ministers) (National Audit Act 1983 s 2). The Commission examines the NAO's work and reports to the House of Commons.

The NAO's investigative role also provides information for the Public Accounts Committee, a select committee of the House of Commons that has been responsible since 1861 for examining the accounts of expenditure of funds granted by Parliament. Both the NAO and the Public Accounts Committee support the constitutional responsibility of Parliament to scrutinize public expenditure.

15.4.3 European Union control over contracting

The control of government procurement is one of the most creative ways in which the European Union has pursued its purpose of creating a single market. Public procurement was an obvious target for EC law because it has enormous economic importance, and member states tended to buy goods and services from private suppliers in their own countries. The EC rules start with the Treaty, because the Articles on free movement of goods and services that were designed to create a single market imply that governments must open up their procurement processes. A variety of directives have been made to require member states to secure open procurement by public authorities in general.

The rules do two very important things, both of which have been implemented in English law by the Public Contracts Regulations 2006 SI 2006/5. First, a contracting authority must award a public contract to the **lowest price or the most economically advantageous** bid—which means that the lowest price bid wins unless there is reason to think that there will be economic advantage in paying more. Secondly, 'economic operators' interested in tendering for public contracts get **process rights**, including the right to know the criteria for a successful bid ahead of time. Criteria for economically advantageous tenders must be specified in advance. The process for the award of the contract must be transparent, and there is a duty to give reasons.

These rules have not abolished local preferences in procurement, but they have had a more general collateral effect, because they create an opportunity for a disappointed bidder to argue that the public authority has not followed its criteria, or has not considered a bid fairly. Companies bidding for a public contract would have no such procedural rights under the ordinary law of due process. The change creates

---

to discuss the standards to be applied: *R (Ealing) v Audit Commission* [2005] EWCA Civ 556. The National Audit Office is different from the Audit Commission because of its relation to Parliament.

a technique for a disappointed tenderer to challenge a decision to award a contract to one of its competitors, by catching the public authority in a breach of the process rules.[32]

In choosing among bids, the public body cannot create new criteria, or even sub-headings within its criteria, and it can only decide what weight to give to the sub-headings of an award criterion if the decision:

- 'does not alter the criteria for the award of the contract set out in the contract documents or the contract notice;

- 'does not contain elements which, if they had been known at the time the tenders were prepared, could have affected that preparation;

- 'was not adopted on the basis of matters likely to give rise to discrimination against one of the tenderers.'[33]

These controls on government contracting were designed to reduce trade barriers between EU member states; but you do not have to come from outside the UK to challenge a contracting decision by a public authority. The effect of the rules is to give English judges a jurisdiction to impose standards of good procedure on public authority contracting decisions in general.

15.4.4 Common law judicial control over contracting

Apart from the EU procurement rules, can you get judicial review of a government decision not to make a contract with you? Or a decision to award or not to award a contract to someone else? It seems to be contrary to the idea of contract, which is a legal device for parties to decide their own rights and obligations. If you are disappointed that Tesco will not enter into a contract with you, you have no legal recourse. Why should you have any recourse if a public authority will not enter into a contract with you?

The reason is really just the **core rationale** for judicial review (see p 65). The considerations are the same as with *any* duty that the law imposes on a public authority but not on Tesco. It is not so remarkable to impose duties of due process, and for the courts to have jurisdiction to prevent abuse of power in contracting. The law allows private contractors to decide their own purposes, as long as they do not commit a crime or a tort, or breach a regulatory requirement. But on the *Padfield* doctrine (see p 45), public authorities do not have an altogether free hand in deciding their purposes. It is undoubtedly the case that a public authority cannot do something by contracting that it has no power to do directly. A contract designed to achieve that would be *ultra vires*. But if a contract is not a way of evading limits on the powers of a public authority, the courts are very restrained in judicial review of contracting. If an authority has the power to enter into an agreement, the courts will defer massively

---

[32]   See, e.g., *Lettings International Limited v Newham* [2007] EWCA Civ 1522 [20].

[33]   Case C-331/04 *ATI EAC Srl v ACTV Venezia SpA* [2005] ECR I-10109 [32].

on the content of the contract, and will even defer to some extent on the process that ought to be pursued in negotiations.

A local council's decisions in setting policy for making contracts with private service providers are subject to judicial review, and a decision to impose a contract term on a nursing home will be quashed if it is contrary to the purpose of the legislation under which the council is acting (R v Cleveland CC, ex p Cleveland Care Homes Association [1994] COD 221). Since the early days of contracting out, the courts have been prepared to ask whether contracting authorities have acted fairly: in R v London Borough of Enfield, ex p T F Unwin (Roydon) Ltd [1989] COD 466, a decision to remove a firm from a council's list of contractors and to prevent it from tendering for renewal of an existing contract was held to be subject to a legal requirement of due process.

In the early days of contracting out, Lord Justice Glidewell suggested that judicial review was only available for certain sorts of contract decisions: those in which there is a 'public law element' in the decision itself (Mass Energy Ltd v Birmingham City Council [1994] ELR 298, 306). And Waller J held in R v Lord Chancellor's Dept, ex p Hibbit & Saunders [1993] COD 326 that 'it would need something additional to the simple fact that the governmental body was negotiating the contract to impose on that authority any public law obligation in addition to any private law obligations or duties there might be...' (328). But that public law element is really surplus, because even in a merely commercial contract to buy paperclips, the courts should be prepared to hear a claim that a public authority has abused its power; every governmental decision to buy something has a public law element, if it is an abuse of power. And in negotiating any contract, the law imposes on a public authority an obligation to use its contracting power for proper purposes and not (e.g.) for a vendetta or for private profit. So in Cookson & Clegg v Ministry of Defence [2005] EWCA Civ 811, the Court of Appeal held that judicial review will be available 'if there were bribery, corruption or the implementation of a policy unlawful in itself, either because it was ultra vires or for other reasons' [18]. A malicious refusal to contract ought to count as the tort of misfeasance and judicial review ought to be available, but only for abuse of power.

Real abuses of power will be rare. It is much more common, though, for a company to invest substantial resources on a good bid for a multimillion-pound contract, and to complain, on coming second, that the process was unfair or that the substance of the decision was irrational. So in Cookson & Clegg, a disappointed bidder for a large clothing contract for the military claimed that the Ministry had broken the regulations implementing the EU directive, but they also sought judicial review, asking the court to strike down the decision to award the contract to a rival for 'irrationality' (see p 228). The company wanted the court to apply standards of public law reasonableness in addition to the regulation requirements. The Court of Appeal refused to allow judicial review to proceed alongside an ordinary claim based on the regulations, because of the **last resort rule** (see p 60): judicial review is not available to hear every allegation that a public authority has acted unlawfully, but is only available where it is necessary in the public interest for the court to impose the rule of law on administration. An ordinary claim based on the regulations gave the claimants fair recourse against the decision they were challenging.

And consider a case that was not subject to the EU procurement rules,[34] brought by the second-place contestant in a very close competition for a contract to provide bailiff services to the Court Service in Wales and Cheshire. In R (Menai Collect) v Department for Constitutional Affairs [2006] EWHC 724, the unsuccessful tenderer claimed that the decision was unlawful because the panel that evaluated the bids did not pass all the information on to the board that took the final decision:

> ‘ It is not every wandering from the precise paths of best practice that lends fuel to a claim for judicial review. It is, I think, for this reason that the examples given of cases where commercial processes such as these are likely to be subject to review are such as they are in the reported cases, namely bribery, corruption, implementation of unlawful policy and the like. ’ [47]

The court will refuse to enter into 'a quasi-regulatory scrutiny' [49] designed to check whether a contracting authority assessed the bids in the right way. The core rationale for judicial review does not require a court to impose its decision on that point in place of the decision made by the contracting public authority.

The result of *Cookson & Clegg* and *Menai Collect* is that permission to bring a claim for judicial review of a decision not to award a contract to a claimant should be refused, unless the claim alleges a serious abuse of power. So if you are angry that a public authority turned you down and accepted a bid from a competitor, you cannot seek judicial review and say that apart from the controls in the regulations implementing the EU directive, you want judicial review for irrationality too. The EU procurement rules are important because they impose much closer judicial control on the contract process than common law judicial review does.

15.5 Contracting out of administrative law?

Who can be subjected to judicial review, for which sorts of decisions? We can ask similar questions about who can be charged with the crime of misconduct in a public office (for which sorts of actions), or sued in the tort of misfeasance in a public office, or investigated by an ombudsman or an auditor, or taken to a tribunal, or who can be required to respond to a freedom of information request. Most controversially, the law needs to determine who can be held to have acted unlawfully by infringing a Convention right under the Human Rights Act 1998 s 6.

This set of questions is important quite apart from contracting. People with grievances have made varied, more or less successful attempts to bring legal controls on abuse of public power to bear on actors that are not part of government, and that have no contract of any kind with government, but are carrying out a role that has a relation to the public interest that, according to the complainant, calls for the controls of

---

34 It was a 'services concession' contract, excluded by Public Contracts Regulations 2006 s 6(2)(m); s 6 provides other exclusions covering, e.g., employment contracts and contracts for the purchase of land, and for financial services.

administrative law. We need to look at those attempts carefully, but this section will focus on a special challenge that arises in determining the scope of judicial review and other administrative law controls: **can the government escape from the controls on its conduct imposed by administrative law, by contracting services out to private actors?**

The important points to start with are that the law must:

(1) decide the scope of the process in question by reference to the **purpose of the standards** to which the process gives effect; and

(2) look at the **kind of decision** being made, and not simply at the **kind of decision maker.**

In addressing those two points, keep in mind the danger that may arise from government by contract: if, for example, a public authority nursing home is controlled by judicial review but a private nursing home providing places under a contract with the public authority is not controlled, then it seems that the authority can escape the rule of law, by contracting out. In R v Servite Houses, ex p Goldsmith (2001) 33 HLR 35, Moses J held that when a local authority contracted out the provision of nursing home care to a private service provider, judicial review was not available against the private company. 'If I am right in my reasoning, it demonstrates an inadequacy of response to the plight of these applicants now that Parliament has permitted public law obligations to be discharged by entering into private law arrangements' [105]. This section concerns what it would take for the law to make an adequate response, when public bodies use contracts to provide services.

15.5.1 The scope of judicial review

If Tesco abuses its power in the market by doing something that no reasonable supermarket would do, there is no recourse in administrative law. Tesco has much greater power (in a variety of respects) than many public agencies, but it is not 'amenable' to judicial review. That is, the court has no jurisdiction to hear a claim for judicial review against it. An abuse of power by Tesco is no better than an abuse of power by a public authority; but the law of contract, tort, and crime, along with any regulatory regimes Parliament may impose (for environmental protection, food safety, fair competition, truth in advertising, fire safety, decent working hours, a minimum wage, etc., etc.), are the law's techniques for preventing abuse of power by private companies. The judges have no general supervisory jurisdiction to pass judgment on whether a private person has abused its power.

The Civil Procedure Rules limit the scope of judicial review to controlling 'the exercise of a public function' (CPR 54.1). The rules do not say what that means. In R v Panel on Take-overs and Mergers, ex p Datafin Plc [1987] QB 815 (CA), the Court of Appeal allowed an application for judicial review to proceed against a body that was not a government agency. The Panel was not even a legal person, according to Lord Donaldson MR (824), yet the Court treated it as a legal person by subjecting its conduct to judicial review. The leading investment banks in the City of London wanted to preserve a form of self-regulation over the conduct of company takeovers; the Panel was a committee of people they appointed to oversee the 'City Code', and to decide whether the Code had been infringed. Lord Donaldson asked, 'what is to happen if the panel goes off the rails? Suppose, perish the thought, that it were to use its powers in a way which was manifestly unfair. What then?' (827). His answer was that the courts would then give judicial review, on the same grounds of lack of natural justice and abuse of power that apply to the conduct of public authorities.

● *Pop Quiz* ●
Was the Panel on Take-overs and Mergers a public authority?

An abuse of power would go unremedied without the judicial willingness to interfere, and it would be the abuse of a kind of power (a disciplinary power over commercial trading) that the Panel had for the public good, so that there is a public interest in preventing its abuse. And the court could effectively impose a legal requirement of procedural fairness, and legal protection against abuse of power, without damaging the Panel's pursuit of its legitimate purposes. The capacity of the court to impose the rule of law on the Panel, without interfering inappropriately, justifies the availability of judicial review; it is an application of the core rationale for judicial review, which does not require that the defendant should be an agency of the state.

Unfortunately, Lord Donaldson did not stop there. He went on to emphasize the ways in which the Government had relied on the industry's self-regulation through the Panel, rather than imposing legal regulation. 'As an act of government' he said, 'it was decided' that the Panel should carry on the regulation of takeovers (835). The suggestion is that it was the Government's relations with the Panel that justified judicial review. But the core rationale for judicial review applies regardless of any particular relation between the Panel and government, because of the Panel's function (the nature of the issues at stake, the reasons for which it is the Panel that is addressing them, and the implications of the decision for the people affected). The real task for the Court in *Datafin* was not to ask (as it seemed to), 'is this body closely enough connected to government that we can review it?', but to ask the following set of questions: 'does this Panel's power need controlling in the public interest, to prevent it from being used arbitrarily? If so, are the courts capable of forming the judgments that would be needed to provide that control? And would the Panel's functioning be unduly damaged by subjecting it to the process of litigation?' But we will see that there is now the prospect that these latter questions can be addressed *not* through judicial review, but in an ordinary claim for a declaration, with no requirement of any connection between the government and the defendant.

Crimes in public office

Does criminal liability depend on whether a person is employed by the government? If a member of the Panel took a bribe to make a disciplinary decision one way or another, would he be guilty of the crime of misconduct in a public office

(see p 544)? The law is still[35] as Lord Mansfield stated it in R v Bembridge (1783) 3 Doug 327, 332: 'Here there are two principles applicable: first, that a man accepting an office of trust concerning the public, especially if attended with profit, is answerable criminally to the King for misbehaviour in his office; this is true, by whomever and in whatever way the officer is appointed.' The question is, whether the King (through the common law courts) can legitimately hold the official to answer for criminally abusing the public trust, and not whether the King appointed the official. But note that Bembridge was a government employee (an accountant in the army paymaster's office), and no one has ever been convicted of misconduct in a public office without being a servant of the government. There is no doubt that office holders who are independent of government (such as judges, ombudsmen, or Crown prosecutors) could be guilty of the offence. But it may be that the courts today would not convict someone who is not even on the government payroll, because of one of the requirements of the **principle of legality** (see p 19): that no one should be held criminally liable for conduct that was not specifically prohibited as criminal at the time of the conduct.

15.5.2 Judicial supervision of private bodies: 'The common law abhors all monopolies'

In the 2002 Gold Cup, Be My Royal crossed the finish line first, but the Jockey Club's discipline committee disqualified the horse for failing a drugs test. The Jockey Club's Appeal Board upheld the decision. William Mullins, the horse's trainer, sought judicial review on the ground that the decision was arbitrary and capricious and was based on a misconstruction of the rules on horse doping.

The Administrative Court refused permission for judicial review (R (Mullins) v Appeal Board of the Jockey Club (No 1) [2005] EWHC 2197). That was unsurprising, given the landmark decision in R v Disciplinary Committee of the Jockey Club, ex p Aga Khan [1993] 1 WLR 909 (CA). The Aga Khan case had decided there was no jurisdiction to give judicial review of Jockey Club disciplinary decisions, because the Club was not a government agency, and because there were adequate remedies for any abuse of power in an action for breach of contract. Bingham LJ emphasized the adequacy of contract remedies, and did not decide that judicial review would be unavailable if the Jockey Club abused its power in its treatment of a claimant who did not have a contract. But Hoffmann LJ said, 'I do not think that one should try to patch up the remedies available against domestic bodies by pretending that they are organs of government' (933)—suggesting that the adequacy of private law remedies was not the main point, and also that it was the Jockey Club's lack of a connection to the government, rather than the nature of its functions, that protected it from judicial review.

Meanwhile, a string of decisions before and after Aga Khan held that judicial review was unavailable against the National Greyhound Racing Club, the Chief Rabbi, and

---

[35] See also R v Bowden [1996] 1 WLR 98, 103 (CA).

the Football Association[36]—although the Advertising Standards Association and a pharmaceutical industry committee were subjected to judicial review as instruments for the same sort of commercial self-regulation of an industry as in *Datafin*.[37]

It may seem that these cases represent an arbitrary judicial refusal to control a potential abuse of power: if the government had regulated horse racing, and a tribunal applied the rules against doping horses, then William Mullins would definitely have had access to all the controls of judicial review (though judicial review would be unavailable, if a claim in contract would provide an adequate remedy—see p 583). And it makes no difference, from Mullins' point of view, whether the committee allegedly abusing its power was a government agency regulating horse racing, or a private club regulating horse racing. The test of governmental connection from the *Aga Khan* case does not reflect the nature of the power, which is what ought to determine whether the courts are prepared to impose the rule of law on its exercise.

But the refusal of permission for judicial review was not the end of the road for the *Be My Royal* litigation. After he had refused judicial review in R (*Mullins*) v *Appeal Board of the Jockey Club*, Stanley Burnton J transferred the claim from the Administrative Court to the Queen's Bench Division, to proceed under CPR 8 as a claim for a declaration that the horse's disqualification was unlawful. And the decision in that case, *Mullins v McFarlane* [2006] EWHC 986, provides support for the view that the Court 'has a supervisory jurisdiction over tribunals such as the Appeal Board, irrespective of the existence of a contract between the claimant and the tribunal or the body appointing it' [38]. *Mullins* represents the rediscovery of a form of control over the private use of power that the courts had forgotten: *Mullins* relied on *Nagle v Feilden* [1966] 2 QB 633, in which the Court of Appeal refused to strike out a claim that the Jockey Club's rule against women trainers was arbitrary and capricious. Lord Denning held that the rule against women horse trainers 'may well be said to be arbitrary and capricious. It is not as if the training of horses could be regarded as an unsuitable occupation for a woman, like that of a jockey or speedway-rider' (647).[38]

What was the legal basis for this action for a declaration that a private organization was acting arbitrarily? Lord Denning excavated the ancient law on the right to work, from Lord Coke's judgment in the famous case of the *Tailors of*

---

[36]   *Law v National Greyhound Racing Club* [1983] 3 All ER 300 (CA) (in which the defendant claimed that it was subject to judicial review, to try to get the court to strike out the ordinary action); R v *Chief Rabbi, ex p Wachmann* [1992] 1 WLR 1036; R v *Football Association, ex p Football League* [1993] 2 All ER 833.

[37]   R v *Advertising Standards Authority, ex p Insurance Service* (1989) 2 Admin LR 77 (DC); R v *Code of Practice Committee of the British Pharmaceutical Industry, ex p Professional Counselling Aids* (1990) 3 Admin LR 697. And the Law Society and the General Council of the Bar are subject to judicial review in their exercise of power in the public interest: *Swain v Law Society* [1983] 1 AC 598 (HL) (618); R v *General Council of the Bar, ex p Percival* [1991] 1 QB 212 (DC).

[38]   It would take the Sex Discrimination Act 1975 to change the law on access to those professions that Lord Denning considered to be unsuitable for a woman.

Ipswich (1614) 11 Co Rep 53a:

> '... at the common law, no man could be prohibited from working in any lawful trade, for the law abhors idleness, the mother of all evil, ... and especially in young men, who ought in their youth, (which is their seed time) to learn lawful sciences and trades, which are profitable to the commonwealth, and whereof they might reap the fruit in their old age, for idle in youth, poor in age; and therefore the common law abhors all monopolies, which prohibit any from working in any lawful trade.' (Lord Coke CJ, 53b)

This rule has three crucial features: (1) the justification Lord Coke offered was the public interest (though the rule also benefited individuals); (2) yet it was a rule made by judges ('at the common law'); and (3) the rule was imposed on private organizations for the benefit of persons who had no other argument of private right (such as a contract) against the organization.

The result is judicial control of private power based on just the same **core rationale** as judicial control of public power: the *mere capacity* of the judges to prevent certain forms of injustice in a way that is itself ruled by law, and that promotes the rule of law (see p 65). So Salmon LJ said in *Nagle*, 'One of the principal functions of our courts is, whenever possible, to protect the individual from injustice and oppression. It is important, perhaps today more than ever, that we should not abdicate that function' (654).

The judges do not have a *general* jurisdiction to do justice (see pp 23–5). In private law just as in public law, they can only protect the individual from injustice and oppression 'whenever possible', and it is not always possible. For example, the common law of contract treats only *certain* forms of injustice and oppression (misrepresentation and duress, but *not* the unfairness of demanding an excessive price for goods or services) as relevant to the enforceability of contracts. So the jurisdiction asserted in *Nagle* and *Mullins* relies on the justiciability of the considerations at stake, and on the court's capacity to operate its process and to give a remedy without unjustifiably interfering with the freedom of the people involved in the Jockey Club, or unjustifiably damaging its work as an organization.

But how did the doctrine extend from Lord Coke's protection of the right to carry on a trade, to protection of a horse's position in the Gold Cup? *Mullins* followed *Bradley v Jockey Club* [2004] EWHC 2164,[39] a case in which a bloodstock agent had given confidential information to a betting syndicate; he challenged his penalty of eight years' disqualification as disproportionate. Crucially, the court insisted that the disciplinary decision could be controlled regardless of any other ground of private right (such as contract). So *Bradley*, like *Mullins*, revives the *Tailors of Ipswich* approach. But the case involved Bradley's freedom to carry out his trade—like *Nagle* and the *Tailors of Ipswich* case. In *Mullins*, Stanley Burnton J moved the law beyond the common law

---

[39] Richard J's reasons were later commended by the Court of Appeal in *Bradley v Jockey Club* [2005] EWCA Civ 1056 [2].

right to work, at least tentatively: 'My provisional view is that there is no jurisdictional (in the narrow sense of the word) boundary to the power of the Court to grant declaratory relief in this context: the jurisdiction of the Court under CPR Part 40.20[40] to grant declaratory relief is unrestricted' [39]. So can the courts control arbitrary private decisions in general? No: the power is restricted to 'this context'. The context includes the fact, as Lord Denning put it, that the Jockey Club has 'a virtual monopoly in an important field of human activity' (*Nagle v Feilden*, 644).

The 'provisional' approach of *Mullins* is to use the procedural flexibility of the Civil Procedure Rules to broaden the ancient doctrine of the *Tailors of Ipswich* case, into a wide jurisdiction to control *some* arbitrary decision making by private bodies. Just how widely the *Mullins* approach will range, if it holds up, will depend on some of the same considerations that limit judicial review of public authorities. For example, the issues at stake in some decisions of private bodies are non-justiciable—just as is the case with public authorities. More importantly, the judges need to hold onto the basic principle that the court's supervisory jurisdiction is only to be used against abuses of power that would otherwise go unremedied (see p 60). That actually represents a drastic restriction on the jurisdiction, because the instances will be rare in which the issues at stake are justiciable, *and* an injustice by one private person against another cannot be remedied by the law of contract, tort, property, trusts, or criminal law, or any regulatory scheme. Moreover, the approach in *Mullins* should be limited by factors that are *not* at work in judicial review of public authorities: for example, the commitment of the law to allow private ordering to flourish by *refraining* from interfering on some grounds of justice (such as whether a seller has asked a fair price for goods).

So the *Mullins* move does not promise a wide-ranging overhaul of English law, but it is radical in principle. It simply circumvents the suggestions in earlier cases such as *Aga Khan* and *Datafin*, that judicial review is not available unless the defendant has a connection with government. It circumvents those cases because it gives courts the same supervisory role as in judicial review, but in a claim for a declaration under CPR 8 (and the rules are flexible enough for a claim for judicial review to be transferred from a claim for judicial review to an ordinary claim, as in *Mullins* itself). Within its limits this radical move is justifiable, because the contexts in which the courts can potentially achieve justice (without illegitimately interfering with a body like the Jockey Club) are not limited to restraints on the right to work. Although the scope of the doctrine is unclear and in flux, we can say the following about the judges' jurisdiction to review the lawfulness of the conduct of private bodies in the administration of schemes that regulate public access to popular activities such as horse racing. While showing deference (just as they should in judicial review of public authorities) to 'the decision of an impartial qualified tribunal whose knowledge and experience of the subject matter in question is likely to exceed those of the Court' (*Mullins v McFarlane*

---

[40] CPR 40.20: 'The court may make binding declarations whether or not any other remedy is claimed.'

[39]), the courts are prepared to apply the familiar grounds in deciding whether to declare that a decision of the private body was unlawful:

- **reasonableness**: 'The court's role, in the exercise of its supervisory jurisdiction, is to determine whether the decision reached falls within the limits of the decision-maker's discretionary area of judgment' (*Bradley v Jockey Club* [2004] EWHC 2164[41]);

- **'legal error in applying the Rules'** (*Mullins v McFarlane* [48]); and

- **bias**[42] and other forms of **procedural unfairness** (*Mullins v McFarlane* [38]).

It's all there, just as in judicial review of public authorities. It seems that if the defendant is the Jockey Club, you simply need to use proceedings for a declaration under CPR 40.20, rather than CPR Part 54 (judicial review). The *Datafin* criteria for availability of judicial review (seemingly requiring some connection to government) must be met for CPR Part 54, even though it allows judicial review 'in relation to the exercise of a public function', and does not require any connection to government (CPR 54.1(2)(a) (ii)). As the *Mullins* litigation shows, the declaration process can allow judicial supervision of private bodies even without judicial review.

● Pop Quiz ●
What good is a declaration against a private body, if it does not order the defendant to do anything, and is not backed up by contempt of court?

Although the doctrine is in flux, it has the potential to right wrongs that are more serious than arbitrarily disqualifying a racehorse. People housed by a public authority in a nursing home are protected from abuse of power (*R v North and East Devon Health Authority, ex p Coughlan* [2001] QB 213—see pp 287–9). Protection from abuse of power has been denied to people housed in a care home by a private agency acting under a contract with a local authority (*R v Servite Houses, ex p Goldsmith* [2001] LGR 55). Unlike Mrs. Coughlan, they have no recourse in judicial review if the private agency unfairly closes their home, after promising that they can stay there for life. Moses J felt constrained to that outcome by *Datafin* and *Aga Khan*, because Servite Houses' relationship with the local authority was 'purely commercial', and the courts 'cannot impose public law standards upon a body the source of whose power is contractual and absent sufficient statutory penetration' (81).

If the common law's historic protection against abuse of private power can be extended beyond the right to work, this is the place to do it. Extending it in this way would not be as great a leap as the leap suggested in *Mullins*. The courts would have to keep to a test of *abuse* of the power that private housing agencies have over the residents of a care home (rather than taking over the general management of private

---

[41] And the Court of Appeal held in *Nagle v Feilden* that arbitrariness or capriciousness in the Jockey Club's rules would be unlawful.

[42] See *Modahl v British Athletic Federation Ltd (No 2)* [2001] EWCA Civ 1447.

care homes). If they can do that,[43] then they have the opportunity to right an injustice without interfering in the commercial arrangement between the housing agency and the local authority. That commercial arrangement becomes purely irrelevant, because there is no reason to think that control *on abuse of power* would damage it.

So is there any difference between the law of public administration, and the law of private administration? Yes—a massive difference in practice: in public administration, the potential is incomparably greater for injustices that can only be remedied by the supervisory jurisdiction (so permission for judicial review against public authorities is given in more than 1,000 cases per year; *Bradley* and *Mullins v McFarlane* are oddities). And the judicial review *process* is still restricted to the control of *public* functions. That is a relatively new development; *R v Master of the Company of Surgeons* (1759) 2 Burr 892, argued on very the same legal basis as the *Tailors of Ipswich* case, was an application for a mandamus (the predecessor of the mandatory order).[44] It is a reminder that in the 18th century, *the prerogative writs (certiorari* [quashing order], *mandamus* [mandatory order], *prohibition* [prohibiting order]) *were not restricted to claims against public authorities.* The great case of *R v Barker* (1762) 3 Burr 1265 (see p 395), after all, was a *mandamus* against the trustees of a Presbyterian meeting-house. In the 19th century this aspect of the prerogative writs withered, so that by the 20th century (when English judges started to think about 'public law' as the law controlling the state), they were thought to be available only against public authorities. The Civil Procedure Rules keep that 20th-century doctrine (CPR 54.1). But it seems that the courts' old capacity to control private abuse of power is returning, by way of the summary process for seeking a declaration in CPR 8, and the power to give a declaration in CPR 40.20. If the courts have that power, then the law controls private decision makers in the same context-sensitive way as it controls public authorities, where there is a public interest in the prevention of arbitrary decision making.

15.5.3 'Public authorities' under the Human Rights Act

The European Convention on Human Rights binds the 'Contracting Parties'—the states—that agreed to it. So a claim in the Strasbourg Court is a claim against 'one of the High Contracting Parties' (e.g., the United Kingdom), alleging that the state has violated a Convention right. All legal responsibility under the Convention lies on the state. But Art 1 of the Convention says that 'the High Contracting Parties shall secure to everyone within their jurisdiction the rights' in the Convention. And the Strasbourg Court has taken a very broad view of what counts as a violation of a right *by the state*: 'The State cannot absolve itself from responsibility . . . by delegating its

---

[43] And, of course, that is what they are committed to doing under the *Coughlan* doctrine (see p 288). In *Coughlan*, it is comity with the health authority that demands that the court not take over the management of the home. In the *Servite Houses* situation, it is a combination of comity with the local authority, and respect for the private agency's ability to enter into a commercial arrangement without having undue obligations superimposed for the public good.

[44] The Company of Surgeons required that even an apprentice should know Latin; Lord Mansfield thought that the justification of that restriction on employment was 'too plain to argue'.

obligations to private bodies or individuals' (*Sychev v Ukraine* (App no 4773/02) ECHR 11 October 2005 [53]).

Because of the positive obligations (see p 89) that the Strasbourg Court has imposed on states under Art 2 (right to life), 3 (prohibition on torture) and Art 8 (right to respect for private and family life), it will often be the case that a private act against an interest protected by the Convention will reflect the violation of a right by the state: for example, if the United Kingdom does not prevent excessive corporal punishment in a private school, the victim can complain in the Strasbourg Court (*Costello-Roberts v UK* (App no 13134/87) 25 March 1993). But the private school will not have violated the Convention, because it is not a Contracting Party. The defendant in the *Costello-Roberts* case was, of course, the United Kingdom. If a private school were to torture you, the UK would have violated your Convention right if (1) it failed to carry out a positive duty to protect you from abuses by private persons (either by a failure to provide the sort of scheme of protection that a state can be expected to provide against the abuse by private persons, or by a failure in implementation of the scheme[45]), or (2) if the school was, in effect, a way in which the UK provided education, so that the state's responsibility to conform to Convention rights ought to be seen as having been delegated to the school. That sort of delegation would take a close connection between the UK Government and the school, and the Strasbourg Court would not find that a school is part of the British state just because education is of public importance. The school would have to be, in effect, *part of* the state.

In the UK, the Human Rights Act 1998 s 6 makes it unlawful for a 'public authority' to act incompatibly with a Convention right. Section 6 defines the phrase 'public authorities', confusingly, to include *anybody* who has 'functions of a public nature' (s 6(3)(b)).[46] It is the same in effect as if the Act made it unlawful for *anyone* to infringe a Convention right in carrying out a function that has a public nature.[47] The judges call real public authorities under s 6 'core public authorities', and they call other people or bodies 'hybrid' or 'functional' public authorities if their functions are public for the purposes of s 6(3)(b) (*Aston Cantlow v Wallbank* [2003] UKHL 37, Lord Nicholls [7]–[9]).

What gives a function a 'public nature'? The question creates a conundrum for the courts, when public authorities contract with private agencies for the provision of public services—especially housing provided under local authorities' statutory duty to arrange nursing home provision for people who need care because of age, illness, or disability (National Assistance Act 1948 s 21). The local authority is, of course, carrying out a public function—a function paid for and organized by government on behalf of the public, giving effect to a decision by Parliament on behalf of the state, that doing so is in the public interest. If the local authority carries out that duty by operating its own nursing home, and a resident is evicted or a home is closed down,

---

[45] *X and Y v The Netherlands* (1985) 8 EHRR 235, *Z v United Kingdom* (2001) 34 EHRR 97.

[46] A person that has some public functions is not a public authority in respect of a particular act, 'if the nature of the act is private' (s 6(5)).

[47] Unless that person is acting in a way required by primary legislation —see p 73.

then she can complain that the decision infringed her Art 8 right to respect for her private and family life, and since the decision certainly affected her private life, the local authority will have to show that its impact on her was not disproportionate to the value of pursuing a legitimate purpose recognized by Art 8 as justifying interference with someone's privacy.

What if the local authority carries out its statutory duty to provide housing by contracting out its housing provision to a private operator of nursing homes? If the private housing association abuses a resident (by, for example, evicting her or shutting down her nursing home arbitrarily), then the local authority would need to take new steps to carry out its duty to provide housing, and if the debacle came about because of a failure to take the steps that government ought to take in those circumstances out of respect for the resident's private and family life (e.g., by regulating nursing homes, and by entering into a responsible agreement with the nursing home), then the resident's Convention right would have been infringed, and the resident would have a remedy against the local authority (or conceivably some other authority that ought to have been regulating the private home) under the Human Rights Act 1998, and she would have a remedy in Strasbourg against the UK.

But there is a remedial gap when a private operator is trying to evict a resident (*Poplar Housing v Donoghue* [2001] EWCA Civ 595), or when the private operator proposes to close the resident's home, and the resident wants to stay there (*R (Heather) v Leonard Cheshire Foundation* [2002] EWCA Civ 366). In those situations, seeking damages from the local authority for any violation of the housing statute or a Convention right would be a distant second-best. For a resident who doesn't want to be thrown out of her home, her rights against the local authority and the United Kingdom won't stop the company from evicting her or closing the home.

So residents in that predicament have asked the courts to hold a private nursing home company to be a 'functional' public authority. In both *Poplar* and *Heather*, the Court of Appeal accepted that carrying out what would certainly be a public function for a public authority does *not* necessarily count (for a private body) as performing a public function. But the housing association in *Poplar* was held to be a 'functional public authority' because its role was 'enmeshed' with the activities of the local authority. Its role was 'so closely assimilated to that of Tower Hamlets [the local authority] that it was performing public and not private functions' (70). The local authority itself set up Poplar to operate homes, and transferred housing stock to Poplar, including the defendant's flat; Poplar was subject to guidance from the local authority. The *Poplar Housing* case very definitely applies a test of connection with government and *not* a test of the nature of the function.

The housing provider in the *Heather* case was not enmeshed with the public authority, and was held *not* to be subject to the Human Rights Act 1998 s 6. The court found that on the facts, there was 'no black hole into which [the residents] would sink' [31]; and perhaps the case would have been decided differently if it had been clear that the residents were being abused.

The result in *Heather* gives every local authority a financial incentive to contract out their care provision to private concerns that will be able to do it cheaper than the local authority could do it, if the Convention rights put expensive constraints on building management. And the availability of Human Rights Act *proceedings* itself means that as a result of *Heather*, local authorities face an expense that private operators would not face, when they want to close a home or move a resident.

The House of Lords' first opportunity to deal with functional public authorities came in *Aston Cantlow PCC v Wallbank* [2003] UKHL 37, which held that a 'core' public authority is a governmental organization of the kind that the United Kingdom is answerable for in the Strasbourg Court. The House of Lords' approach to functional public authorities was not based on an organized account of the purpose of s 6, but on the vague goal of 'giving a generously wide scope to the expression "public function"' to 'further the statutory aim of promoting the observance of human rights values' (Lord Nicholls [11]). The result was not a 'single test', but a list of factors to be considered, including 'the extent to which in carrying out the relevant function the body is publicly funded, or is exercising statutory powers, or is taking the place of central government or local authorities, or is providing a public service' [12]. Only the 'public service' factor moves beyond the *Poplar* approach of focusing on relations with government. And that factor did not help to resolve the question in *Heather* of whether a private nursing home operator is providing a public function when it provides housing under a contracting-out agreement with a local authority.

Here is the conundrum the courts face. The function of the private nursing home in *Heather* is clearly, definitely a public function when you look at it one way: the resident is receiving social housing at state expense for a public purpose adopted on behalf of the public by authority of Parliament. And the function is clearly, definitely *not* a public function in another way: the provider is simply housing and caring for a person for money. The home is carrying out just the same function, as if the resident were paying for her own care. If the company provides the same services to customers who pay their own way, it is not providing a public function, and its function does not change its nature when the cheque for housing a particular resident comes from a local authority. 'Function of a public nature' is ambiguous, because the same function is public in one sense and is not public in another sense. And the Human Rights Act 1998 s 6 cannot be applied without a resolution to the ambiguity. It ought to be resolved in a way that gives effect to the purpose of treating a private body as a 'public authority' under s 6. But even that purpose is unclear. It was extraordinary for the drafters of the Human Rights Act to put such a strain on the words 'public function', but they evidently did so to leave it to the judges to decide the reach of the Human Rights Act.

YL v Birmingham [2007] UKHL 27 is the landmark case in which the House of Lords took on this conundrum. And the Law Lords were sharply divided. The claimant, an 84-year-old woman with Alzheimer's disease, was placed in a private nursing home under a three-way agreement between the local council, her family, and the home. The home threatened to evict her because of the conduct of her daughter and husband during visits. If the nursing home company, Southern Cross, was carrying out functions of a public nature under that agreement, then she could use Art 8 of the Convention to challenge her eviction. To Baroness Hale and Lord Bingham, it was obvious that Southern Cross was fulfilling a public function: 'The performance by private body A by arrangement with public body B, and perhaps at the expense of B, of what would undoubtedly be a public function if carried out by B is, in my opinion, precisely the case which section 6(3)(b) was intended to embrace' (Lord Bingham [20]). To the majority, it was obvious that Southern Cross was *not* fulfilling a public function: 'Southern Cross is a company carrying on a socially useful business for profit. It is neither a charity nor a philanthropist. It enters into private law contracts with the residents in its care homes and with the local authorities with whom it does business' (Lord Scott [26]).

The tantalizing feature of the judges' reasoning is that both sides are right, in a sense. Southern Cross was of course carrying out a public function in a sense, because the arrangement was a public authority's way of carrying out a public function (state provision of housing for vulnerable people who don't have the money to pay for themselves), and it is a function that is at the heart of the welfare state. Described another way, Southern Cross was obviously *not* carrying out a public function: its purpose was to make a profit for its private owners, and it was acting for that private purpose.

The majority judges considered it very important to treat YL the same as residents in the private nursing home who were paying for themselves (who would evidently not be able to assert the abstract Convention right to respect for their family and private life against Southern Cross). The dissenters considered it very important to treat YL the same as residents in a nursing home run by the council (who would without any doubt be able to assert Convention rights against the council).

Imagine that Alice, Beatrice, and Candice live on Care Street. In Number 1, Southern Cross houses Alice, who is paying for her own care. In Number 2, Southern Cross houses Beatrice, under an agreement with the council in which the council pays for her care. In Number 3, the council houses Candice.[48]

The majority in YL thought that it would be arbitrary for Beatrice to have legal protection against the home's decisions that Alice did not have, just because the council is paying for Beatrice and Alice is paying for herself. The dissenters in YL thought that it would be arbitrary to deprive Beatrice of legal protection that Candice has, just because the council contracted out Beatrice's housing.

The solution to the practical problem is obvious: Alice ought to be protected from abuses as well as Candice is. That would erase the conundrum about how to treat Beatrice under the Human Rights Act 1998 s 6(3)(b), because it wouldn't matter any more. Justice demands that the law protect Alice from abuse when she pays her private nursing home for her care, and there is nothing about the community's relationship (through the local authority, with or without Southern Cross helping out) with Beatrice and Candice that requires that the law protect them better than it protects Alice.

[48] If Denise in Number 4 is housed by a 'registered social landlord' (RSL), she can use the Human Rights Act, because registered social landlords *are* functional public authorities: R (Weaver) v London & Quadrant Housing Trust [2008] EWHC 1377. That decision is compatible with YL because, although they are private bodies, RSLs are subsidized by the state and play a role in policy implementation; they are 'enmeshed' in the work of local authority. Doubt was cast on *Poplar Housing* in YL, but the relationship between a private organization and government can still provide a basis for the court to hold that the private partner in a PPP is a functional public authority. In spite of *Servite Houses*, *Weaver* holds that Denise can bring a claim for judicial review against an RSL, too.

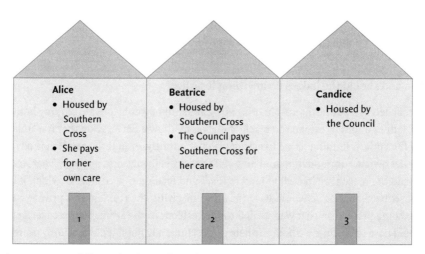

Figure 15.3 **Public and private functions on Care Street**

The care conundrum

The question of whether the private nursing home is carrying out a public function in caring for people on behalf of a local authority *only* matters if the Human Rights Act gives Candice more protection than Alice has. If that is the case, either Alice is not properly protected from abuse in her private relationship with the nursing home company, or Candice is getting more protection than she needs (i.e., the combination of the substance of the Convention rights and the Human Rights Act processes impose too great a burden on the operation of nursing homes).

How should the judges resolve the conundrum? Given what amounts to an extraordinary delegation of power to the judges through the ambiguity of s 6(3)(b), they ought to impose the protections of the Human Rights Act if that is what it takes to prevent an abuse of public power through the contracting-out process. The majority decision in YL does an injustice, *if* it merely hands to local authorities a technique for evading protections that residents of nursing homes need. But that is only the case, if Beatrice is exposed to genuine abuse as a result; and if Alice is exposed to genuine abuse by her private nursing home, then the failing is just as bad. So the problem *ought* to be immaterial (because Alice ought to have good protection from abuse), and if it is immaterial, then the majority decision was right, and YL only lost a legal technique for fighting the nursing home that she did not need to protect her from a genuine abuse.

Of course, the ideology of the Human Rights Act is that everyone needs the techniques of the Act to protect them from genuine abuses, and Lord Bingham and Baroness Hale were simply extending the ideology of the Act. But the majority decision does no injustice to Beatrice, if Alice has protection from abuse of private power. On the other hand, the majority were allowing local authorities to subvert the Act, if Alice is not protected from abuse of private power. In that case, their decision in YL abandons equity in the social provision of care, because it allows a council to leave Beatrice to be abused. So what can be done for Alice?

Can and should the judges do anything for Alice?

Since there is a public interest in preventing abuse of power by private nursing homes, the judges ought to extend the reach of *Mullins* to allow a declaration that it is unlawful for a *private* nursing home to evict a resident unfairly, even if the resident is paying for her own accommodation and no public agency is involved in any way. That would extend the reasoning in *Mullins* (and in *Nagle* and *Bradley*) to a context in which it has not yet been applied. It would have the effect of giving the resident in a private nursing home protection that was denied to the resident in the *Servite Houses* case. And it would have to be done without the help of the Human Rights Act, which only protects people against public authorities. But it would be entirely compatible with the reasoning in *Mullins*.

But the judges should only do this if it is necessary in the public interest for protection of vulnerable people from abuse. And it should not be necessary: the home is regulated under the Care Standards Act 2000 and the Care Homes Regulations 2001 SI 2001/3965, by the Care Quality Commission. The nationwide standards require residents to be able to have visitors at any reasonable time, so the basis on which Southern Cross threatened to evict the resident in YL could be the matter of a complaint to the Commission.

> **The Care Quality Commission** (see p 501) is an independent regulator that can investigate services provided by the private sector. So *unlike the courts*, the commissioner offers a response to injustice in the provision of contracted-out services. But the Commission cannot stop the closure of a home.

Meanwhile, Beatrice has the following protections, after the House of Lords' decision:

- she has a contract with Southern Cross, which they would breach by mistreating her, but which may or may not give her a remedy against an unreasonable decision to evict her;

- the council has a contract that requires Southern Cross to respect residents' Convention rights. That does not enable YL to assert Convention rights against Southern Cross when they threaten to evict her. But it would give her a basis for a complaint to the council; and

- she has a right under the Human Rights Act (which she can pursue in the English courts) to a remedy against Birmingham for breach of her Convention rights (including compensation—see section 14.6, or an order for different accommodation to be provided if that is what it takes for the Council to show respect for her private and family life).

The following process:	Is available against a body or person that:
a claim for judicial review—	—exercises a 'public function' (CPR 54.1); the defendant must meet the ambiguous criteria in *Datafin*[49] of public function, *and/or* connection (of some kind) to government (*Datafin*, *Aga Khan*[50]), **but only if:**
	—there is no adequate legal control and right to redress in private law.[51]
an ordinary claim for a declaration or injunction—	—interferes with the right to carry on a trade (*Tailors of Ipswich*[52]) or has a virtual monopoly in an important field of human activity (*Nagel*,[53] *Mullins*[54]) **if:**
	—the issues are justiciable, and
	—an abuse of power would go unremedied if the court were not prepared to make a declaration.
a claim in tort—	—is alleged to be the tortfeasor.
a prosecution for misconduct in a public office—	—has an 'office of trust concerning the public, especially if attended with profit ... by whomever and in whatever way the officer is appointed'.[55]
proceedings under the Human Rights Act—	—has functions of a public nature, in an unexplained sense that the courts have been left to work out[56] (but each House of Parliament is excluded).
proceedings in the Strasbourg Court for infringement of the Convention rights—	—is a Contracting Party to the Convention (i.e., the UK or one of the other nations that have signed the Convention).
proceedings for breach of an EU directive—	—is an organ (very broadly construed) of the member state.
proceedings in an English court for breach of the EU's procurement rules—	—is on a long list of 'contracting operators' that includes central government department, local authorities, fire and police authorities, and NDPBs.[57]
a complaint to the Parliamentary ombudsman—	—is on the list in the Parliamentary Commissioner Act 1967 covering government departments, Executive Agencies, and other bodies fulfilling public functions.[58]
a request for information under the Freedom of Information Act—	—is a 'public authority', defined by a very long list, with the addition of publicly owned companies.[59]

Figure 15.4 Summary: who or what is subject to administrative law processes

---

[49]   R v Panel on Take-overs and Mergers, ex p Datafin Plc [1987] QB 815 (CA).

[50]   R v Disciplinary Committee of the Jockey Club, ex p Aga Khan [1993] 1 WLR 909 (CA).

[51]   Evans v The University of Cambridge [2002] EWHC 1382.

[52]   (1614) 11 Co Rep 53a.

[53]   Nagel v F [1966] 2 QB 633.

[54]   Mullins v McFarlane [2006] EWHC 986 (QB).

[55]   R v Bembridge (1783) 3 Doug 327 (332).

[56]   Human Rights Act 1998 s 6(3)(b); see YL v Birmingham [2007] UKHL 27.

[57]   Public Contracting Regulations 2006 s 3(1)(w).

[58]   Parliamentary Commissioner Act 1967 Sch 2.

[59]   Freedom of Information Act 2000 s 3.

The difficulty of the controversy in the House of Lords over YL only arises because of the extraordinary remedy that YL wanted, of a judicial decision that her eviction could not proceed. That remedy could be obtained in a claim under CPR 8 for a declaration under CPR 40.20, if the reasoning in *Mullins* were extended. But it would be an unprecedented remedy, and it ought to be given only in the case of an abusive eviction.

15.5.4 Public authorities in European law

Directives of the EC bind the member states but not private parties, so the ECJ has had to decide how to draw the line around the bodies whose acts count as acts of a member state. It did so first in Case 152/84 *Marshall v Southampton and South West Hampshire Area Health Authority* [1986] QB 401, in which the decisive principle was that no body should be able to act incompatibly with a directive, if its doing so would represent a way for the member state to avoid the effect of the directive. So 'the "state" must be taken broadly, as including all the organs of the state' (413). Which organs are those? In Case C-188/89 *Foster v British Gas* [1991] 2 WLR 258, the ECJ endorsed two criteria offered by the Commission: 'both the criterion "exercise of a public function" and that of "real control" can bring a person, in this case an employer, within the concept of "the state"' [20]. The 'public function' criterion was meant to catch bodies such as police services that act independently of the government; the point in *Foster* was that the ECJ also wanted to catch any body controlled by the member state: 'the state may not benefit from its default in respect of anything that lies within the sphere of responsibility which by its own free choice it has taken upon itself, irrespective of the person through whom that responsibility is exercised' [21].

This problem is different from the domestic problems of identifying public authorities for the sake of judicial review, or even under the Human Rights Act. The difference is that the ECJ's purpose is to hold *member states* to their obligations under directives. So in this context, the connection with government really matters.

15.6 Conclusion: private law and public law

Accountability does not simply mean more control of public decision making by government ministers, or by Parliament, or by courts. As regards courts in particular, it is a remarkable fact that unfair, unreasonable, arbitrary uses of power are *not necessarily* subject to judicial control. Claimants may quite rightly face all sorts of potential obstacles to using the impressive grounds of judicial review to secure redress against an arbitrary use of power. We saw them in Chapter 10 on how to sue the government (time limits, the discretions of the courts, and the problems created by *O'Reilly v Mackman* [1983] 2 AC 237), and in Chapter 11 on standing, and in this chapter (the need to establish that the defendant (or its decision) is 'public' in the relevant sense). And a claimant needs to use other processes and remedies *instead of* judicial review, if doing so will secure a just result (see p 583).

Non-judicial forms of accountability are in some ways, for some purposes, more useful than judicial review. Specification of criteria and procedural transparency in contracting-out processes, with oversight by auditors, give a more impressive set of accountability techniques than is provided by the rather hands-off judicial review that is available to control contracting-out decisions. And public information as to whether policy is being carried out in practice doesn't just reduce costs; it can enhance responsibility in delivering services. The government plays up that potential by calling the users of services 'customers'.

If government is accountable for the cost efficiency of its spending decisions, *and that's all*, then there is a dangerous lack of integrity-accountability, and equity-accountability. The Labour Government's response to this danger, through the Best Value regime (see p 575), has been to couple efficiency-accountability with performance targets that are meant to achieve *good* public services.

Those government-by-contract accountability techniques, though, remain focused on what auditors are good at, and judges still have a role in controlling abuse of power in government by contract.

15.6.1 Where does the rule of law come in?

If the rule of law does not require judges to control everything, can we say that it *does* require them to control all abuse of *public* power? In the 1980s and 1990s, it seemed crucial to distinguish between public law and private law. Lord Diplock in *O'Reilly v Mackman*, 275, Lord Bridge in *Cocks v Thanet DC* [1983] 2 AC 286, 292, and Lord Wilberforce in *Davy v Spelthorne* [1984] 1 AC 262, 276 started talking about 'public law'—or as Lord Scarman called it, 'the newly fledged distinction in English law between public and private law' (*Gillick v West Norfolk and Wisbech Area Health Authority* [1986] 1 AC 112, 178). But the distinction between public law and private law is ancient.[60] And in fact, the Law Lords did not really mean 'public law' when they started talking about 'public law' as something new in the 1980s.

15.6.2 What is public law?

Law in general is public, in a sense: it is available for members of the community to know (at least, it ought to be, and in England it is). It is enforced (and disputes are adjudicated) by public officials. What's more, law is (at least, it ought to be) made for the public good. That includes the law of contract, which benefits the public (that is, the people of the community) by enabling them to enter into binding agreements on reasonable terms, and by providing public techniques for enforcement and dispute resolution. So if all law is public in these respects, what is the sense of distinguishing public law from private law?

---

[60] E.g.: it is an ancient rule of the common law, as Lord Mansfield put it, that 'all kinds of crimes of a public nature, all misdemeanors whatsoever of a public evil example against the common law, may be indicted; but no injuries of a private nature, unless they some way concern the King' (*R v Bembridge*, 332).

People call the law of contract 'private law', because it regulates a private transaction (such as the purchase of a car). A type of transaction is private if it does not necessarily impose on the parties to the transaction any legal duty to the community. Tort law is private law, because even though it serves the public good, the duties it imposes are duties owed by one person to another, and not necessarily[61] to the community, and the rights that it provides are rights held by one person against another, and not necessarily against the community. So, for example, if you vandalize my car, you are liable in tort law to compensate me, whether you are acting for a public authority or not, and whether I am a public authority or not. The transaction does not necessarily involve the community. The vandalism may be a crime, too (and criminal law is public law—it imposes duties to the community, and if they are breached, the community can bring legal proceedings for the imposition of sanctions to enforce the duties). Criminal law regulates the relation between the community and the vandal; tort law regulates the relation between the vandal and the victim. Lawyers use the term 'private law' for legal standards that regulate types of transaction and relationship that need involve no duties owed to the public. A legal dispute is a dispute over private law, if neither party has any legal duty to the public that is relevant to the dispute.

In the Court of Appeal in *O'Reilly v Mackman*, Lord Denning said that 'Private law regulates the affairs of subjects as between themselves. Public law regulates the affairs of subjects *vis-à-vis* public authorities' (255). But that is unhelpful, because as Lord Denning knew, private law regulates the affairs of subjects vis-à-vis public authorities, whenever the public authority has a contract or alleges a tort by a private person. If you buy a used car from a car dealer, and you buy a used car from a government agency, it makes no difference at all that one transaction is an affair between subjects and the other is an affair *vis-à-vis* a public authority. Your legal rights are just the same in the two cases. And we saw in Chapter 14 that tort law is *generally the same* whether the defendant is private or public, with the exception of the tort of misfeasance in a public office.

The courts emerged from Lord Diplock's era with an artificial view of judicial review as the unique and exclusive forum for 'public law'. By 'public law', Lord Diplock roughly meant, the judicially administered aspects of administrative law: the legal standards for the use of the power of public authorities that are applied in claims for the prerogative remedies. After the *Roy*[62] and *Mercury*[63] cases (see pp 357–8), it seemed fiendishly difficult to distinguish public from private. Largely because of the *O'Reilly* fiasco (see p 351), the courts thought that they had to draw a boundary in the twilight zone between the public and the private. But if a claimant alleges that a public authority has abused its power to determine a contract term, the issue is not *in between* the public and the private. Those cases involve *both* public law and private law at the same time: the parties in *Roy* and *Mercury* had contracts, *and* the content of

---

[61] Tort law protects bodies too, incidentally, since a public body may make a claim in tort.

[62] *Roy v Kensington & Chelsea FPC* [1992] 1 AC 624.

[63] *Mercury Communications v Director General of Telecommunications* [1996] 1 WLR 48.

that private law relationship was determined by a public authority's decision (which was controlled by the standards of lawful administration that have been developed in judicial review). It was the combination that made the distinction between public law and private law seem mysterious in those cases. In fact, the distinction is simple and clear. Public law *requires people to act in the public interest*. Criminal law is public law (because the duties it imposes are owed to the community). So is the law of taxation, and the law of planning, and the law of building regulations, and environmental protection law.

> **Public law and private law**
> It is sometimes said that private actors are not subject to **public law**. But Tesco is subject to all sorts of public law: tax law, criminal law, health and safety regulations, planning law...Tesco is subject to **public law**, but is not subject to **administrative law**, which, in England, is a branch of **constitutional law**.

Public law imposes duties to serve the public interest; *administrative law* creates institutions and processes through which one public authority may exercise legal authority to control another public authority. Administrative law requires the courts to oversee the integrity of decision making by persons and bodies that the law ought to require to act on behalf of the public.

But although the distinction between private and public is *simple*, it is also *vague*. And in one respect, there actually is a twilight zone between public and private, and the courts must be prepared to draw the line: it concerns whether the standards imposed on public authorities in judicial review are to be imposed on non-governmental organizations. As we have seen, the practical effects of this boundary-drawing exercise are less important than they seemed to be twenty years ago, when the courts had decided that judicial review was 'public', and had not yet developed the scope of the action for a declaration as a tool for imposing justice in private administration. The courts had lost track of the heritage of Lord Mansfield, who was prepared to use *mandamus*—an instrument of administrative law, in which the courts take responsibility for the integrity of decision making—without reckoning whether it was being used against a public authority.[64]

Tony Blair's vision for the British State was 'to provide the same level of customer service as the public have come to expect in every other aspect of their lives'.[65] In that approach, contract does not just regulate PPPs, and serve as a model for relations between departments and executive agencies. By treating people as 'customers', government also uses contract as a model for its relation with the people. A customer is a contractor.

That vision needs to be reconciled with the principle of proportionate administration—the principle that administrative structures and techniques should

[64] R v Barker (1762) 3 Burr 1265—see p 592.

[65] See the quotation at the beginning of this chapter.

be crafted in a way that provides sufficient accountability and efficiency for the purpose at hand. If people are the state's customers, then the state should certainly provide good customer service. But the state long ago privatized most of the services that involved customers (such as coal mining, gas, water, electricity, and telephone service).

Prisoners, the homeless, and the disabled are not customers of the state, and neither are public employees or taxpayers. In carrying on its relations with those people, the state needs partnerships with private service providers. And Public Private Partnerships do not need to result in an accountability disaster. But they will do so whenever accountability for some particular public interest (say, efficiency) is given priority over accountability for equity.

TAKE-HOME MESSAGE • • •

- Government may be able to serve the community better and at less cost by contracting with private companies for a service, than by delivering a service itself. Or it may end up damaging the community by treating the people it serves as if they were **customers**.

- If political accountability is damaged through government by contract, the courts cannot make up for it. But they can do some basic tasks that provide *legal* **accountability**:
  - controlling government by just decisions as to whether a particular agency has **capacity** to enter into a particular contract;
  - providing judicial review against contracting decisions that judges can identify as an **abuse of power**; and
  - providing a check on the unjust avoidance of public law obligations through contracting out.

- The law of the **European Union** gives judges a remarkable role in controlling spending decisions. It does so because of the distinctive EU project of creating and sustaining a single market for goods and services, and not because judges should generally be controlling government expenditure.

- **Auditors** are generally better equipped to investigate the effectiveness of government spending than judges are.

- It is difficult for judges to define the scope of their control over public power. But the difficulty and the importance of this problem are limited, because courts should also be controlling **purely private uses of power**, where an abuse of power calls for control in the public interest.

- **Public law** imposes legal obligations to serve the public interest.

···· *Critical reading* ···

Nagle v Feilden [1966] 2 QB 633
Crédit Suisse v Allerdale BC [1997] QB 306
R v Panel on Take-overs and Mergers, ex p Datafin Plc [1987] QB 815 (CA)

R v Disciplinary Committee of the Jockey Club, ex p Aga Khan [1993] 1 WLR
909 (CA)
Poplar Housing v Donoghue [2001] EWCA Civ 595
R v Servite Houses, ex p Goldsmith [2001] LGR 55
R (Heather) v Leonard Cheshire Foundation [2002] EWCA Civ 366
Aston Cantlow v Wallbank [2003] UKHL 37
Mullins v McFarlane [2006] EWHC 986
YL v Birmingham [2007] UKHL 27
Critical viewing: Robocop 1987

CRITICAL QUESTIONS • • •

1   Would you be able to get judicial review of a decision by the Government to privat-
    ize the British army by selling it to a company and paying the company for security
    services?

2   How is an auditor different from an ombudsman?

3   No public authority should be able to expand its powers by making an *ultra vires*
    contract. No public authority should be able to get out of a contract by claiming
    that it had no power to make the contract. Can you reconcile these two ideas?

4   Does the common law of due process require courts to decide the process by which
    public authorities decide whether to enter into a contract?

Further questions:

5   Is a private nursing home carrying out a public function, when it houses a resident
    whose accommodation is paid for by a public authority?

6   Is a private boarding school a 'functional public authority' in respect of students
    whose families pay for their board and education? If a public educational authority
    pays a private school for a student's board and education, is the school a 'func-
    tional public authority' in respect of that student?

online resource centre
Visit the online resource centre to access the following resources which
accompany this chapter: links to legislation and online reports of judicial
decisions, summaries of key cases and legislation, updates in the law,
suggestions for answering the pop quizzes and questions, and links to useful
websites.

Glossary

The index shows where you can find further explanation of these terms.

Abuse of power: A use of public power that is blameworthy (either because it oppresses some person, or grabs a private advantage against the public interest). Judges generally distinguish abusing a power from merely using it wrongly. Abuse of power is generally a ground of judicial review; using a power wrongly is generally not a ground of judicial review.

Action: The old term (before the Civil Procedure Rules 1998) for a claim in which a party asserts a legal right to a remedy in a civil court (now called an ordinary claim).

Administration: The running of the executive branch of government. Administration includes both the making and implementing of policies, so far as it can be done without primary legislation or judicial decision. 'The administration' is a general term for the institutions and officers that carry out administration.

Administrative justice: Buzzword for processes operated by the administration, designed to do justice between complainants and the administration.

Administrative law: An array of legal processes and techniques for controlling the conduct of public authorities (not only administrators, but also many others). Administrative law is reflexive: it controls the conduct of institutions such as tribunals and ombudsmen that were themselves designed to control the administration.

ADR = Alternative dispute resolution

Alternative dispute resolution: A way of resolving a dispute without taking it to a court or tribunal for a binding determination.

Appeal: A proceeding in which a higher tribunal or court re-examines the decision of a lower tribunal or court, or of an administrative authority. The point is not to repeat the initial proceeding, but to determine whether there is ground for reversing it. Appeal processes are created by statute; the **judicial review** process has been developed through the common law.

Application for judicial review: The term used for a claim for judicial review (see **claim**), before the Civil Procedure Rules 1998.

Bias: The attitude of a decision maker who is hostile towards one side, in a process or proceeding in which the decision maker ought to be impartial.

Cause of action = Right of action.

Certiorari ('to be certified'): A prerogative writ developed at common law, which has been replaced by the order called a 'quashing order' in the Civil Procedure Rules 1998.

Civil servant: A servant of the Crown employed by a department of central government ('public servant' is the term for everyone who works for a public authority, including civil servants, police, local authority employees, employees of executive agencies and non-departmental public bodies, employees of the armed forces, etc).

Claim: A judicial proceeding in which a claimant seeks a remedy. In an ordinary claim, the claimant must establish a right to a remedy; the claimant has no right to proceed with the claim if he or she does not assert grounds on which such a right to a remedy could be established (a 'right of action').

In a *claim for judicial review*, the claimant asks the Court for permission to commence a proceeding in which the Court will review the lawfulness of a decision 'in relation to the exercise of a public function' (CPR 54.1). The claimant must have **standing** (which requires a 'sufficient interest' in the matter; see section 11.1.2), and must show that there is a ground for judicial review, but need not show any right to a remedy.

Comity: Respect that one public authority ought to show for the good functioning of another.

Complainant: A person who has a complaint against a public authority.

Court of specific jurisdiction: Court whose jurisdiction is limited to a particular size or type of claim. They are also called inferior courts (a term at least as old as R v Cowle (1759) 2 Burr 834 (861) Lord Mansfield), because their decisions are normally subject to appeal or review in a superior court.

CPR: The Civil Procedure Rules 1998: http://www.dca.gov.uk/civil/procrules_fin/index.htm.

Council of Europe (http://www.coe.int): The treaty organization, set up in 1949, that is responsible for the European Convention on Human Rights. The Council of Europe and the European Union are independent of each other, though they cooperate on joint programmes.

Crown: The crown was a symbol for the power of the state, which the monarch wielded. Today, the Queen herself is a symbol for the power of the state, which is wielded by the Government. 'The Crown' is a name for the Government of the United Kingdom as a legal personality. Governmental acts of Secretaries of State—and of government departments in general—are acts of the Crown.

Deference: A reviewing decision maker defers to an initial decision maker if he or she declines to interfere with a decision because of the fact that it was made by the initial decision maker, unless there are special grounds (i.e., grounds *other* than merely that the reviewing decision maker would have taken a different decision).

Derogate: To suspend the effect of a law in a specific situation or class of situations; see p 6.

Discretion: A public authority has discretion to the extent that the law authorizes or requires it to choose between courses of action, without requiring a particular choice.

District Judge: A judge in the county courts.

Due process: The decision-making procedures that are required to be followed in making a decision. They may be required by legislation, or by the decision maker's own rules or practice, or by **natural justice**.

ex gratia: as a favour (i.e., even though the law does not require it).

European Union (http://europa.eu/index_en.htm): In 1950, Belgium, France, Germany, Italy, Luxembourg, and the Netherlands set up a free-trade arrangement for coal and steel, which has evolved into a unique interstate political and legal system. In 1957, the Treaty of Rome created the European Economic Community. Britain joined in 1973. The Single Market was really completed in the 1990s, and the term 'European Union' was adopted in 1993. Today there are 27 member states. The major institutions of the EU are the European Parliament, the Council of the European Union, the European Commission, the European Court of Justice, the European Court of Auditors, and the European Ombudsman.

Executive agency: Semi-independent agency operating at arm's length from day-to-day ministerial control, but with a framework agreement setting out its accountability to a department (cf **non-departmental public body**).

Fairness: A public authority acts unfairly if it wrongly neglects an interest of a person affected by the decision. The neglected interest may be an interest in the outcome (substantive unfairness), or in participation in the making of the decision (procedural unfairness; see **natural justice**). Because of the special legal protections for participation in processes (see chapter 4), the term 'fairness' is sometimes used in public law as a shorthand for procedural fairness. Procedural unfairness is a ground of judicial review. Substantive unfairness is not a ground of judicial review *in itself*, but certain forms of substantive unfairness ground judicial review.

Government: In the traditional English sense, 'the Government' means the ministers of the Crown and the departments they administer. The word can also be used in the broad sense for all public authorities including the courts and Parliament; 'the Government' in the traditional English sense is the central leadership of the executive branch of 'government' in the broad sense.

Grounds for judicial review: Features of a decision which courts treat as reasons (subject to the court's discretion) for interfering with the decision in judicial review.

Habeas corpus **('get the body'):** Early prerogative writ from a court of common law or equity, requiring a person to be brought to the court; it developed into a technique for judges to inquire into the lawfulness of detention.

Human right: A right that persons have because they are human. The European Convention on Human Rights uses the term to mean, roughly, rights that are so fundamental to a civilized community that the Contracting States have a duty to protect them in law (see p 85). According to the Council of Europe, 'Human rights are inalienable rights which guarantee the fundamental dignity of the human being. The European Convention on Human Rights guarantees civil and political human rights. The European Social Charter, its natural complement, guarantees social and economic human rights.'[1]

Inferior court = Court of specific jurisdiction

Inherent jurisdiction: The power of the High Court to create new remedies, or processes, or doctrines to do justice between the parties before it. The power is limited in various ways by common law and statute; it is not a power to ignore the law, but a power to develop the law in the interest of the good administration of justice. The development of *habeas corpus* is one dramatic and important instance of the exercise of inherent jurisdiction. Its constitutional source is delegation from the Crown to the Queen's judges of the sovereign power to administer justice.

Interest: A reason for wanting to challenge a decision in the courts (for example, the fact that the decision determines your legal position). In order to challenge a decision in judicial review, the claimant's interest in the decision must be 'sufficient'.

Issue: A disputed question that a court must answer in order to decide a **claim**.

Irrationality: An action is irrational if it cannot be understood as the action of someone acting for a purpose. But in administrative law the term is given a special meaning, which is roughly, 'extremely unreasonable'. 'Irrationality' in that technical sense is often (but not always: see p 247) a ground of judicial review.

Judicial review: Consideration by a court of the lawfulness of administrative conduct. But the phrase is sometimes used as a term for the act of interfering with a decision, or as a term for a **claim for judicial review.**

Jurisdiction: Legal power of decision (as in *Anisminic v Foreign Compensation Commission* [1969] 2 AC 147) or action (as in *Entick v Carrington* (1765) 19 Howell's State Trials 1029, concerning whether the Secretary of State had 'a jurisdiction' to seize Entick's papers). Courts, tribunals, and administrative decision makers all have jurisdiction to make legally binding decisions, although the doctrine of review for error of law (see p 302) has made English lawyers hesitate to talk about the jurisdiction of administrative decision makers. Lord Reid used the term in a 'narrow sense' (for power to address an issue) and in a 'broad sense' (for power not only to address an issue, but to reach a particular decision on it): see p 316.

Justice: Appropriateness in conduct. Just administrative action promotes the public good (which includes the overriding public good of respecting the rights not only of citizens but of people in general). Justice is not, in itself, a ground of judicial review (see pp 23–4), because the rule of law often requires that a public authority abide by

[1]   http://www.coe.int/t/dghl/monitoring/socialcharter/presentation/aboutcharter_EN.asp

rules which may prevent it from acting justly, or may prevent a court from quashing an unjust decision. But the rule of law itself is valuable only insofar as it serves justice. So justice is the point of the grounds of judicial review, and of law in general.

Justiciability: An issue is justiciable if it is suitable for resolution by judges, through a judicial process.

Legitimate expectation: An expectation that deserves legal protection. The form of protection can vary. The reason for giving legal protection may be that it is procedurally unfair for an administrative authority to disappoint your expectation without giving you a hearing, or that disappointing your expectation would involve substantive unfairness that a court ought to prevent.

Locus standi: see Standing

Maladministration: Bad administration. It is not generally a ground of judicial review, although some forms of bad administration give grounds for judicial review. Ombudsmen have the task of investigating complaints of maladministration, and maladministration can infringe Article 8 of the European Convention (but only in very tightly limited circumstances).

Mandamus ('we command'): A prerogative writ developed at common law, which has been replaced by the order called a 'mandatory order' in the Civil Procedure Rules 1998.

Misfeasance: An abuse of power that is done in bad faith. Misfeasance in a public office is the only tort that can only be committed by public officials.

Natural justice: Legal jargon for procedures that the common law requires. Usually interchangeable with **procedural fairness**; see pp 109, 121.

New public management: Management of public projects and government programmes through techniques learned from the management of private enterprise.

Non-departmental public body (NDPB): A public authority that is somewhat independent of government. An **executive agency** is set up to implement policy set by a department under a framework agreement (an example is Jobcentre Plus, which implements policy set by the Department for Work and Pensions); NDPBs are typically more independent than executive agencies, and set policy at arm's length from a department (but some NDPBs are called 'Executive NDPBs' because they provide government services; the Environment Agency is an example).

Non-justiciable: See **Justiciability.**

Obiter dicta: See **ratio**.

Ombudsman: An officer who investigates a complaint of bad administration, and reports on what happened and what, if anything, should be done about it. There is a Parliamentary Ombudsman, also referred to as the Parliamentary Commissioner for Administration (the PCA; she also serves as the Health Service Ombudsman), and three Local Government Ombudsmen.

Order in Council: A legislative instrument made by the **Privy Council**; the Privy Council's role is to rubber-stamp legislation drafted by government departments and presented by ministers. An Order in Council can be an exercise of the prerogative, or it can be a statutory instrument (where a statute provides that delegated legislation under the statute is to be made by Order in Council). An Order in Council made in the exercise of the prerogative counts as primary legislation under the Human Rights Act (s 21).

Ouster clause: A statutory provision purporting to prevent the courts from interfering with a decision of a public authority.

Parliamentary sovereignty: The basis of the UK constitution, which imposes no legal limits on Parliament's power to make laws. Acts of Parliament cannot be overruled by any other institution, and Parliament cannot bind its successor as to the content of legislation.

Plaintiff: The term used for a **claimant** in an action, before the changes in the Civil Procedure Rules 1998.

Policy: A course of action that the government adopts, or a reason for a course of action. But the term is commonly used for the sort of governmental purpose on which judges (or ombudsmen...) should defer (to some extent) to administrative officials.

Prerogative powers: Powers that belong exclusively to the Crown, and are exercised by the Government. They allow Ministers to make certain decisions without an Act of Parliament.

'Prerogative is nothing but the power of doing public good without a rule.'—John Locke, *Of Civil Government* (1689) Chapter XIV [166].

'Prerogative: A sovereign's right to do wrong.' –Ambrose Bierce, *The Devil's Dictionary* (1911).

Prima facie: 'At first glance' or presumptively; a ruling is *prima facie* valid, or a *prima facie* right or duty exists, if the ruling is valid or the right or duty exists *unless* some special reason defeats the presumption that it is valid or exists.

Principles: Starting points for reasoning. The principles of administrative law are basic starting points for reasoning about how the law ought to control public action for the good of the public and to give effect to claims of right. See sections 1.5 and 1.6.

Private Finance Initiative ('PFI'): A form of Public-Private Partnership in which the private partner invests in a large building project such as a school or a hospital. The private partner typically owns the facility that is built, and the public partner agrees to provide the private partner with a stream of future income from the service that the facility will be used to provide.

Private law: Law designed to promote the interests of private persons. It includes the law that gives rights to public authorities and private persons in contract and the law of property, and the rules of tort law that impose duties to respect interests of private persons and of public authorities, and the rules and processes for giving judicial remedies for breach of private law rights and duties. There may, of course, be reasons of public policy for making such laws.

Privatization: The sale of a public enterprise to private owners, accompanied by (1) a government decision not to carry on a public enterprise in the industry in question, and (2) (typically) new forms of licensing and regulation of the resulting enterprise. Beware that people sometimes use the word 'privatization' more loosely, for any move by the Government to involve private actors in public administration.

Privy Council: A council that advises the **Crown**; Cabinet ministers and some other ministers are appointed to the Privy Council for life. There are hundreds of Privy Councillors, but advice of the Privy Council is given by those members currently holding ministerial office. Judicial decisions are made on behalf of the Privy Council by a committee of Law Lords and senior commonwealth judges; that committee serves as the court of final appeal for overseas territories and for those Commonwealth countries that have not abolished appeals. See http://www.privy-council.org.uk/.

Procedural fairness: A decision is procedurally unfair if the decision is biased, or if the process by which it is made wrongly disregards the interest that an affected person has in participating in the decision. Since *Ridge v Baldwin* [1964] AC 40 (see Chapter 4), it has been clear that an administrative decision is unlawful if it is made by an unfair process. Fairness is the primary requirement of **due process**.

Procedure: A step that a decision maker takes to get information for making a decision, or to hear argument as to what decision it ought to make, or to communicate its decision, or to reconsider its decision, or to entertain an appeal from a decision of another decision maker.

Proceeding: The process by which a case is heard by a tribunal or court.

Process: The set of procedures by which a decision is made (and, potentially, communicated, and reconsidered or made subject to appeal...).

Prohibition: A prerogative writ developed at common law, which has been replaced by the order called a 'prohibiting order' in the Civil Procedure Rules 1998.

Proportionality: A just relation between legitimate ends that a public authority pursues, and the means by which it pursues them. Ordinarily, it means not imposing a burden on a person that is out of proportion to the value of the public authority's action.

Public authority: A person or institution with a power that is exercised on behalf of the community, and subject to controls for the good of the community. The question of who or what counts as a public authority may have different answers in different contexts, depending on the purposes of a particular doctrine of public law (see section 15.5).

Public law: Law designed to serve the public interest directly (private law promotes the public interest indirectly, by enabling members of the community to make just legal arrangements with each other, and to seek vindication of their rights against each other). Public law gives legal powers for the administration of government and for the making of law, and controls the use of those powers, and imposes duties on private persons in the public interest. So it includes, e.g., tax law, criminal law, and constitutional law (contrast **administrative law**).

Public-Private Partnership: An ongoing arrangement between a public authority (often a government department or executive agency) and a private company for the provision of a public service.

Quasi-judicial: A decision or function of a public authority that is similar to the decision or function of a judge, so that it requires the public authority to act similarly to the way in which a judge would act. The term has not been used very much since *Ridge v Baldwin* [1964] AC 40 restored the ancient rule that an administrative decision does not need to be quasi-judicial in order to be subject to the law of due process.

Ratio or *ratio decidendi* ('reasoning' or 'reason for decision'): In the common law, the legal basis on which a court decides a case. It determines the effect of the decision as a precedent. A decision binds future courts (subject to powers such as that of the House of Lords to overrule earlier decisions) only as to the *ratio*. Common law courts have jurisdiction only to adjudicate claims, and not to make general enactments, so the *ratio* is restricted to the statements of law that a court makes in order to explain why it decided the case as it did. Any further statements of law that the court makes are *obiter dicta* ('things said along the way').

Reasonableness: It is unreasonable to act in a way that is not guided by the appropriate reasons. The public authorities to whom a decision-making responsibility was assigned are often better able to assess those reasons than the judges (who are responsible for the rule of law, but not for good decision making in general). Unreasonableness is not a general ground of judicial review. An action is unreasonable in the special, restricted sense that does provide a ground of judicial review, if it is not guided by reasons that the law requires judges to insist on. A decision should be quashed as unreasonable on judicial review when it is inconsistent with reasons that it is right for judges to impose on other decision makers.

Relator proceeding: A claim brought by the Attorney General at the request of a person. These proceedings reflect the general standing of the **Crown** to ask its courts to determine the lawfulness of official conduct. But they have become obsolete because the courts have become willing to give standing to private litigants to seek judicial review in (it seems) all circumstances in which they might have asked the Attorney General to bring a claim.

Res judicata: The rule that judicial decisions are final (subject to appeal). There is no such general rule for administrative decisions; a public authority generally has authority to reconsider an administrative decision, subject to the doctrine of legitimate expectations.

Right: An entitlement of a person that must be respected regardless of benefits that could be achieved by acting contrary to the person's interest. A legal right is a legal entitlement that the law protects by imposing duties on other persons. See **human right**.

Right of action: The right that a claimant has to a remedy in an ordinary claim, if the facts are proved. In an ordinary claim, the claimant's statement of case must assert a right of action; if it 'discloses no reasonable grounds for bringing or defending the claim', the court may strike out the statement (CPR 3.4(2)). A claimant for judicial review need not assert a right of action.

Secretary of State: They really were secretaries under Elizabeth I; under Elizabeth II they are cabinet ministers who head the major departments. There are Secretaries of State for the Home Department; Foreign and Commonwealth Affairs; Trade and Industry; Health; Culture, Media and Sport; Constitutional Affairs; International Development; Education and Skills; Communities and Local Government; Work and Pensions; Environment, Food and Rural Affairs; Defence; Transport; Northern Ireland; and Scotland. The phrase, 'the Secretary of State' is a common term in legislation for whatever secretary of state heads the department in question. So, for example, legislation saying 'the Secretary of State may...' gives a power to the department.

Standing = locus standi: The right to bring proceedings. To have standing to bring a claim for judicial review, the claimant must have a 'sufficient interest' in the matter.

Strasbourg Court: The European Court of Human Rights in Strasbourg.

Subsidiarity: Allocation of power to the level of government (e.g., a local council, a regional assembly, a national legislature, or the institutions of the European Union) at which it can be exercised most effectively and responsibly.

Substance: The content of a decision (that is, *what is decided*); cf. **Process**.

Tariff: The period of time that a prisoner must spend in prison for punitive purposes, before being considered for parole (parole is then to be granted if release would not be dangerous to the community or to particular people).

Tribunal: Any decision-making forum is a tribunal (courts are tribunals). But the word 'tribunal' is used in a special sense in English administrative law to refer to a quasi-independent decision-making authority that is separate from the courts service, but hears a dispute between two parties (so it is different from an ombudsman, who investigates a complaint).

Ultra vires: Latin for 'outside [someone's] lawful powers'. In administrative law, English lawyers and judges sometimes talk as if acting *ultra vires* meant acting in a way *that Parliament intended* to be outside the public authority's powers. But no public authority has lawful power to act contrary to law, so an action of a public authority is *ultra vires* if it is unlawful for any reason (because Parliament has prohibited such action, or because some other rule of law prohibits it).

Upper Tribunal: The new appellate and judicial review body for the tribunal system, set up by the Tribunals, Courts and Enforcement Act 2007.

Wednesbury grounds (= Wednesbury principles): Lord Greene's explanation, in *Associated Provincial Picture Houses v Wednesbury* [1948] 1 KB 223, of some of the restricted grounds on which a court will quash an unreasonable decision of a public authority.

Wednesbury unreasonableness: A decision is *Wednesbury*-unreasonable if it is 'so unreasonable that no reasonable authority could ever have come to it' (*Associated Provincial Picture Houses v Wednesbury Corporation* [1948] 1 KB 223, 230, 234 (Lord Greene)) (Beware: the phrase is used in various other ways by different judges and writers!) It is essential to remember that Lord Greene mentioned other grounds of control of discretion too: they are often called the **Wednesbury principles.**

White Paper: A document produced by the Government or a Parliamentary committee outlining a policy or a legislative proposal.

Index